Nigel Cottier

Alphabetical Playground

slanted

AF105560

Nigel Cottier

Alphabetical Playground

Slanted
ISBN: 978-3-948440-87-9

For L

022 Foreword

024 Introduction

A Alphanumeric 027

027 A.A An alphabet formed of numbers based on its letter's alphanumeric code

032 A.B A sans serif alphabet with letterforms slanted based on its letter's alphanumeric code

034 A.C An all-caps sans serif, with letterforms weighted based on its letter's alphanumeric code

036 A.D An all-caps alphabet formed of units of letters based on its letter's alphanumeric code

040 A.E An all-caps alphabet with repeated concentric contours based on its letter's alphanumeric code

044 A.F An all-caps alphabet with repeated letterform based on its letter's alphanumeric code

046 A.G An all-caps alphabet with repeated horizontals based on its letter's alphanumeric code

049 A.H An alphabet formed of horizontal lines, weighted based on its letter's alphanumeric code

050 A.I An all-caps alphabet formed of units of dots based on its letter's alphanumeric code

051 A.J An alphabet formed of grids of dots based on its letter's alphanumeric code

052 A.K An alphabet formed of dots, each scaled down from the centre based on its letter's alphanumeric code

053 A.L An alphabet formed of squares, each scaled down from the centre based on its letter's alphanumeric code

054 A.M An alphabet formed of squares, each scaled down from the bottom-right corner based on its letter's alphanumeric code

		056	A.N	An alphabet formed of squares split horizontally based on its letter's alphanumeric code
B	Bisect	065	B.A	An all-caps alphabet with letters formed of two equal congruent parts bisected by a single line
		070	B.B	An all-caps alphabet with letters formed of a single line bisecting two equal congruent parts
		072	B.C	An all-caps alphabet with letters formed of two equal congruent parts bisected by a single curved line
		074	B.D	An alphabet formed of units of letters based on its letter's alphanumeric code
C	Cursive	083	C.A	A continuous single line all-caps cursive with a squared path
		087	C.B	A continuous single line all-caps cursive with a squared intersecting path
		088	C.C	A continuous single line all-caps cursive with a rounded intersecting path
		089	C.D	A continuous single line all-caps cursive with a squared coiling path
		090	C.E	A continuous single line all-caps cursive with a detailed squared intertwining path
		091	C.F	A continuous single line all-caps cursive with a detailed rounded intertwining path
		092	C.G	A continuous single line all-caps cursive with an intricate squared coiling path
		093	C.H	A continuous single line all-caps cursive with an intricate squared intertwining path*
		094	C.I	A continuous single line all-caps cursive with an intricate rounded intertwining path
		095	C.J	A continuous single line all-caps cursive with a 9 phase labyrinthine path

	096	C.K	A continuous single line cursive with a highly intricate coiling path
	097	C.L	A continuous single line cursive with a detailed squared decoratively intersecting path
	098	C.M	A continuous single line cursive with letterforms revealed though a skirting, meandering sine wave path
	099	C.N	A continuous single line cursive with a rounded decoratively intersecting path
	100	C.O	A continuous single line all-caps cursive with a horizontally meandering path
	101	C.P	A continuous single line cursive with an 8 phases horizontally coiling path
	102	C.Q	A continuous single line cursive with a detailed rounded decoratively intersecting path
	103	C.R	A continuous single line cursive with letterforms revealed through a shifting, meandering sine wave path
	104	C.S	A continuous single line all-caps cursive with an intricate rounded mazing path
	105	C.T	A continuous single line cursive with letterforms revealed though a concentrated, meandering sine wave path
	107	C.U	A continuous single line all-caps cursive with an intricate squared coiling path
D Dimensional	115	D.A	A dimensional serif to sans serif alphabet rendered to appear blurred through a square dot grid
	120	D.B	A dimensional alphabet formed of a wireframe extruded through an isometric projection from its YZ plane
	121	D.C	A dimensional alphabet formed of a wireframe extruded through an isometric projection from its XY plane
	124	D.D	A dimensional all-caps alphabet rendered to appear engraved through horizontal lines

E	Embedded Geometry	131	E.A	A 2-part unit based type system formed of expanding and contracting superellipse curves
		138	E.B	A 2-part unit based type system formed of decreasing unit hyperbola to parabolic curves
		142	E.C	A 2-part unit based type system formed of expanding quadrifolium curves
		144	E.D	A 2-part unit based type system formed of iterated space-filling curves
F	Frameworks	159	F.A	A Framework writing system formed of a grid where plotted dots decrease in size consecutively within each word
		166	F.B	A Framework writing system formed of a grid with plotted dots connected with lines consecutively within each word
		168	F.C	A Framework writing system formed of a grid with plotted points connected with overlapping squares consecutively within each word
G	Gradated	179	G.A	An all-caps alphabet formed of gradating lines decreasing in weight from the centre
		184	G.B	An all-caps alphabet formed of gradating lines increasing in weight from the centre
		186	G.C	An all-caps alphabet formed of gradating lines that decrease then increase in weight from the centre
		188	G.D	An all-caps alphabet formed of gradating lines that increase then decrease in weight from the centre
		190	G.E	An all-caps alphabet formed of gradating lines that first decrease then increase in weight vertically and increase then decrease horizontally from the centre
		192	G.F	An all-caps alphabet formed of gradating lines that first increase then decrease in weight vertically and decrease then increase horizontally from the centre
		194	G.G	An All-caps alphabet formed of gradating lines, light in weight vertically and heavy in weight horizontally
		196	G.H	An all-caps alphabet formed of gradating lines, heavy in weight vertically and light in weight horizontally

H Horizontal

207	H.A	A	A wide width alphabet formed of horizontal lines, bold in foreground weight
211	H.A	B	A wide width alphabet formed of horizontal lines, light in foreground weight
212	H.A	C	A wide width alphabet formed of horizontal lines, bold in background weight
213	H.A	D	A wide width alphabet formed of horizontal lines, bold in foreground weight and bold in background weight
214	H.A	E	A blurred wide width alphabet formed of horizontal lines, bold in foreground weight and light in background weight
215	H.A	F	A blurred wide width alphabet formed of horizontal lines, light in foreground weight and bold in background weight
220	H.A	G	A regular width alphabet formed of horizontal lines, bold in foreground weight
221	H.A	H	A regular width alphabet formed of horizontal lines, light in foreground weight
222	H.A	I	A regular width alphabet formed of horizontal lines, bold in background weight
223	H.A	J	A regular width alphabet formed of horizontal lines, bold in foreground weight and bold in background weight
224	H.A	K	A blurred regular width alphabet formed of horizontal lines, bold in foreground weight and light in background weight
225	H.A	L	A blurred regular width alphabet formed of horizontal lines, light in foreground weightand bold in background weight
226	H.A	M	A narrow width alphabet formed of horizontal lines, bold in foreground weight
227	H.A	N	A narrow width alphabet formed of horizontal lines, light in foreground weight
228	H.A	O	A narrow width alphabet formed of horizontal lines, bold in background weight

229	H.A	P		A narrow width alphabet formed of horizontal lines, bold in foreground weight and bold in background weight
230	H.A	Q		A blurred narrow width alphabet formed of horizontal lines, bold in foreground weight and light in background weight
231	H.A	R		A blurred narrow width alphabet formed of horizontal lines, light in foreground weight and bold in background weight

I Inverting

239

	I.A	A	An ultra-light rounded inverting alphabet, alternating between negative and positive space from character to character
245	I.A	B	An ultra-light squared inverting alphabet, alternating between negative and positive space from character to character
246	I.A	C	A light weight rounded outline inverting alphabet, alternating between negative and positive space from character to character
247	I.A	D	A light weight squared outline inverting alphabet, alternating between negative and positive space from character to character
248	I.A	E	A medium weight rounded inverting alphabet, alternating between negative and positive space from character to character
251	I.A	F	A medium weight squared inverting alphabet, alternating between negative and positive space from character to character
252	I.A	G	A medium rounded outline inverting alphabet, alternating between negative and positive space from character to character
253	I.A	H	A medium squared outline inverting alphabet, alternating between negative and positive space from character to character
254	I.A	I	A bold weight rounded inverting alphabet, alternating between negative and positive space from character to character
255	I.A	J	A bold weight squared inverting alphabet, alternating between negative and positive space from character to character
256	I.A	K	A bold rounded outline inverting alphabet, alternating between negative and positive space from character to character
257	I.A	L	A bold squared outline inverting alphabet, alternating between negative and positive space from character to character

			262	I.B	A	A rounded inverting alphabet alternating between standard and reverse contrast from character to character
			263	I.B	B	A squared inverting alphabet alternating between standard and reverse contrast from character to character
			268	I.C	A	A rounded inverting alphabet alternating in both contrast and space from character to character
			269	I.C	B	A squared inverting alphabet alternating in both contrast and space from character to character
J	Justified	281		J.A	A	An all-caps justified type system set to justify text to one column
			285	J.A	B	An all-caps justified type system set to justify text to two columns
			287	J.A	C	An all-caps justified type system set to justify text to three columns
			288	J.A	D	An all-caps justified type system set to justify text to four columns
			289	J.A	E	An all-caps justified type system set to justify text to five columns
			290	J.A	F	An all-caps justified type system set to change proportion incrementally from character to character
			292	J.B	A	An all-caps justified type system changing proportion exponentially from character to character
K	Kinetic	301		K.A		An alphabet formed of delineated lines, shifting in proportion in order to create an effect of optical kinetic movement
			310	K.B		An alphabet formed of dots and outline squares creating an effect of optical kinetic movement
			315	H.C		An alphabet formed of outline squares and dots creating an effect of optical kinetic movement
			318	H.D		An alphabet formed of letters with a fluctuating central axis to create the effect of optical kinetic movement from character to character

365	M.A	N	An all-caps matrix alphabet formed of a range of shapes on a 3×3 grid
366	M.A	O	An all-caps matrix alphabet with letters formed of a range of shapes on a 3×3 grid
368	M.B	A	An all-caps matrix alphabet formed of dots on a 4×4 grid
369	M.B	B	An all-caps matrix alphabet formed of outline circles on a 4×4 grid
370	M.B	C	An all-caps matrix alphabet formed of squares intersected with circles on a 4×4 grid
371	M.B	D	An all-caps matrix alphabet formed of diagonal rounded crosses on a 4×4 grid
372	M.B	E	An all-caps matrix alphabet formed of octagons on a 4×4 grid
373	M.B	F	An all-caps matrix alphabet formed of pinched quatrefoils on a 4×4 grid
374	M.B	G	An all-caps matrix alphabet formed of rounded diamonds inset with rounded squares on a 4×4 grid
375	M.B	H	An all-caps matrix alphabet formed of quatrefoils inset with dots on a 4×4 grid
376	M.B	I	An all-caps matrix alphabet formed of rounded crosses on a 4×4 grid
377	M.B	J	An all-caps matrix alphabet formed of diagonal quatrefoils inset with squares on a 4×4 grid
378	M.B	K	An all-caps matrix alphabet formed of quatrefoils inset with elongated crosses on a 4×4 grid
379	M.B	L	An all-caps matrix alphabet formed of astroid curves on a 4×4 grid
380	M.B	M	An all-caps matrix alphabet formed of a range of dots inset with squares on a 4×4 grid

381	M.B	N	An all-caps matrix alphabet formed of a range of shapes on a 4×4 grid
382	M.B	O	An all-caps matrix alphabet with letters formed of a range of shapes on a 4×4 grid
383	M.C	A	An all-caps matrix alphabet formed of dots trefoils on a 5×5 grid
384	M.C	B	An all-caps matrix alphabet formed of rounded squares on a 5×5 grid
385	M.C	C	An all-caps matrix alphabet formed of diagonal pinched rounded quatrefoils on a 5×5 grid
386	M.C	D	An all-caps matrix alphabet formed of rounded quatrefoils on a 5×5 grid
387	M.C	E	An all-caps matrix alphabet formed of circle lattice units on a 5×5
388	M.C	F	An all-caps matrix alphabet formed of astroid curves on a 5×5 grid
389	M.C	G	An all-caps matrix alphabet formed of pinched pointed quadrifolium on a 5×5 grid
390	M.C	H	An all-caps matrix alphabet formed of diagonal rounded quatrefoils on a 5×5 grid
391	M.C	I	An all-caps matrix alphabet formed of diagonal quatrefoils inset with squares on a 5×5 grid
392	M.C	J	An all-caps matrix alphabet formed of pinched quatrefoils on a 5×5 grid
393	M.C	K	An all-caps matrix alphabet formed of diagonal rounded crosses on a 5×5 grid
394	M.C	L	An all-caps matrix alphabet formed of squares intersected with circles on a 5×5 grid
395	M.C	M	An all-caps matrix alphabet formed of dots inset with squares on a 5×5 grid

		449	O.G	An oblique negative space tessellating type system formed of hexagonal letterforms slanted to 30°
		450	O.H	An oblique extreme Ultra-Black alphabet slanted to 45.2°
		451	O.I	An oblique shifting pattern alphabet formed of a rounded diagonal chequerboard slanted to 33.7°
		452	O.J	An oblique all-caps shifting pattern alphabet formed of a shifted hazard stripe pattern slanted to 20.55°
		453	O.K	An oblique all-caps matrix alphabet formed of dots on a 3×3 grid slanted to 18.2°
		454	O.L	An oblique shifting pattern alphabet formed of a shifted square grid pattern slanted to 20.55°
		455	O.M	An oblique shifting pattern alphabet formed of a rotated cross pattern slanted to 21.8°
		456	O.N	An oblique regular width alphabet formed of vertical lines, bold in foreground weight slanted to 18.43°
		457	O.O	An oblique rounded inverting alphabet alternating in both contrast and space from character to character slanted to 22°
		458	O.P	An oblique all-caps Neo-Matrix alphabet formed of rounded quatrefoils on a 3×3 grid with dot nodes slanted to 23°
		459	O.Q	An oblique quadrisected All-caps alphabet with letters formed of 4 equal congruent rectangles slanted to 19°
P	Phonetic	467	P.A	An alphabet formed of its letter's syllabic phoneme
		472	P.B	An alphabet formed of its letter's NATO phonetic code word
		476	P.C	An alphabet formed of its letter's Flaghoist communication flag
		478	P.D	An alphabet formed of its letter's semaphore positioning

Q Quadrisect 489

Q.A An all-caps quadrisected alphabet with letters formed of 4 equal congruent rectangles

492 Q.B An all-caps quadrisected alphabet with letters formed of 4 equal congruent stadium shapes

493 Q.C An all-caps quadrisected alphabet with letters formed of 4 equal congruent shapes

R Recontextualised 503

R.A A Roman all-caps alphabet formed of characters recontextualised from other modern alphabets

507 R.B Another Roman all-caps alphabet formed of characters recontextualised from other modern alphabets

510 R.C A Roman All-caps alphabet formed of sigils recontextualised from Pagan writing systems

S Shifted Pattern 519

S.A An all-caps shifting pattern alphabet formed of a shifted hazard stripe pattern

523 S.B An all-caps shifting pattern alphabet formed of a shifted square grid pattern

526 S.C A shifting pattern alphabet formed of a rounded diagonal chequerboard pattern

530 S.D A shifting pattern alphabet formed of a rotated quarter circle pattern

533 S.E A shifting pattern alphabet formed of a shifted dot pattern

536 S.F A shifting pattern alphabet formed of a rotated cross pattern

T Tessellation 547

T.A A tessellating type system formed of hexagonal letterforms

552 T.B A negative space tessellating type system formed of hexagonal letterforms

554 T.C A tessellating type system formed of trapezoid letterforms on a hexagonal grid

			615	V.A J	A regular width alphabet formed of vertical lines, bold in foreground weight and bold in background weight
			616	V.A K	A blurred regular width alphabet formed of vertical lines, bold in foreground weight and light in background weight
			617	V.A L	A blurred regular width alphabet formed of vertical lines, light in foreground weight and bold in background weight
			622	V.A M	A narrow width alphabet formed of vertical lines, bold in foreground weight
			623	V.A N	A narrow width alphabet formed of vertical lines, light in foreground weight
			624	V.A O	A narrow width alphabet formed of vertical lines, bold in background weight
			625	V.A P	A narrow width alphabet formed of vertical lines, bold in foreground weight and bold in background weight
			626	V.A Q	A blurred narrow width alphabet formed of vertical lines, bold in foreground weight and light in background weight
			627	V.A R	A blurred narrow width alphabet formed from vertical lines, light in foreground weight and bold in background weight
W	Woven	635		W.A A	A woven alphabet formed of meshing vertical and horizontal lines, bold in foreground and light in background weight
			638	W.A B	A woven alphabet formed of meshing vertical and horizontal lines, light in foreground and bold in background weight
			639	W.B A	A woven alphabet formed of detailed meshing vertical and horizontal lines, bold in foreground and light in background weight
			640	W.B B	A woven alphabet formed of detailed meshing vertical and horizontal lines, light in foreground and bold in background weight
			641	W.C A	A woven alphabet formed of intricate meshing vertical and horizontal lines, bold in foreground and light in background weight
			642	W.C B	A woven alphabet formed of intricate meshing vertical and horizontal lines, light in foreground and bold in background weight

XYZ Mixed system

649 XYZ. A
Gradated × Alphanumeric × Dimensional. An alphabet formed of letterforms gradated in weight, repeated based on each letter's alphanumeric code through a cavalier projection

654 XYZ. B
Kinetic × Shifting Pattern × Gradated. An optically shifting alphabet formed of a rounded gradated square grid

656 XYZ. C
Letters within letters × Embedded geometry × Dimensional. A 2 layer letters within letters writing system with a macro layer formed of superellipse curves with a blurred effect

657 XYZ. D
Inverting × Letters-within-Letters × Matrix. An inverting in prominence, 2 layer letters within letters matrix writing system formed of a range of shapes

660 XYZ. E
Matrix × Gradated × Inverting. A matrix alphabet formed of circles gradating in weight, alternating between negative and positive space from character to character

661 XYZ. F
Neo-Matrix × Gradated × Inverting. A Neo-Matrix alphabet formed of conjoining circles gradating in weight, alternating between negative and positive space from character to character

664 XYZ. G
Shifting Pattern × Gradated × Inverting. A shifting pattern alphabet formed of a gradating cross pattern alternating between negative and positive space from character to character

665 XYZ. H
Neo-Matrix × Shifting Pattern × Inverting. A Neo-Matrix shifting pattern alphabet formed of a rotated stadium curve cross pattern alternating between negative and positive space from character to character

666 XYZ. I
Alphanumeric × Gradated × Dimensional. An alphabet formed of gradated outline squares repeated based on its letter's alphanumeric code through a cavalier projection

668 XYZ. J
Tessellation × Matrix + Dimensional. An alphabet formed of tessellating pinched trefoils with a blurred effect

672	XYZ. K	Vertical × Shifting Pattern × Inverting. An alphabet formed of an interupted vertical line pattern alternating between negative and positive space from character to character
673	XYZ. L	Dimensional × Matrix × Inverting. A blurred Matrix alphabet formed of rounded crosses alternating between negative and positive space from character to character
674	XYZ. M	Kinetic × Shifting Pattern × Inverting. An optically shifting alphabet formed of scaled dots on a diagonal grid alternating between negative and positive space from character to character
675	XYZ. N	Gradated × Dimensional × Quadrisect. An alphabet with repeated gradated letters through a cavalier projection from 4 equal outline stadium curves
676	XYZ. O	Dimensional × Neo-Matrix × Inverting. A blurred Neo-Matrix alphabet formed of rounded crosses with inverting dot nodes alternating between negative and positive space from character to character
680	XYZ. P	Vertical × Shifting Pattern × Kinetic. An alphabet formed of a vertical line pattern shifted within units to reaveal modular letterforms with an optical kinetic effect
682	XYZ. Q	Cursive × Shifting Pattern × Gradated. A cursive alphabet formed of a square pattern with rotated diagonal units revealing letterforms with gradated strokes

With heartfelt thanks to Paul McNeil for his eloquence, knowledge, and generosity—without his help, this book would be far less coherent. Sincere thanks also to Hamish Muir for his generously written Foreword. Above all, my deepest gratitude goes to my wife, Martha—without her, this book would not exist.

Foreword

What's remarkable about the Roman alphabet is its exceptional resilience. Despite being reworked in a million different ways – bent, stretched, fragmented, and mangled – its core shapes remain instantly recognisable, lodged deep in the consciousness of the reader. Think of the countless variations that must exist across all the typefaces in use today. How do we make sense of them all? What exactly is the essence of a letter? What actually happens when we read?

We're so fluent in the visual grammar of written language that we are able to decode meaning from wildly divergent forms, the alphabet always remaining remarkably impervious. You can push its basic structure to breaking point, and it still communicates. So where does that leave legibility? Perhaps nowhere. Or maybe it's just wildly overrated.

In Alphabetical Playground, Nigel Cottier gleefully explores the outer limits of readability, where each turn of the page brings something new and unexpected. Guiding us through this space is Cottier's meticulously structured, methodical approach, one that demonstrates the full potentials of both advanced type design and radical experimentation. With every new outcome, Cottier offers insights into his process, deepening our appreciation of the inventive, unprecedented forms that fill this bold and absorbing publication.

Hamish Muir

Hamish Muir was co-founder of the London-based graphic design studio 8vo (1985–2001), and co-editor of Octavo, journal of typography (1986–92). In 2009, with Paul McNeil, he co-founded MuirMcNeil, a studio which focusses on exploring systematic approaches to type and graphic design.

Introduction

Driven by a fascination with the alphabet as a vessel for unlimited ideas, systems and languages, Alphabetical Playground explores a wide range of themes concerning expression in text. It presents a playful series of graphic experiments that investigate and manipulate the building blocks of language. Each section introduces a uniquely structured exploratory theme, signposted throughout by an alphabetic index code system.

Some sections feature interpretations or abstractions of established typographic classifications such as Cursive, Matrix and Ultra, functioning as attempts to push beyond their boundaries. However, most of the themes fall outside of traditional type categories. Other approaches are grounded in graphic techniques or methods used to render the alphabet, such as Gradated, Dimensional, Horizontal, Vertical, and Woven. These sections focus on how such methods can transform the representation of letterforms, much like the way that an artist's or calligrapher's choice of brush influences the character of their strokes.

Other themes explore constraints imposed on textual or systemic structures. These rules shape letterforms through their affordances and limitations, often leading to unexpected outcomes, as seen in the Alphanumeric, Bisect, Justified, Quadrisect, and Tessellation sections. More conceptual possibilities are explored in the Recontextualised, Letters-within-Letters and Phonetic sections, where glyphs are shaped or selected as discreet interpretations of specific ideas. Some themes involve obscuring or revealing the letterforms through modifications to a predetermined system or framework, such as Shifting Pattern, Embedded Geometry, and Inverting. Within these sections, linguistic information becomes increasingly blurred, sometimes becoming recognizable only through interpretation of the underlying contextual system from which it was created.

While the work on these pages may seem abstract, every mark the reader encounters is, in some way, a letterform. The relationship between the letters becomes just as significant as the recognition of the letters themselves. Through these interactions, a kind of beauty emerges, not from the meaning of the text but from the glyph shapes, their component parts, and the overarching systems that contain and constrain them. The results often lean towards the cultural tradition of asemic writing, where text no longer serves as a vehicle for language but as a pure expression of visual form. This is evidenced clearly in Frameworks which focuses on mechanisms created to store linguistic information without regard for legibility, the visual form serving as the sole container of meaning.

The final section, XYZ Mixed System, extends these themes by combining any three of the approaches outlined to venture into new graphical and alphabetical territories. The same materials can be reconfigured or reversed to produce entirely new outcomes. This cross-pollination of themes emphasises the potential for even more intricately formulated visual codes.

Ultimately – although it may not always be immediately apparent – everything on these pages is language. This work demonstrates how text allows us to embed our thoughts, beliefs and systems within it: a code within a code, a game within a game, a system within a system. It serves as a reminder of the alphabet's enormous potential to transcend its fundamental purpose as a tool for communication and instead become a limitless space for creative expression.

Nigel Cottier

Nigel Cottier is a designer with an ongoing interest in experimental typography and creating work of beauty using formulae, hidden systems and data as tools for creation.

Glossary of Abbreviations

	abbreviation	definition
typesetting	s.	point size
	l.	leading
	t.	tracking
variable parameters	w.	weight
	sf.	serif
	e.	extrusion
	r.	roundness
	fw.	foreground weight
	bw.	background weight
	wd.	width
	b.	blur
	sl.	slant
	h.	horizontal emphasis
	v.	vertical emphasis
type styling	UC	Uppercase
	OL	Outline

027

A Alphanumeric

A set of alphabets constructed using alphanumeric codes where each letter is either formed, influenced, or substituted by a corresponding number. By embedding secondary numerical inputs into the body of the alphabet, a symbiotic relationship emerges between letter codes and number codes. In each alphabet this relationship is interpreted differently, with some using numerical values to shape the letterforms and others reducing the letters to purely numerical representations. These systems constitute a form of pseudo-writing — patterned encodings that express the language they contain as abstractions.

code:

A - 1	H - 8	O - 15	V - 22
B - 2	I - 9	P - 16	W - 23
C - 3	J - 10	Q - 17	X - 24
D - 4	K - 11	R - 18	Y - 25
E - 5	L - 12	S - 19	Z - 26
F - 6	M - 13	T - 20	
G - 7	N - 14	U - 21	

1 14 1 12 16 8 1 2 5 20
6 15 18 13 5 4 15 6
14 21 13 2 5 18 19
2 1 19 5 4 15 14 5 1 3 8
12 5 20 20 5 18 19
1 12 16 8 1 14 21 13 5 18 9 3
3 15 4 5

A.A An alphabet formed of numbers based on its letter's alphanumeric code*

*

s. 34
l. 40
t. 0

1 2 3 4 5 6 7 8
9 10 11 12 13 14
15 16 17 18 19 20
21 22 23 24 25
26 - A B C D E
F G H I

A.A

A-Z 0-9

s. 58
l. 68
t. 0

1 12 16 8 1
14 15 22 –
5 13 2 –
5 18

A.A

Alpha November

s. 102
l. 102
t. -25

A SANS SERIF ALPHABET WITH LETTERFORMS, SLANTED BASED ON EACH LETTER'S ALPHANUMERIC CODE.

A.B A sans serif alphabet with letterforms slanted based on its letter's alphanumeric code.*

*

s. 42
l. 42
t. 0

UC

Alpha Lima Papa Hotel Alpha

A.B

Alpha Lima Papa
Hotel Alpha

s. 94
l. 76
t. 0

ABCDEF
GHIJKLM
NOPQRS
TUVWX
YZ

A.C

An all-caps sans serif, with letterforms weighted based on its letter's alphanumeric code

A–Z

s. 78
l. 65
t. 0

NOV EM BER

A.C

November

s. 170
l. 130
t. 0

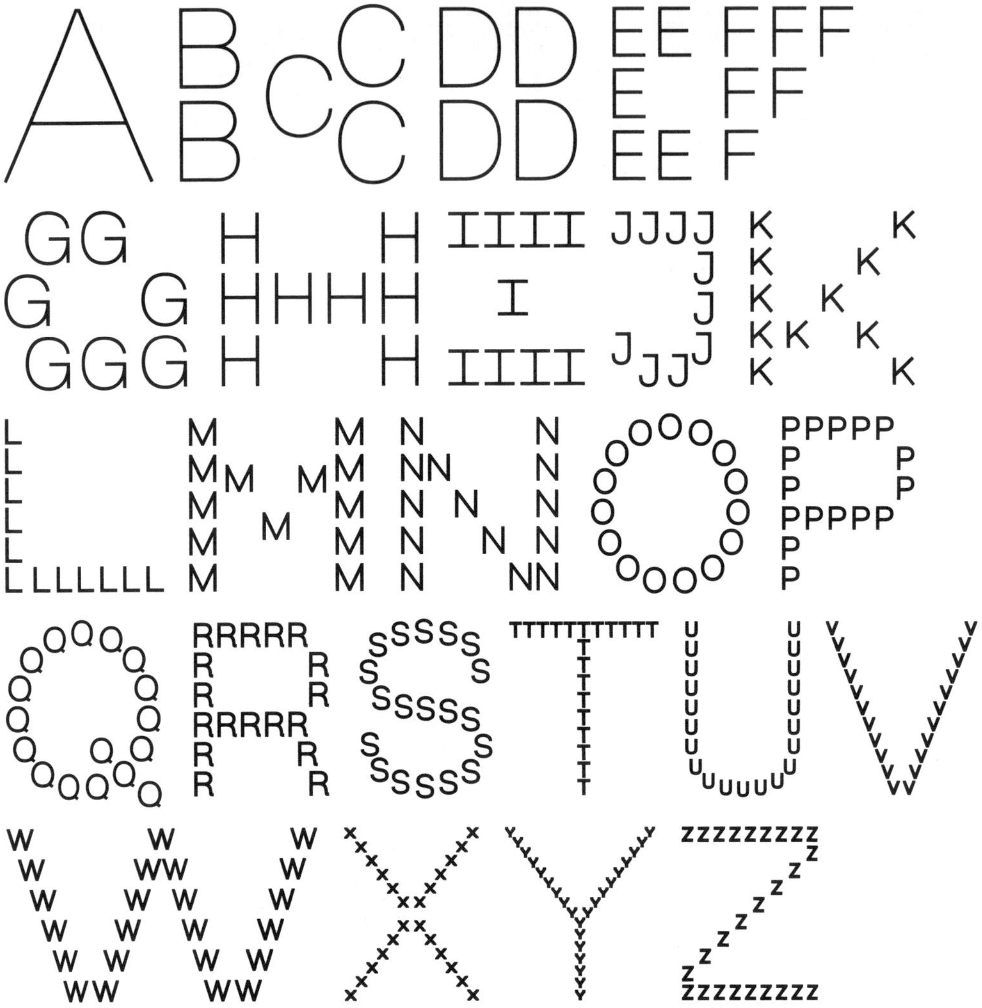

A.D

An all-caps alphabet formed of units of letters based on its letter's alphanumeric code.*

A–Z

s. 88
l. 77
t. 50

AN ALL-CAPS ALPHABET FORMED OF UNITS OF LETTERS BASED ON ITS LETTER'S ALPHANUMERIC CODE.

A.D

*

s. 40
l. 40
t. 50

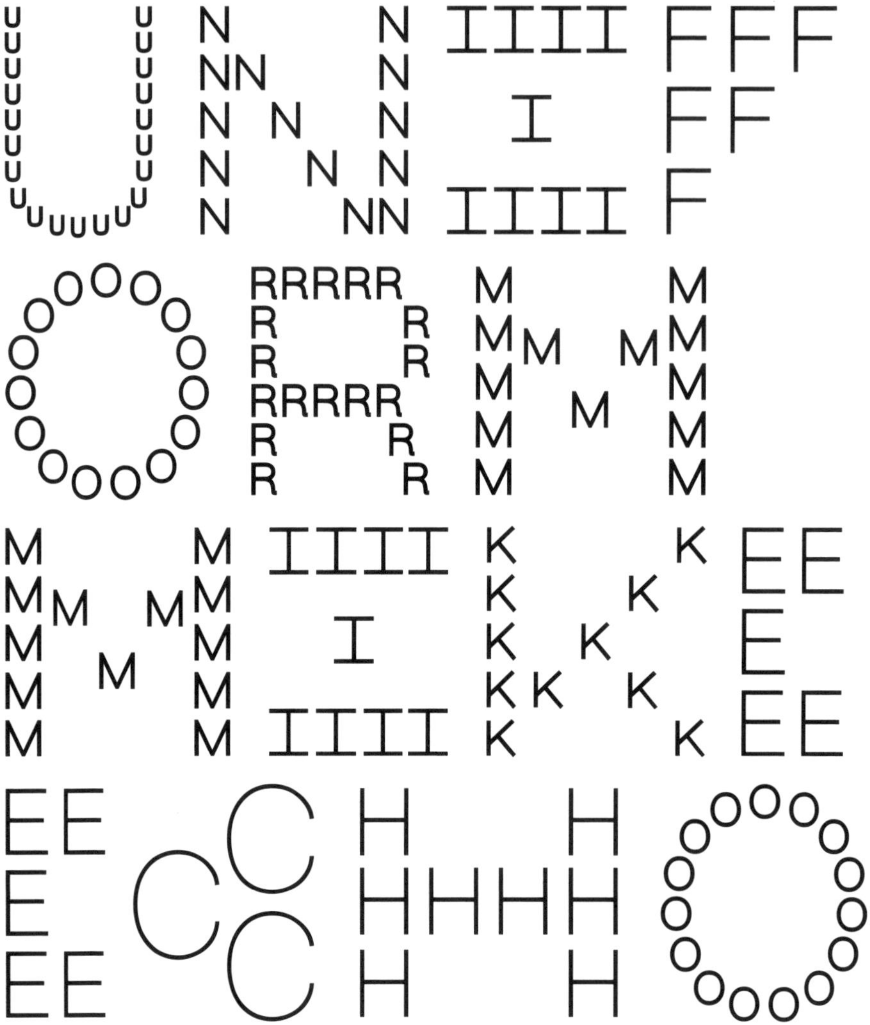

A.D

Uniform Mike Echo

s. 116
l. 98
t. 30

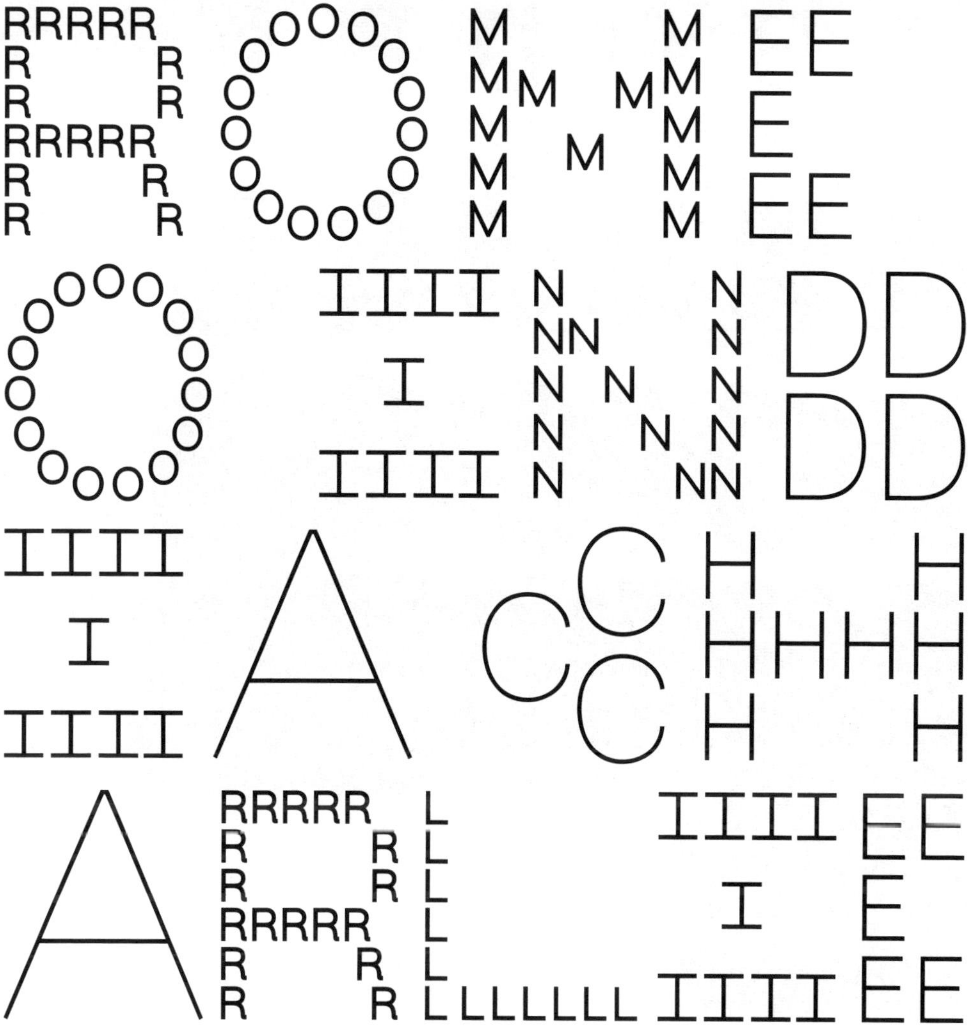

A.D

Romeo India Charlie

s. 116
l. 98
t. 30

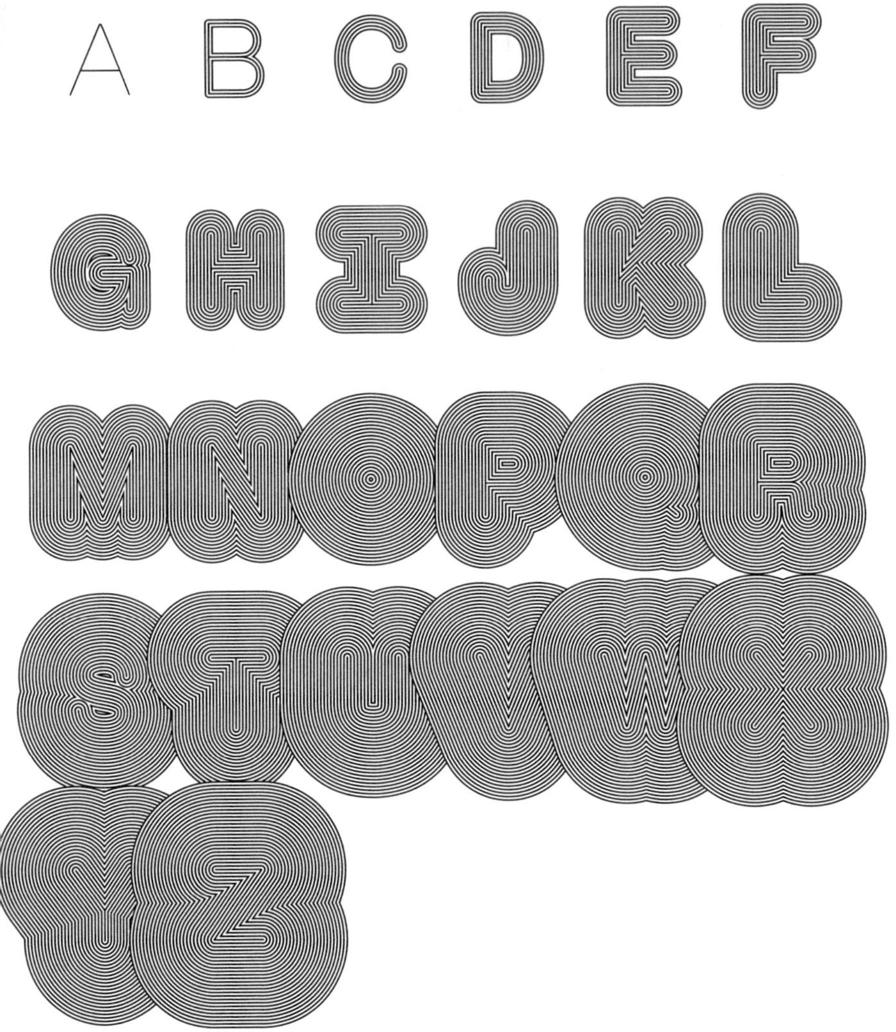

A.E An all-caps alphabet with repeated concentric contours based on its letter's alphanumeric code*

A–Z

s. 42
l. 80
t. 0

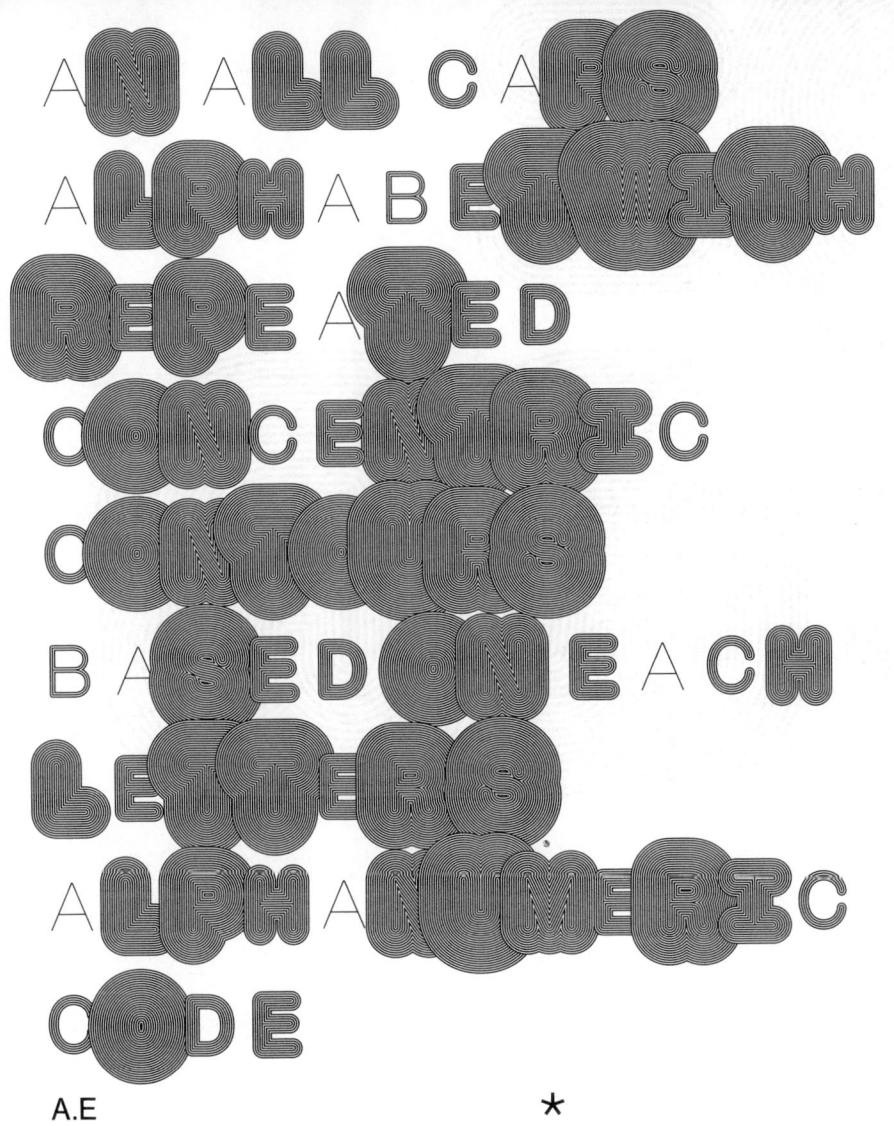

AN ALL CAPS
ALPHABET WITH
REPEATED
CONCENTRIC
CONTOURS
BASED ON EACH
LETTERS
ALPHANUMERIC
CODE

A.E

*

s. 26
l. 44
t. 0

A.E

Sierra

s. 100
l. 150
t. 0

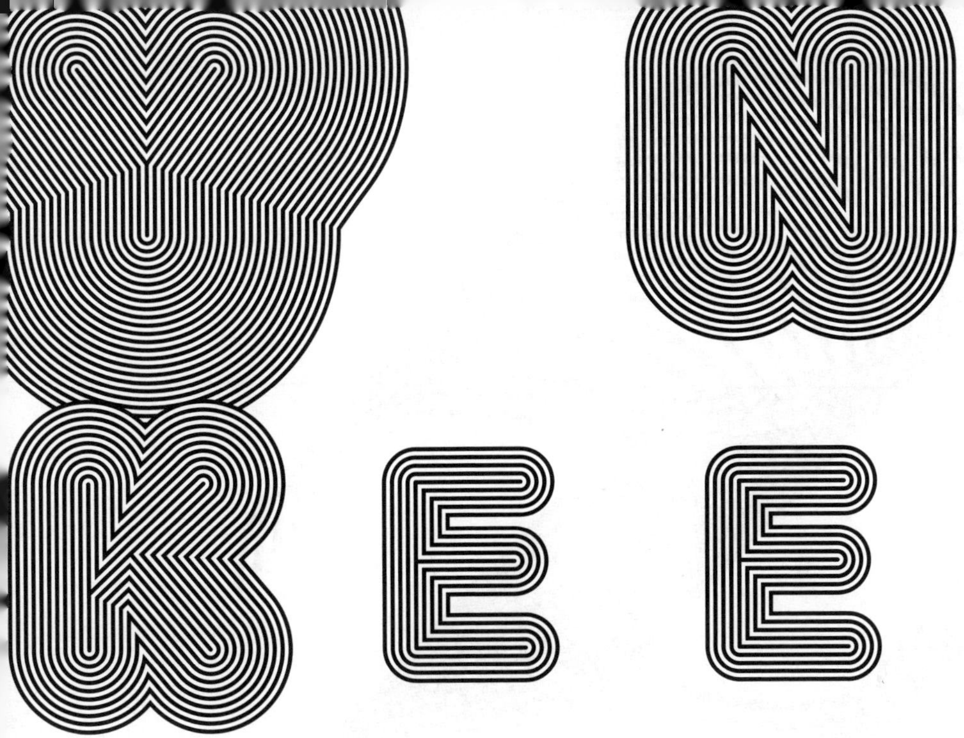

A.E

Yankee

s. 100
l. 150
t. 0

A.F An all-caps alphabet with repeated letterform based on its letter's alphanumeric code

Sierra

s. 382
l. 382
t. 0

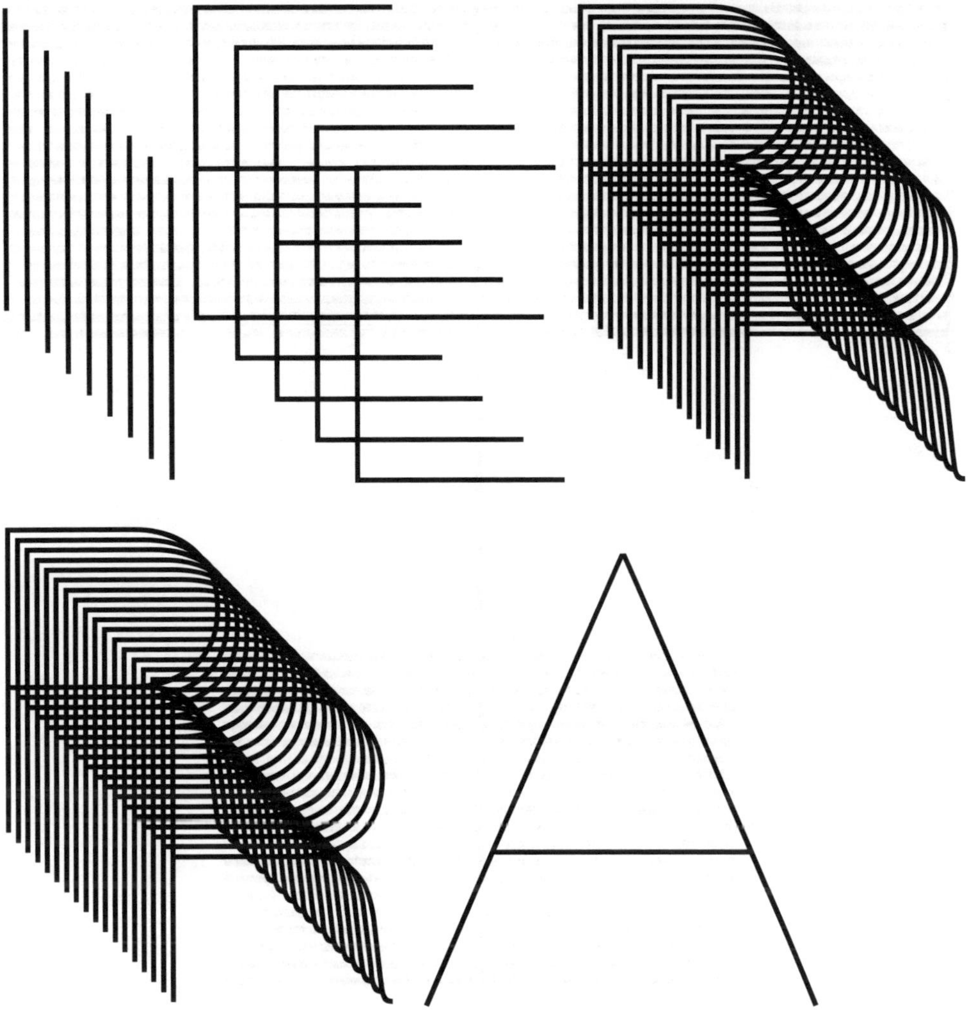

s. 184
l. 196
t. 0

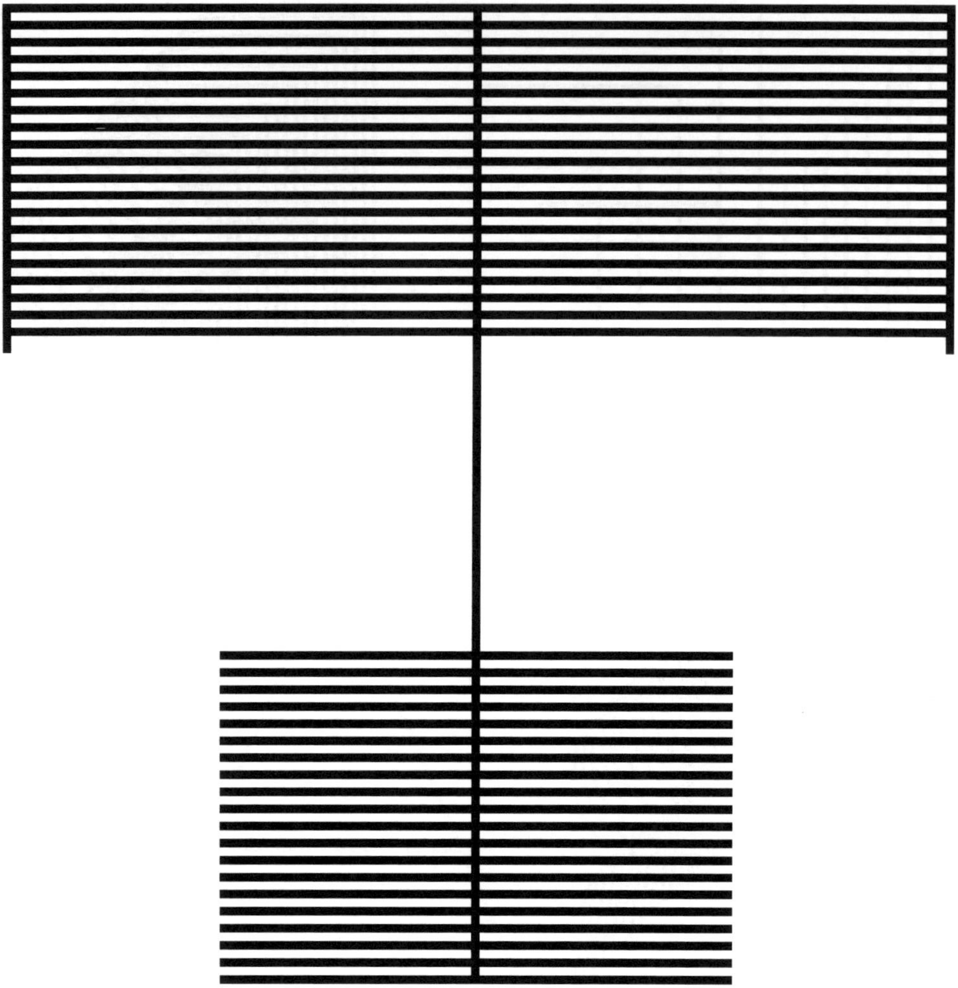

A.G

An all-caps alphabet with repeated horizontals based on its letter's alphanumeric code

Tango

s. 382
l. 382
t. 0

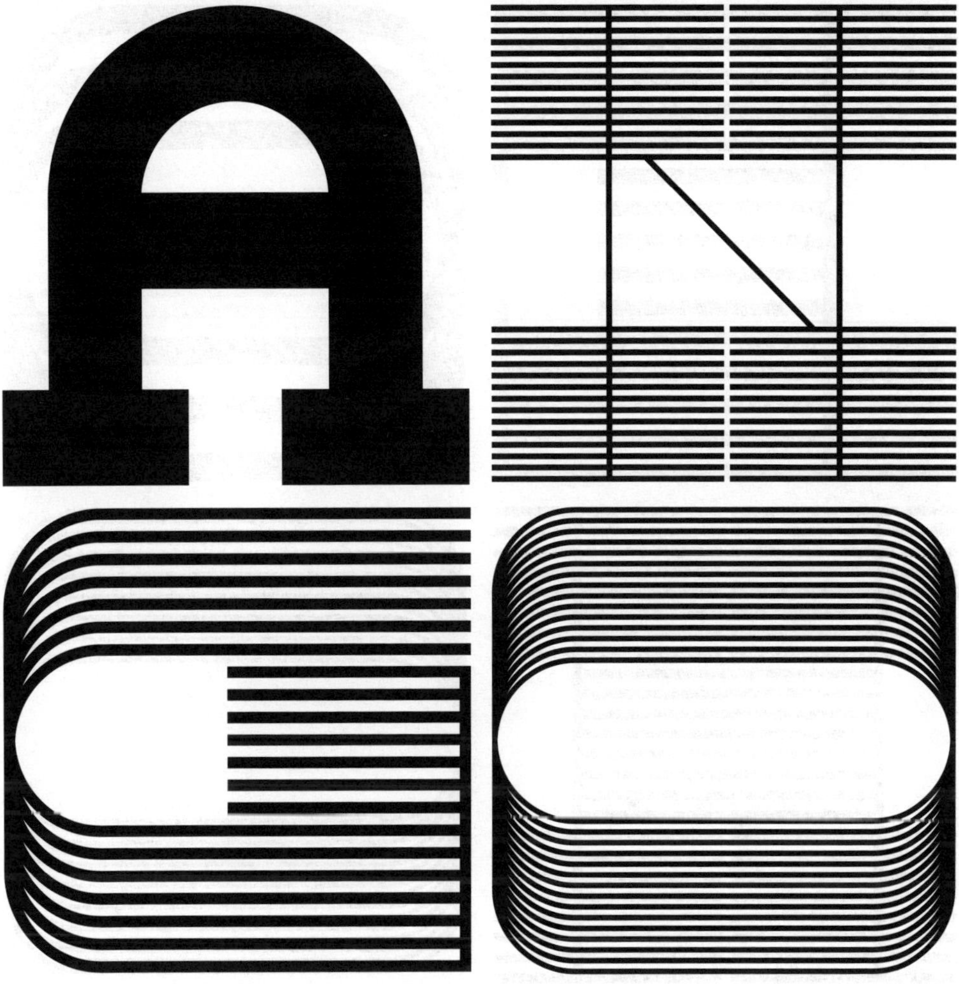

s. 184
l. 176
t. -25

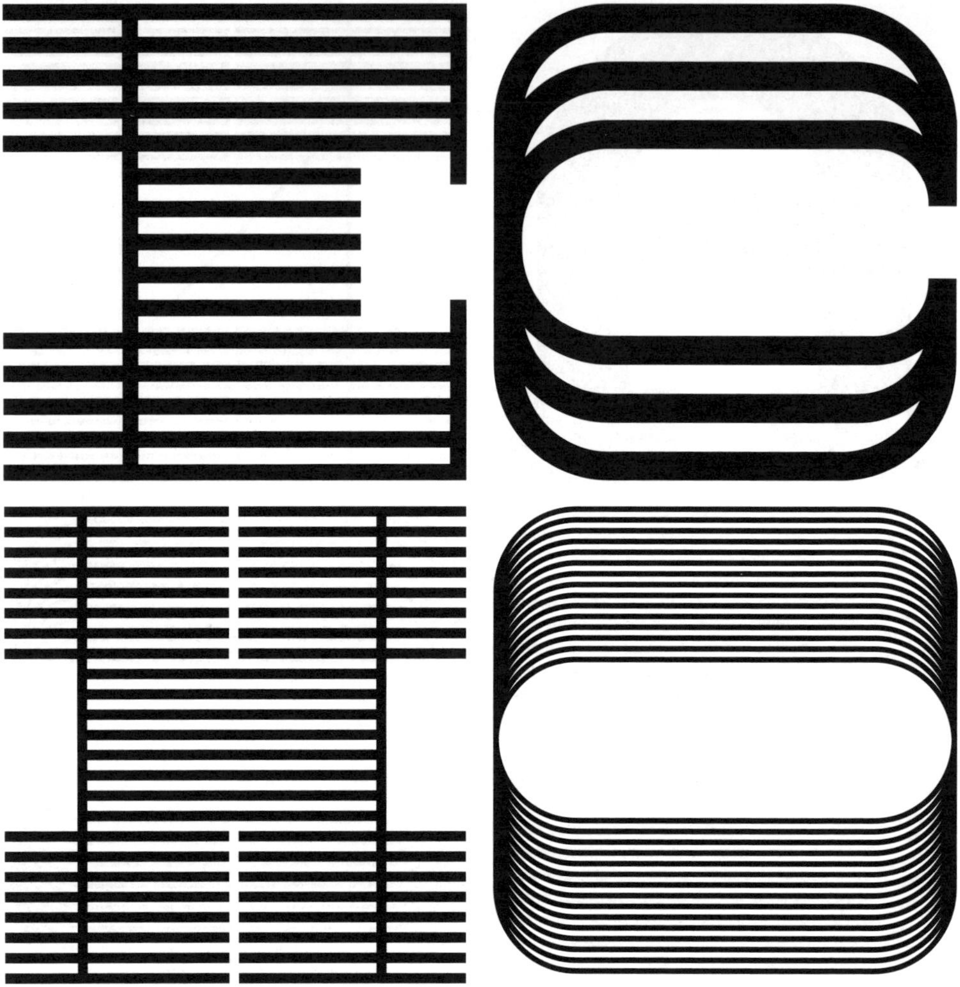

A.G

Echo

s. 184
l. 176
t. -25

A.H

An alphabet formed of horizontal lines, weighted based on its letter's alphanumeric code

Mike

s. 184
l. 184
t. 0

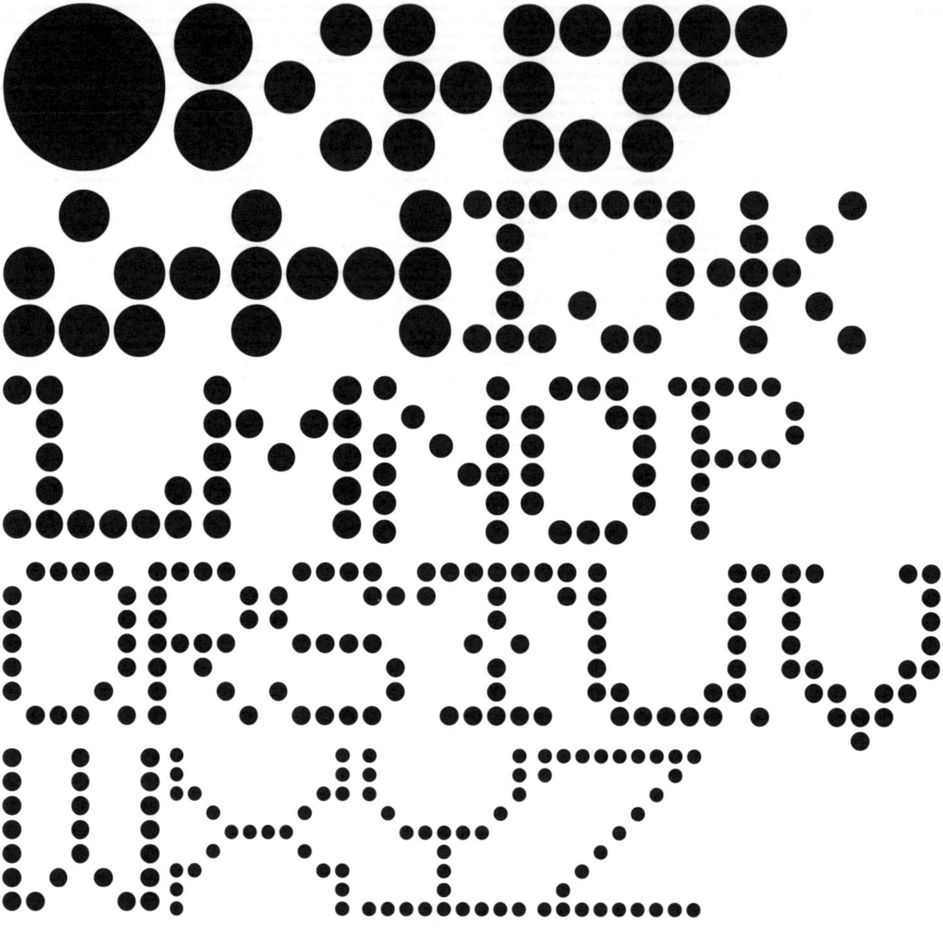

A.I

An all-caps alphabet formed of units of dots based on its letter's alphanumeric code

A–Z

s. 90
l. 70
t. 0

A.J An alphabet formed of grids of dots based on its letter's alphanumeric code*

*

s. 35
l. 35
t. 0

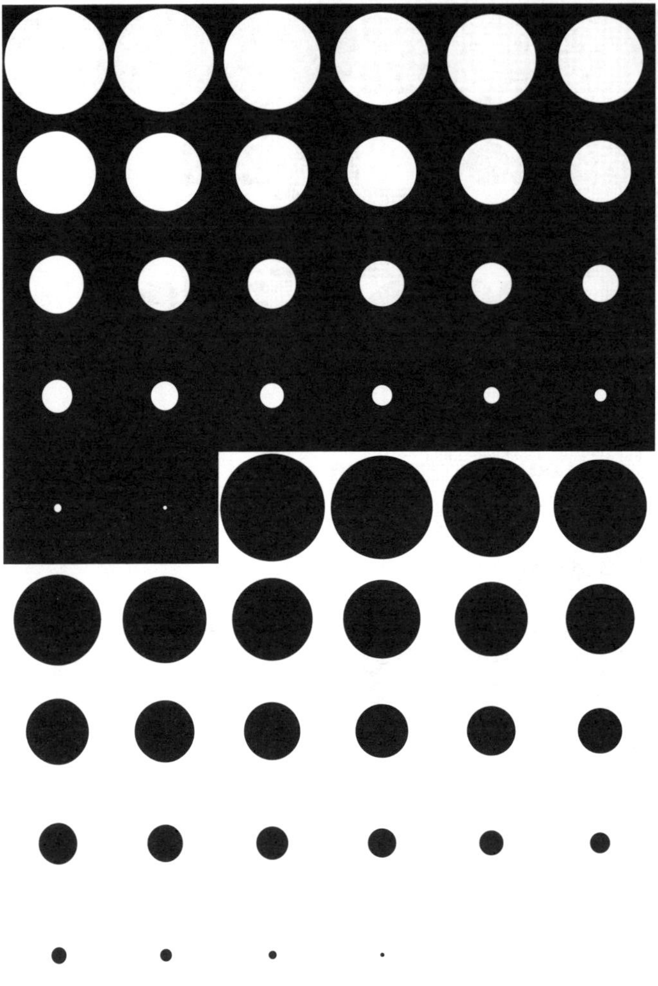

A.K An alphabet formed of dots, each scaled down from the centre based on its letter's alphanumeric code

A–Z, a–z

s. 42
l. 42
t. 0

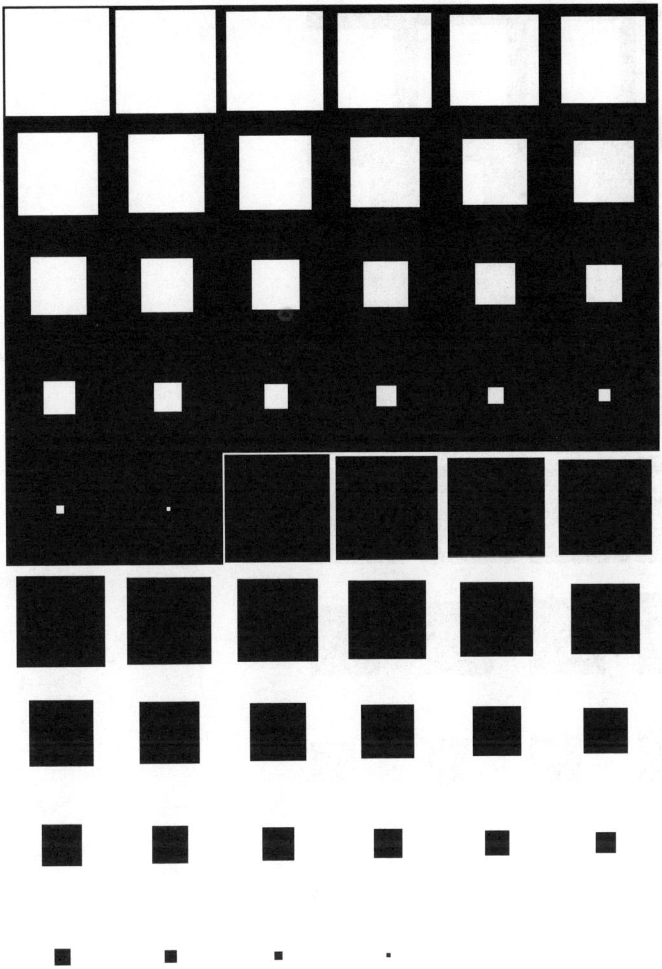

A.L An alphabet formed of squares, each scaled down from the centre based on its letter's alphanumeric code

A–Z, a–z

s. 42
l. 42
t. 0

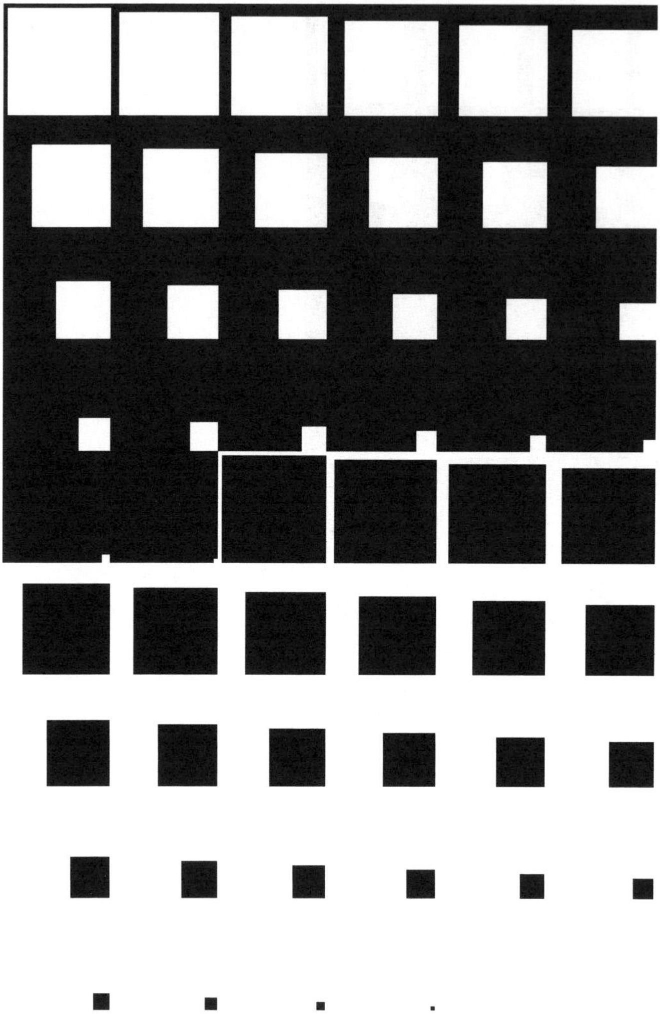

A.M An alphabet formed of squares, each scaled down from the bottom-right corner based on its letter's alphanumeric code*

A–Z, a–z

s. 42
l. 42
t. 0

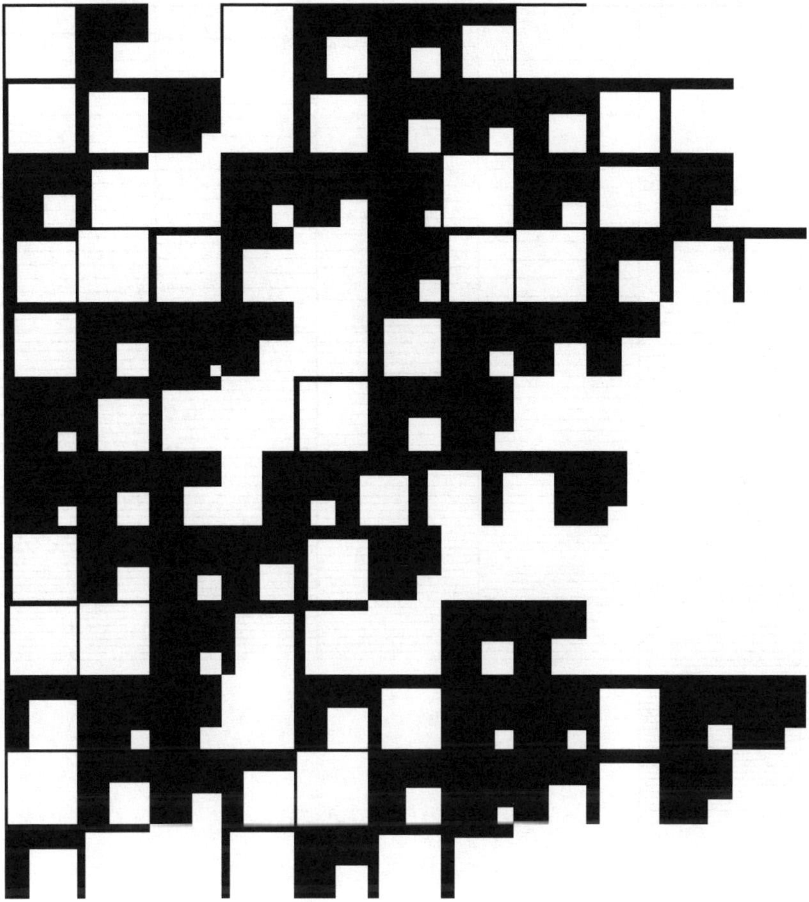

A.M

*

s. 28
l. 28
t. 0

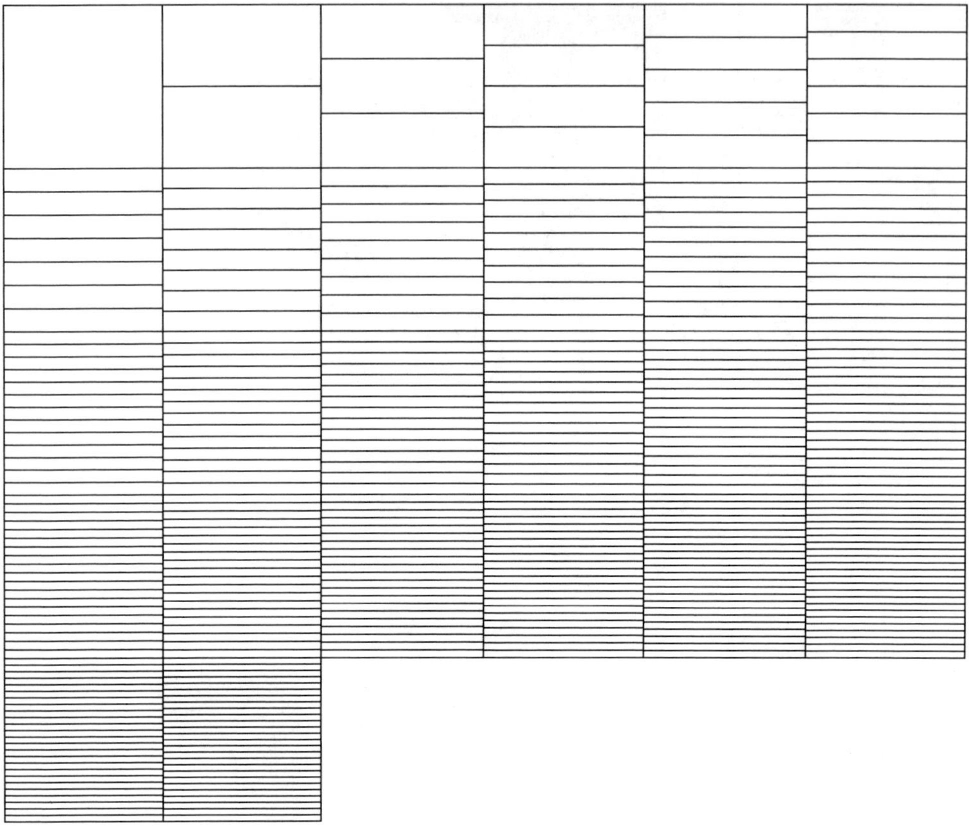

A.N An alphabet formed of squares split horizontally based on its letter's alphanumeric code*

A–Z

s. 62
l. 62
t. 0

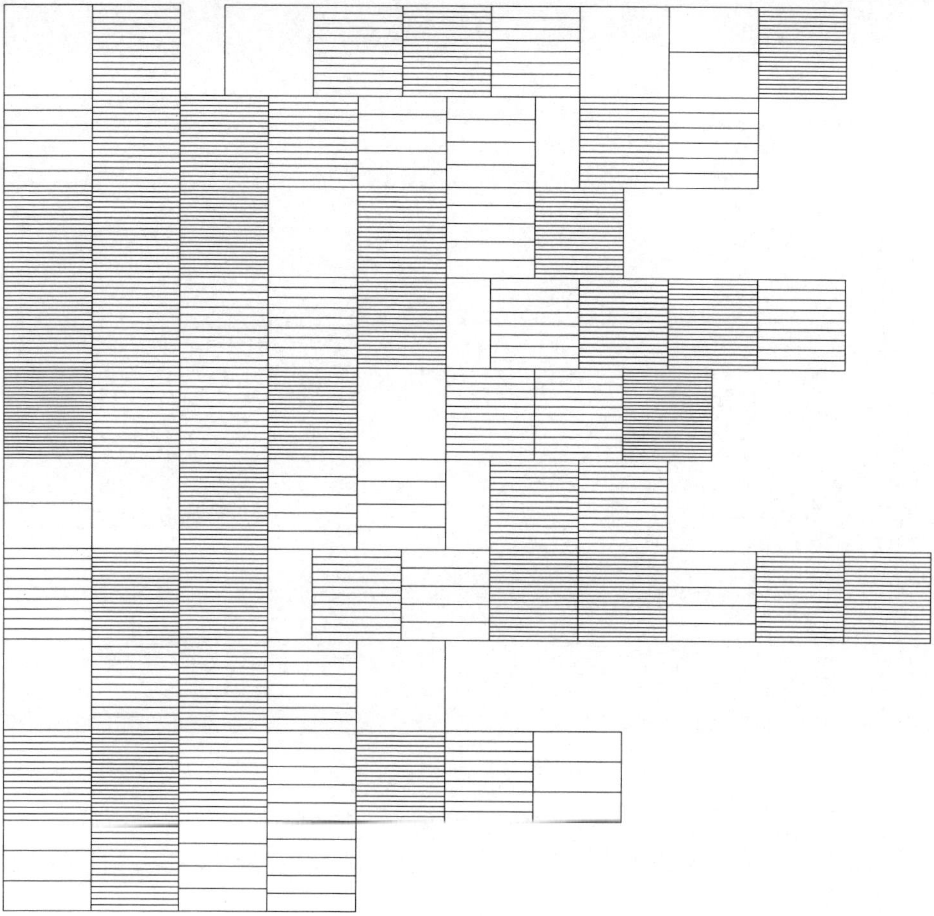

A.N

*

s. 34
l. 34
t. 0

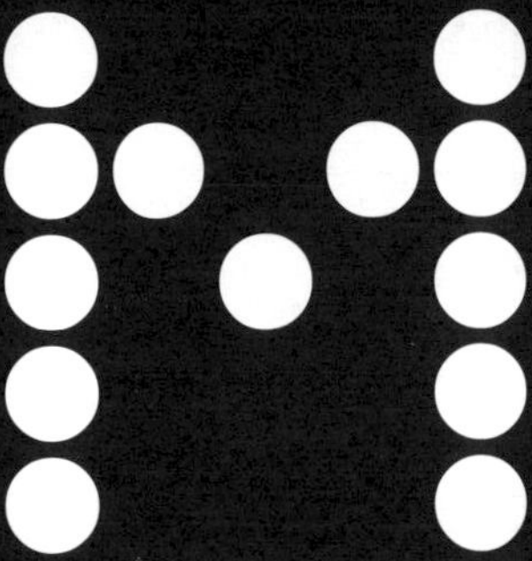

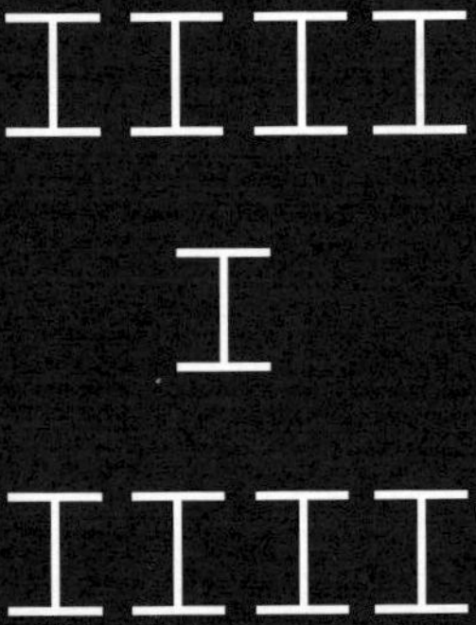

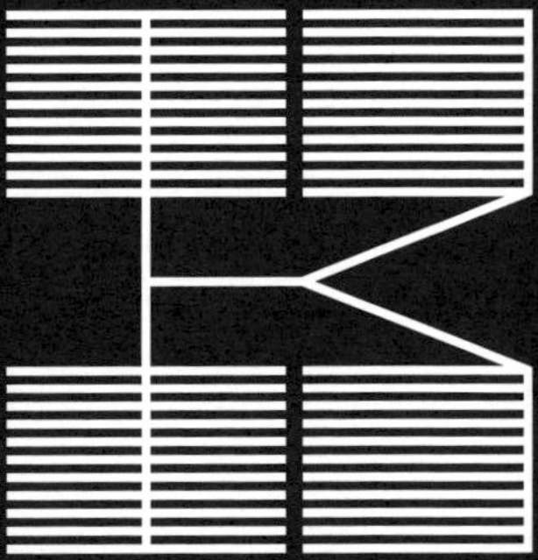

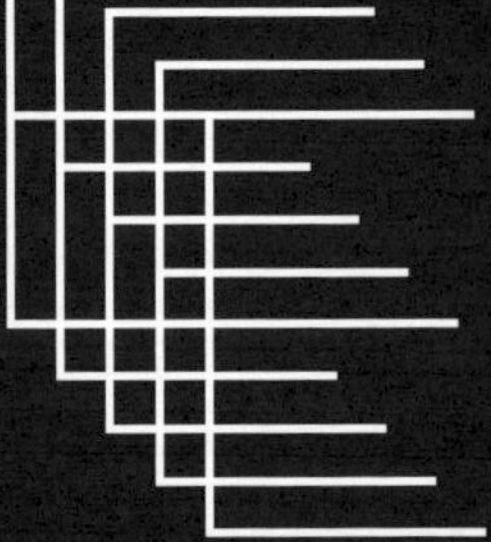

A Alphanumeric

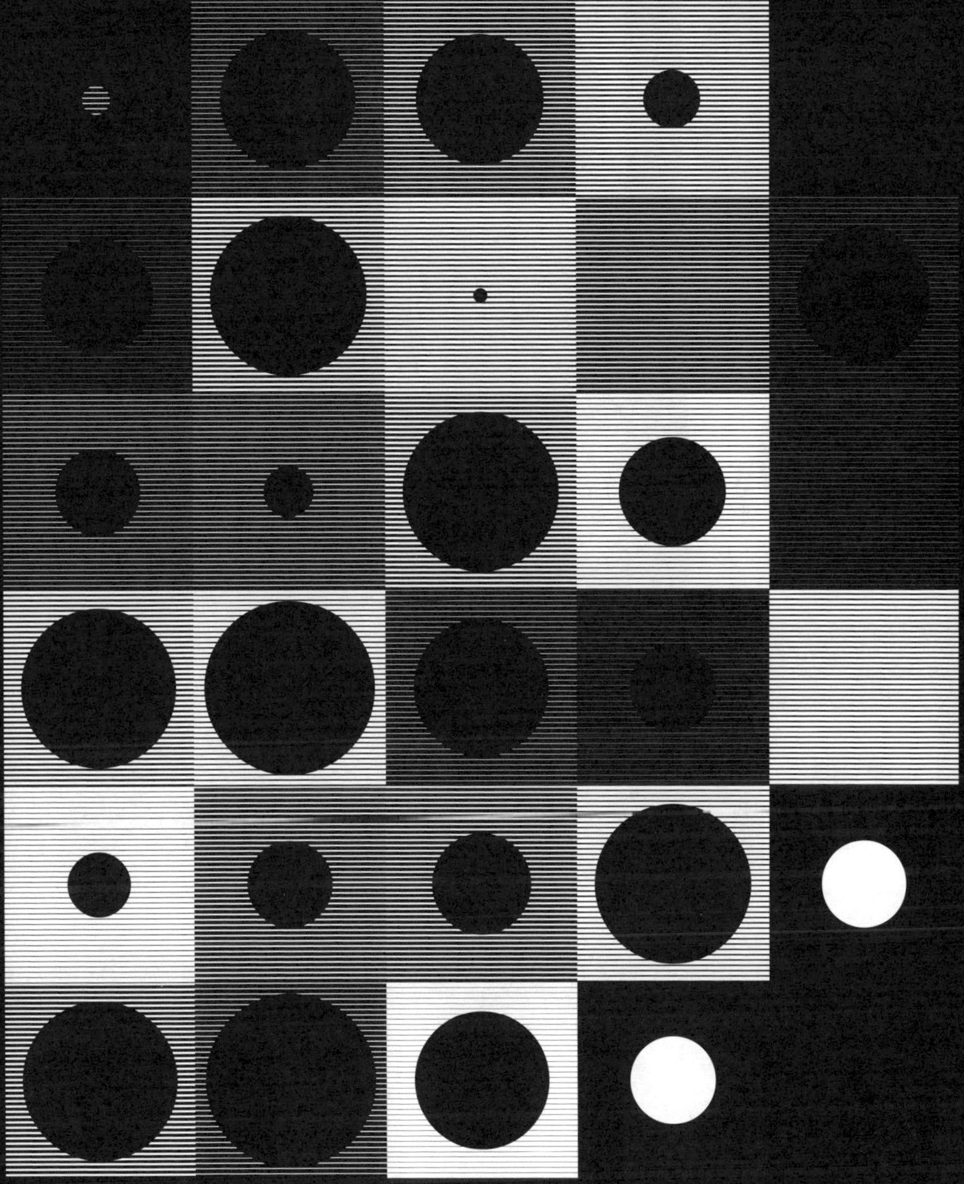

A Alphanumeric

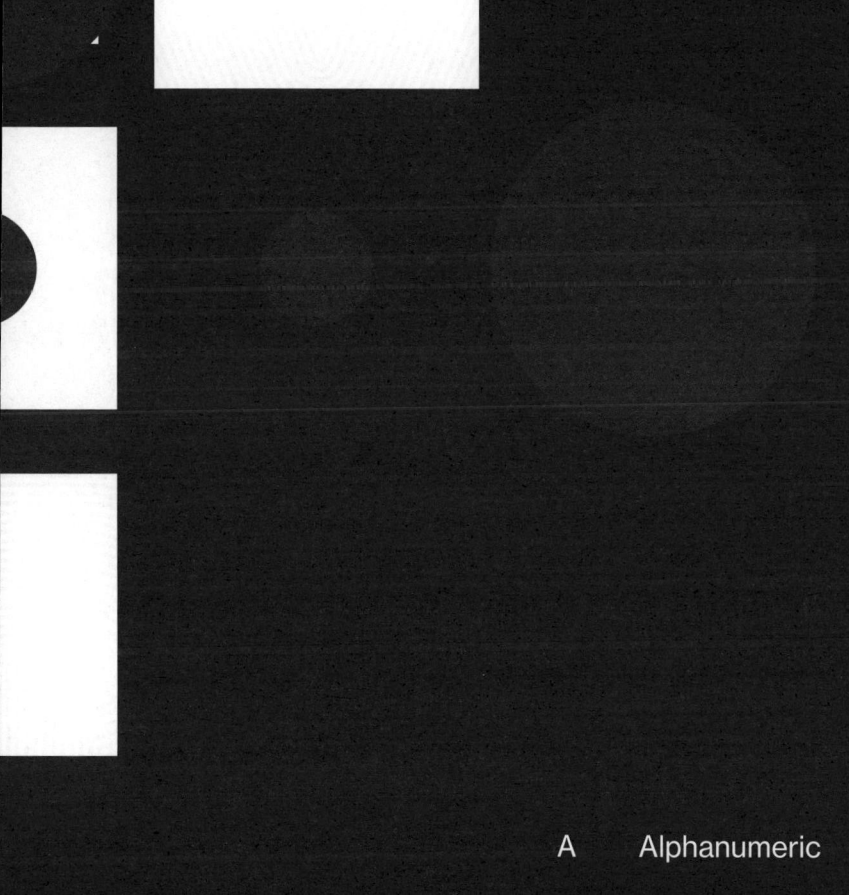

A Alphanumeric

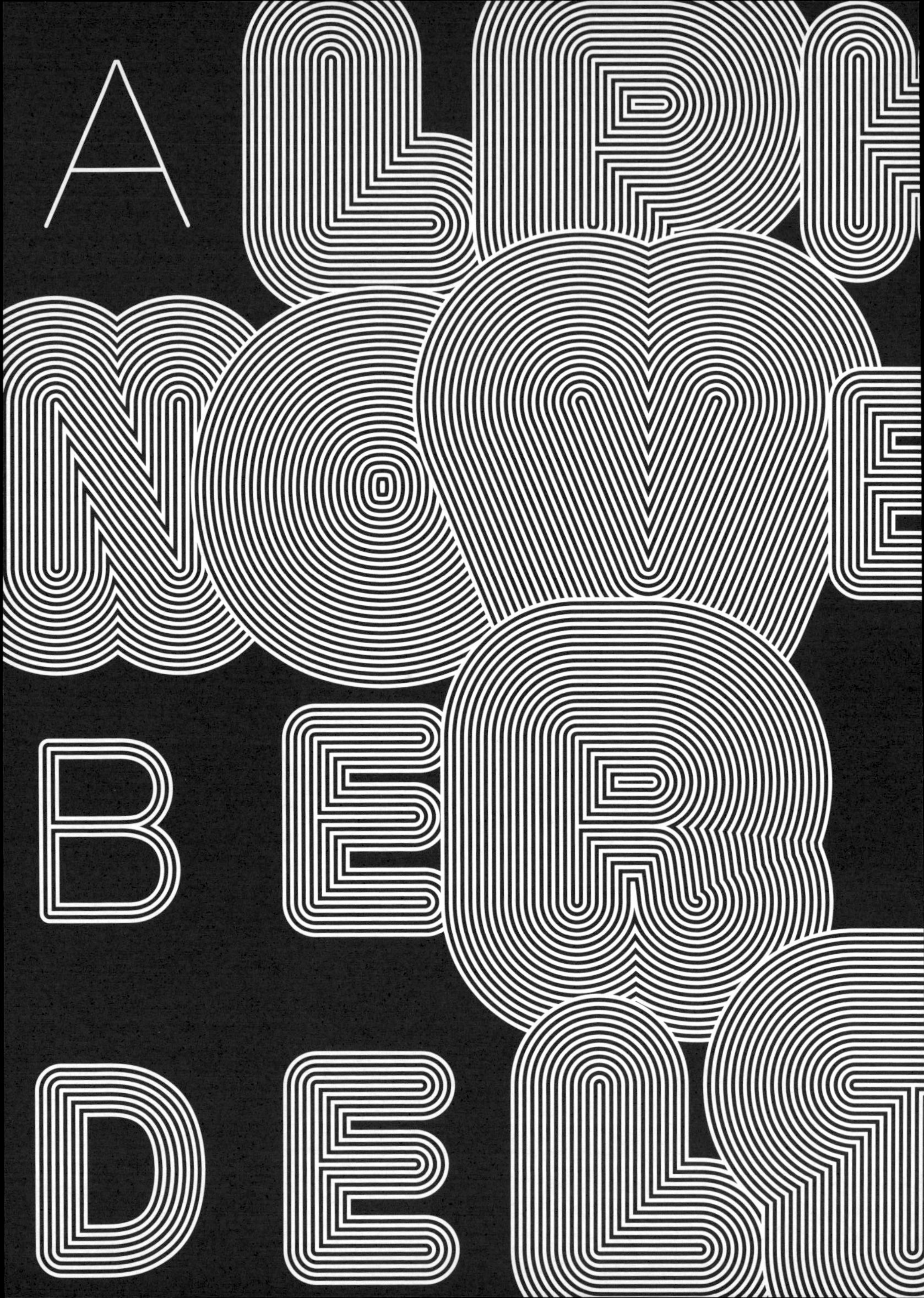
A
NOVE
BER
DE

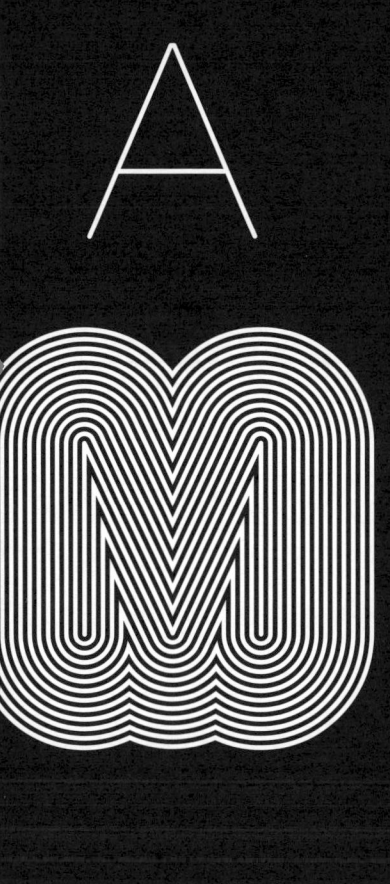

A Alphanumeric

Section Notes:

With the exception of A.E all alphabets within Alphanumeric were created using Glyphs font software and consist of single weight font files. A.E exists as a set of vector based components allowing them to be overlaid concecutively within a peice of text. Although all alphabets use the outlined alphanumeric code, A.K, A.L and A.M use the code in reverse, the form within each letter scaling down throughout the alphabet.

A.D and A.I are redrawn
from Process-Pattern Basic
Numerals released in 2019

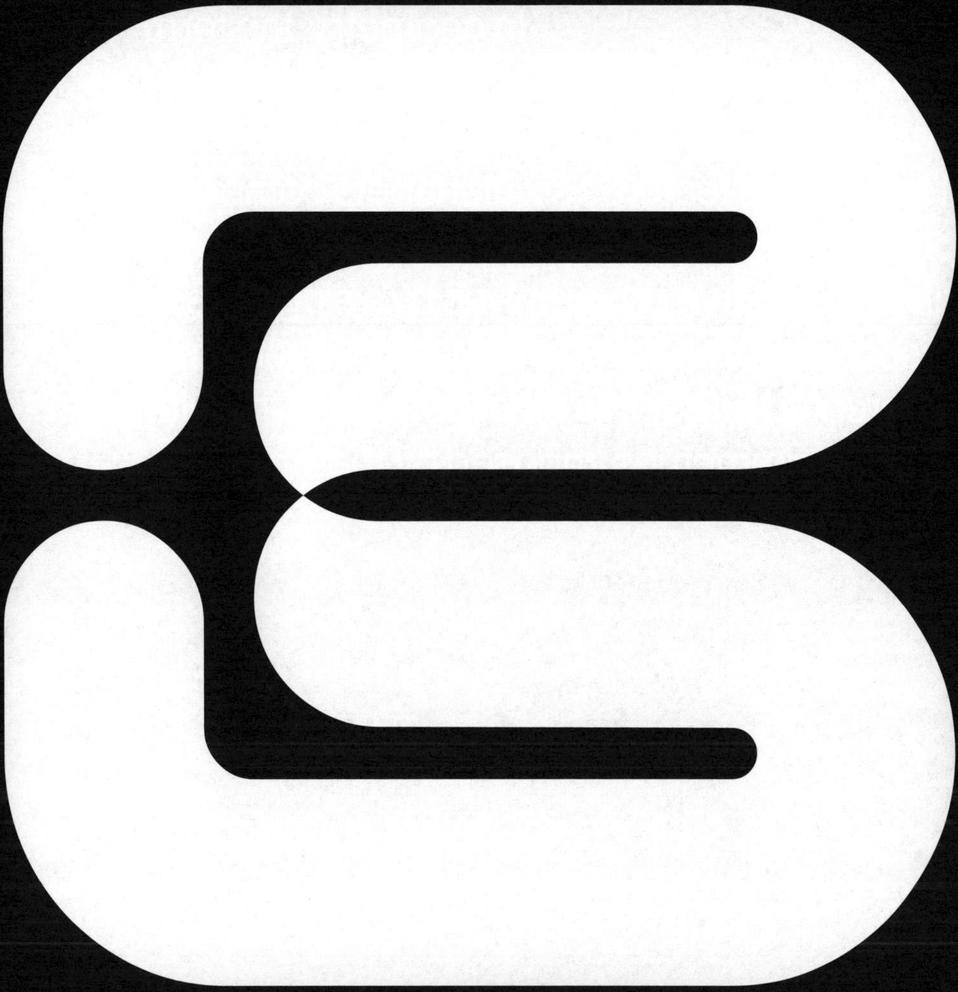

065

In geometry, the term bisection refers to the division of objects into two equal parts, typically by a bisecting line or bisector. This section features six alphabets composed of perfectly symmetrical letterforms that are each divided into two equal halves by a single bisector. Bisect explores the ways in which letterforms can be created under this strict constraint, resulting in natural symmetries imposed by the limitation.

Bisect is also the name of a geometric type system designed by Natasha Lucas and published by MuirMcNeil in 2018. While Lucas's system also employs a two-part structure, the letterforms are not limited to perfectly equal segments.

B.A

An all-caps alphabet with letters formed of two equal congruent parts bisected by a single line.*

Bravo India Sierra
Echo Charlie Tango

s. 53
l. 53
t. 0

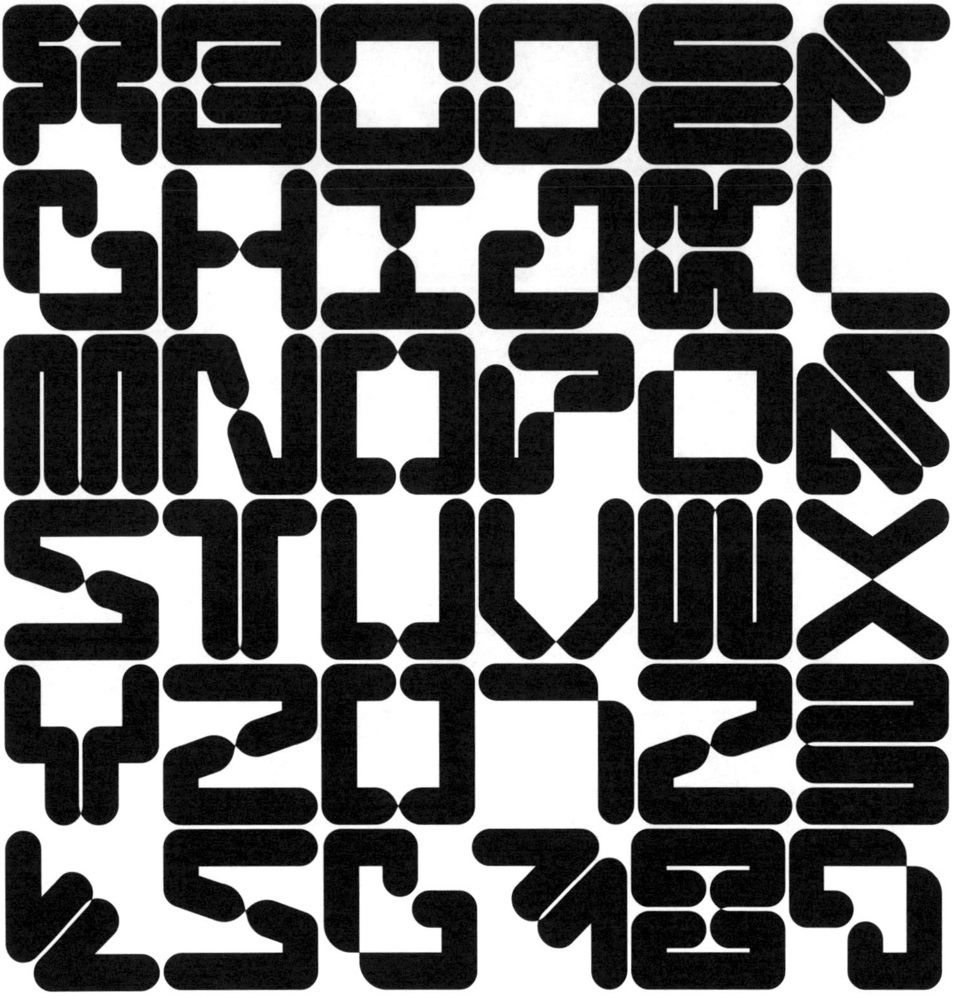

B.A

A–Z, 0–9

s. 62
l. 62
t. 0

AN ALL-CAPS ALPHABET WITH LETTERS FORMED OF TWO EQUAL CONGRUENT PARTS BISECTED BY A SINGLE LINE.

B.A

*

s. 34
l. 34
t. 0

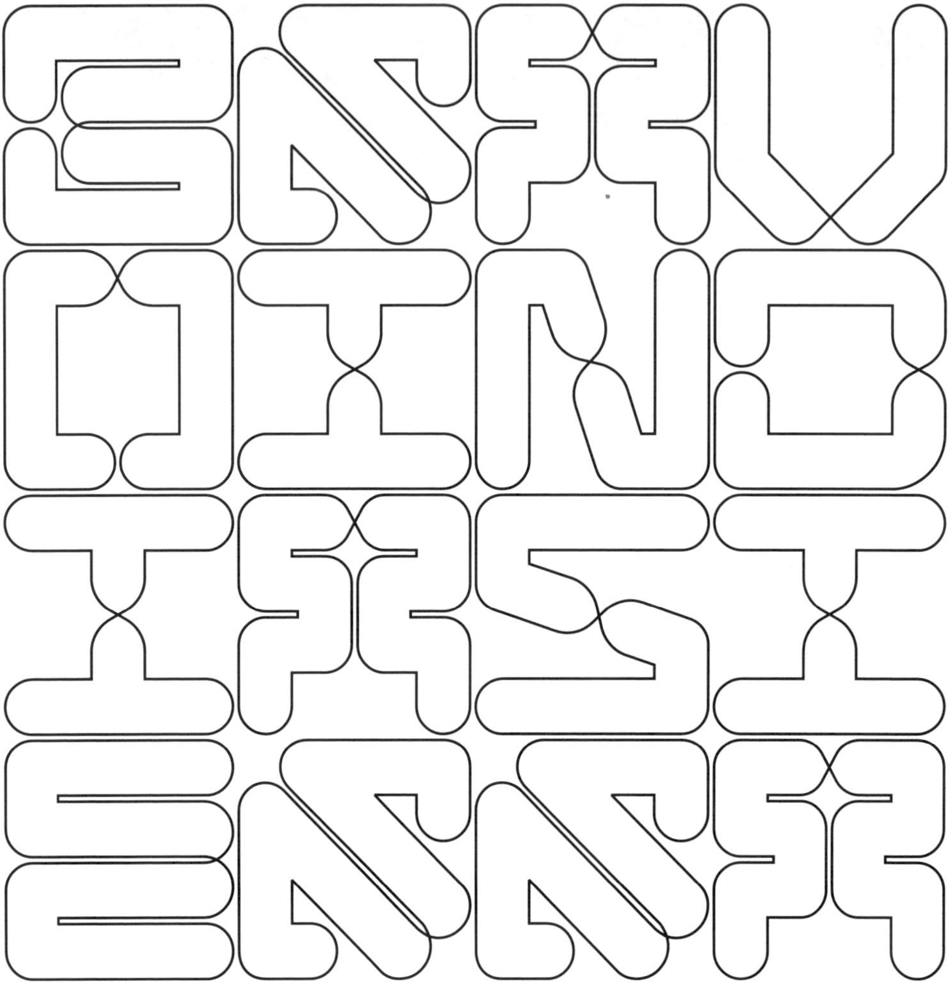

B.B An all-caps alphabet with letters formed of a single line bisecting two equal congruent parts

Bravo India Sierra

s. 92
l. 92
t. 0

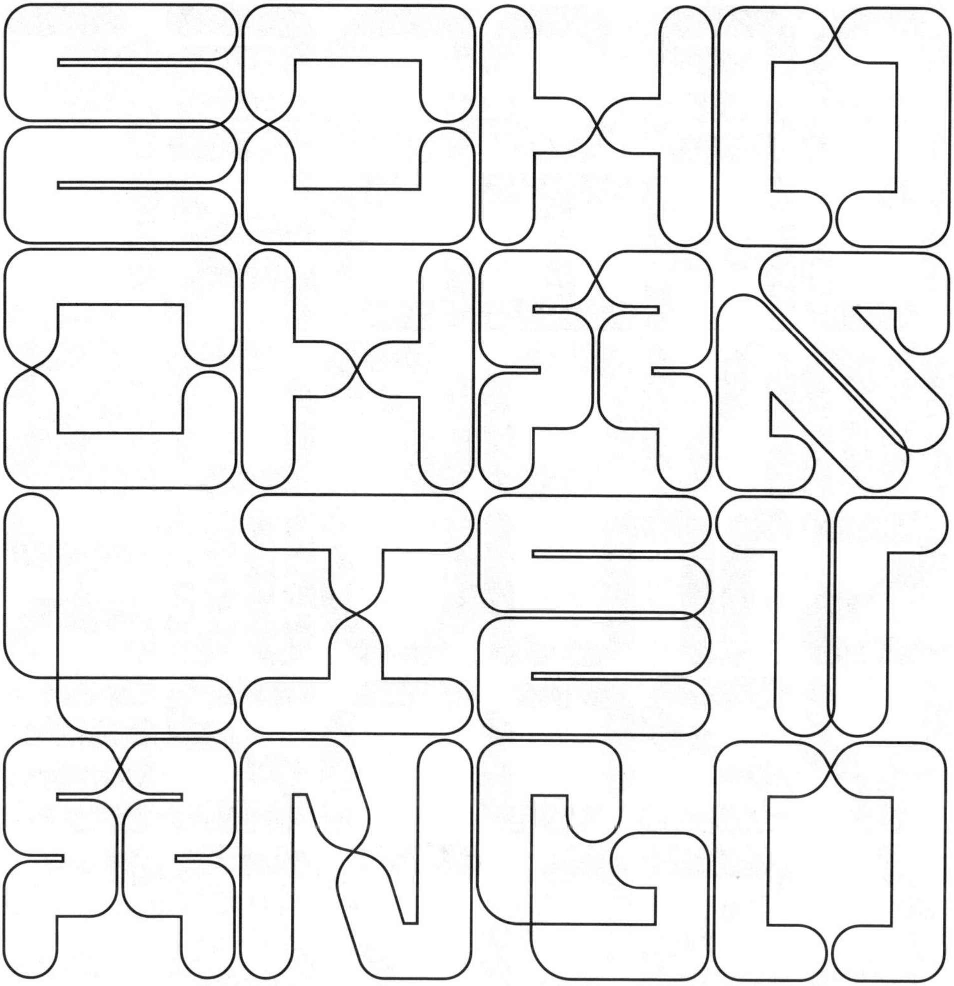

B.B

Echo Charlie Tango

s. 92
l. 92
t. 0

B.C

An all-caps alphabet with letters formed of two equal congruent parts bisected by a single curved line*

A–Z, 0–9

s. 63
l. 63
t. 0

AN ALL-CAPS ALPHABET WITH LETTERS FORMED OF TWO EQUAL CONGRUENT PARTS BISECTED BY A SINGLE CURVED LINE.

B.C

*

s. 34
l. 34
t. 0

B.D A heavy all-caps alphabet with letters formed of two equal congruent parts bisected by a single curved line

A–T

s. 74
l. 76
t. 0

UVWX
YZ01
2345
6789

B.E

U–Z, 0–9

s. 74
l. 76
t. 0

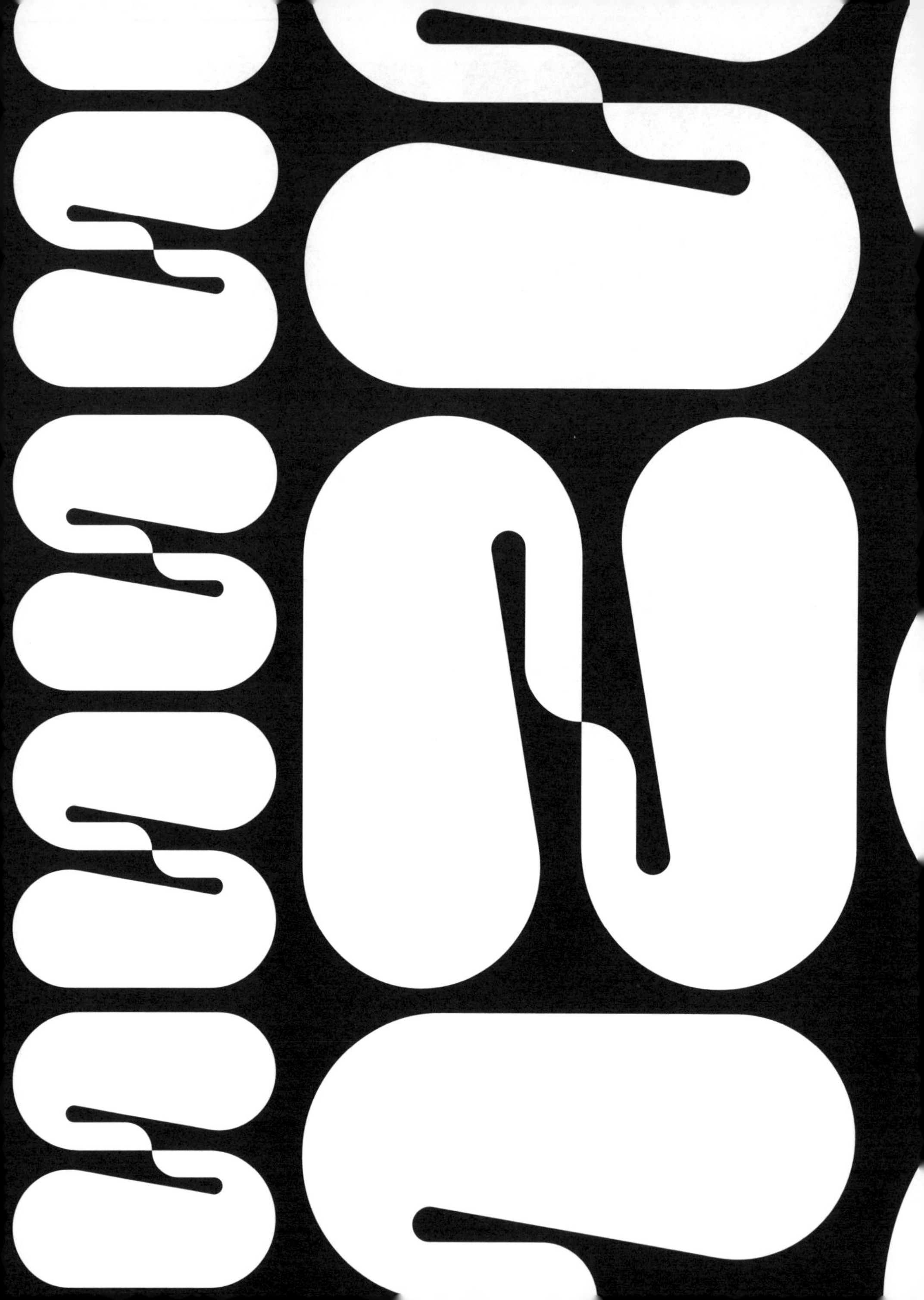

B Bisect

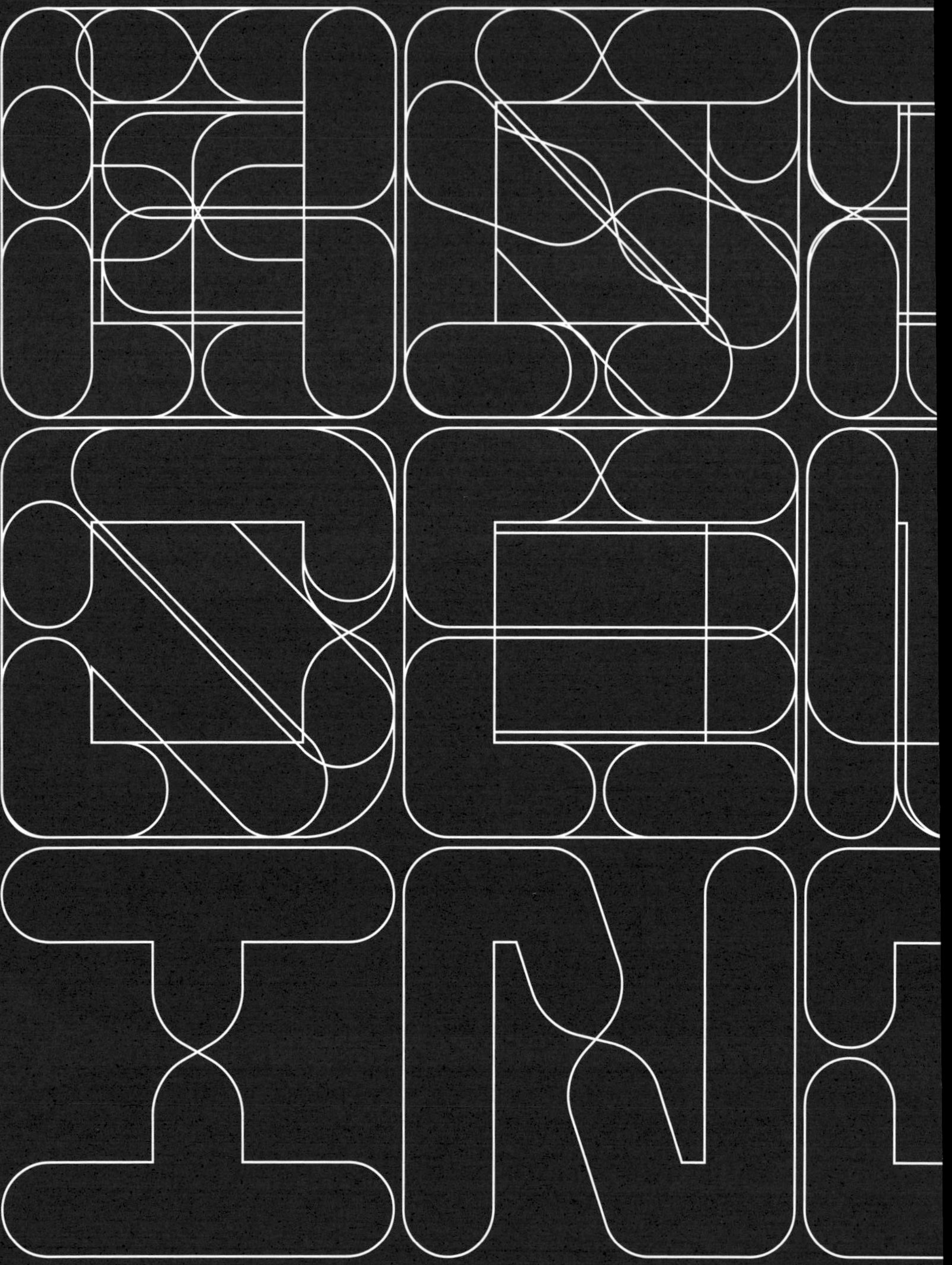

B Bisect

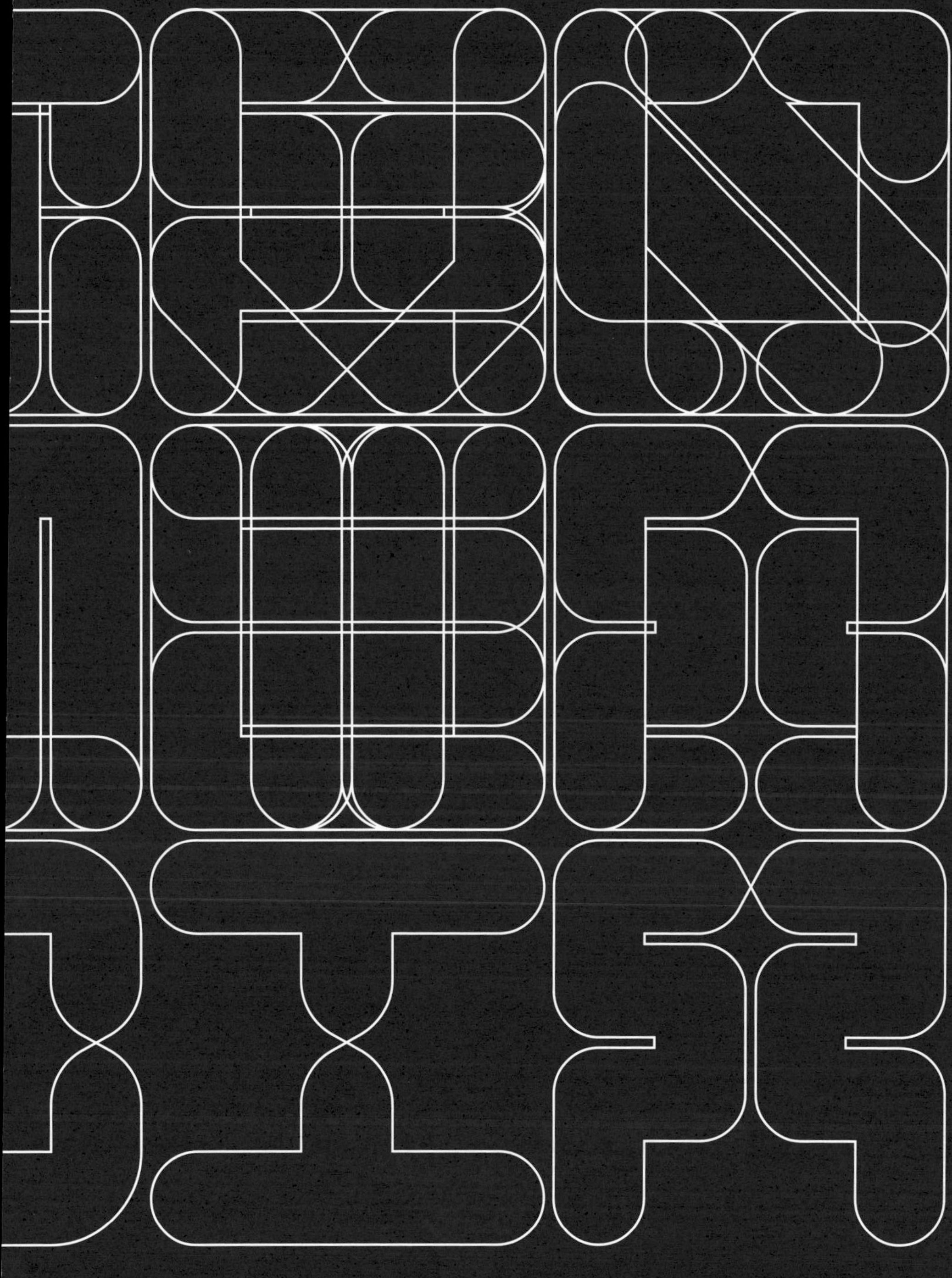

B Bisect

B Bisect

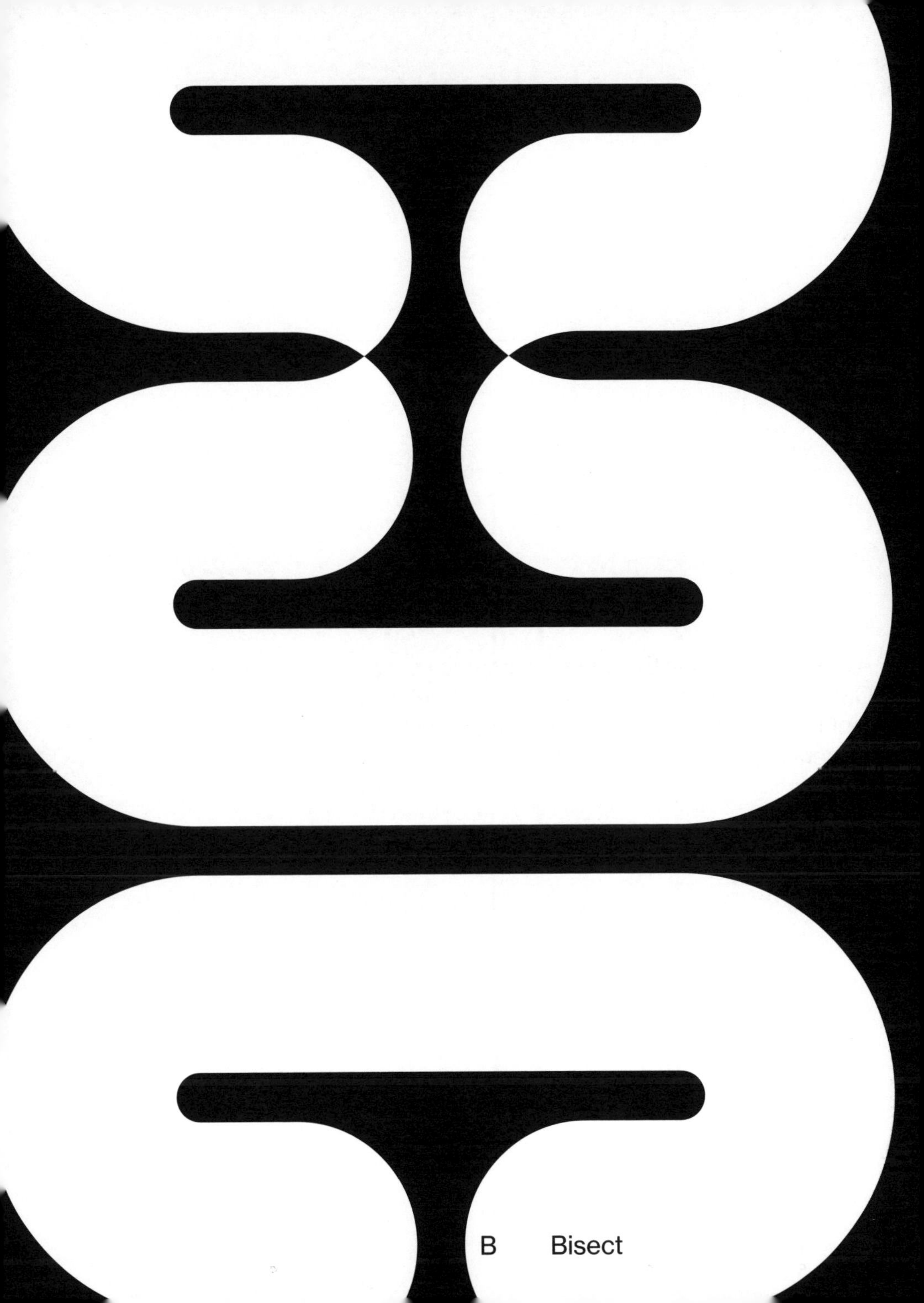

B Bisect

Section Notes:

All alphabets within Bisect were created using Glyphs font software and consist of single weight font files that include uppercase characters, numerals, and basic punctuation.

A geometric response to traditional cursive handwriting, Cursive explores scripts in which each letter is formed using a single, continuous stroke, allowing for extensive variations in complexity and structure. Each Cursive alphabet interprets this constraint differently, demonstrating the diverse possibilities within the cursive framework. The unifying rule throughout is that each letter must be drawn with a single unbroken line which must also connect it to the next letter.

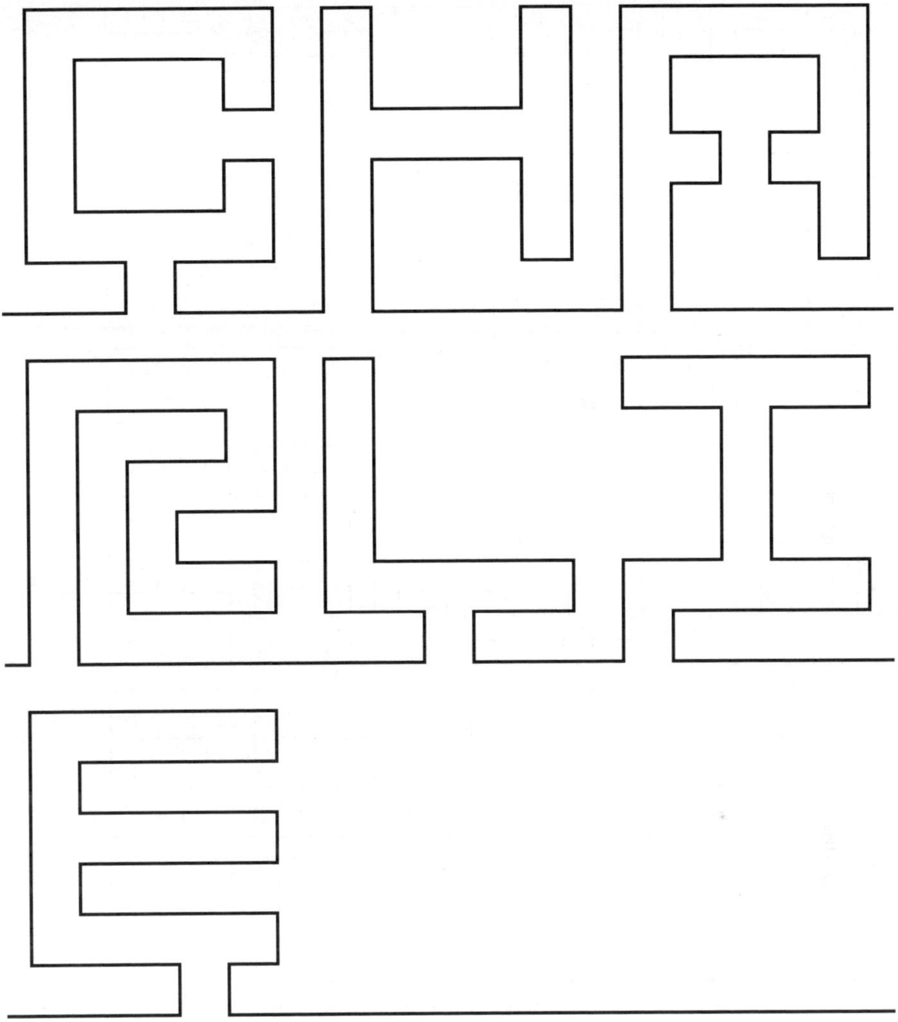

C.A

A continuous single line all-caps cursive
with a squared path

Charlie

s. 120
l. 120
t. 0
w. 100

C.A

A–Z, 0-9

s. 60
l. 60
t. 0
w. 100

C.B A continuous single line all-caps cursive with a squared intersecting path

A–Z, 0-9

s. 60
l. 60
t. 0
w. 200

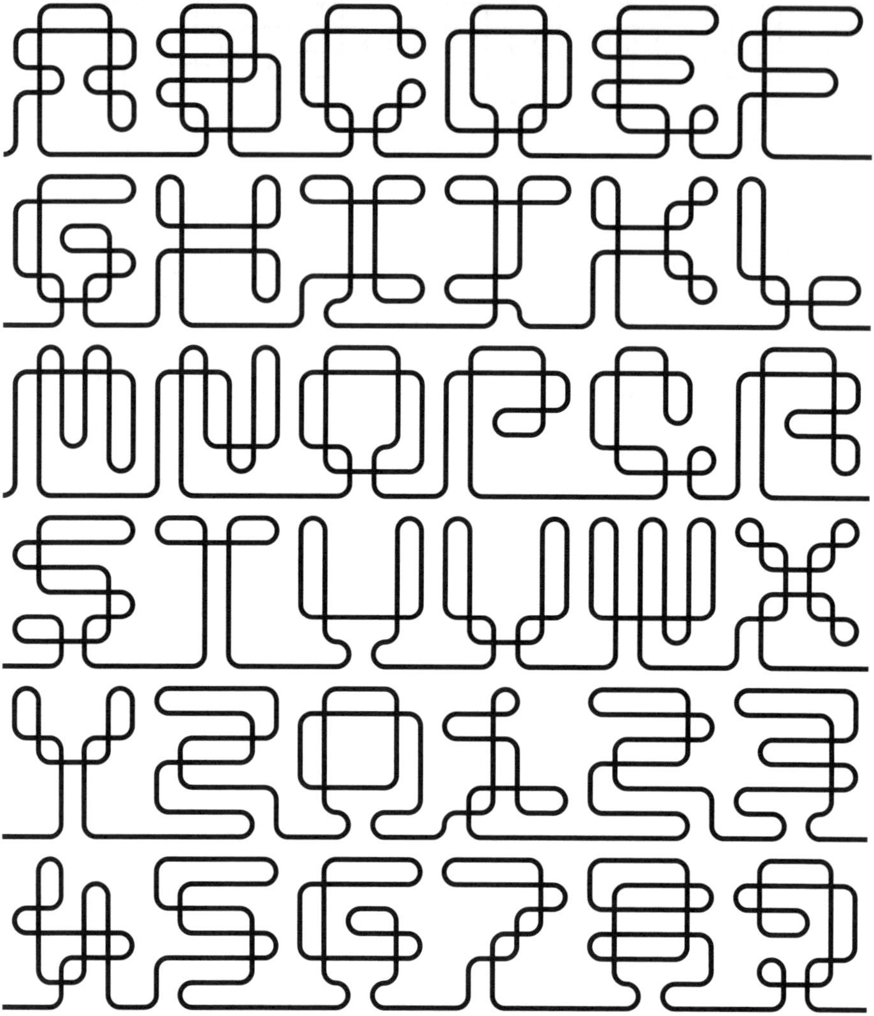

C.C A continuous single line all-caps cursive with a rounded intersecting path

A–Z, 0-9

s. 60
l. 60
t. 0
w. 300

C.D A continuous single line all-caps cursive with a squared coiling path

Uniform

s. 120
l. 120
t. 0
w. 300

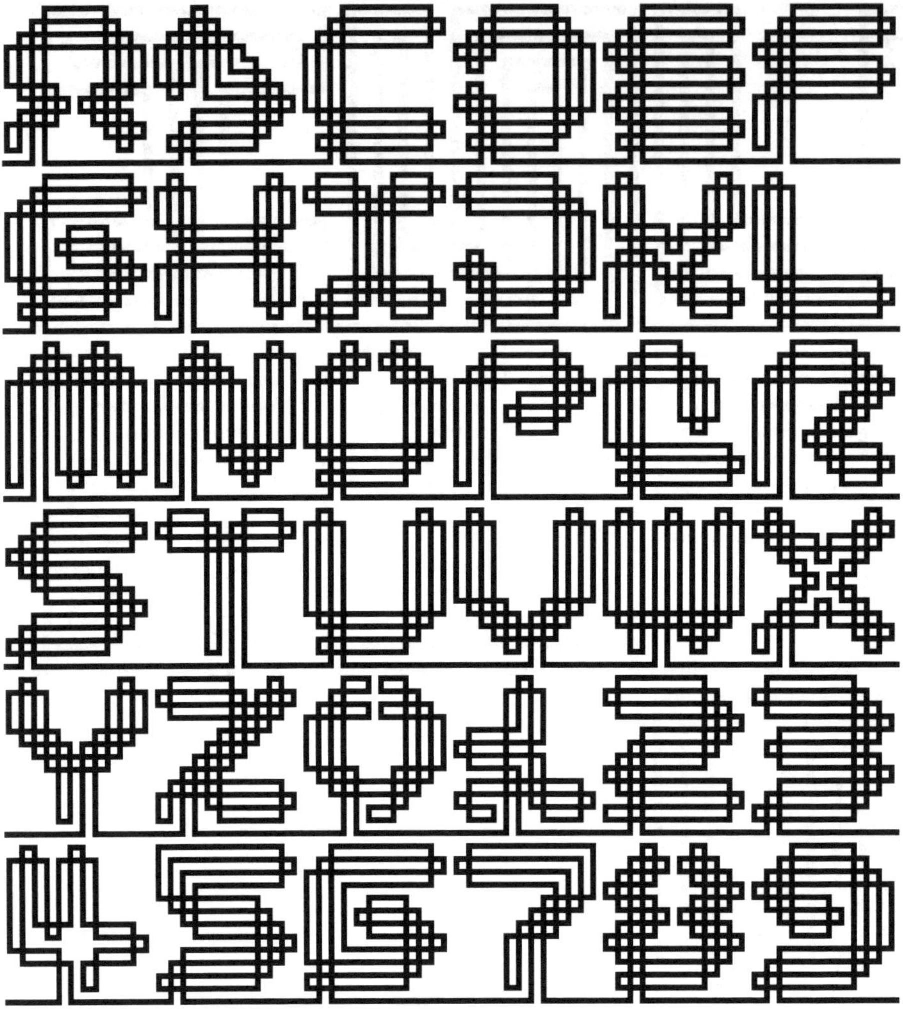

C.E

A continuous single line all-caps cursive with a detailed squared intertwining path

A–Z, 0-9

s. 60
l. 60
t. 0
w. 400

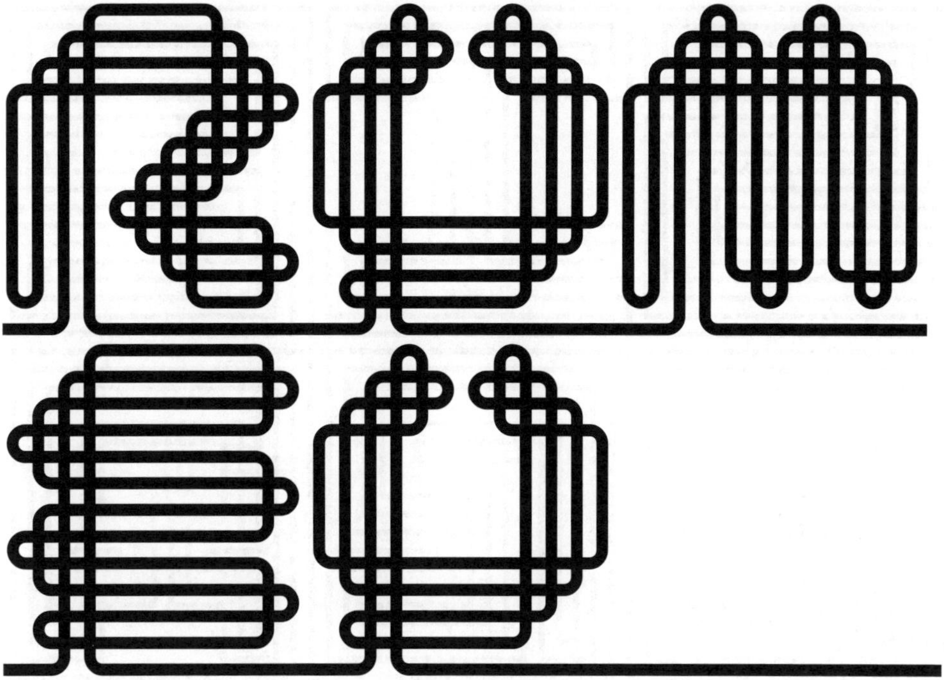

C.F

A continuous single line all-caps cursive with a detailed rounded intertwining path

Romeo

s. 120
l. 120
t. 0
w. 400

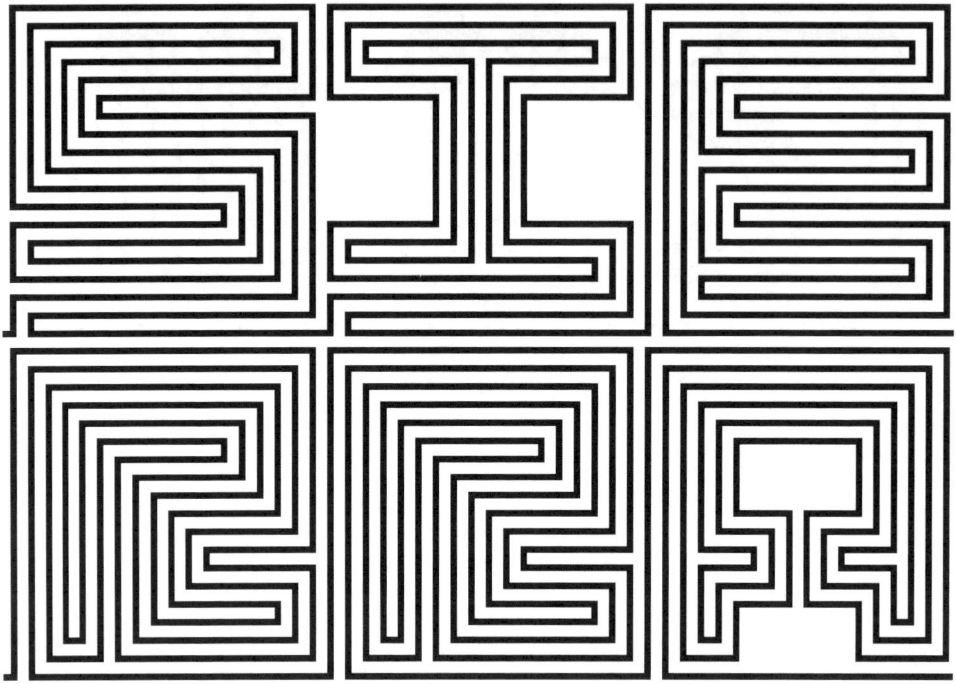

C.G A continuous single line all-caps cursive with an intricate squared coiling path

Sierra

s. 120
l. 120
t. 0
w. 300

A CONTINUOUS
SINGLE LINE
ALL-CAPS
CURSIVE WITH
A INTRICATE
SQUARED
INTERTWINING
PATH

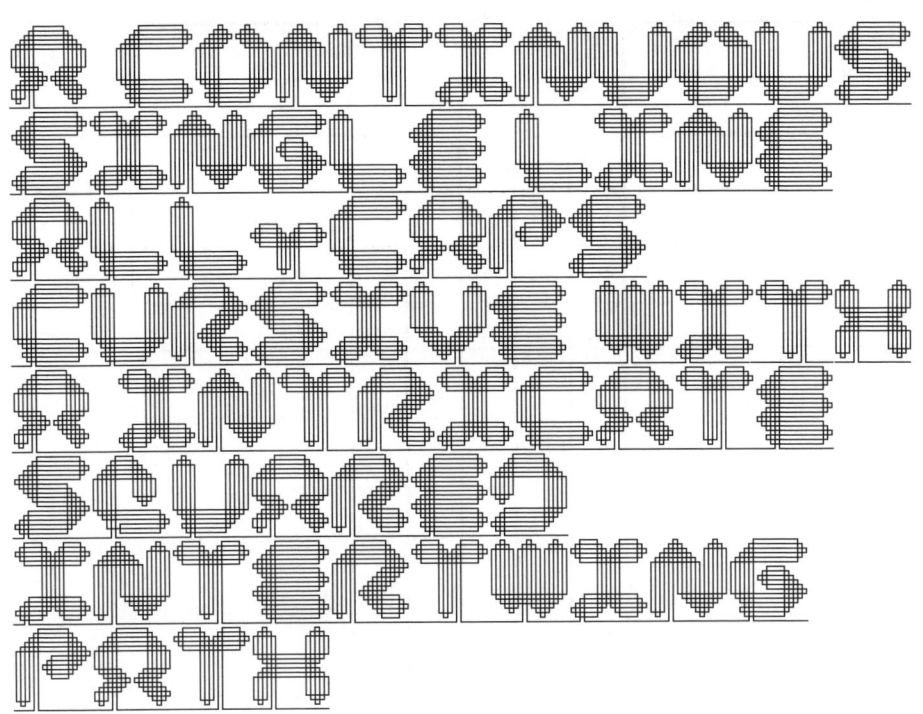

C.H A continuous single line all-caps cursive
with an intricate squared intertwining path*

*

s. 34
l. 34
t. 0
w. 200

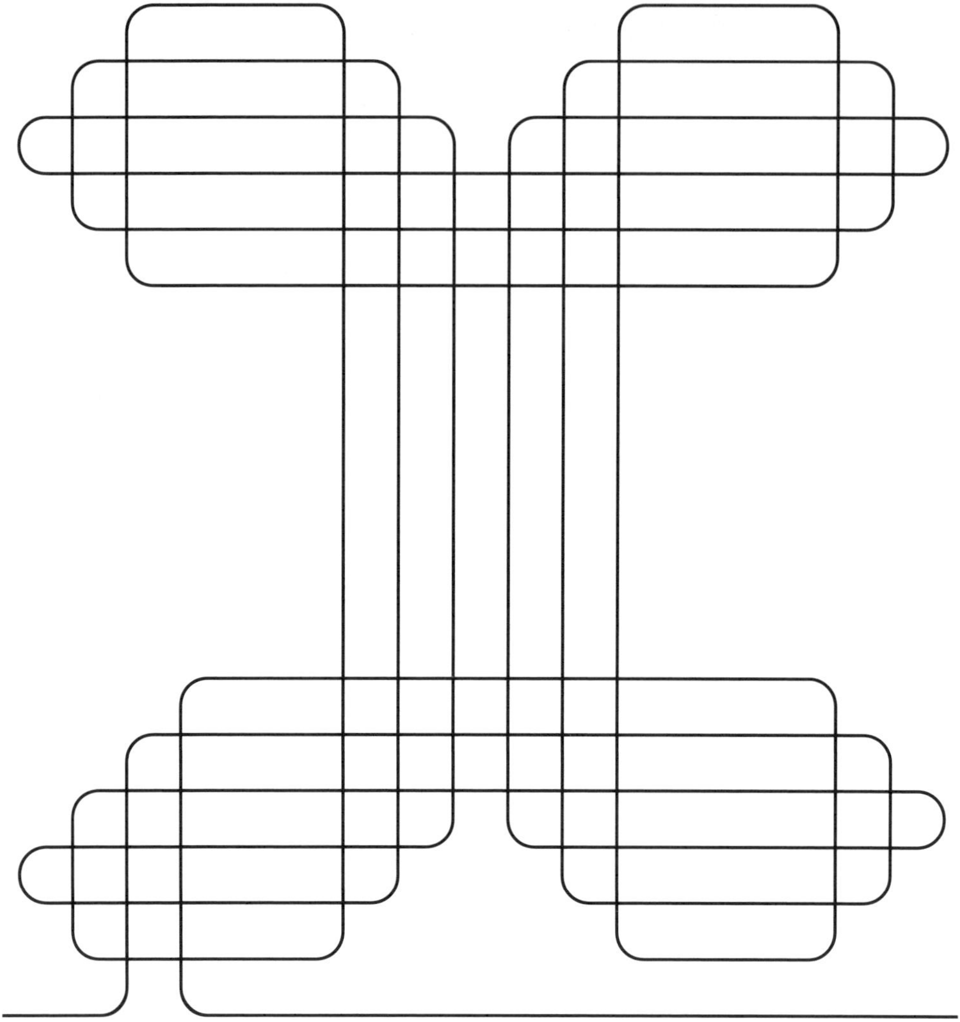

C.I

A continuous single line all-caps cursive with an intricate rounded intertwining path

I

s. 400
l. 400
t. 0
w. 40

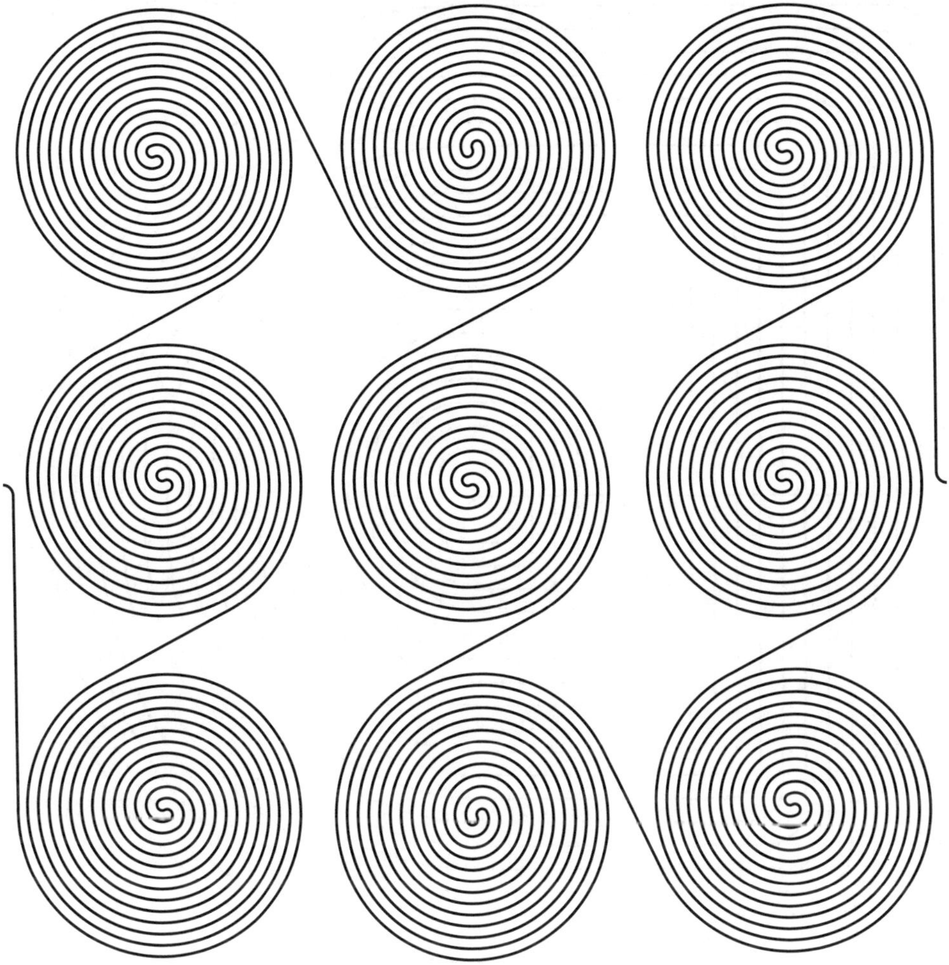

C.J A continuous single line all-caps cursive with a 9 phase labyrinthine path

N

s. 400
l. 400
t. 0

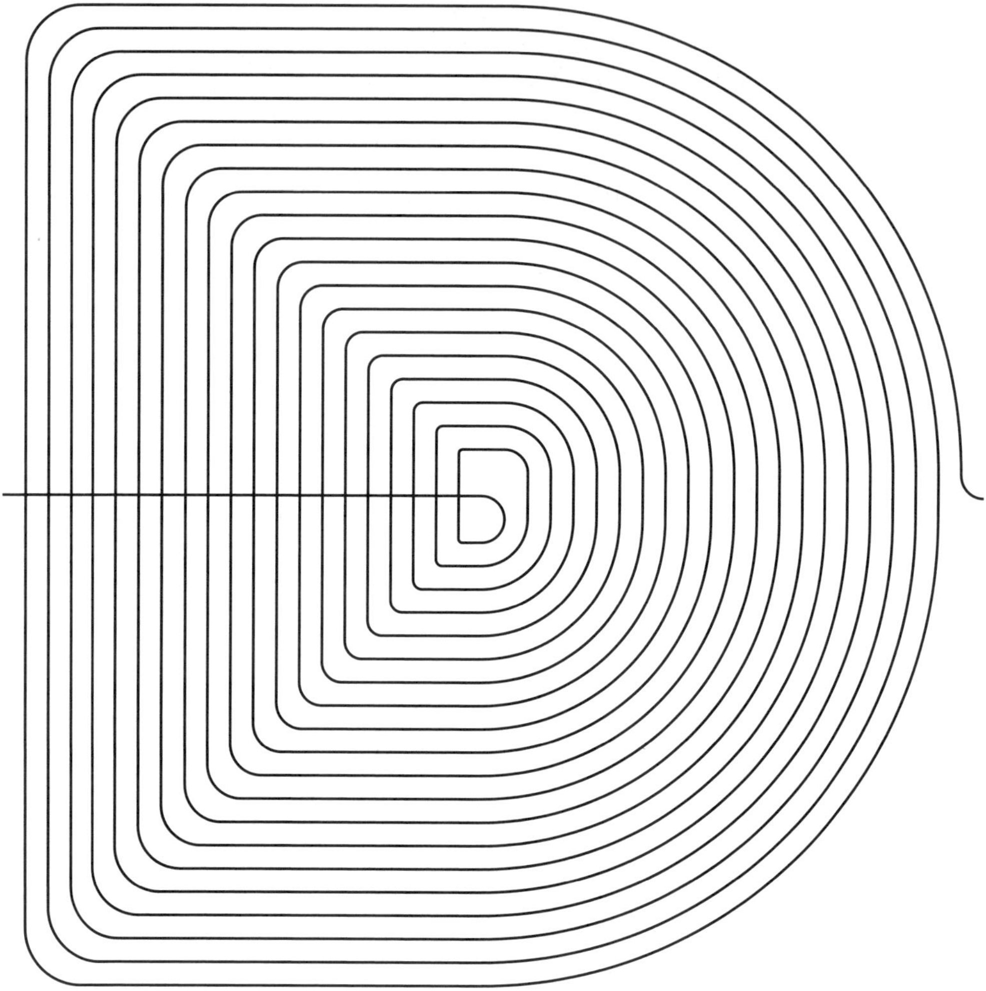

C.K A continuous single line cursive with a highly intricate coiling path

D

s. 400
l. 400
t. 0

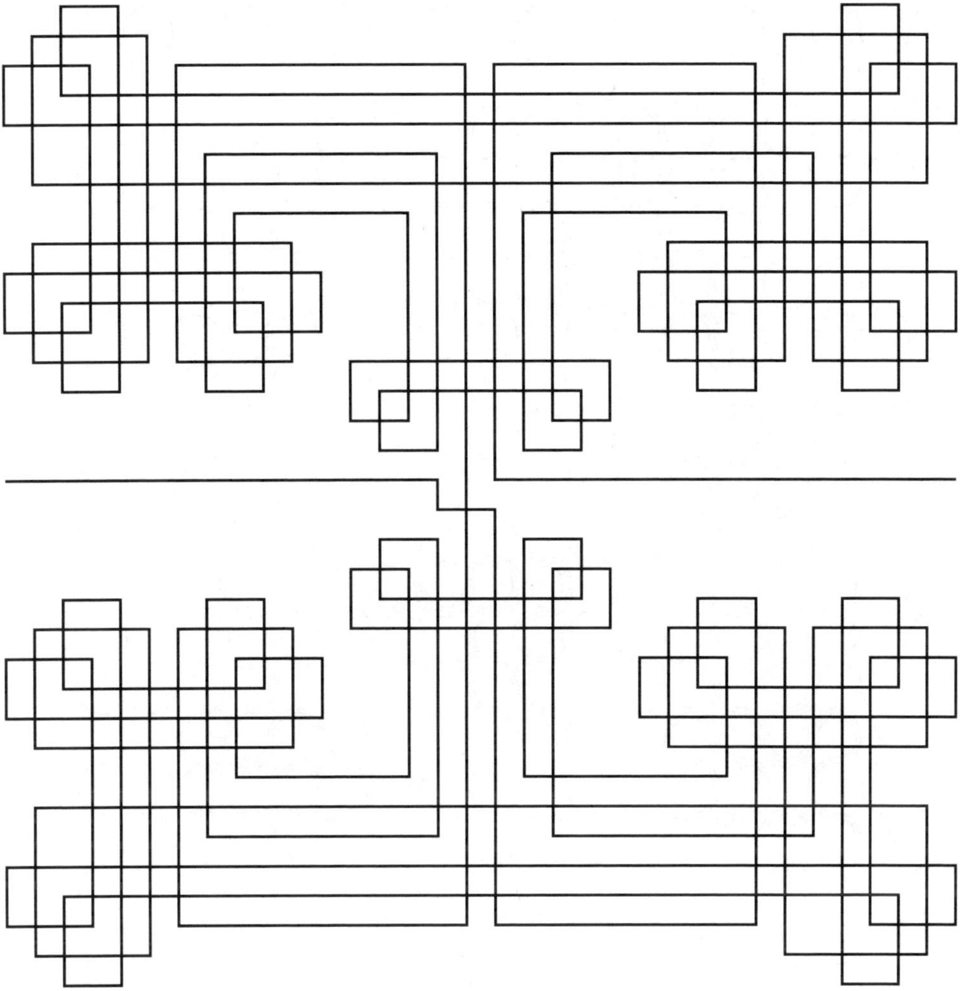

C.L

A continuous single line cursive with a detailed squared decoratively intersecting path

I

s. 400
l. 400
t. 0

C.M A continuous single line cursive with letterforms revealed though a skirting, meandering sine wave path

A

s. 400
l. 400
t. 0

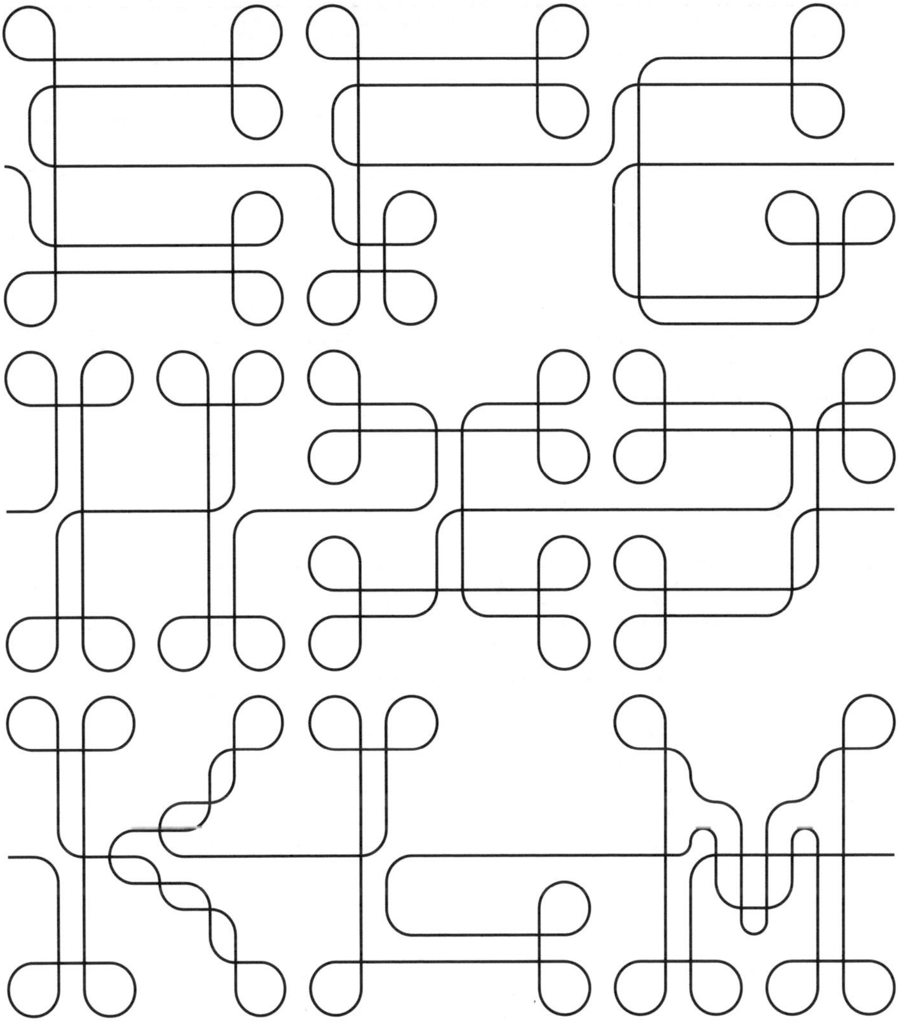

C.N A continuous single line cursive with a rounded decoratively intersecting path

E–M

s. 120
l. 120
t. 0

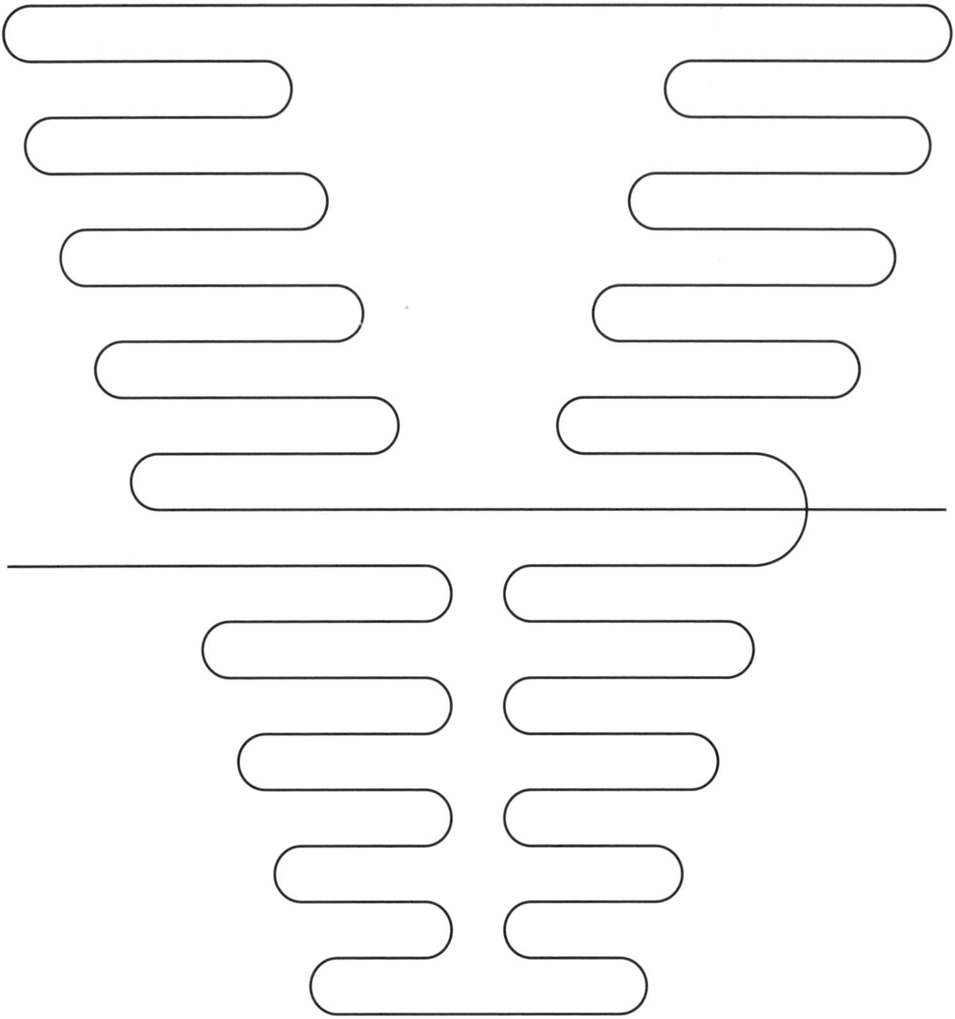

C.O A continuous single line all-caps cursive with a horizontally meandering path

V

s. 400
l. 400
t. 0

C.P A continuous single line cursive with an 8 phases horizontally coiling path

I

s. 400
l. 400
t. 0

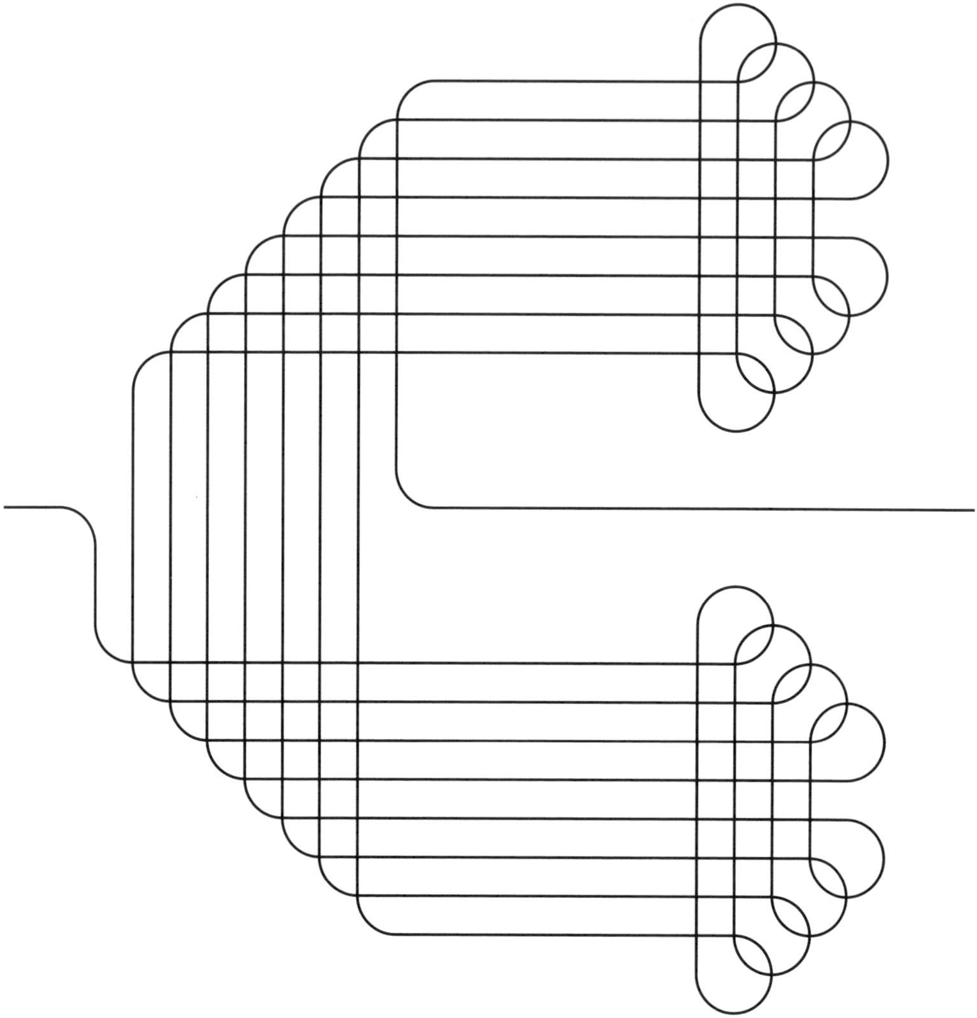

C.Q A continuous single line cursive with a detailed rounded decoratively intersecting path

C

s. 400
l. 400
t. 0

C.R A continuous single line cursive with letterforms revealed through a shifting, meandering sine wave path

T

s. 400
l. 400
t. 0

C.S

A continuous single line all-caps cursive
with an intricate rounded mazing path

O

s. 400
l. 400
t. 0

C.T A continuous single line cursive with letterforms revealed though a concentrated, meandering sine wave path

R

s. 400
l. 400
t. 0

C.T

Echo

s. 190
l. 190
t. 0

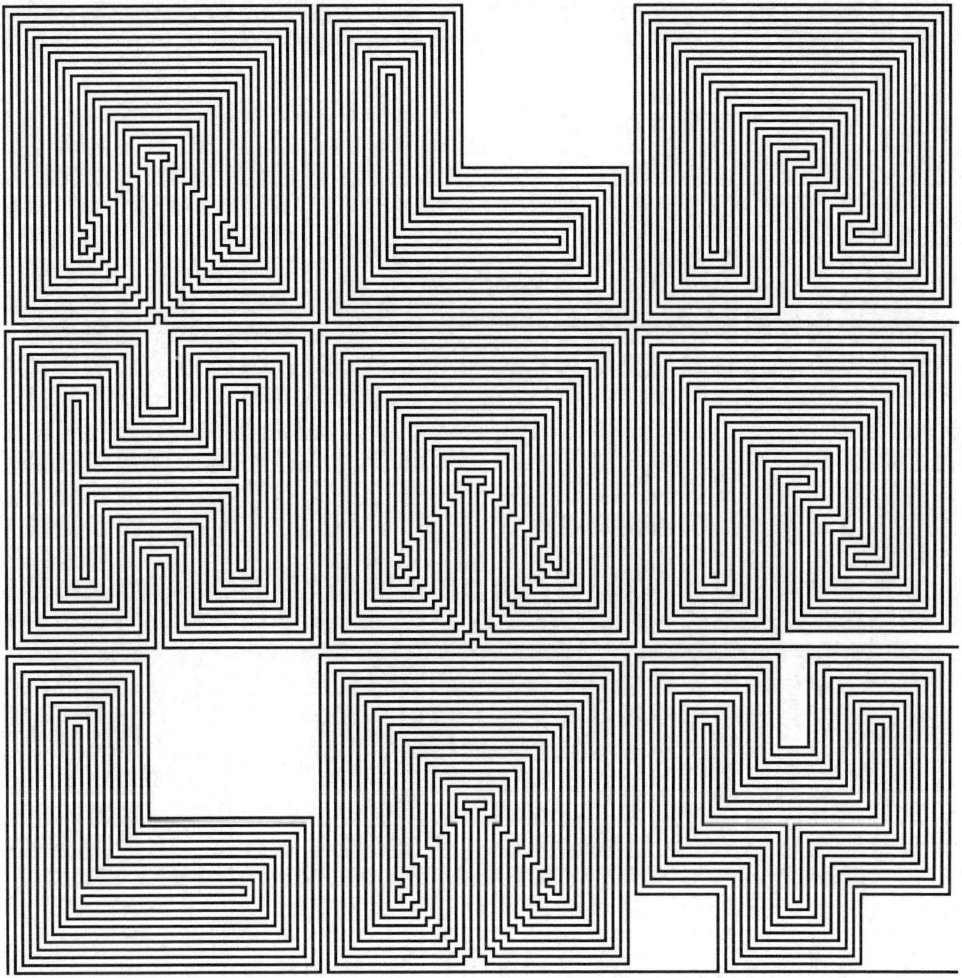

C.U A continuous single line all-caps cursive with an intricate squared coiling path

AlphaPlay

s. 120
l. 120
t. 0

C Cursive

C Cursive

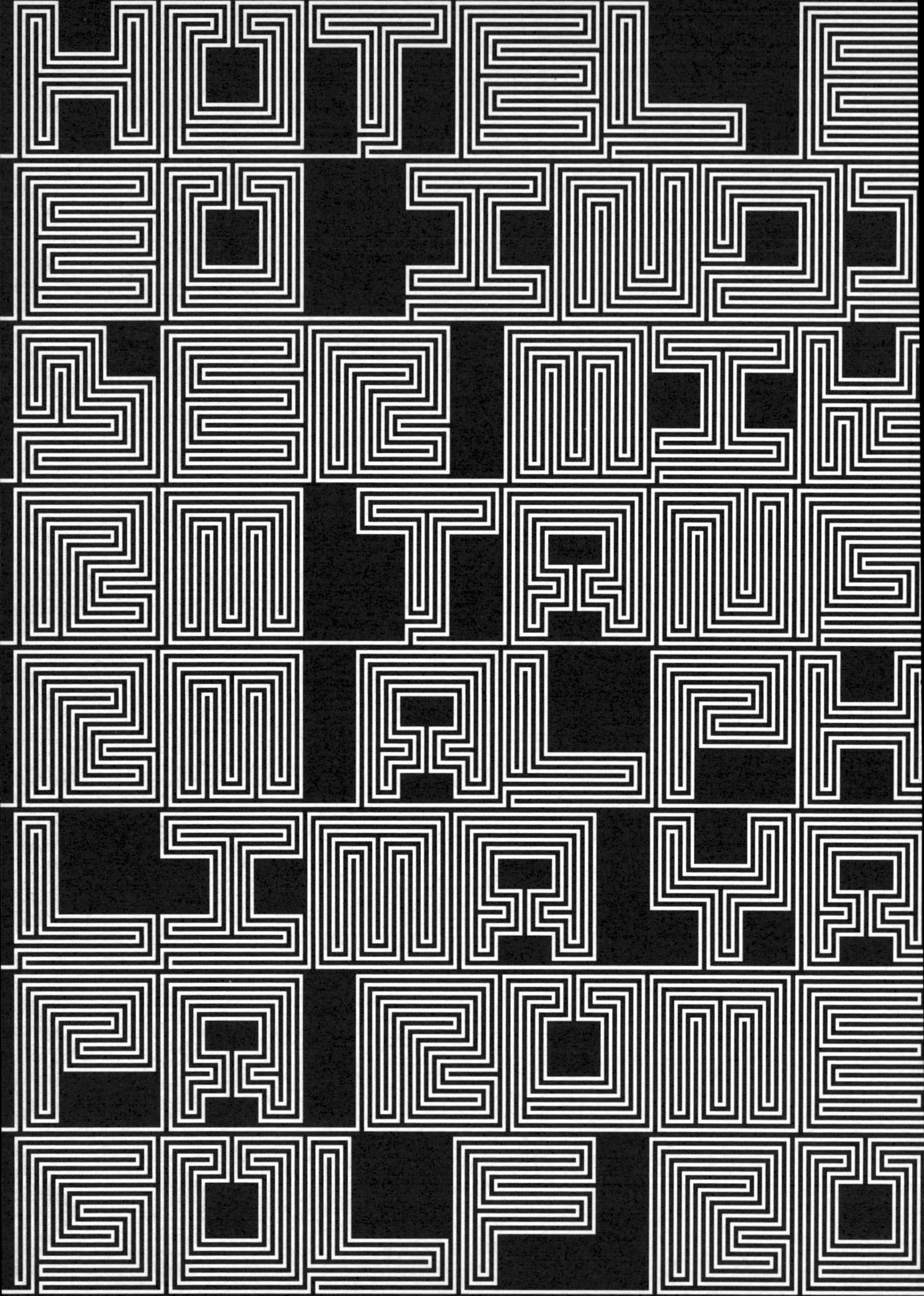
HOTEL

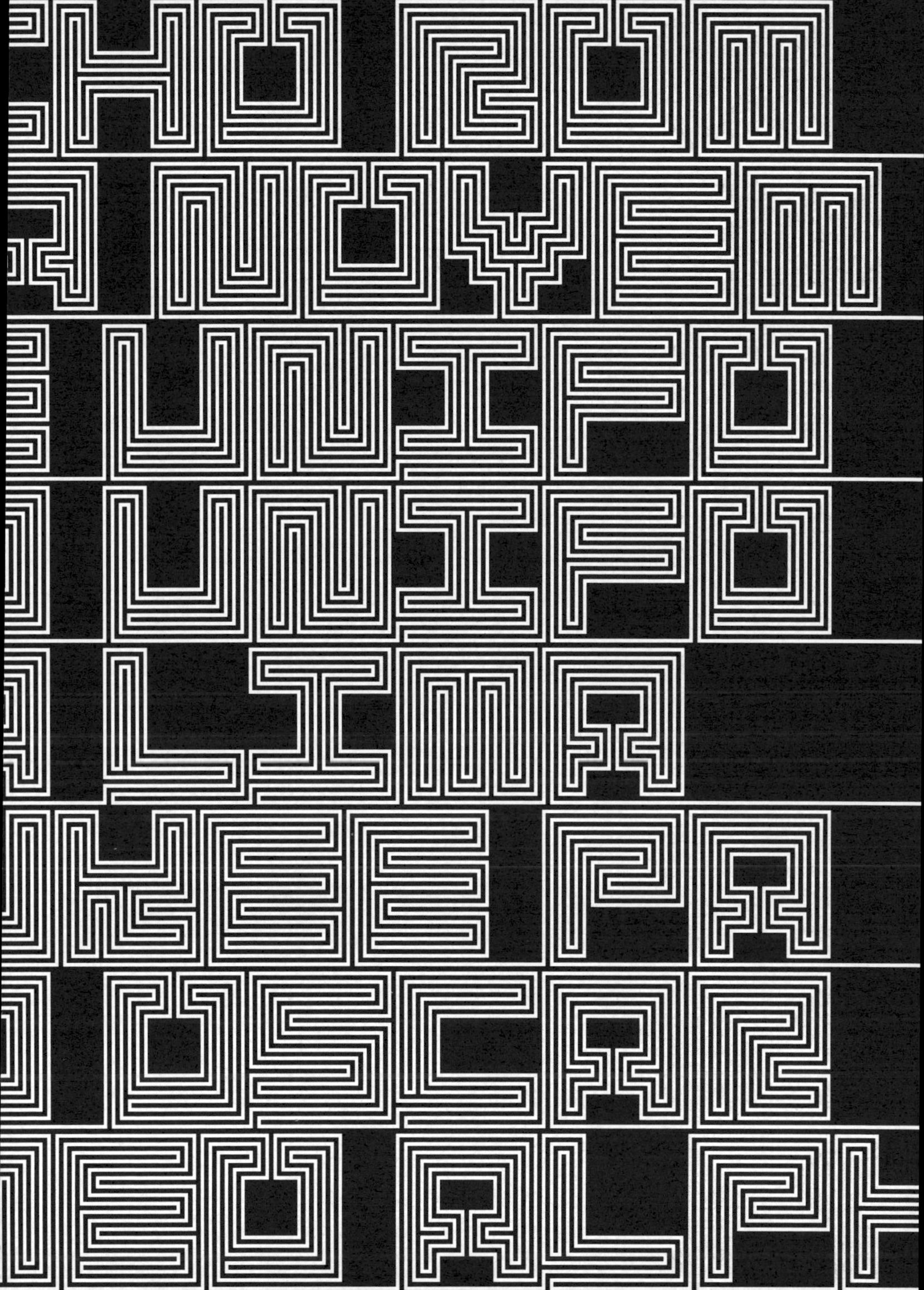

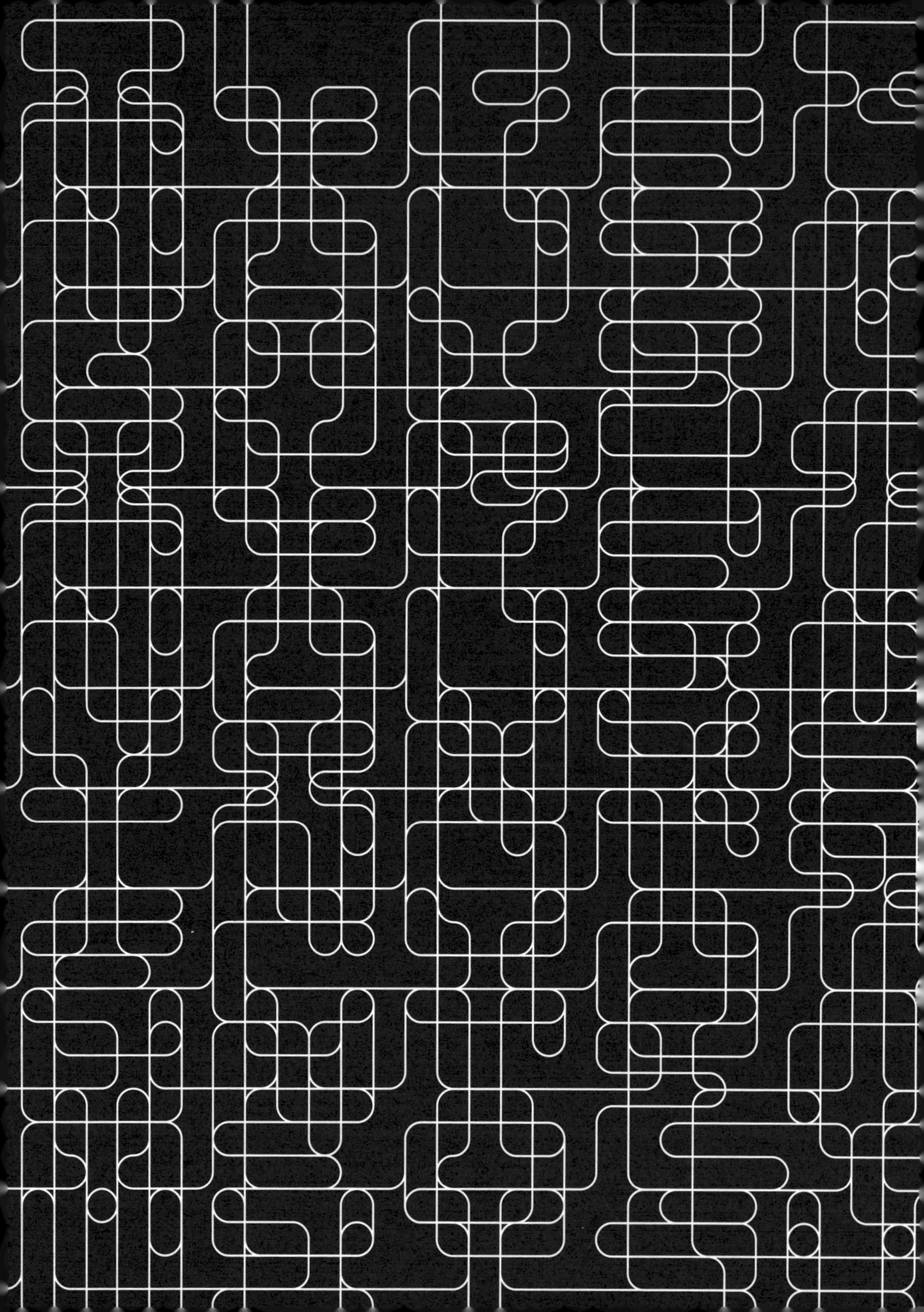

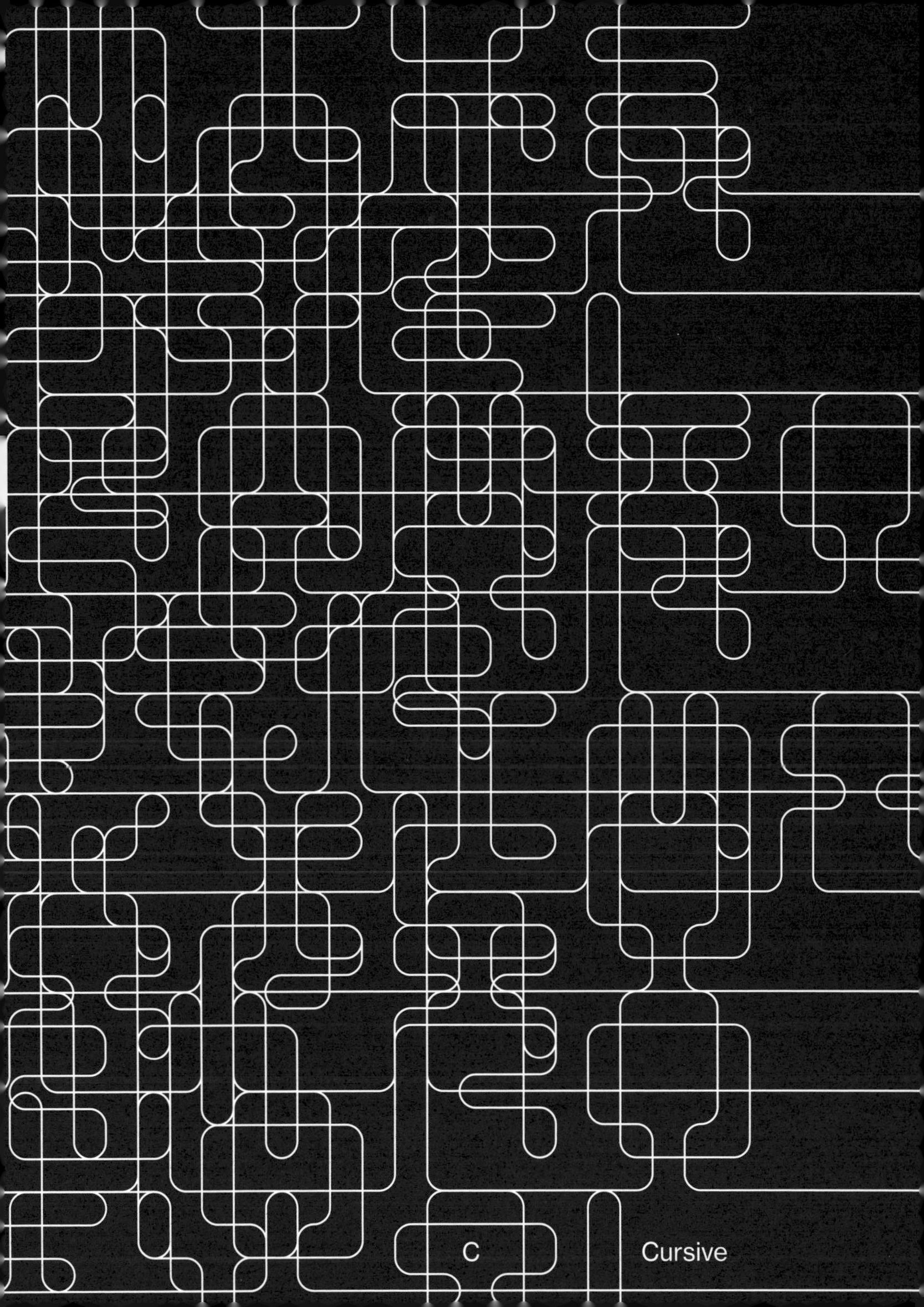

C

Cursive

Section Notes:

Created using Glyphs, C.A, C.B, C.C, C.D, C.E, C.F, C.G, C.H, C.I, C.N, and C.T are fully developed alphabets that include uppercase and lowercase charcter sets, numerals, and basic punctuation. Each is available as a variable font with adjustable weight. C.K, C.L, C.M, C.O, C.P, C.Q, C.R, C.S, and C.U exist only as conceptual sketches—preliminary designs illustrating potential directions for the cursive theme.

D

The Dimensional set of alphabets investigates various methods for simulating three-dimensional letterforms within two-dimensional spaces. These optical illusions are achieved through various visual strategies, including graphical projection to mimic depth, tonal variation to suggest light and shade, and effects that simulate focal distortions where letters appear more or less blurred. These approaches generate receding and projecting forms that challenge the flatness of the page.

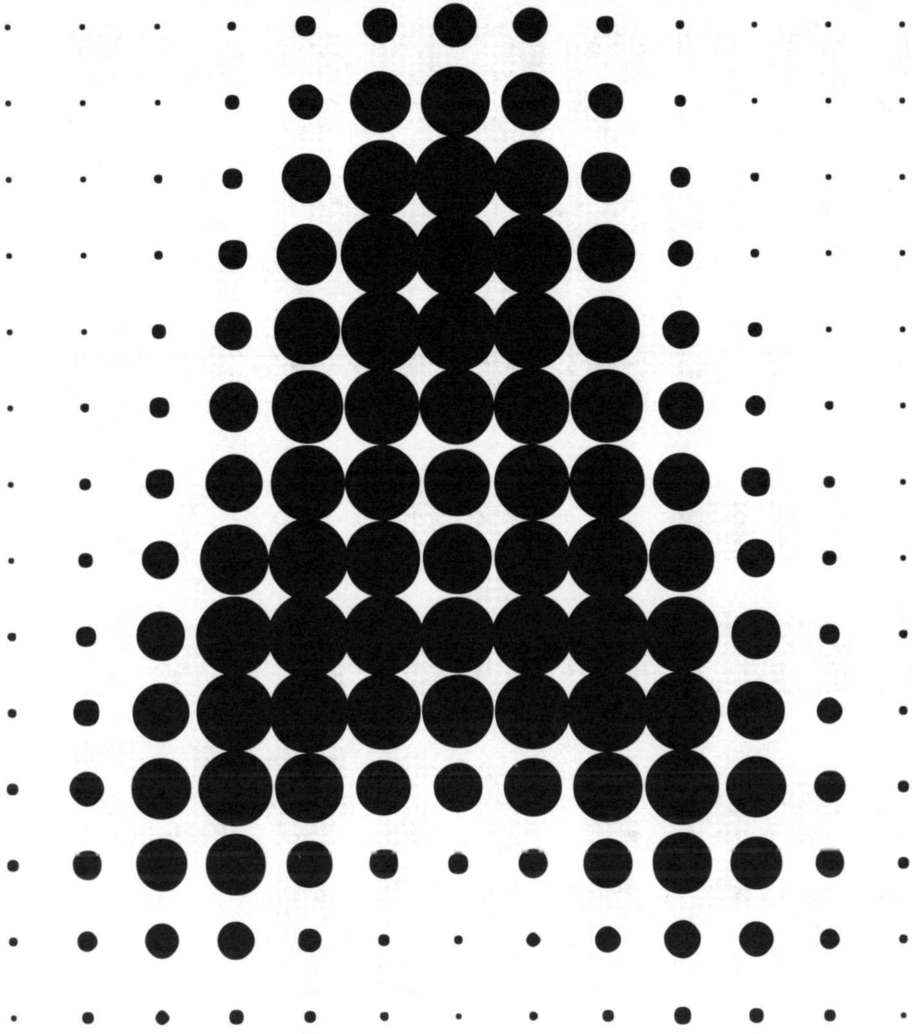

D.A A

A dimensional serif to sans serif alphabet rendered to appear blurred through a square dot grid

A

s. 550
l. 550
t. 0
sr. 0
b. 100

D.A

A–Z a–z 0–9

s. 68
l. 52
t. 0
sf. 0
bl. 100

D.A

A–Z a–z 0–9

s. 68
l. 52
t. 0
sf. 100
bl. 100

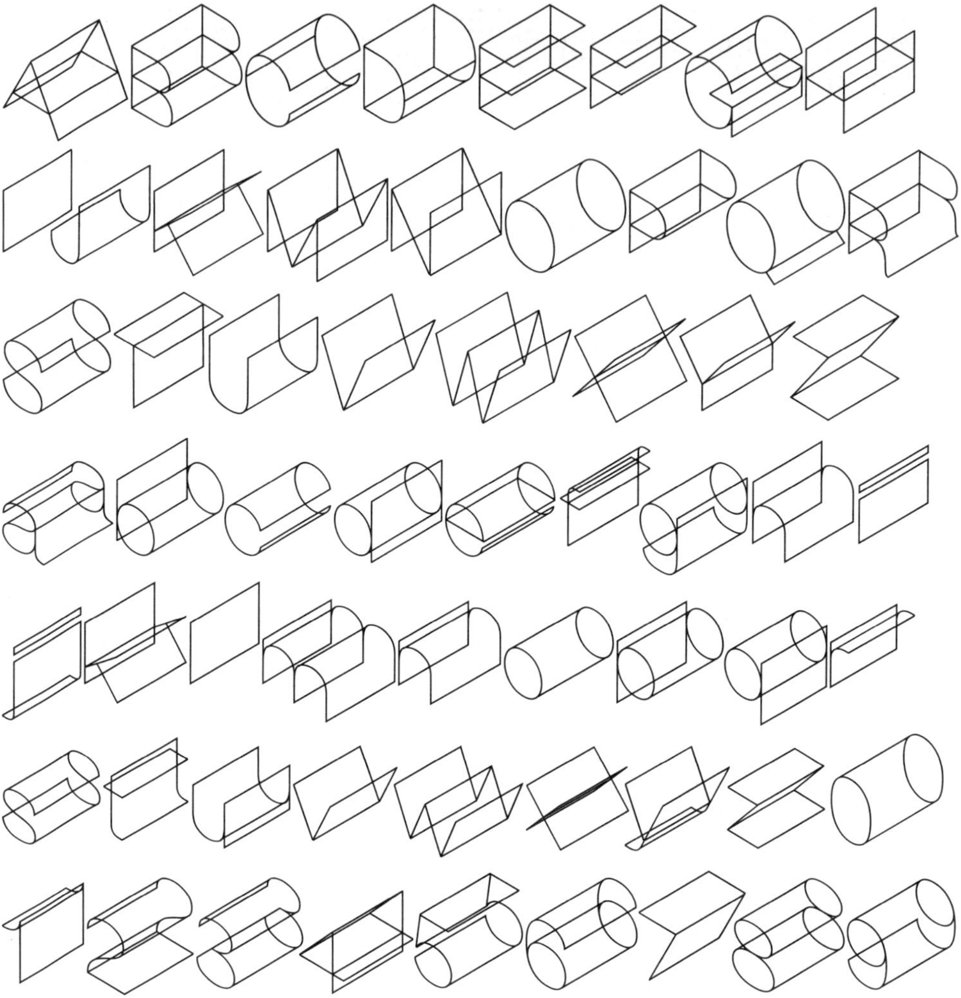

D.B A dimensional alphabet formed of a wireframe extruded through an isometric projection from its YZ plane

A–Z a–z 0–9

s. 55
l. 54
t. 0
w. 300
e. 100

D.C

A dimensional alphabet formed of a wireframe extruded through an isometric projection from its XY plane

A–Z a–z 0–9

s. 63
l. 62
t. 0
w. 300
e. 100

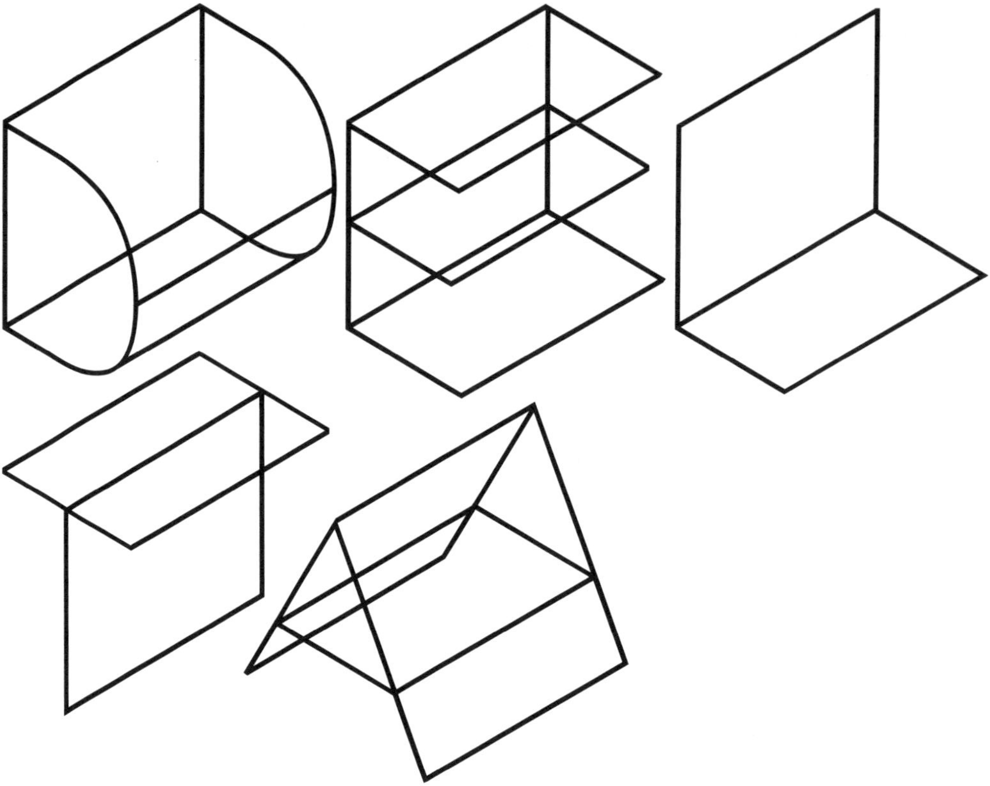

D.B

Delta

s. 180
l. 130
t. 0
w. 300
e. 100

UC

D.C

India Mike Echo
November Sierra India
Oscar November
Alpha Lima

s. 70
l. 54
t. 0
w. 300
e. 100

D.D

A dimensional all-caps alphabet rendered to appear engraved through horizontal lines

A–Z 0–9

s. 63
l. 63
t. 0

D.D

Delta India Mike Echo
November

s. 63
l. 63
t. 0

SIERRA
INDIA
OSCAR
NOVEM
BER
ALPHA

D.D

Sierra India Oscar
November Alpha

s. 63
l. 63
t. 0

D.D

Lima

s. 198
l. 187
t. -40

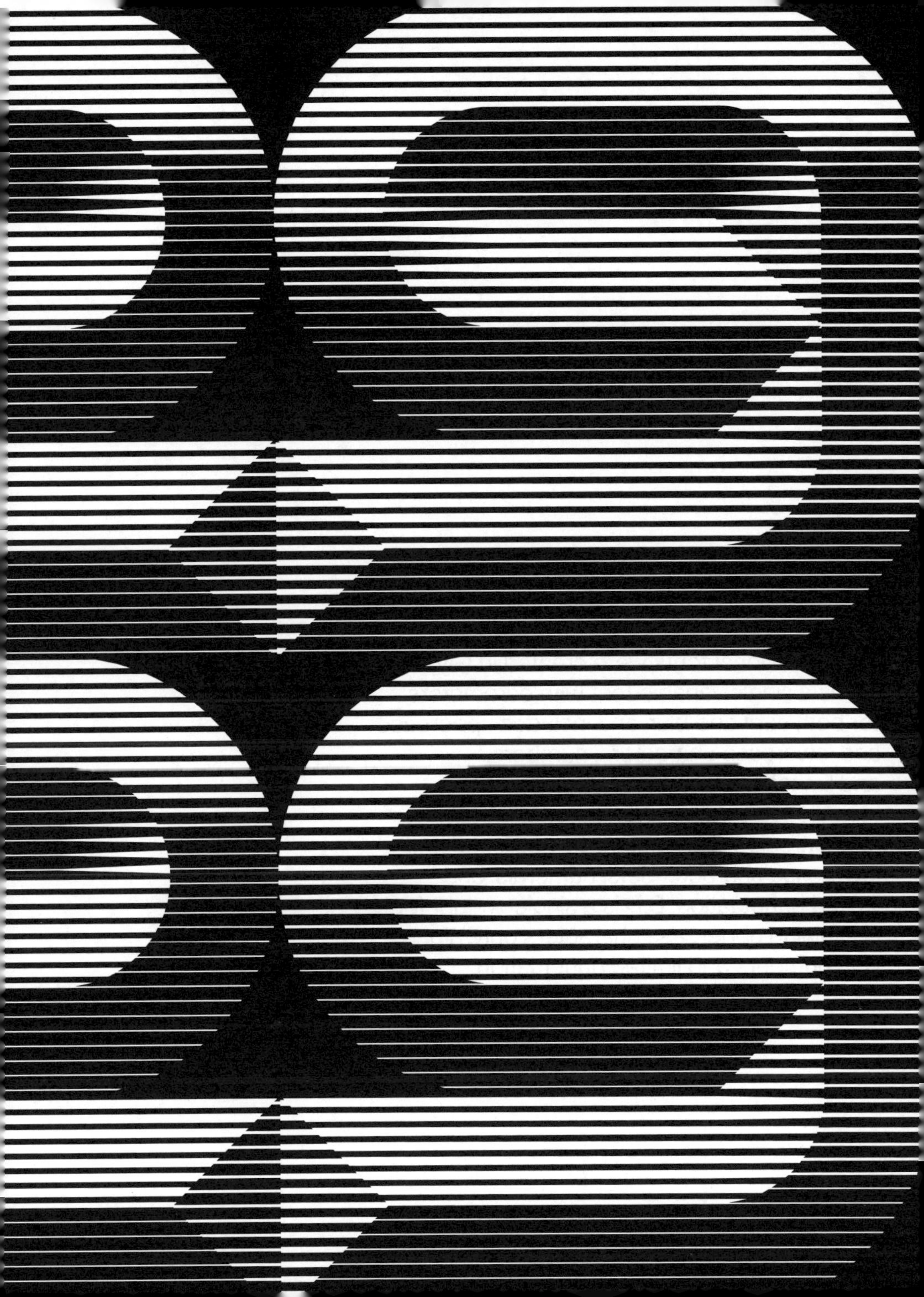

Section Notes:

All Dimensional fonts were created in Glyphs. D.A is a single variable font with parameters for both serif and blur, and includes uppercase and lowercase characters, numbers, and limited punctuation. D.B and D.C are variable fonts with parameters for weight and extrusion, also featuring uppercase and lowercase character sets, numerals, and limited punctuation. D.D is a single-weight font containing uppercase characters only, along with numbers and limited punctuation.

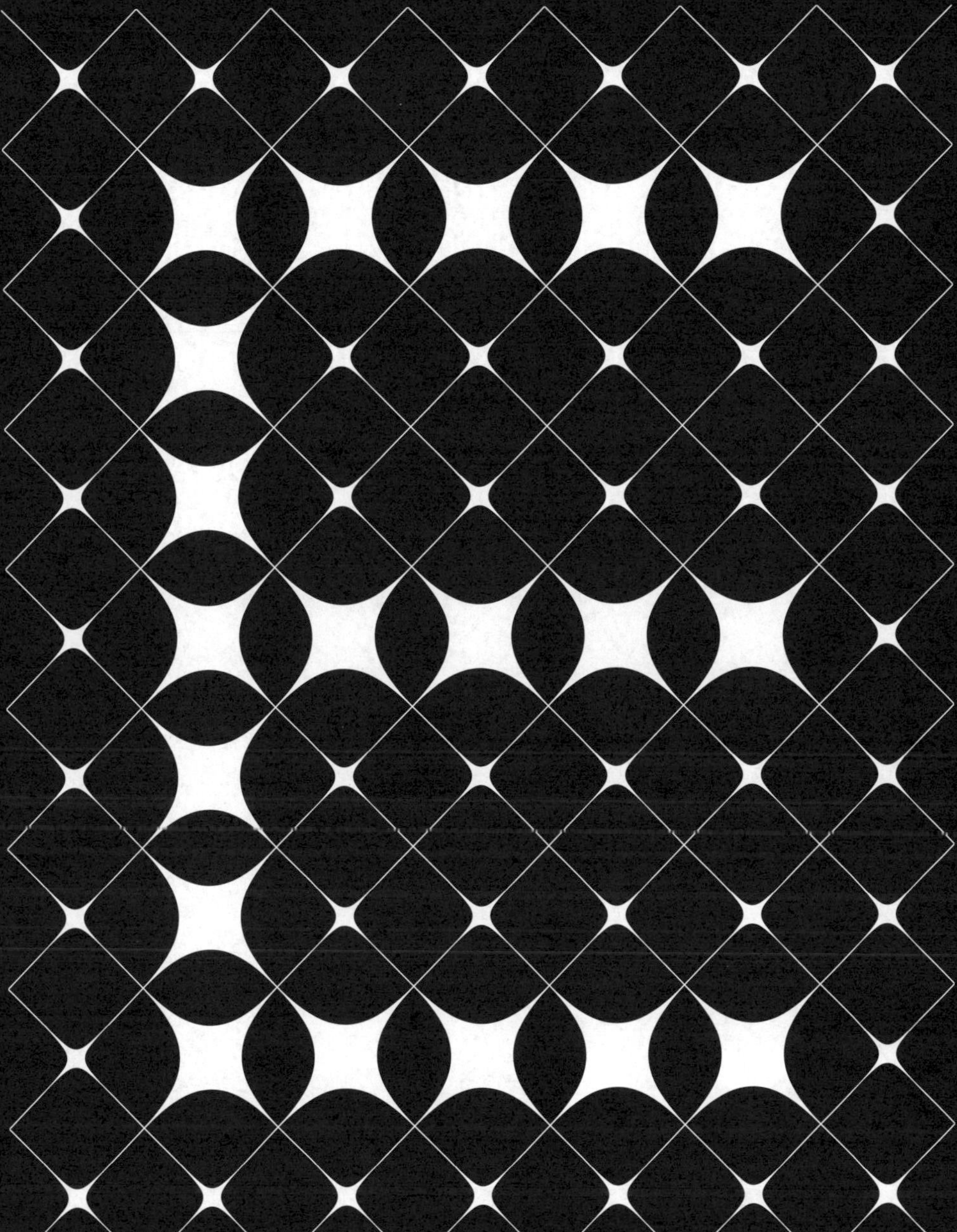

E Embedded Geometry

A series of four two-part type systems constructed from curved modular components that expand and contract to reveal characters and words. Each system consists of a foreground and background layer — a 'male' and 'female' group of components — through which letters emerge by means of variations in the density of the geometric field. As the figure-and-ground components are manipulated within a body of text, intricate visual textures emerge that maintain different degrees of emphasis even at a distance.

Superellipse:

Hyperbolic to parabolic:

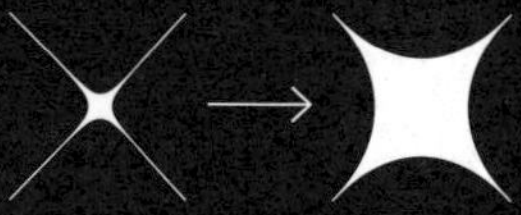

Quadrifolium

Space-filling:

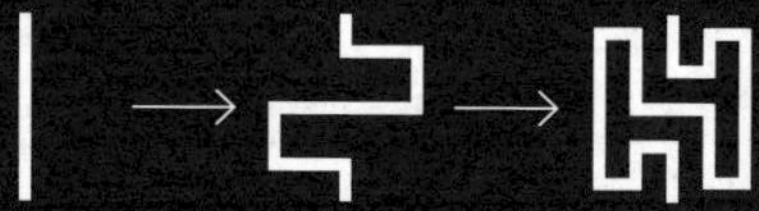

E.A

A 2-part unit based type system formed of expanding and contracting superellipse curves*

Superellipse

s. 102
l. 122
t. 0
w. ±

abcdef w. 150

ghijkl w. 200

mnopqr w. 300

stuvwx w. 500

yz0123 w. 550

456789 w. 600

E.A A

a–z 0–9

s. 53
l. 63
t. 0

w. 150

w. 200

w. 300

w. 500

w. 550

w. 600

E.A B

A–Z 0–9

s. 53
l. 63
t. 0

E.A

AaBbCcDd1234

s. 102
l. 122
t. 0
w. ±

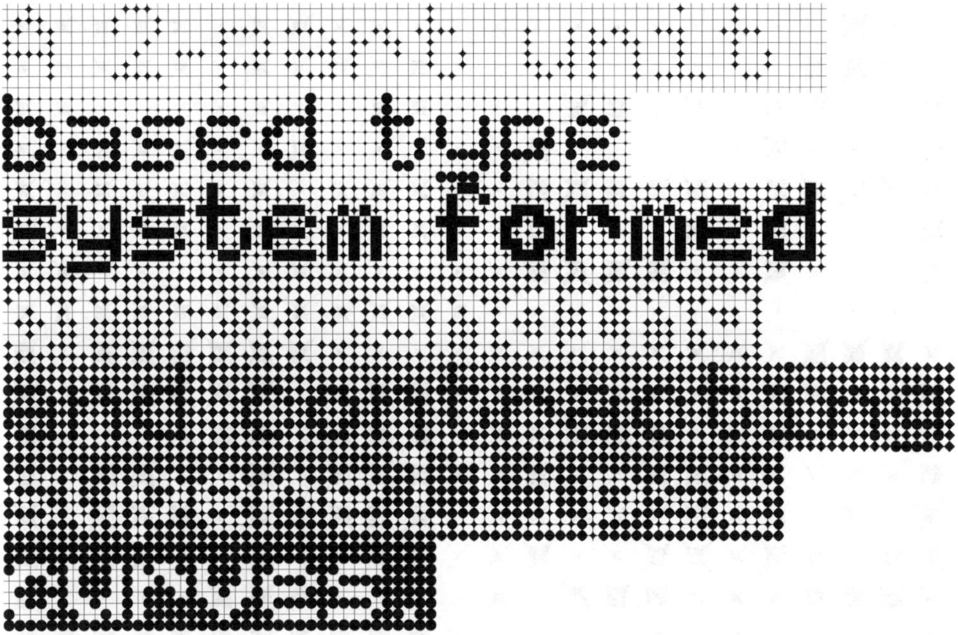
a 2-part unit
based type
system formed
of expanding
and contracting

E.A

*

s. 28
l. 33
t. 0
w. ±

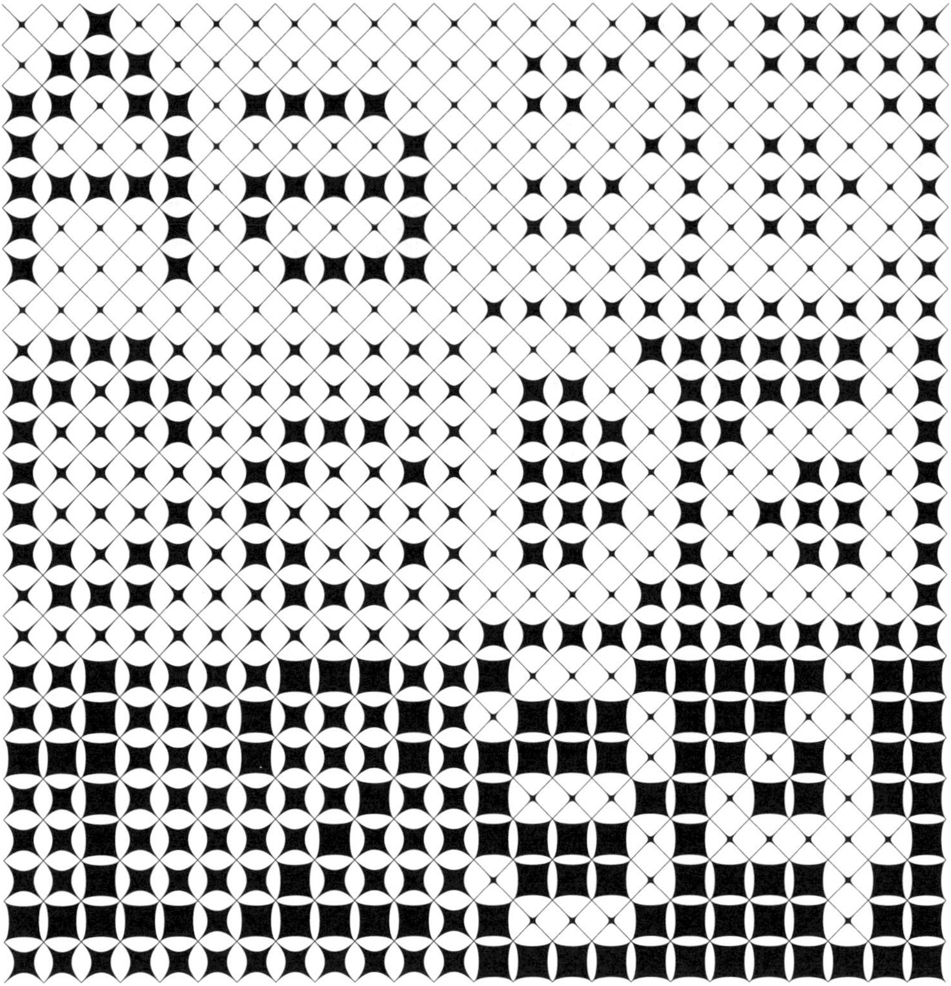

E.B

A 2-part unit based type system formed of decreasing unit hyperbola to parabolic curves.*

AaBbCcDd1234

s. 102
l. 122
t. 0
w. ±

a 2-part unit
based type
[illegible]
of decreasing
and hyperbola
to parabolic
curves

E.B *

s. 28
l. 33
t. 0
w. ±

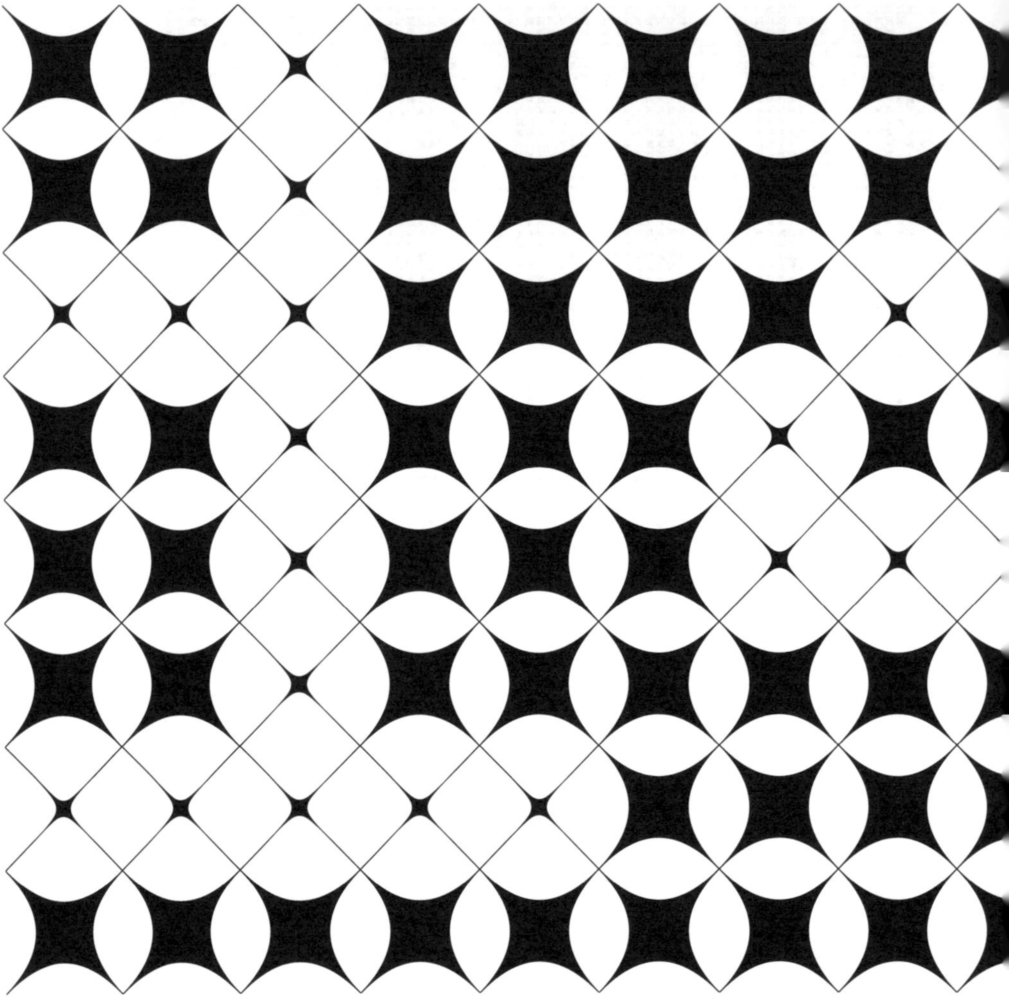

E.B

141

s. 309
l. 370
t. 0
w. ±

E.C

A 2-part unit based type system formed of expanding quadrifolium curves*

AaBbCcDd1234

s. 102
l. 122
t. 0
w. ±

E.C

*

s. 28
l. 33
t. 0
w. ±

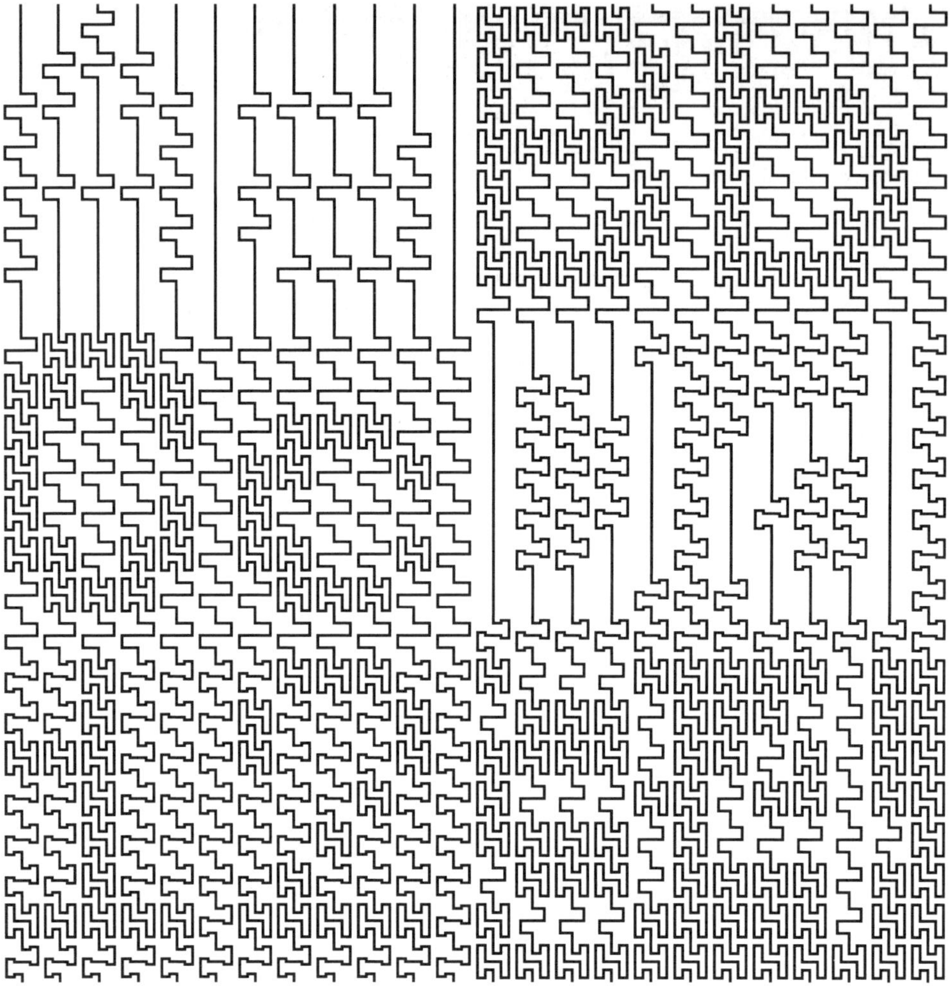

E.D A 2-part unit based type system formed of iterated space-filling curves*

AaBbCcDd1234

s. 102
l. 122
t. 0
w. ±

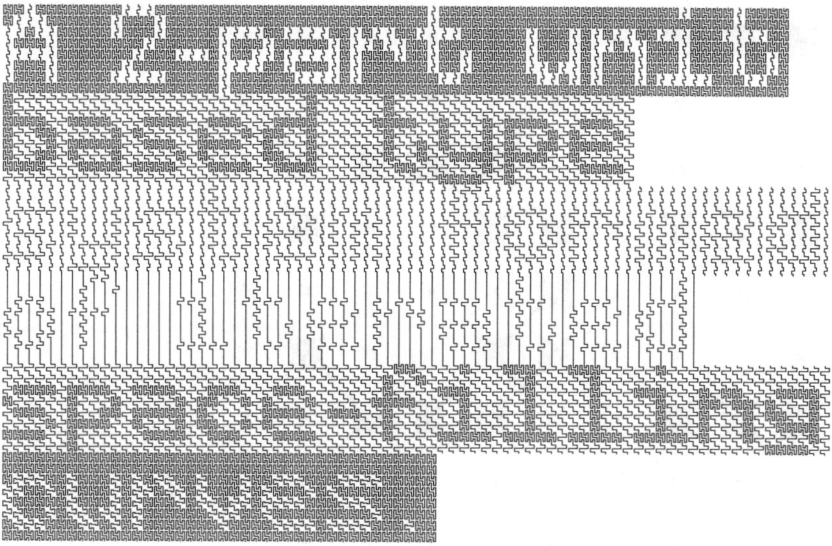

E.D

*

s. 28
l. 33
t. 0
w. ±

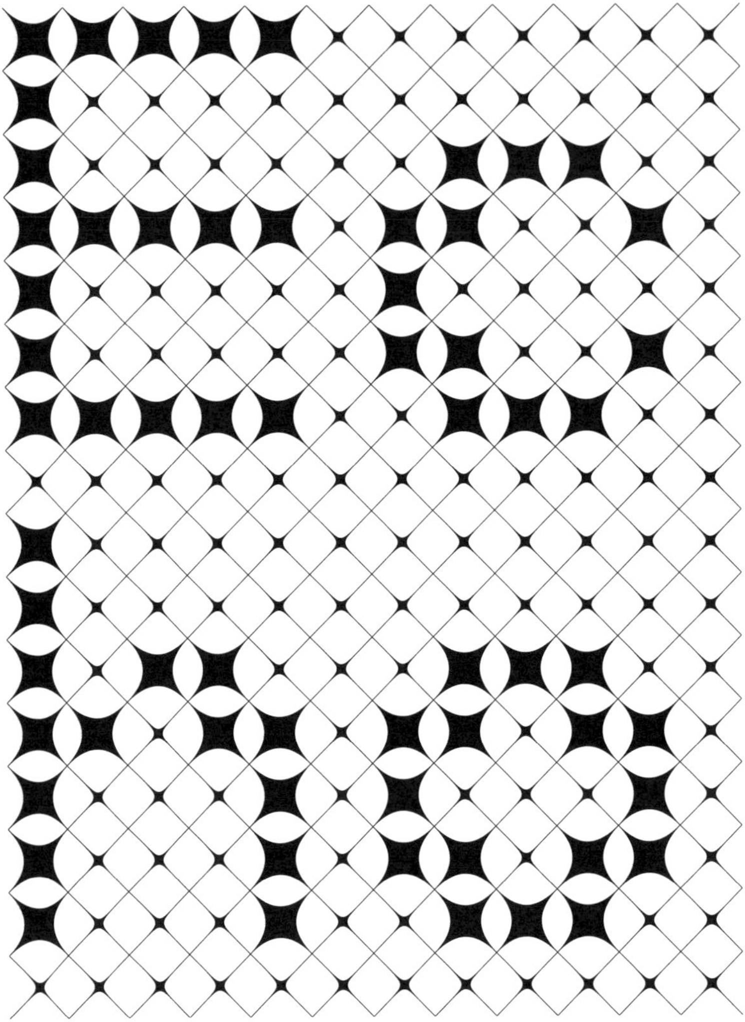

E.B

Echo

s. 158
l. 189
t. 0
w. ±

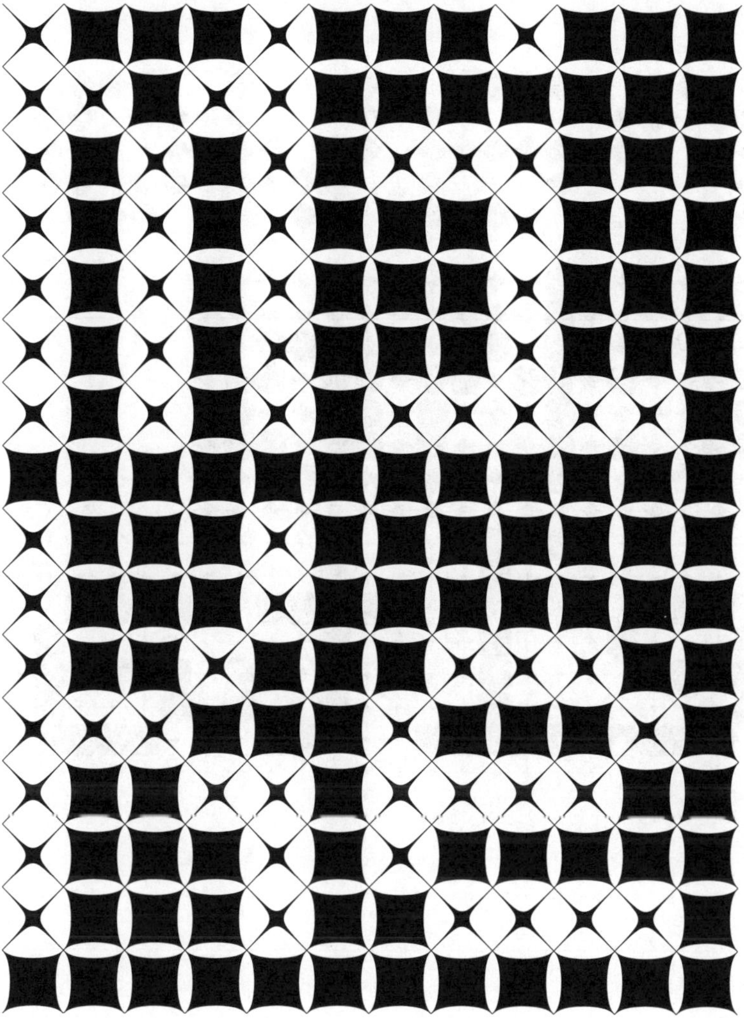

E.B

Mike

s. 158
l. 189
t. 0
w. ±

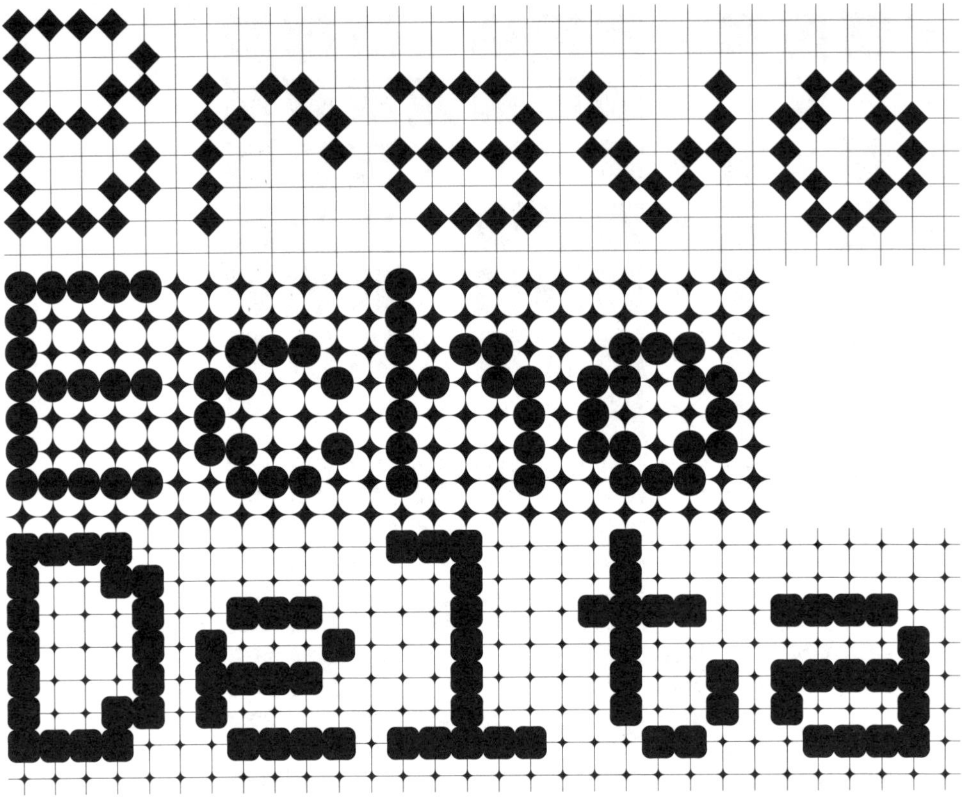

E.A

Bravo Echo Delta

s. 82
l. 98
t. 0
w. ±

E.A

Delta Echo Delta

s. 82
l. 98
t. 0
w. ±

E.C

Golf Echo Oscar
Mike Echo

s. 63
l. 75
t. 0
w. ±

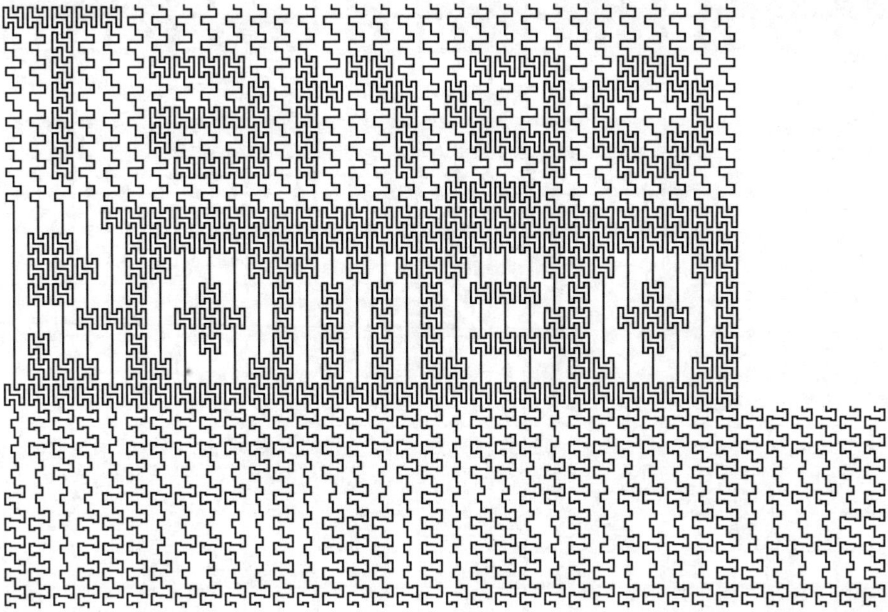

E.D

Tango Romeo
Yankee

s. 63
l. 75
t. 0
w. ±

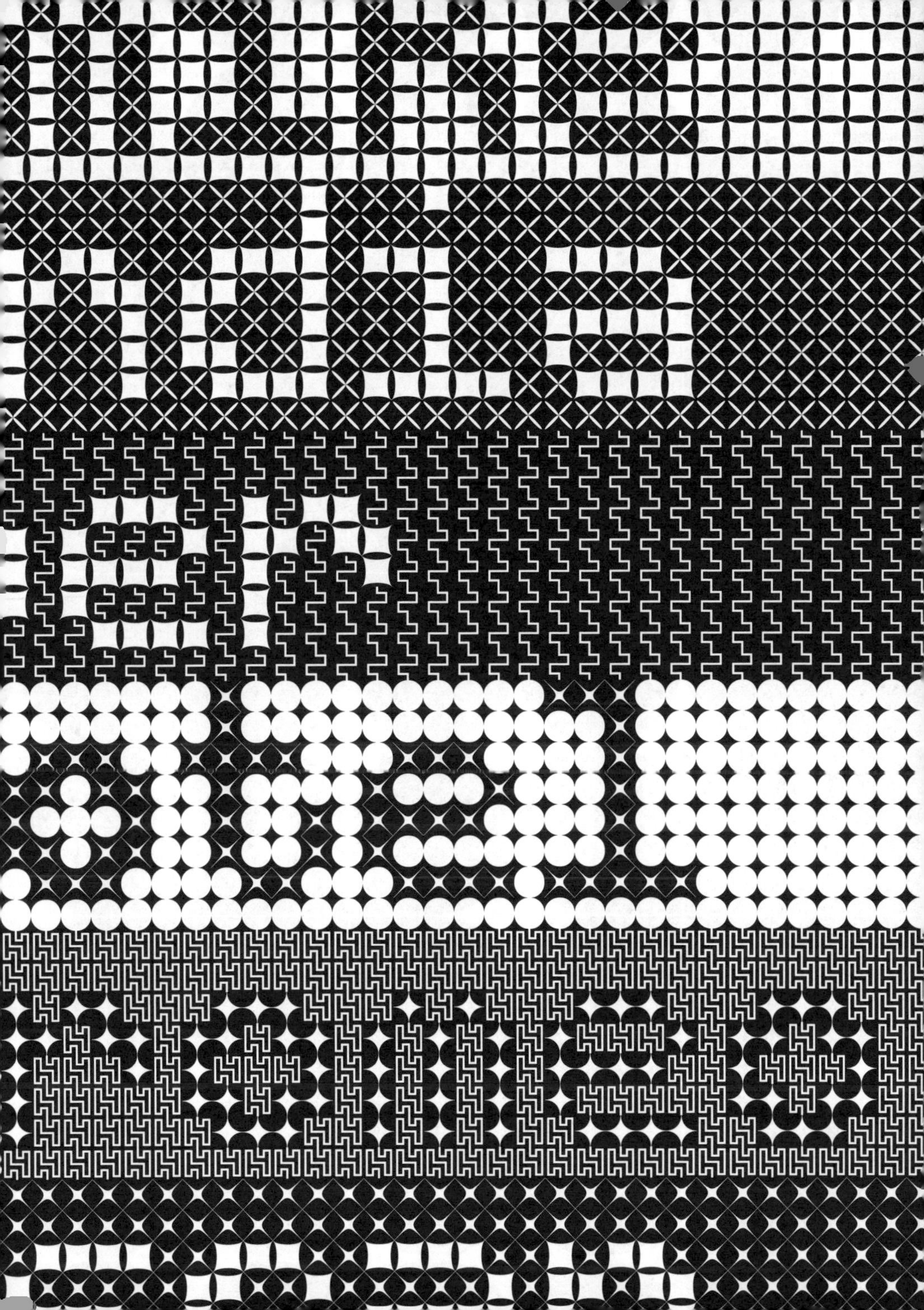

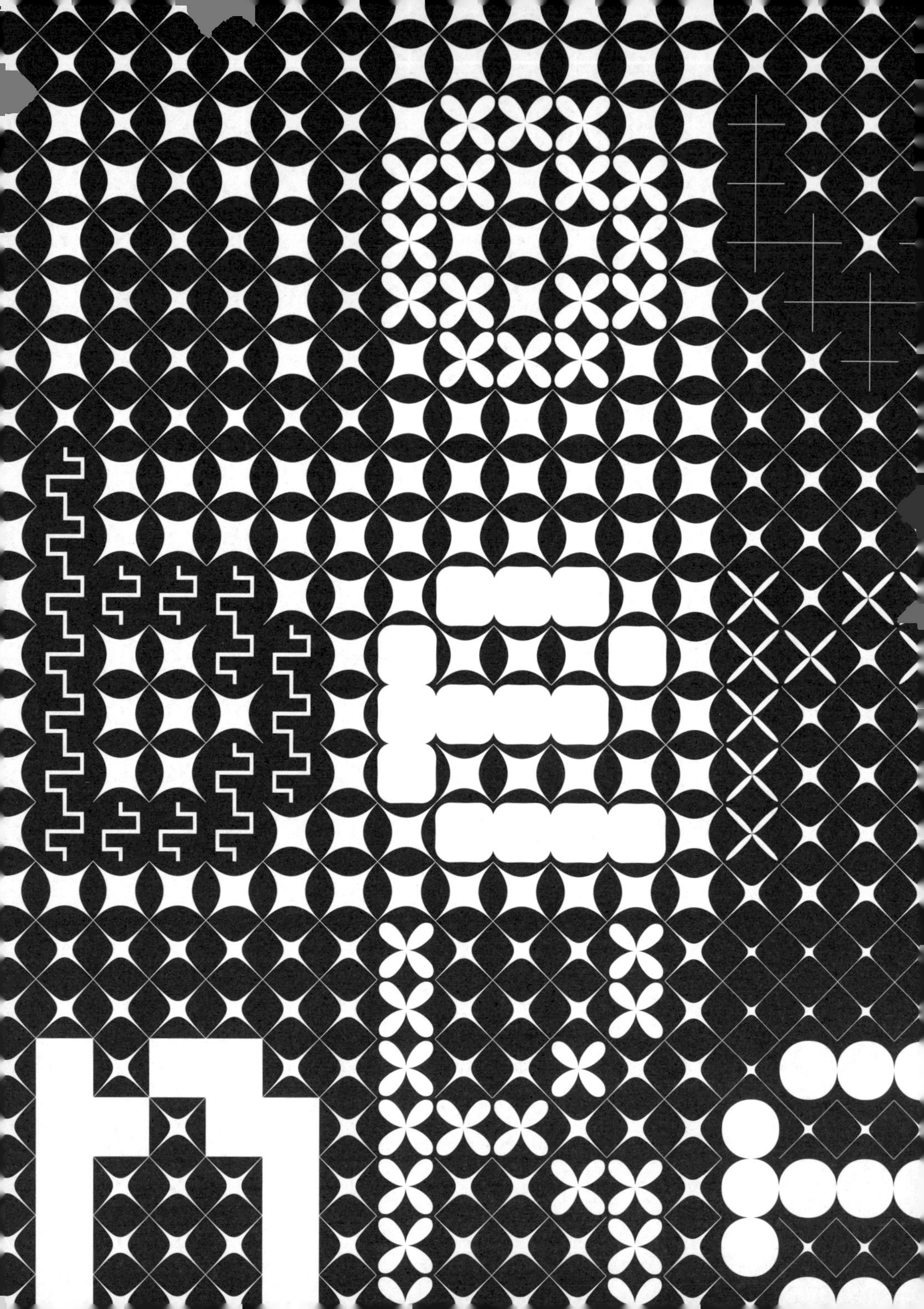

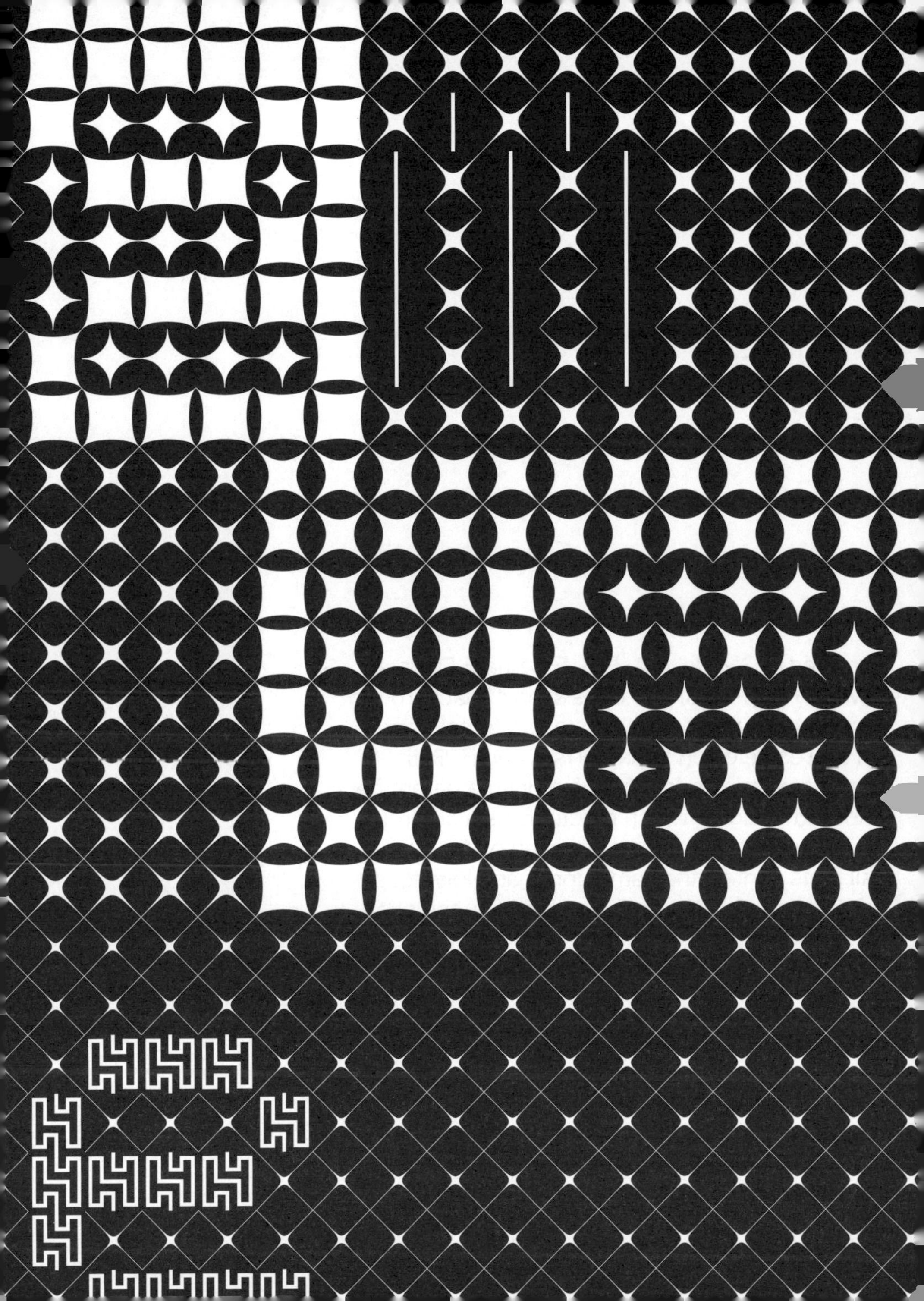

Section Notes:

Created in Glyphs. E.A, E.B, E.C and E.D are all two-part type systems consisting of background and foreground fonts–a male and female array of curves, referred to as Parts A and B. Both parts are variable font files featuring a parameter labelled "weight," which functions as a control for the expansion and contraction of the curves. All fonts contain the same upper and lowercase character sets, numerals and basic punctuation.

E.A has been redrawn from
Process-Pattern Minkowski
Variable released in 2021

An exploration of systems that encode linguistic information without being shackled to conventional legibility, this section presents three alternative writing systems in which encryption functions as the driving logic. Glyph forms are determined by their positions within the alphabet or their spatial relationships to adjacent forms. These systems serve as visual frameworks for encoded data, where meaning is embedded within form but is not immediately decipherable through the reading process.

Framework:

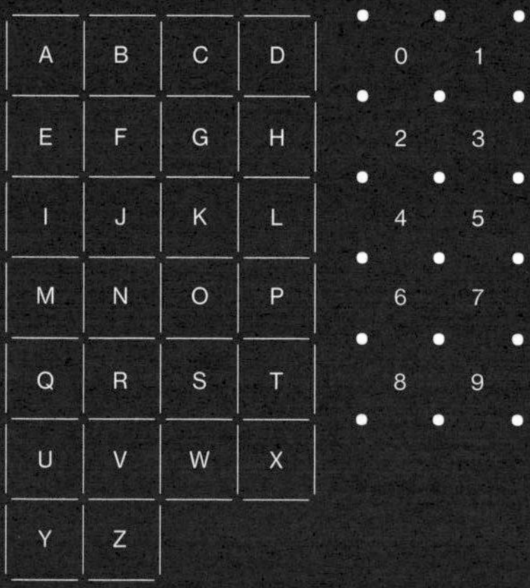

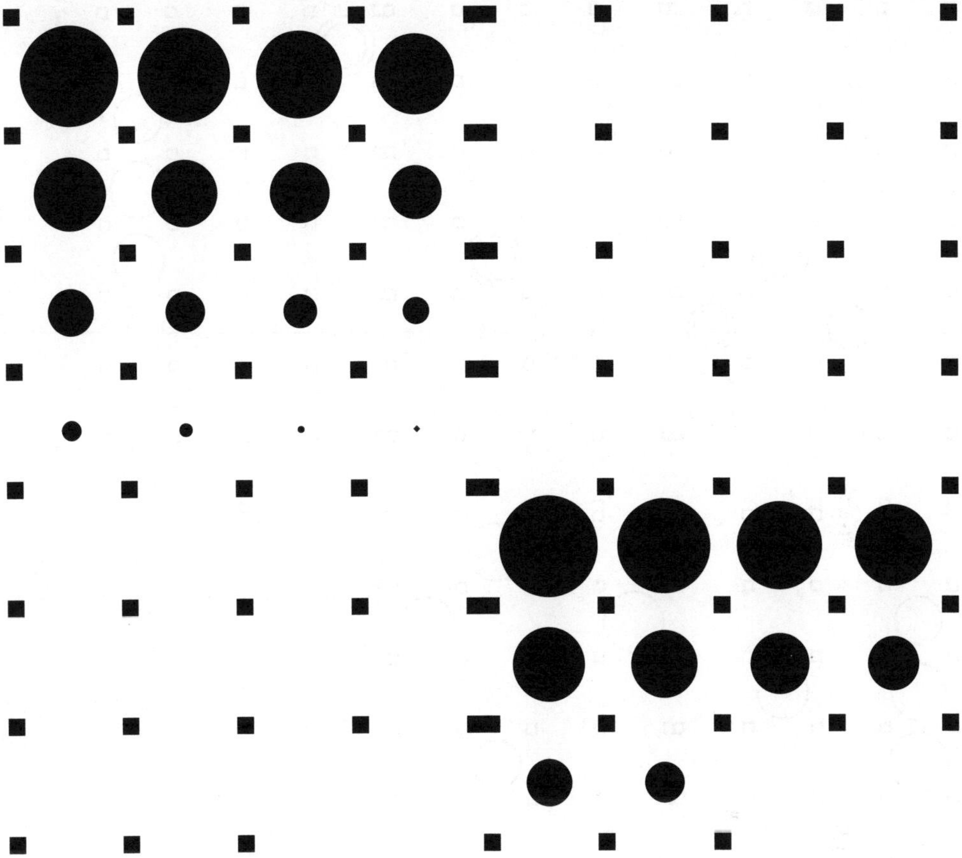

F.A

A Framework writing system formed of a grid where plotted dots decrease in size consecutively within each word

A–P Q–Z

s. 317
l. 317
t. 0

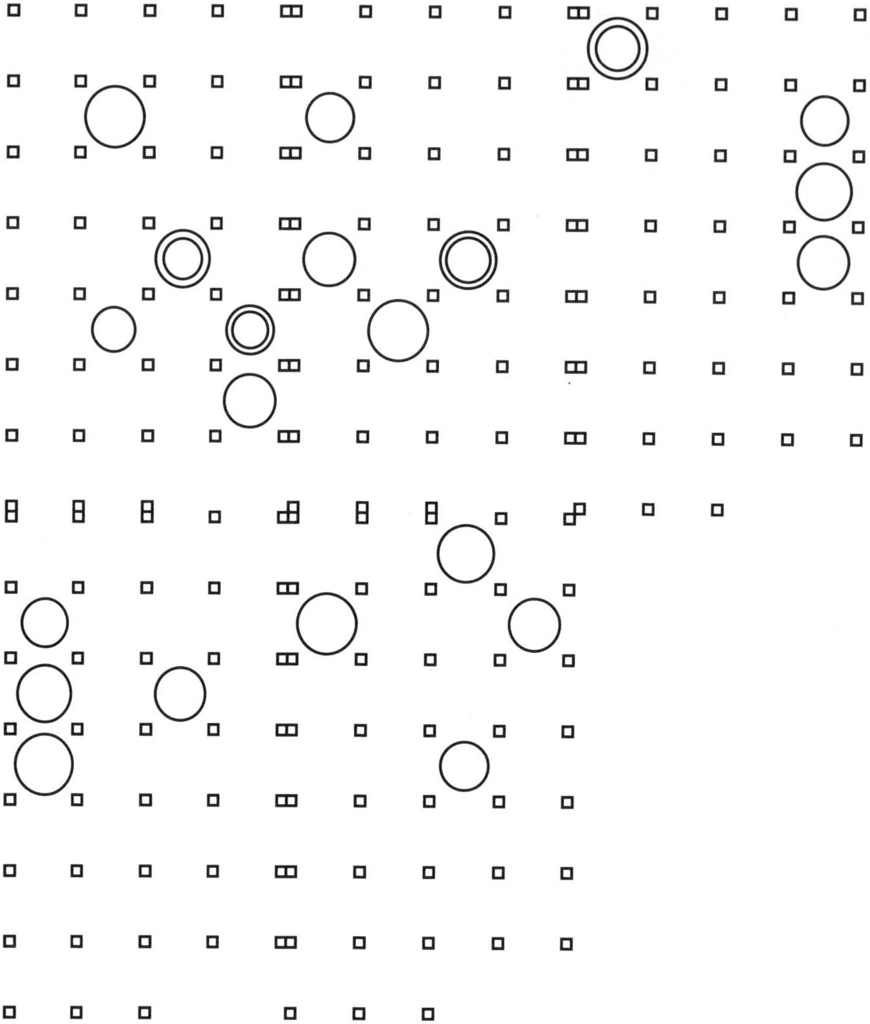

F.A

Foxtrot Romeo Alpha
Mike Echo

s. 190
l. 190
t. 0

OL

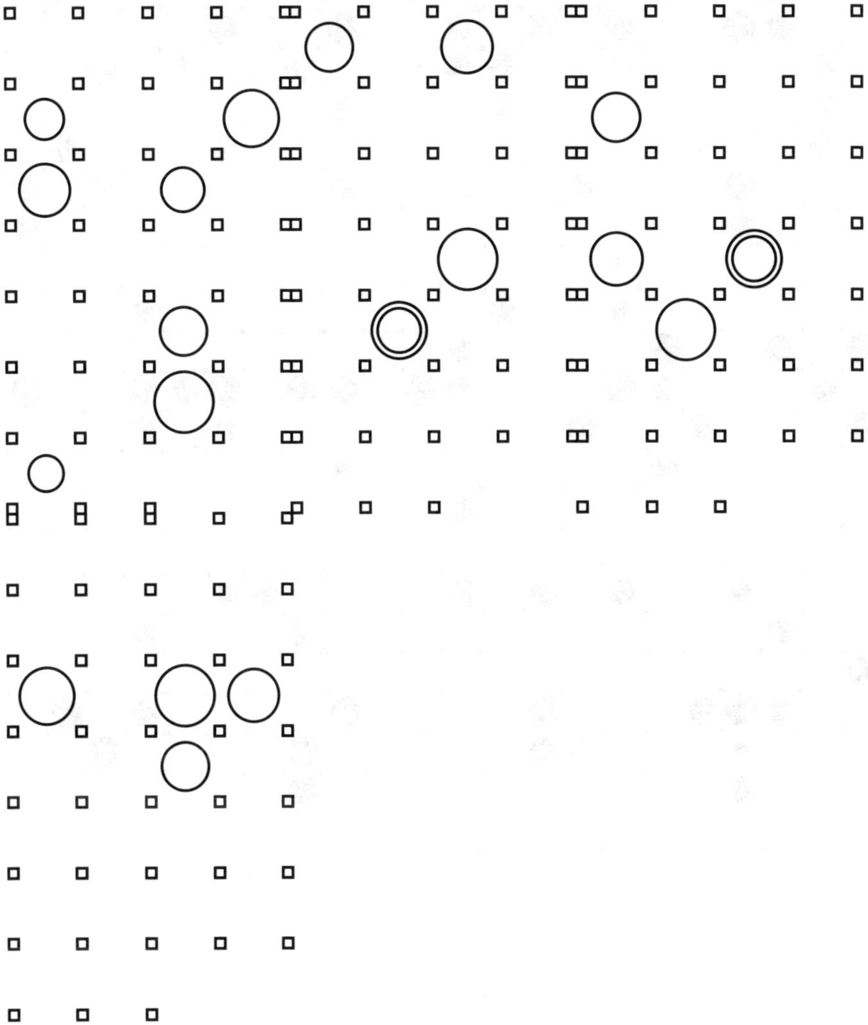

F.A

Whiskey Oscar
Romeo Kilo

s. 190
l. 190
t. 0

OL

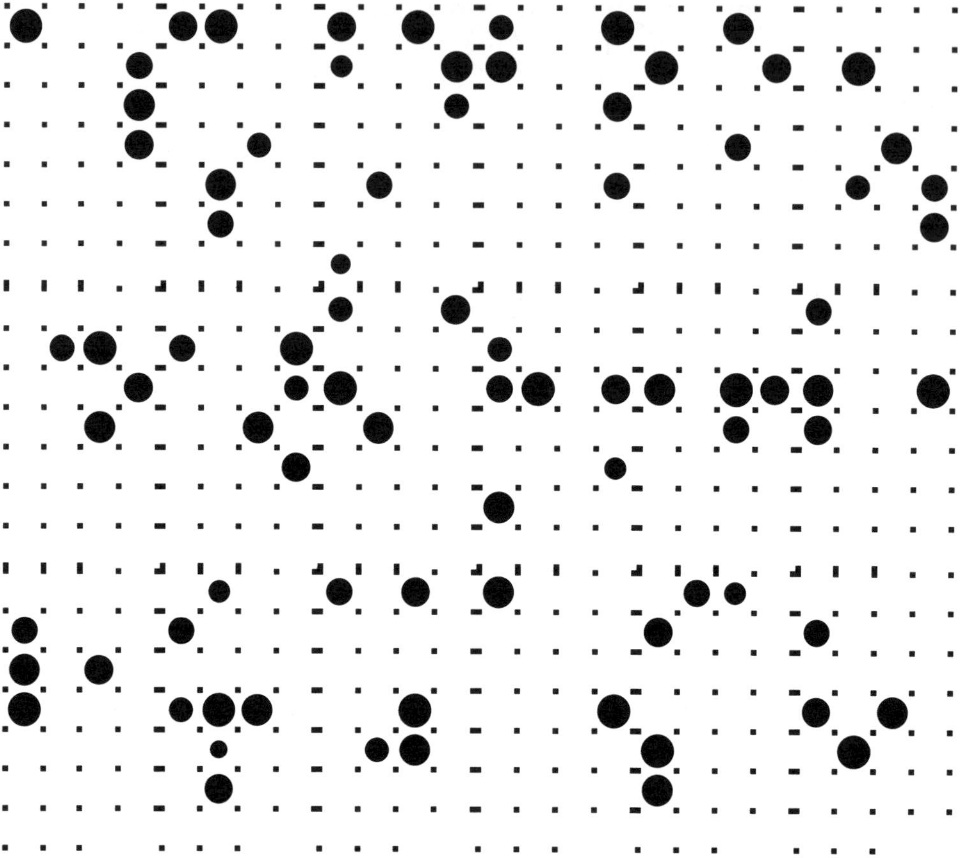

F.A

Alpha Bravo Charley Delta
Echo Foxtrot Golf Hotel
India Juliet Kilo Lima Mike
November Oscar Papa
Quebec Romeo

s. 106
l. 106
t. 0

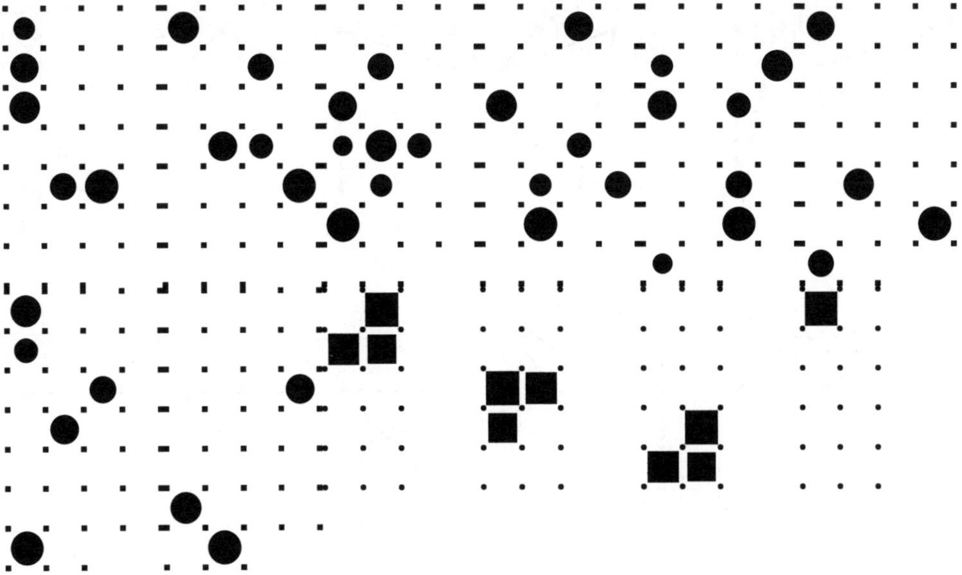

F.A

Sierra Tango Uniform Victor
Whiskey Xray Yankee Zulu
123 456 789 0

s. 106
l. 106
t. 0

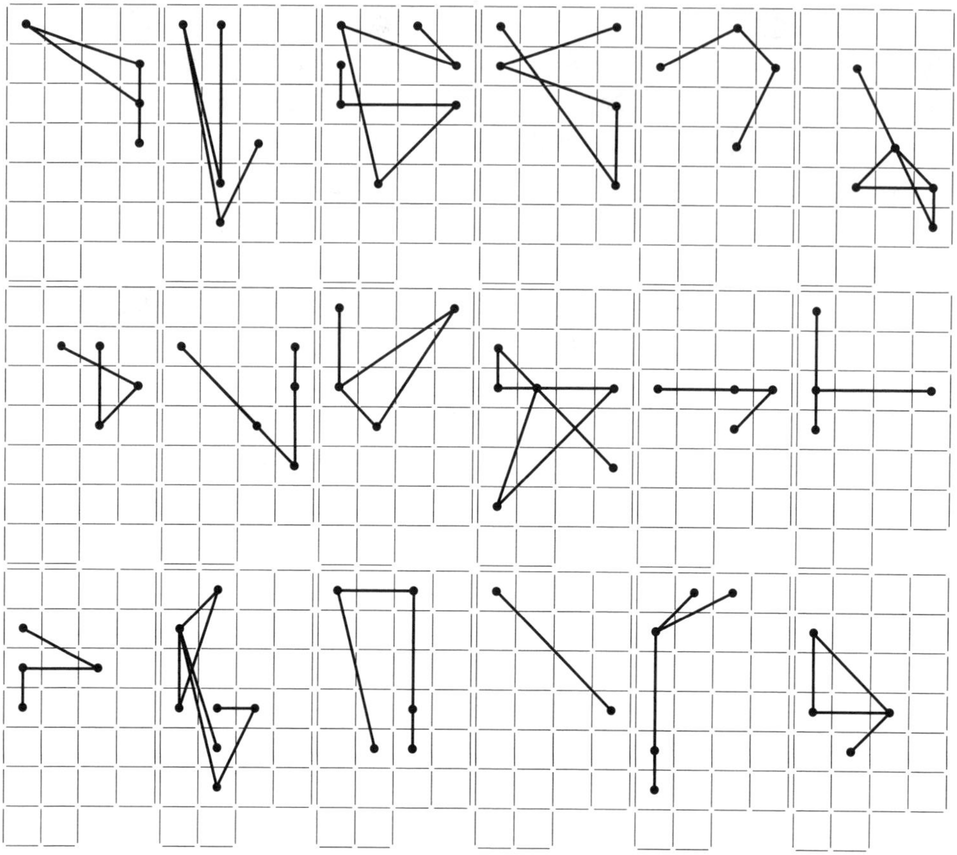

F.B

A Framework writing system formed of a grid with plotted dots connected with lines consecutively within each word

Alpha Bravo Charley Delta
Echo Foxtrot Golf Hotel
India Juliet Kilo Lima Mike
November Oscar Papa
Quebec Romeo

s. 106
l. 106
t. 0

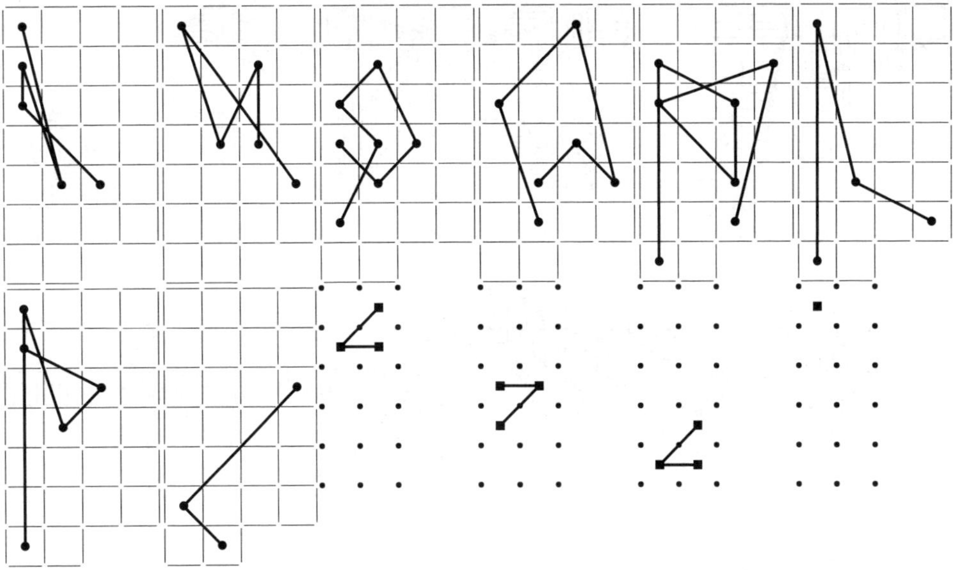

F.B

Sierra Tango Uniform Victor
Whiskey Xray Yankee Zulu
123 456 789 0

s. 106
l. 106
t. 0

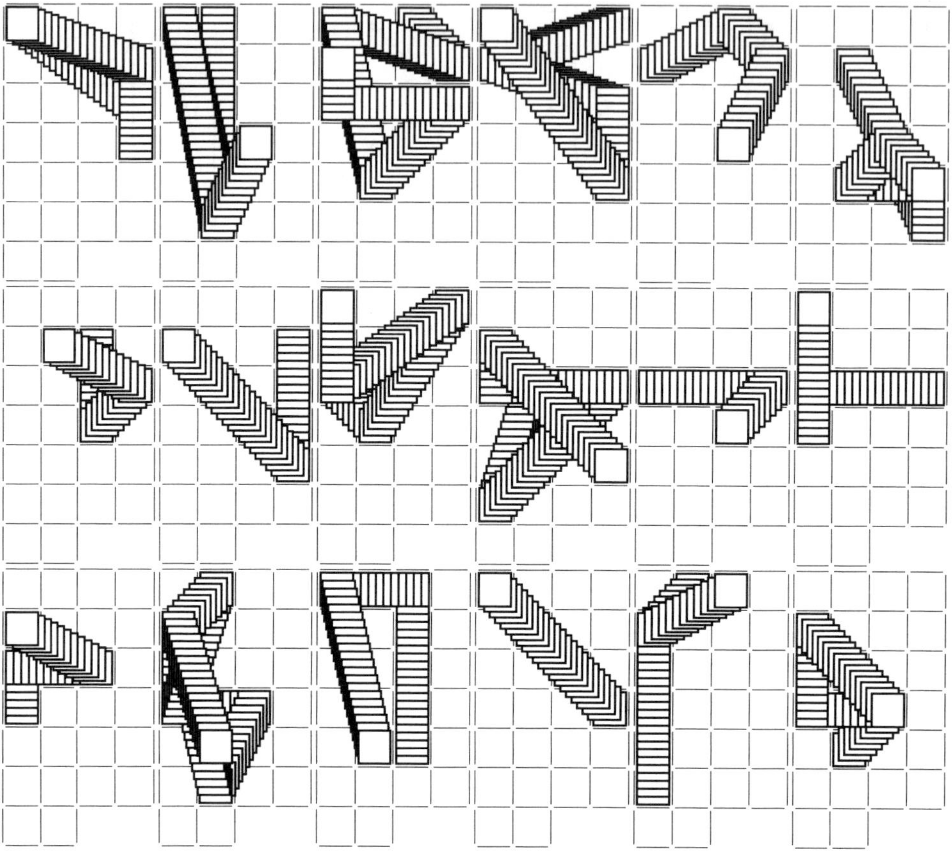

F.C A Framework writing system formed of a grid with plotted points connected with overlapping squares consecutively within each word

Alpha bravo charlie delta
echo foxtrot golf hotel
india juliet kilo lima mike
november oscar papa
quebec romeo

s. 106
l. 106
t. 0

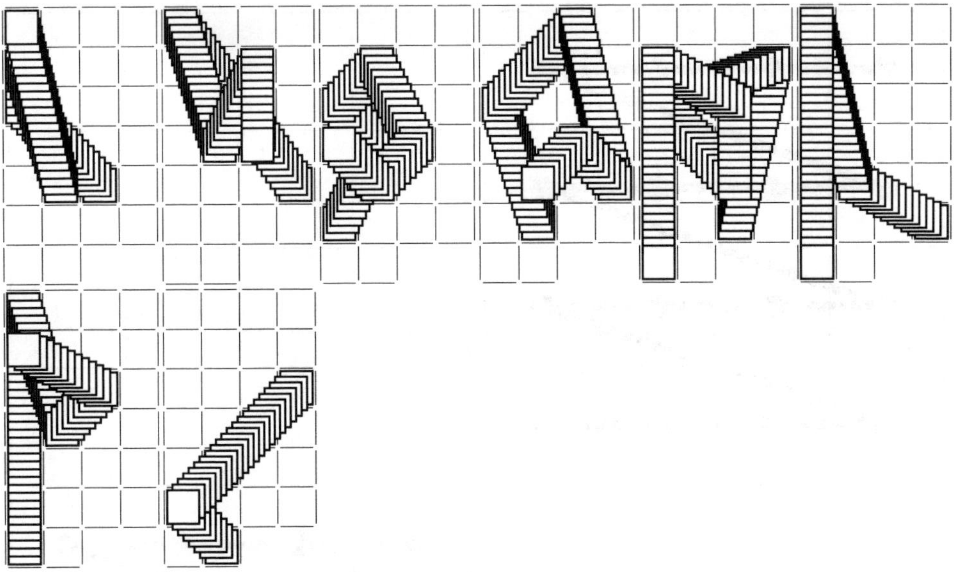

F.C

Sierra Tango Uniform Victor
Whiskey Xray Yankee Zulu

s. 106
l. 106
t. 0

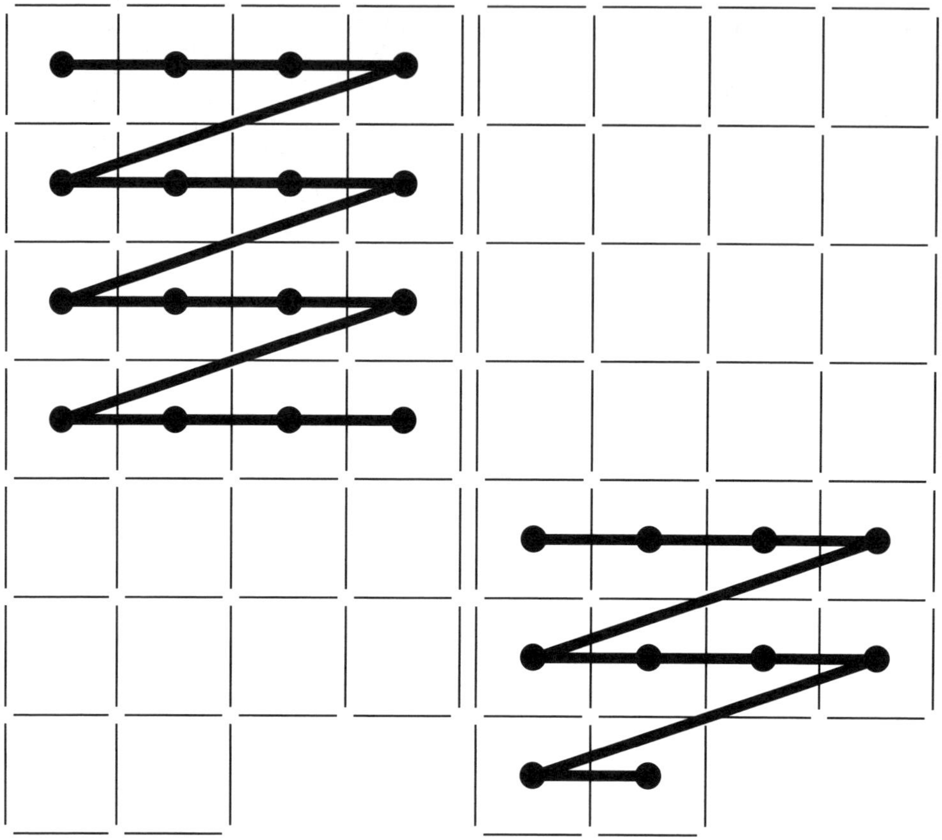

F.B

A–P Q–Z

s. 317
l. 317
t. 0

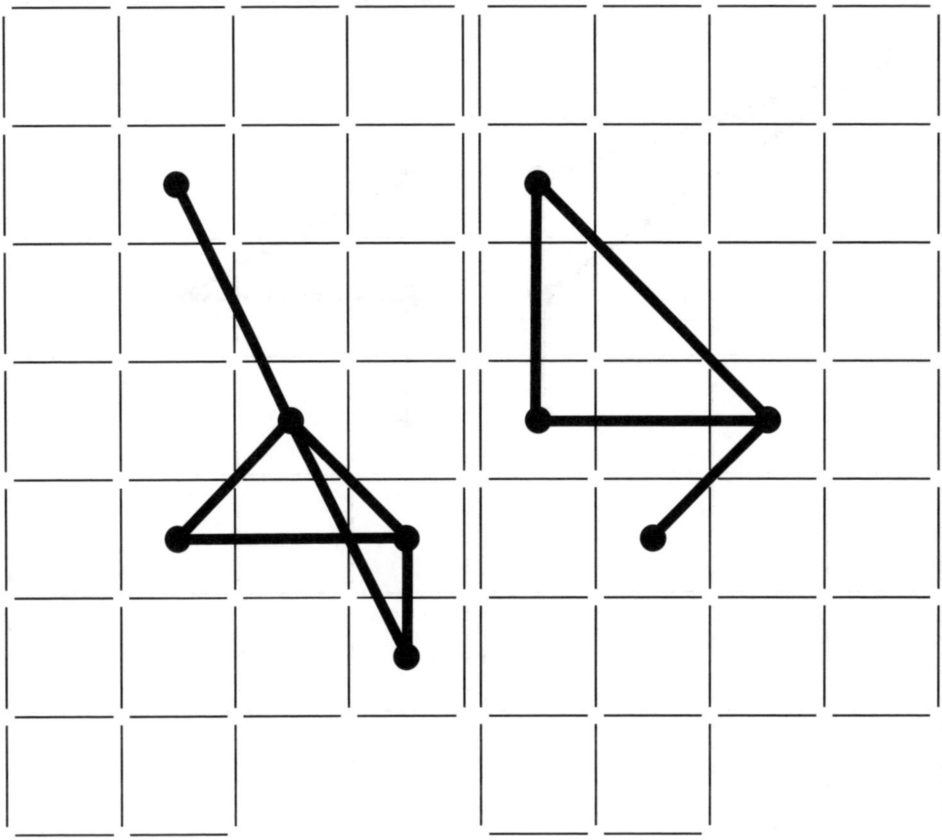

F.B

Foxtrot Romeo

s. 317
l. 317
t. 0

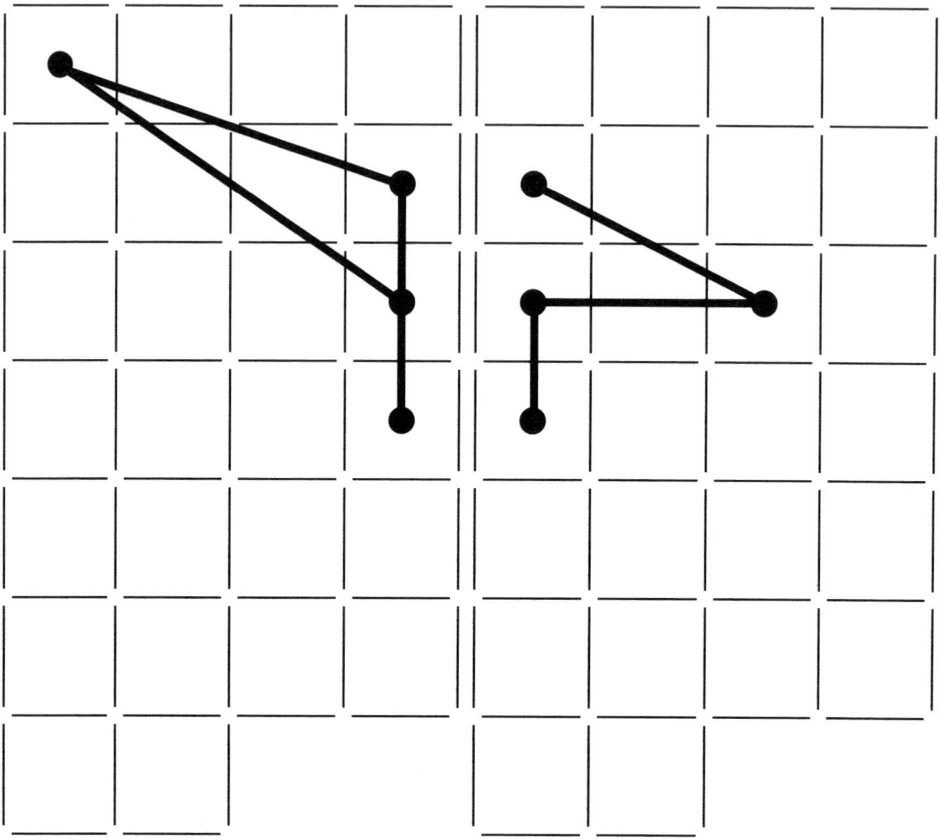

F.B

Alpha Mike

s. 317
l. 317
t. 0

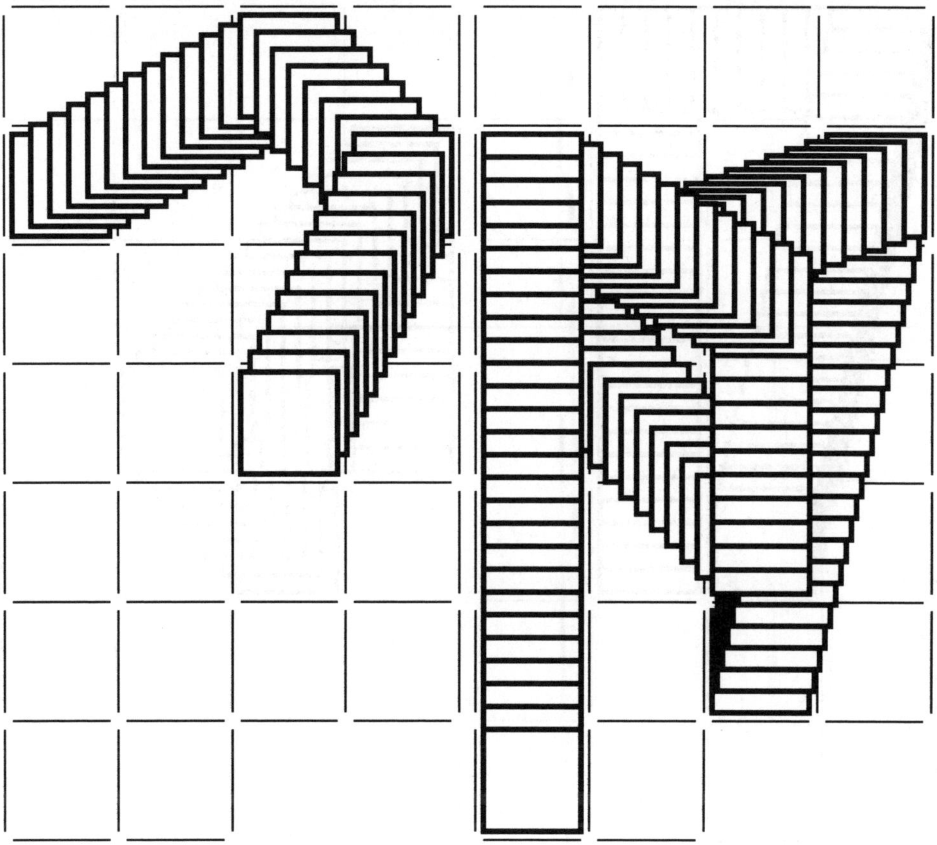

F.C

Echo Whiskey

s. 317
l. 317
t. 0

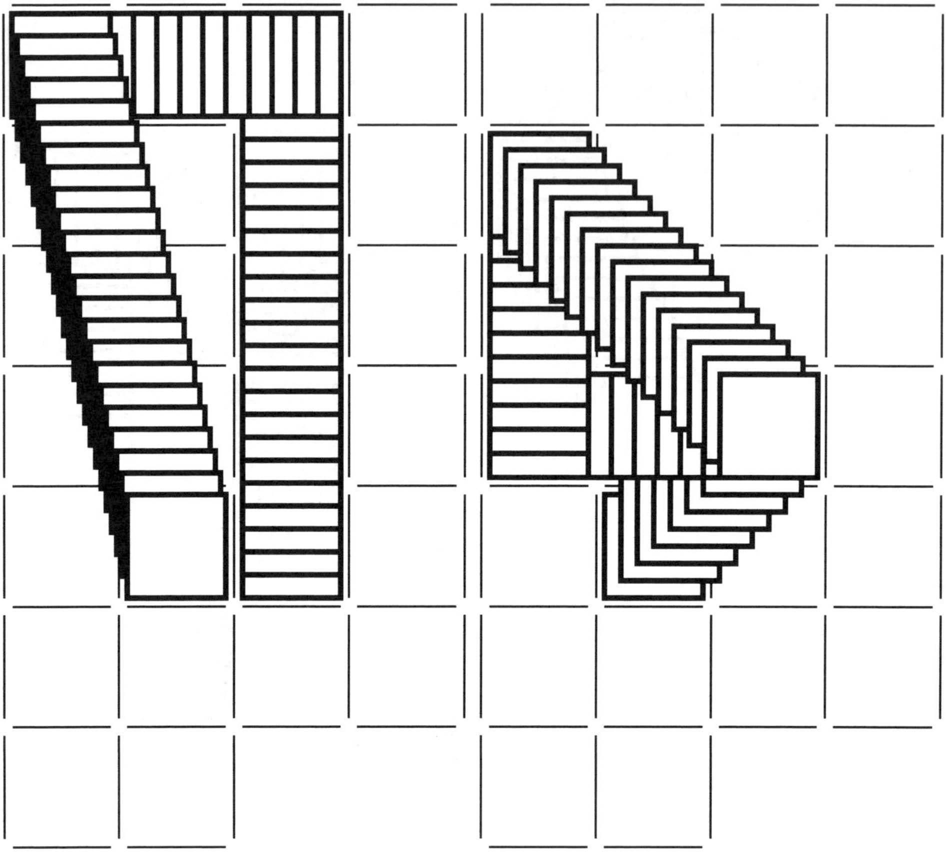

F.C

Oscar Romeo

s. 317
l. 317
t. 0

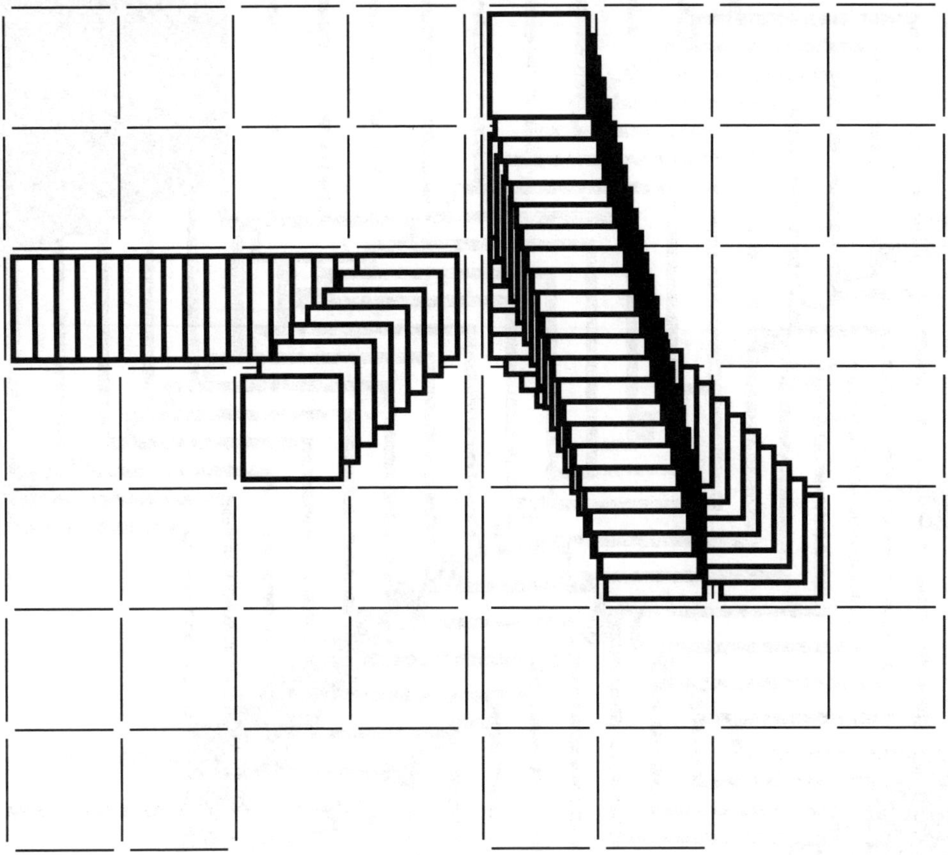

F.C

Kilo Sierra

s. 317
l. 317
t. 0

F Frameworks

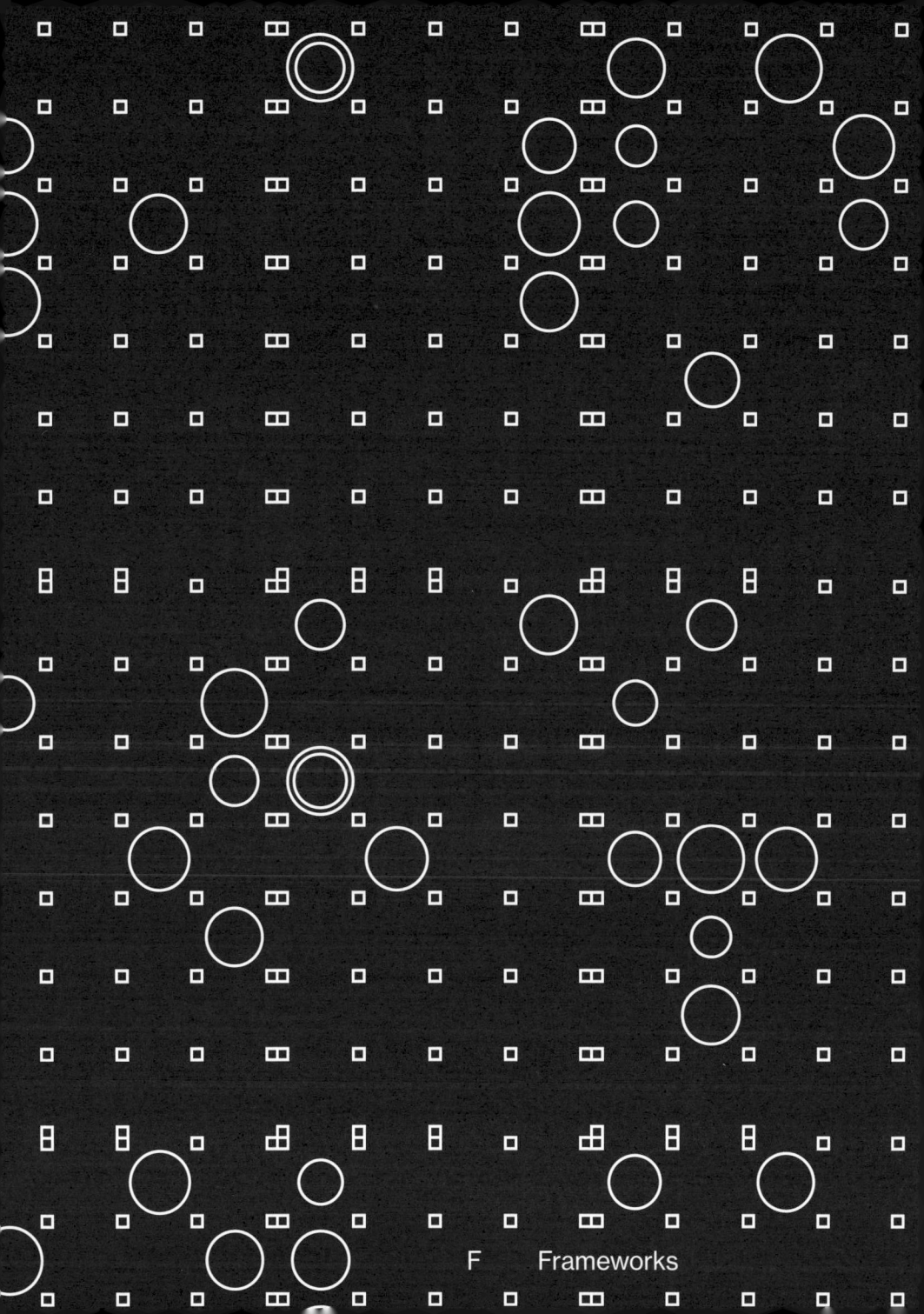

Section Notes:

Created in Glyphs, F.A consists of a single font file containing characters with zero width, functioning as non-spacing marks—similar to diacritics in a standard font. This design allows each character frame to occupy the same space, or word-space. The width of the space character is determined by the word-space, enabling the font to shift to a new frame with each new word. Contextual alternates enable one of 15 stylistic sets within each character profile to be applied based on the letter's position within a word, allowing the reader to decipher the embedded linguistic information. F.B and F.C combine F.A with vector based components allowing them to be overlaid consecutively within a word-space.

179

A set of alphabets investigating the visual effects of gradated line weights on the perception of letterforms. Through the progressive modulation of stroke thicknesses — in both vertical and horizontal axes — between inner and outer contours, the typefaces appear to shift in curvature and shape, despite consistent structure, positioning and stroke frequency.

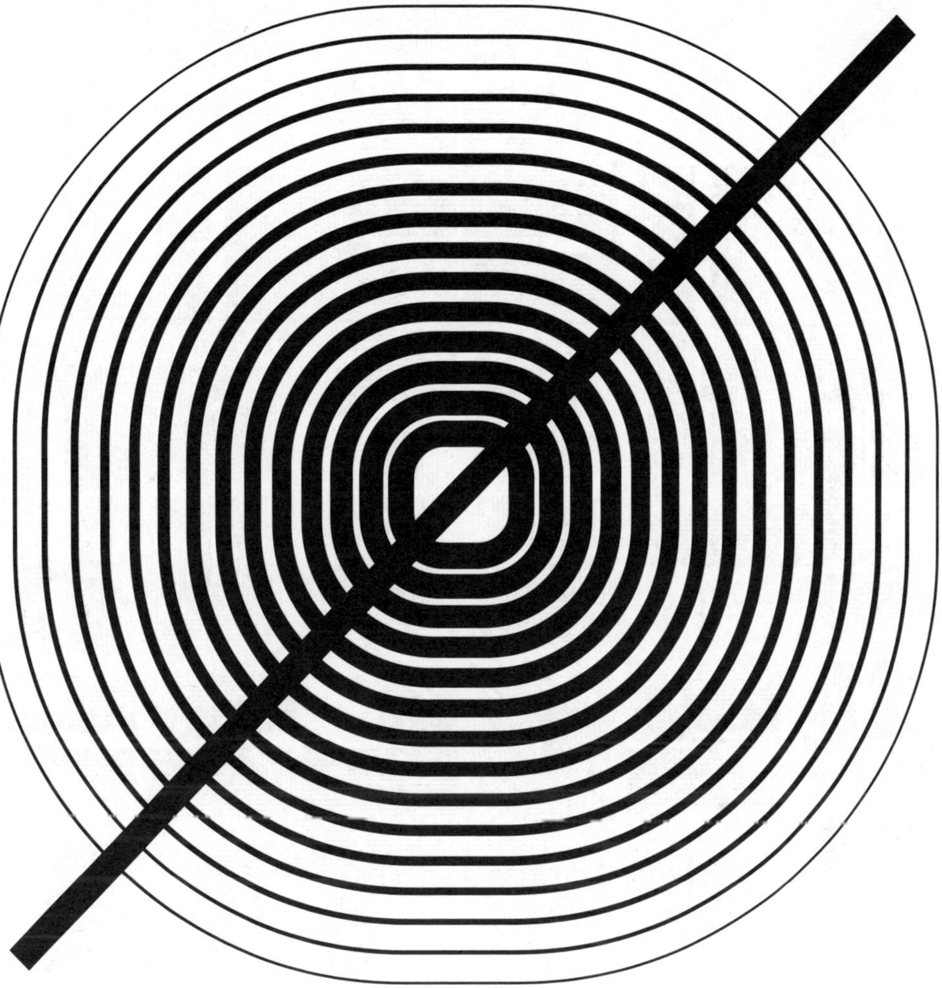

G.A An all-caps alphabet formed of gradating lines decreasing in weight from the centre

0

s. 380
l. 380
t. 0
w. 700

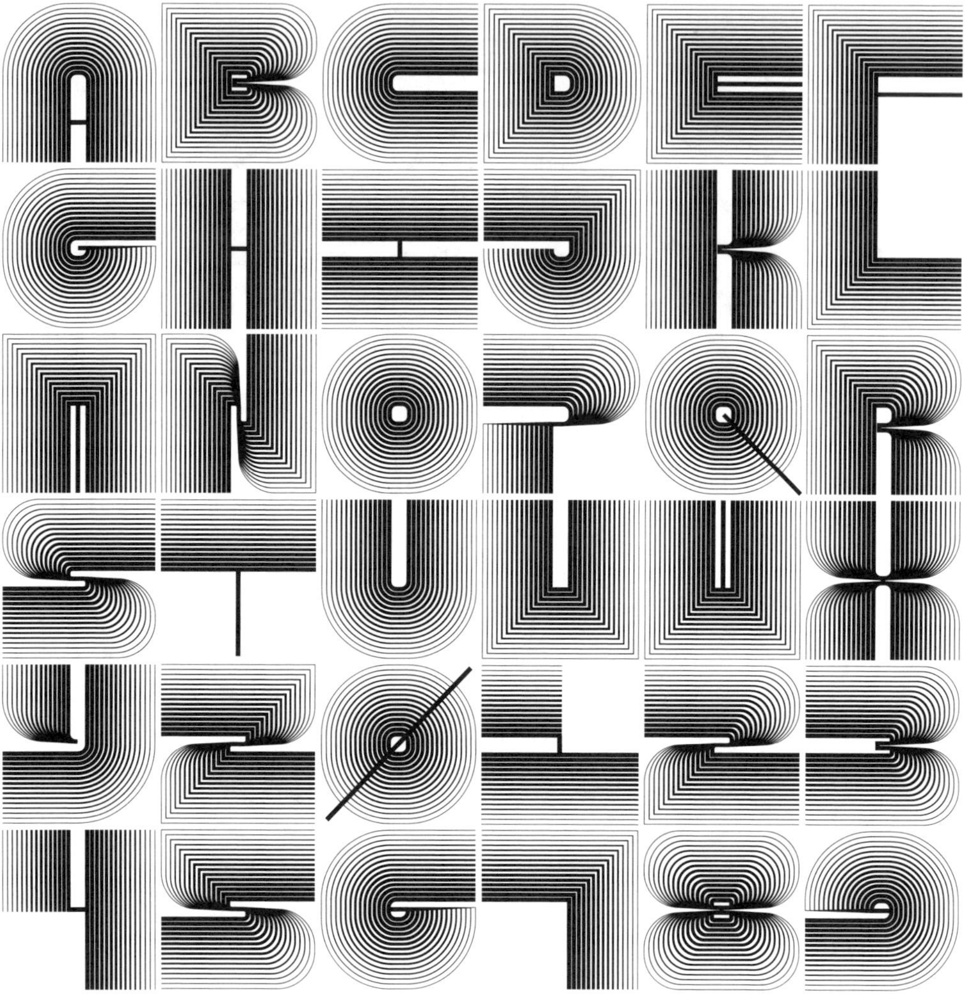

G.A

A–Z 0–9

s. 62
l. 62
t. 0
w. 700

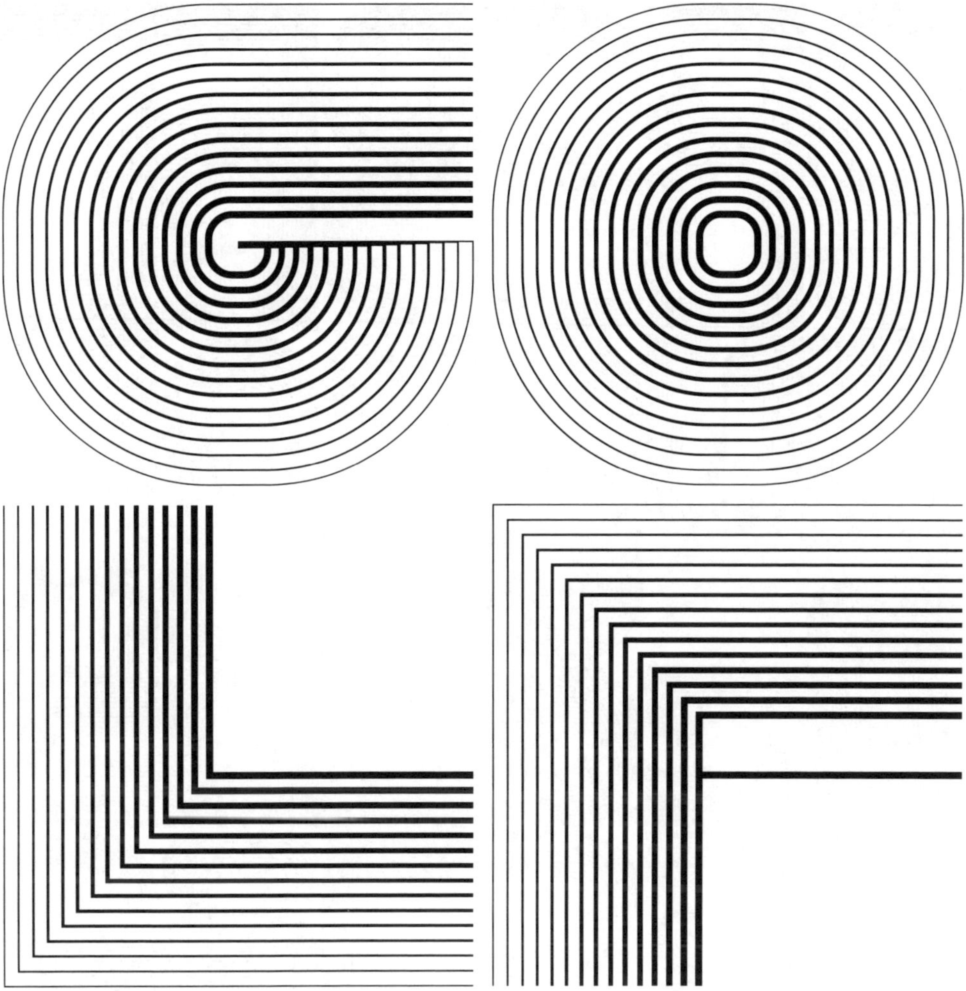

G.A

Golf

s. 188
l. 188
t. 0
w. 400

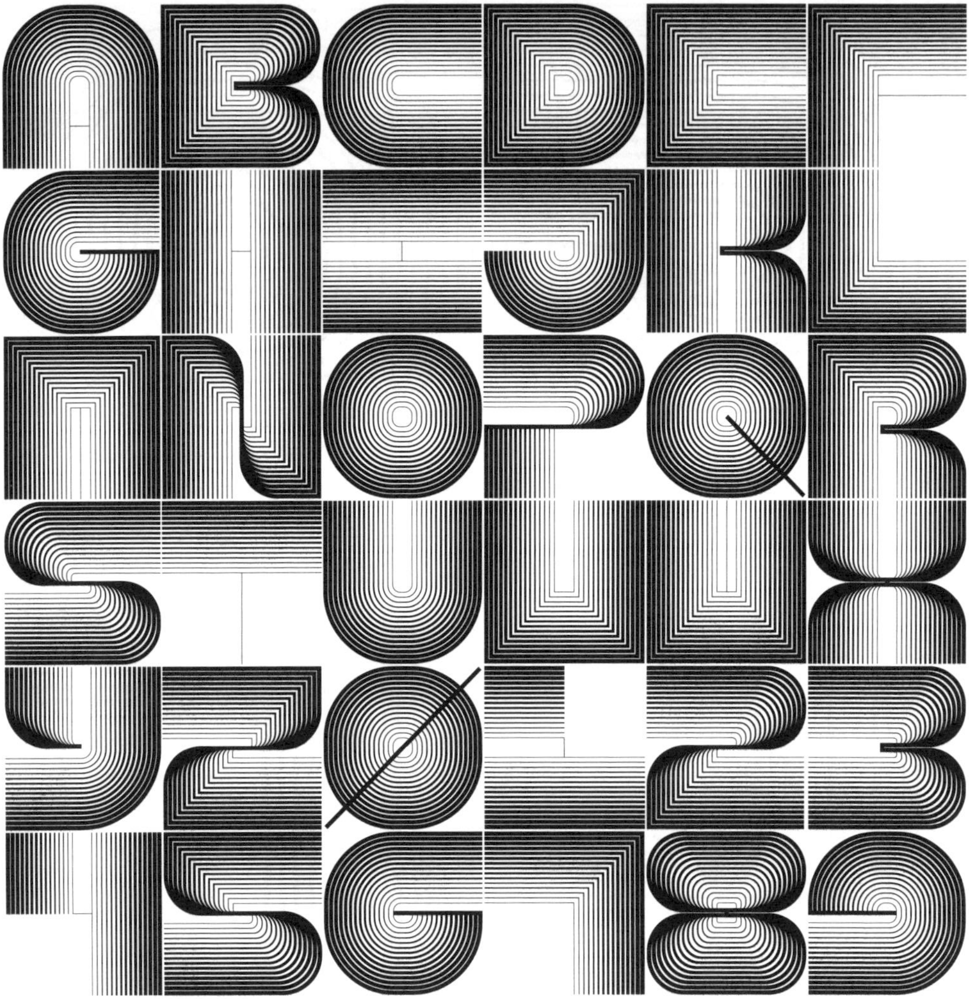

G.B An all-caps alphabet formed of gradating lines increasing in weight from the centre

A–Z 0–9

s. 62
l. 62
t. 0
w. 700

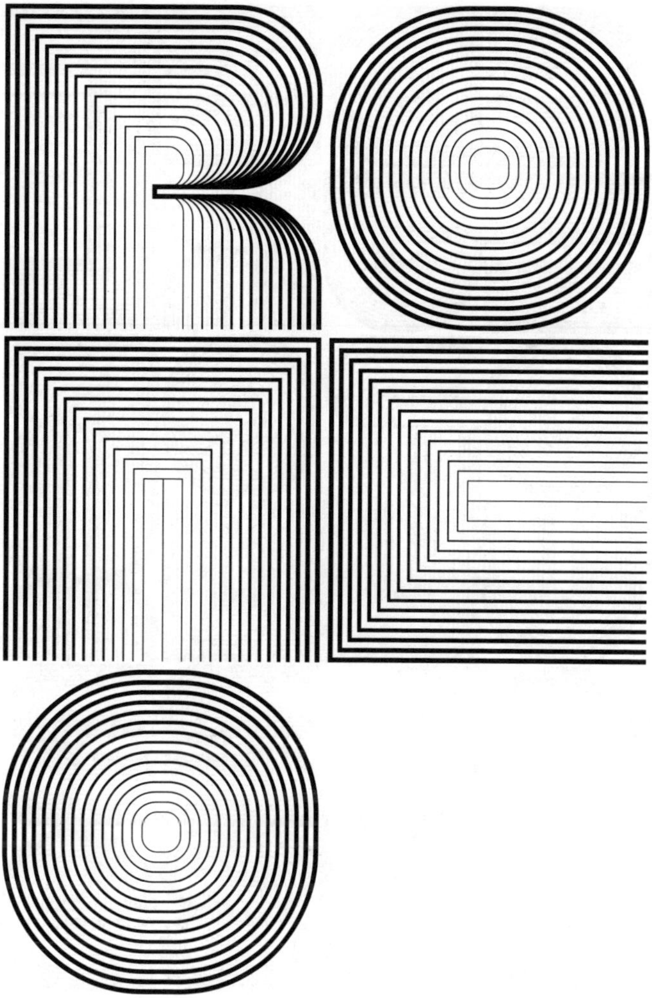

G.B

Romeo

s. 125
l. 125
t. 0
w. 400

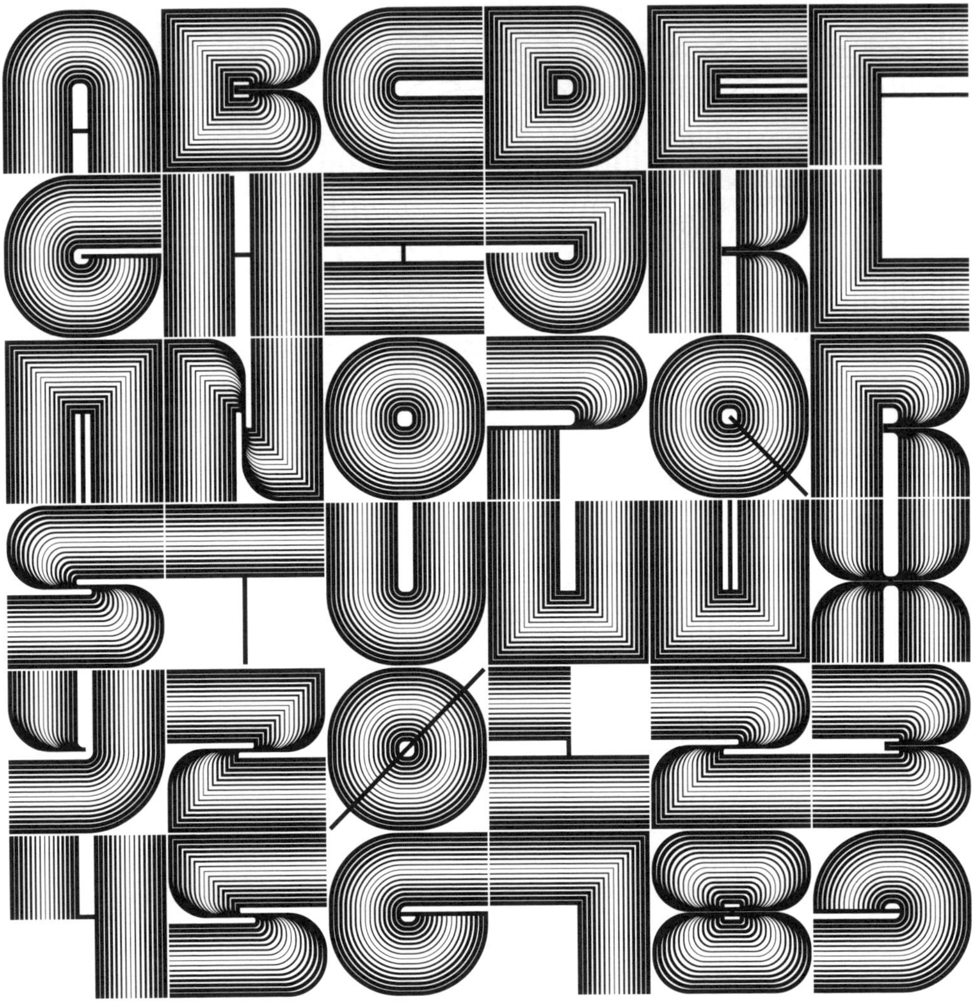

G.C

An all-caps alphabet formed of gradating lines that decrease then increase in weight from the centre

A–Z 0–9

s. 62
l. 62
t. 0
w. 700

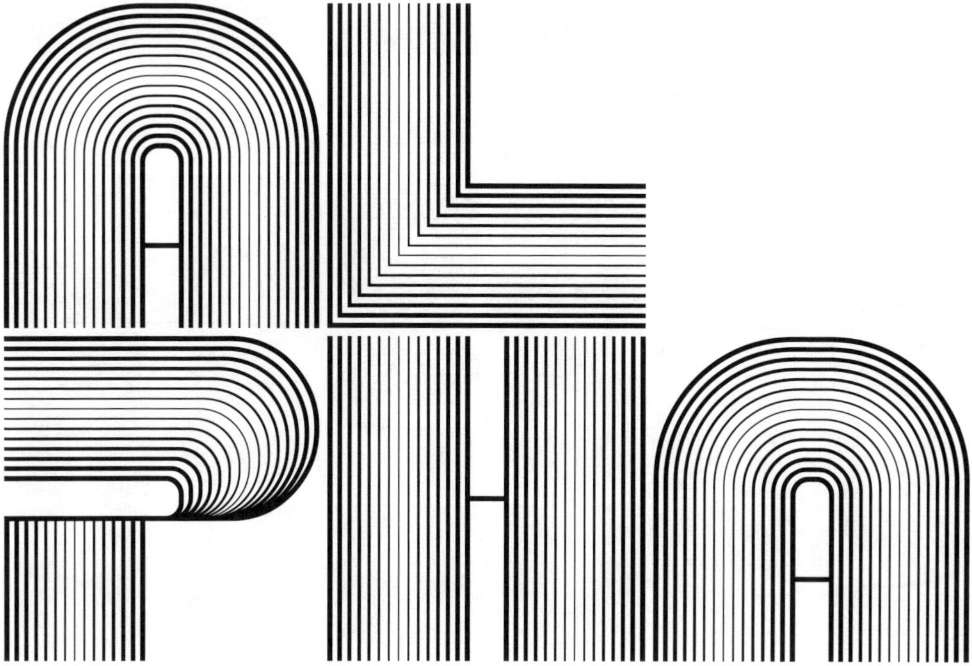

G.C

Alpha

s. 125
l. 125
t. 0
w. 400

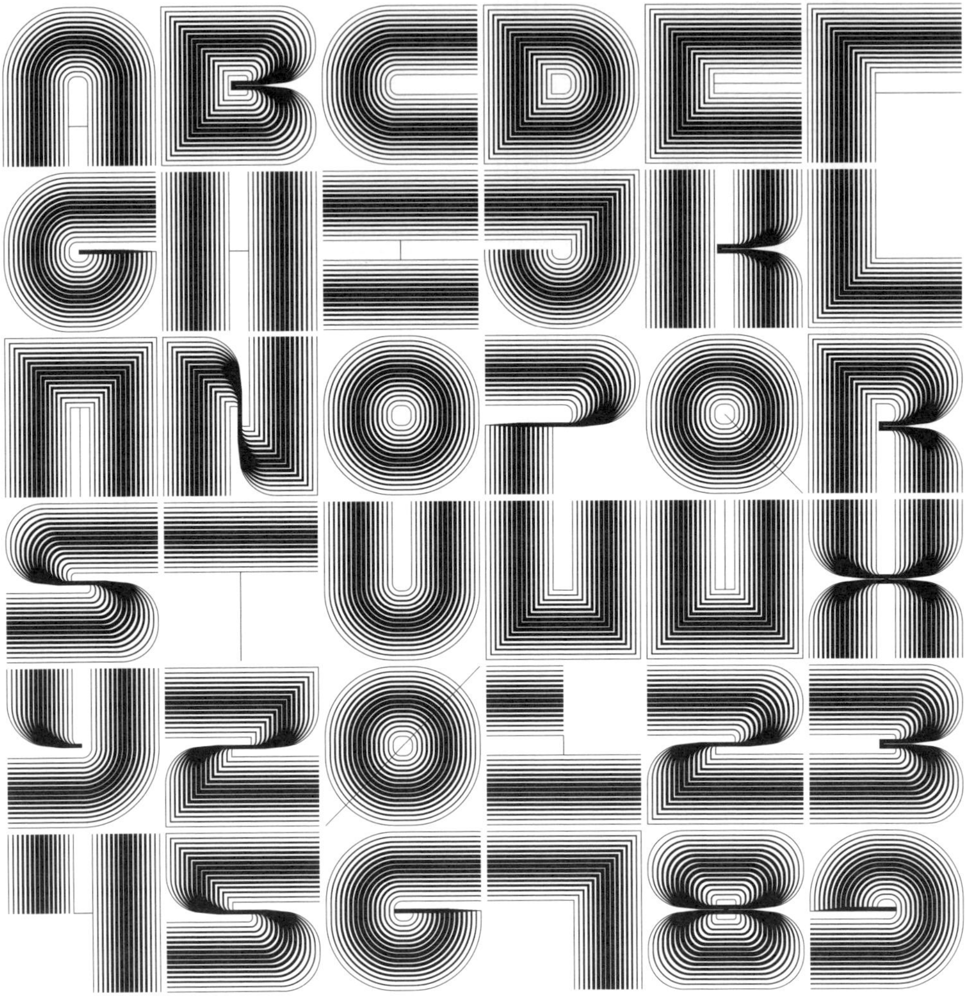

G.D

An all-caps alphabet formed of gradating lines that increase then decrease in weight from the centre

A–Z 0–9

s. 62
l. 62
t. 0
w. 700

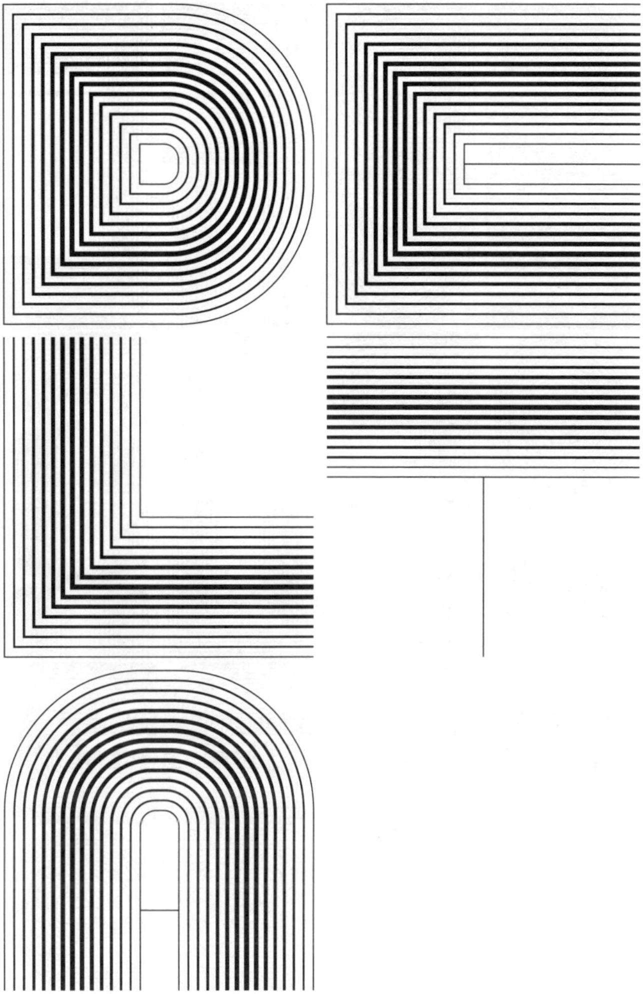

G.D

Delta

s. 125
l. 125
t. 0
w. 400

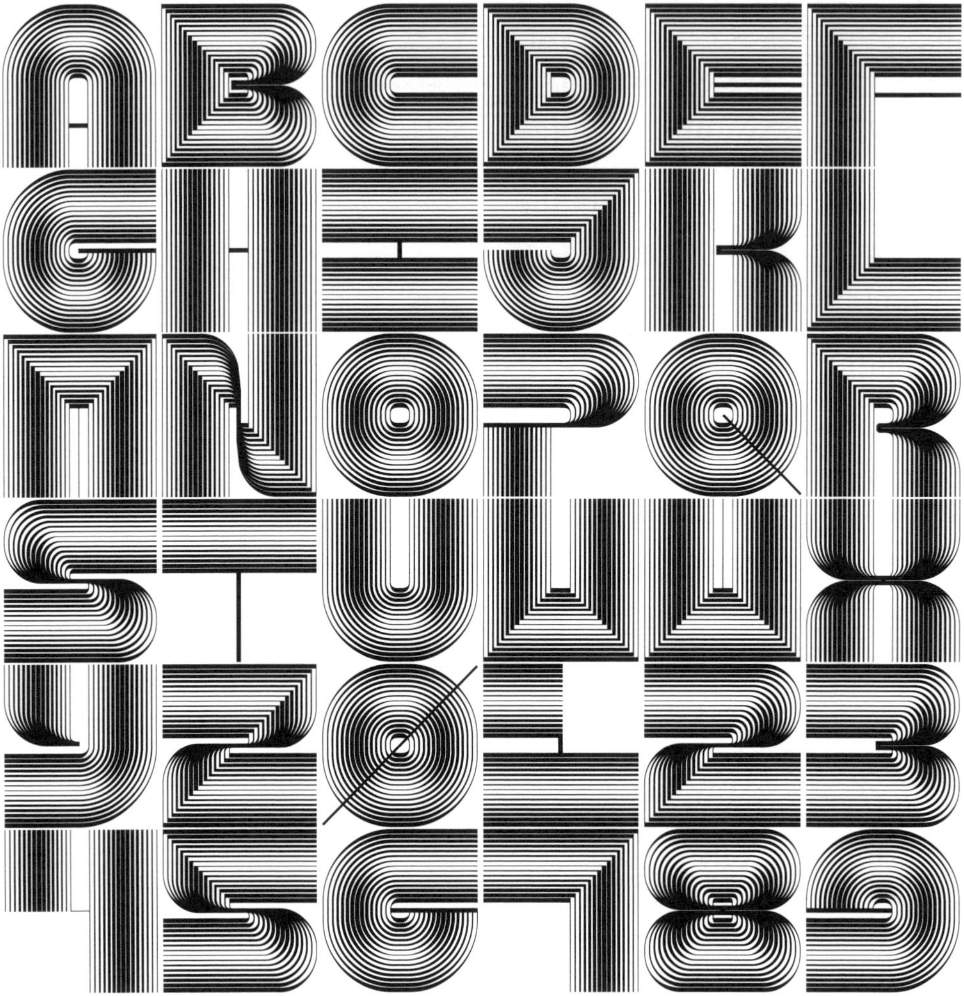

G.E An All-caps alphabet formed of gradating lines that first decrease then increase in weight vertically and increase then decrease horizontally from the centre

A–Z 0–9

s. 62
l. 62
t. 0

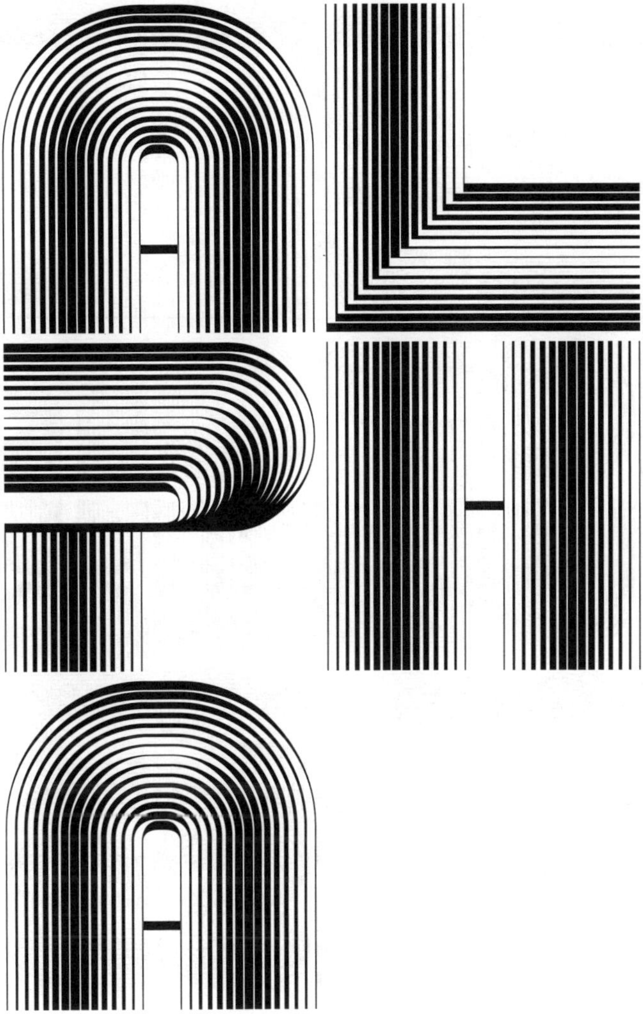

G.E

Alpha

s. 125
l. 125
t. 0

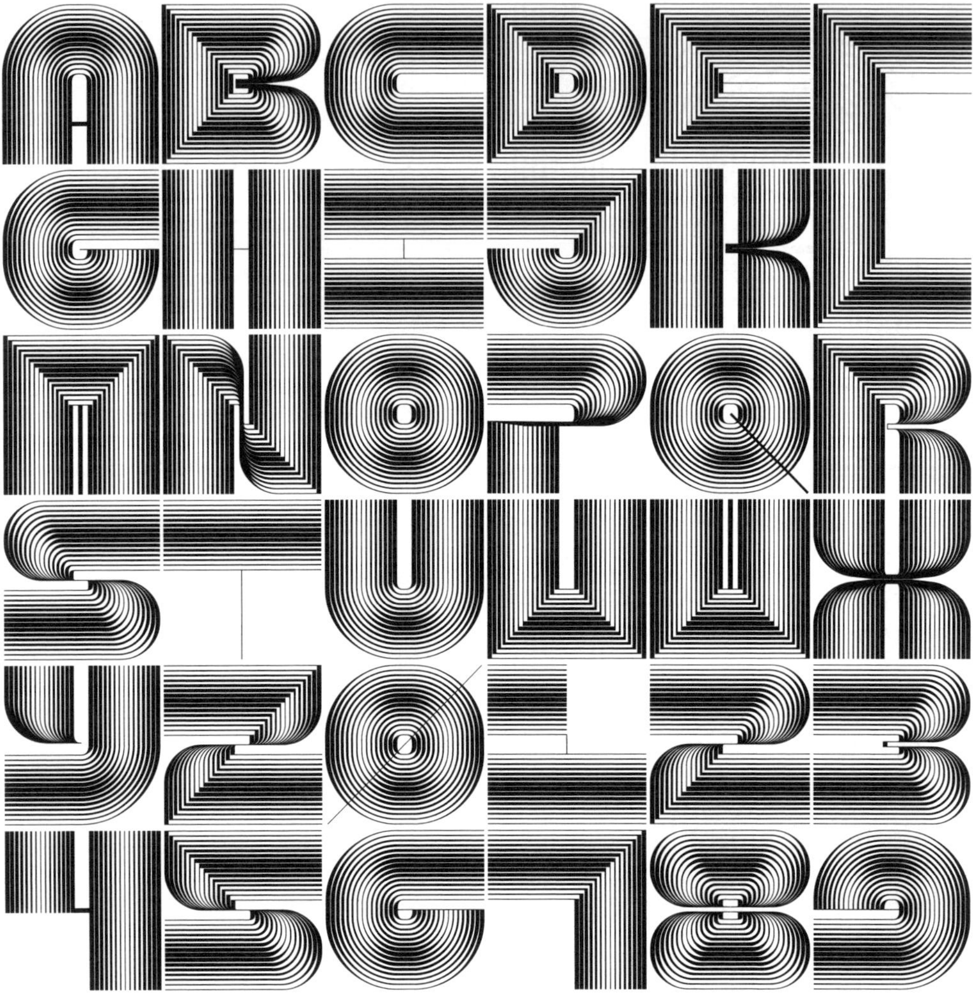

G.F An All-caps alphabet formed of gradating lines that first increase then decrease in weight vertically and decrease then increase horizontally from the centre

A–Z 0–9

s. 62
l. 62
t. 0

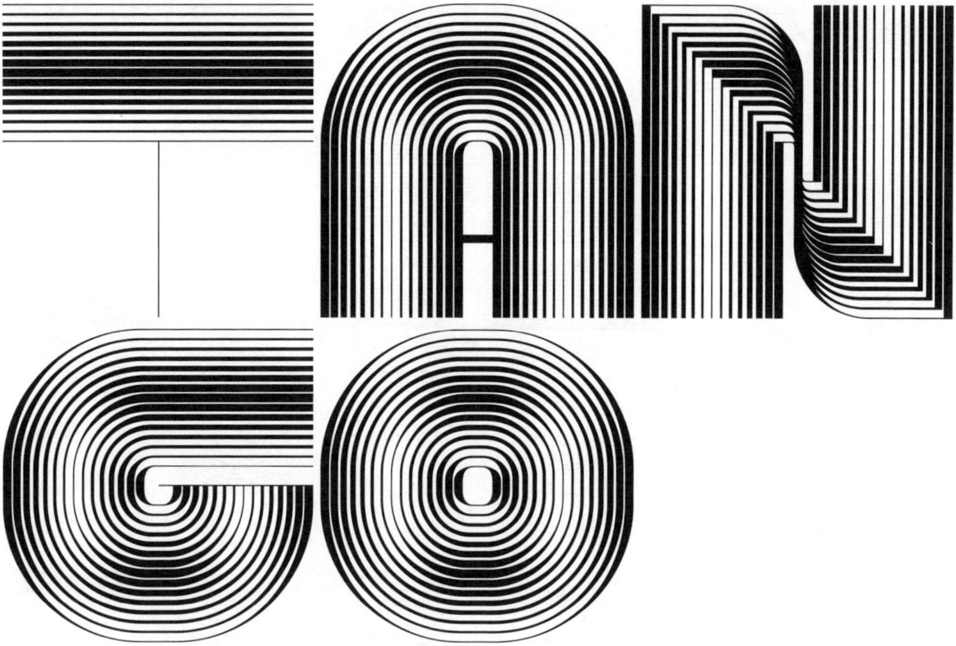

G.F

Tango

s. 125
l. 125
t. 0

G.G

An All-caps alphabet formed of gradating lines, light in weight vertically and heavy in weight horizontally

A–Z 0–9

s. 63
l. 63
t. 0
w. 500

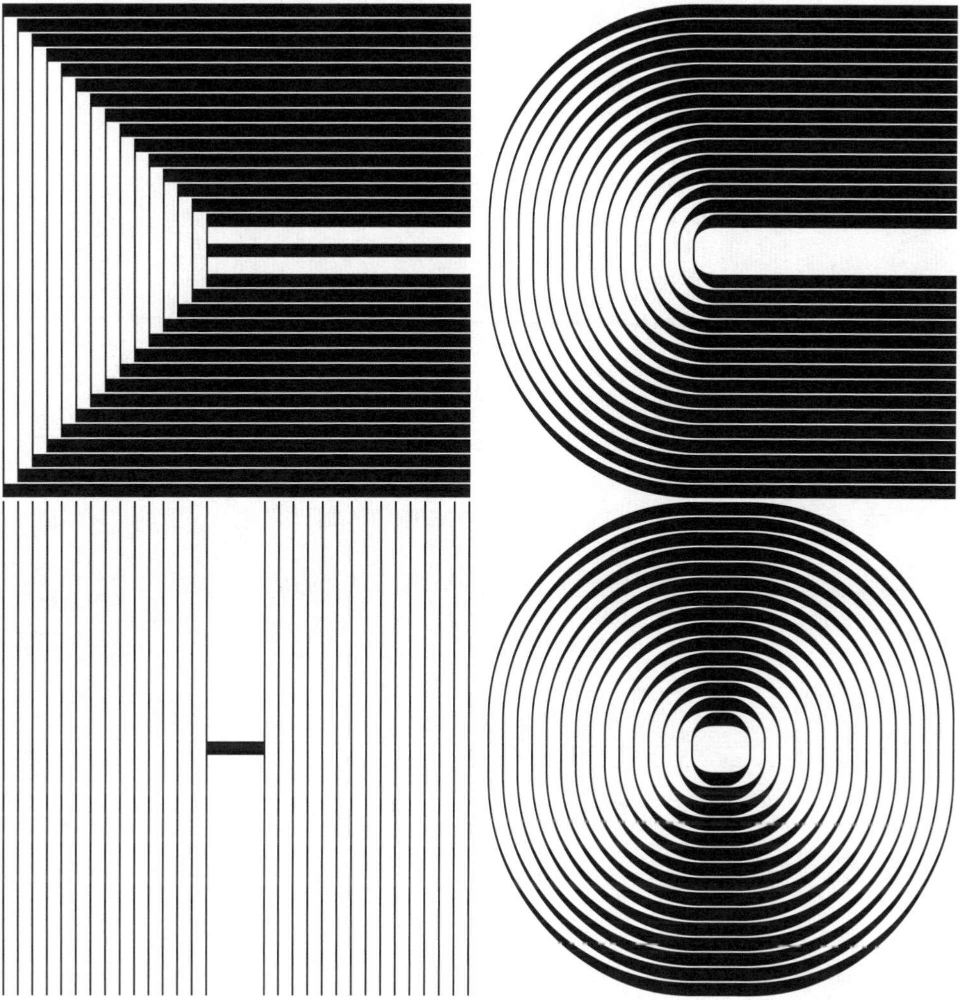

G.G

Echo

s. 188
l. 188
t. 0
w. 700

G.H An all-caps alphabet formed of gradating lines, heavy in weight vertically and light in weight horizontally

A–Z 0–9

s. 63
l. 63
t. 0
w. 500

G.H

Delta

s. 125
l. 125
t. 0
w. 500

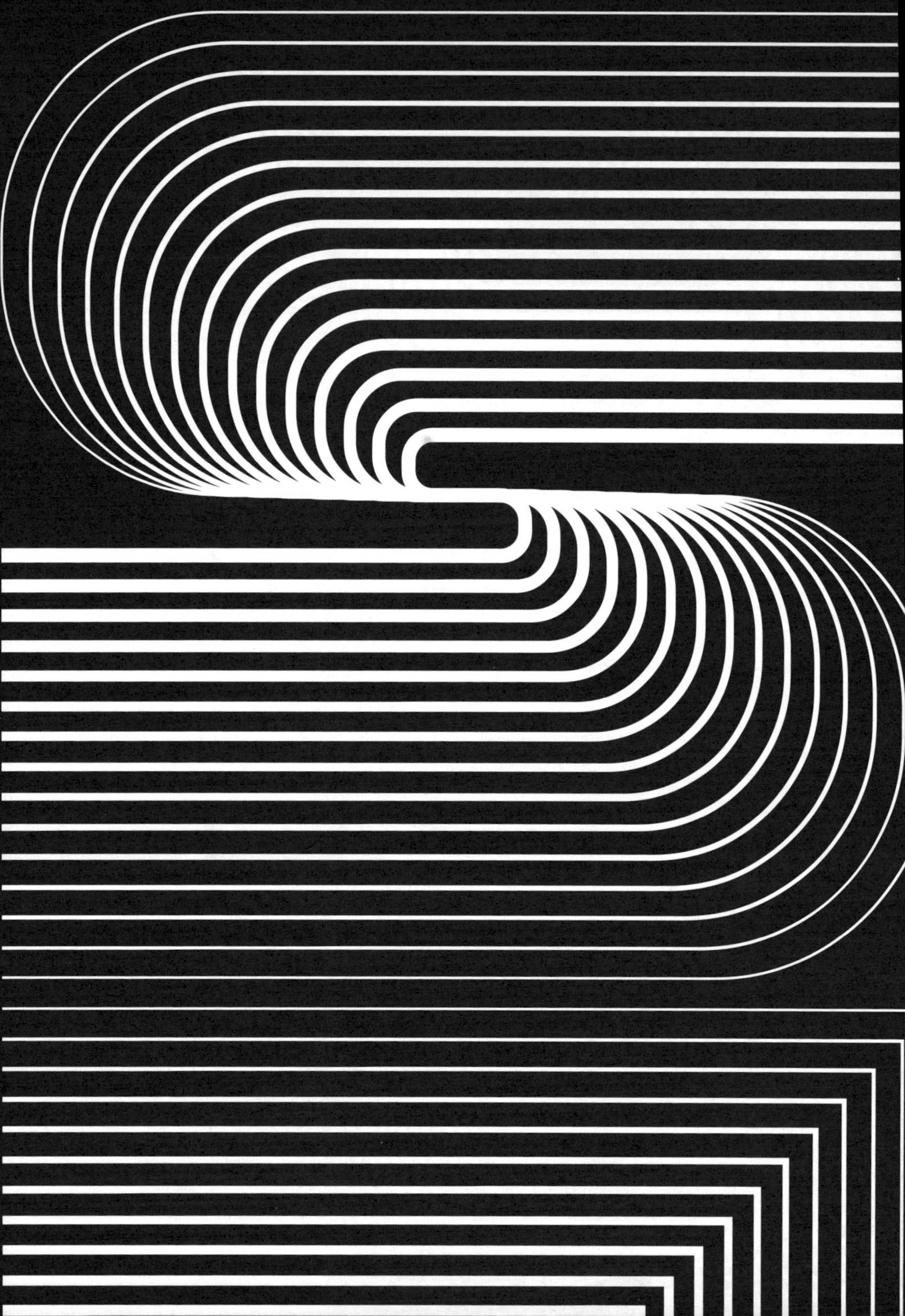

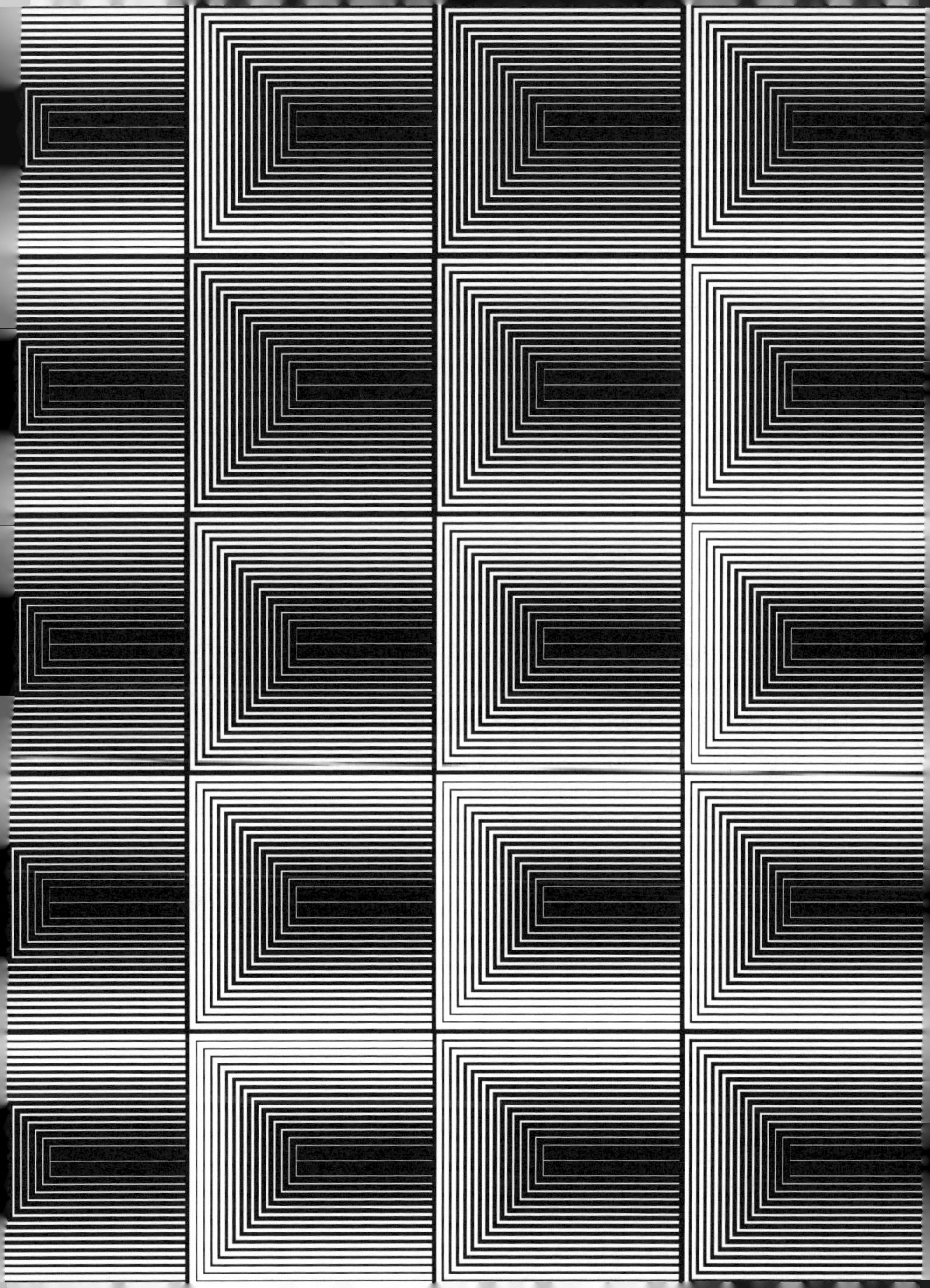

Section Notes:

Created in Glyphs, each alphabet within Gradated includes uppercase characters, numerals, and minimal punctuation. All have been developed as variable fonts with a weight parameter that controls the contrast of gradation. While all alphabets share the same underlying skeletal structure, their forms are defined by the sequence and contrast of line gradation.

H Horizontal

A highly reductive type system constructed exclusively from horizontal blocks arranged within a fixed unit grid. Letterforms are constructed through variations in parameters such as foreground line weight, background line weight, width, and simulated focus. Initially recognisable as abstract linear patterns, glyphs become decipherable only through relationships between the underlying parametric constraints.

H.A A

A wide width alphabet formed of horizontal lines, bold in foreground weight

Hotel Oscar Romeo

s.	69
l.	57
t.	0
fw.	820
bw.	100
wd.	900
b.	0

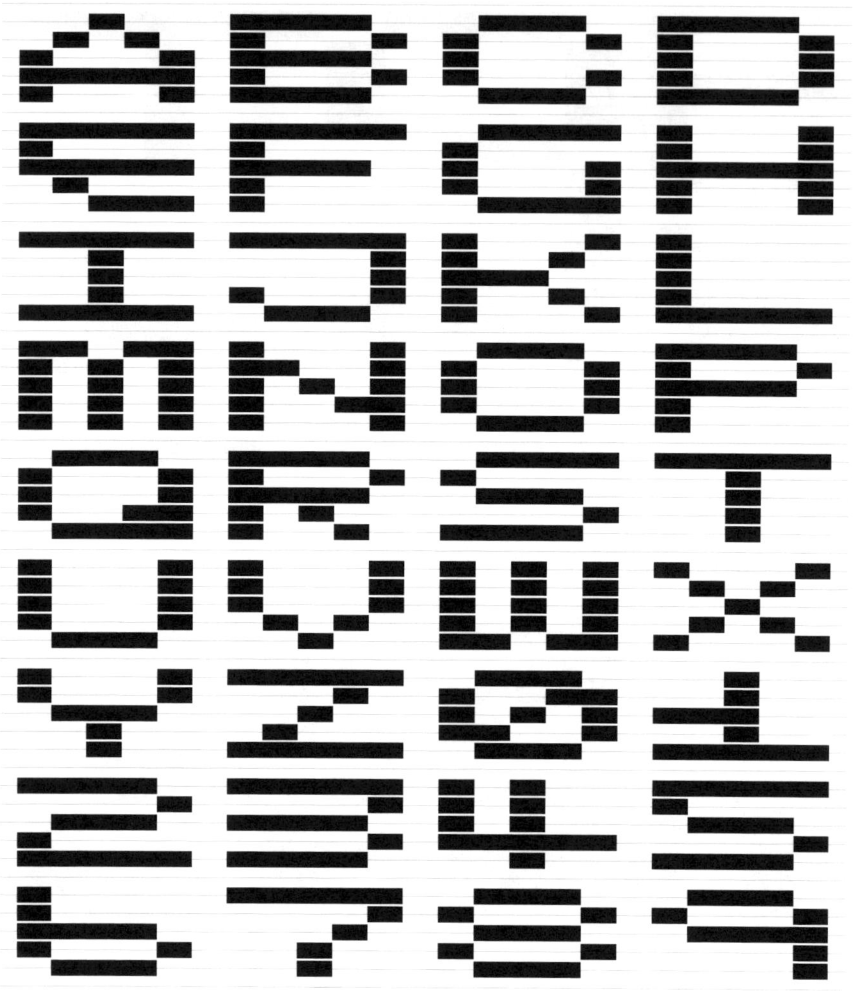

H.A A

A–Z 0–9

s. 41
l. 41
t. 0
fw. 800
bw. 100
wd. 900
b. 0

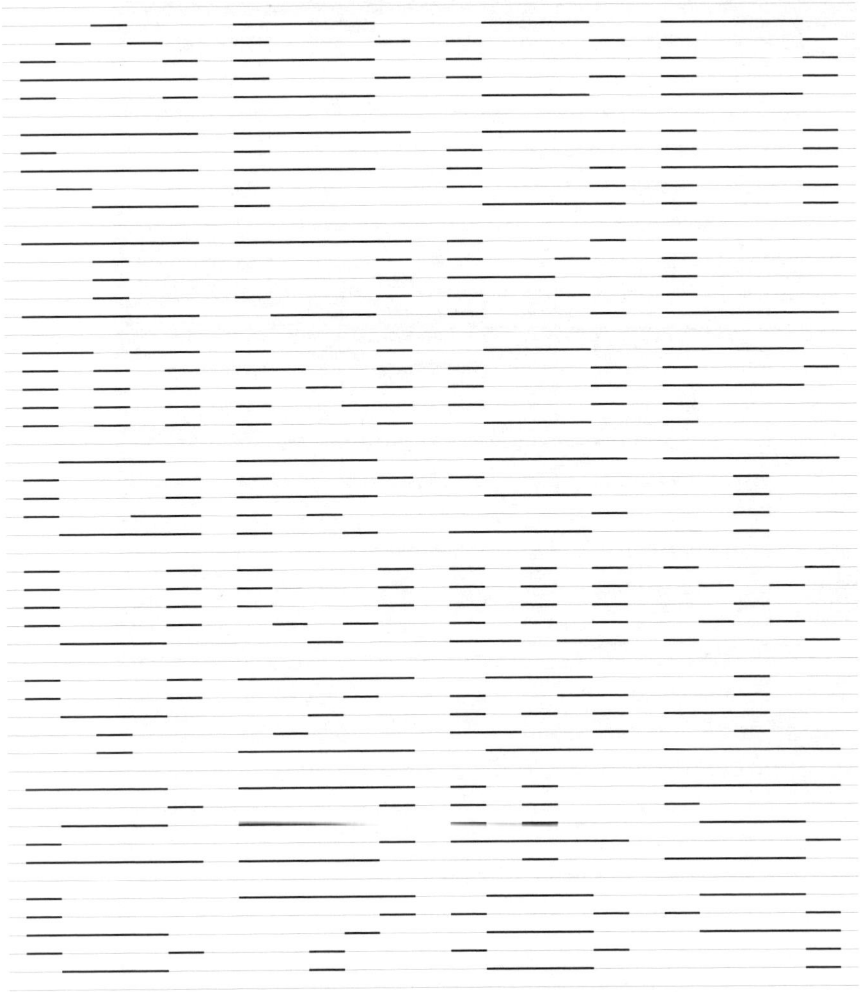

H.A B

A wide width alphabet formed of horizontal lines, light in foreground weight

A–Z 0–9

s. 41
l. 41
t. 0
fw. 100
bw. 100
wd. 900
b. 0

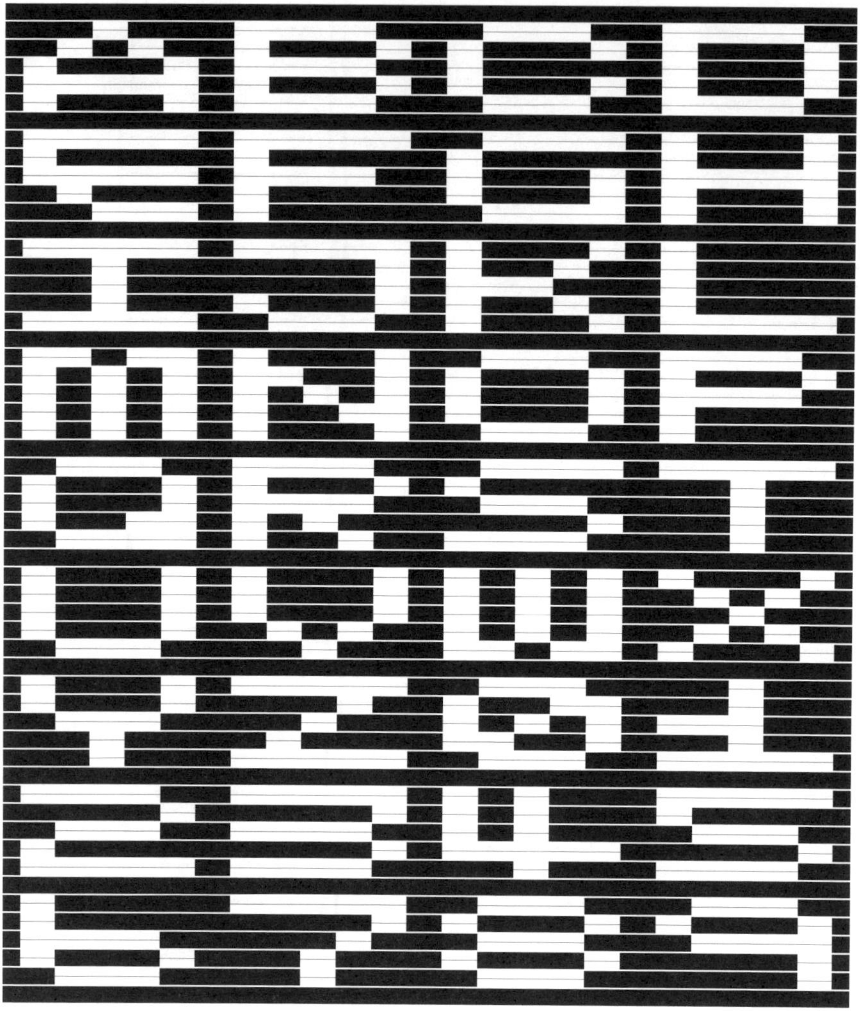

H.A C

A wide width alphabet formed of horizontal lines, bold in background weight

A–Z 0–9

s. 41
l. 41
t. 0
fw. 100
bw. 800
wd. 900
b. 0

H.A D

A wide width alphabet formed of horizontal lines, bold in foreground weight and bold in background weight

A–Z 0–9

s. 41
l. 41
t. 0
fw. 100
bw. 100
wd. 900
b. 0

H.A E

A blurred wide width alphabet formed of horizontal lines, bold in foreground weight and light in background weight

A–Z 0–9

s. 41
l. 41
t. 0
fw. 900
bw. 100
wd. 900
b. 100

H.A F

A blurred wide width alphabet formed of horizontal lines, light in foreground weight and bold in background weight

A–Z 0–9

s.	41
l.	41
t.	0
fw.	100
bw.	900
wd.	900
b.	100

H.A B

India Zulu Oscar

s. 108
l. 90
t. -150
fw. 140
bw. 100
wd.900
b. 0

H.A A

November

s. 100
l. 83
t. -150
fw. 800
bw. 124
wd. 900
b. 0

H.A E

Tango Alpha Lima

s. 67
l. 56
t. -150
fw. 900
bw. 100
wd.900
b. 100

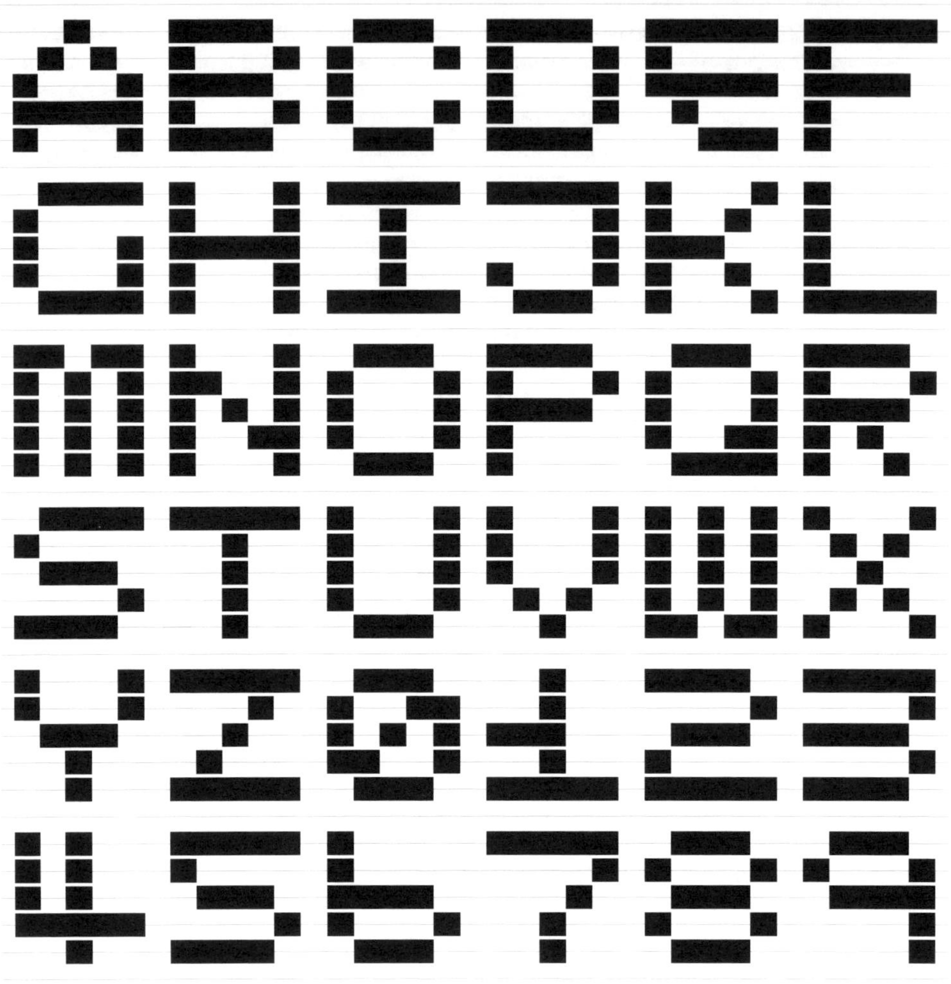

H.A G

A regular width alphabet formed of horizontal lines, bold in foreground weight

A–Z 0–9

s. 61
l. 61
t. 0
fw. 800
bw. 100
wd. 500
b. 0

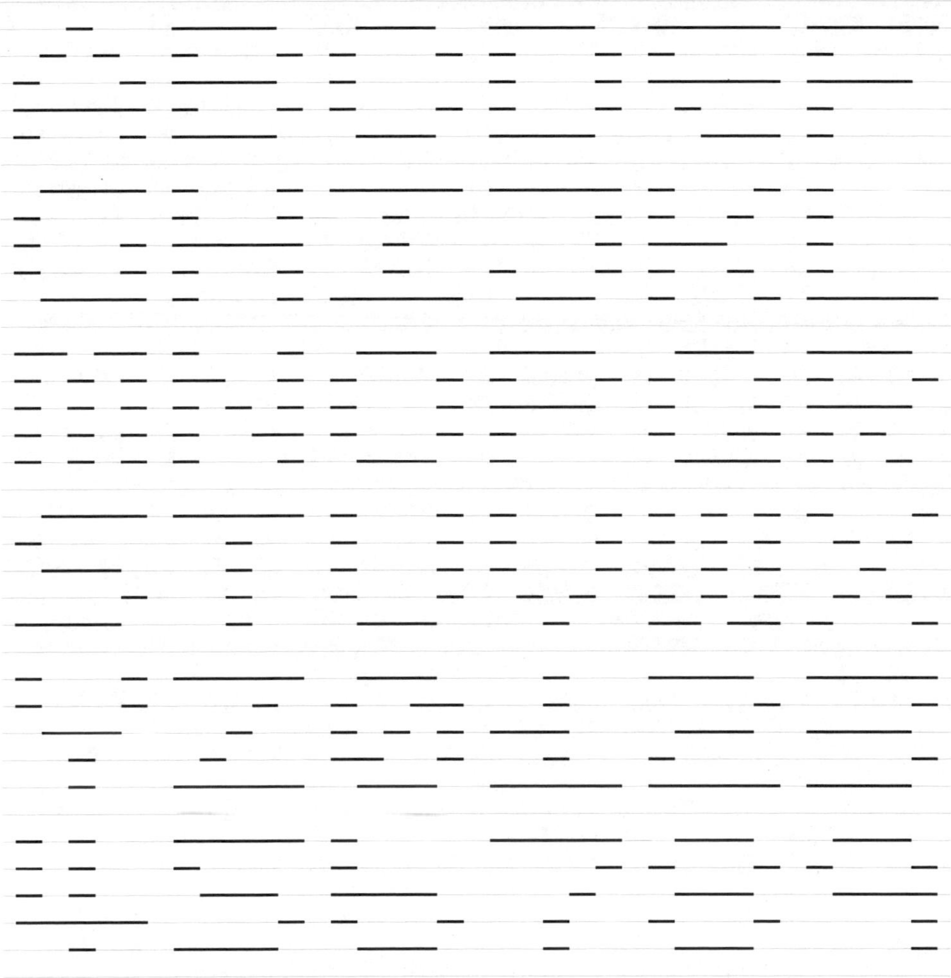

H.A H

A regular width alphabet formed of horizontal lines, light in foreground weight

A–Z 0–9

s. 61
l. 61
t. 0
fw. 100
bw. 100
wd. 500
b. 0

H.A I

A regular width alphabet formed of horizontal lines, bold in background weight

A–Z 0–9

s.	61
l.	61
t.	0
fw.	100
bw.	800
wd.	500
b.	0

H.A J

A regular width alphabet formed of horizontal lines, bold in foreground weight and bold in background weight

A–Z 0–9

s. 61
l. 61
t. 0
fw. 900
bw. 800
wd. 500
b. 0

H.A K

A blurred regular width alphabet formed of horizontal lines, bold in foreground weight and light in background weight

A–Z 0–9

s. 61
l. 61
t. 0
fw. 900
bw. 100
wd. 500
b. 100

H.A L

A blurred regular width alphabet formed of horizontal lines, light in foreground weightand bold in background weight

A–Z 0–9

s. 61
l. 61
t. 0
fw. 100
bw. 900
wd. 500
b. 100

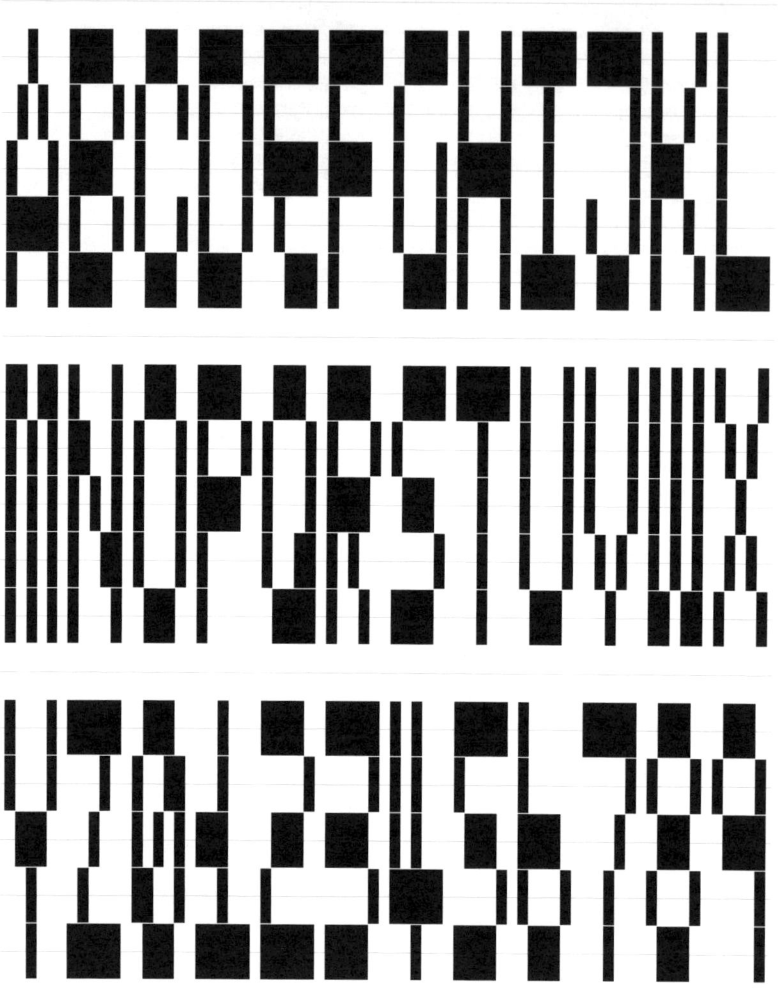

H.A M

A narrow width alphabet formed of horizontal lines, bold in foreground weight

A–Z 0–9

s. 126
l. 126
t. 0
fw. 800
bw. 100
wd. 100
b. 0

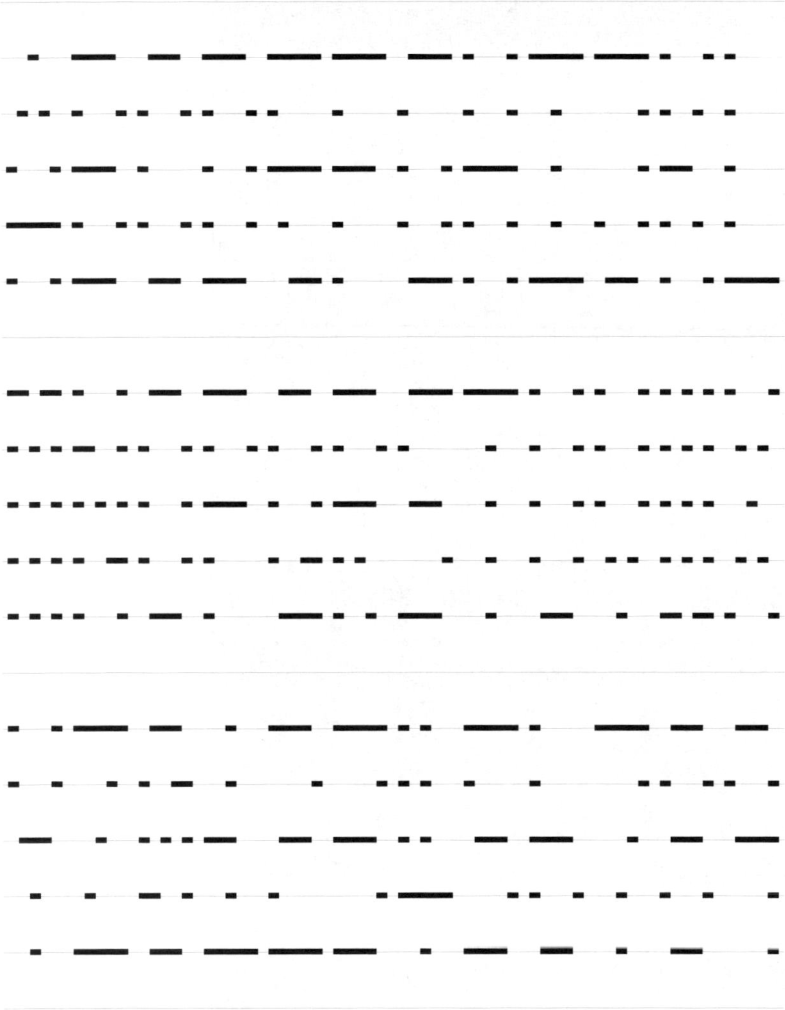

H.A N

A narrow width alphabet formed of horizontal lines, light in foreground weight

A–Z 0–9

s. 126
l. 126
t. 0
fw. 100
bw. 100
wd. 100
b. 0

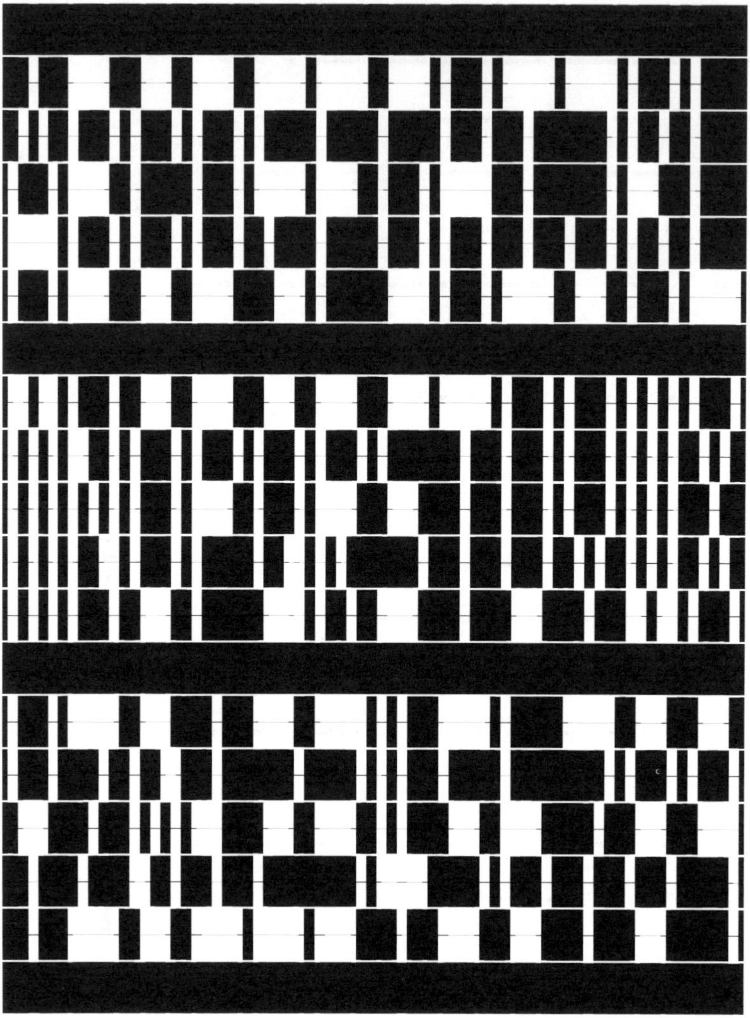

H.A O

A narrow width alphabet formed of horizontal lines, bold in background weight

A–Z 0–9

s. 126
l. 126
t. 0
fw. 100
bw. 800
wd. 100
b. 0

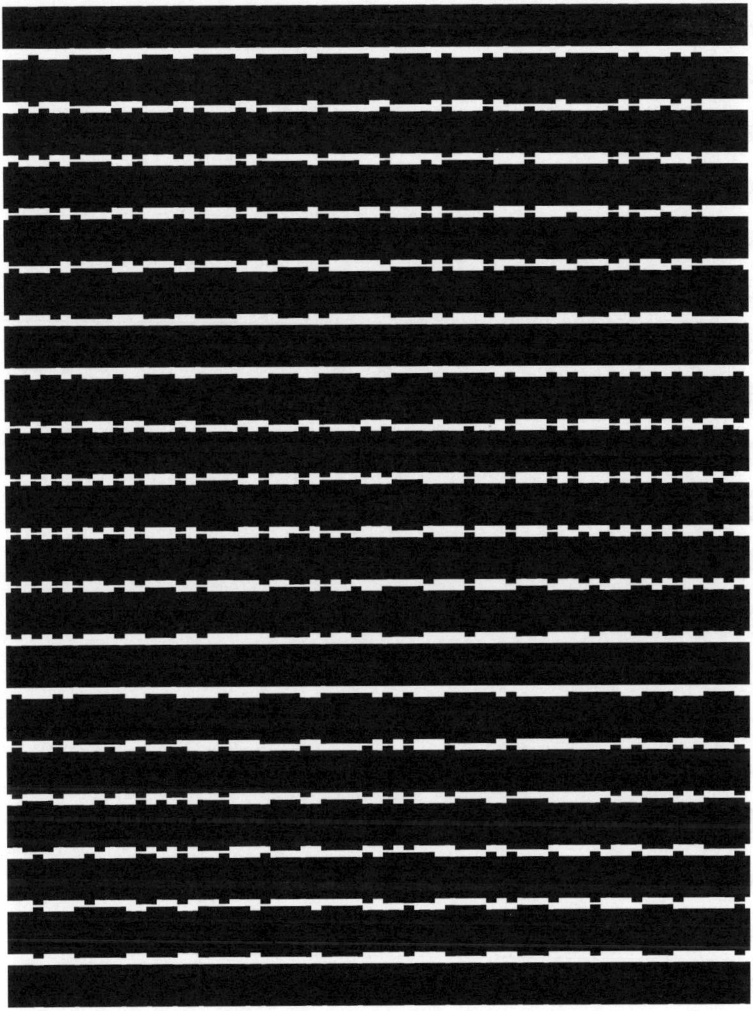

H.A P

A narrow width alphabet formed of horizontal lines, bold in foreground weight and bold in background weight

A–Z 0–9

s.	126
l.	126
t.	0
fw.	800
bw.	800
wd.	100
b.	0

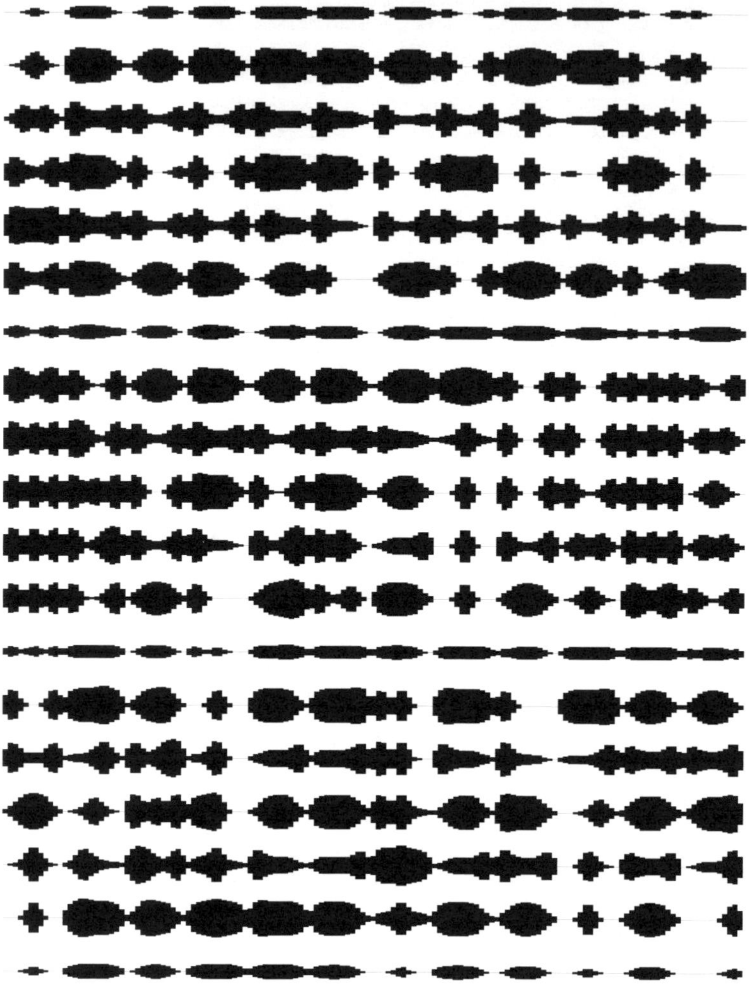

H.A Q

A blurred narrow width alphabet formed of horizontal lines, bold in foreground weight and light in background weight

A–Z 0–9

s. 126
l. 126
t. 0
fw. 900
bw. 100
wd. 100
b. 100

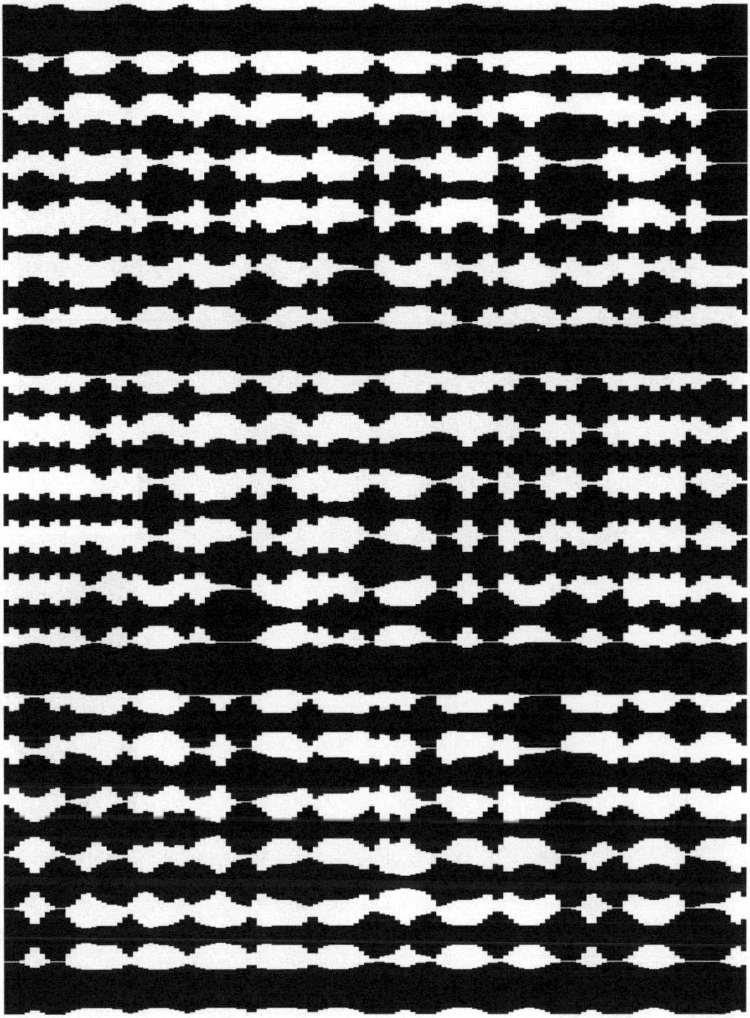

H.A R

A blurred narrow width alphabet formed of horizontal lines, light in foreground weight and bold in background weight

A–Z 0–9

s. 126
l. 126
t. 0
fw. 100
bw. 900
wd. 100
b. 100

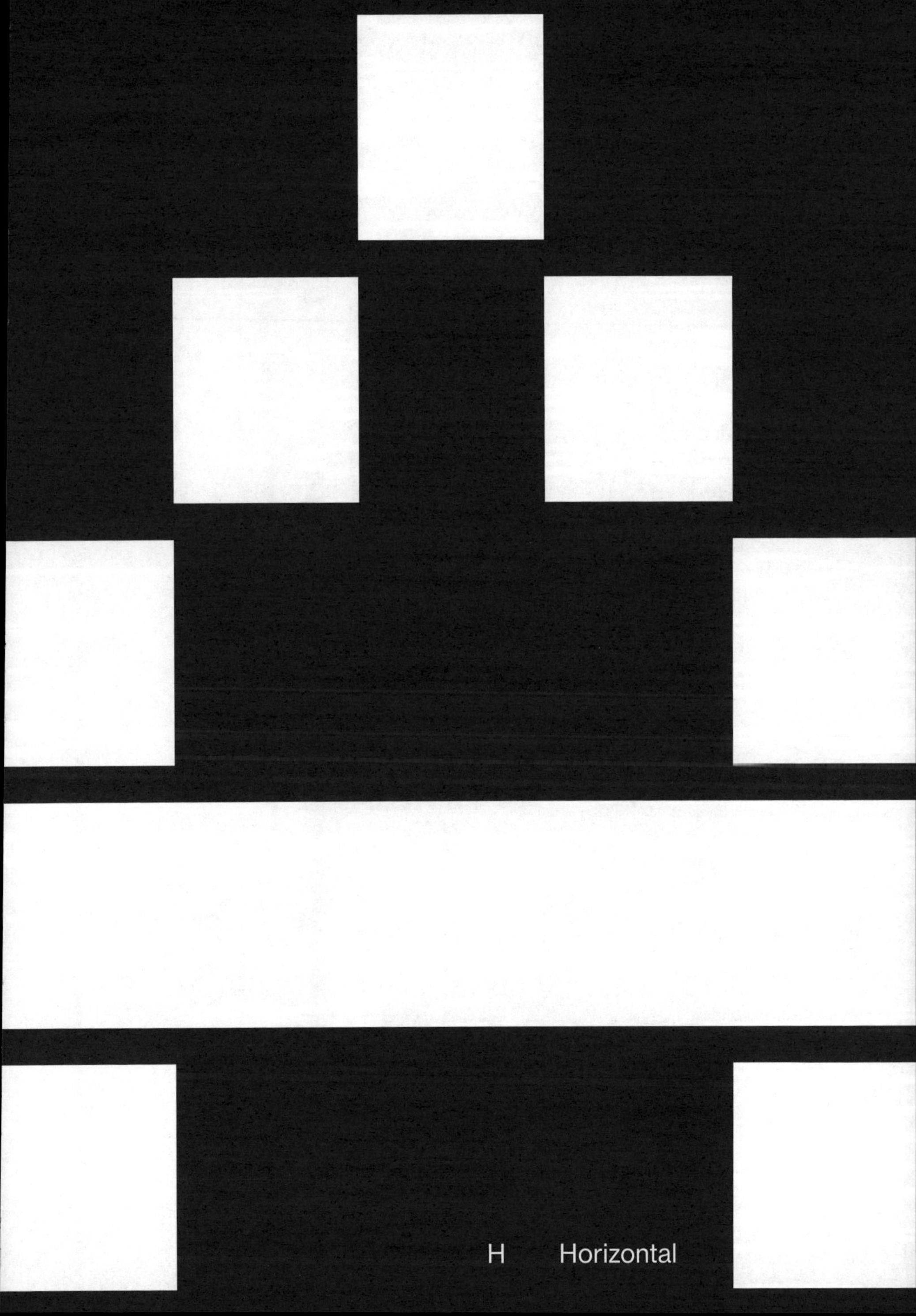

H Horizontal

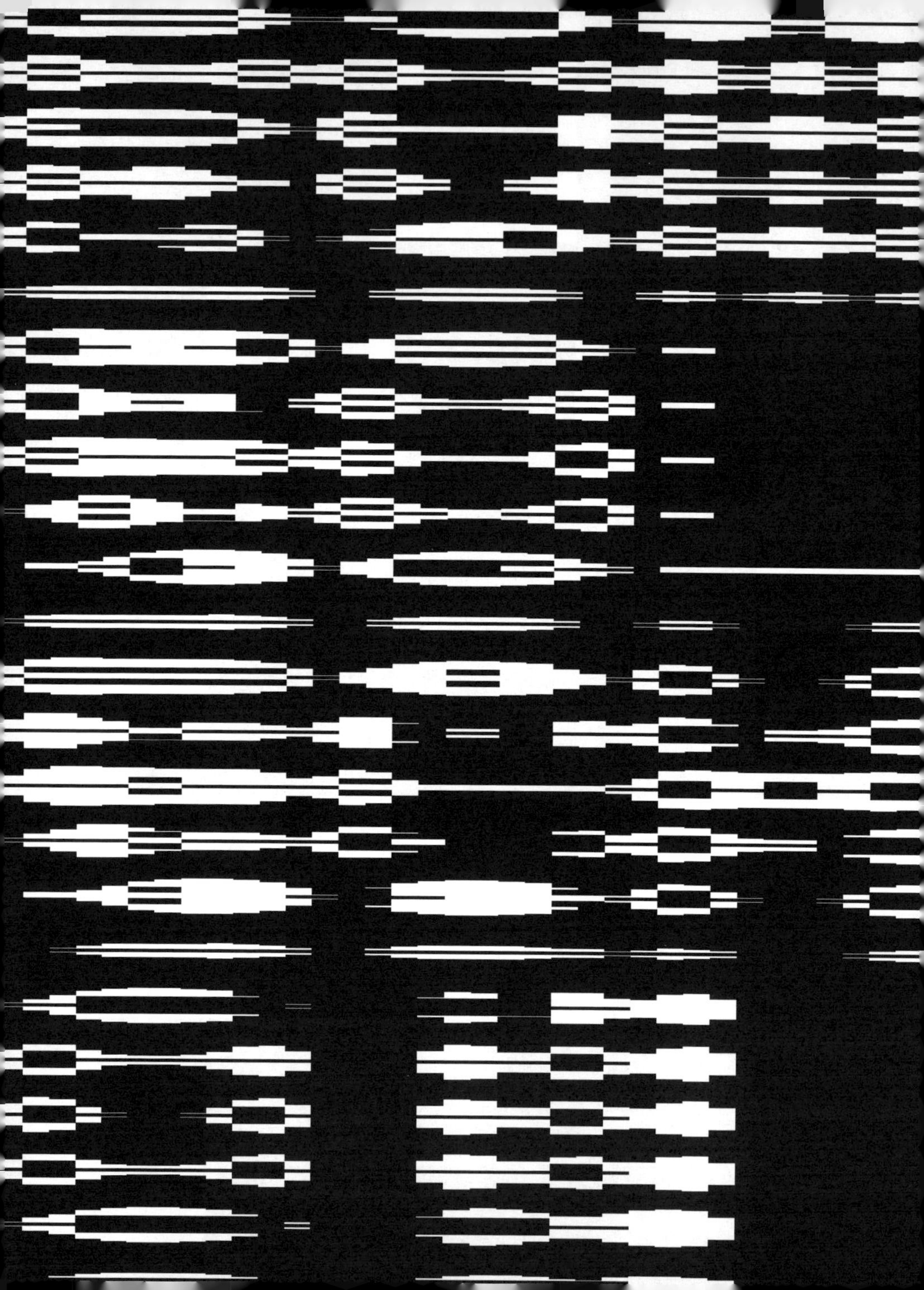

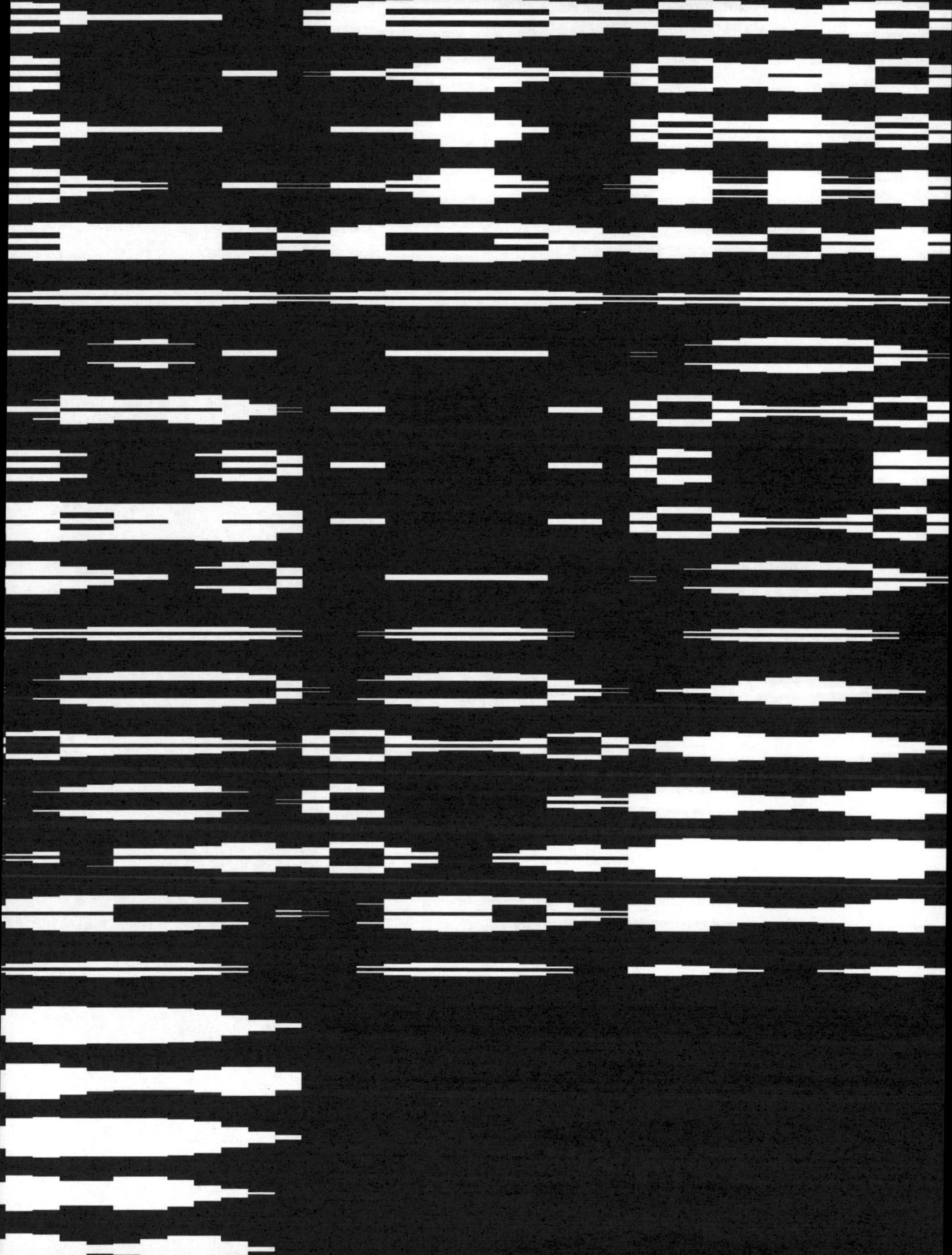

H Horizontal

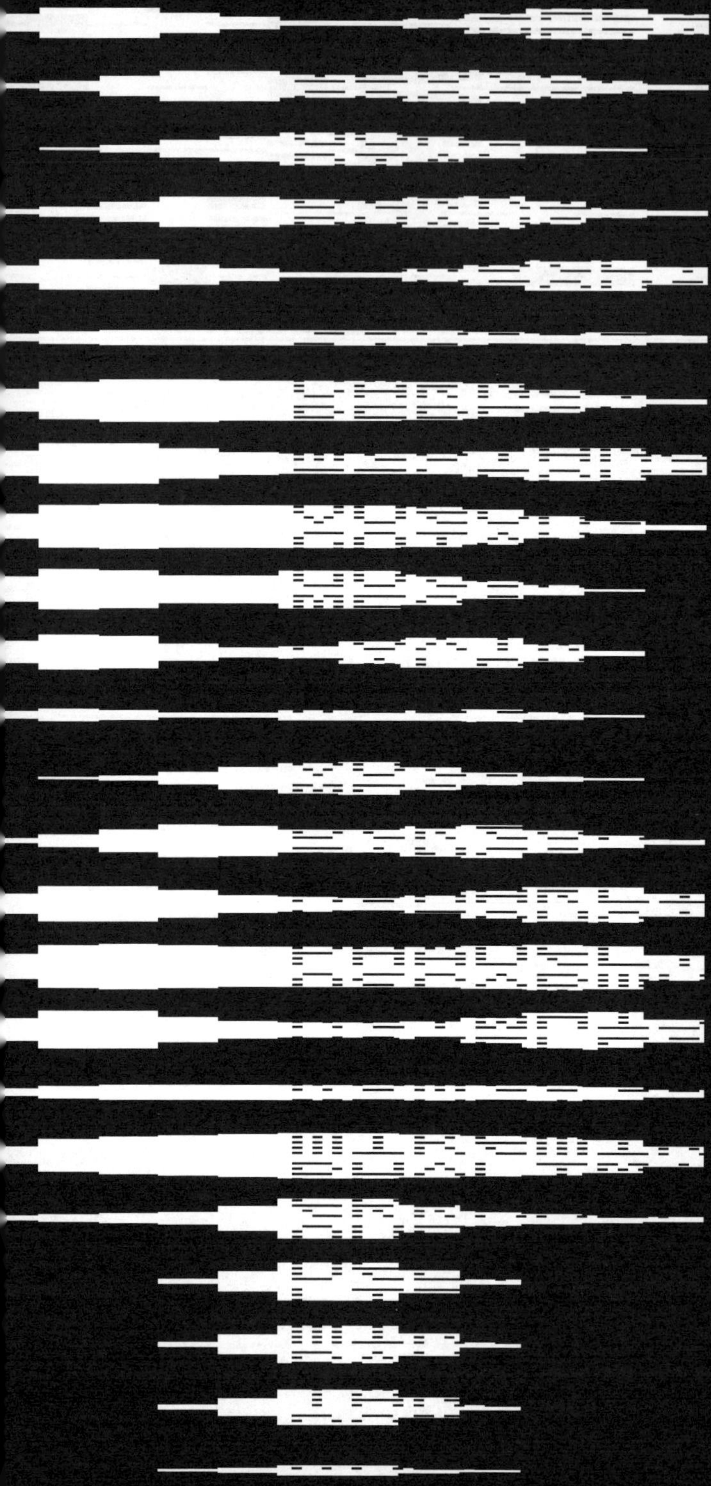

Section Notes:

Created in Glyphs, H.A consists of a single font file containing variable parameters for foreground weight, background weight, width and simulated blur, it includes uppercase characters, numerals, and minimal punctuation.

I Inverting

A set of three type systems defined by variable parameters. Each system incorporates alternating stylistic sets that produce spatial or contrast-based variations across character strings. Text is encrypted through these inversions, requiring readers to interpret glyphs as either positive or negative spaces, or through shifts in contrast. The simplicity of the geometric letterforms provides a rhythmic interchange of figure and ground patterns that offset reading and abstraction.

I.A A

An ultra-light rounded inverting alphabet, alternating between negative and positive space from character to character*

India

s. 123
l. 123
t. 0
w. 100
r. 900

I.A A

November

s. 123
l. 123
t. 0
w. 100
r. 900

UC

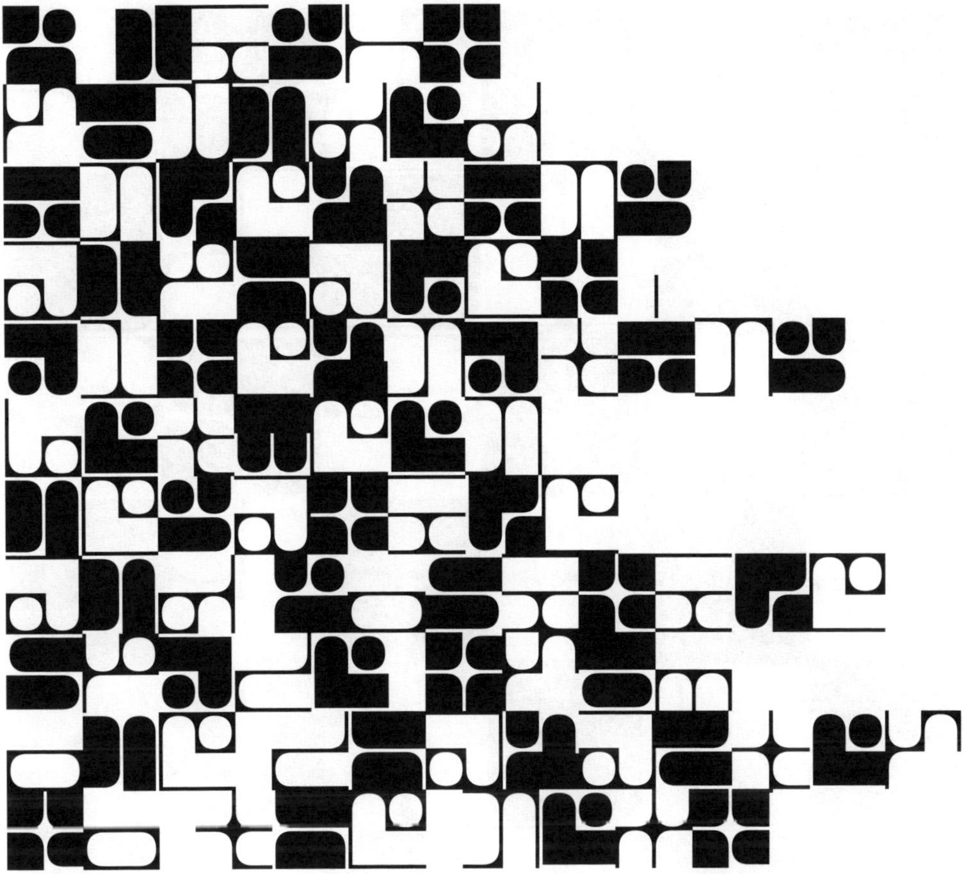

I.A A *

s. 30
l. 30
t. 0
w. 300
r. 900

I.A A

A–Z 0–9

s. 62
l. 62
t. 0
w. 100
r. 900

I.A B

An ultra-light squared inverting alphabet, alternating between negative and positive space from character to character

a–z !#%$/&£€?@

s. 62
l. 62
t. 0
w. 100
r. 900

I.A C

A light weight rounded outline inverting alphabet, alternating between negative and positive space from character to character

A–Z 0–9

s. 62
l. 62
t. 0
w. 300
r. 900

I.A D

A light weight squared outline inverting alphabet, alternating between negative and positive space from character to character

a–z !#%$/&£€?@

s. 62
l. 62
t. 0
w. 300
r. 900

I.A E

A medium weight rounded inverting alphabet, alternating between negative and positive space from character to character

Victor

s. 123
l. 123
t. 0
w. 400
r. 900

UC

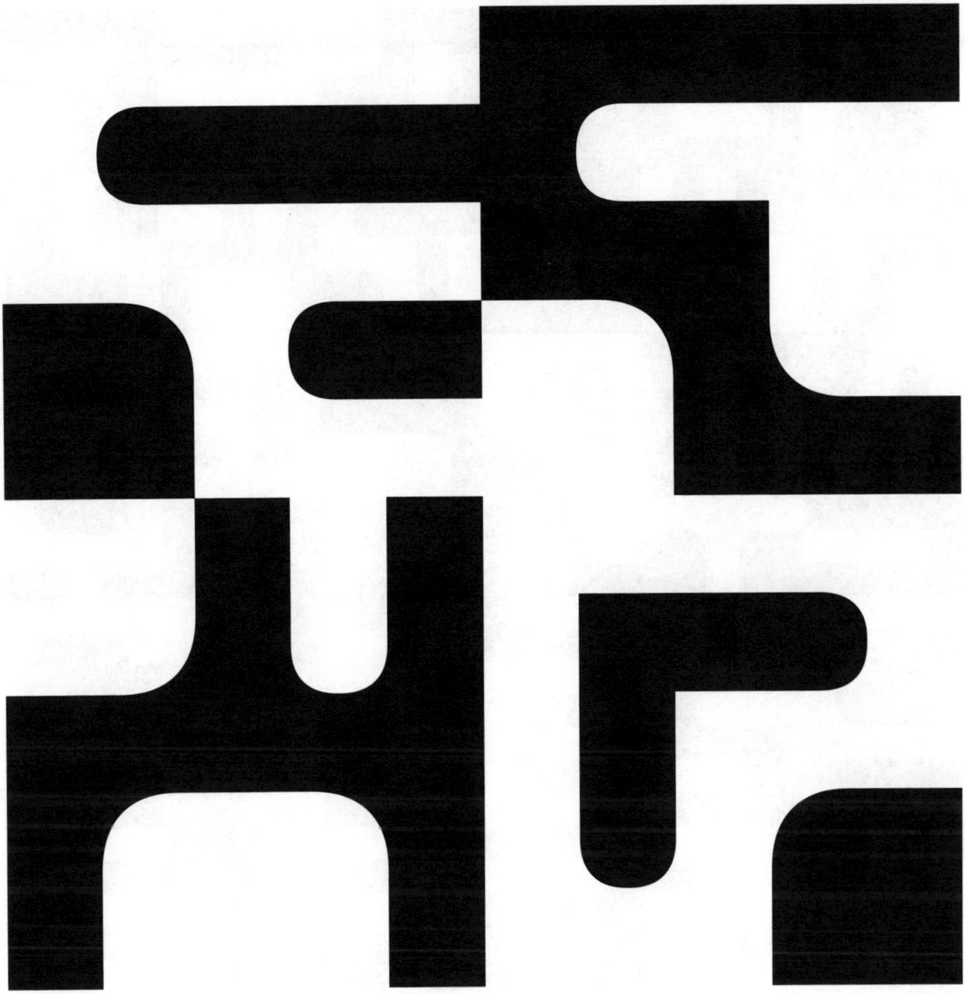

I.A E

Echo

s. 184
l. 184
t. 0
w. 400
r. 900

UC

I.A E

A–Z 0–9

s. 62
l. 62
t. 0
w. 400
r. 900

I.A F

A medium weight squared inverting alphabet, alternating between negative and positive space from character to character

a–z !#%$/&£€?@

s. 62
l. 62
t. 0
w. 400
r. 100

I.A G

A medium rounded outline inverting alphabet, alternating between negative and positive space from character to character

A–Z 0–9

s. 62
l. 62
t. 0
w. 400
r. 900

I.A H

A medium squared outline inverting alphabet, alternating between negative and positive space from character to character

a–z !#%$/&£€?@

s. 62
l. 62
t. 0
w. 400
r. 100

I.A I

A bold weight rounded inverting alphabet, alternating between negative and positive space from character to character

A–Z 0–9

s. 62
l. 62
t. 0
w. 900
r. 900

I.A J

A bold weight, squared and outline inverting alphabet, alternating between negative and positive space from one character to the next*

a–z !#%$/&£€?@

s. 62
l. 62
t. 0
w. 900
r. 100

I.A K

A bold rounded outline inverting alphabet, alternating between negative and positive space from character to character

A–Z 0–9

s. 62
l. 62
t. 0
w. 900
r. 900

I.A L

A bold squared outline inverting alphabet, alternating between negative and positive space from character to character

a–z !#%$/&£€?@

s. 62
l. 62
t. 0
w. 900
r. 100

I.A B

Romeo Tango India

s. 123
l. 123
t. 0
w. 100
r. 900

UC

I.A J November

s. 184
l. 184
t. 0
w. 900
r. 900

UC

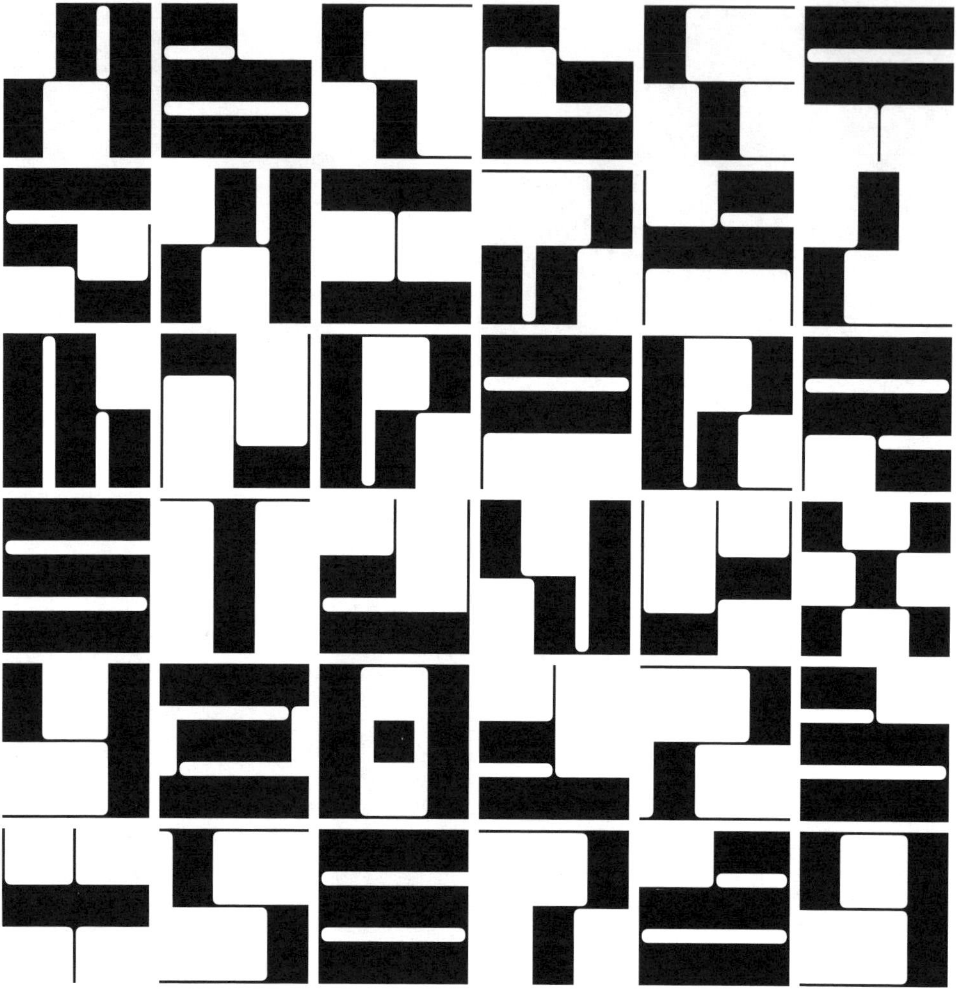

I.B A

A rounded inverting alphabet alternating between standard and reverse contrast from character to character*

A–Z 0–9

s. 58
l. 62
t. 70
w. 900
r. 900

I.B B

A squared inverting alphabet alternating between standard and reverse contrast from character to character

a–z !#%$/&£€?@

s. 58
l. 62
t. 70
w. 900
r. 100

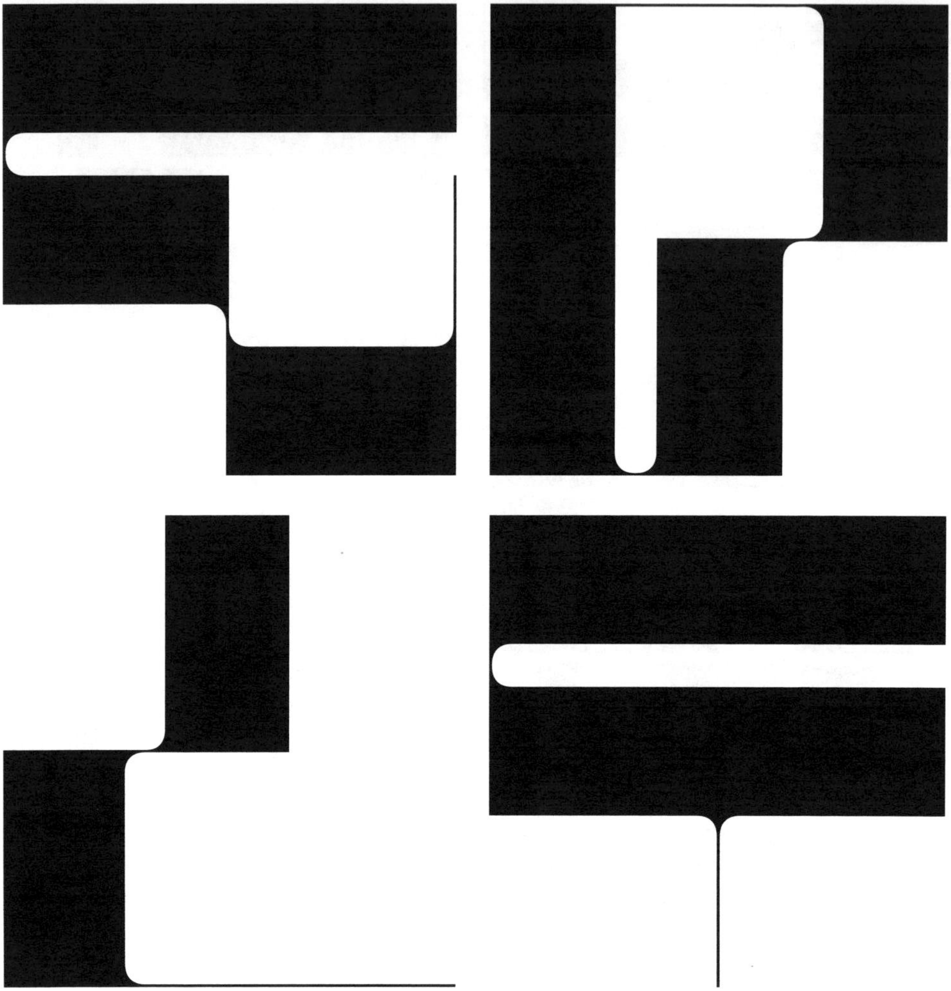

I.B A

Golf

s. 177
l. 190
t. 70
w. 100
r. 900

UC

a modular
inverting
alphabet
alternating
between
standard
and reverse
contrast
from
character
to character

I.B A *

s. 29
l. 30
t. 40
w. 300
r. 900

I.B A Charlie

s. 177
l. 190
t. 70
w. 100
r. 900

I.C A

A rounded inverting alphabet alternating in both contrast and space from character to character*

A–Z 0–9

s. 62
l. 62
t. 0
w. 300
r. 900

I.C B

A squared inverting alphabet alternating in both contrast and space from character to character

a–z !#%$/&£€?@

s. 62
l. 62
t. 0
w. 300
r. 100

I.C

Oscar November Tango
Romeo Alpha Sierra

s. 62
l. 62
t. 0
w. 300
r. 900

UC

I.C

*

s. 62
l. 62
t. 0
w. 900
r. 100

I.C Tango

s. 184
l. 184
t. 0
w. 100
r. 900

UC

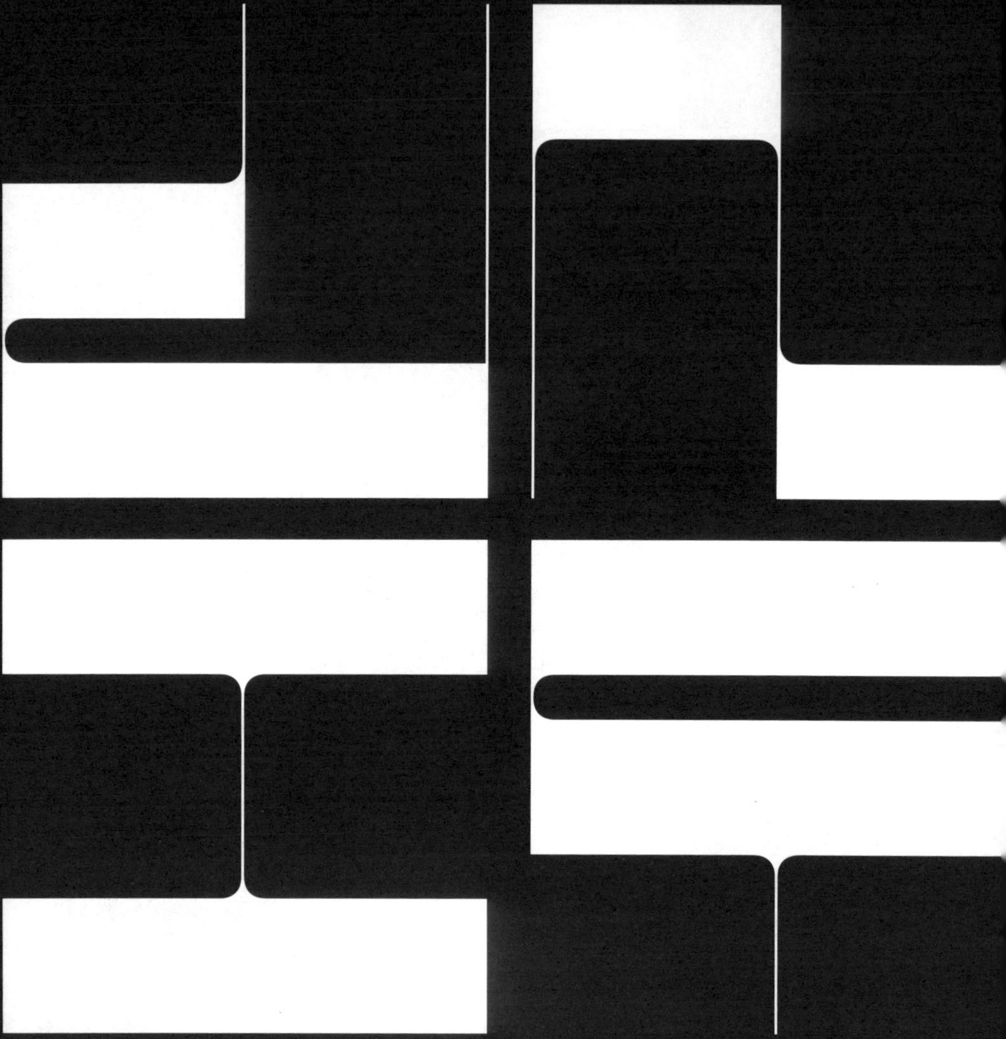

I Inverting

I Inverting

I Inverting

Section Notes:

Created in Glyphs, I.A, I.B, and I.C each consist of a single font file containing both uppercase and lowercase character sets, numerals, and basic punctuation. Each system includes variable parameters for weight and roundness. Contextual alternates enable stylistic variation within each system, allowing alternation between spatial (I.A), contrast-based (I.B), or combined (I.C) styles across character strings.

J

A pair of type systems composed of non-proportional, fixed-width glyphs, all of which allow for justified 'shrink-to-fit' settings that can fill the proportions of any layout or grid. Rather than adjusting inter-character spacing, justification* is achieved through the expansion or contraction of character widths. Each set can operate independently or as part of a system of contextual alternates, scripted to create dynamic columns adjusted at will. The page, frame or screen functions as a responsive field of typographic density, using width variation alone to articulate structure, rhythm, and emphasis.

*While "justification" usually refers to the adjustment of spacing between letters and words in order to align both left and right margins of consecutive lines of text, in this instance the term refers to the expansion and contraction of the letters themselves to fit text blocks, grids or pages.

JUSTIFIED

J.A A

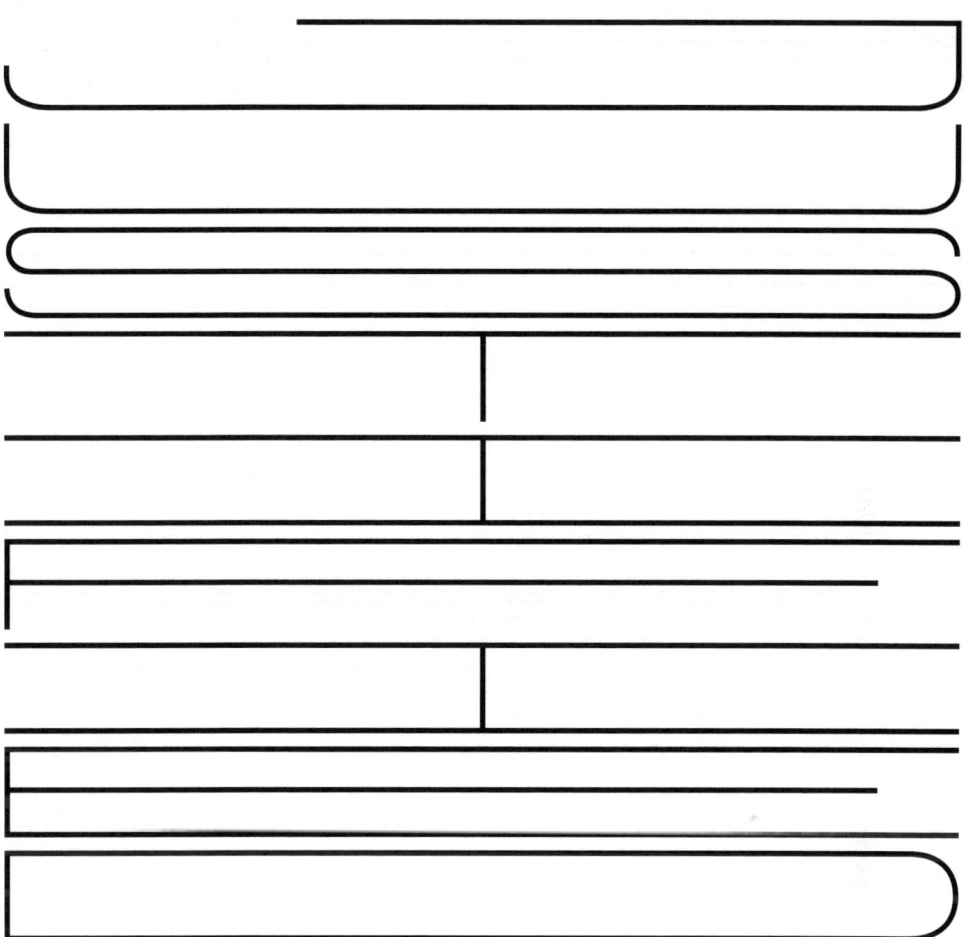

An all-caps justified type system set to justify text to one column

Justified

s. 40
l. 39
t. 0

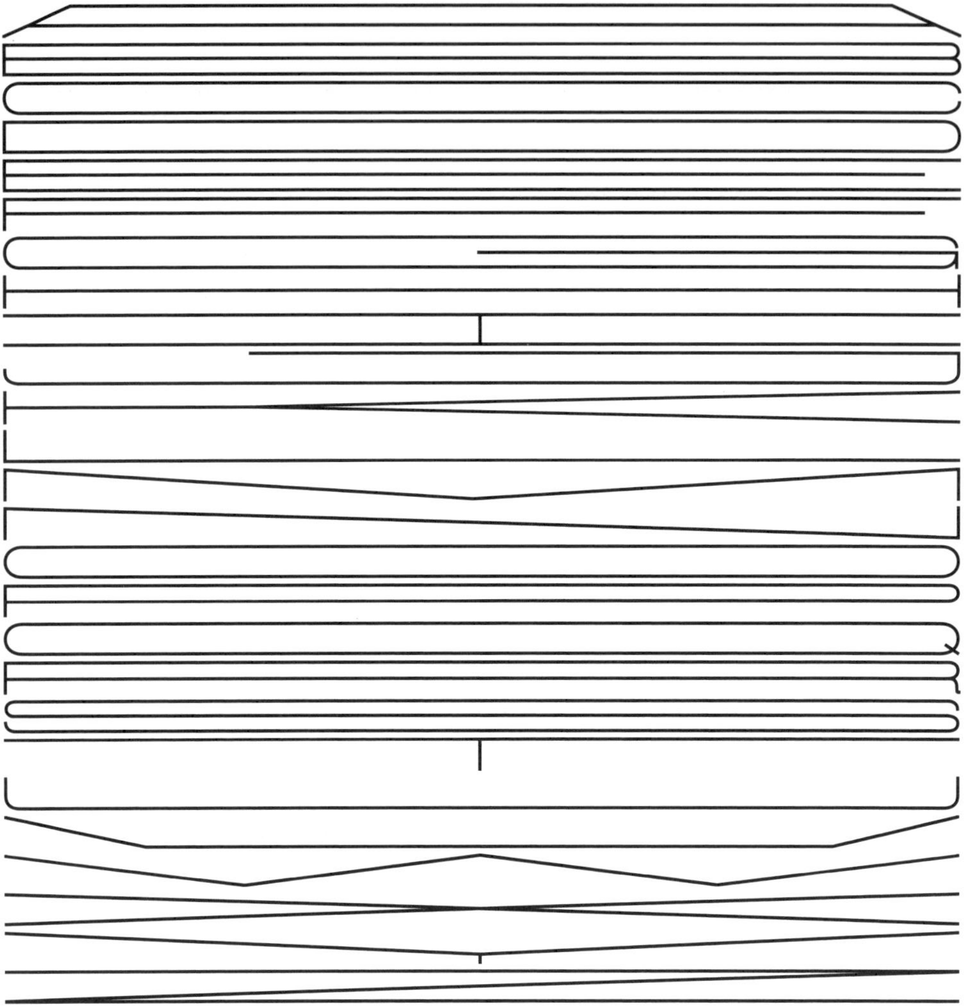

J.A A A–Z

s. 14
l. 14.5
t. 0

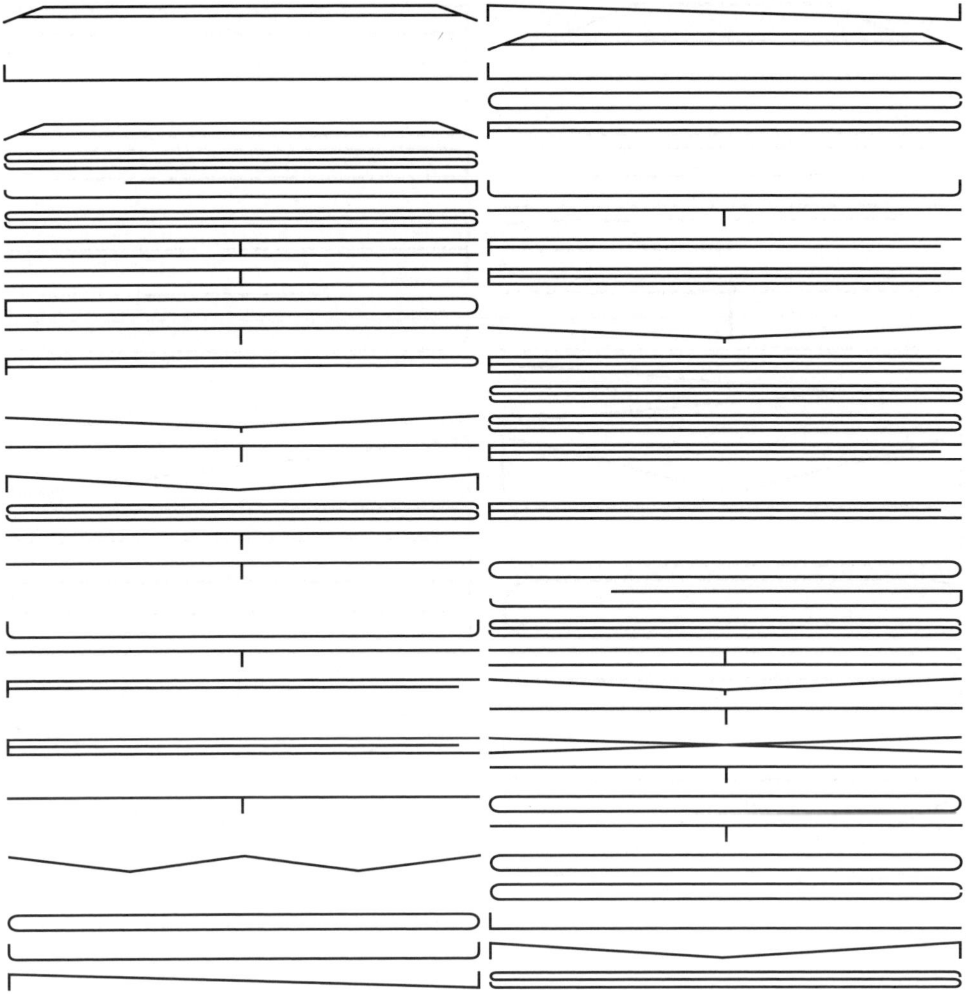

J.A B

An all-caps justified type system set
to justify text to two columns

*

s. 7
l. 11
t. 0

A B
C D
E F
G H
I J
K L
M N
O P
Q R
S T
U V
W X
Y Z

J.A B

A–Z

s. 27
l. 27
t. 0

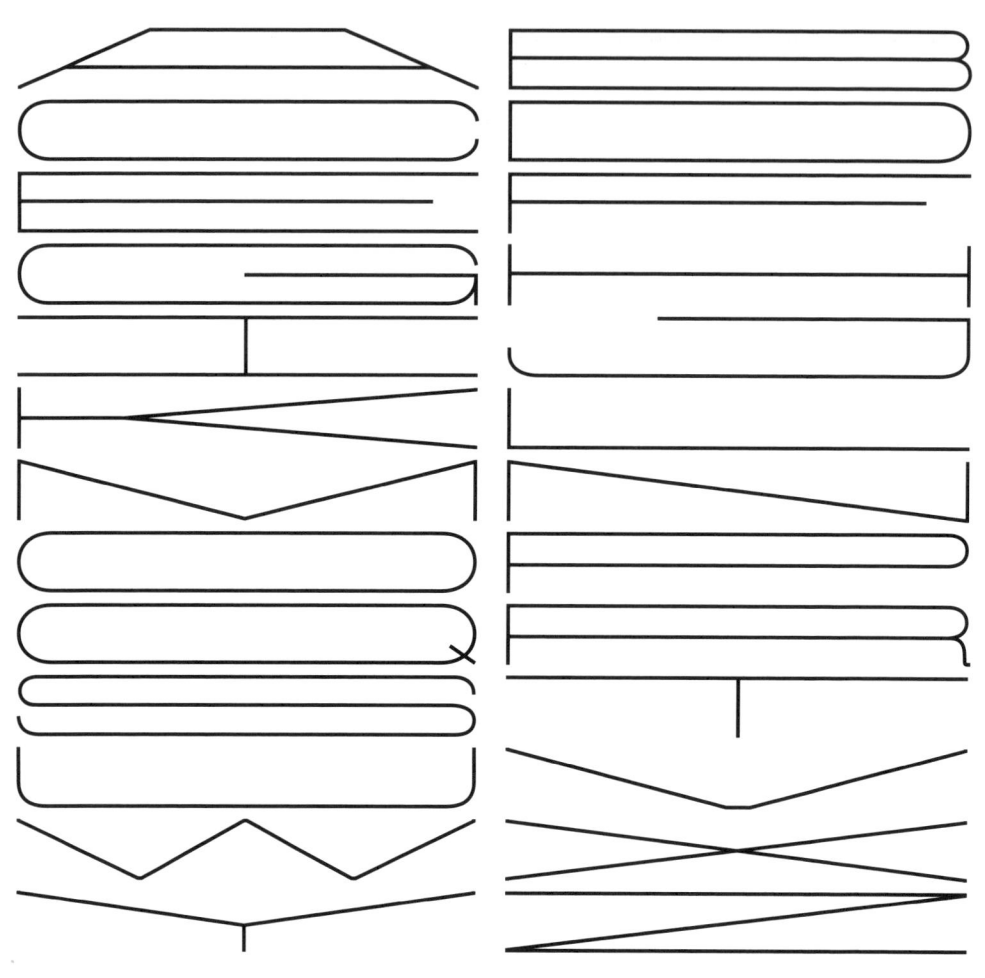

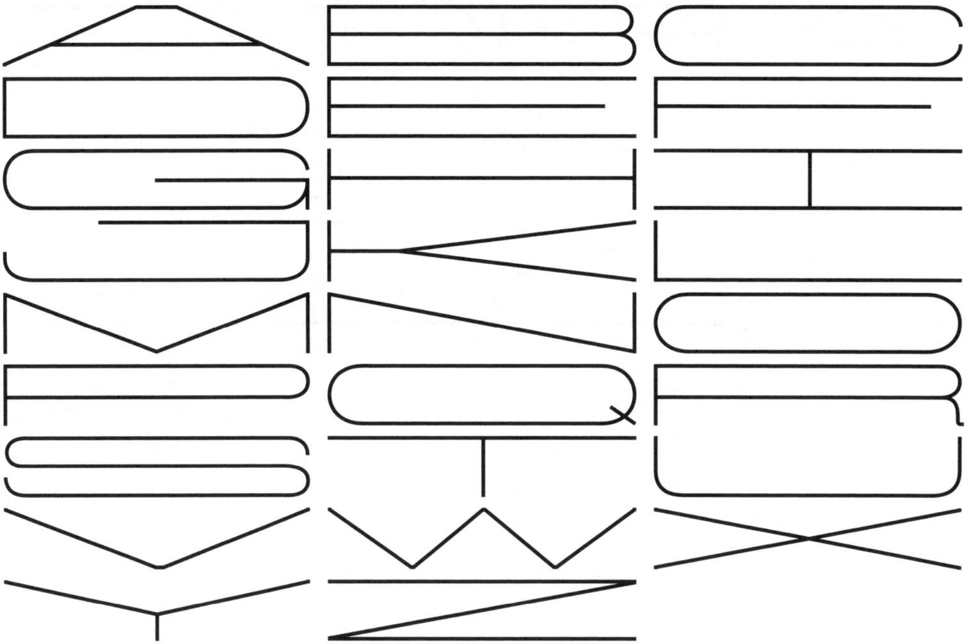

J.A C

An all-caps justified type system set to justify text to three columns

A–Z

s. 27
l. 27
t. 0

ABCD
EFGH
IJKL
MNOP
QRST
UVWX
YZ

J.A D

An all-caps justified type system set to justify text to four columns

A–Z

s. 27
l. 27
t. 0

AN AL
LCAPS
JUST
IFIED
TYPE
SYST
EM SE
T TO
JUSTI
FY TE
XT TO
FIVE
COLUM
NS

J.A E

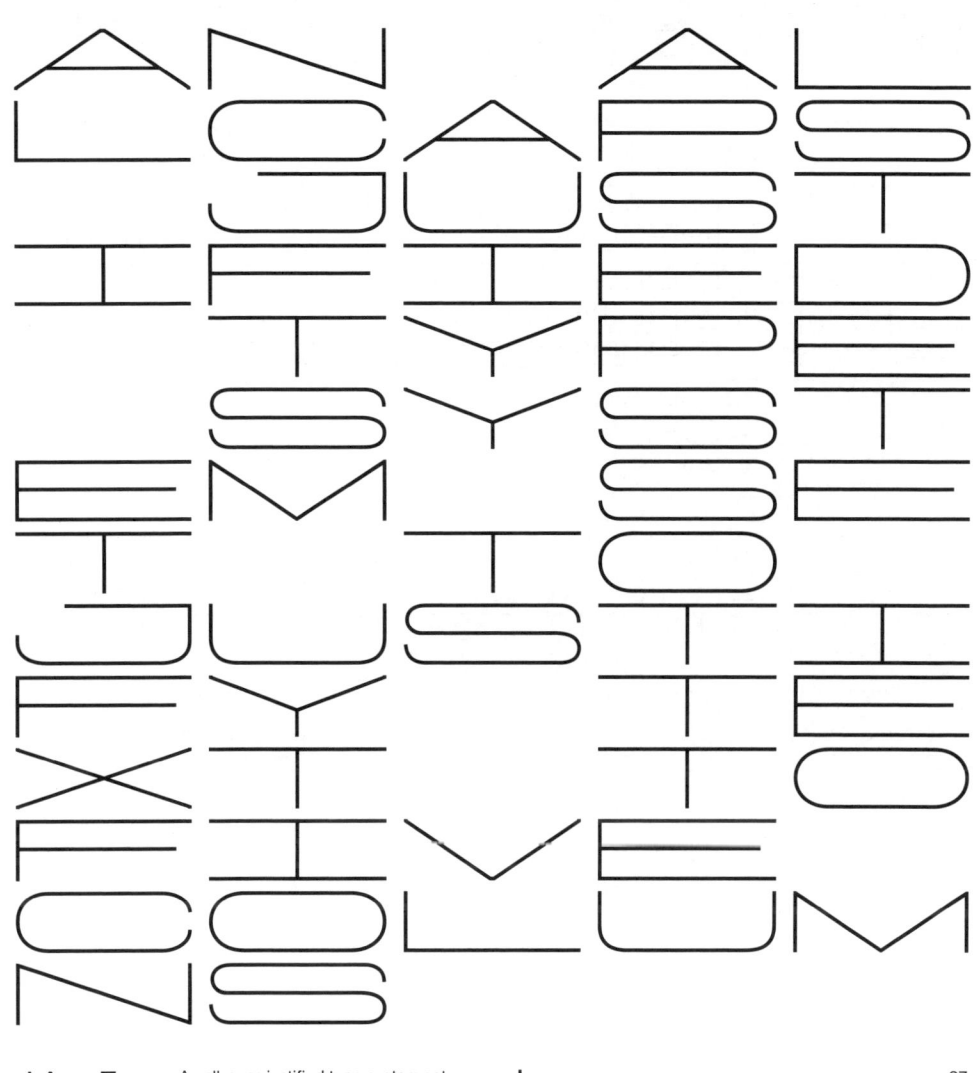

An all-caps justified type system set to justify text to five columns

*

s. 27
l. 27
t. 0

A TYPE SYSTEM THAT USES AN ARRAY OF NON PROPORTIONAL CHARACTERS WITH SET FIXED WIDTHS. THE USE OF THESE SETS ALLOWS FOR FULLY JUSTIFIED LETTERFORM TEXT TO ANY PROPORTION OF PAGE LAYOUT.

EACH OF THESE FIXED WIDTH SETS CAN BE USED TOGETHER AS CONTEXTUAL ALTERNATES, SCRIPTED TO AN ORDER FOR TEXT TO BE SET WITH COLUMNS OF LETTERS THAT SHIFT IN RATIO CREATING COMPOSITIONS OF TYPE THAT DEVIATE ACROSS THE PAGE.

ALTHOUGH THE TERM JUSTIFICATION USUALLY REFERS TO THE SPACING

J.A F

An all-caps justified type system set to change proportion incrementally from character to character

–

s. 12
l. 14
t. 0

BETWEEEN
LETTERS AND
WORDS IN
ORDER TO
ALIGN BOTH
LEFT AND
RIGHT ENDS OF
CONSECUTIVE
LINES OF TEXT.
IN THIS
INSTANCE
THE TERM
REFERS TO
THE JUSTI-
FICATION OF
THE LETTERS
THEMSELVES
ACROSS THE
ENTIRE OR
PORTION OF
THE PAGE.

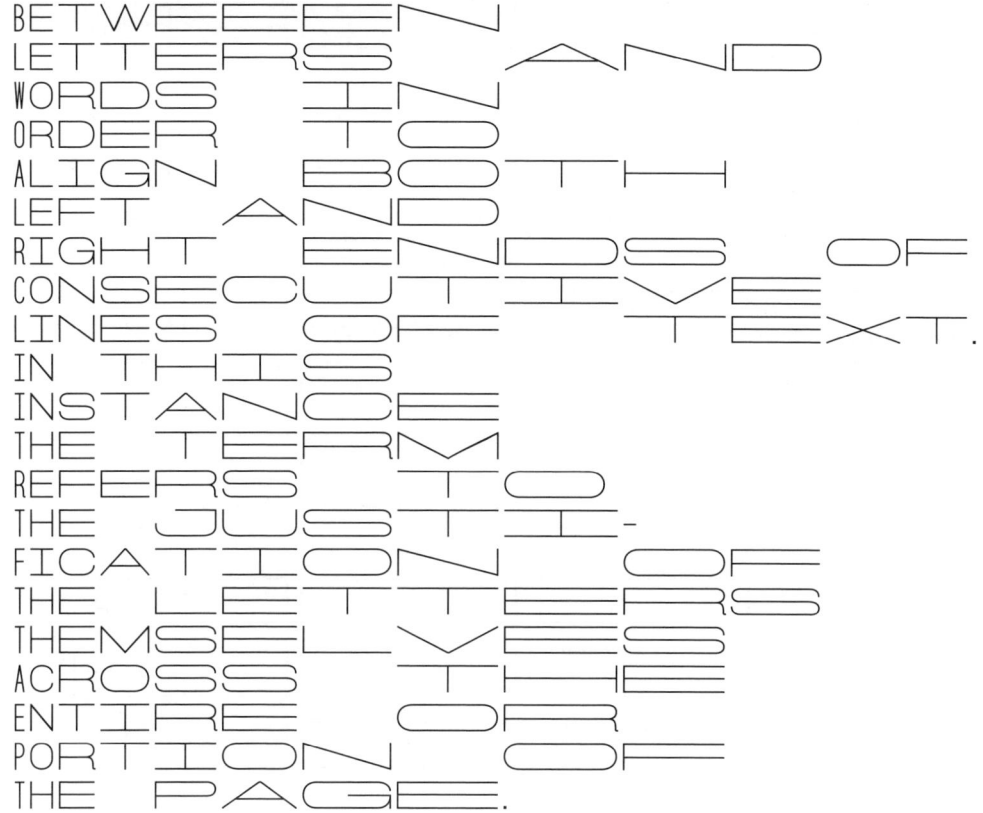

J.A F

s. 12
l. 14
t. 0

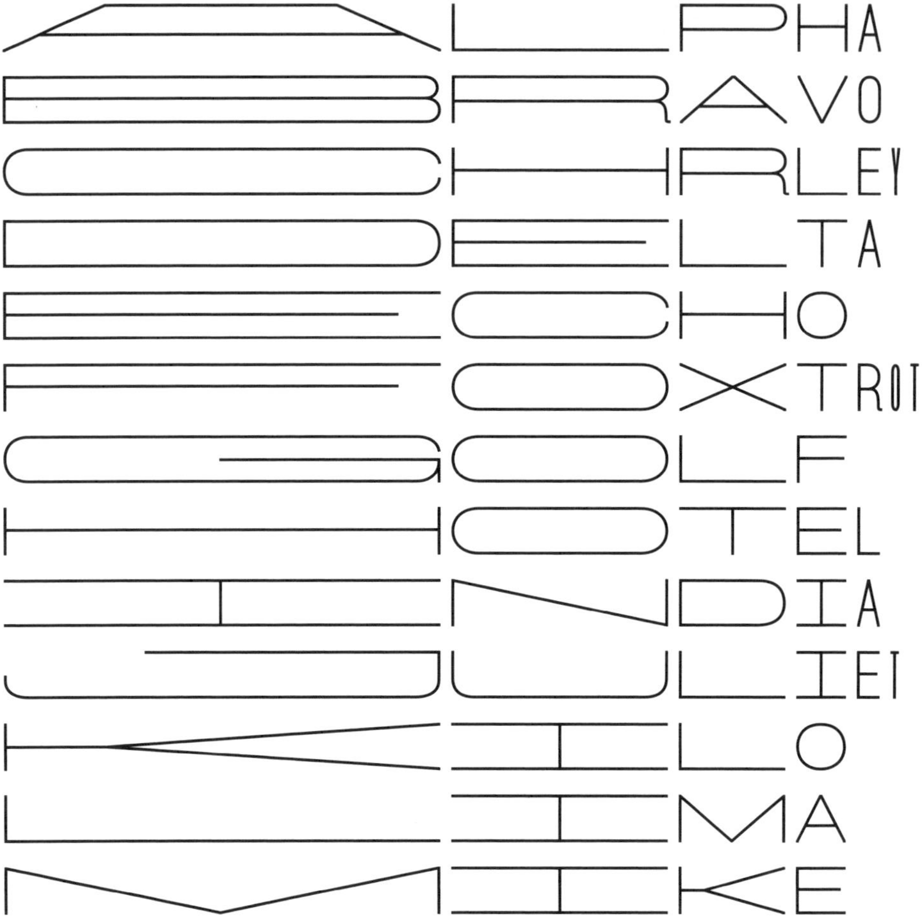

J.B A

An all-caps justified type system changing proportion exponentially from character to character

Alpha Bravo Charlie Delta
Foxtrot Golf Hotel India
Juliet Kilo Lima Mike

s. 21
l. 27
t. 0

NOVEMBER
OSCAR
PAPA
QUEBEC
ROMEO
SIERRA
TANGO
UNIFORM
VICTOR
WHISKEY
XRAY
YANKEE
ZULU

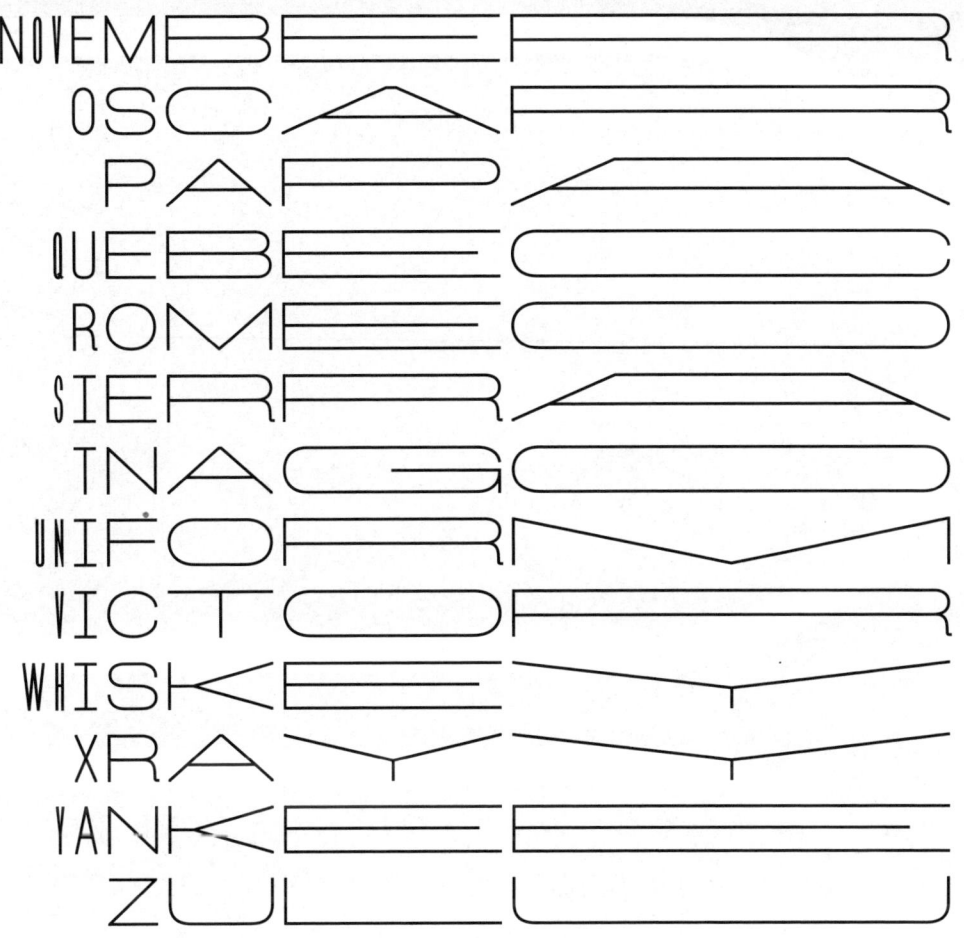

J.B A

November Oscar Papa
Quebec Romeo Sierra
Tango Uniform Victor
Whiskey Xray Yankee Zulu

s. 21
l. 27
t. 0

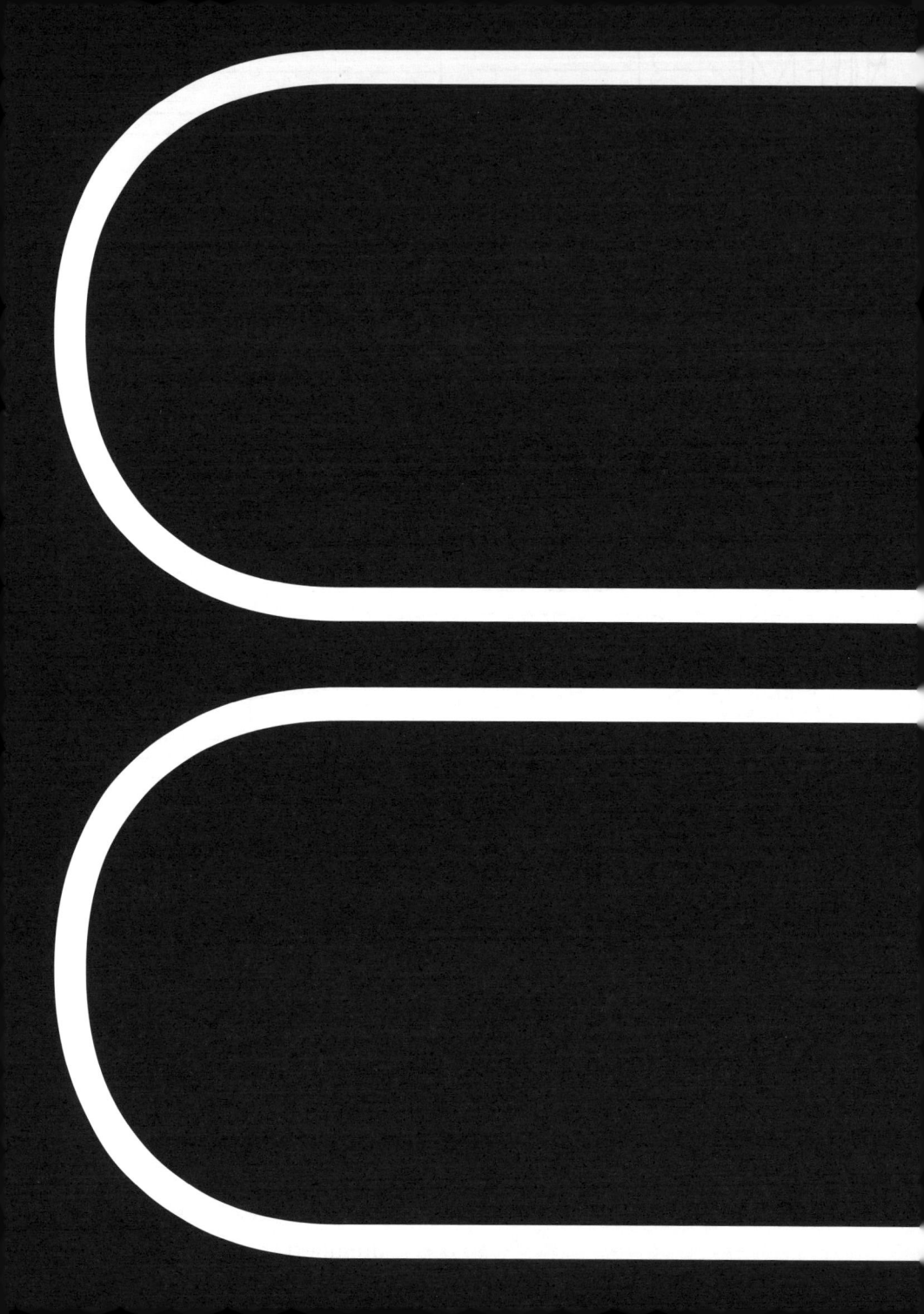

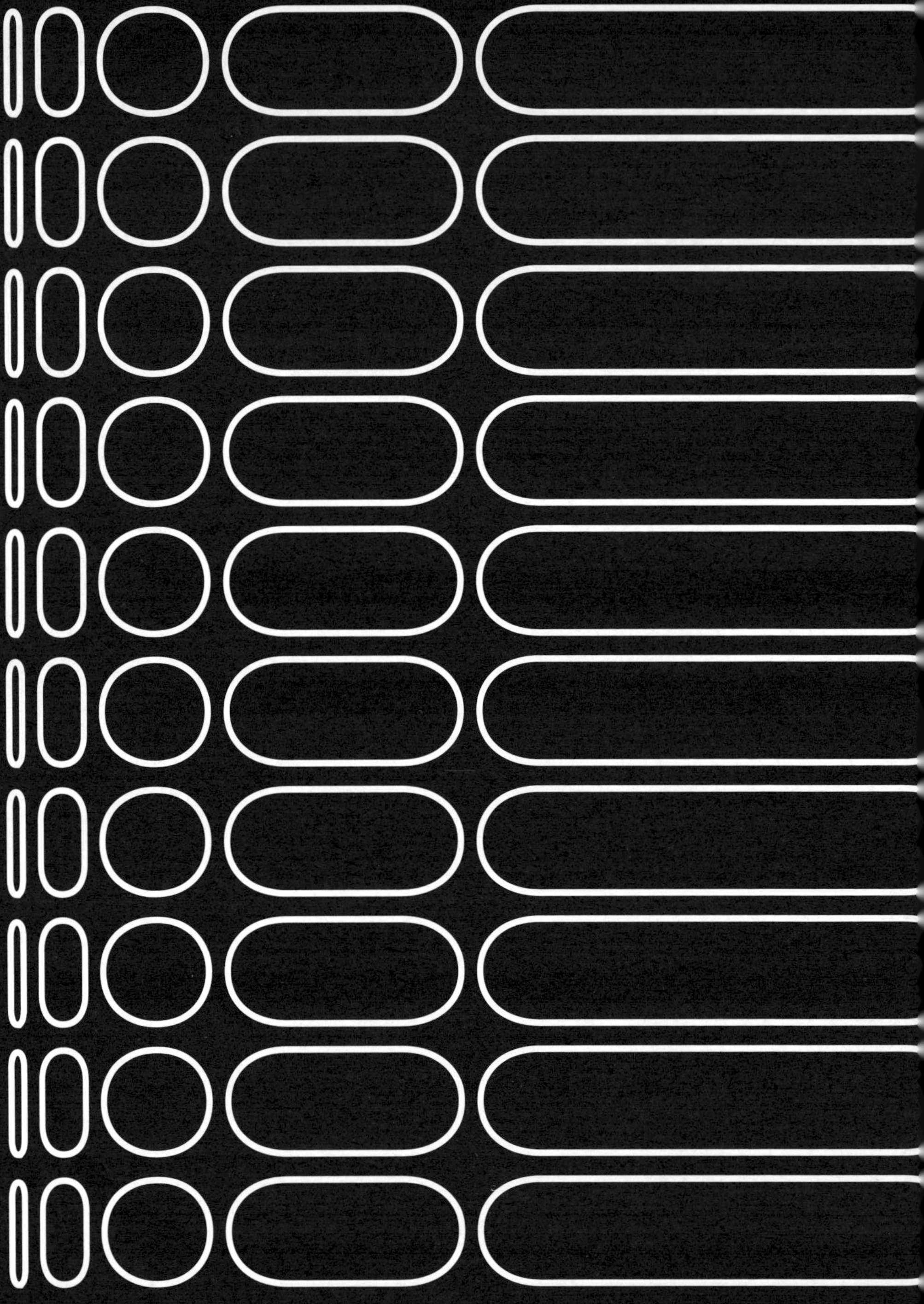

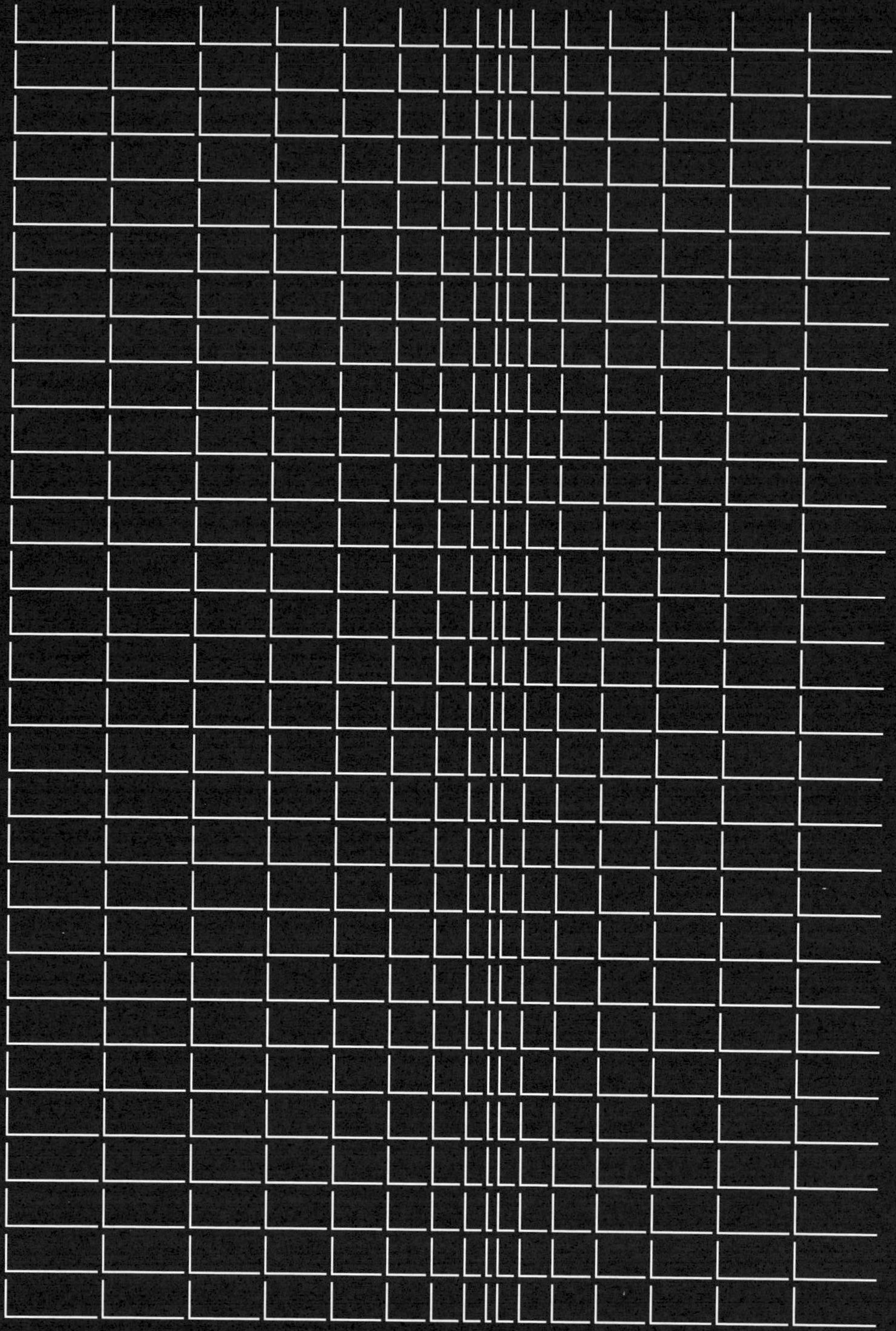

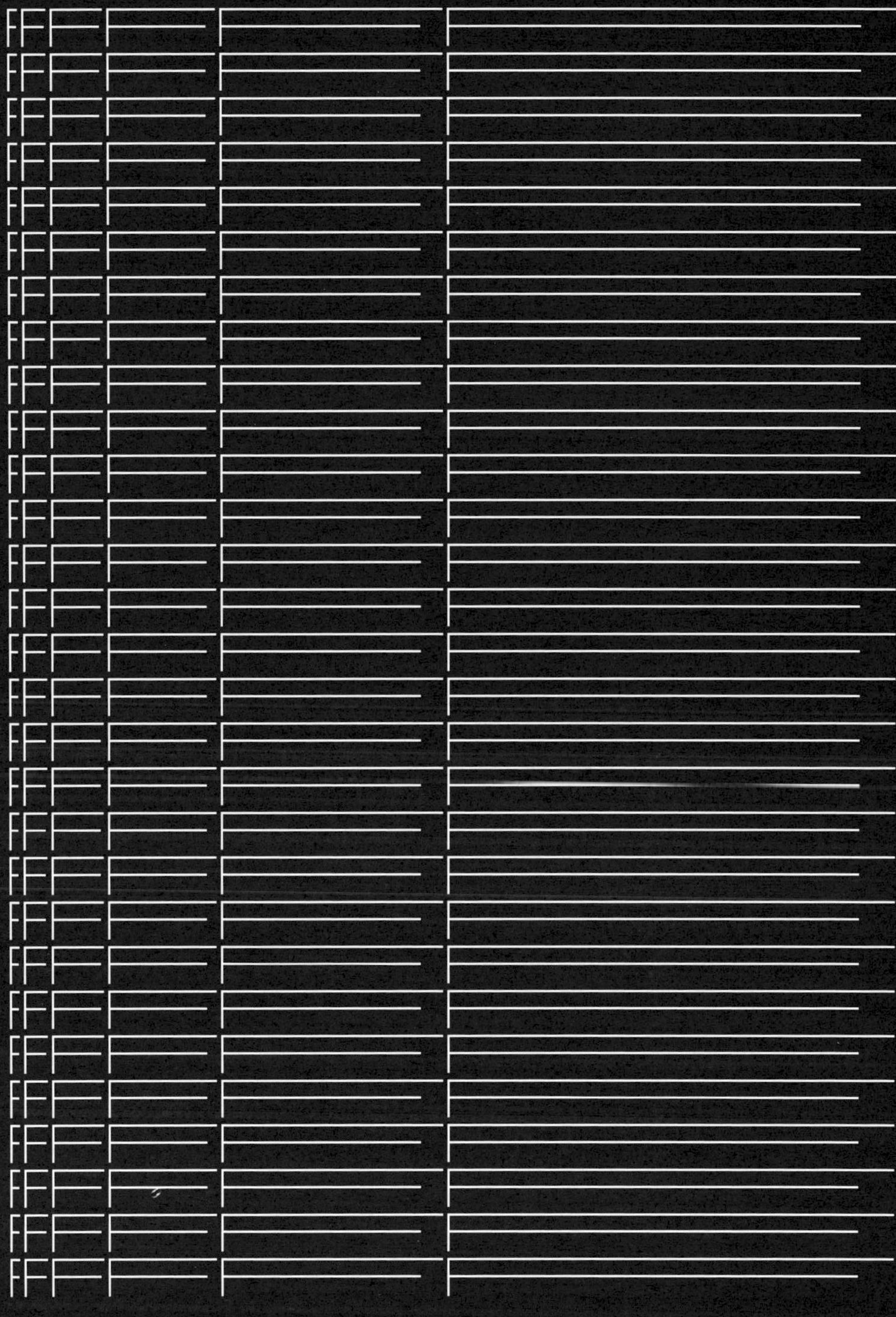

Section Notes:

Created in Glyphs, J.A and J.B each consist of a single font file. Containing uppercase character sets, numerals, and basic punctuation, each type system is designed with an array of stylistic sets featuring proportionally differing widths. Each set can operate independently or as part of a system of contextual alternates, scripted to create dynamic columns. J.A can be set to change proportion incrementally, while J.B is set to change exponentially from character to character. An additional variable width parameter can be used to fine-tune the overall composition to the desired layout width.

A set of three type systems that explore optical illusions, perceptual instability, and kinaesthetic effects to simulate motion within static letterform sequences. Drawing inspiration from the Kinetic Art and Op Art movements, these systems investigate the ways in which typography can evoke movement through linear interference, pattern frequency and directional distortion. The resulting forms animate language through the interplay of successive glyphs.

K.A An alphabet formed of delineated lines, shifting in proportion in order to create an effect of optical kinetic movement*

*

s. 33
l. 33
t. 0

K.A

A–Z 0–9

s. 62
l. 620
t.

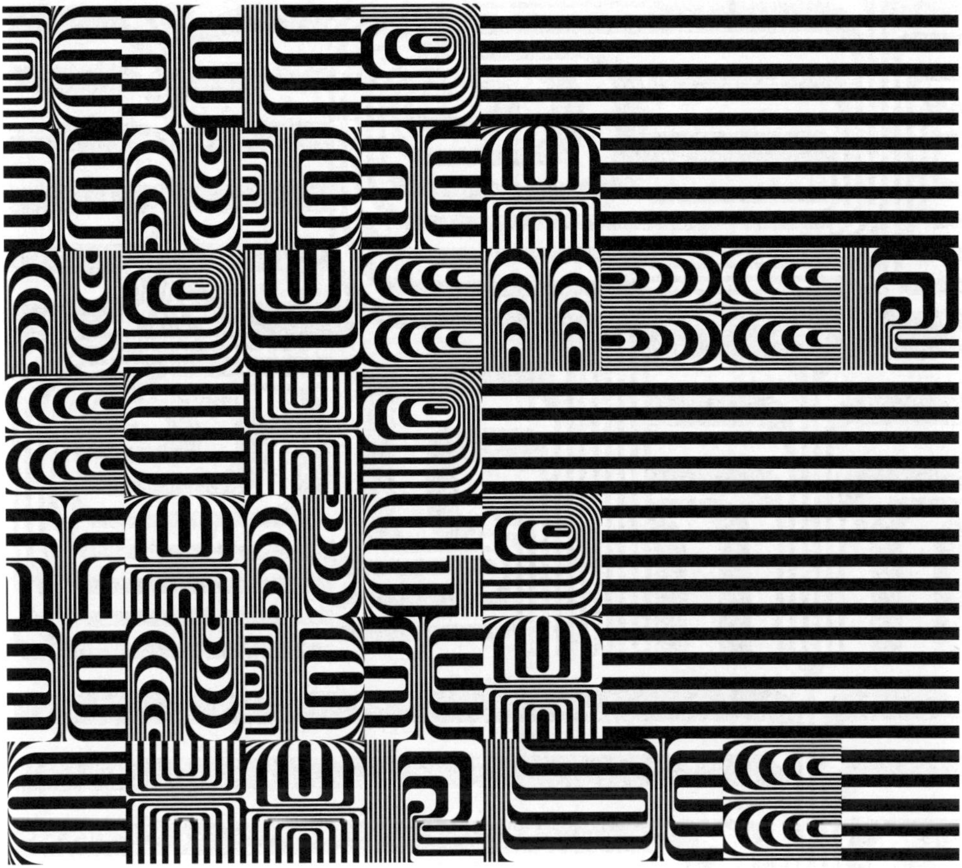

K.A

Kilo India November Echo
Tango India Charlie

s. 46
l. 46
t. 0

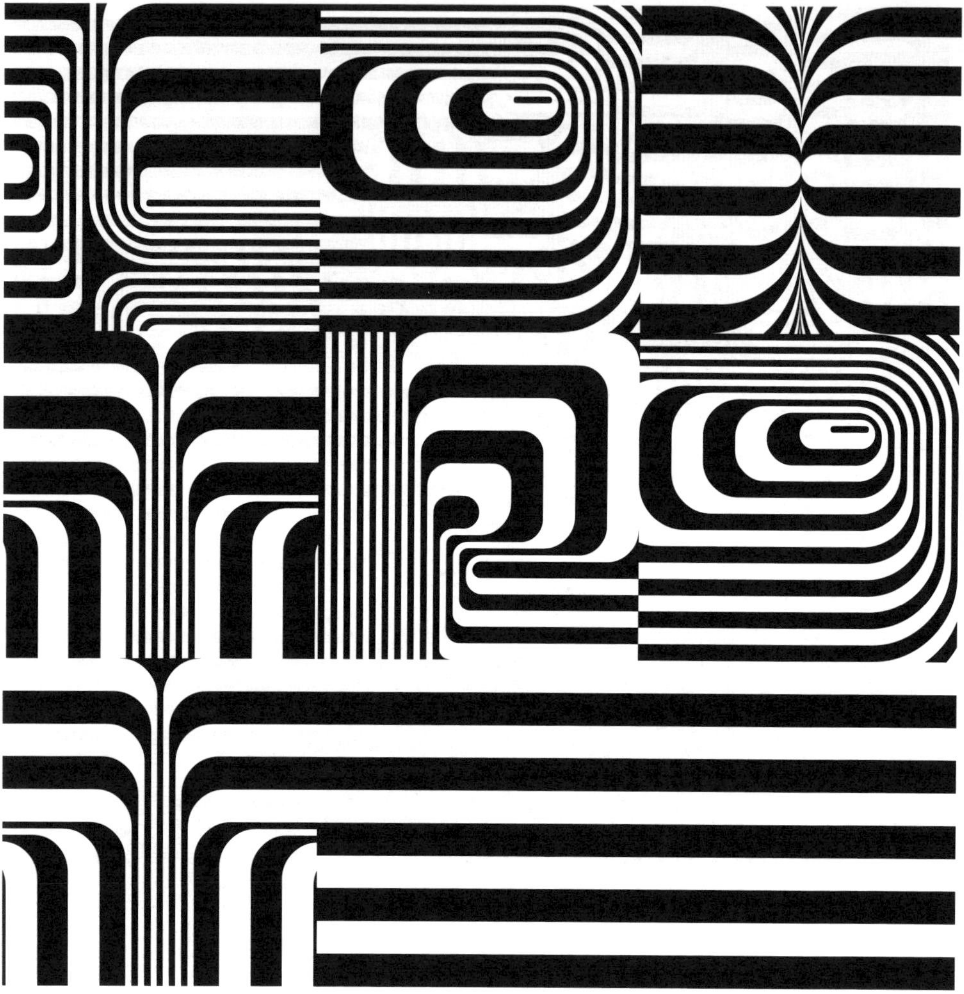

K.A

Foxtrot

s. 123
l. 123
t. 0

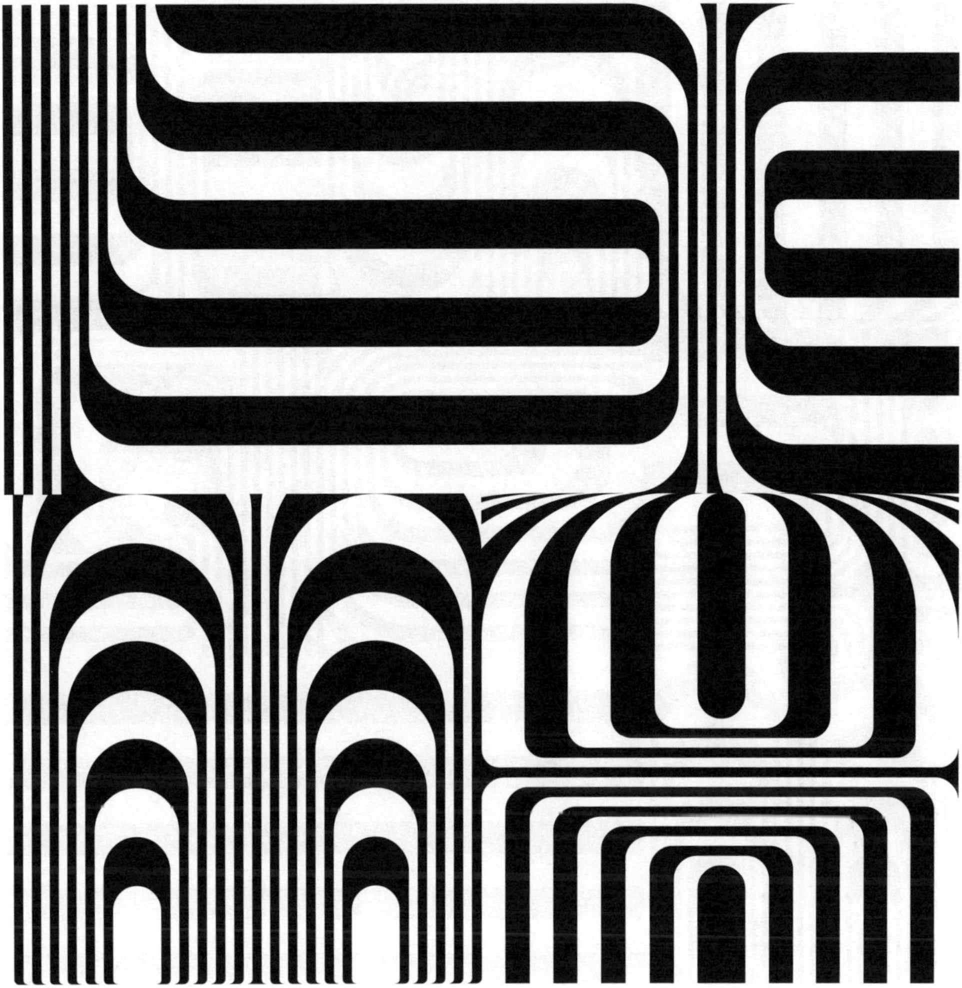

K.A Lima

s. 184
l. 184
t. 0

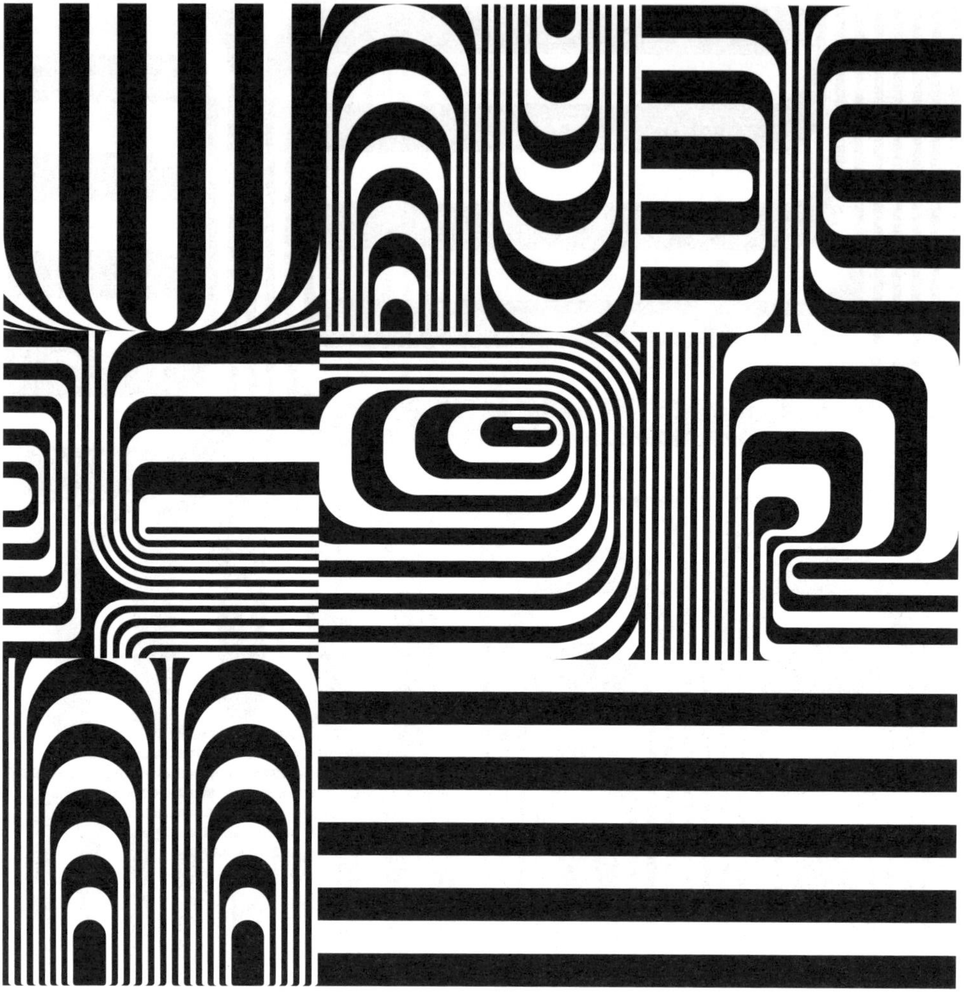

K.A

Uniform

s. 123
l. 123
t. 0

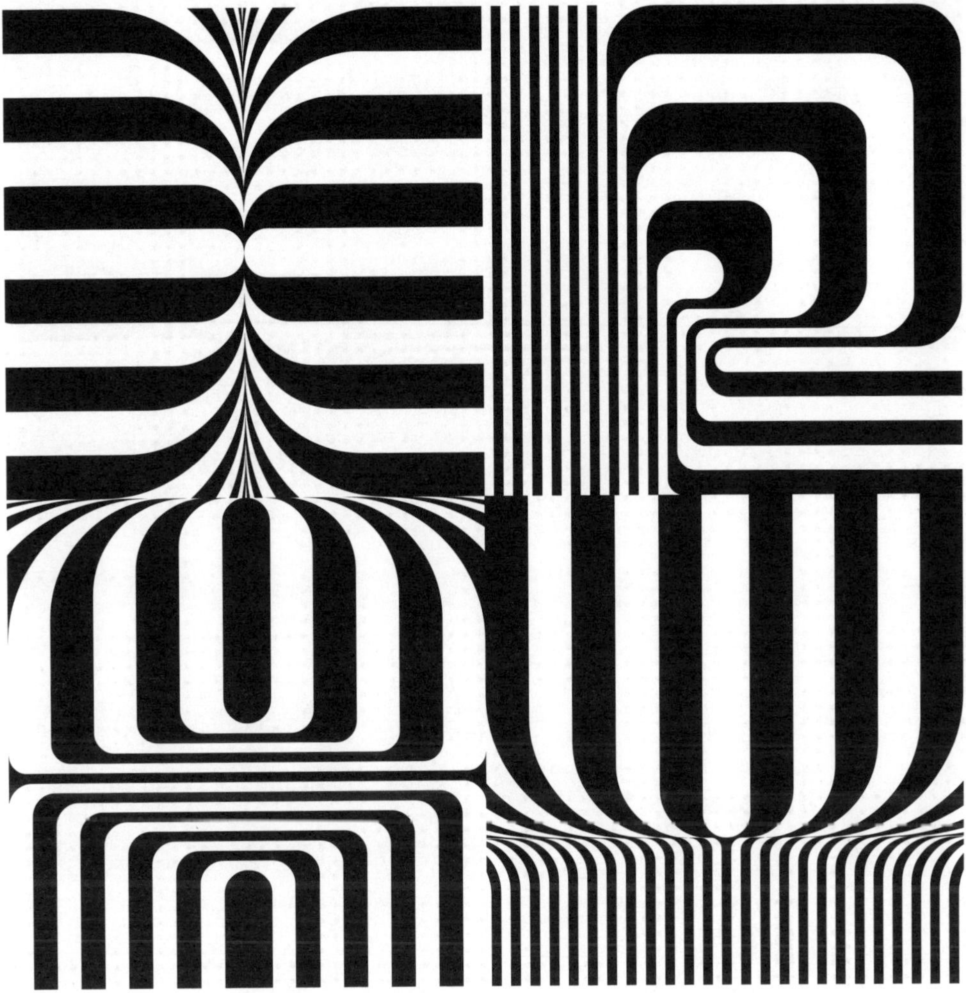

K.A

Xray

s. 184
l. 184
t. 0

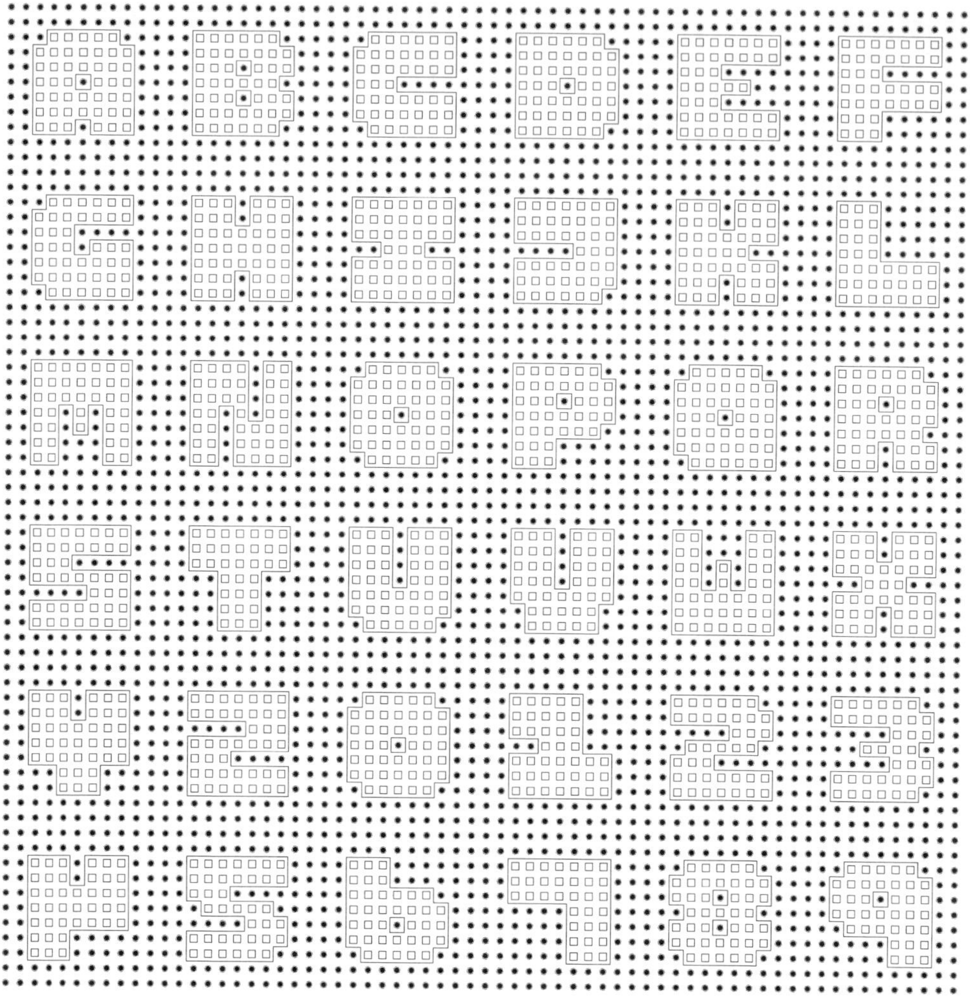

K.B An alphabet formed of dots and outline squares creating an effect of optical kinetic movement*

A–Z 0–9

s. 62
l. 62
t. 0

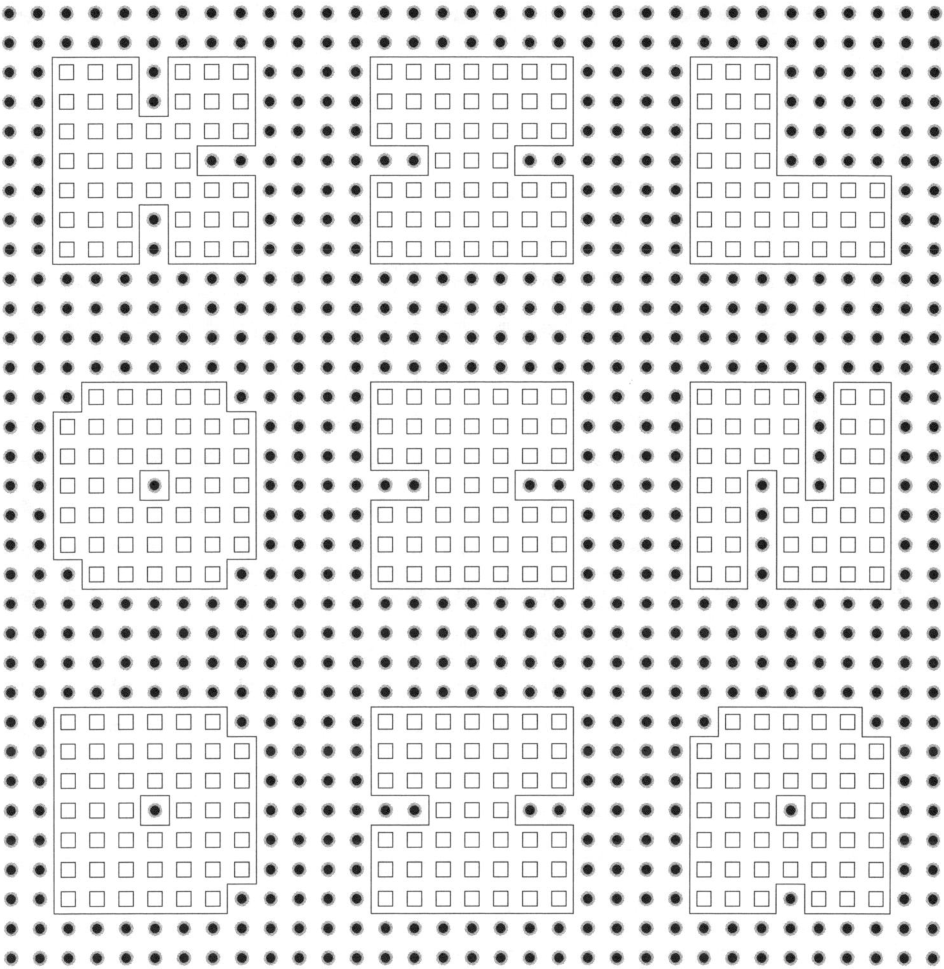

K.B

Kilo India

s. 122
l. 122
t. 0

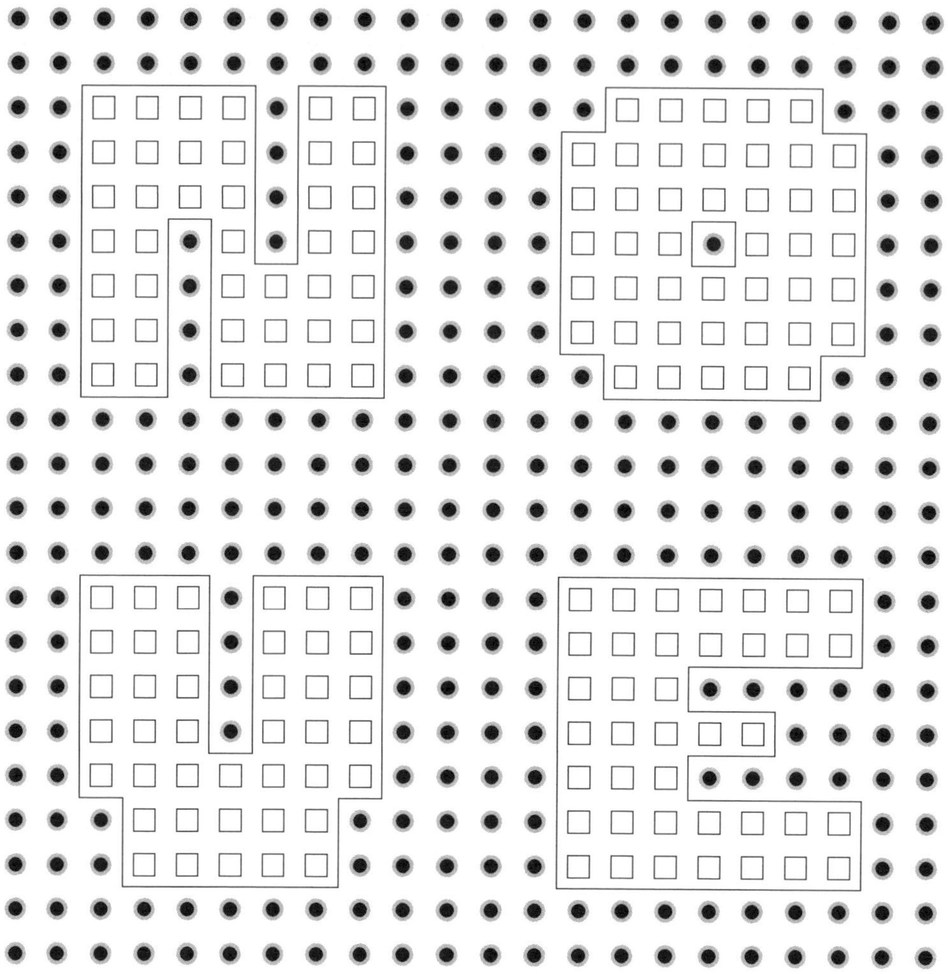

K.B

November

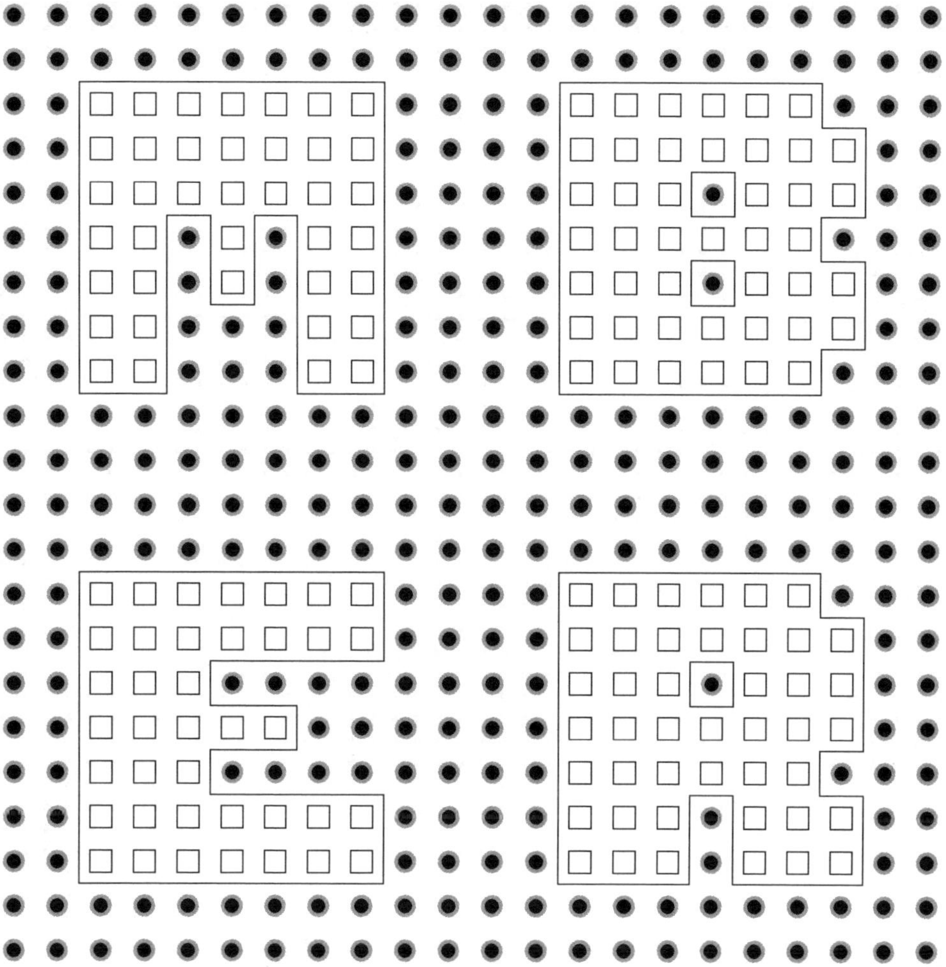

s. 184
l. 184
t. 0

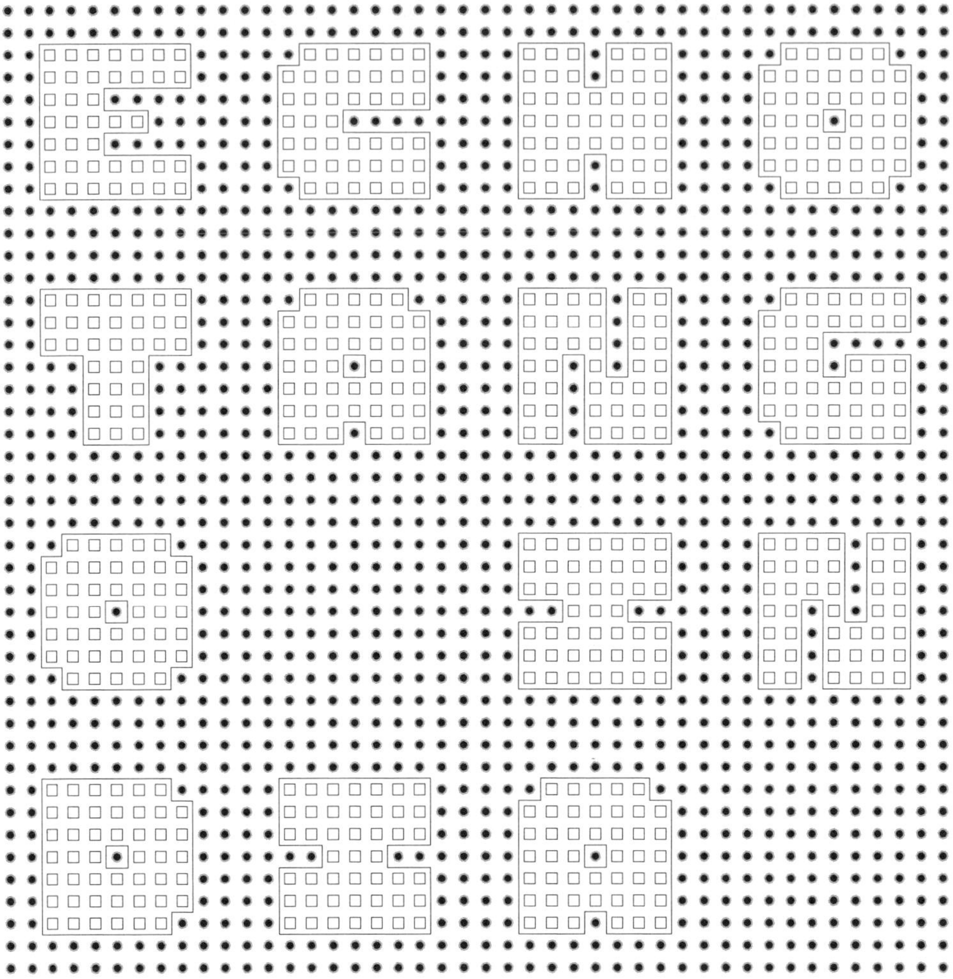

K.B

Echo Tango India

s. 92
l. 92
t. 0

K.C An alphabet formed of outline squares and dots creating an effect of optical kinetic movement*

A–Z 0–9

s. 62
l. 62
t. 0

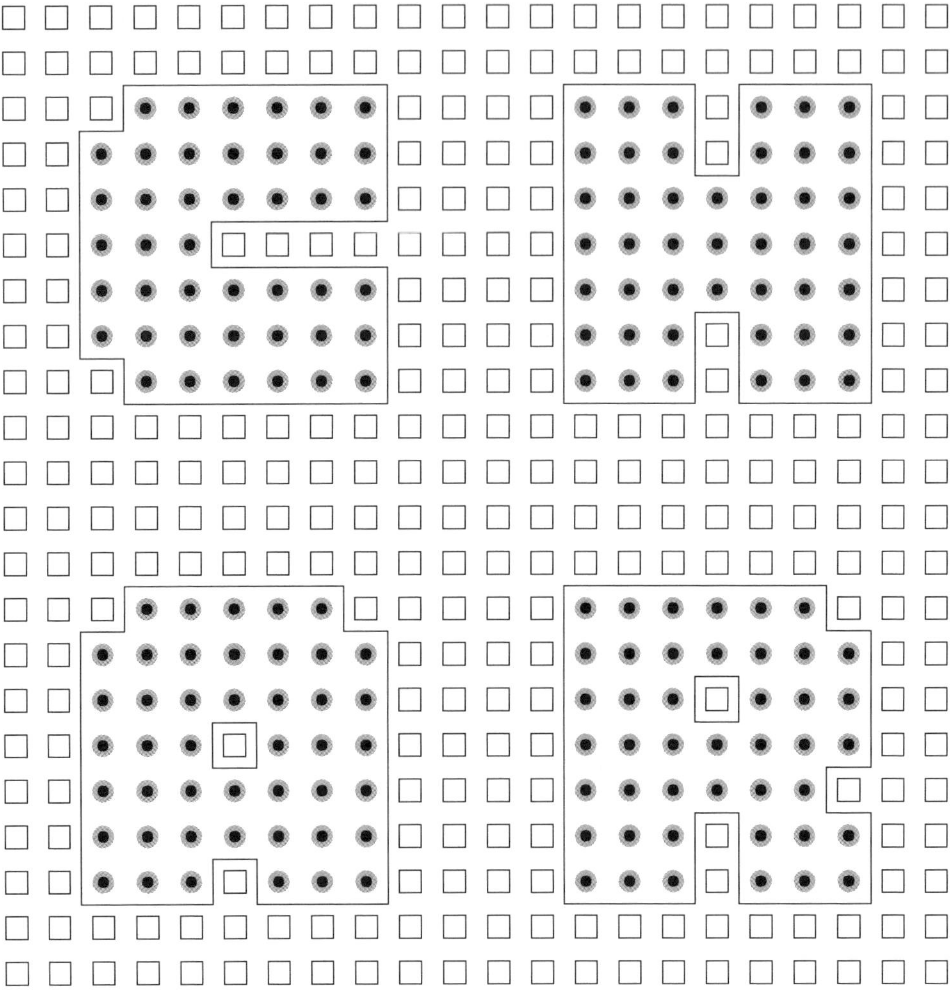

K.C

Charlie

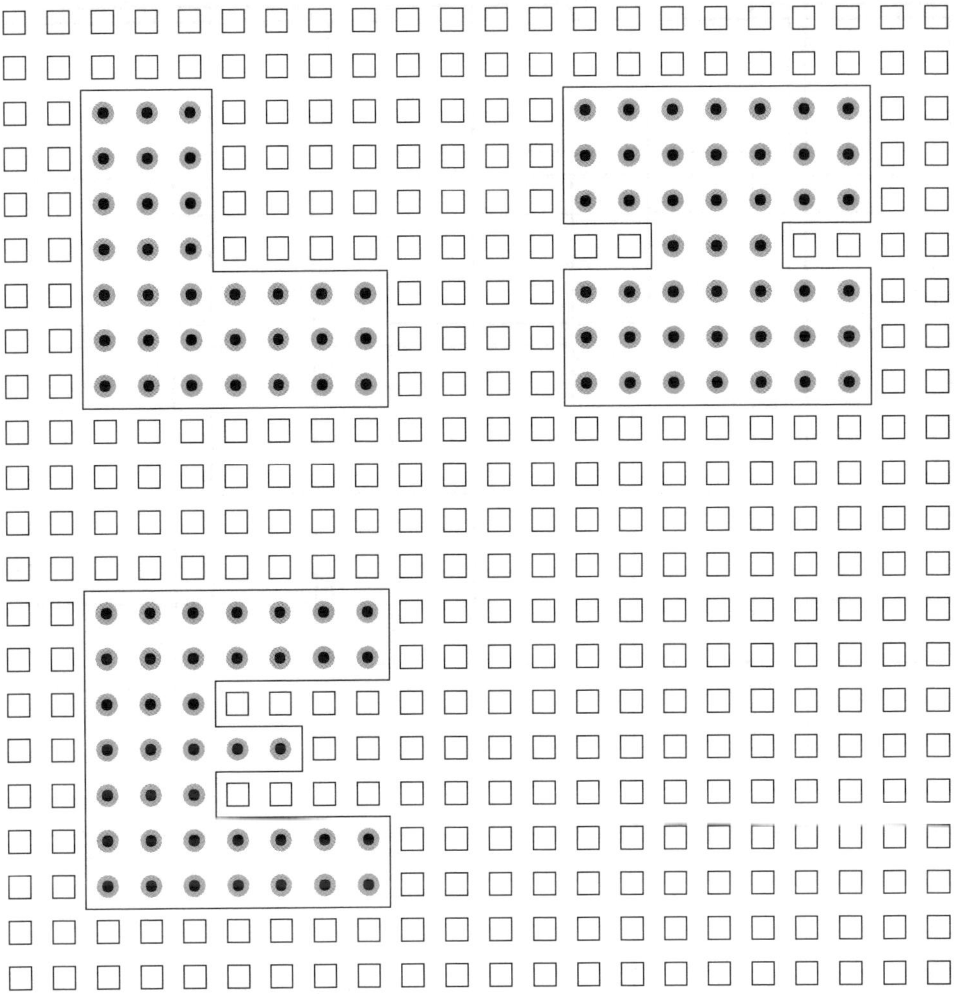

s. 184
l. 184
t. 0

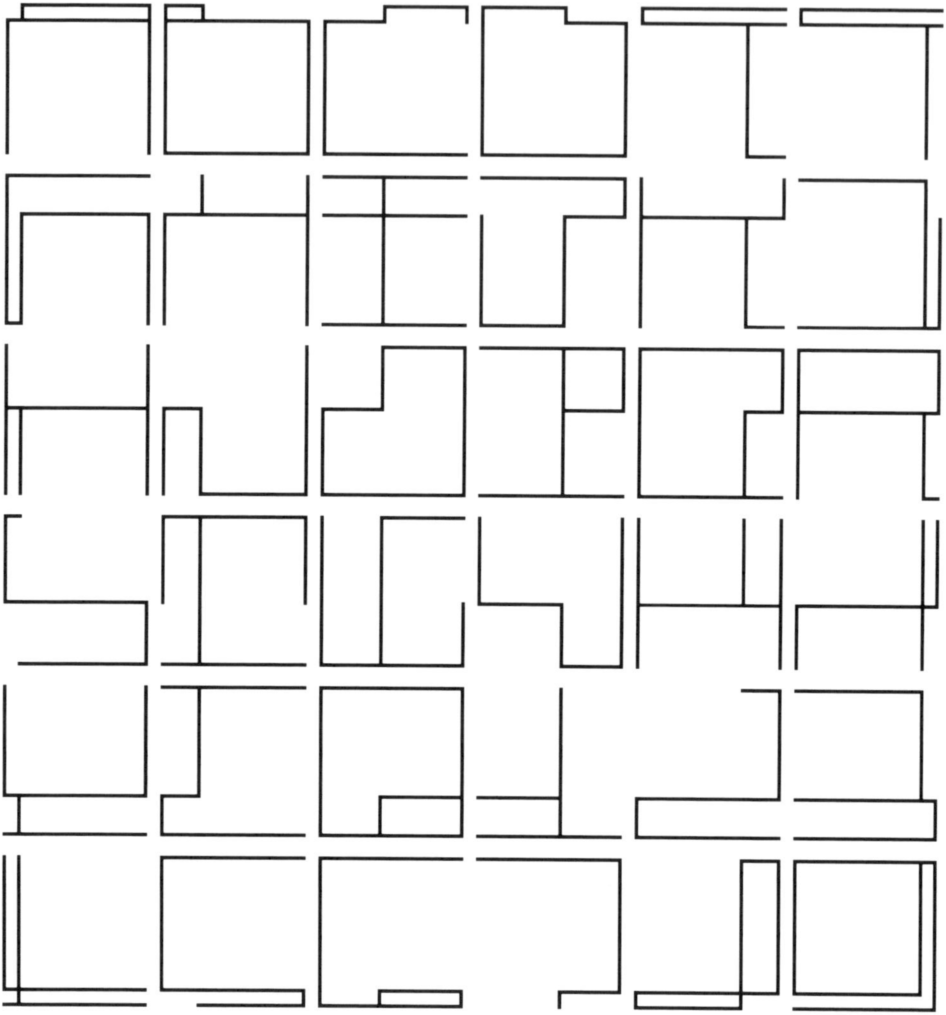

K.D

An alphabet formed of letters with a fluctuating central axis to create the effect of optical kinetic movement from character to character

A–Z 0–9

s.	62
l.	63
t.	0
r.	100
h.	±
v.	±

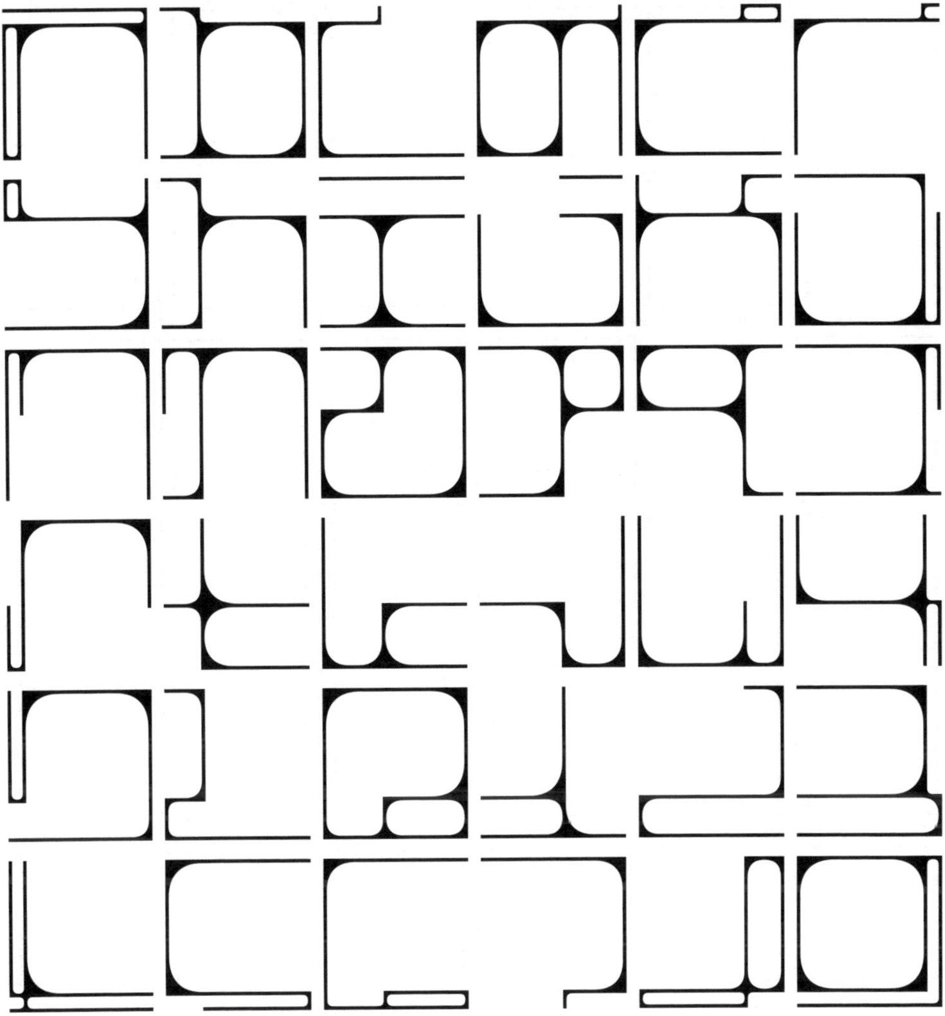

K.D

a–z 0–9

62
63
0
900
±
±

K.D

Kilo India November Echo
Tango India Chalie Papa
Romeo Oscar Papa Oscar
Romeo Tango

s. 62
l. 63
t. 0
r. 100
h. ±
v. ±

UC

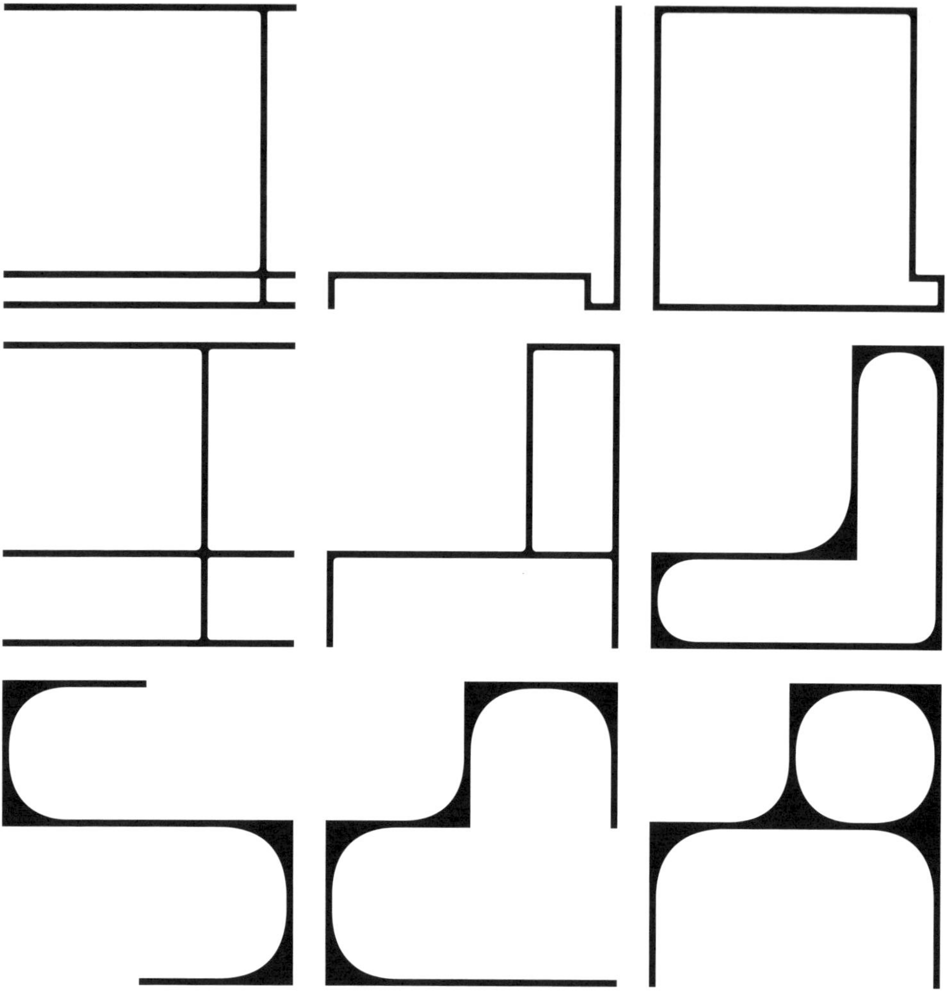

K.D

India Oscar November

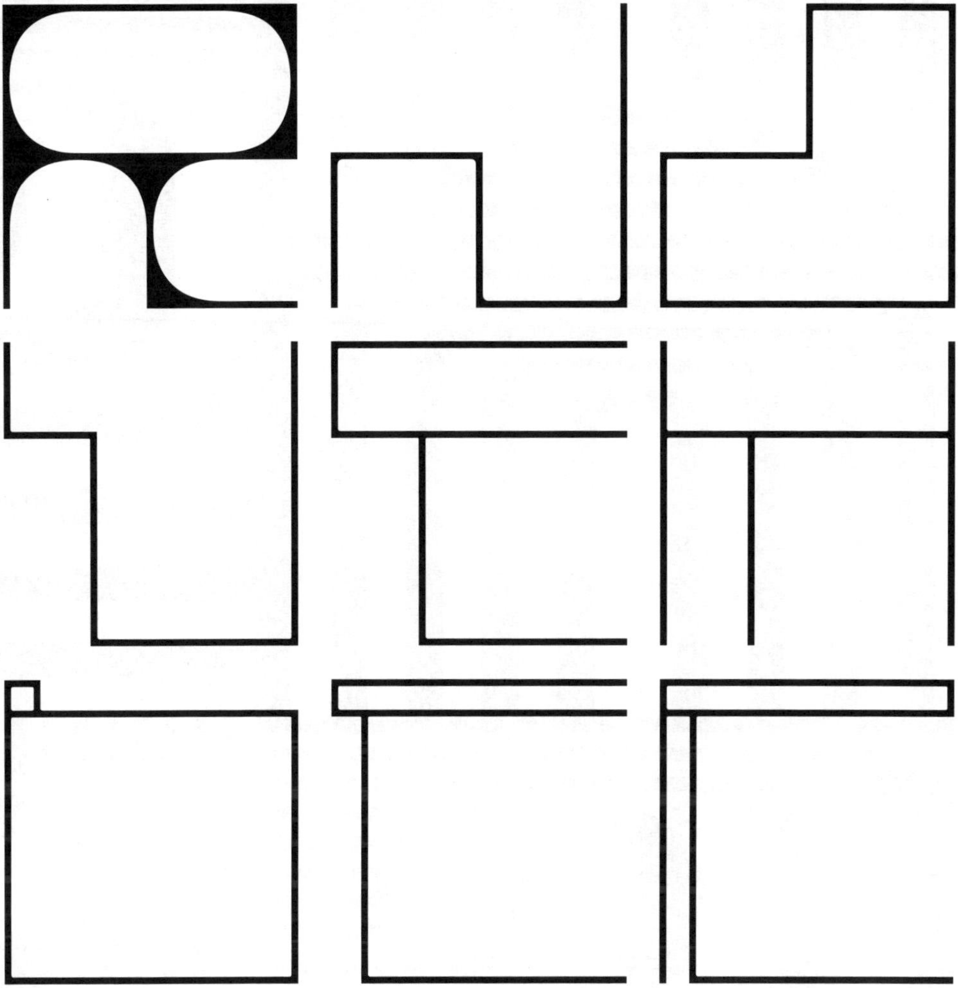

s. 127
l. 127
t. 0
r. ±
h. ±
v. ±

UC

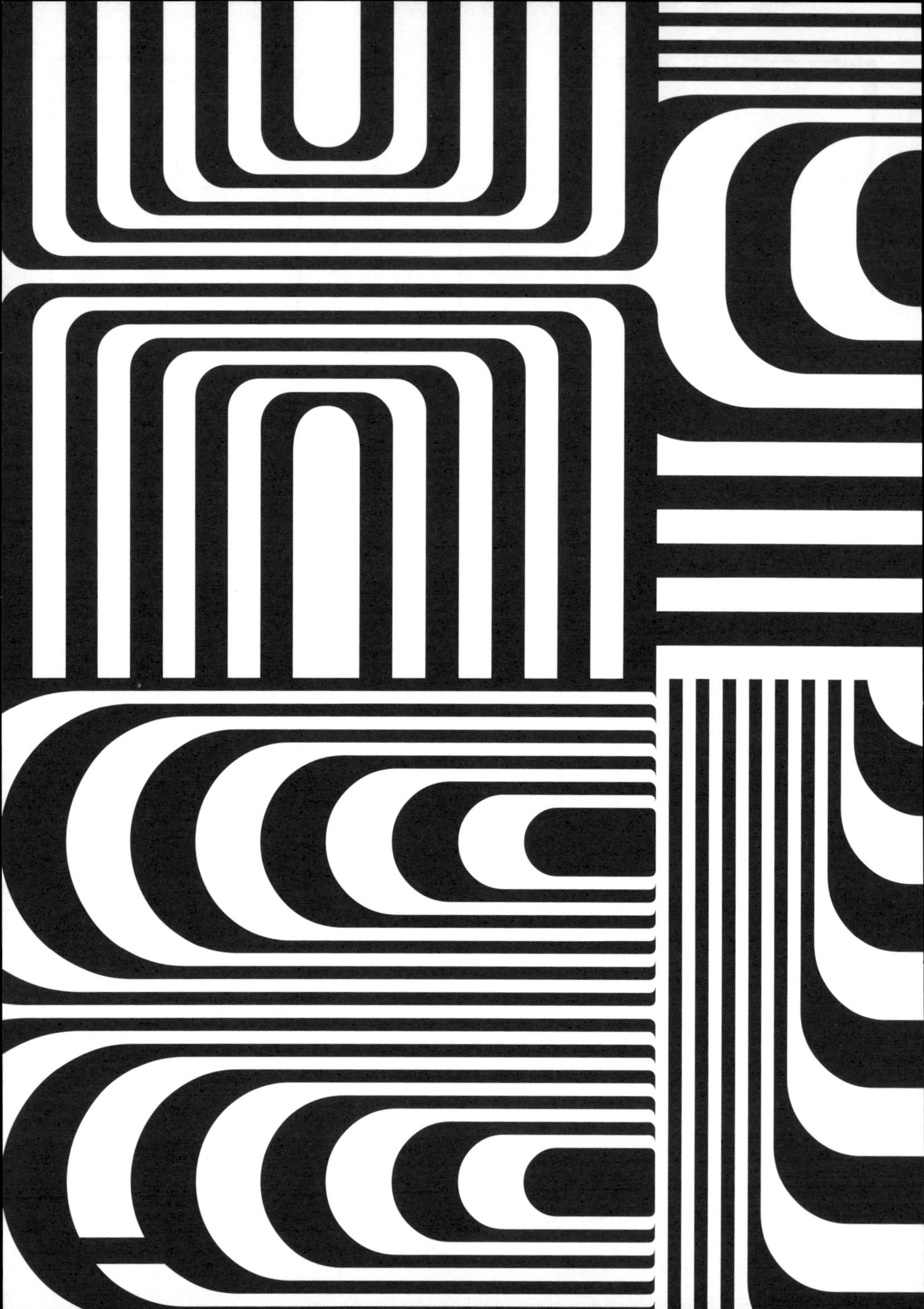

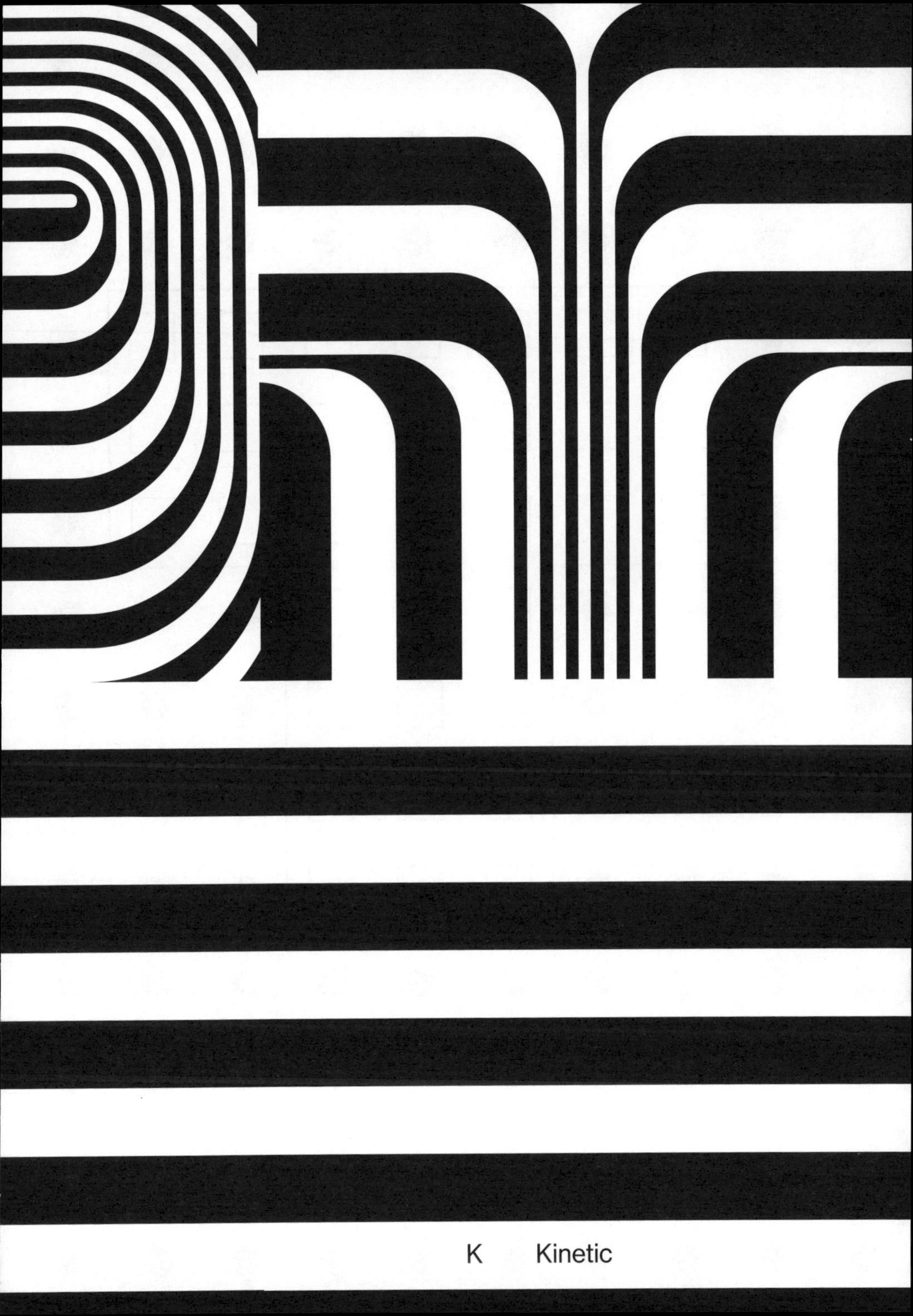

K Kinetic

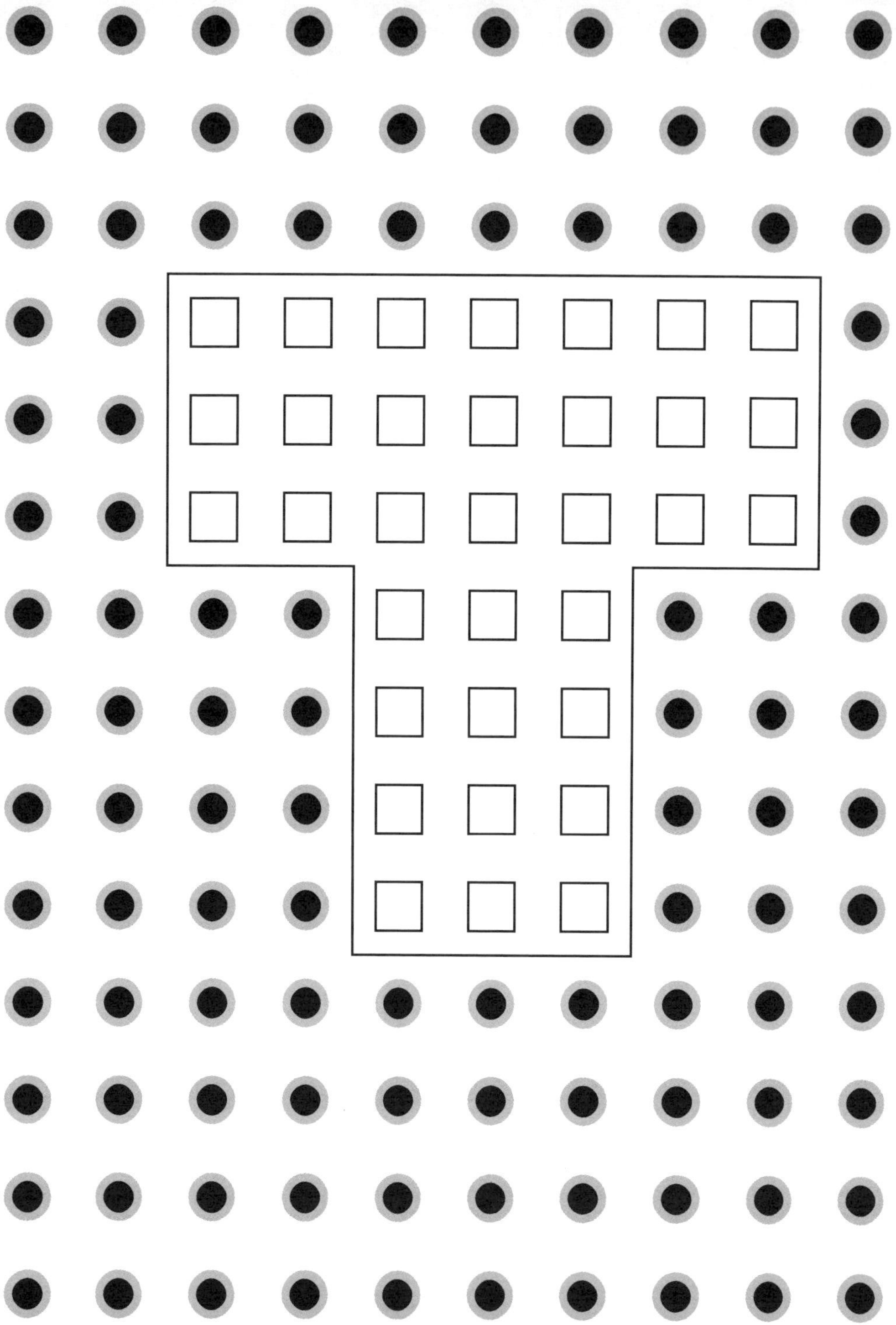

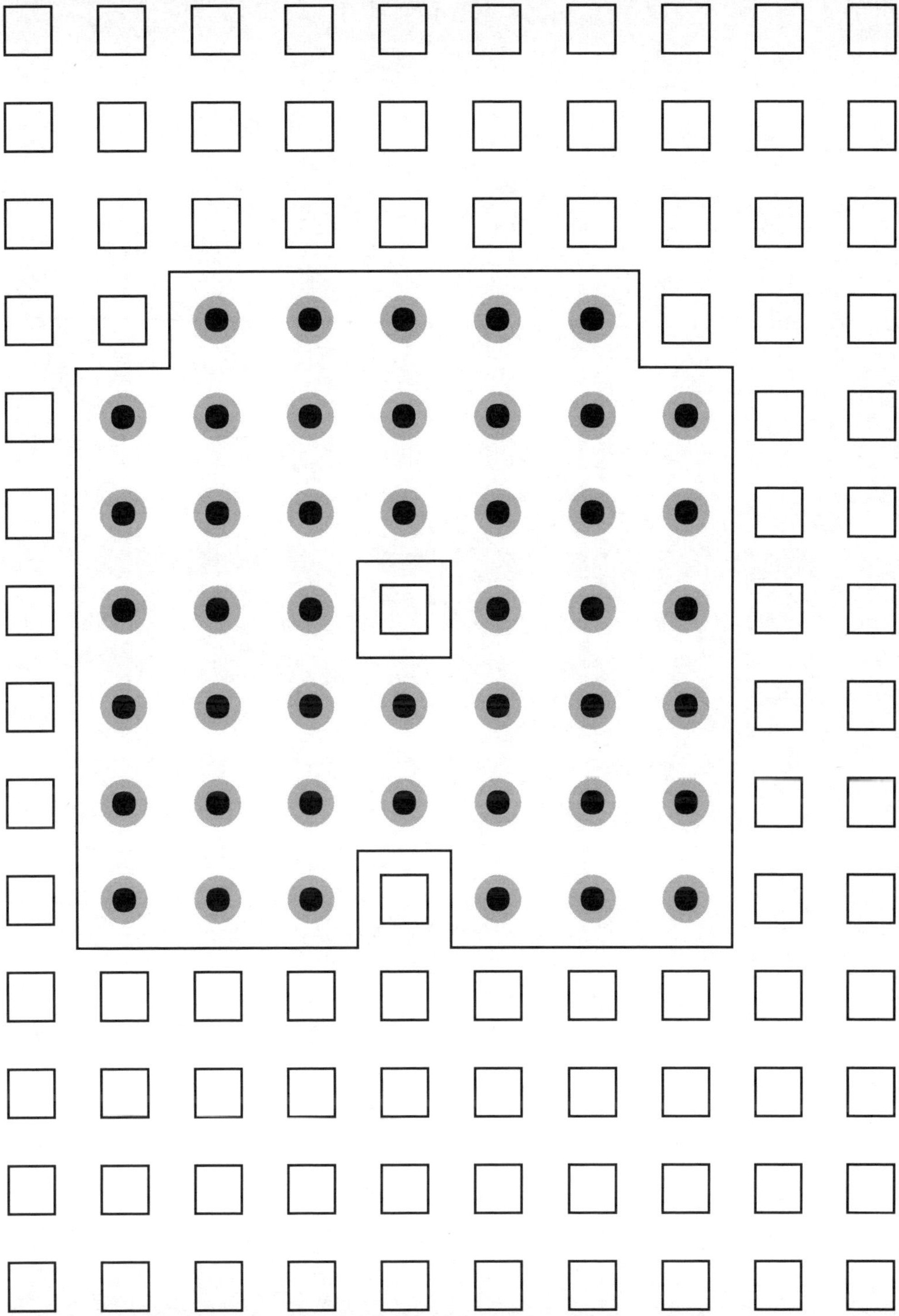

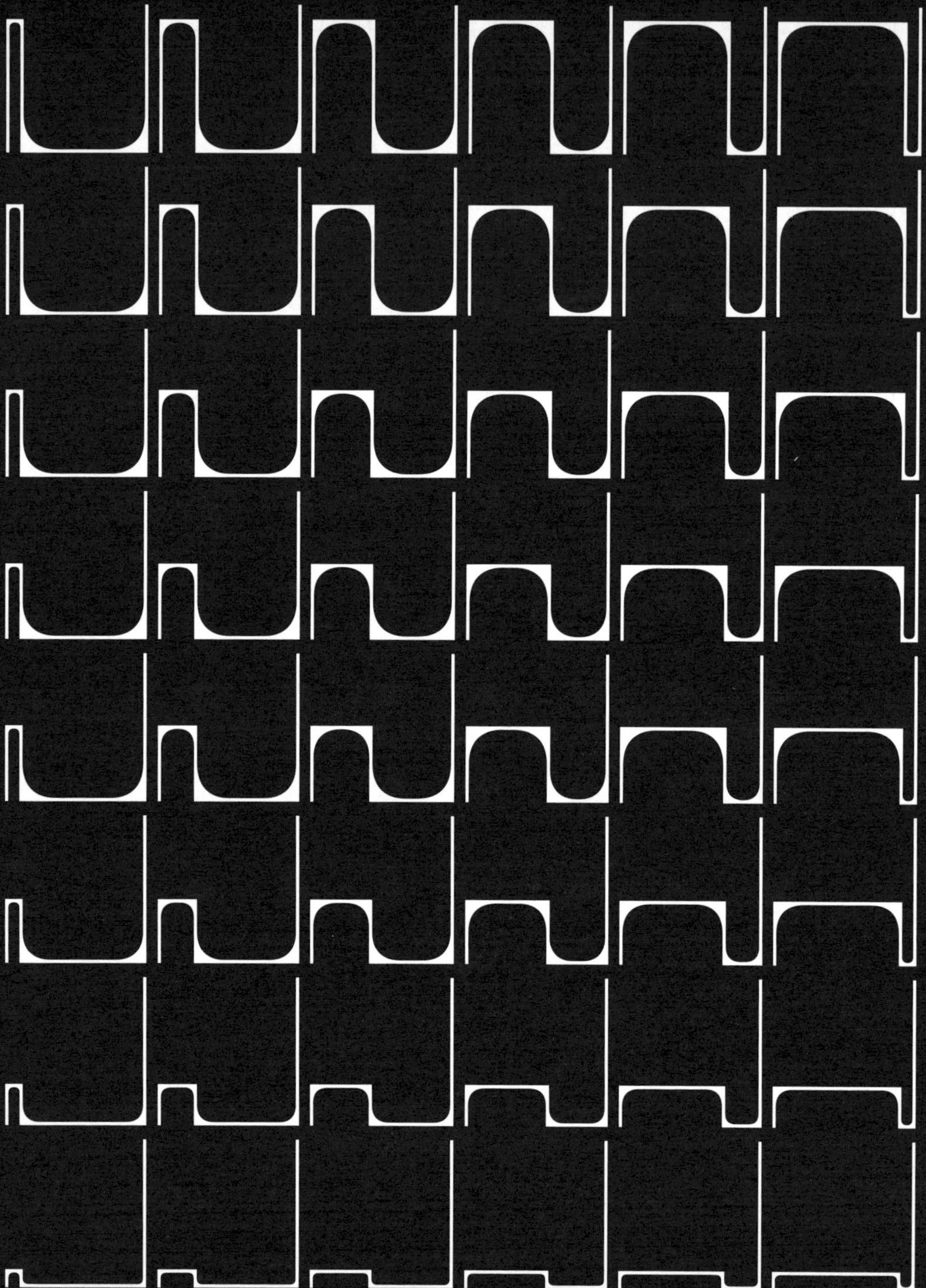

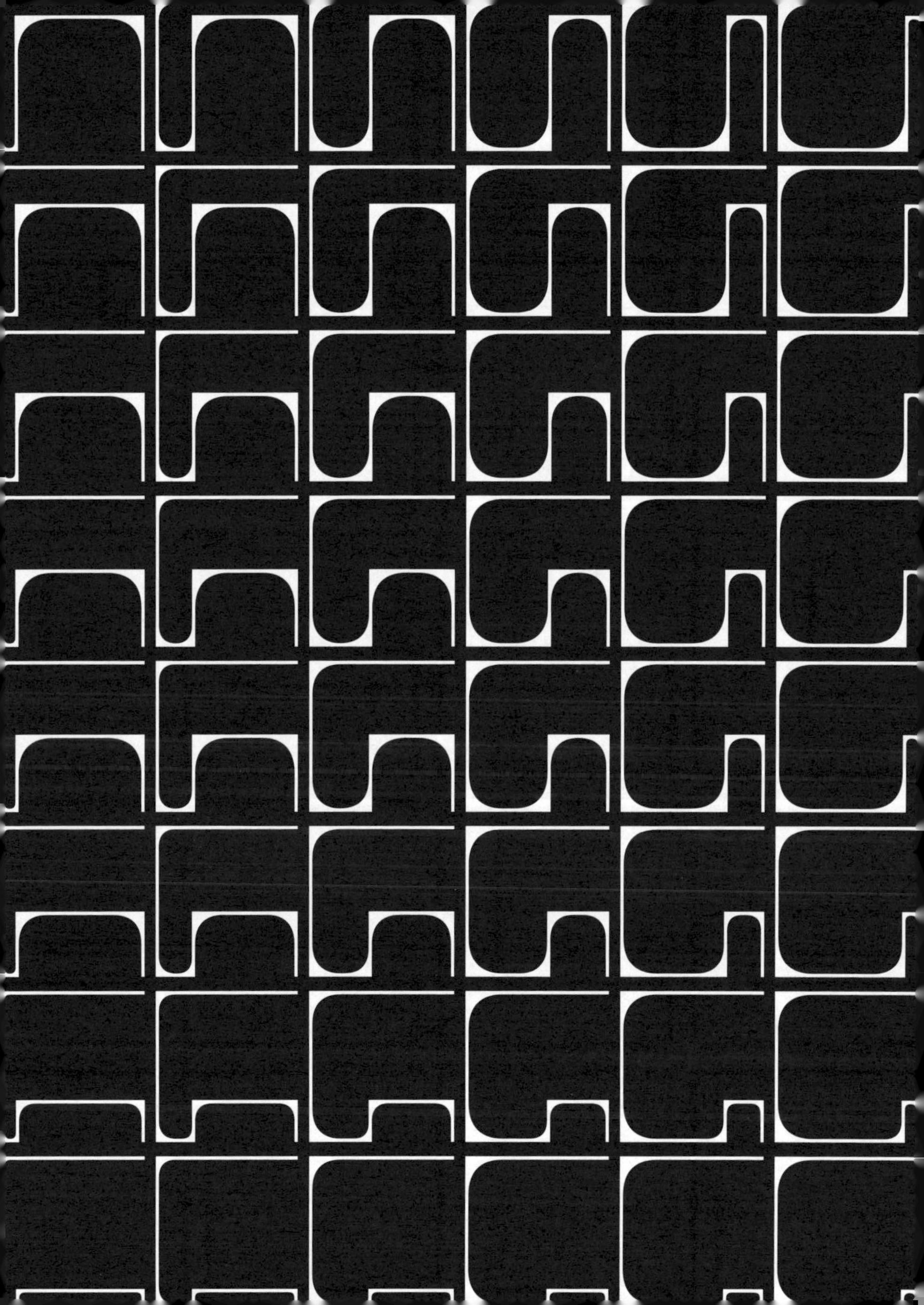

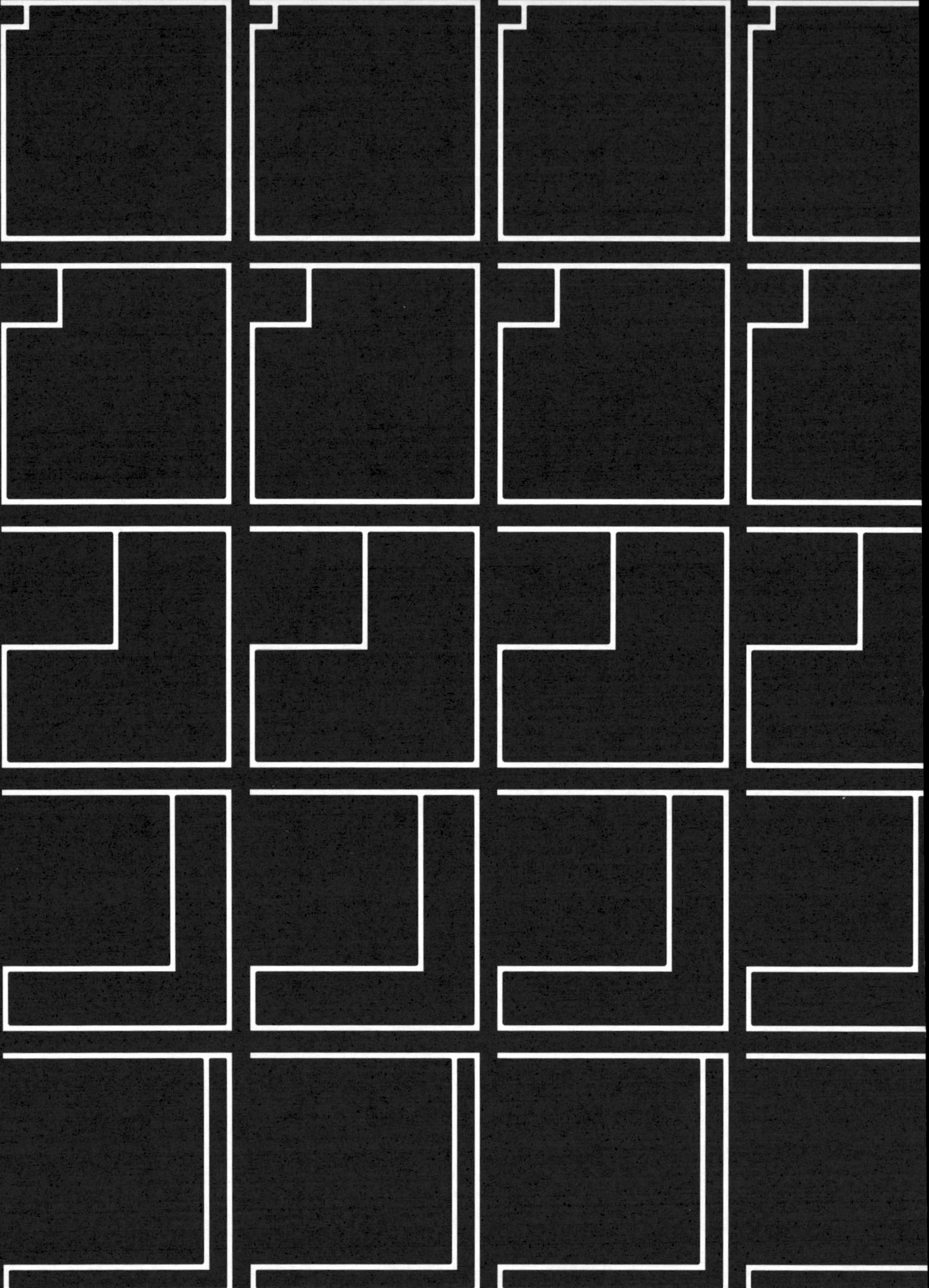

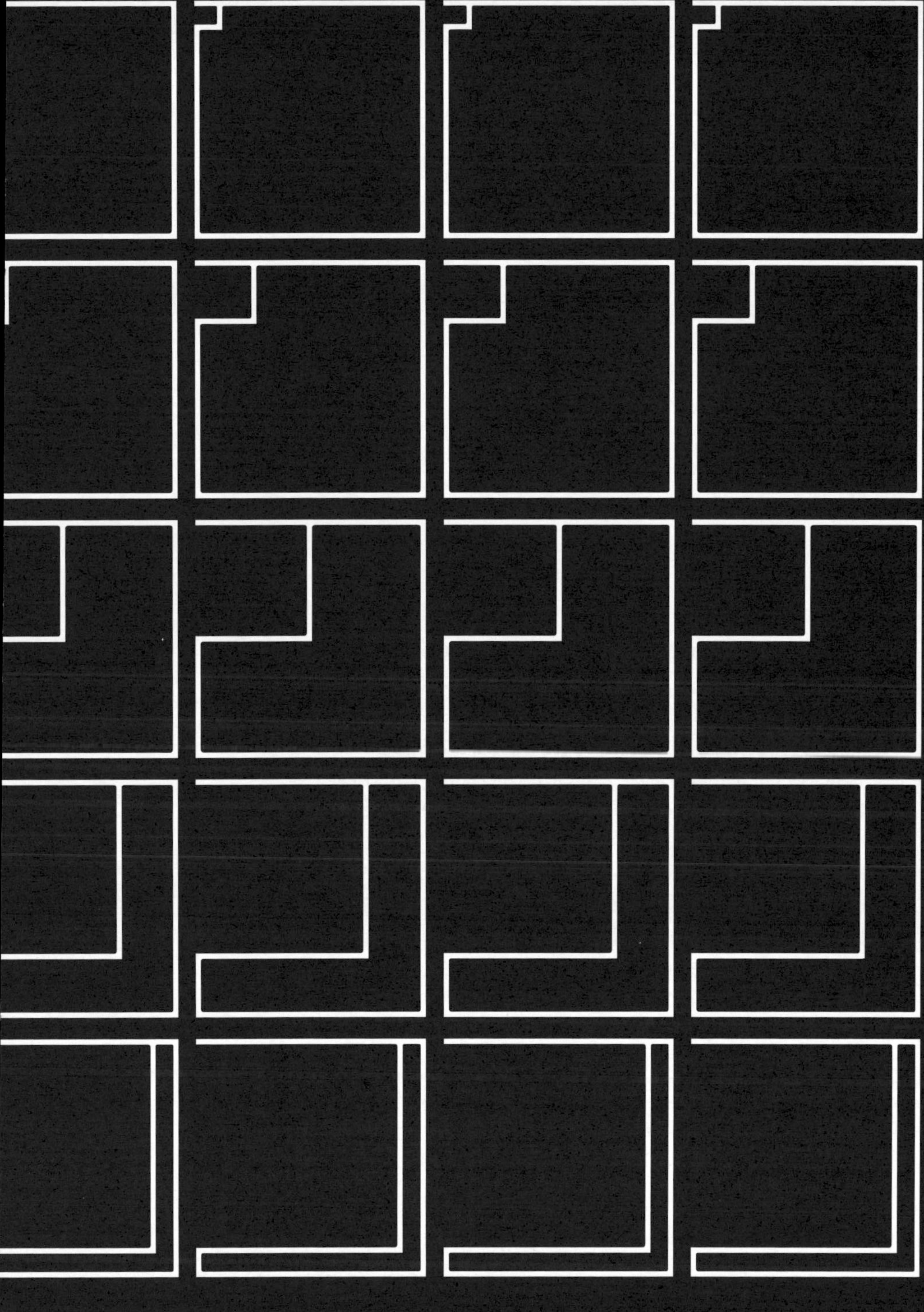

Section Notes:

All alphabets in the Kinetic section were created in Glyphs. K.A is a single, static font file containing uppercase characters, numerals, and basic punctuation. Its lowercase characters are inversions of the uppercase set, allowing for more or less differentiation between characters. K.B and K.C are two-part type systems: Part A is placed beneath Part B in a grey tone, while Part B uses a near-identical set with a slightly finer dot pattern. Together, they form a softer dot grid that creates a sense of depth and a subtle kinaesthetic effect. K.D is a single variable font file with parameters for the internal roundness of connectors and the central axis–one controlling horizontal shift, the other vertical. These parameters produce varying internal distortions across characters, generating a sense of kinetic movement within the text.

LETTERS·WIT
HIN·LETTERS
·WITHIN·LET
TERS·WITHIN
·LETTERS·WI
THIN·LETTER
S·WITHIN·LE
TTERS·WITHI
N·LETTERS·W
ITHIN·LETTE
RS·WITHIN·L

L Letters-within-letters A layered typographic system in which multiple letters can be nested inside larger individual letters, thus embedding several levels of textual information within a single space. This approach enables simultaneous macro- and micro-level communication — allowing, for instance, a heading to contain a subtext, or one word to contain another word. By stacking visual and linguistic layers within the same frame, the system provides a stratified, non-linear model of encoded language.

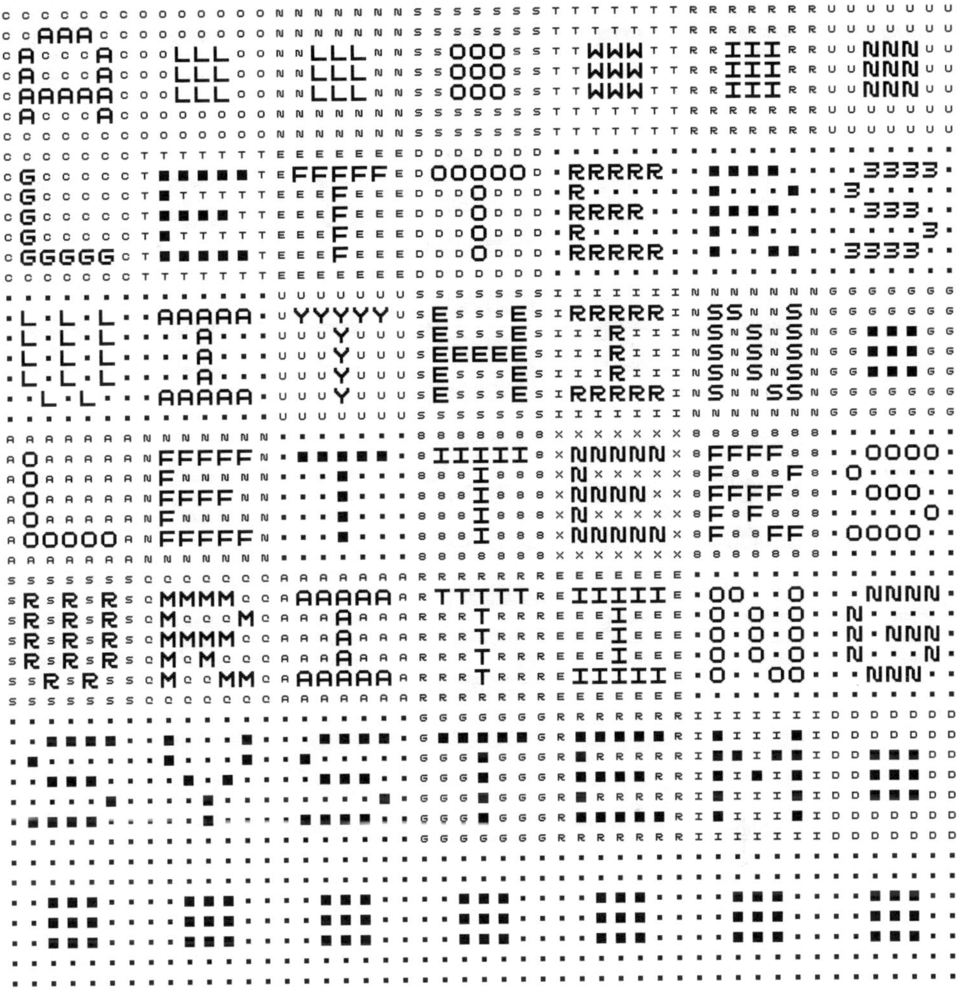

L.A

A Letters-within-Letters writing system constructed using an 7x7 square grid allowing for 3 layers of information with a prominent positive space*

*

s. 53
l. 53
t. 0

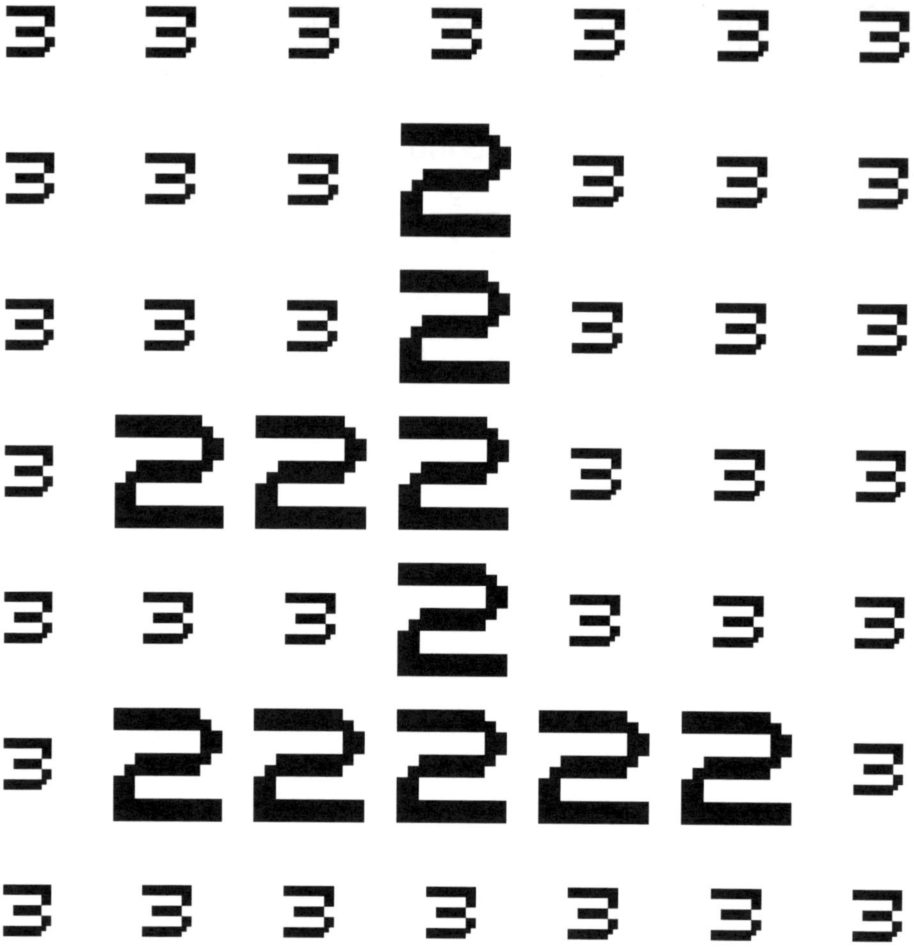

L.A

123

s. 385
l. 385
t. 0

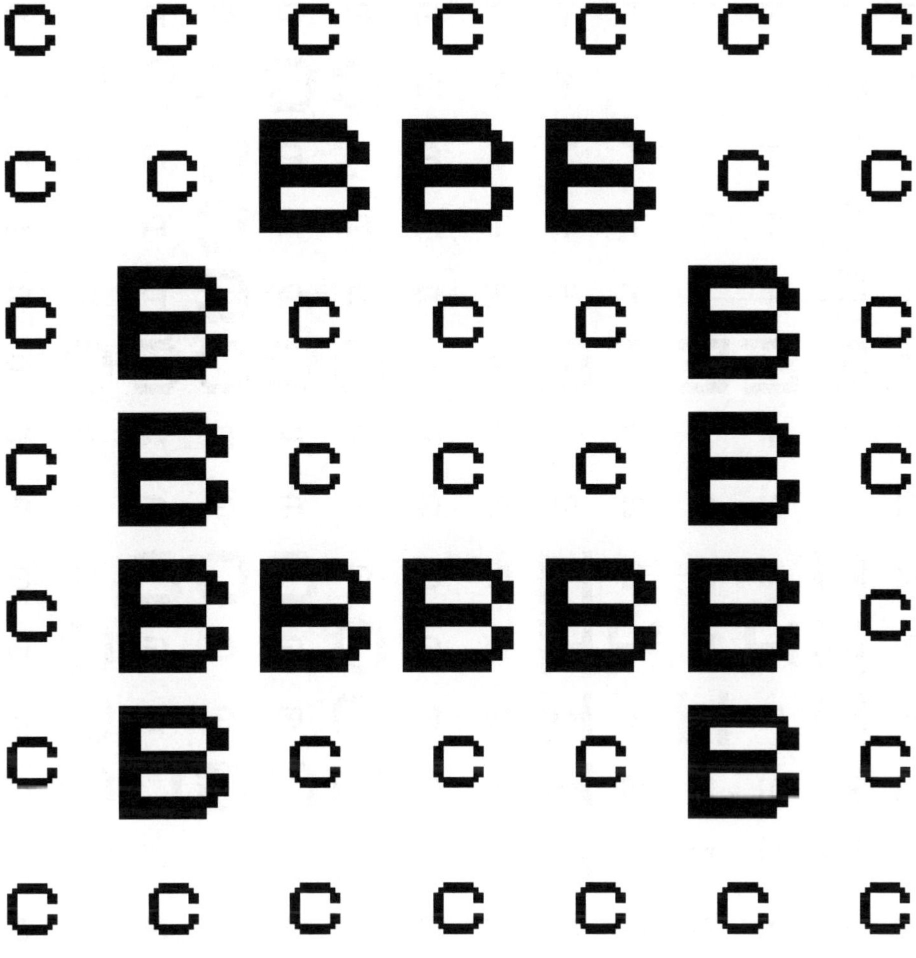

L.A

ABC

s. 385
l. 385
t. 0

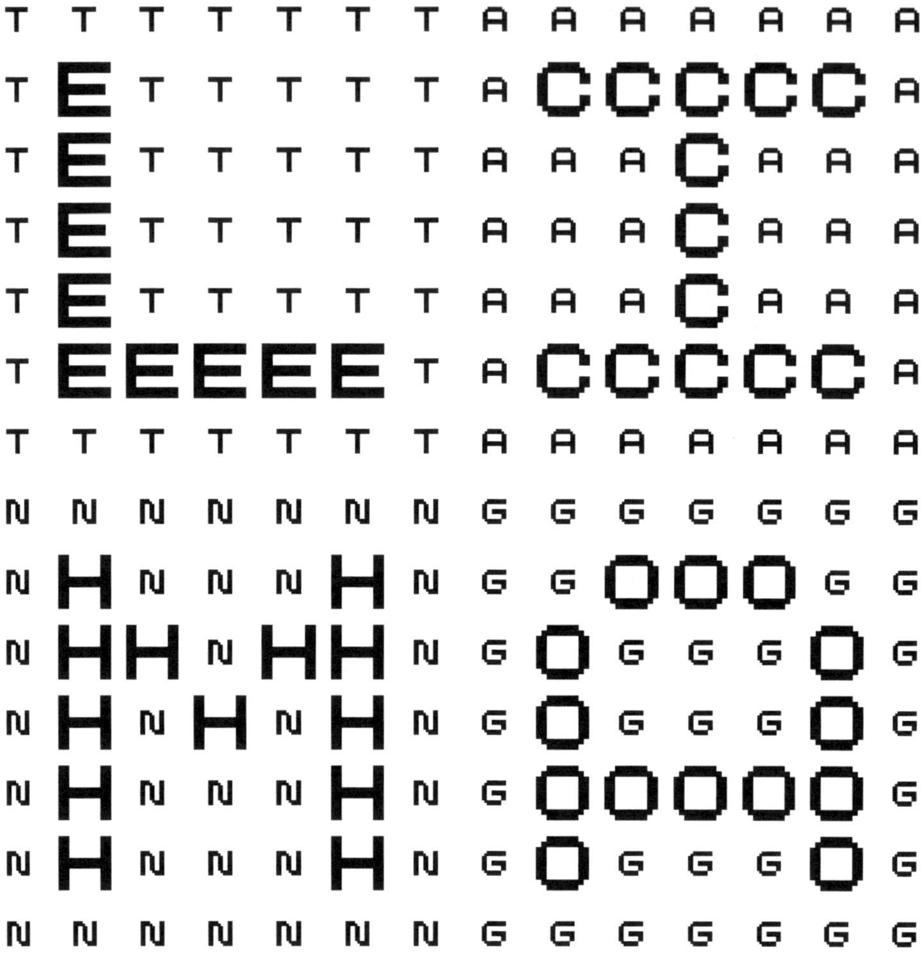

L.A

Lima Echo Tango
Tango Echo

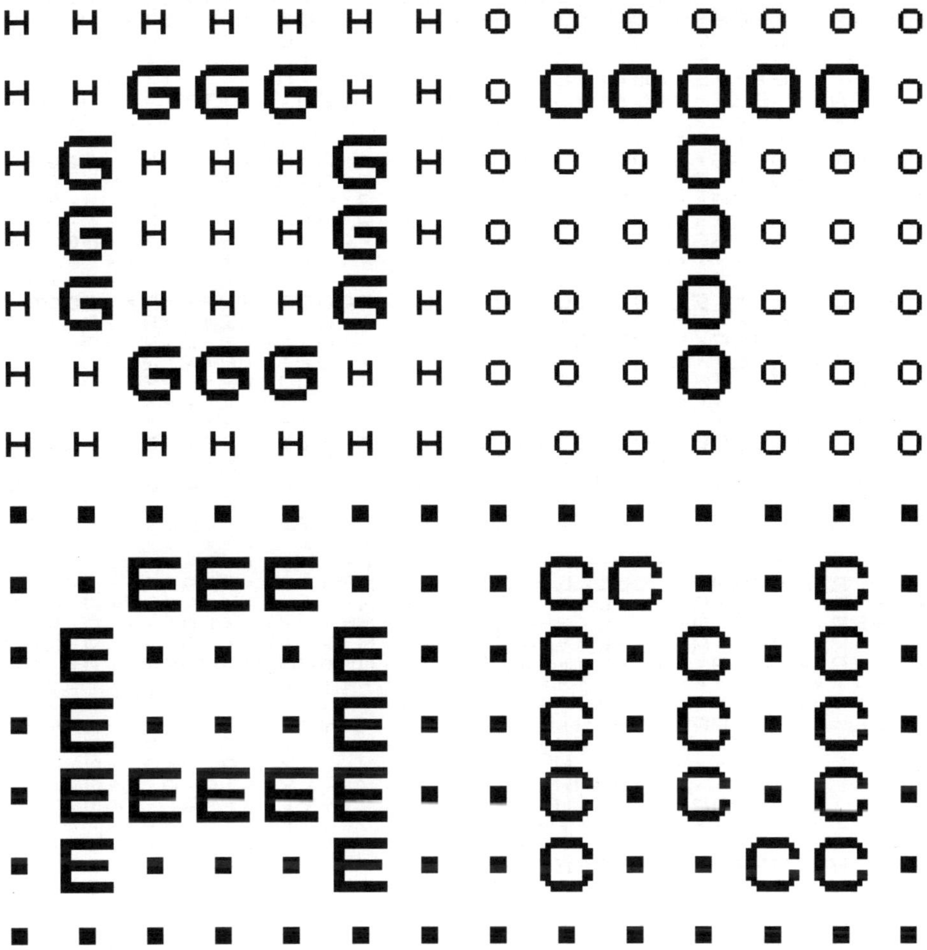

s. 185
l. 185
t. 0

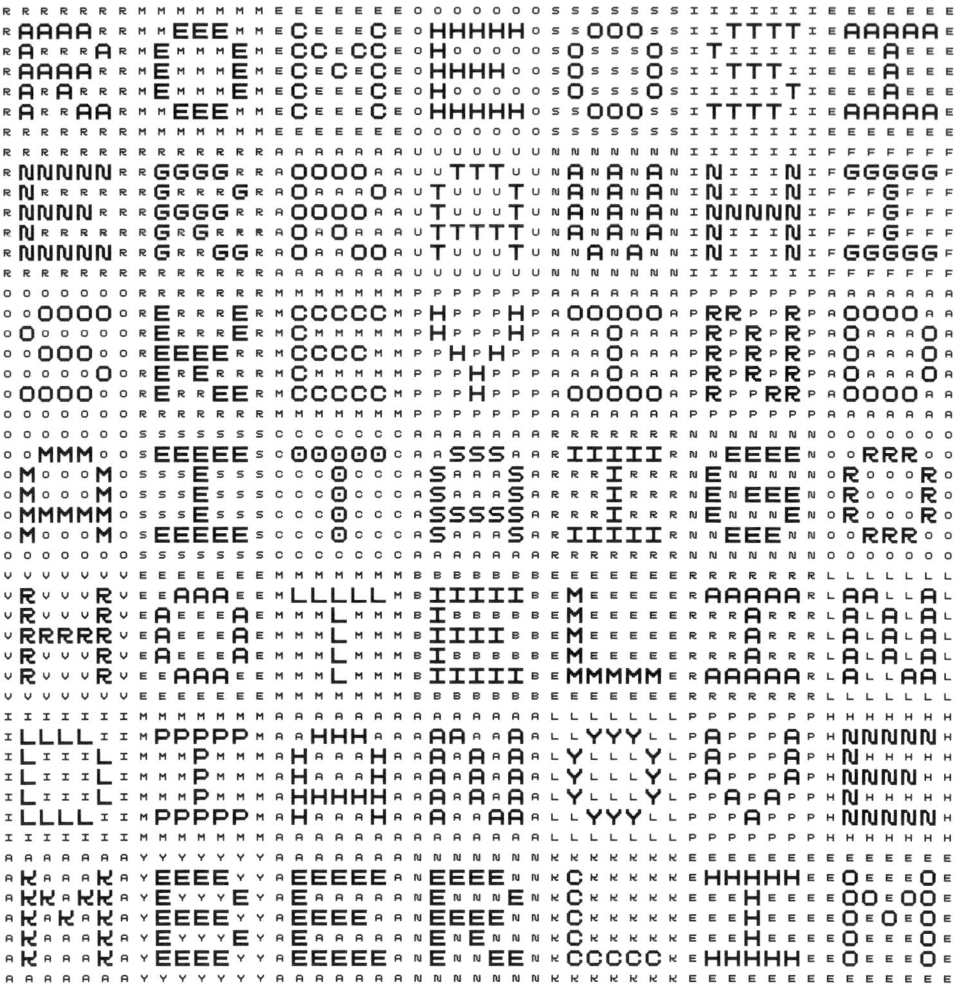

L.A

Romeo Sierra Whiskey India Tango Hotel
India November Lima Echo Tango Tango Echo
Romeo Sierra Lima Alpha Yankee Echo Romeo
Sierra Uniform Papa Oscar November Lima
Alpha Yankee

s. 53
l. 53
t. 0

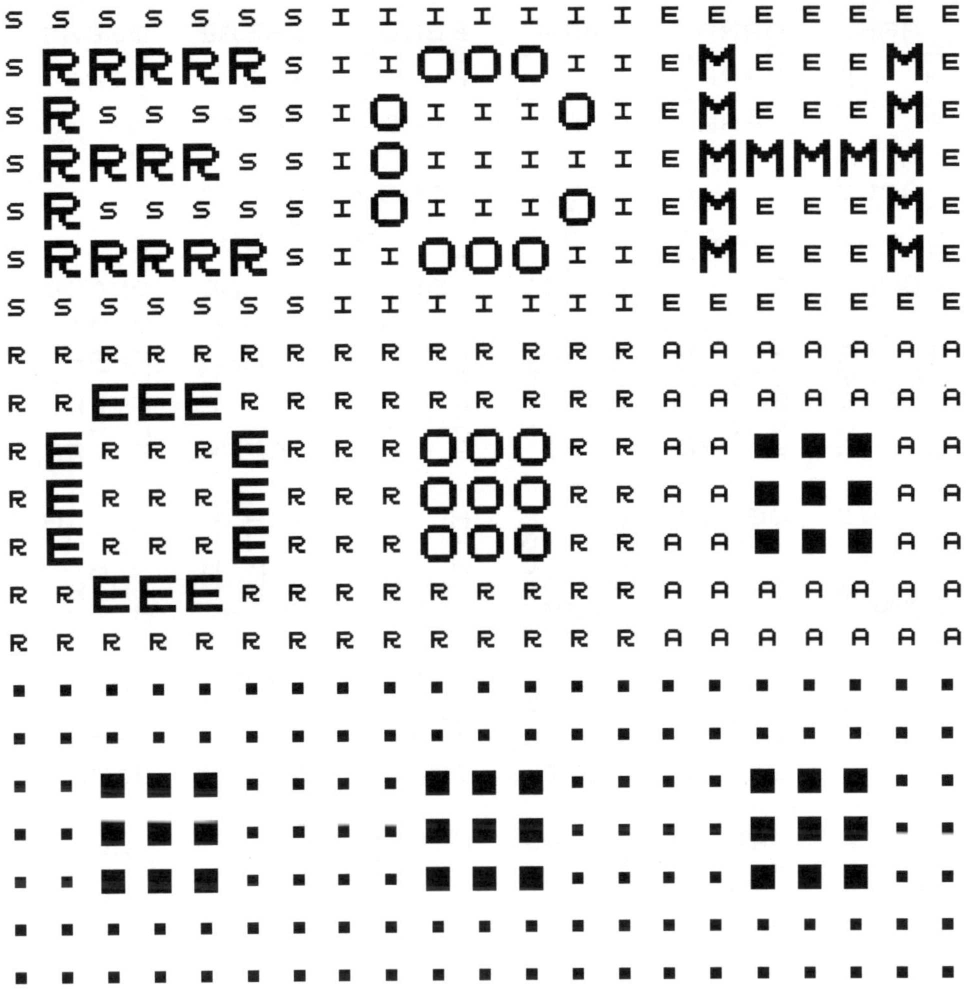

L.A

Echo Romeo Sierra

s. 126
l. 126
t. 0

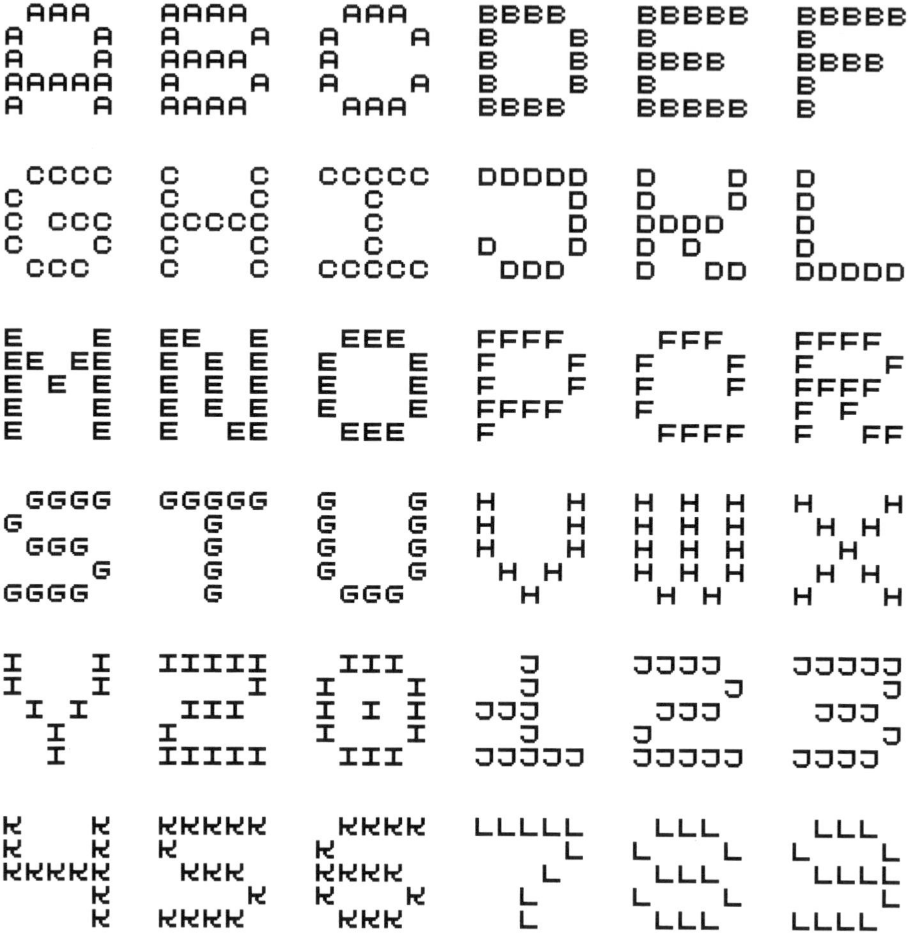

L.A A

A–Z 0–9

AAABBB
CCCDDD
EEEFFF
GGGHHH
IIIJJJ
KKKLLL

s. 61
l. 61
t. 0

L.A B

A–Z 0–9

MMMNNN
OOOPPP
QQQRRR
SSSTTT
UUUVVV
WWWXXX

s. 61
l. 61
t. 0

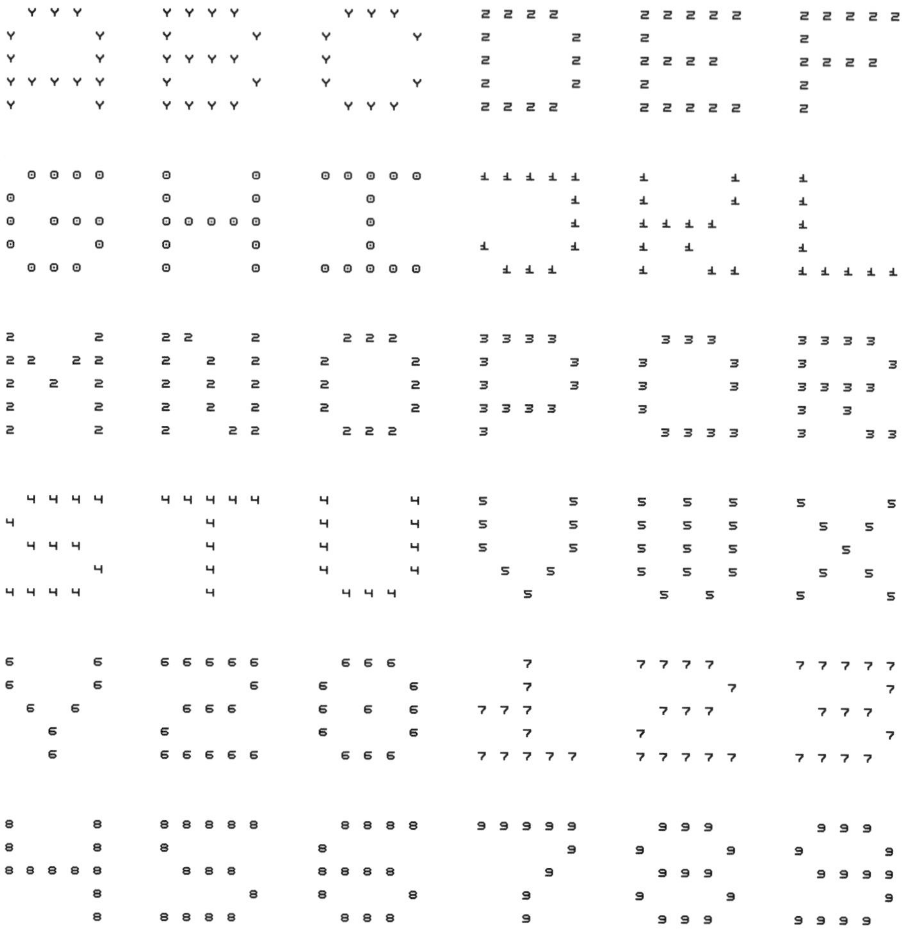

L.B A

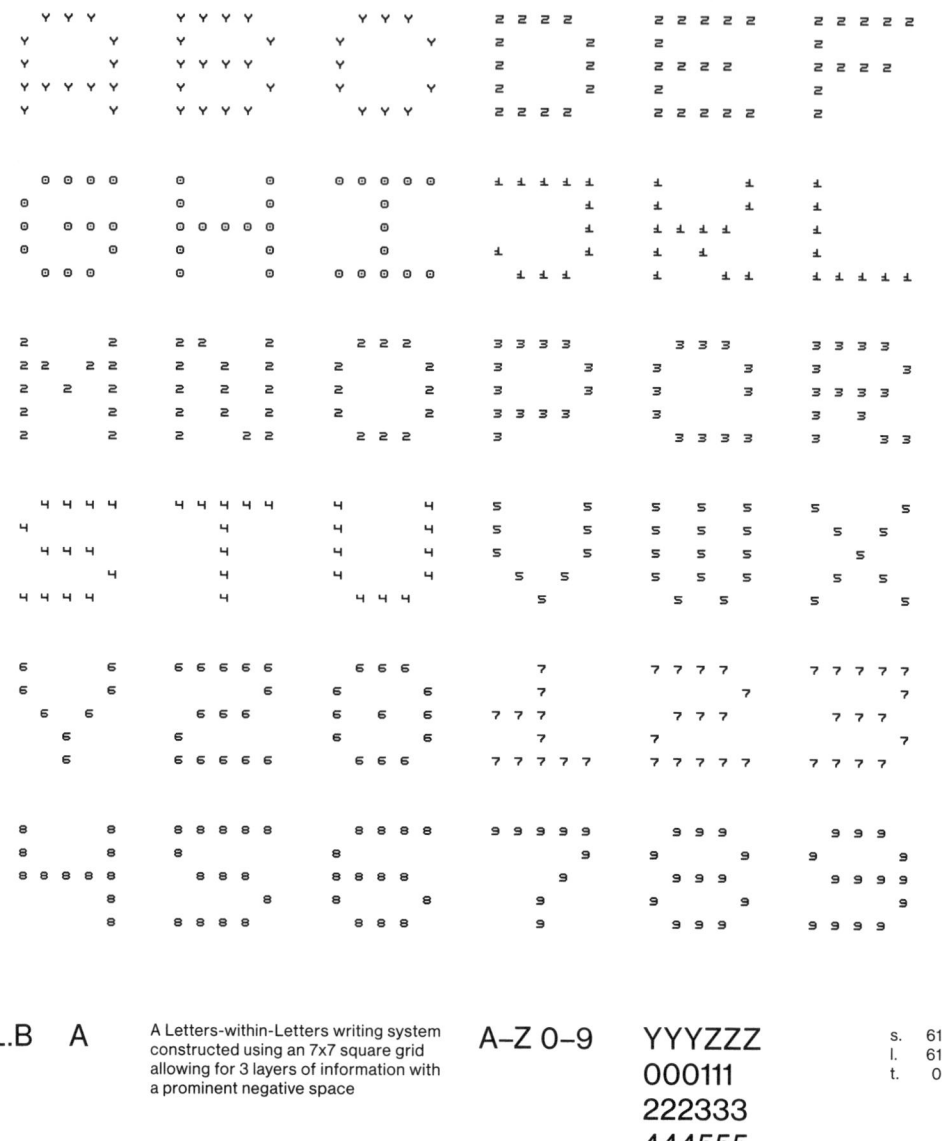

A Letters-within-Letters writing system constructed using an 7x7 square grid allowing for 3 layers of information with a prominent negative space

A–Z 0–9

YYYZZZ
000111
222333
444555
666777
888999

s. 61
l. 61
t. 0

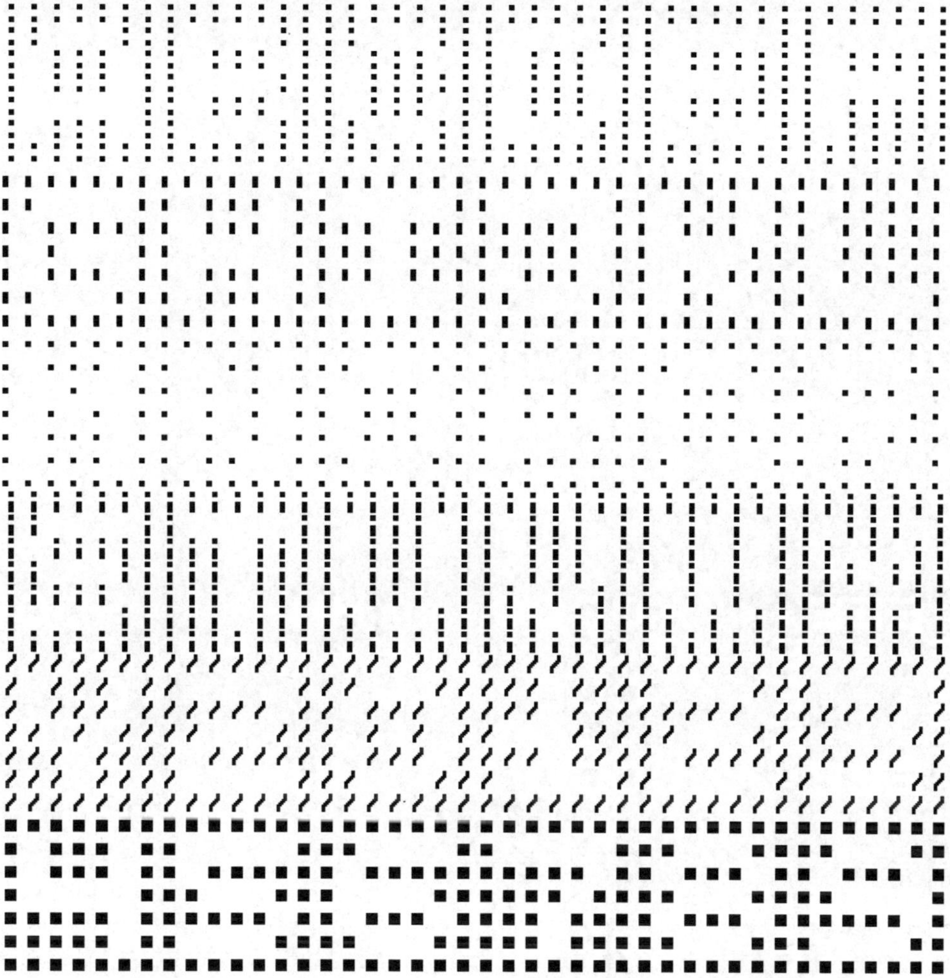

L.B B

A–Z 0–9

::::::

,,,,,,

......

::::::
,,,,,,

••••••

s. 61
l. 61
t. 0

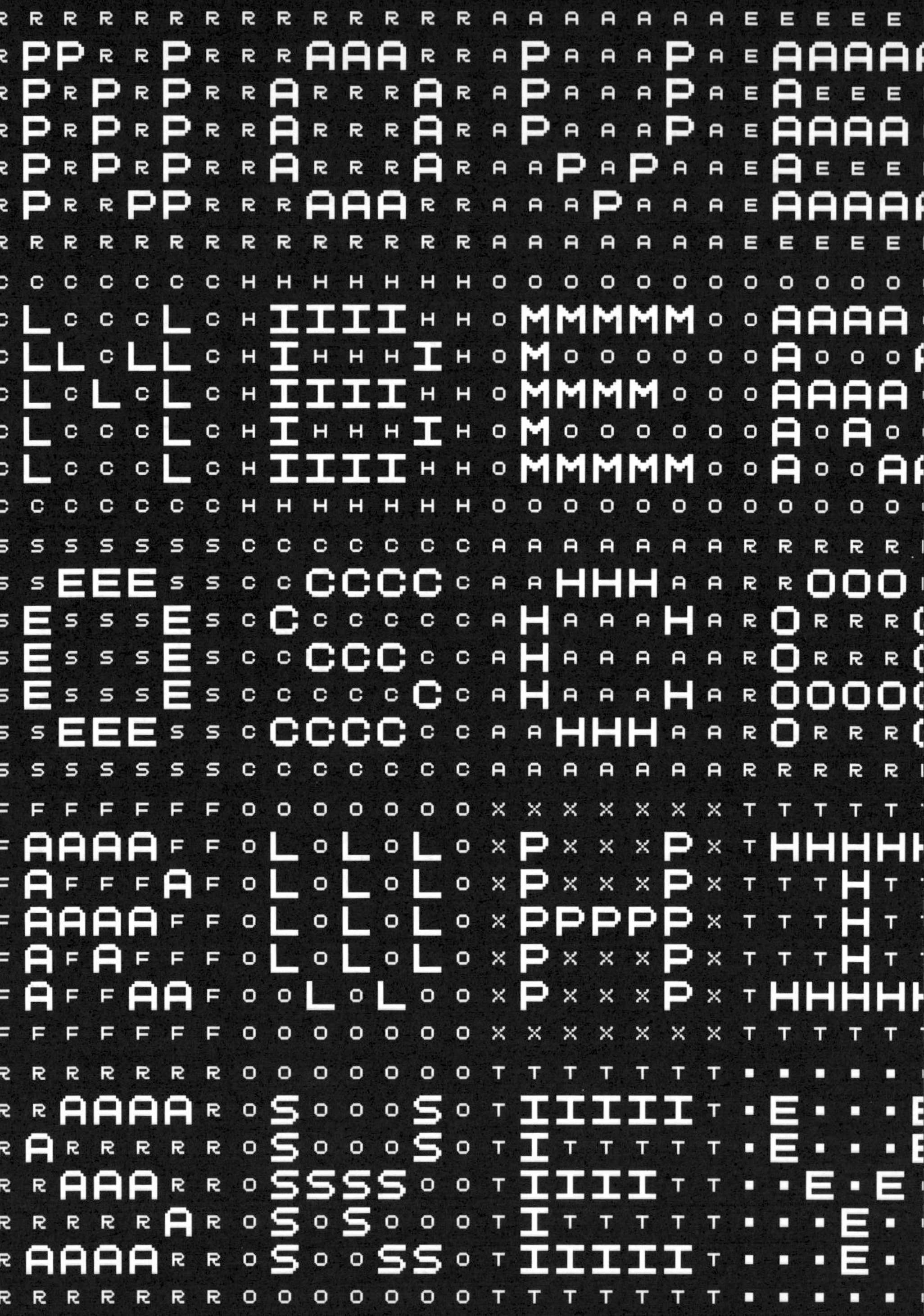

ALPHA·CH
CHARLEY·
YANKEE·B
RAVO·ECH
O·ROMEO·
NOVEMBER
ECHO·TAN
GO·INDIA
CHARLEY·
FOXTROT·

Section Notes:

Created in Glyphs, both L.A and L.B are two-part type systems: Part A displays the foreground of each character unit, and Part B the background. Each part includes a font style for every letterform, allowing the micro-character to be individually assigned. This two-part system enables three layers of information.

Inspired by conventional dot matrix technologies, Matrix explores three distinct typographic systems that vary in linguistic fidelity. Instead of using traditional dots, each system's characters are constructed from unique geometric components. While they draw from functional matrix-based typography, these designs prioritise the interactions between the individual subcomponents of letterforms and their adjacent characters. By also eliminating spacing between glyphs, emphasis shifts away from conventional legibility and towards the abstraction of intricate patterns.

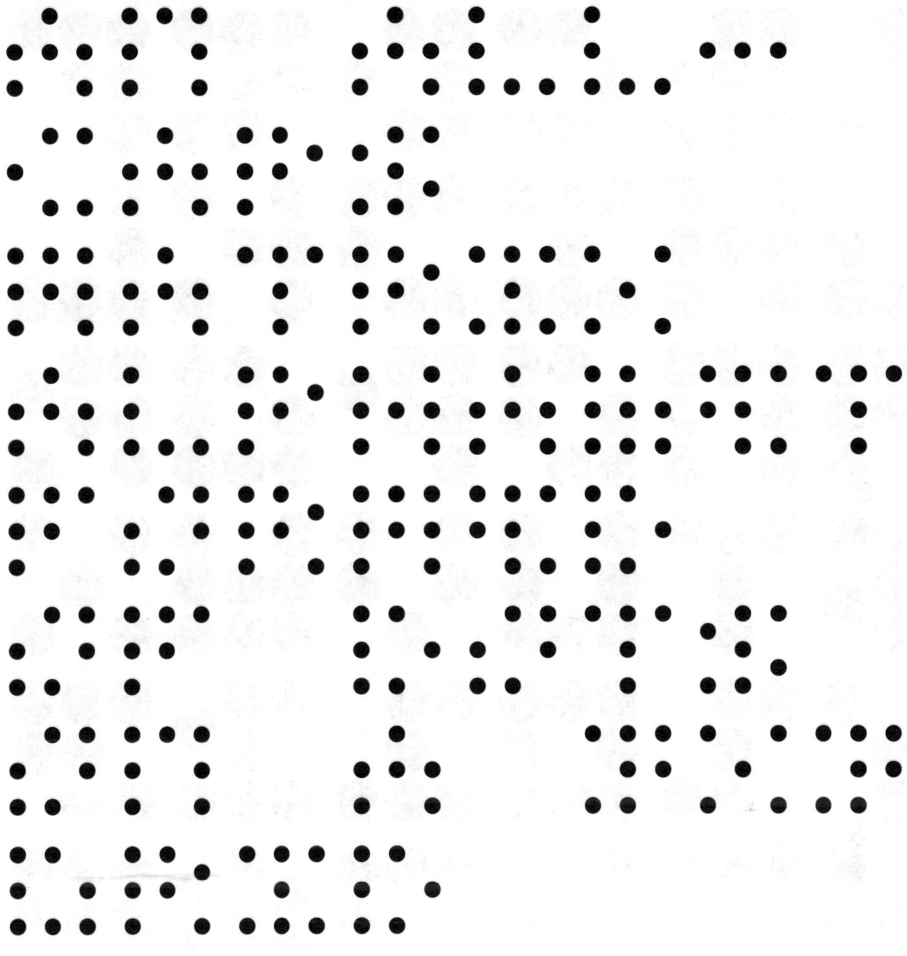

M.A A

An all-caps matrix alphabet
formed of dots on a 3×3 grid*

*

s. 41
l. 45
t. 100
w. 400

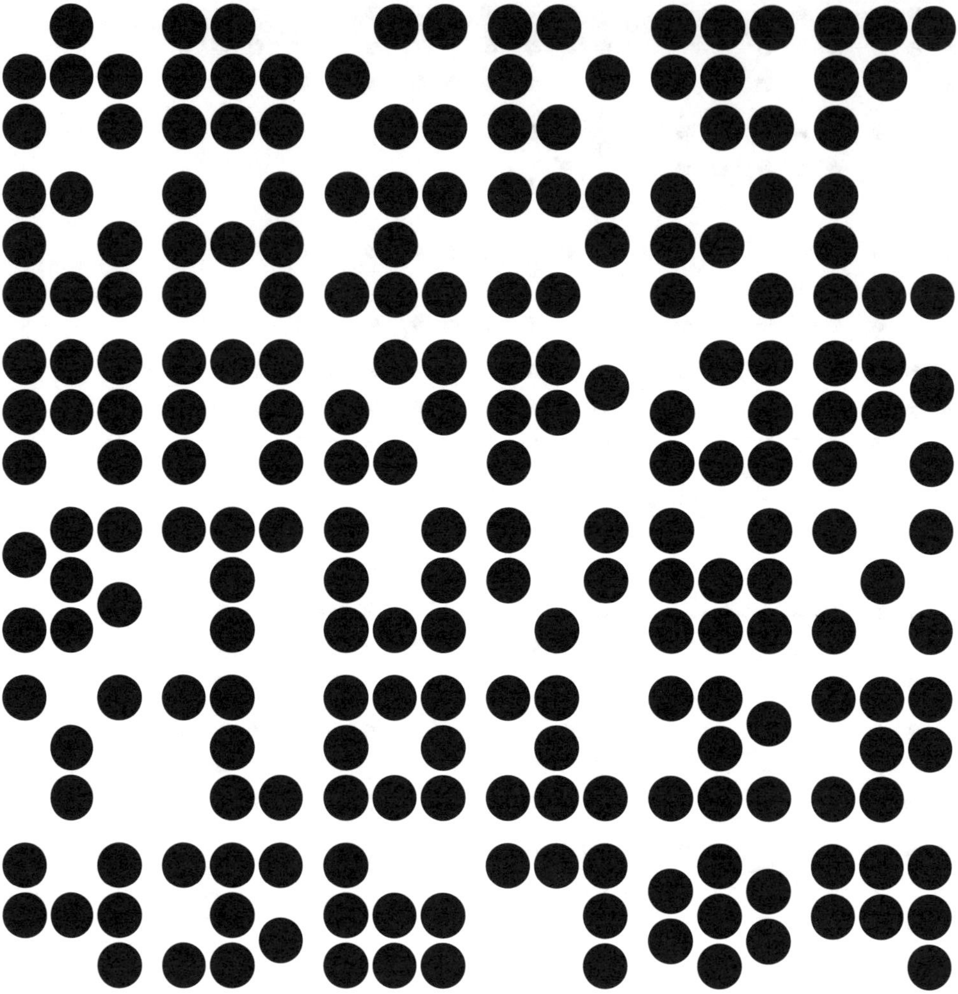

M.A A

A–Z 0–9

s. 57
l. 63
t. 100
w. 900

M.A B

An all-caps matrix alphabet formed of rounded squares on a 3×3 grid

A–Z 0–9

s. 57
l. 63
t. 100
w. 900

M.A C

An all-caps matrix alphabet formed of rounded diamonds on a 3×3 grid

Mike

s. 185
l. 185
t. 0
w. 900

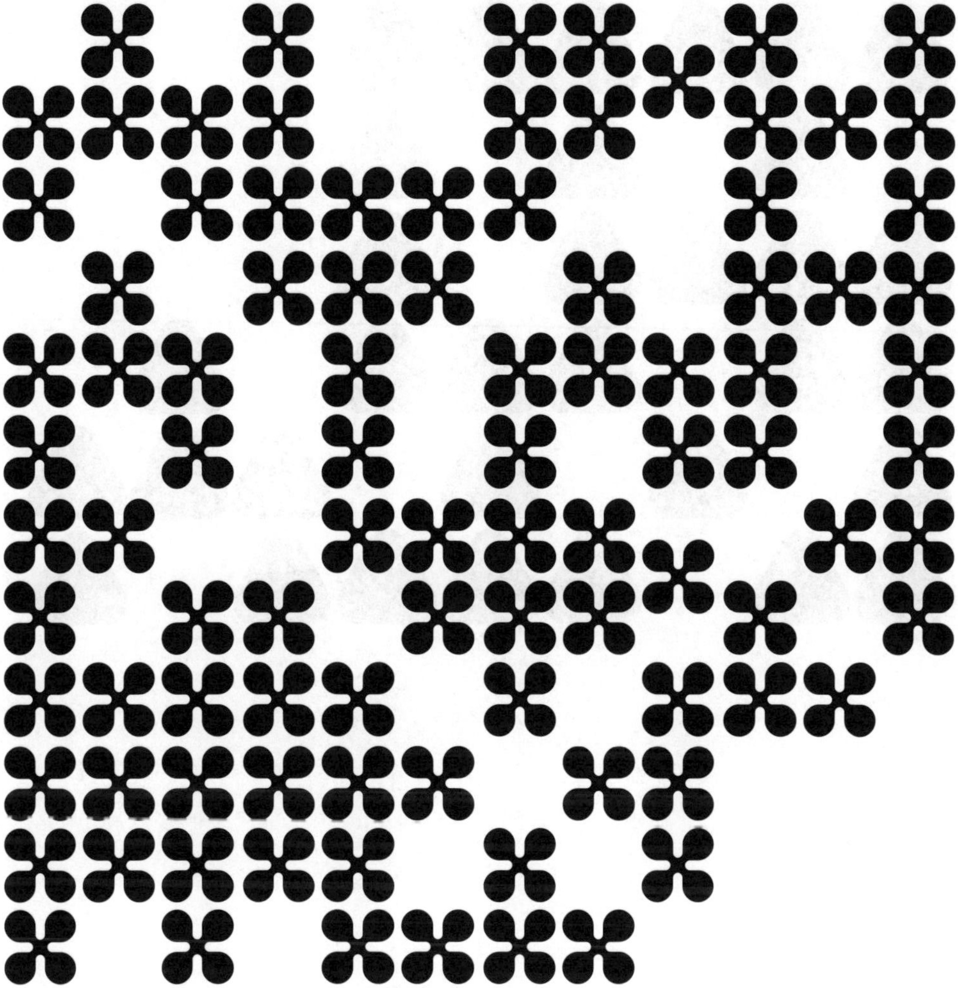

M.A D

An all-caps matrix alphabet formed of diagonal pinched rounded quatrefoils on a 3×3 grid

Alpha Tango Romeo

s. 93
l. 93
t. 0
w. 900

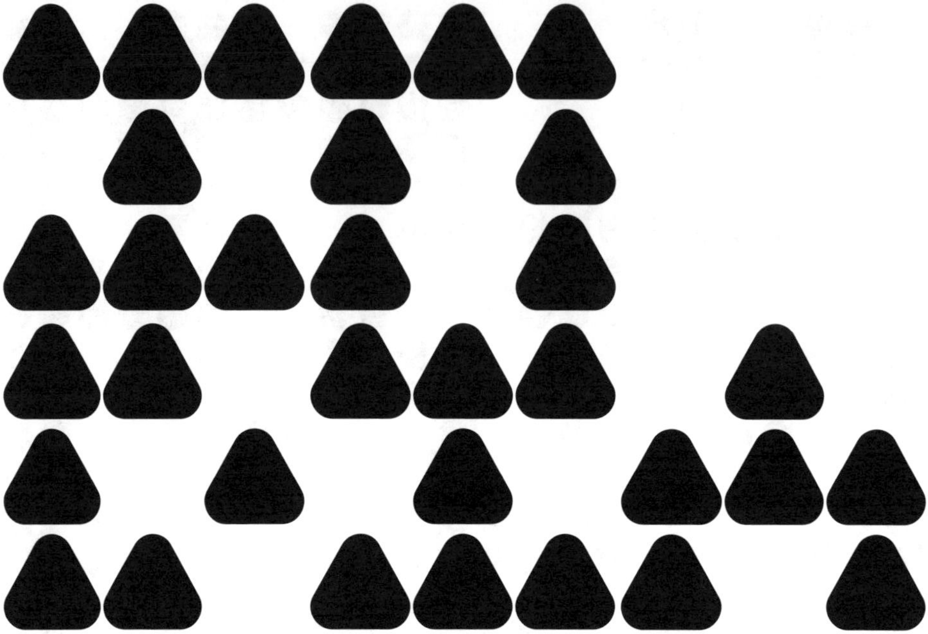

M.A E

An all-caps matrix alphabet formed of rounded triangles on a 3×3 grid

India

s. 120
l. 120
t. 0
w. 900

AN ALL…
CAPS
MATRIX
ALPHABET
FORMED OF
DIAGONAL
QUATRE…
FOIL ON A
3X3 GRID

M.A F

An all-caps matrix alphabet formed of diagonal rounded quatrefoils on a 3×3 grid*

*

s. 34
l. 38
t. 100
w. 900

M.A G

An all-caps matrix alphabet formed of rounded quatrefoils on a 3×3 grid

Xray

s. 185
l. 185
t. 0
w. 900

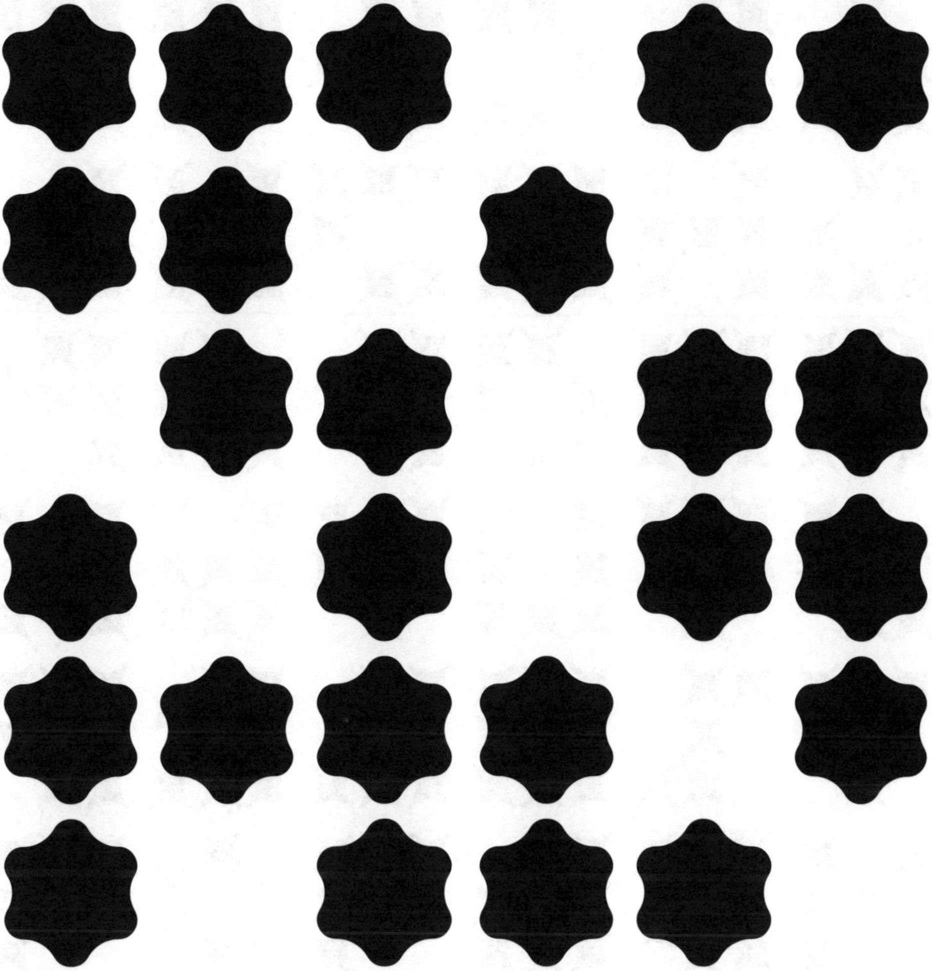

M.A H

An all-caps matrix alphabet formed of rounded six pointed stars on a 3×3 grid

Echo

s. 185
l. 185
t. 0
w. 900

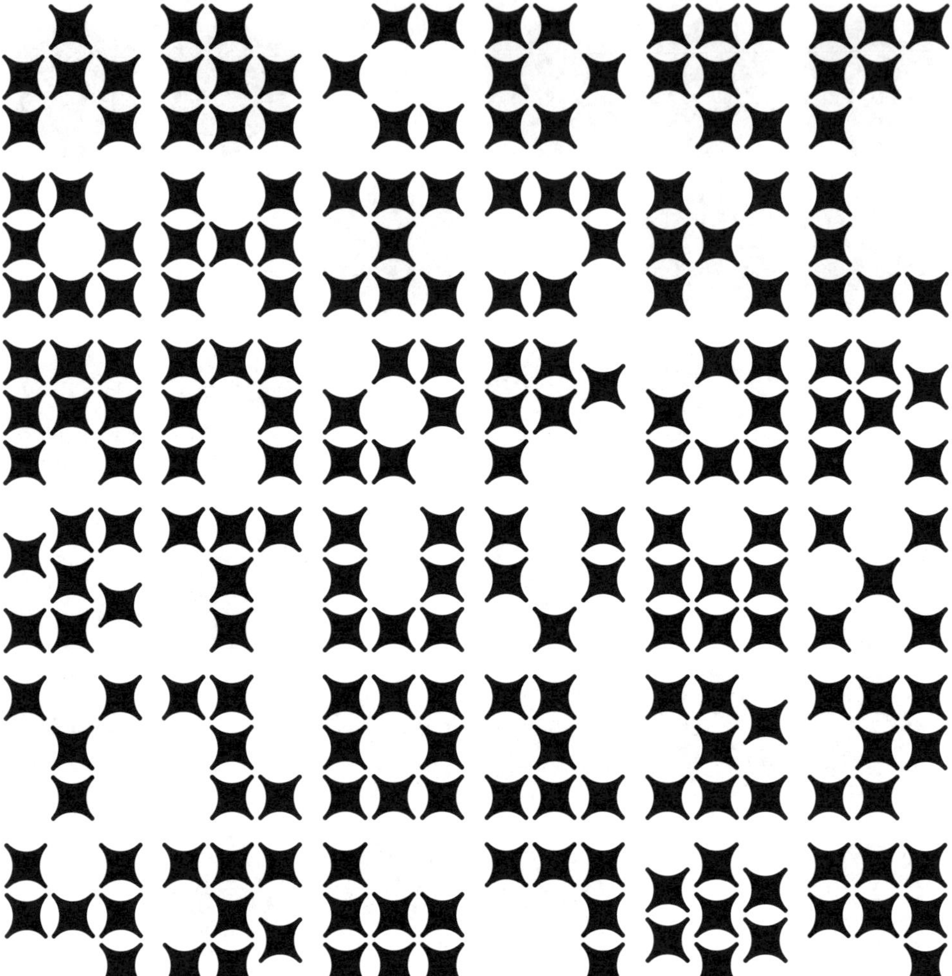

M.A I

An all-caps matrix alphabet formed of diagonal astroid curves on a 3×3 grid

A–Z 0–9

s. 57
l. 63
t. 100
w. 900

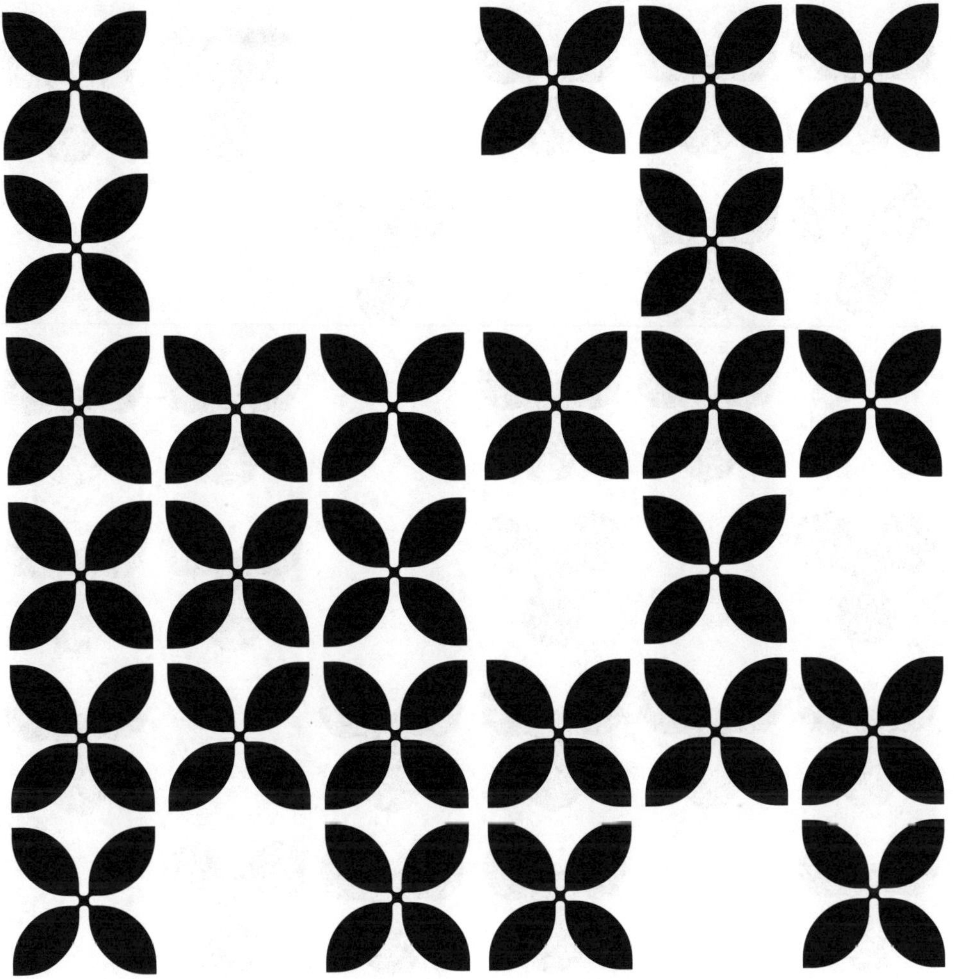

M.A J

An all-caps matrix alphabet formed of pinched pointed quadrifolium on a 3×3 grid

Lima

s. 185
l. 185
t. 0
w. 900

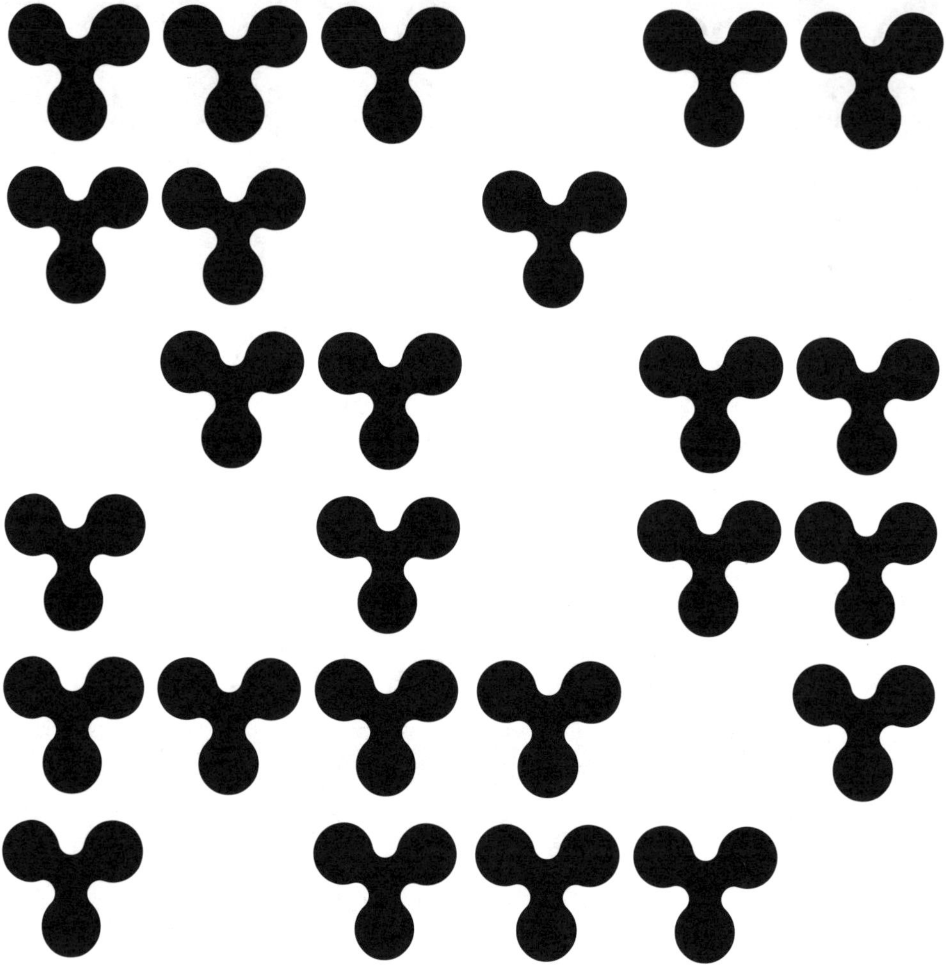

M.A K

An all-caps matrix alphabet formed of pinched rounded trefoils on a 3×3 grid

Echo

s. 185
l. 185
t. 0
w. 900

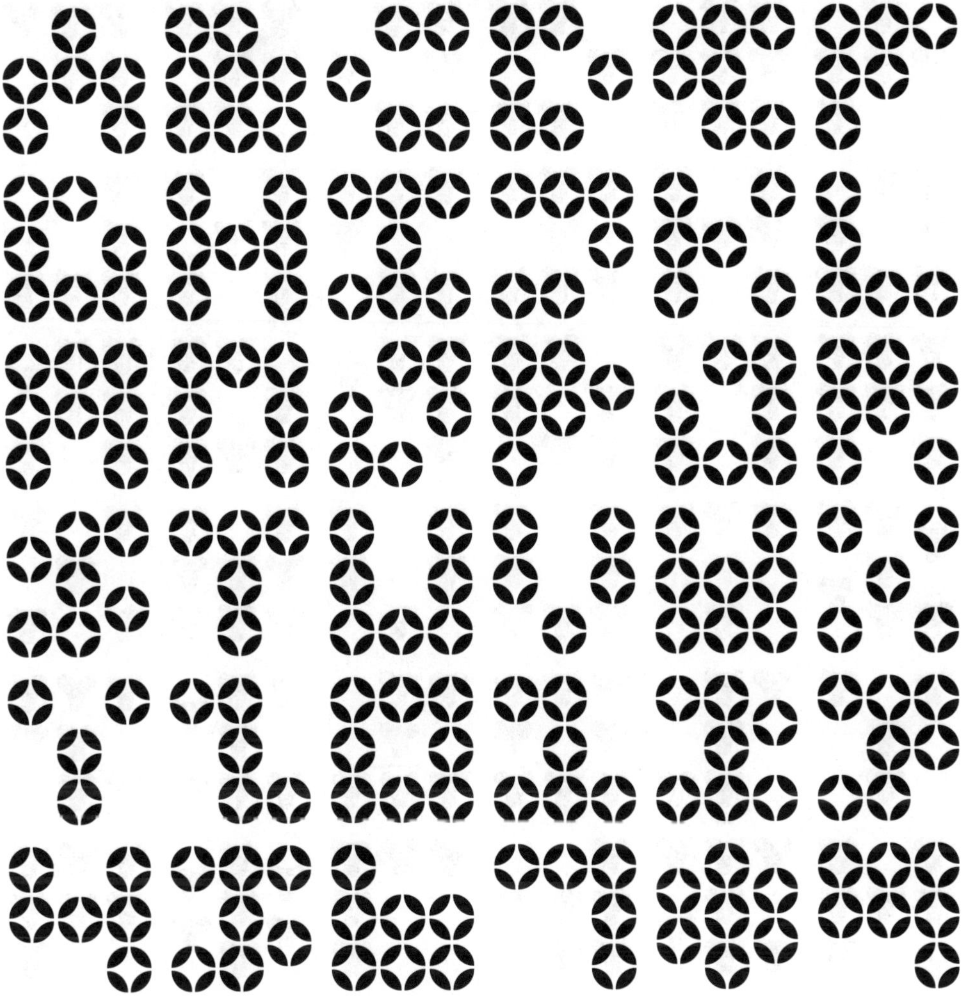

M.A L

An all-caps matrix alphabet formed of circle lattice units on a 3×3 grid

A–Z 0–9

s. 57
l. 63
t. 100
w. 900

M.A M

An all-caps matrix alphabet formed of rounded trefoils on a 3×3 grid

A–Z 0–9

s. 57
l. 63
t. 100
w. 900

M.A N

An all-caps matrix alphabet formed of a range of shapes on a 3×3 grid

Mike

s. 185
l. 185
t. 0
w. 900

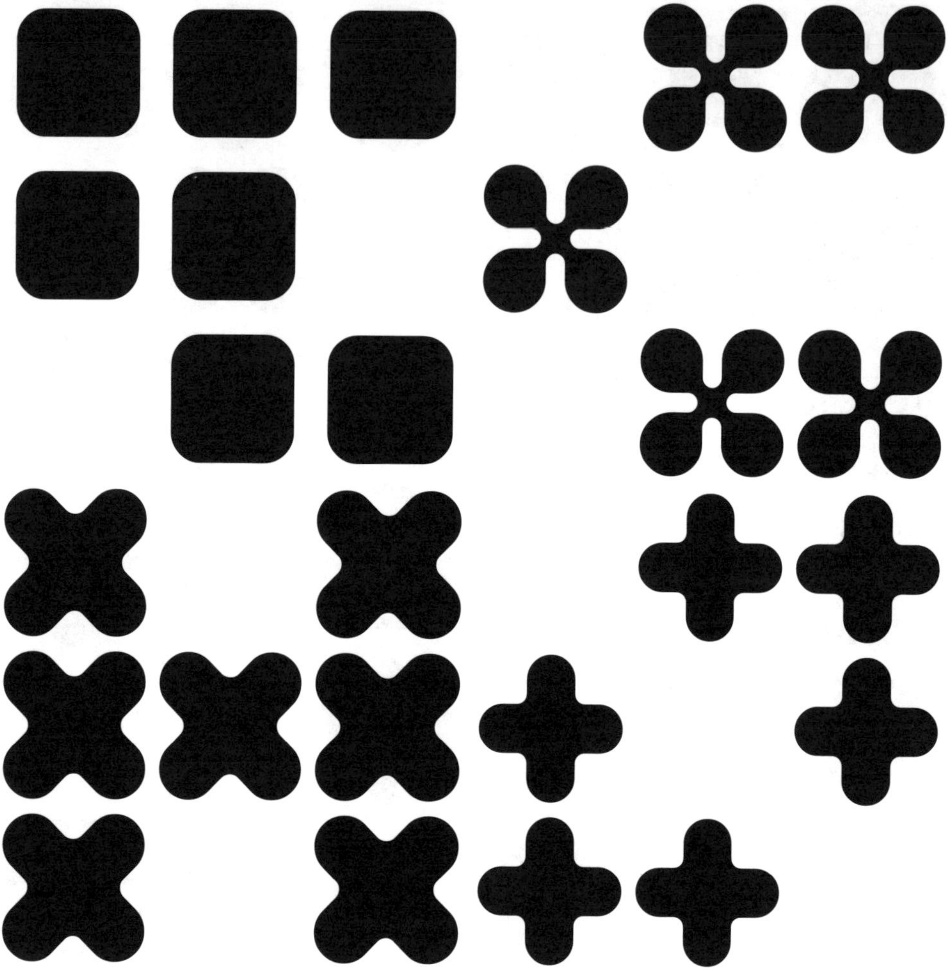

M.A O

An all-caps matrix alphabet with letters formed of a range of shapes on a 3×3 grid

Echo

s. 185
l. 185
t. 0
w. 900

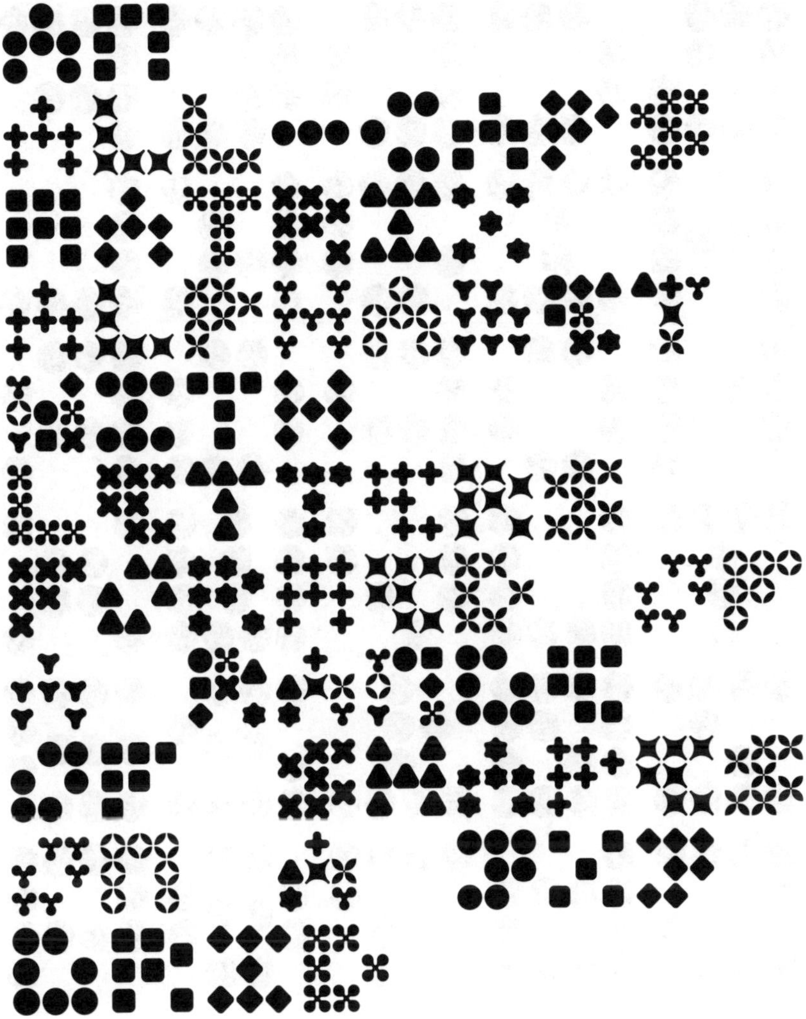

M.A O

*

s. 31
l. 34
t. 100
w. 900

M.B A

An all-caps matrix alphabet formed of dots on a 4×4 grid

A–Z 0–9

s. 57
l. 63
t. 100
w. 900

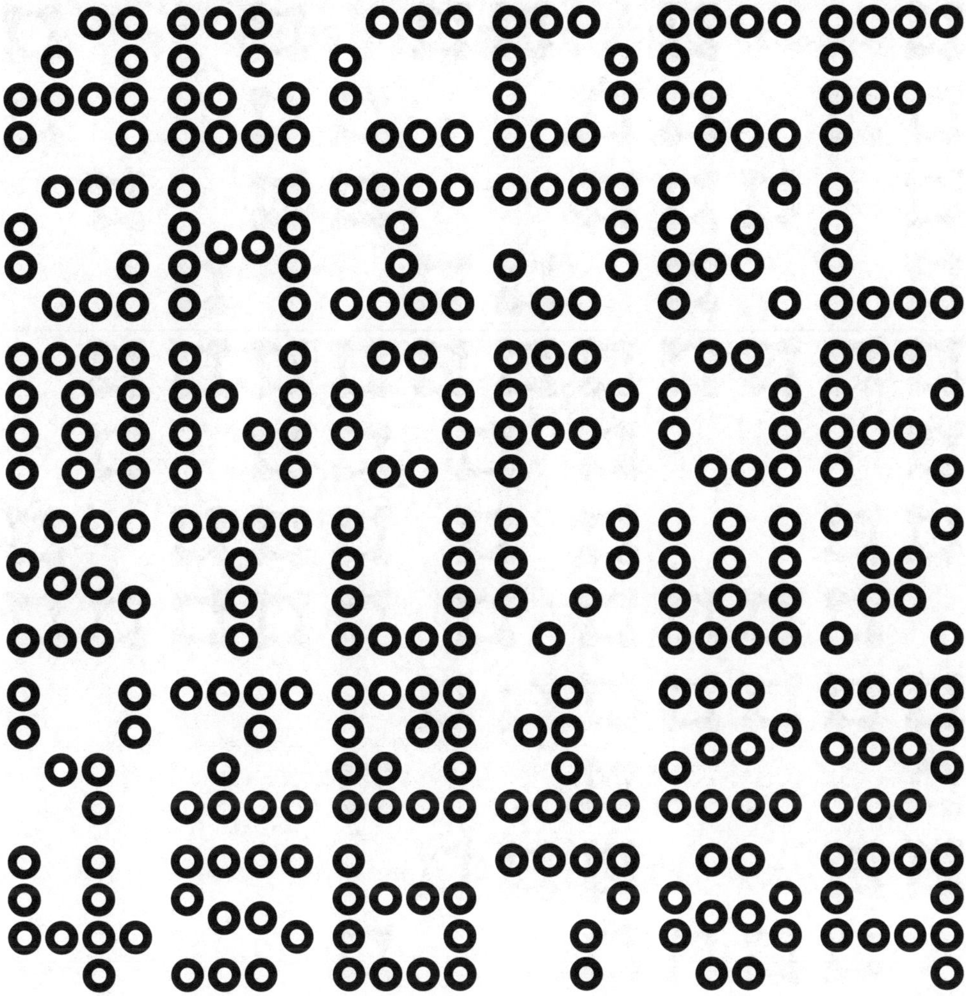

M.B B

An all-caps matrix alphabet formed of outline circles on a 4×4 grid

A–Z 0–9

s. 57
l. 63
t. 100
w. 900

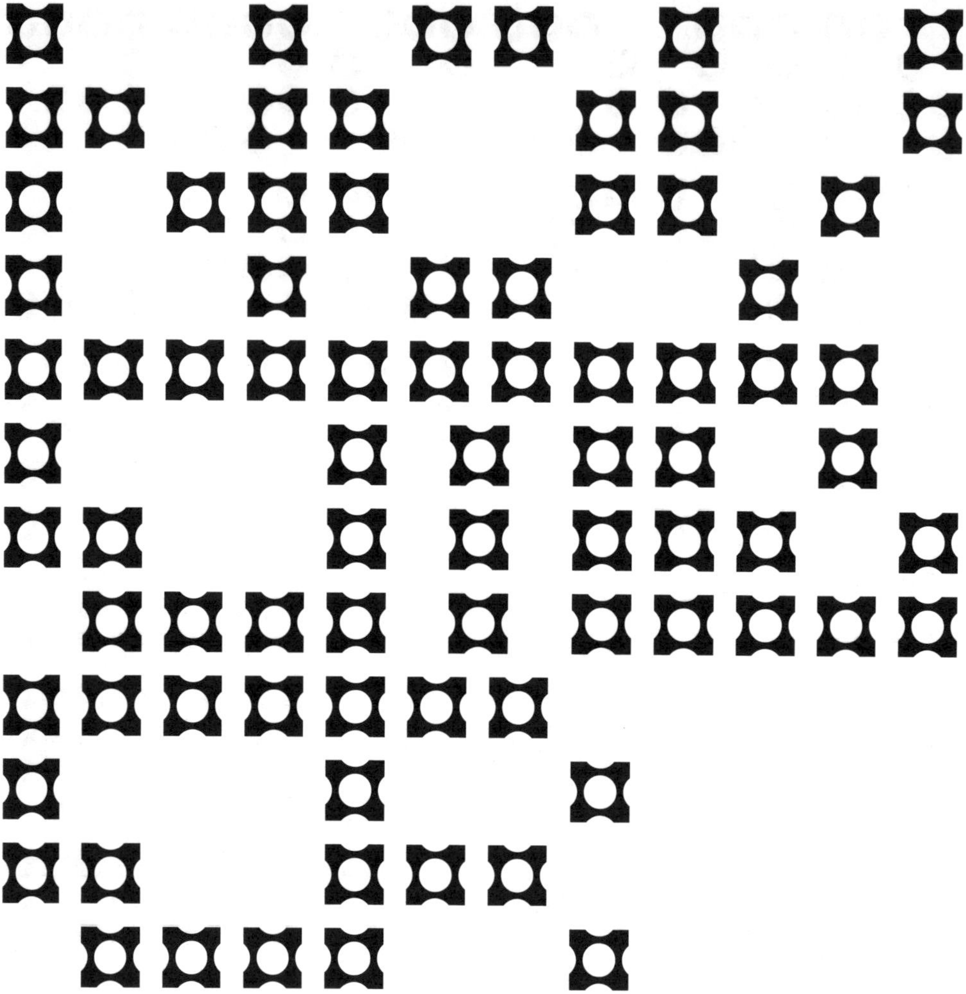

M.B C

An all-caps matrix alphabet formed of squares intersected with circles on a 4×4 grid

November

s. 126
l. 126
t. 0
w. 900

M.B D

An all-caps matrix alphabet formed of diagonal rounded crosses on a 4×4 grid

Tango Sierra

s. 92
l. 92
t. 0
w. 900

AN
ALL-CAPS
MATRIX
ALPHABET
FORMED OF
OCTAGONS
ON A 4X4
GRID

M.B E

An all-caps matrix alphabet formed of octagons on a 4×4 grid*

*

s. 37
l. 41
t. 100
w. 900

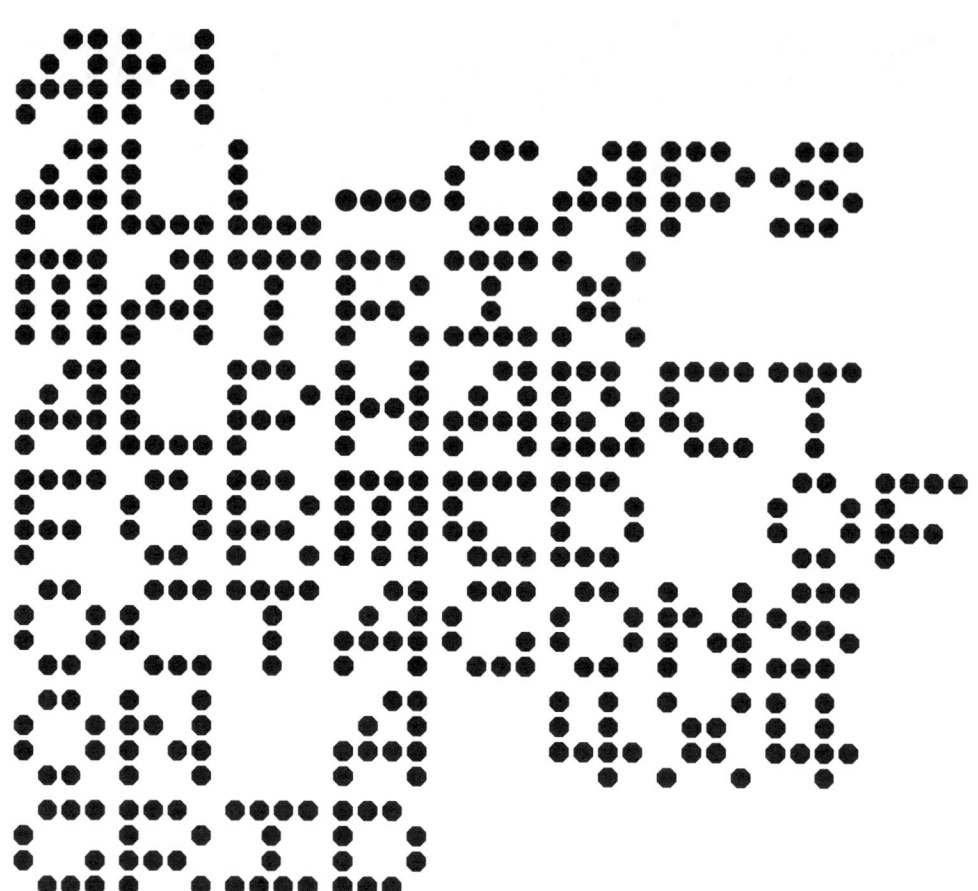

GF

M.B F

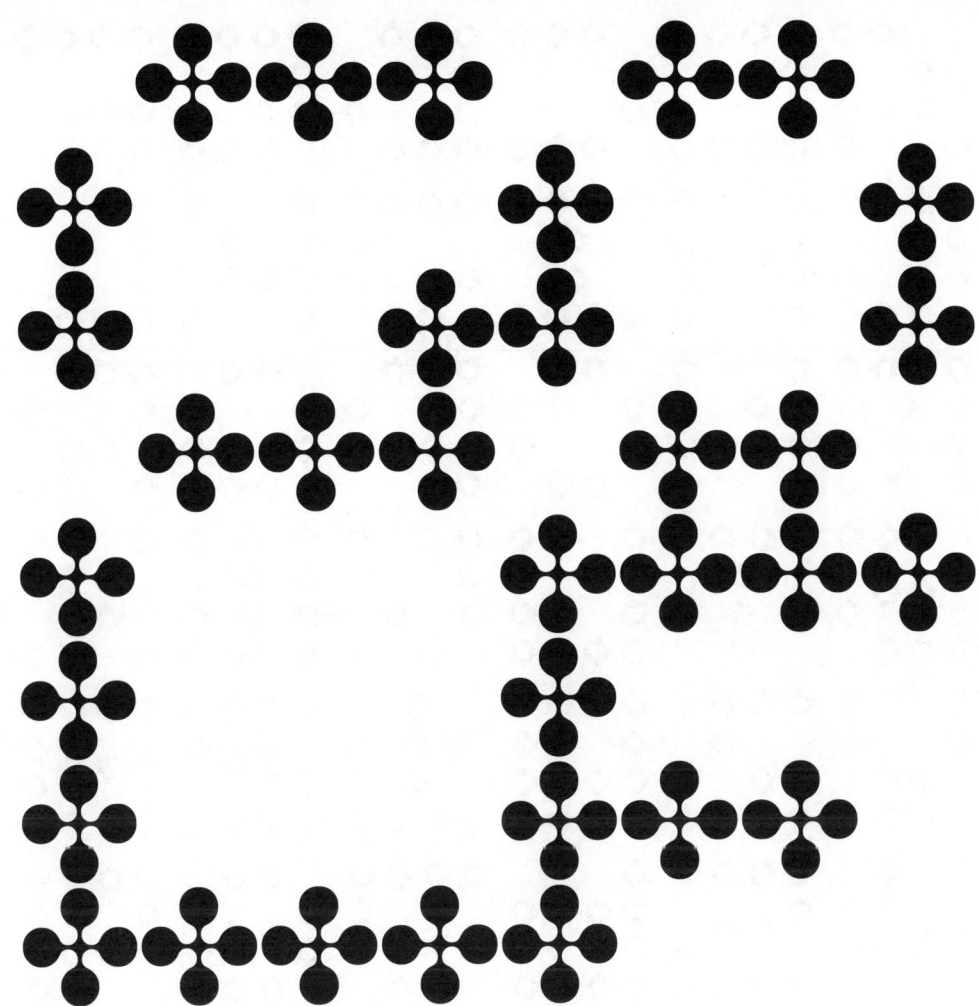

An all-caps matrix alphabet formed of pinched quatrefoils on a 4×4 grid

Golf

s. 184
l. 184
t. 0
w. 900

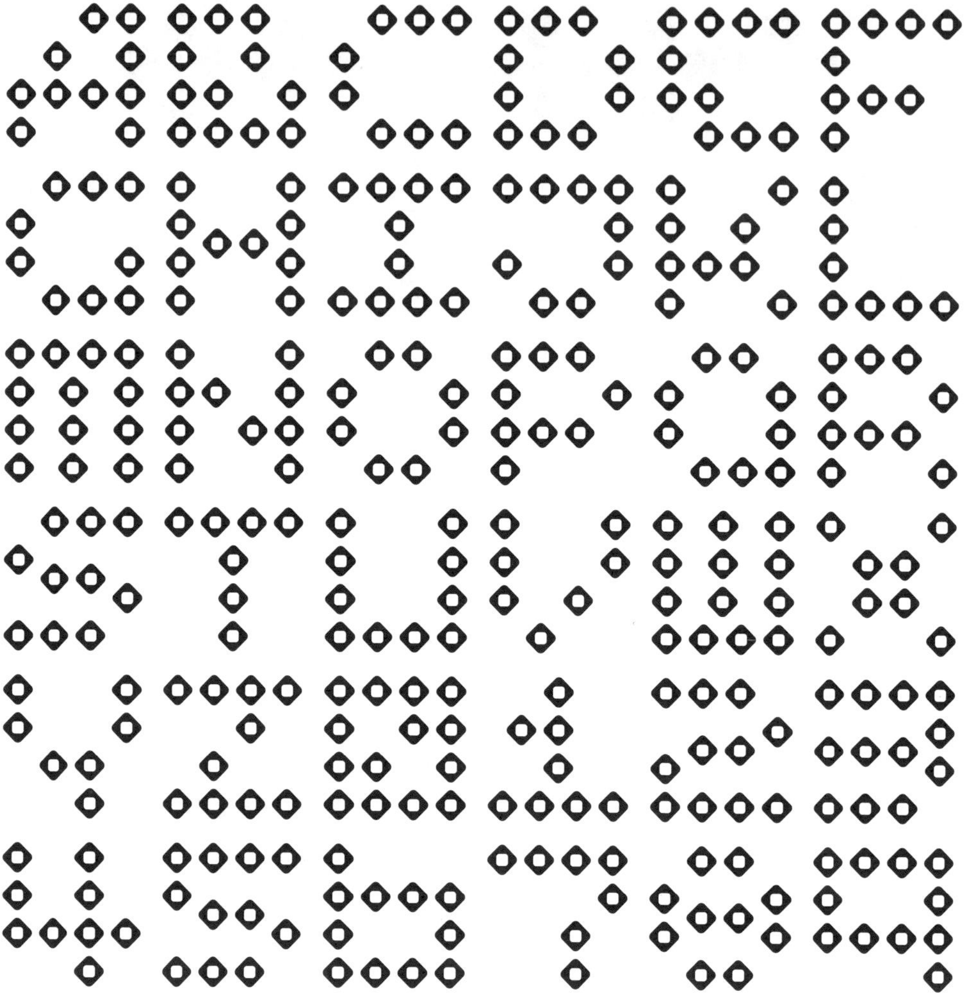

M.B G

An all-caps matrix alphabet formed of rounded diamonds inset with rounded squares on a 4×4 grid

A–Z 0–9

s. 57
l. 63
t. 100
w. 900

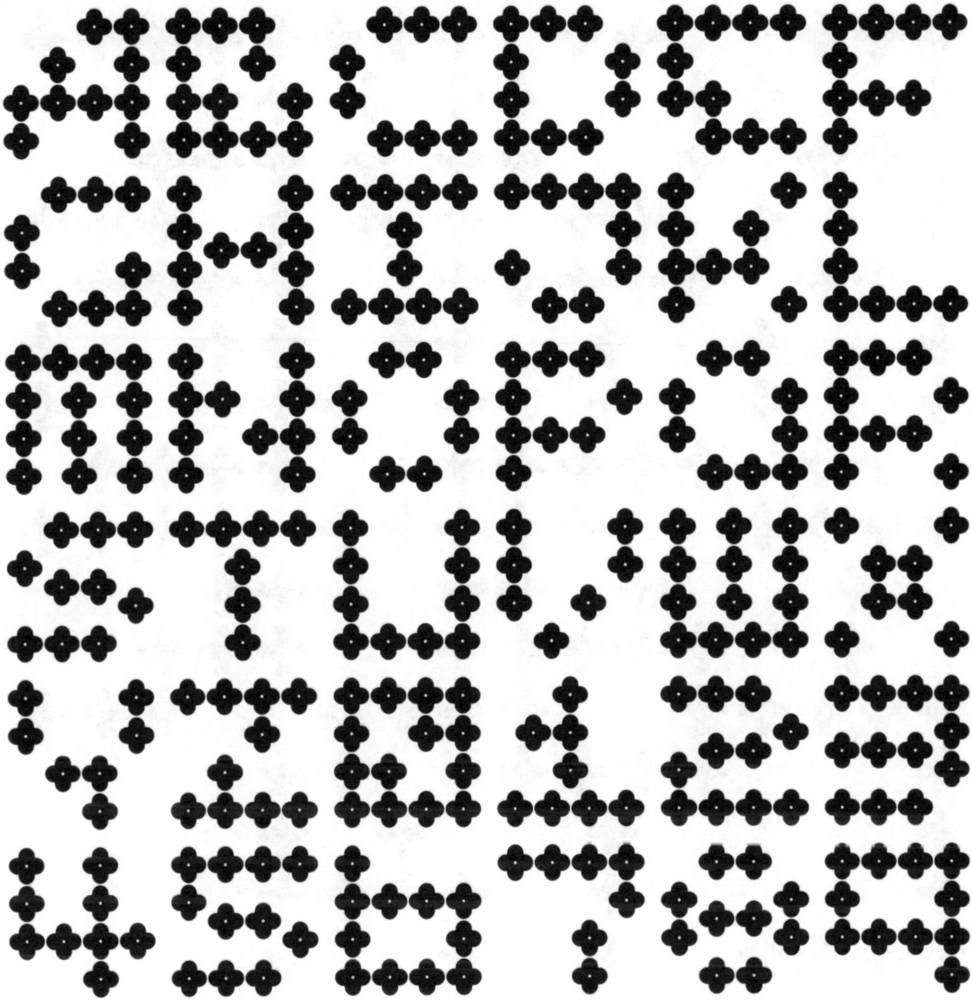

M.B H

An all-caps matrix alphabet formed of quatrefoils inset with dots on a 4×4 grid

A–Z 0–9

s. 57
l. 63
t. 100
w. 900

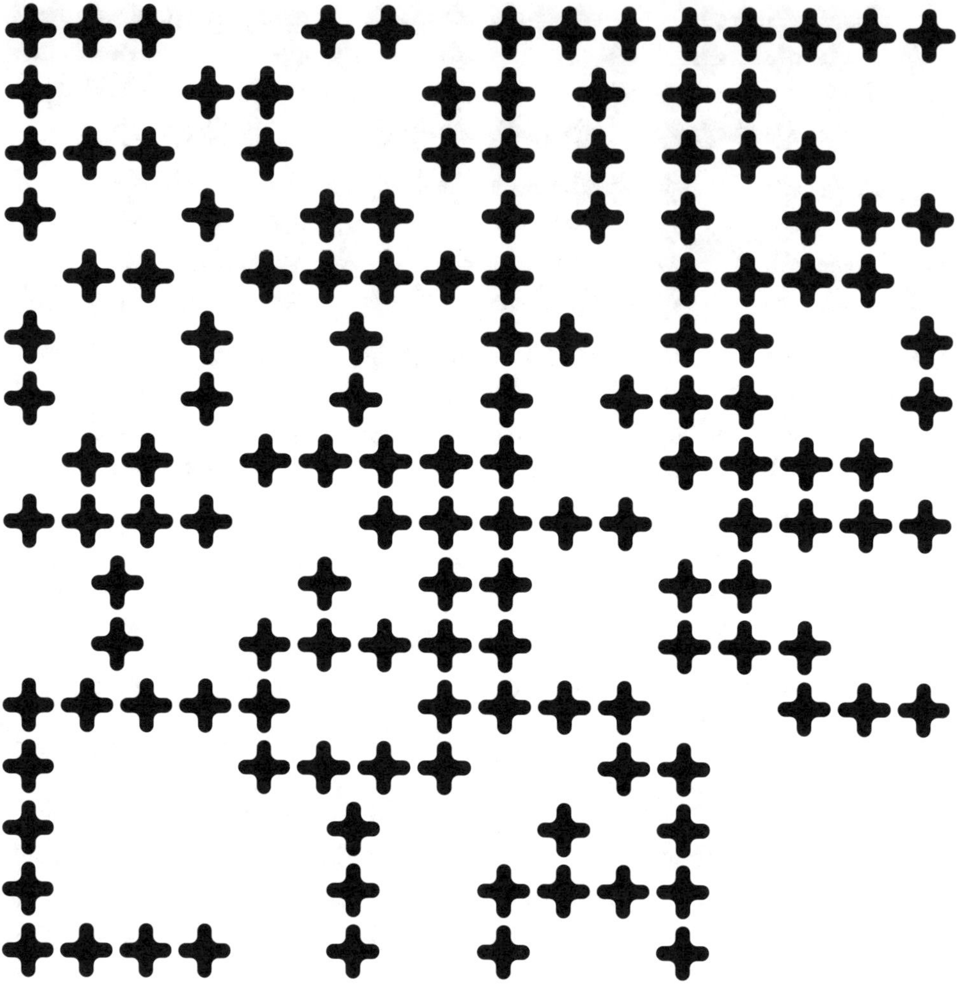

M.B I

An all-caps matrix alphabet formed of rounded crosses on a 4×4 grid

Romeo India Delta

s. 92
l. 92
t. 0
w. 900

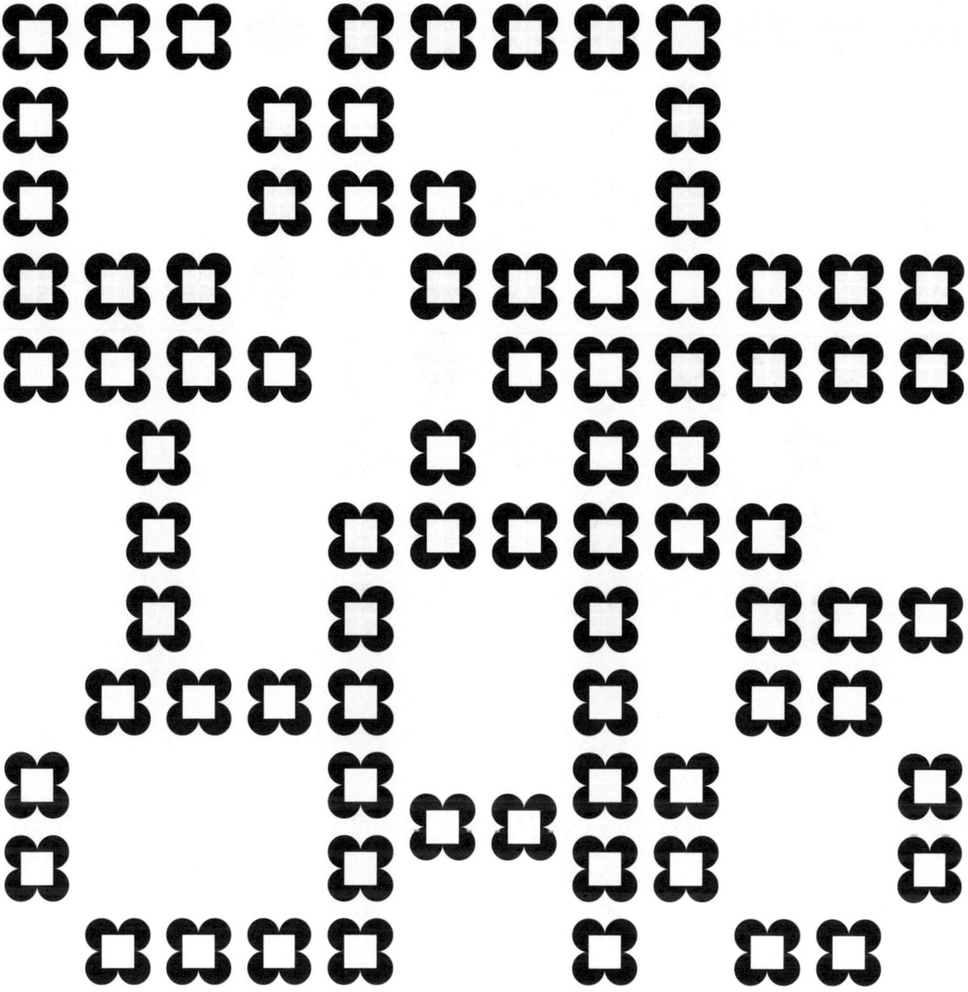

M.B J

An all-caps matrix alphabet formed of diagonal quatrefoils inset with squares on a 4×4 grid

Delta Echo

s. 125
l. 125
t. 0
w. 900

M.B K

An all-caps matrix alphabet formed of quatrefoils inset with elongated crosses on a 4×4 grid

Delta

s. 125
l. 125
t. 0
w. 900

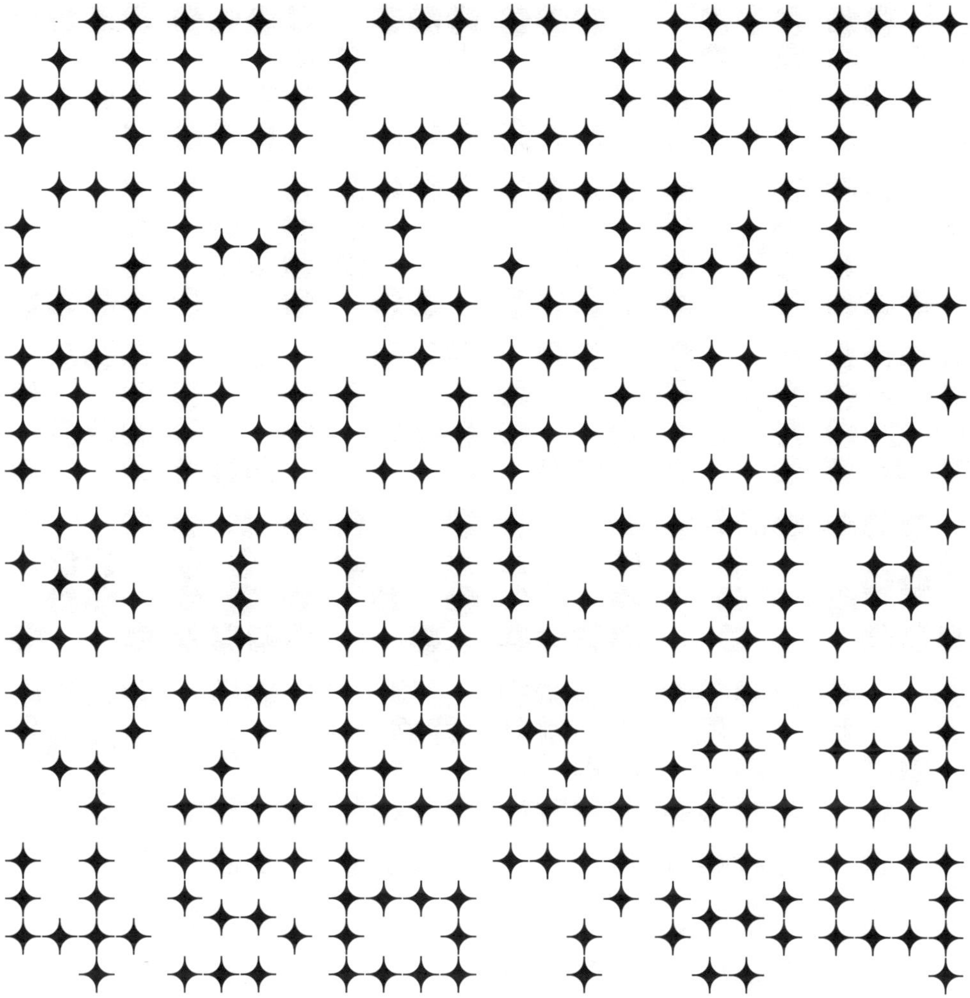

M.B L

An all-caps matrix alphabet formed of astroid curves on a 4×4 grid

A–Z 0–9

s. 57
l. 63
t. 100
w. 900

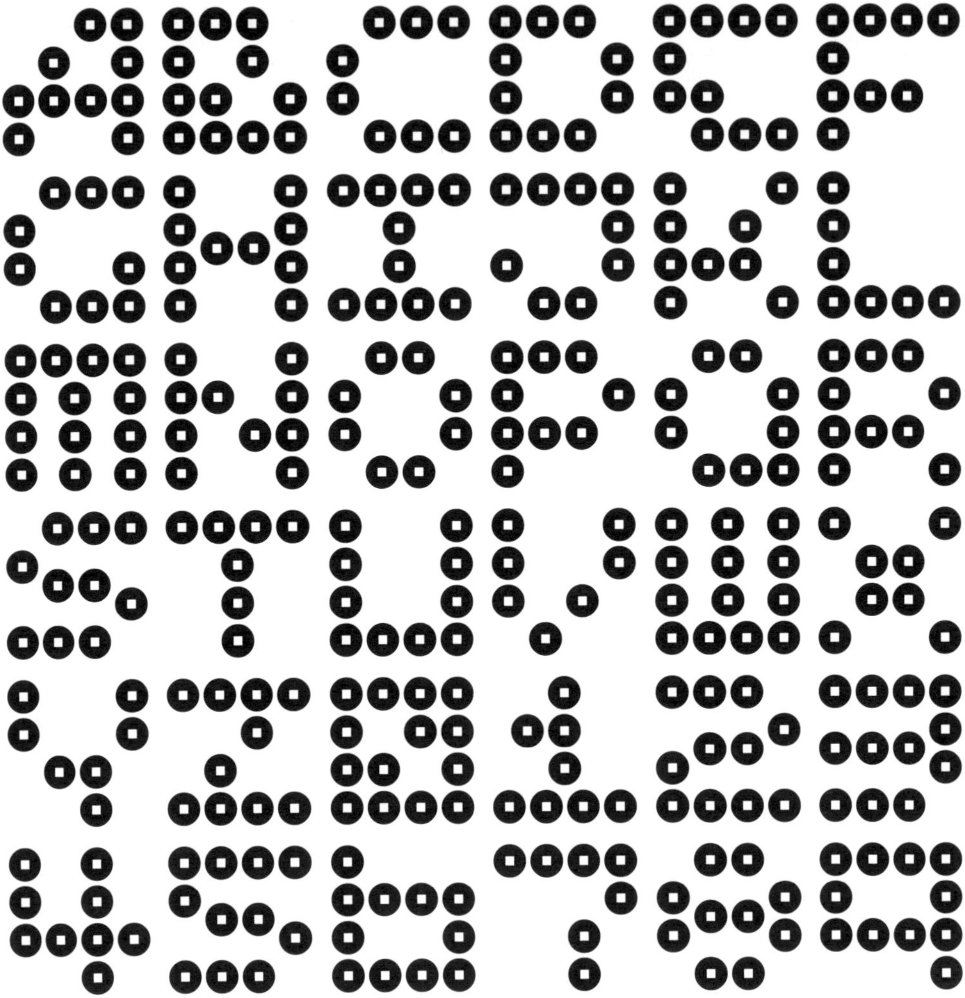

M.B M

An all-caps matrix alphabet formed of a range of dots inset with squares on a 4×4 grid

A–Z 0–9

s. 57
l. 63
t. 100
w. 900

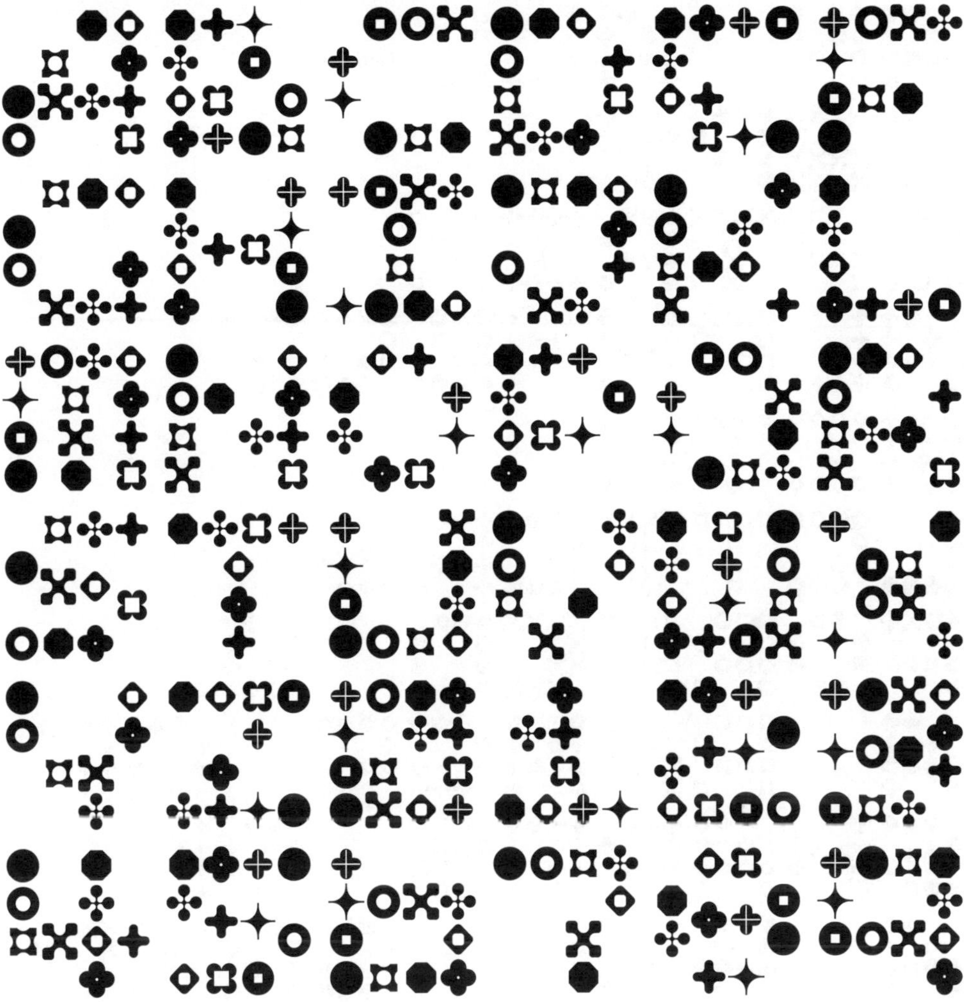

M.B N

An all-caps matrix alphabet formed of a range of shapes on a 4×4 grid

A–Z 0–9

s. 57
l. 63
t. 100
w. 900

AN ALL-
CAPS
MATRIX
ALPHABET
WITH
LETTERS
FORMED OF
A RANGE OF
SHAPES ON
A 4X4 GRID

M.B O

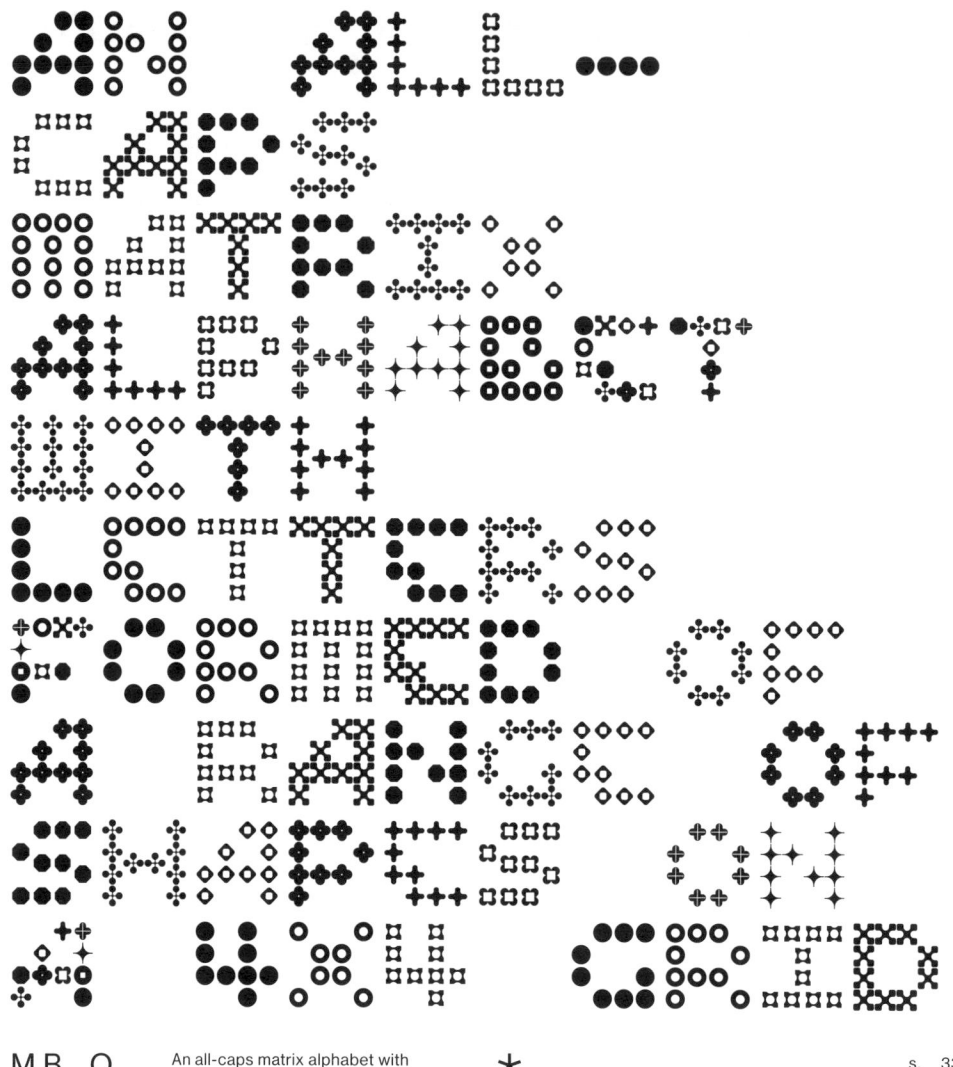

An all-caps matrix alphabet with letters formed of a range of shapes on a 4×4 grid*

*

s. 33
l. 38
t. 100
w. 900

AN ALL-
CAPS
MATRIX
ALPHABET
FORMED OF
DOTS ON A
5X5 GRID

M.C A

An all-caps matrix alphabet formed of dots trefoils on a 5×5 grid*

*

s. 37
l. 41
t. 100
w. 400

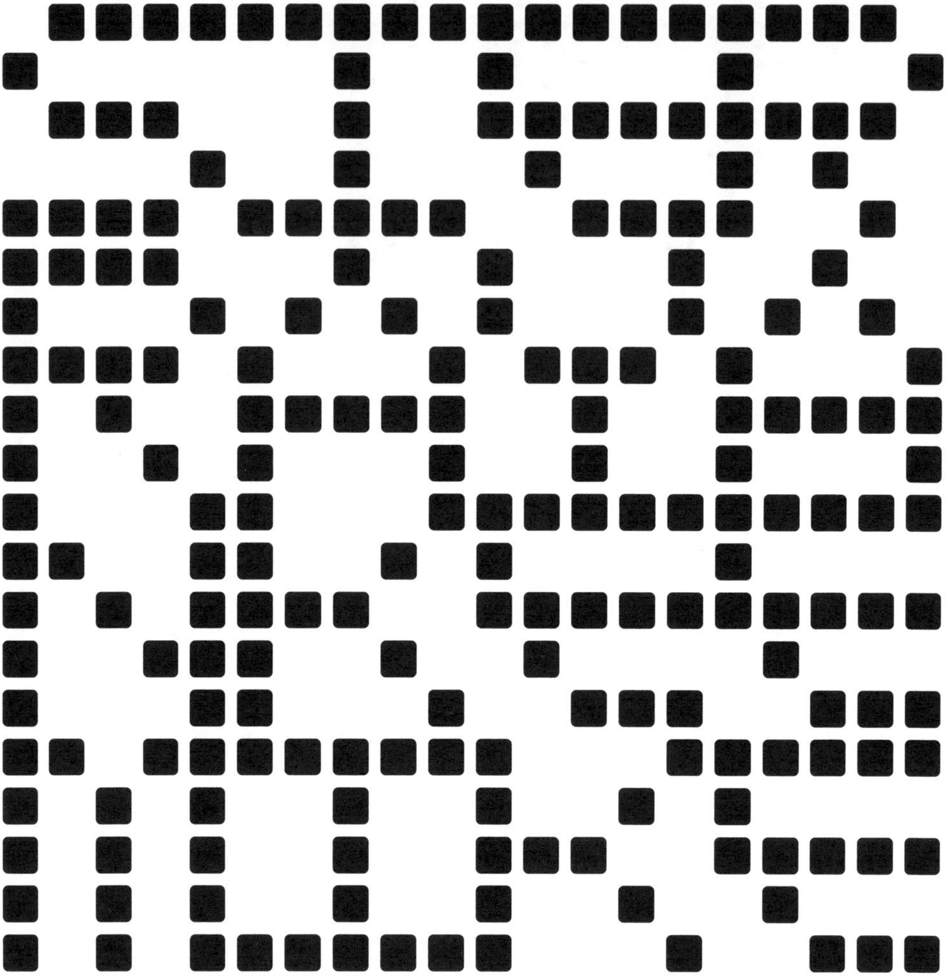

M.C B

An all-caps matrix alphabet formed of rounded squares on a 5×5 grid

Sierra Yankee Mike

s. 92
l. 92
t. 0
w. 900

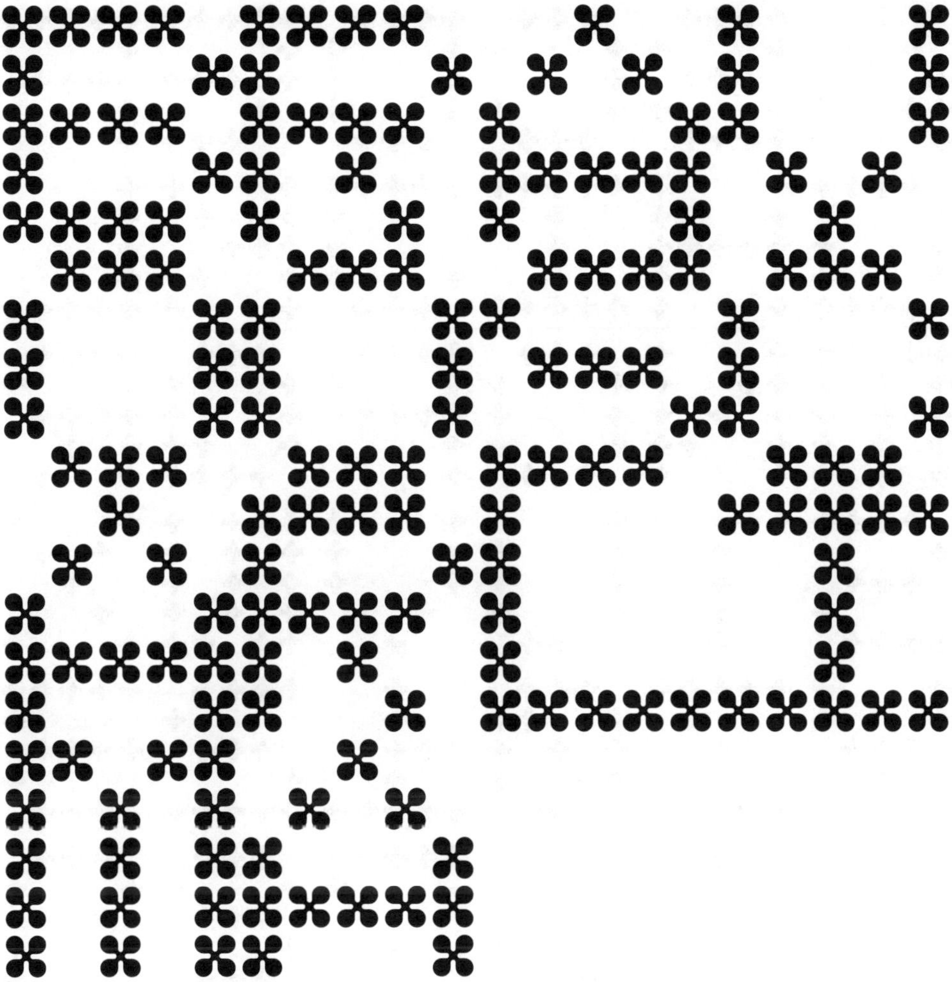

M.C C

An all-caps matrix alphabet formed of diagonal pinched rounded quatrefoils on a 5×5 grid

Bravo Oscar Lima

s. 92
l. 92
t. 0
w. 900

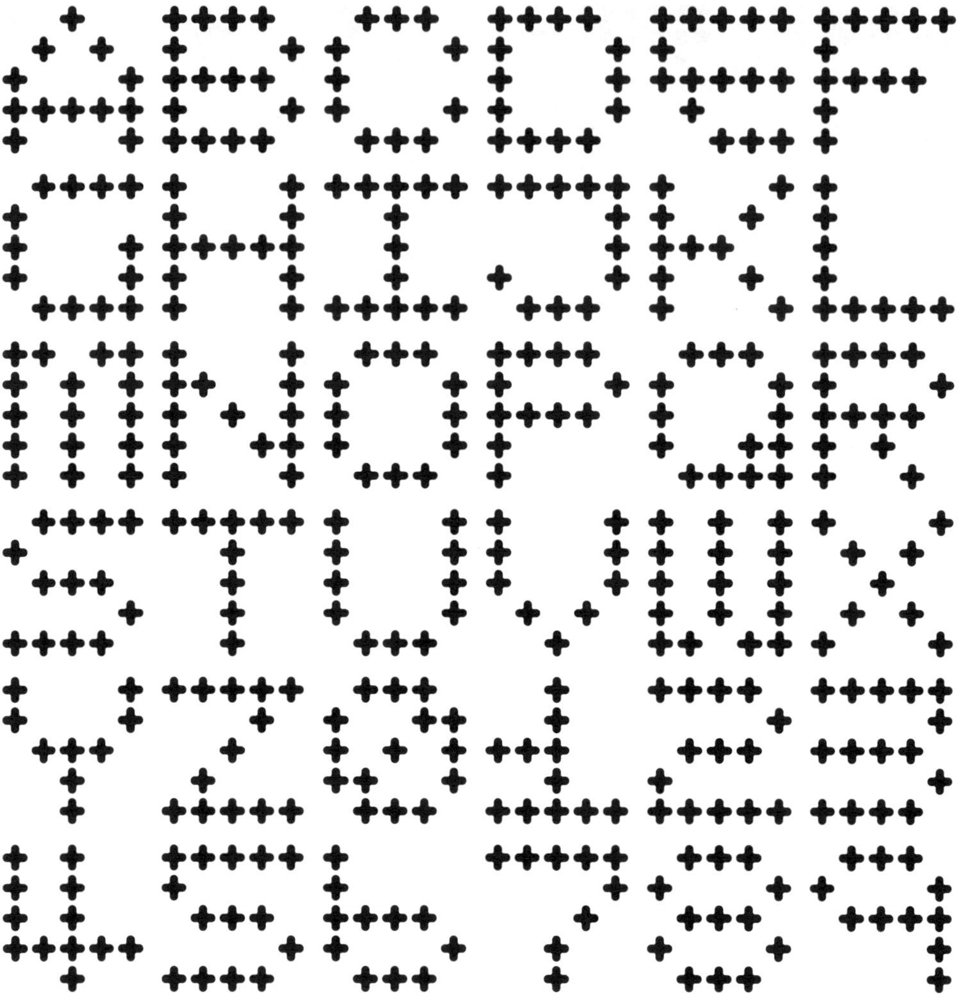

M.C D

An all-caps matrix alphabet formed of rounded quatrefoils on a 5×5 grid*

A–Z 0–9

s. 57
l. 63
t. 100
w. 900

AN
ALL-CAPS
MATRIX
ALPHABET
FORMED OF
CIRCLE
LATTICE
UNITS
ON A SXS
GRID

M.C E

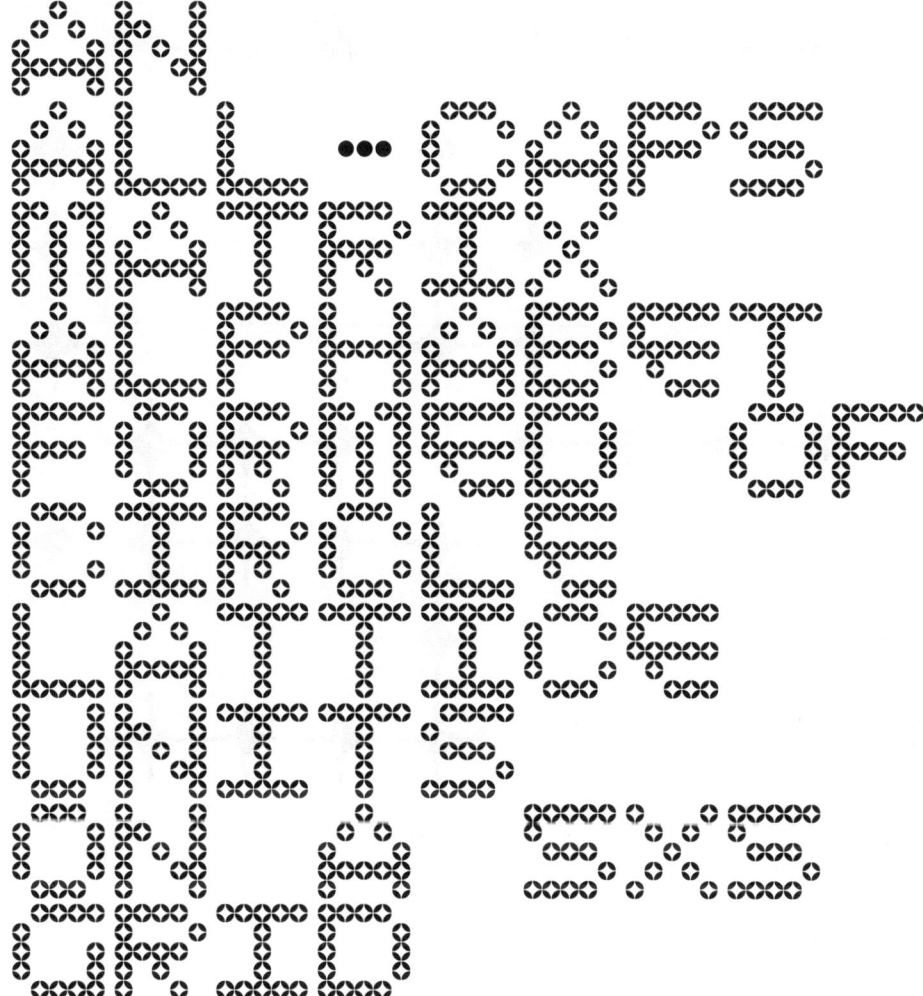

An all-caps matrix alphabet formed of circle lattice units on a 5×5*

*

s. 37
l. 41
t. 100
w. 400

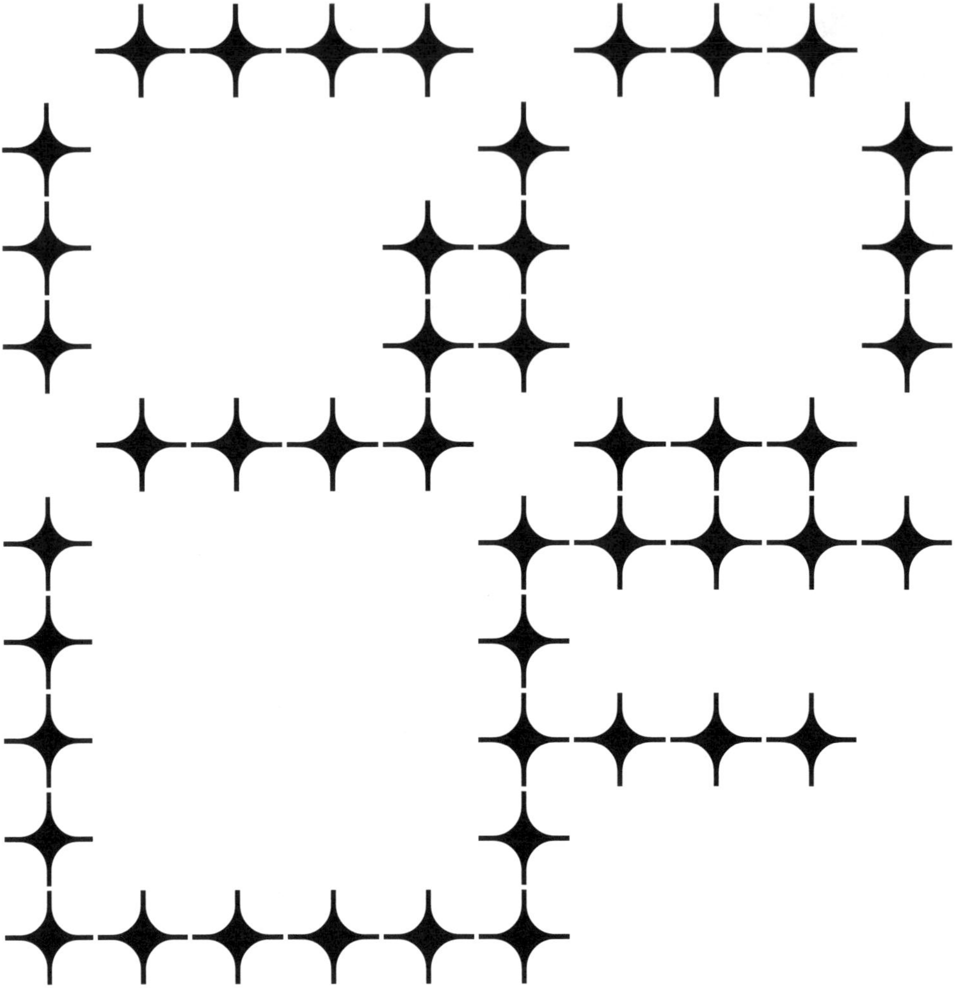

M.C F

An all-caps matrix alphabet formed of astroid curves on a 5×5 grid

Golf

s. 184
l. 184
t. 0
w. 900

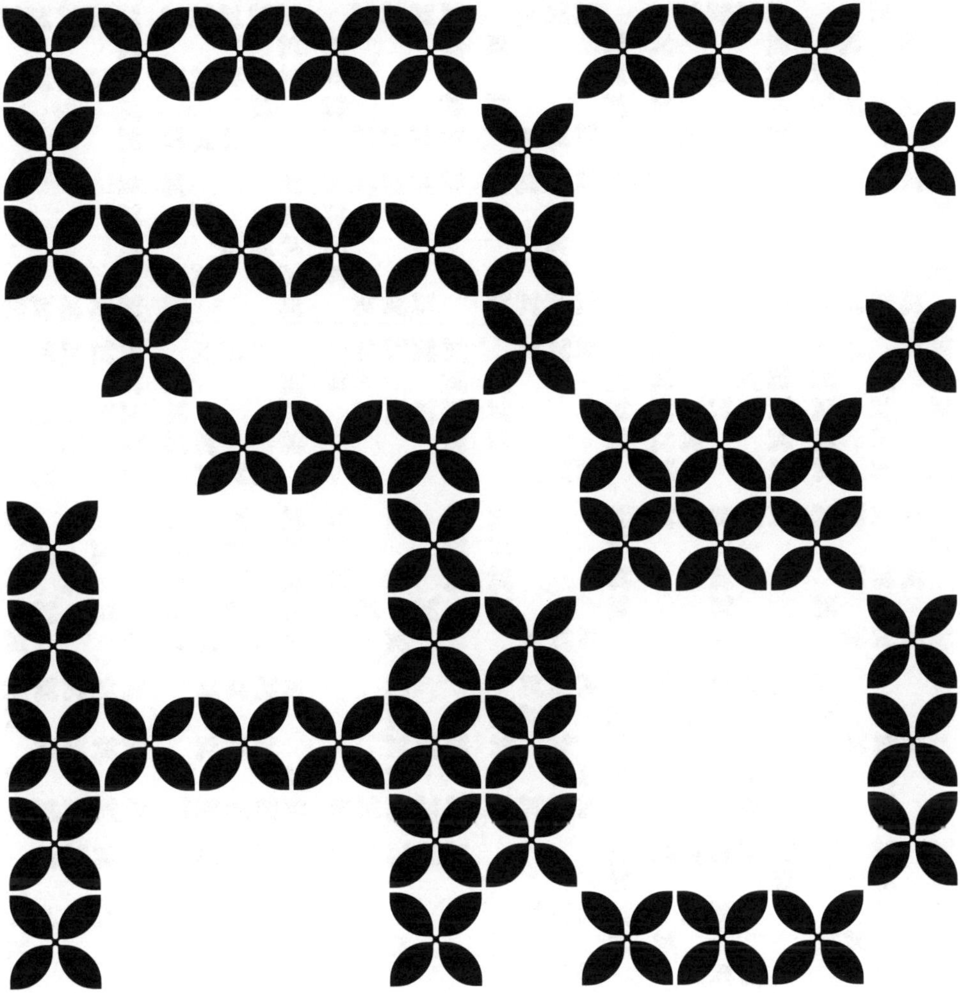

M.C G

An all-caps matrix alphabet formed of pinched pointed quadrifolium on a 5×5 grid

Echo

s. 184
l. 184
t. 0
w. 900

ABCDEF
GHIJKL
MNOPQR
STUVWX
YZ0123
456789

M.C H

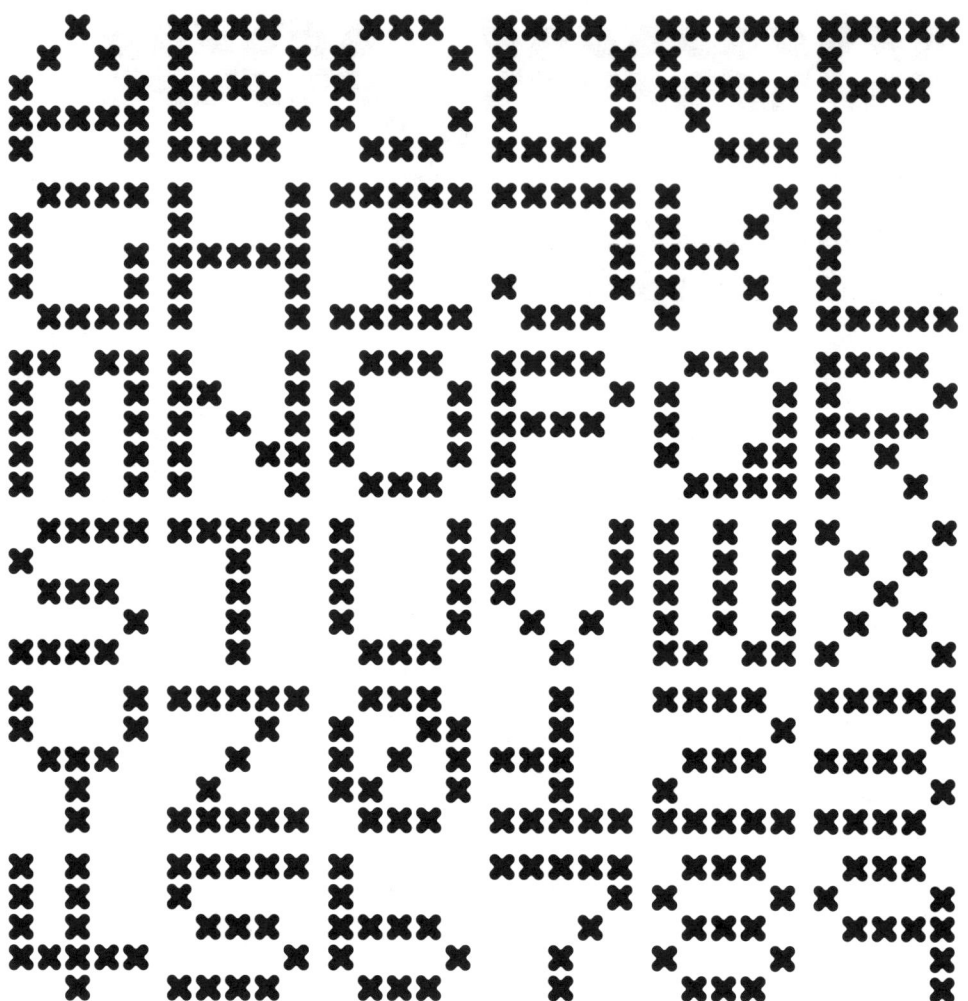

An all-caps matrix alphabet formed of diagonal rounded quatrefoils on a 5×5 grid

A–Z 0–9

s. 57
l. 63
t. 100
w. 900

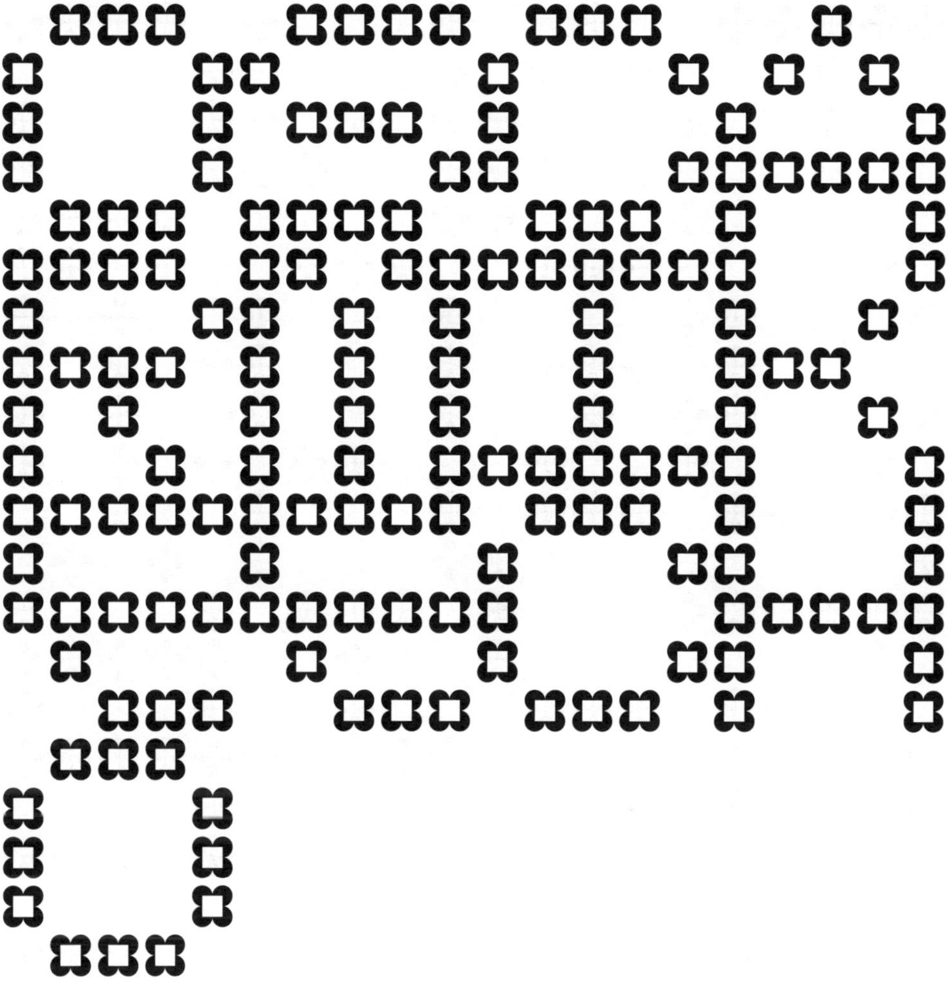

M.C I

An all-caps matrix alphabet formed of diagonal quatrefoils inset with squares on a 5×5 grid

Oscar Mike Echo

s. 92
l. 92
t. 0
w. 900

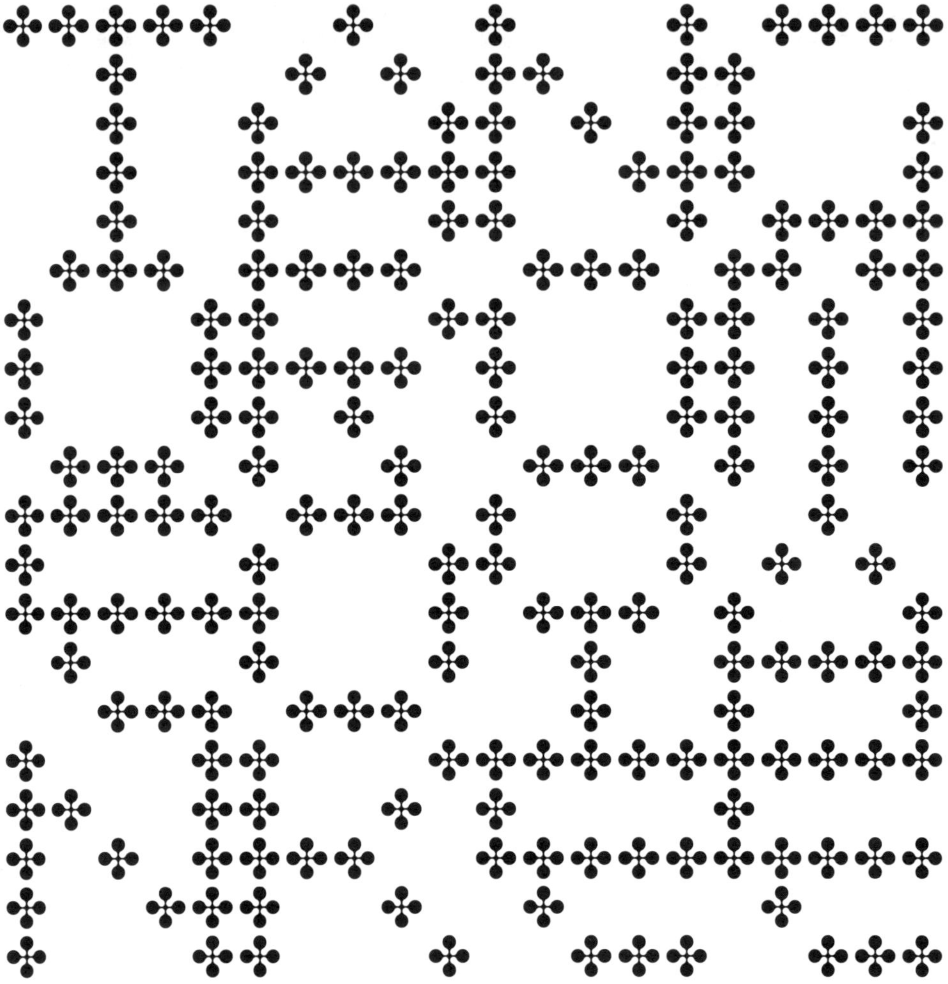

M.C J

An all-caps matrix alphabet formed of pinched quatrefoils on a 5×5 grid

Tango Romeo Yankee

s. 92
l. 92
t. 0
w. 900

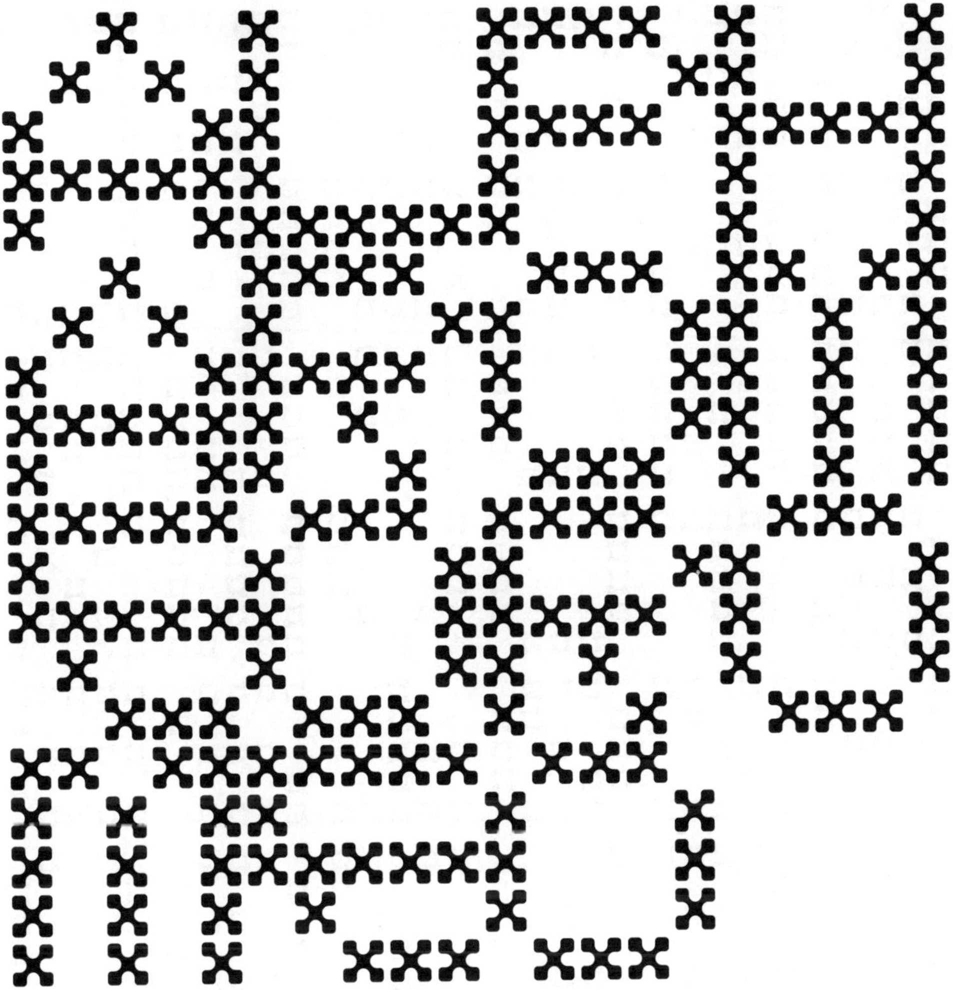

M.C K

An all-caps matrix alphabet formed of diagonal rounded crosses on a 5×5 grid

Alpha Romeo Romeo

s. 92
l. 92
t. 0
w. 900

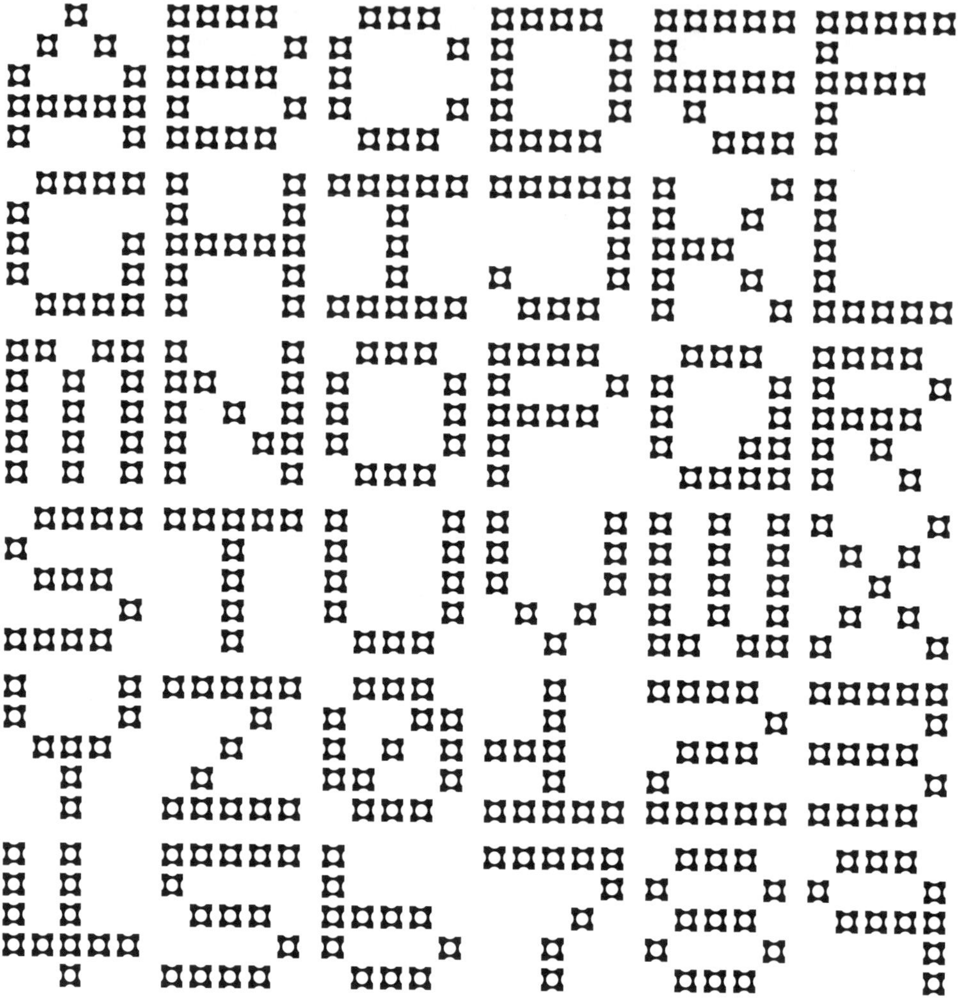

M.C L

An all-caps matrix alphabet formed of squares intersected with circles on a 5×5 grid

A–Z 0–9

s. 57
l. 63
t. 100
w. 900

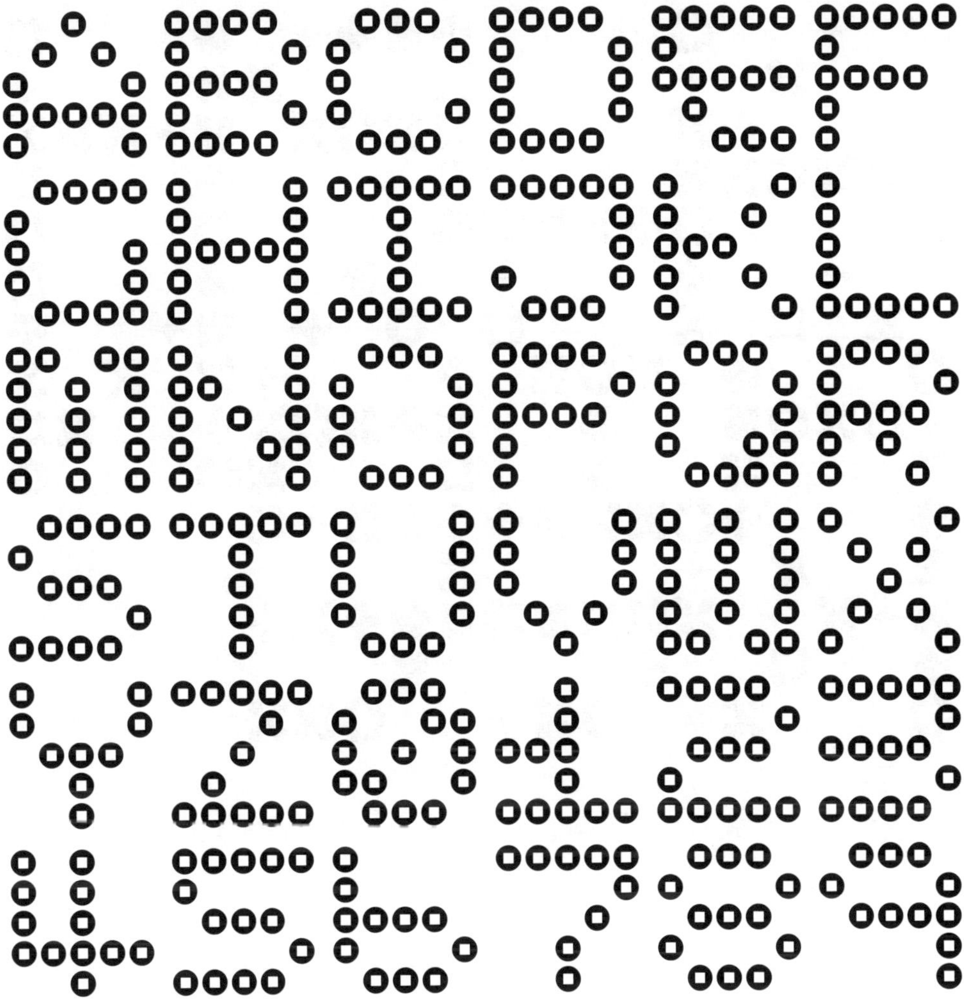

M.C M

An all-caps matrix alphabet formed of dots inset with squares on a 5×5 grid

A–Z 0–9

s. 57
l. 63
t. 100
w. 900

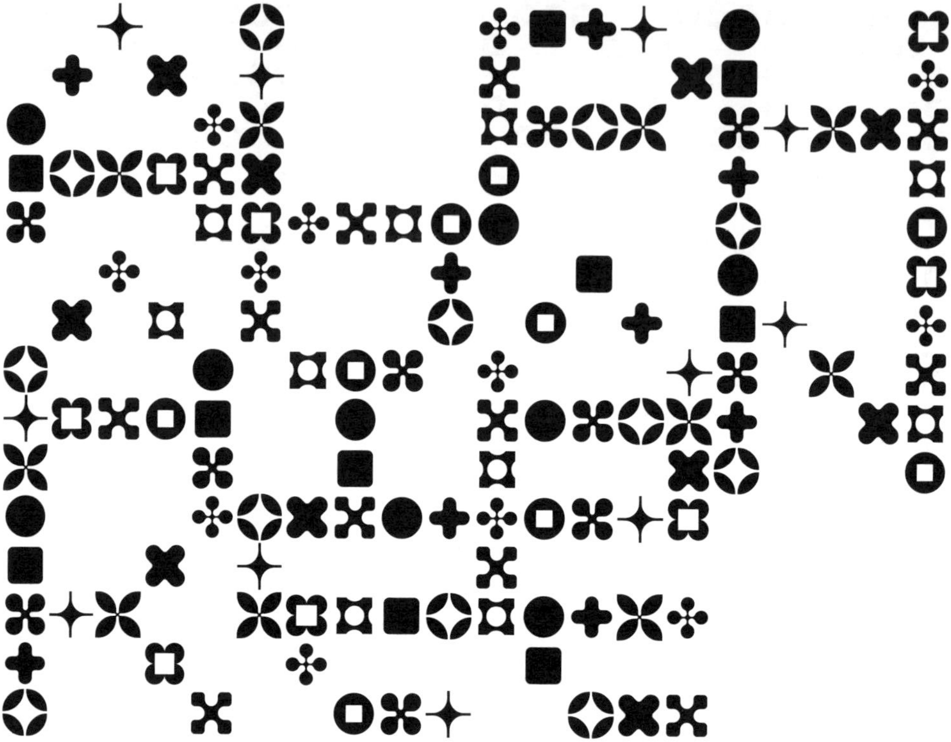

M.C N

An all-caps matrix alphabet formed of a range of shapes on a 5×5 grid

Alpha Yankee

s. 92
l. 92
t. 0
w. 900

AN ALL-
CAPS
MATRIX
ALPHABET
WITH
LETTERS
FORMED OF
A RANGE OF
SHAPES ON
A 5X5 GRID

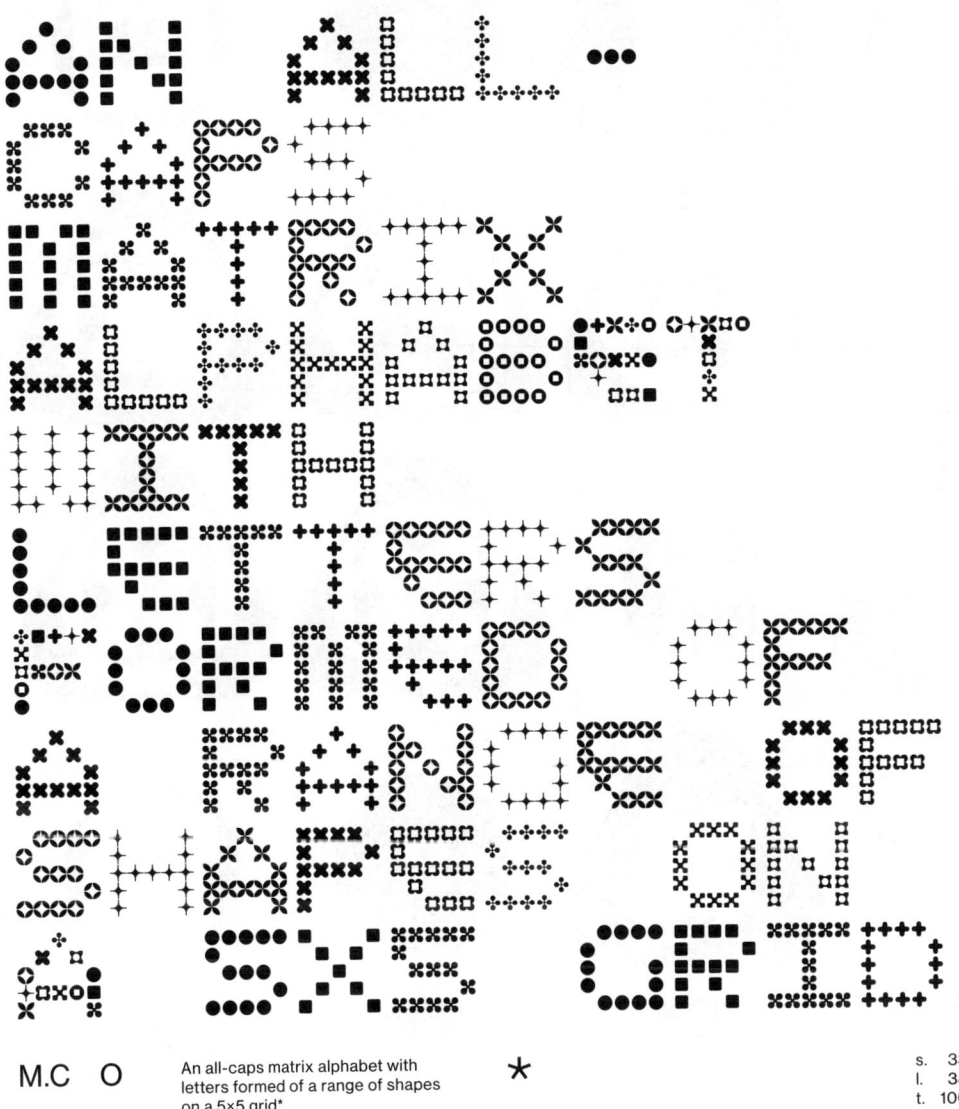

M.C O

An all-caps matrix alphabet with letters formed of a range of shapes on a 5×5 grid*

*

s. 33
l. 38
t. 100
w. 400

M

Matrix

M Matrix

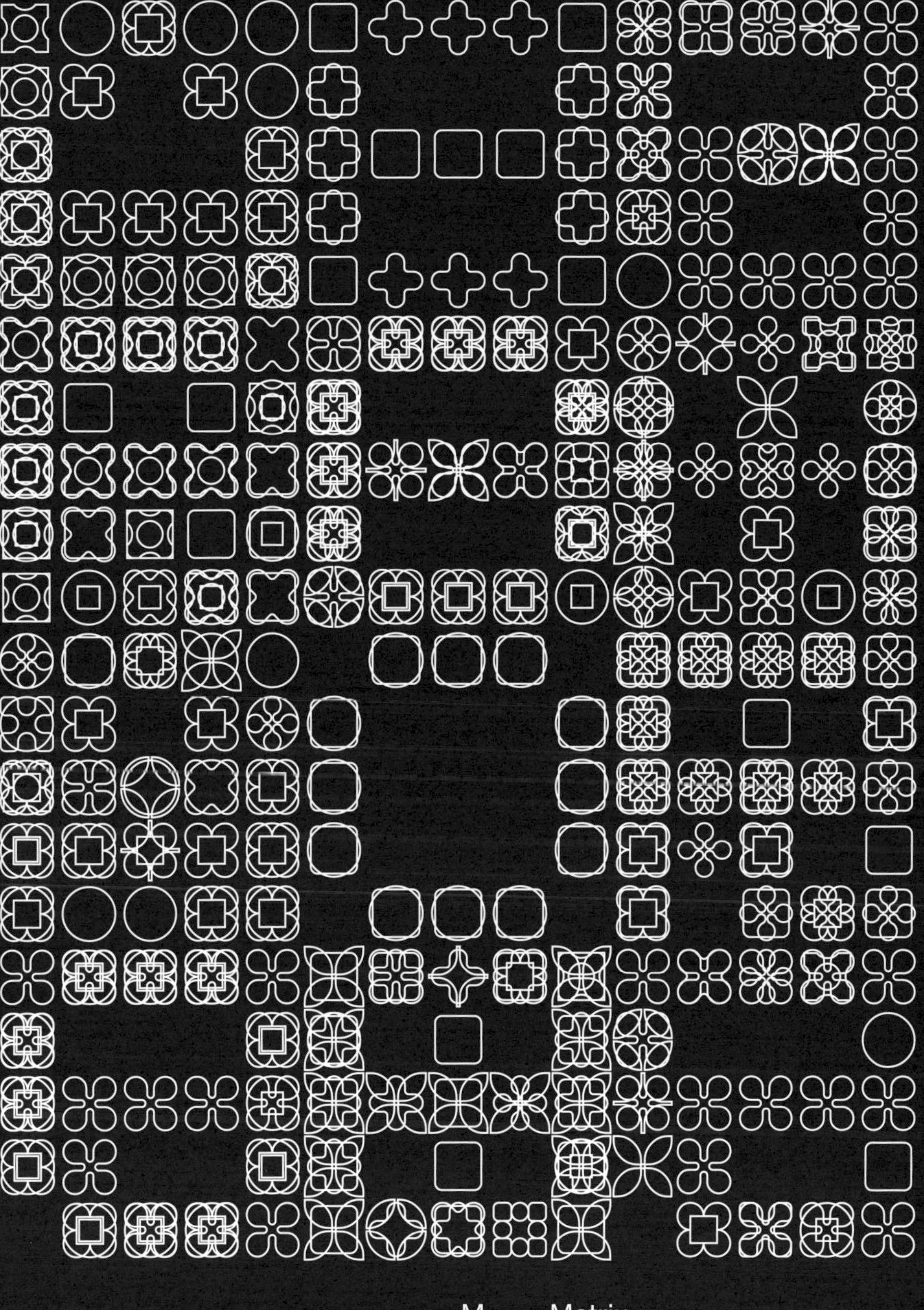

M Matrix

Section Notes:

Created in Glyphs, M.A, M.B, and M.C each consist of a single variable font file with a weight parameter that controls the scale of the matrix units. Each font is built on a different grid resolution: M.A uses a 3×3 grid, M.B a 4×4 grid, and M.C a 5×5 grid. Within each font, stylistic sets allow different geometric shapes to be placed within the matrix. A combined set, N, merges these shapes. These stylistic sets can also be used in combination via a contextual alternates script, referred to as set O.

N Neo-Matrix

A development of the Matrix system, Neo-Matrix features a set of alphabetic forms built from geometric shapes. These units exceed the limits of the original matrix system. Where shapes overlap or merge, they generate to new configurations and geometric relationships. The points of connection between units are emphasised, becoming key visual and structural features of the type, giving visual cohesion to the overall design.

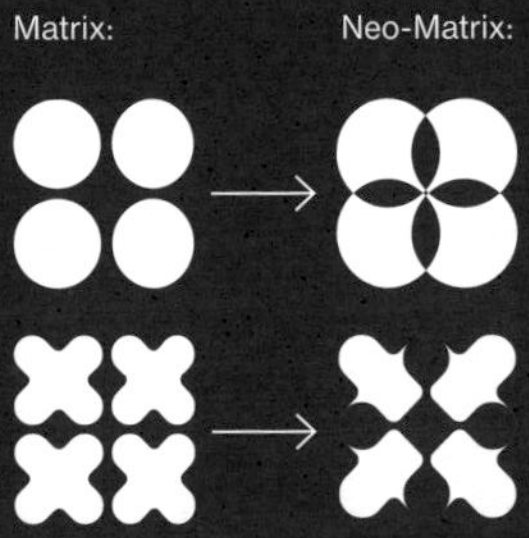

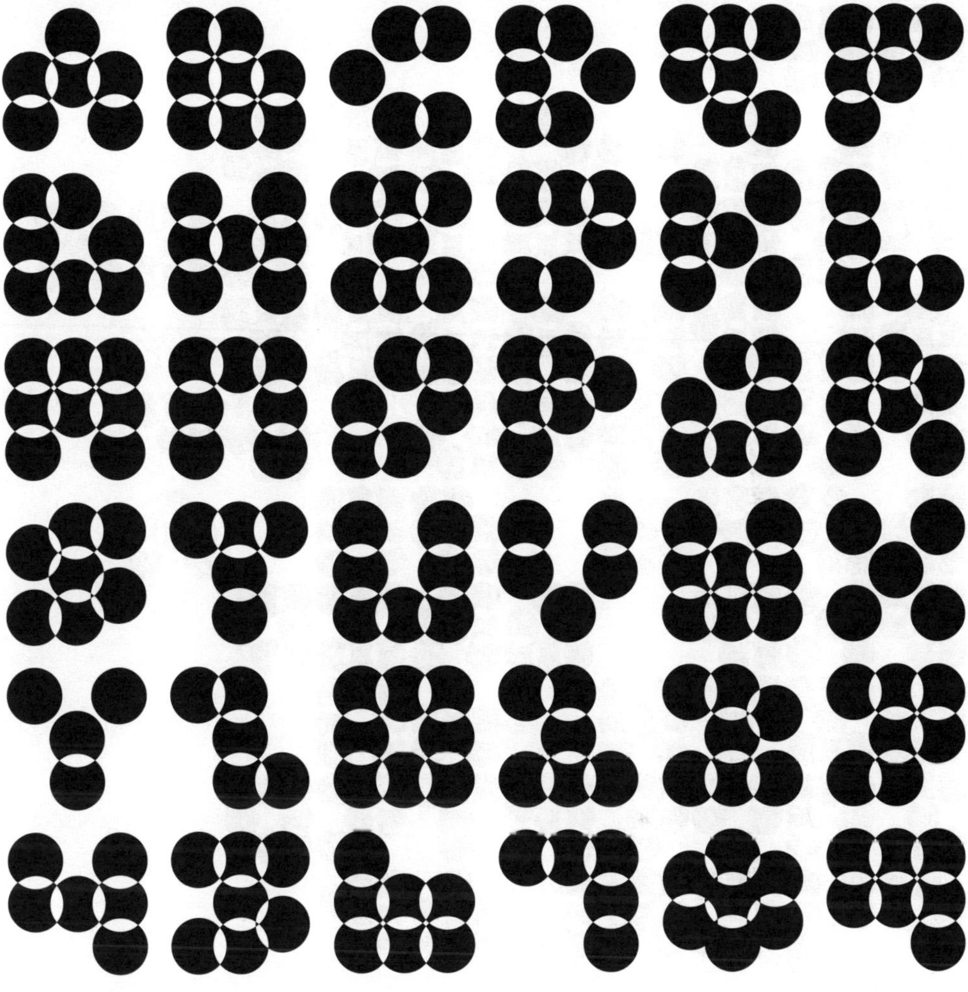

N.A An all-caps Neo-Matrix alphabet formed of dots on a 3×3 grid with an inverted overlap

A–Z 0–9

s. 56
l. 62
t. 125
w. 900

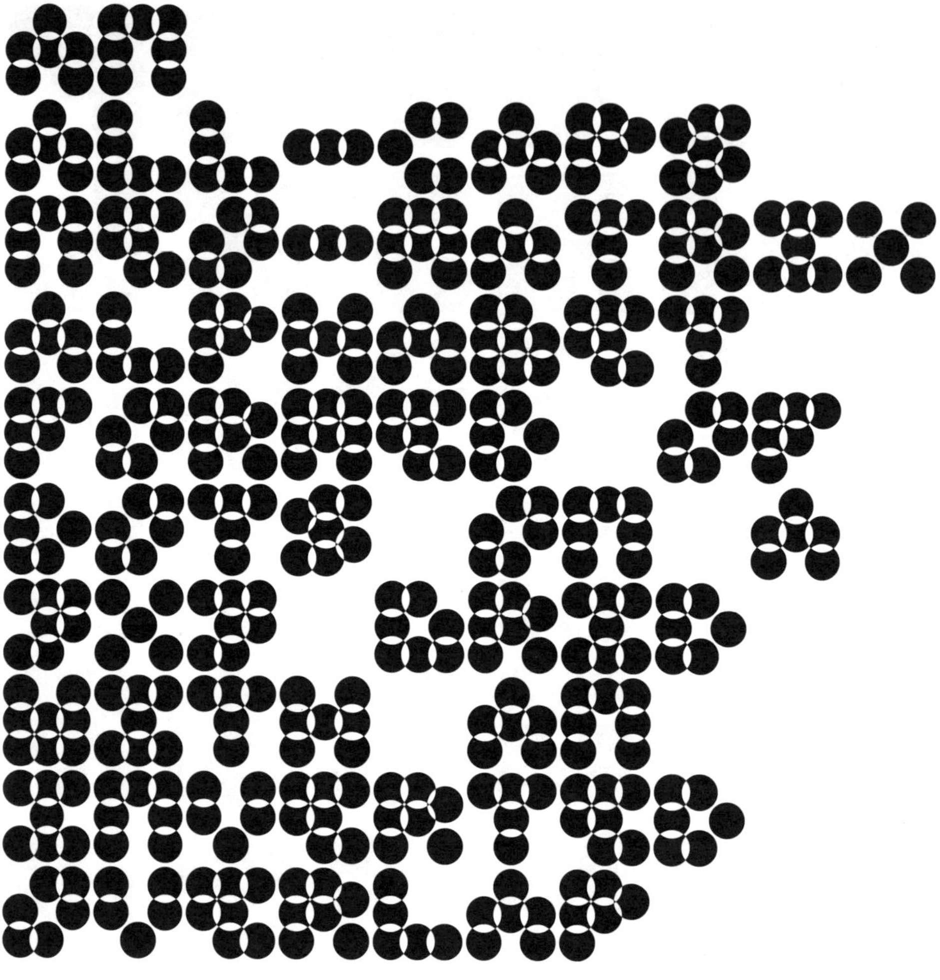

N.A

*

s. 36
l. 36
t. 0
w. 900

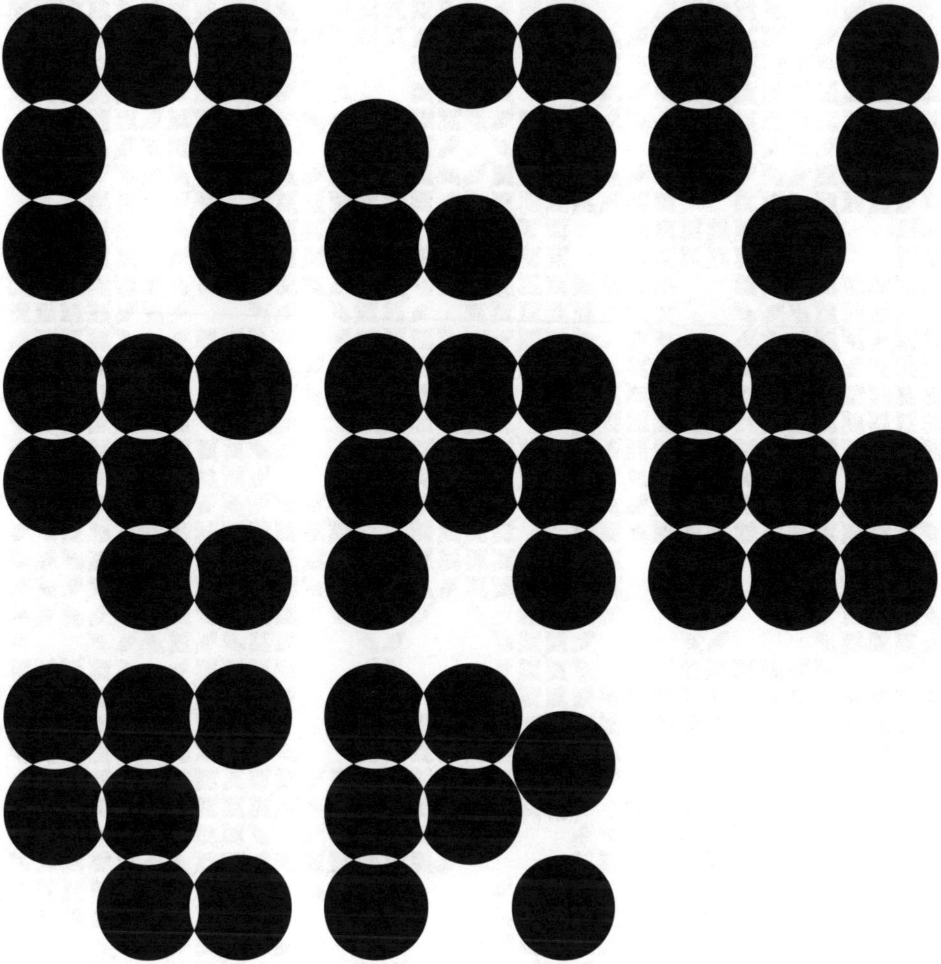

N.A

November

s. 124
l. 124
t. 0
w. 450

N.B An all-caps Neo-Matrix alphabet formed of circle lattice units on a 5×5 grid with an inverted overlap

A–Z 0–9

s. 62
l. 62
t. 0
w. 800

N.B

Echo

s. 184
l. 184
t. 0
w. 100

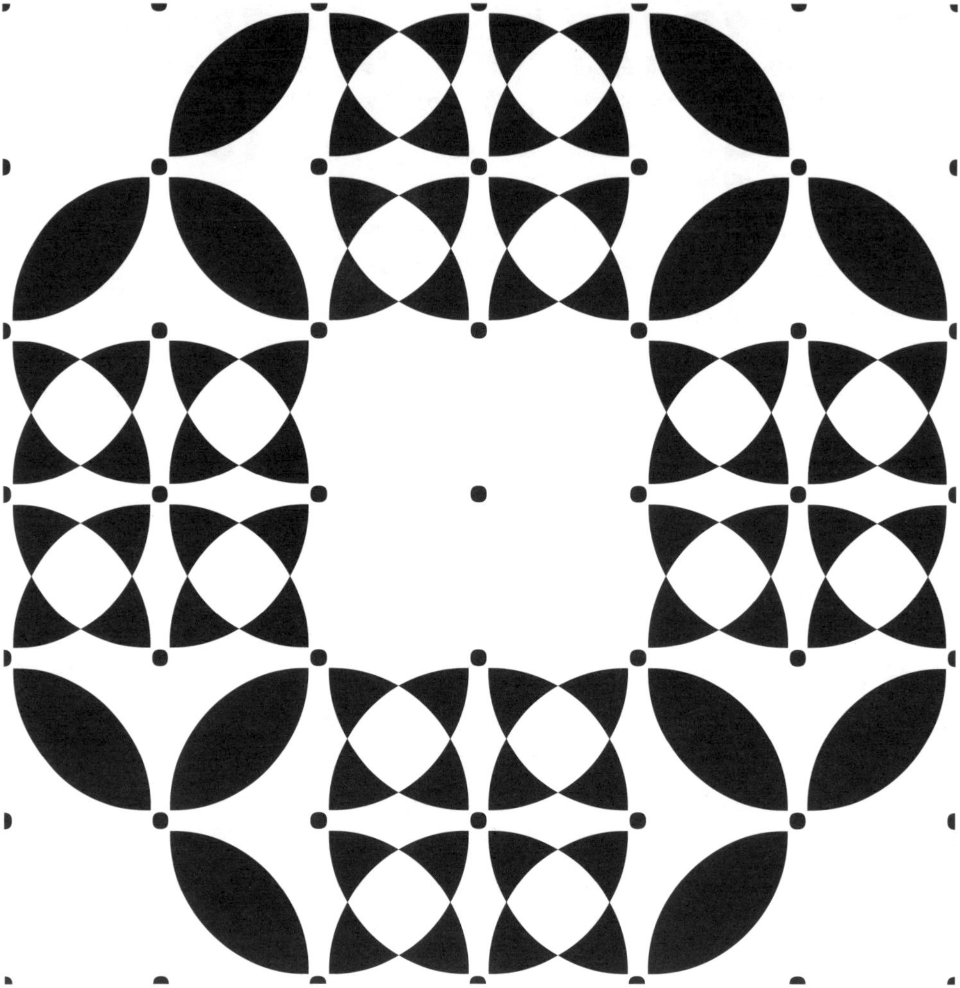

N.B

Oscar

s. 368
l. 368
t. 0
w. 100

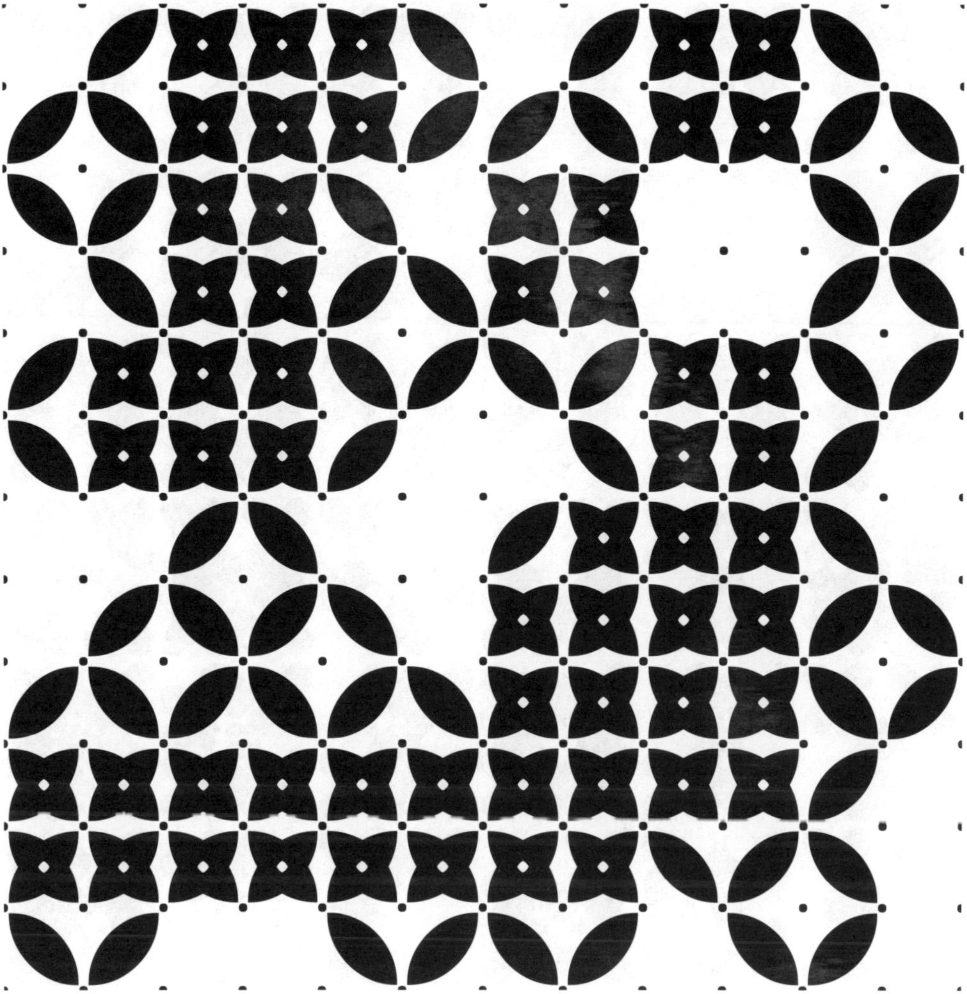

s. 184
l. 184
t. 0
w. 750

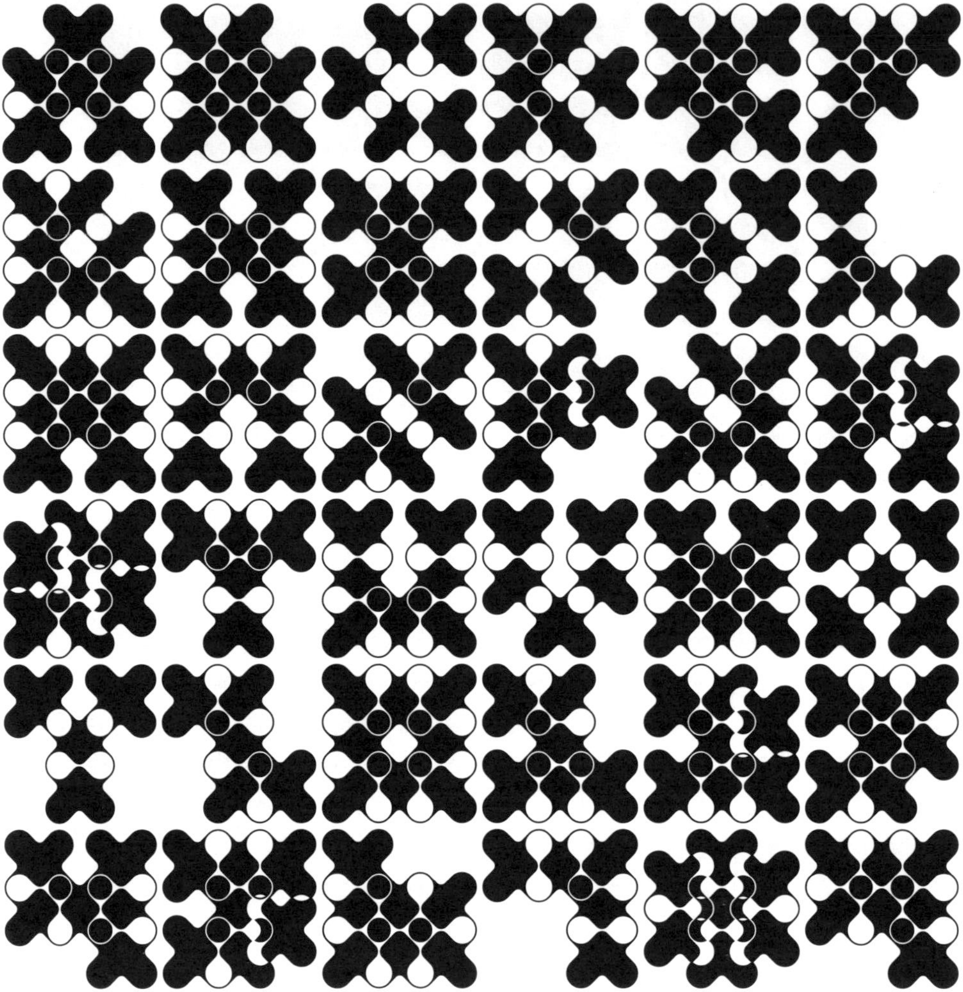

N.C An all-caps Neo-Matrix alphabet formed of diagonal rounded quatrefoils on a 3×3 grid with an inverted overlap

A–Z 0–9

s. 62
l. 62
t. 0
w. 500

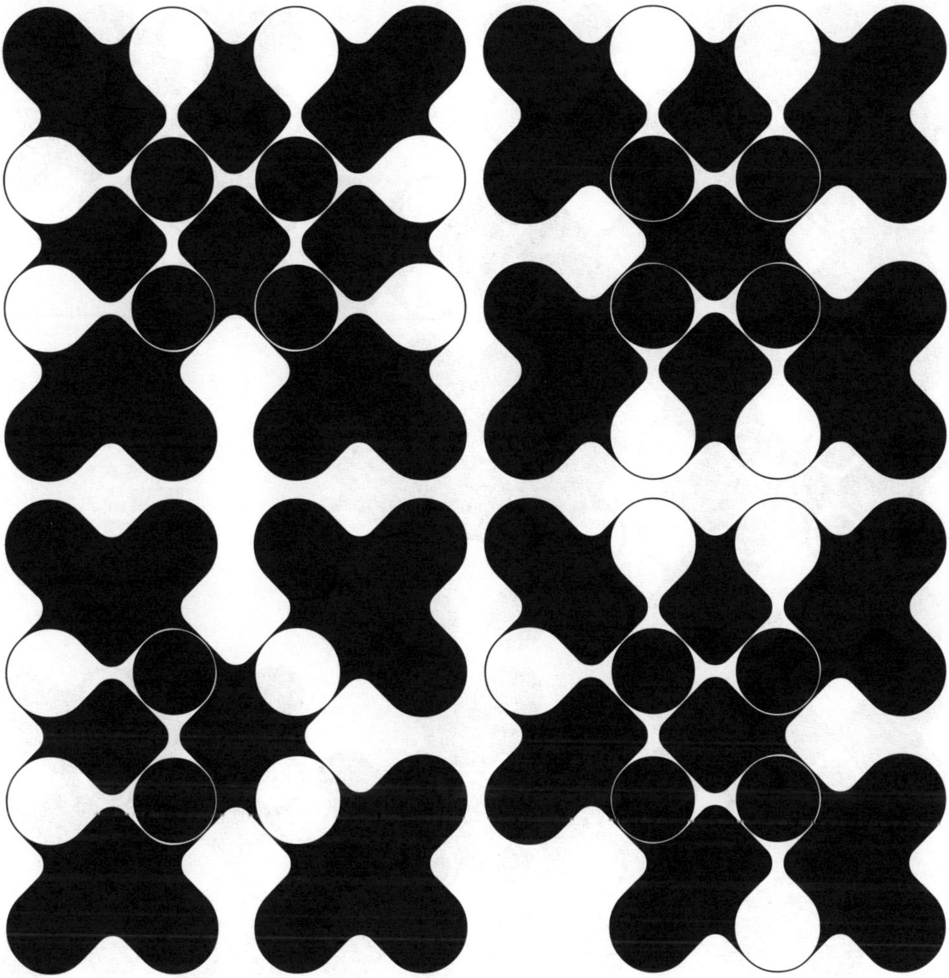

N.C

Mike

s. 184
l. 184
t. 0
w. 900

N.C

Alpha Tango Romeo

s. 124
l. 124
t. 0
w. 100

N.D

An all-caps Neo-Matrix alphabet formed of linking pinched pointed quadrifolium on a 4×4 grid with dot nodes

A–Z 0–9

s. 61
l. 61
t. 0

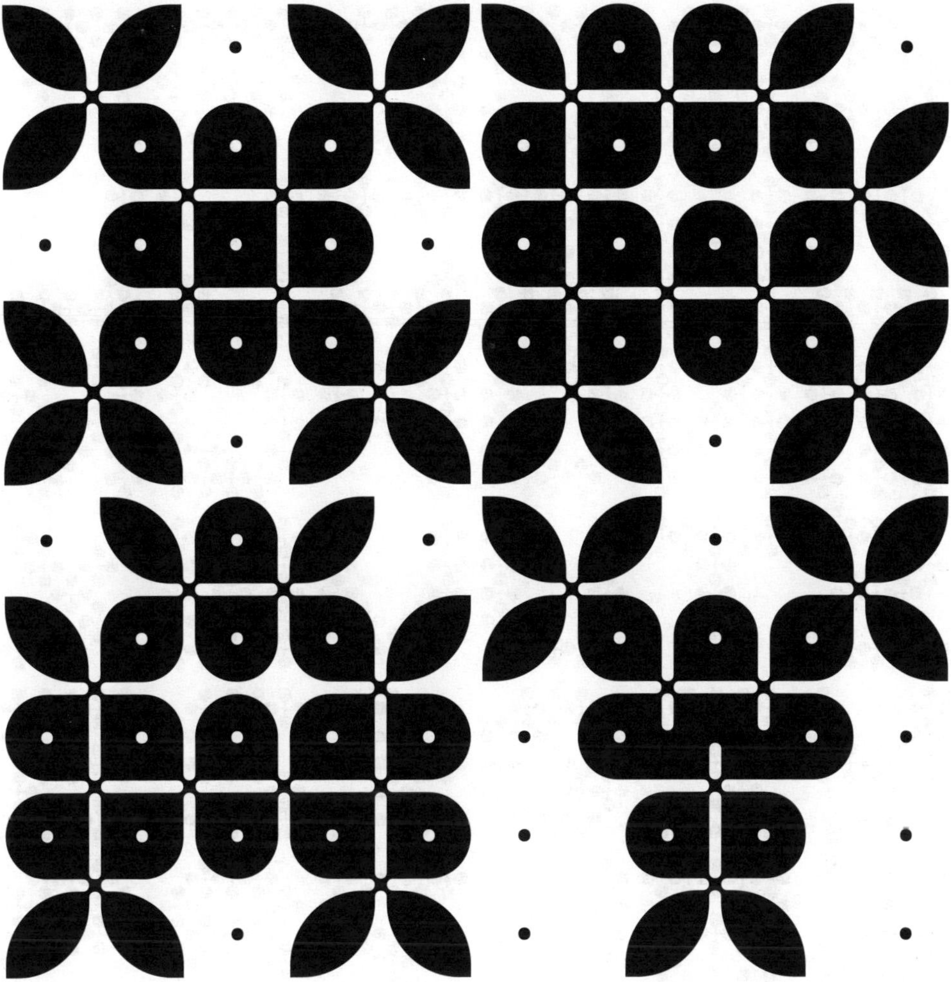

N.D

Xray

s. 184
l. 184
t. 0

N.E

An all-caps Neo-Matrix alphabet formed of linking pinched quatrefoils on a 5×5 grid with dot nodes*

A–Z 0–9

s. 58
l. 64
t. 75
w. 100

A NEO-MATRIX
ALL-CAPS
FORMED OF
LINKING
PINCHED
QUATREFOILS
ON A 5X5
GRID WITH
DOT NODES

N.E *

s. 29
l. 31
t. 75
w. 900

N.F

An all-caps Neo-Matrix alphabet formed of linking diagonal pinched quatrefoils on a 3×3 grid with dot nodes*

A–Z 0–9

s. 62
l. 62
t. 0

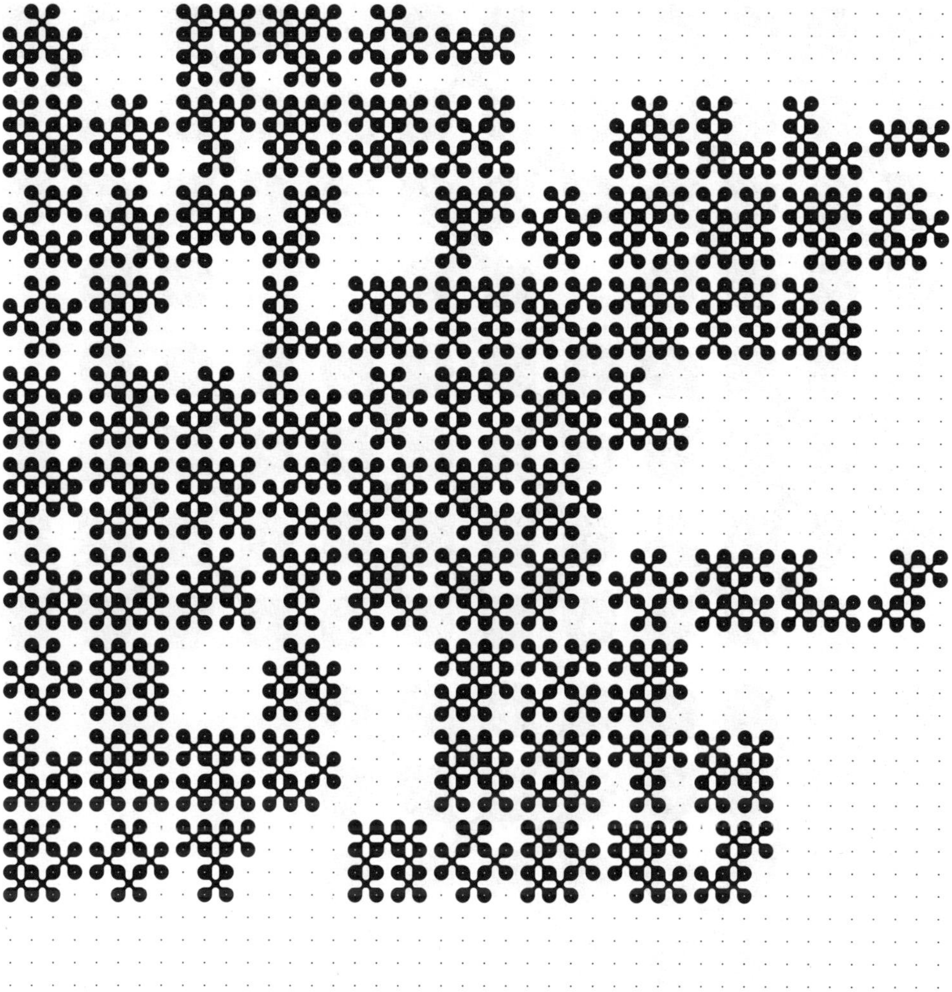

N.F

*

s. 34
l. 34
t. 0

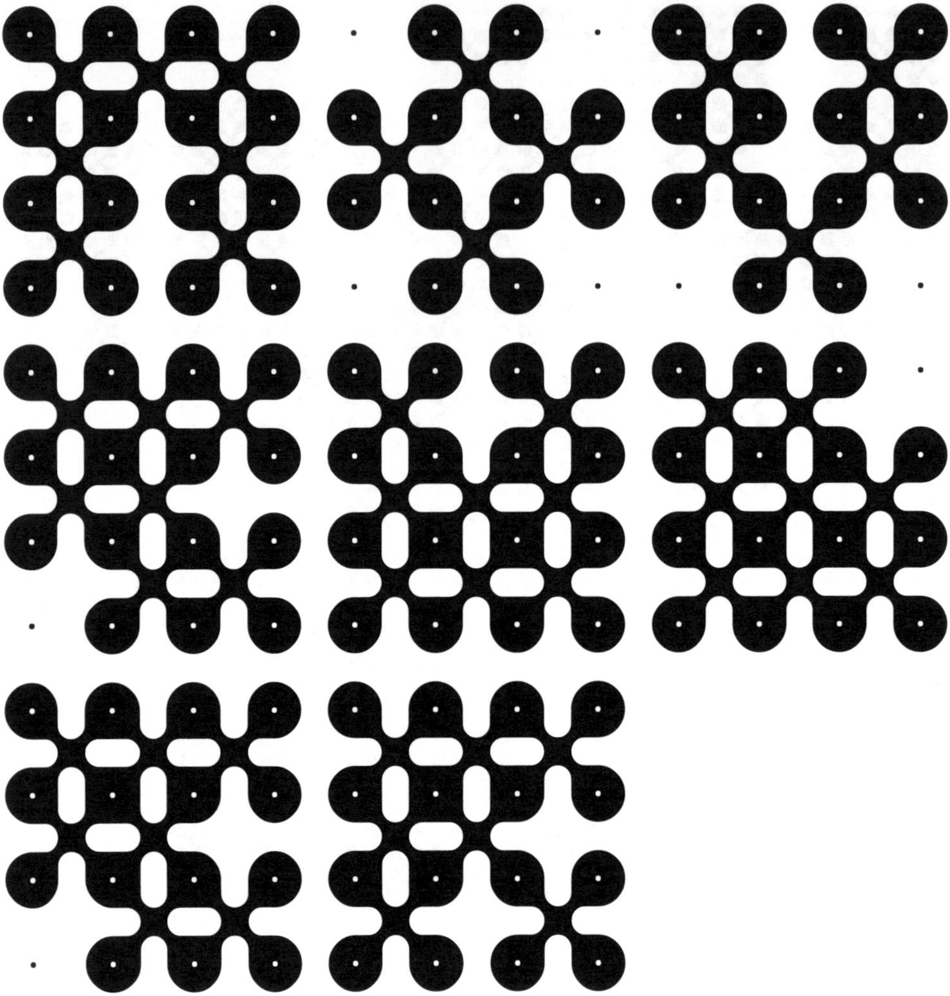

N.F

November

s. 126
l. 126
t. 0

N.G An all-caps Neo-Matrix alphabet formed of rounded quatrefoils on a 3×3 grid with dot nodes

A–Z 0–9

s. 70
l. 62
t. -125
w. 500

N.G

Echo

s. 242
l. 180
t. -250
w. 100

N.G

Oscar Mike Alpha
Tango Romeo

s. 83
l. 73
t. -125
w. 750

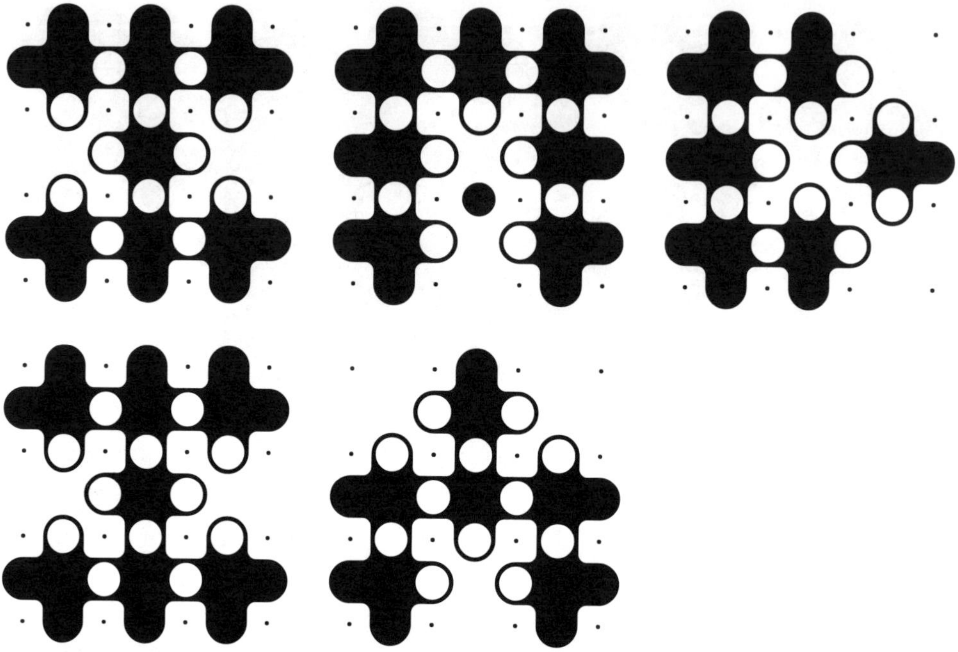

N.G

India

s. 128
l. 128
t. 0
w. 500

N.G

Xray

s. 243
l. 176
t. -240
w. 300

N Neo-Matrix

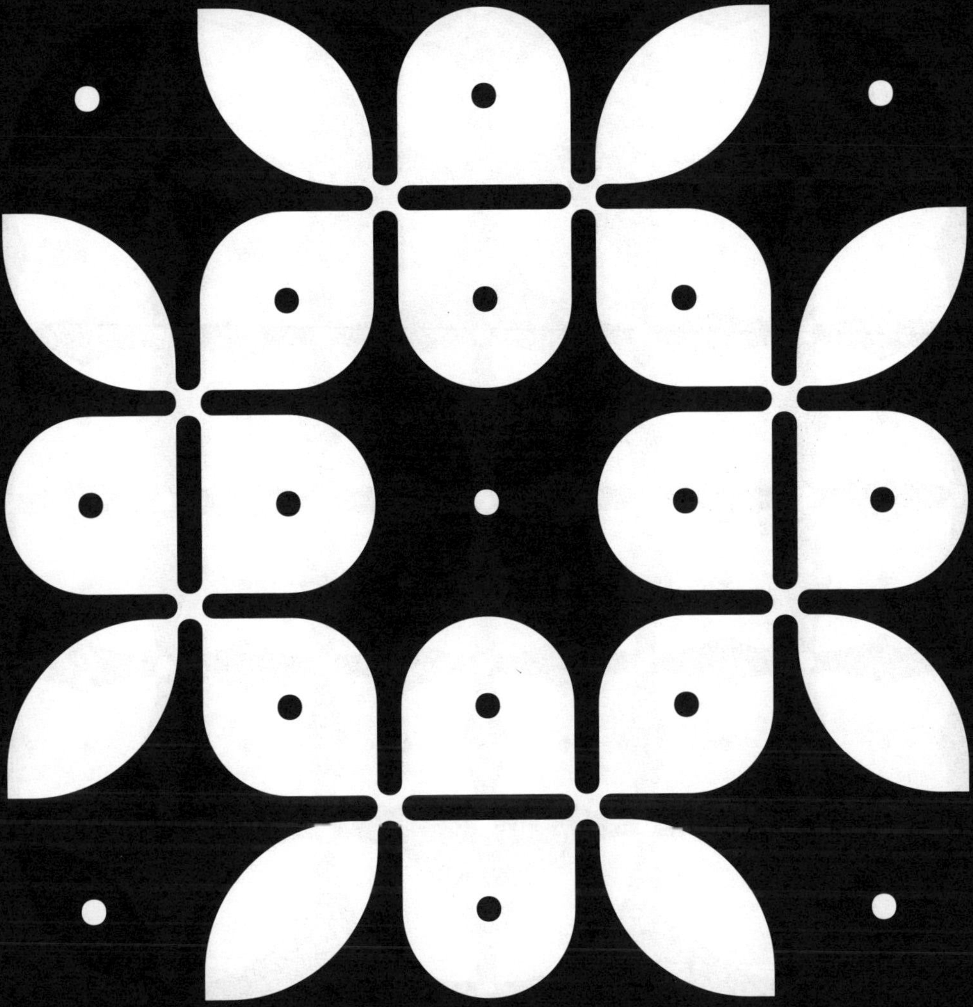

N Neo-Matrix

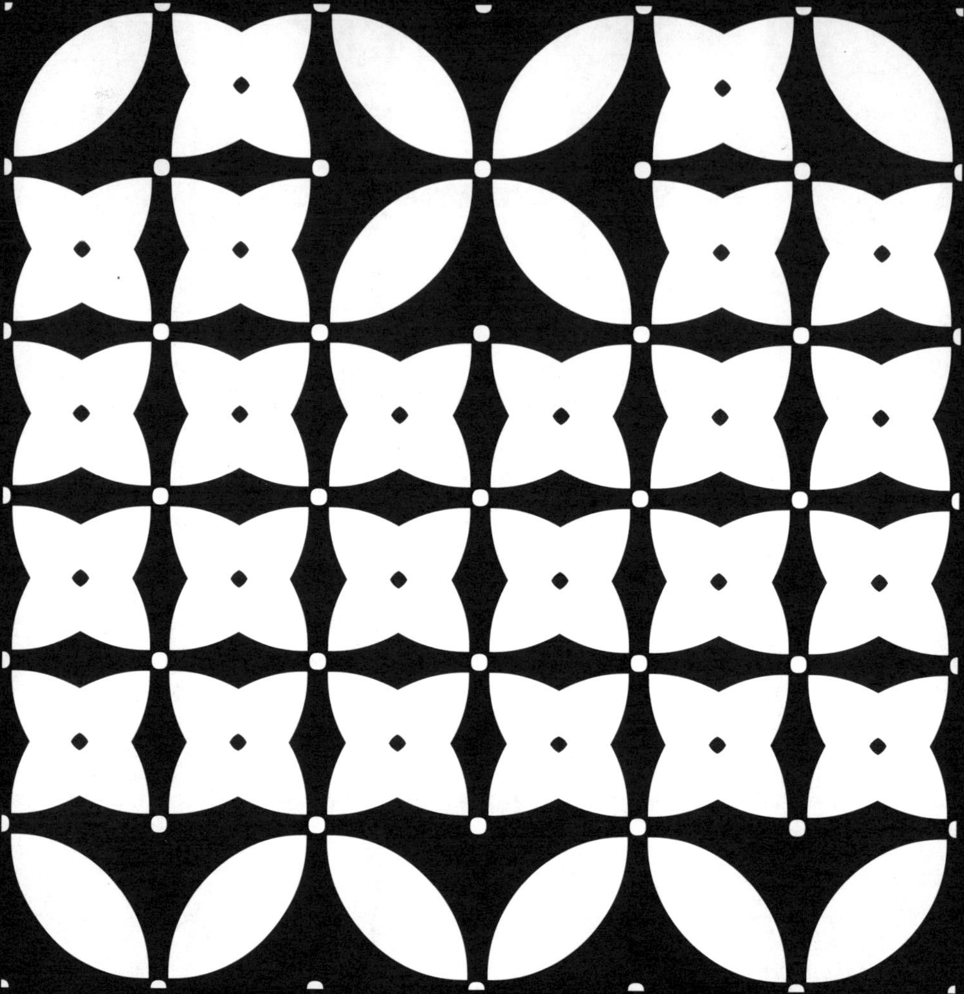

N Neo-Matrix

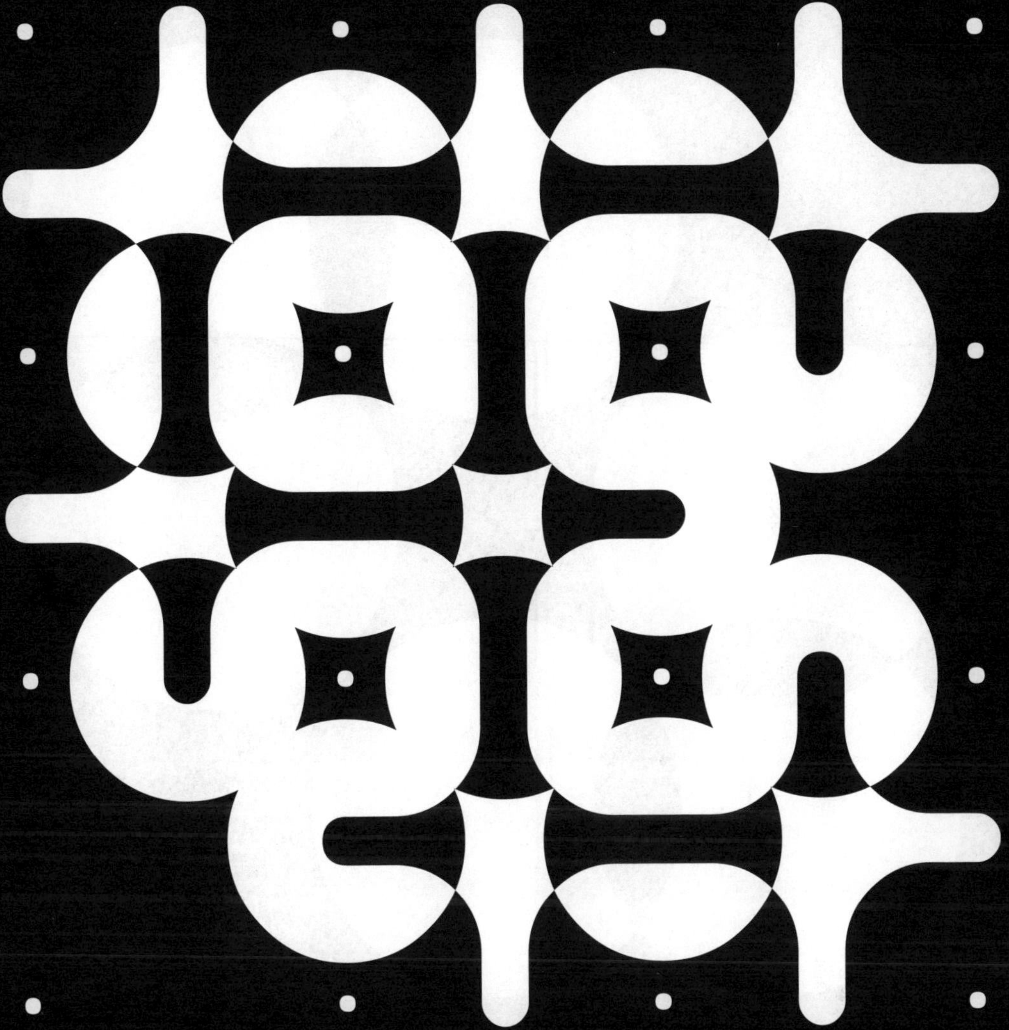

N Neo-Matrix

N Neo-Matrix

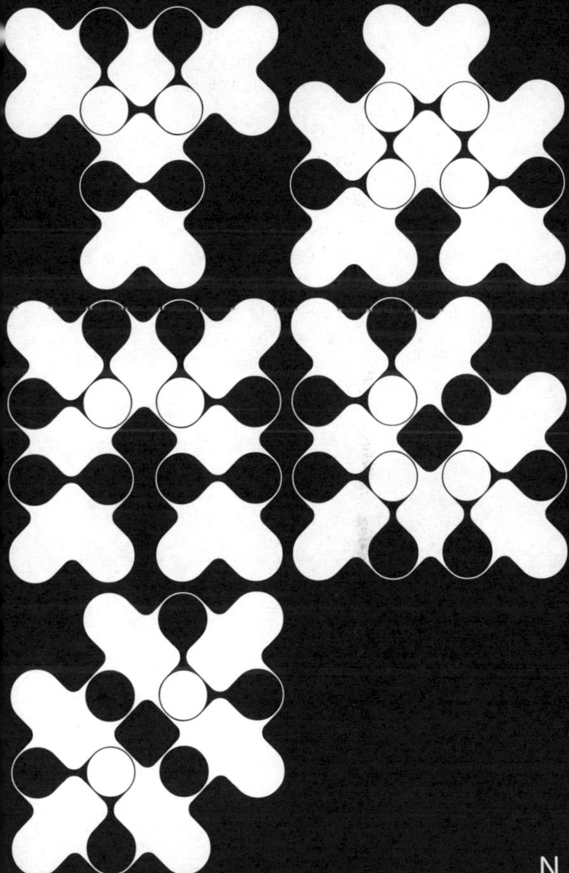

N Neo-Matrix

N Neo-Matrix

N Neo-Matrix

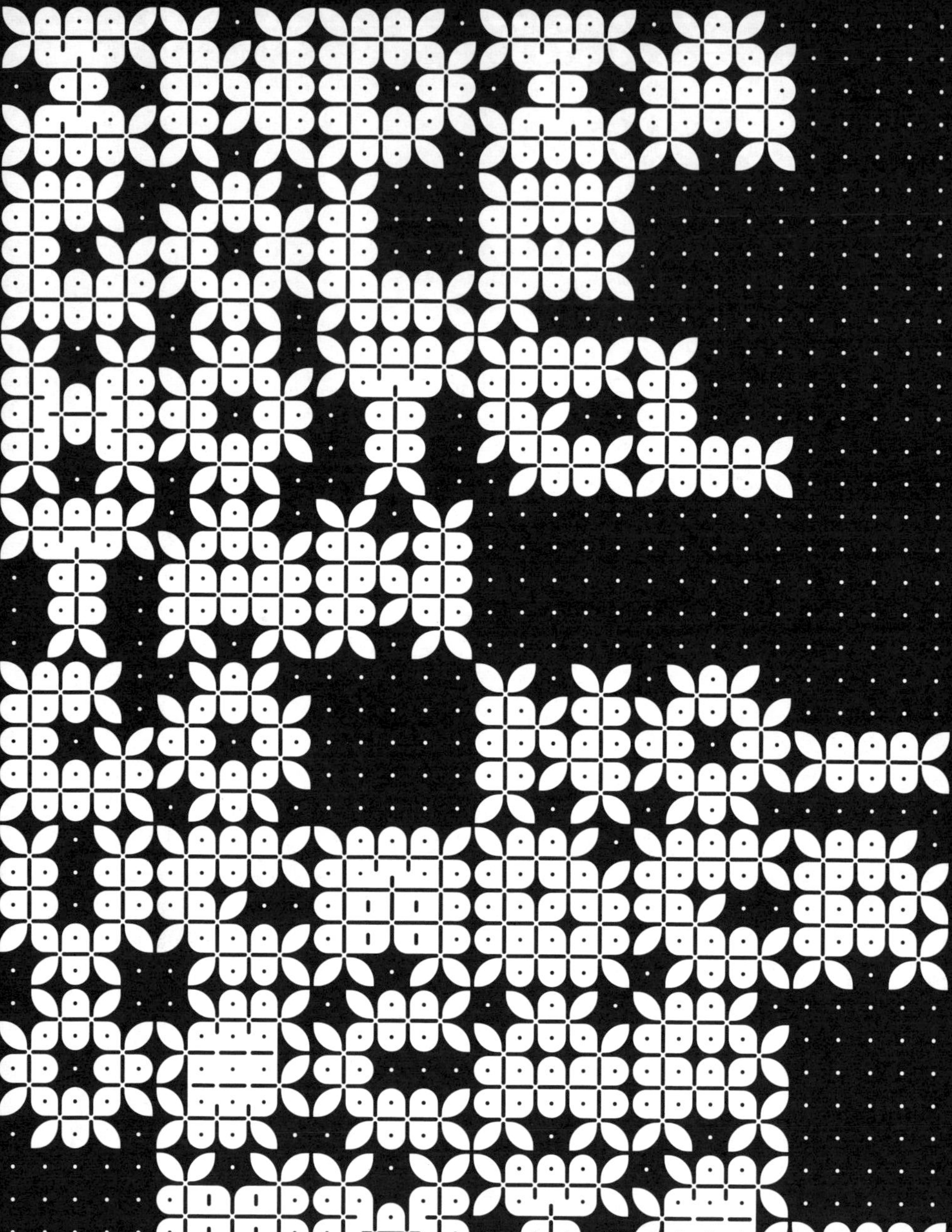

N Neo-Matrix

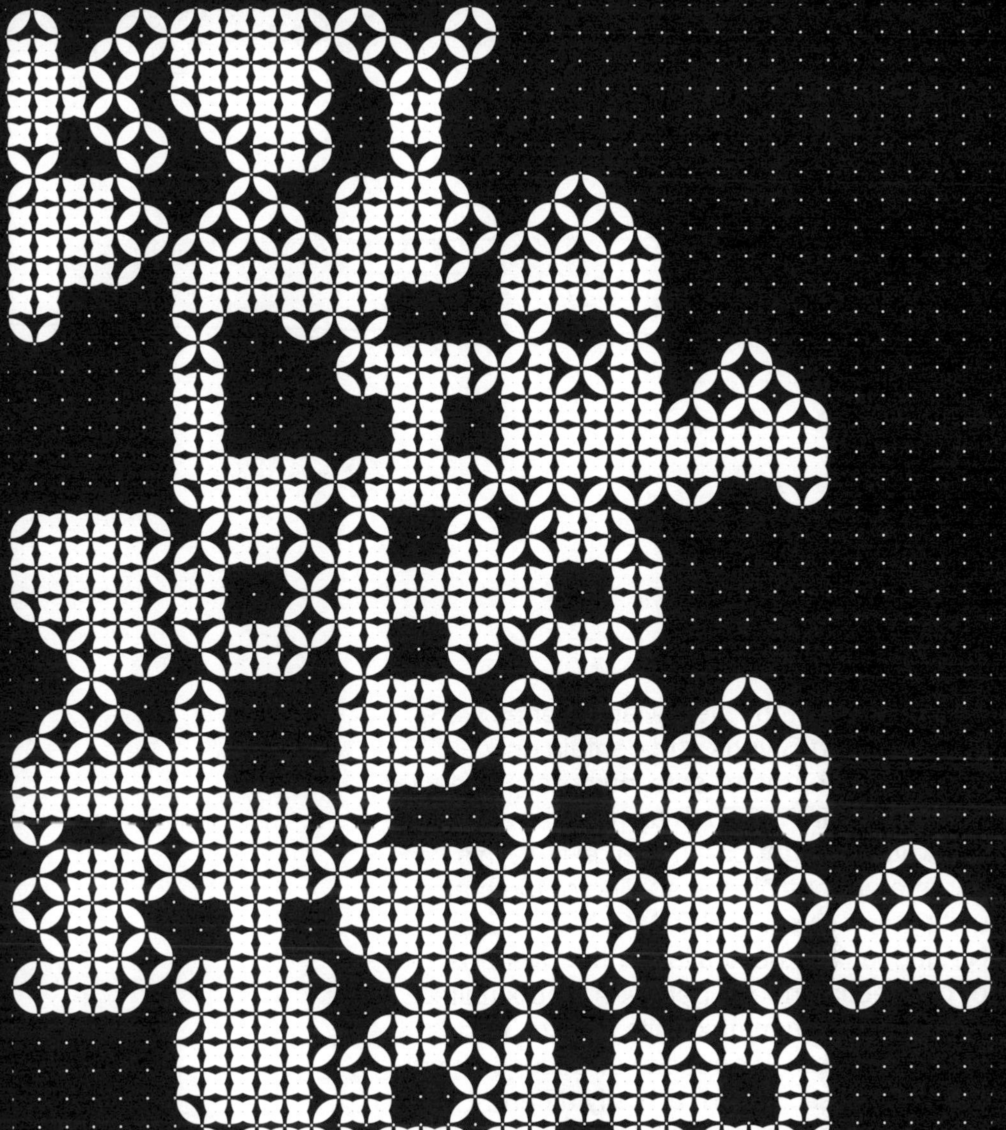

N Neo-Matrix

Section Notes:

All alphabets in the Neo-Matrix series were created using Glyphs and contain only uppercase character sets, numerals, and basic punctuation. Each alphabet is a variable font with a weight parameter. In N.A, this parameter controls the scaling of the matrix units themselves. In N.B, N.C, N.D, N.E, and N.F, it controls the scaling of the overlaps or connecting nodes between matrix units. In N.G, both the matrix units and the nodes are scaled—but in opposite directions along the slider—resulting in radically different geometries within a single font file.

This set comprises selected alphabets slanted at various angles. Drawn from other sections of Alphabetical Playground, each form is chosen for its adaptability and correspondence to an overarching slanted framework. Many designs are constructed on a grid or composed of gridded units which, when slanted, align seamlessly with adjacent columns. This creates a vertical rhythm and interlocking structure between lines, resulting in a dynamic text flow.

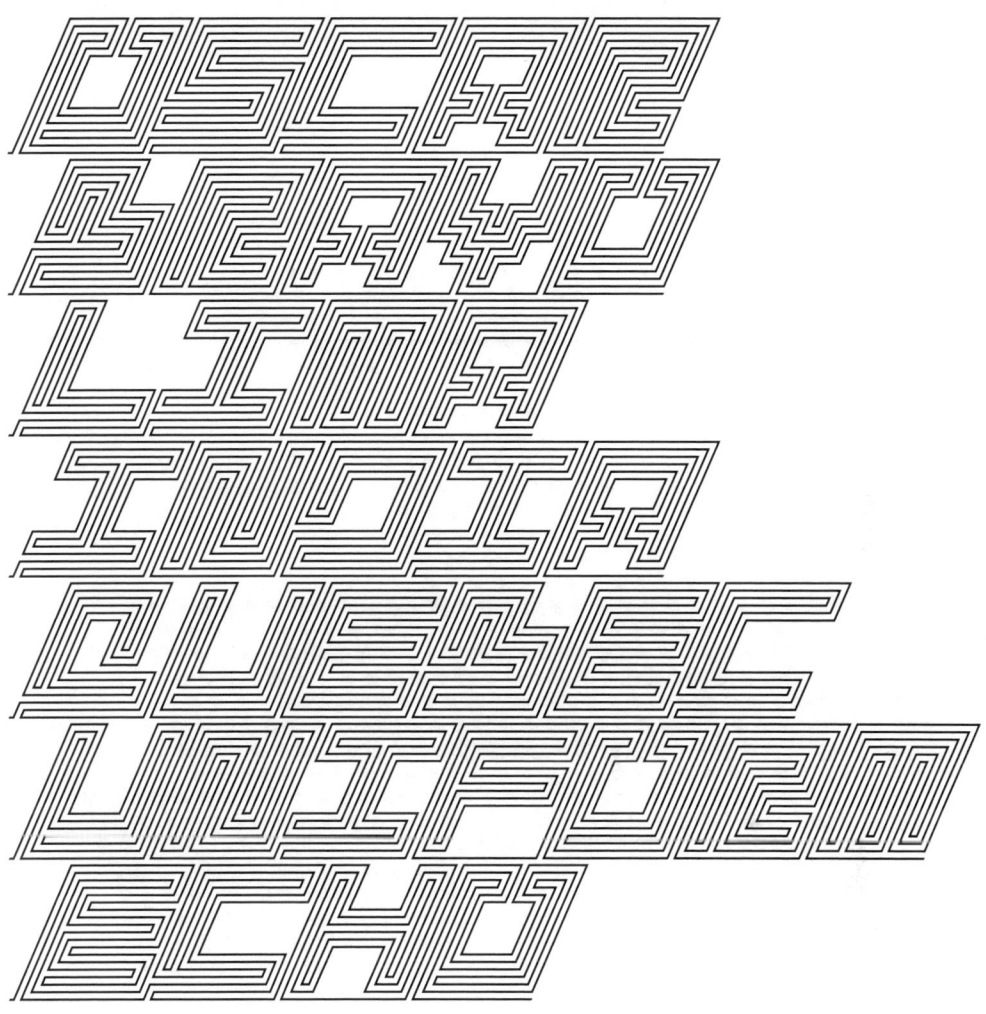

OSCAR
BRAVO
LIMA
INDIA
QUEBEC
UNIFORM
ECHO

O.A

An oblique continuous single line all-caps cursive with an intricate squared coiling path slanted to 24°

Oscar Bravo Lima India
Quebec Uniform Echo

s. 56
l. 56
t. 0
w. 230

O.B

An oblique 2-part unit based type system formed of expanding and contracting superellipse curves slanted to 20.5°

Oscar Bravo Lima
India Quebec

s. 60
l. 72
t. 0
w. ±

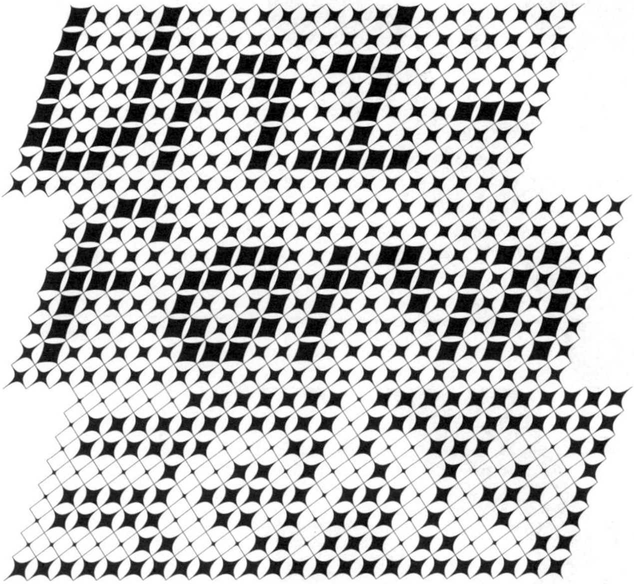

O.C An oblique 2-part unit based type system formedof decreasing unit hyperbola to parabolic curves slanted to 20.5°

Uniform Echo

s. 60
l. 72
t. 0
w. ±

O.D

An oblique ultra-light rounded inverting alphabet, alternating between negative and positive space from character to character slanted to 26.5°

Oscar Bravo Lima India
Quebec Uniform Echo

s. 50
l. 50
t. 0
w. 100
r. 900

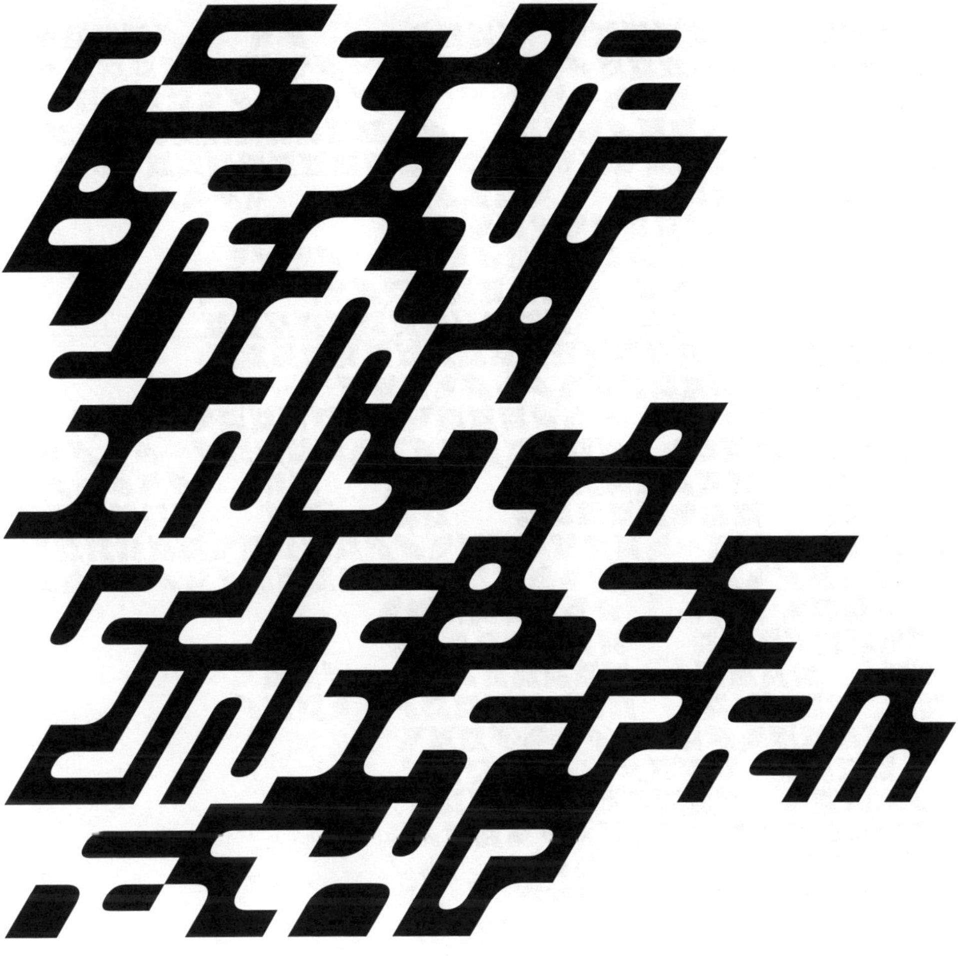

O.E

An oblique medium weight rounded inverting alphabet, alternating between negative and positive space from character to character slanted to 26.5°

Oscar Bravo Lima India
Quebec Uniform Echo

s. 50
l. 50
t. 0
w. 400
r. 900

O.F

An oblique all-caps Neo-Matrix alphabet formed of circle lattice units on a 5×5 grid with an inverted overlap slanted to 9.42°

Oscar Bravo Lima
India Quebec

s. 72
l. 72
t. 0
w. 600

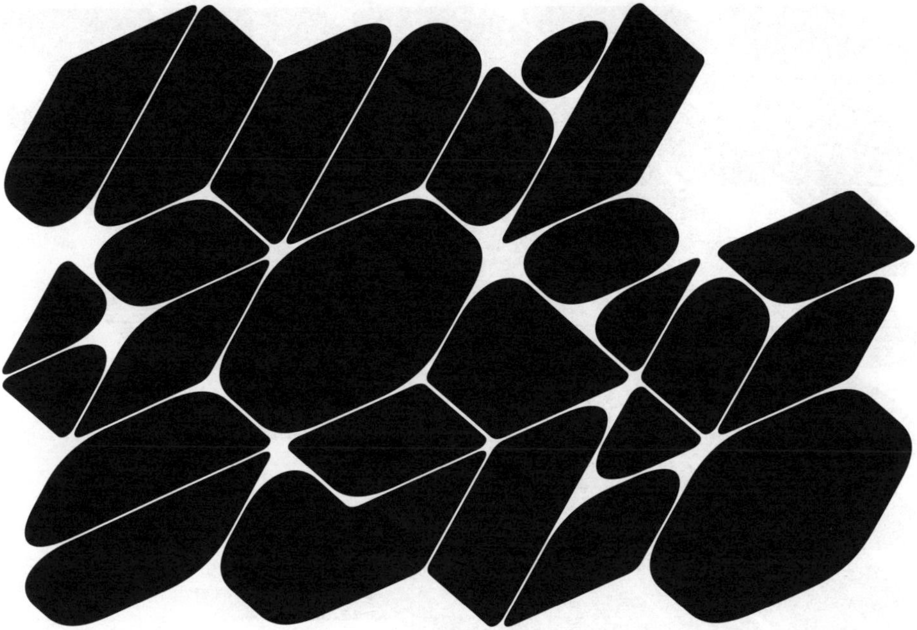

O.G An oblique negative space tessellating type system formed of hexagonal letterforms slanted to 30°

Uniform Echo

s. 72
l. 72
t. 0

OSCAR
BRAVO
LIMA
INDIA
QUE-
BEC
UNI-
FORM
ECHO

O.H An oblique extreme Ultra-Black alphabet slanted to 45.2°

Oscar Bravo Lima India
Quebec Uniform Echo

s. 42
l. 35
t. 0
w. 600

O.I

An oblique shifting pattern alphabet formed of a rounded diagonal chequerboard slanted to 33.7°

Oscar Bravo Lima India
Quebec Uniform Echo

s. 70
l. 52
t. 0
w. 440

O.J

An oblique all-caps shifting pattern alphabet formed of a shifted hazard stripe pattern slanted to 20.55°

Oscar Bravo Lima India
Quebec Uniform Echo

s. 51
l. 51
t. 0

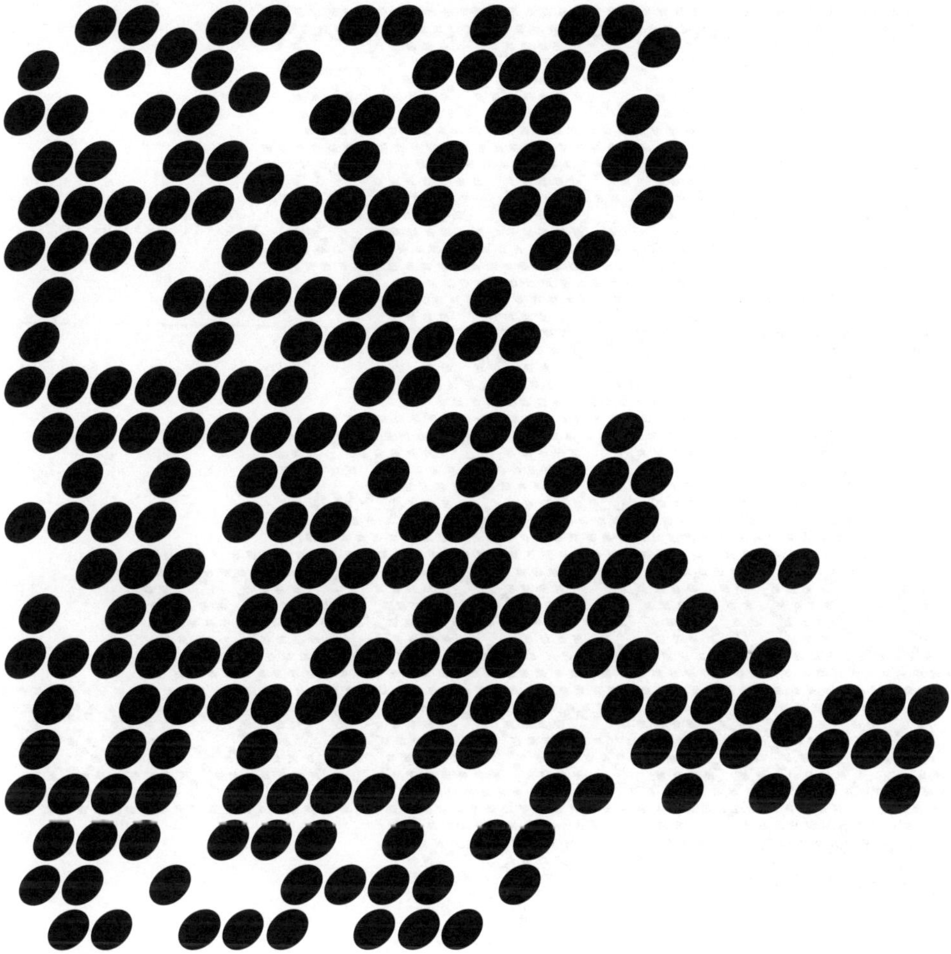

O.K

An oblique all-caps matrix alphabet formed of dots on a 3×3 grid slanted to 18.2°

Oscar Bravo Lima India
Quebec Uniform Echo

s. 51
l. 51
t. 0
w. 900

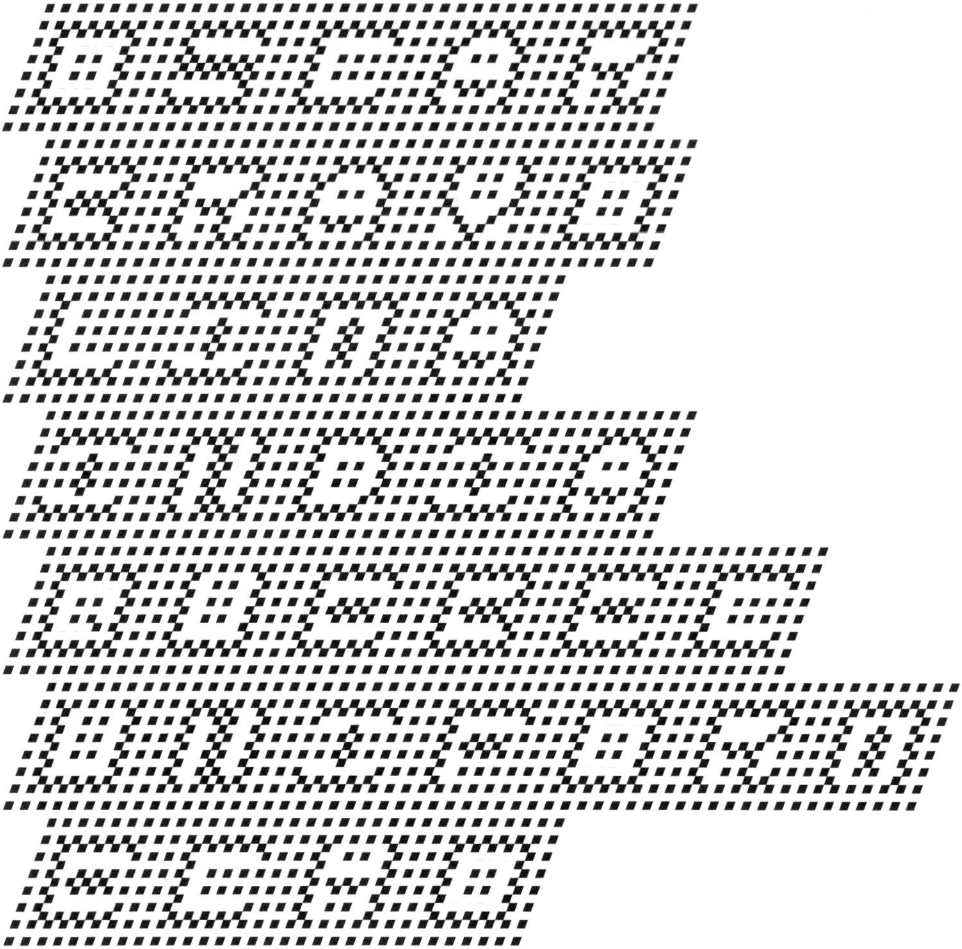

O.L

An oblique shifting pattern alphabet formed of a shifted square grid pattern slanted to 20.55°

Oscar Bravo Lima India
Quebec Uniform Echo

s. 51
l. 51
t. 0

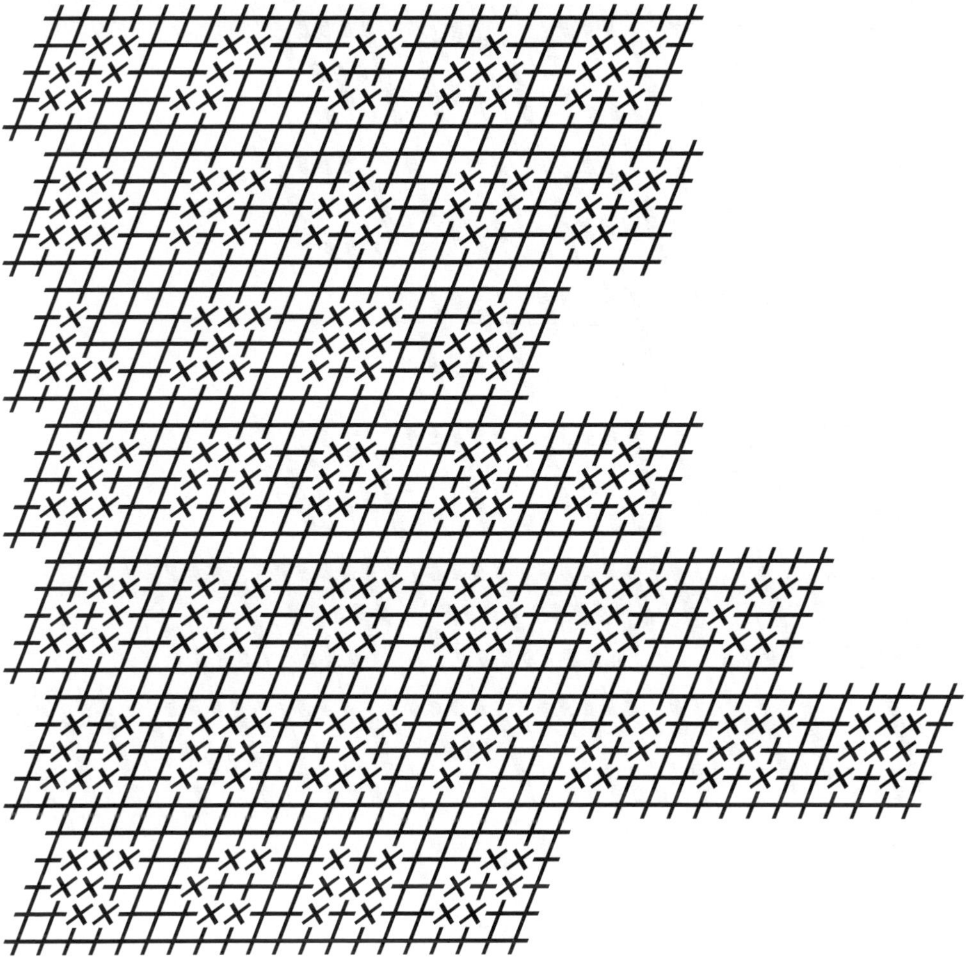

O.M An oblique shifting pattern alphabet formed of a rotated cross pattern slanted to 21.8°

Oscar Bravo Lima India
Quebec Uniform Echo

s. 51
l. 51
t. 0
w. 400
wd.900

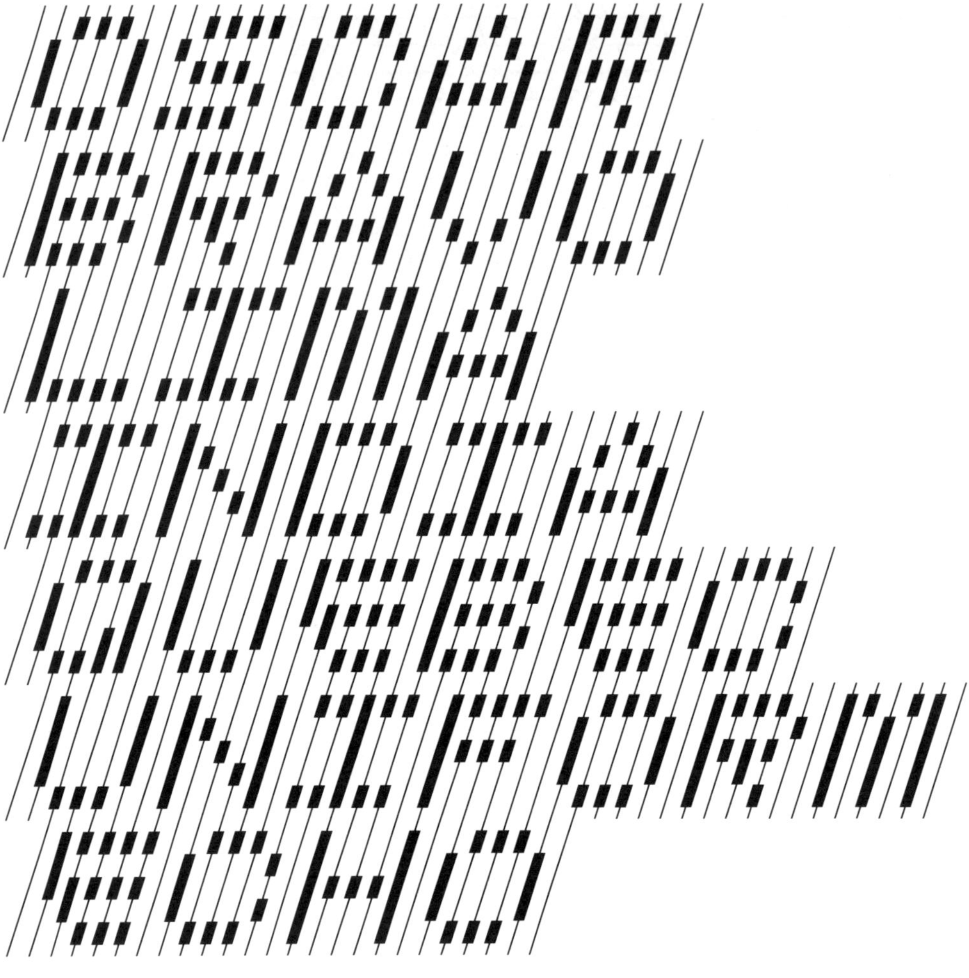

O.N

An oblique regular width alphabet formed of vertical lines, bold in foreground weight slanted to 18.43°

Oscar Bravo Lima India Quebec Uniform Echo

s. 51
l. 51
t. 0
fw. 500
bw. 150
wd.500

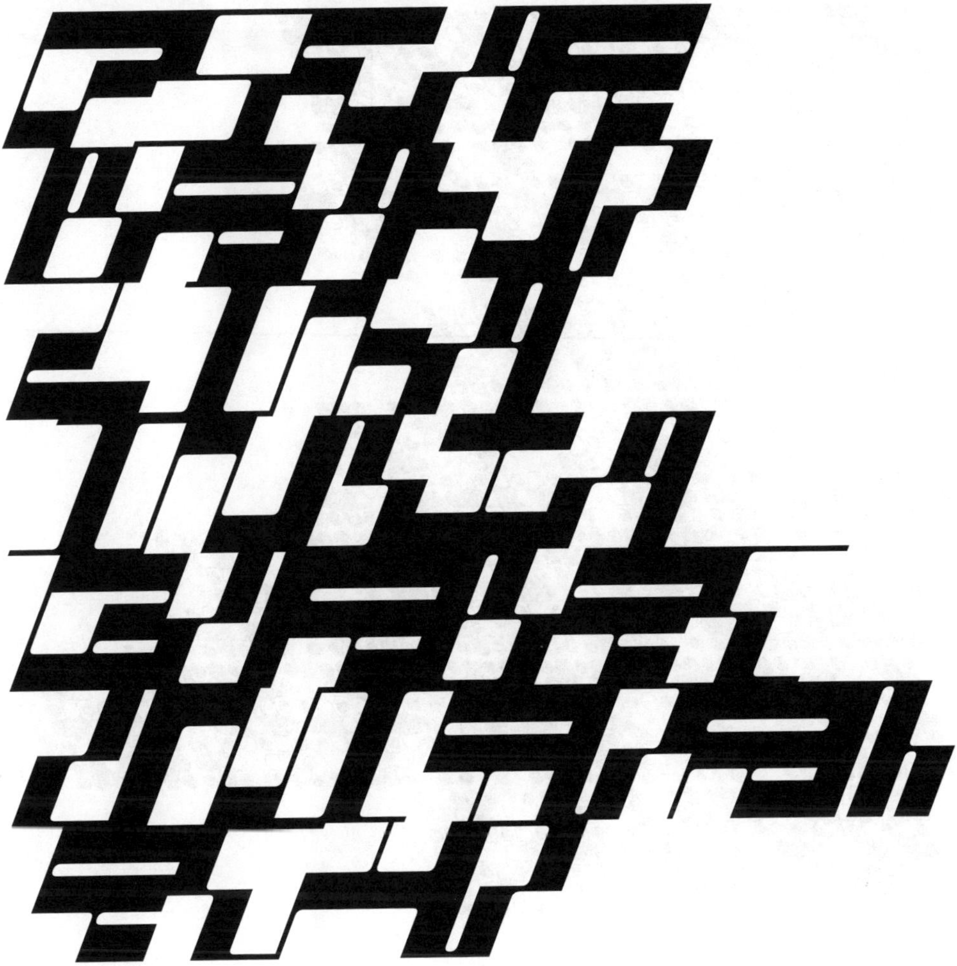

O.O An oblique rounded inverting alphabet alternating in both contrast and space from character to character slanted to 22°

Oscar Bravo Lima India
Quebec Uniform Echo

s.	51
l.	51
t.	0
w.	82
r.	900

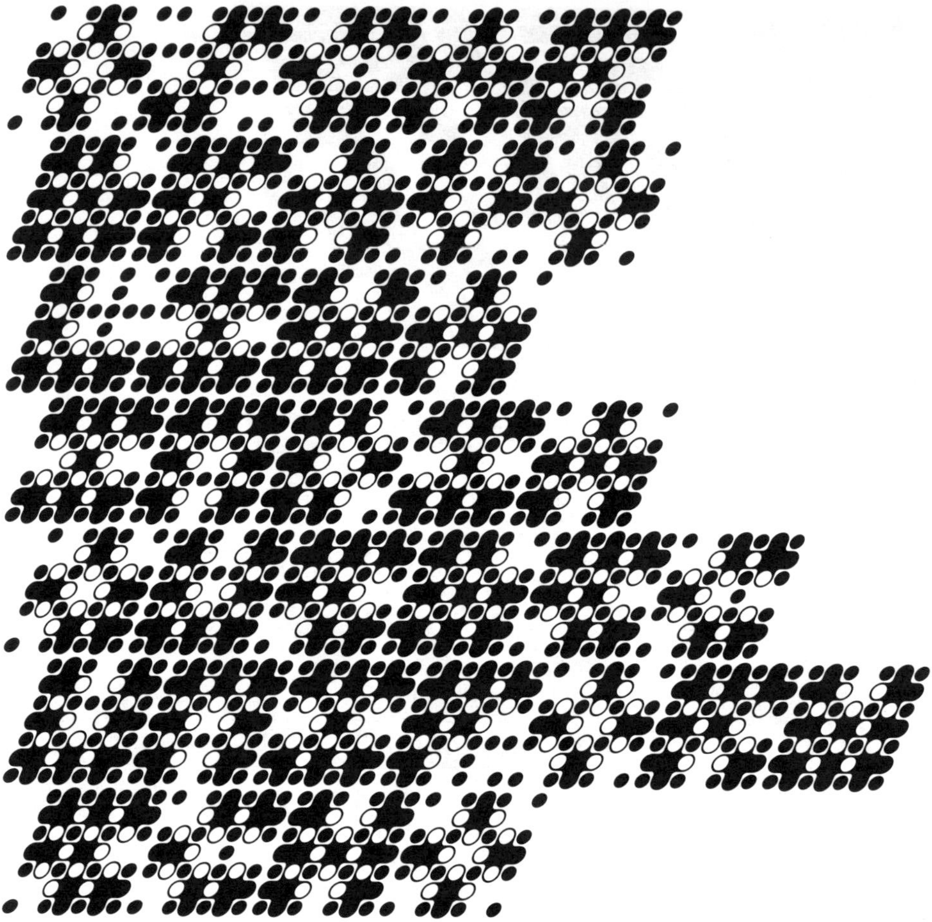

O.P

An oblique all-caps Neo-Matrix alphabet formed of rounded quatrefoils on a 3×3 grid with dot nodes slanted to 23°

Oscar Bravo Lima India
Quebec Uniform Echo

s. 55
l. 49
t. -110
w. 500

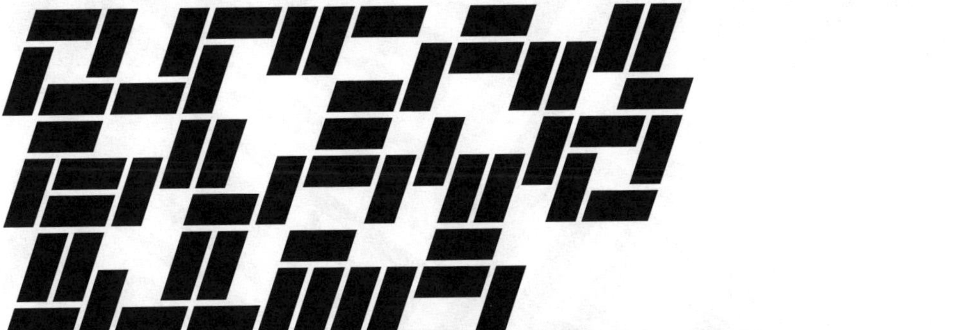

O.Q

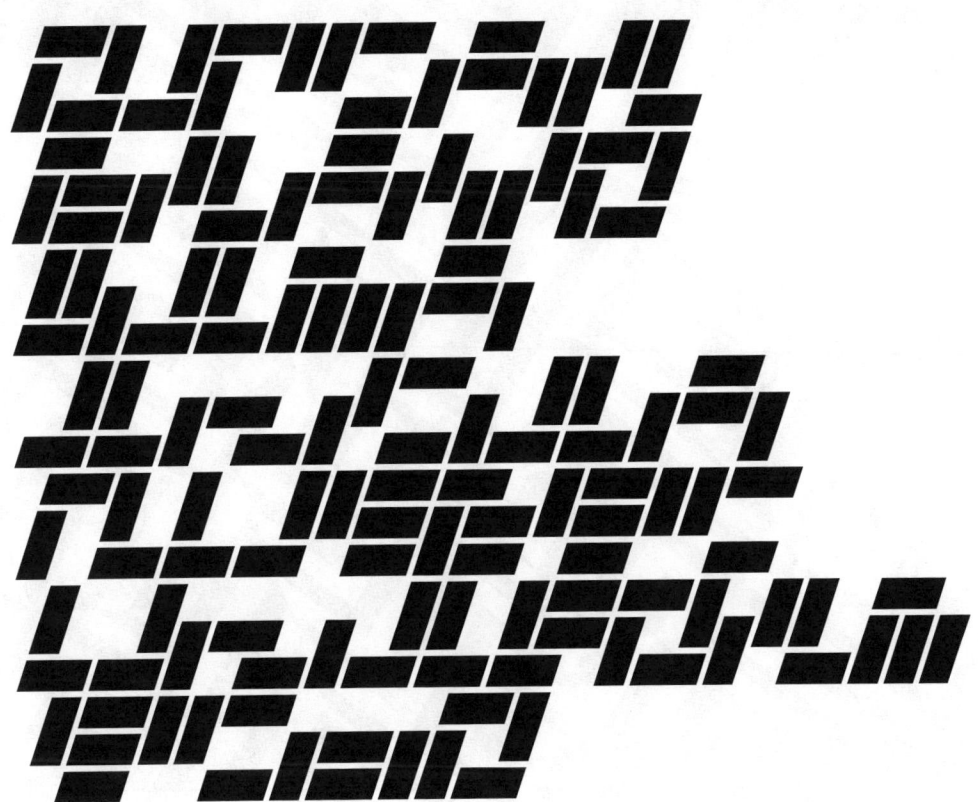

An oblique quadrisected All-caps alphabet with letters formed of 4 equal congruent rectangles slanted to 19°

Oscar Bravo Lima India
Quebec Uniform Echo

s. 42
l. 42
t. 0

Section Notes:

Drawn from other sections of Alphabetical Playground, each form is chosen for its adaptability and correspondence to an overarching slanted framework. Each original source alphabet and corresponding slant value is list below.

O.A=(24°)(C.G)
O.B=(20.5°)(E.A)
O.C=(20.5°)(E.B)
O.D=(26.5°)(I.A A)
O.E=(26.5°)(I.A E)
O.F=(9.42°)(N.B)
O.G=(30°)(T.B)
O.H=(45.2°)(U.A)
O.I=(33.7°)(S.C)
O.J=(20.55°)(S.A)
O.K=(18.2°)(M.A)
O.L=(20.55°)(S.B)
O.M=(21.8°)(S.F)
O.N=(18.43°)(V.A)
O.O=(22°)(I.C)
O.P=(23°)(N.G)
O.Q=(19°)(Q.A)

[pʰiː]

467

This set of five alphabets reimagines the Latin script through systems of phonetics, acrophony, and semiotic encoding. Phonetic structures are abstracted into visual forms that imply sound; acrophonic principles evoke early writing systems where letters referenced speech; and semiotic systems like braille or Morse code are recontextualized as typographic expressions. Removed from their original purposes, these systems become symbolic, with re-translation acting as both method and mode of perception.

[eɪ] [bi:] [si:] [di:] [i:] [ɛf]
[dʒi:] [eɪtʃ] [aɪ] [dʒei:]
[kʰei:] [ɛl] [ɛm] [ɛn]
[oʊ] [pʰi:] [kʲu:] [ɑɭ] [ɛs]
[ti:] [ju:] [vi:] [dʌbəl ju:]
[ɛks] [waɪ] [zed]

P.A An alphabet formed of its letter's syllabic phoneme*

A–Z

s. 48
l. 50
t. 0

[pʰiː][eɪ]
[pʰiː][eɪ]

P.A

Papa

s. 140
l. 140
t. 0

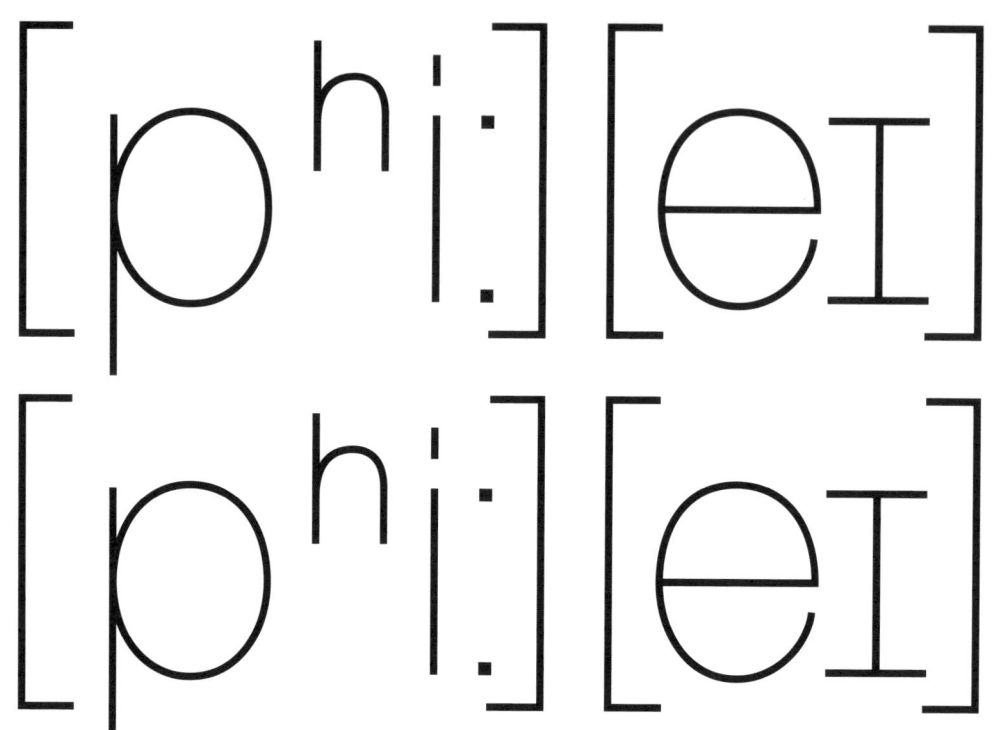

[eɪ][ɛn] [eɪ][ɛl][pʰiː]
[eɪtʃ][eɪ][biː][iː][tiː]
[ɛf][oʊ][ɑɹ][ɛm][iː][diː]
[oʊ][ɛf] [iː][eɪ][siː][eɪtʃ]
[ɛl][iː][tiː][tiː][iː][ɑɹ][ɛs]
[ɛs][waɪ][ɛl][ɛl][eɪ][biː]
[aɪ][siː] [pʰiː][eɪtʃ][oʊ][ɛn]
[iː][ɛm][iː]

P.A

*

s. 40
l. 40
t. 0

Papa Hotel
Oscar
November
Echo Tango
India Charlie

P.B An alphabet formed of its letter's NATO phonetic code word*

Phonetic

s. 77
l. 70
t. 0

Alpha November   Alpha Lima Papa
Hotel Alpha Bravo Echo Tango
Foxtrot Oscar Romeo Mike Echo Delta
Oscar Foxtrot   Echo Alpha Charlie Hotel
Lima Echo Tango Tango Echo
Romeo Sierra   November Alpha
Tango Oscar   Papa Hotel Oscar
November Echo Tango India Charlie
Charlie Oscar Delta Echo
Whiskey Oscar Romeo Delta

P.B

*

s. 22
l. 23
t. 0

Alpha Lima Papa Hotel Alpha Papa Lima Alpha Yankee

P.B

Alphaplay

s. 77
l. 70
t. 0

Alpha Bravo Charlie
Delta Echo Foxtrot
Golf Hotel India Juliet
Kilo Lima Mike
November Oscar
Papa Quebec Romeo
Sierra Tango Uniform
Victor Whiskey Xray
Yankee Zulu

P.B

A–Z

s. 40
l. 40
t. 0

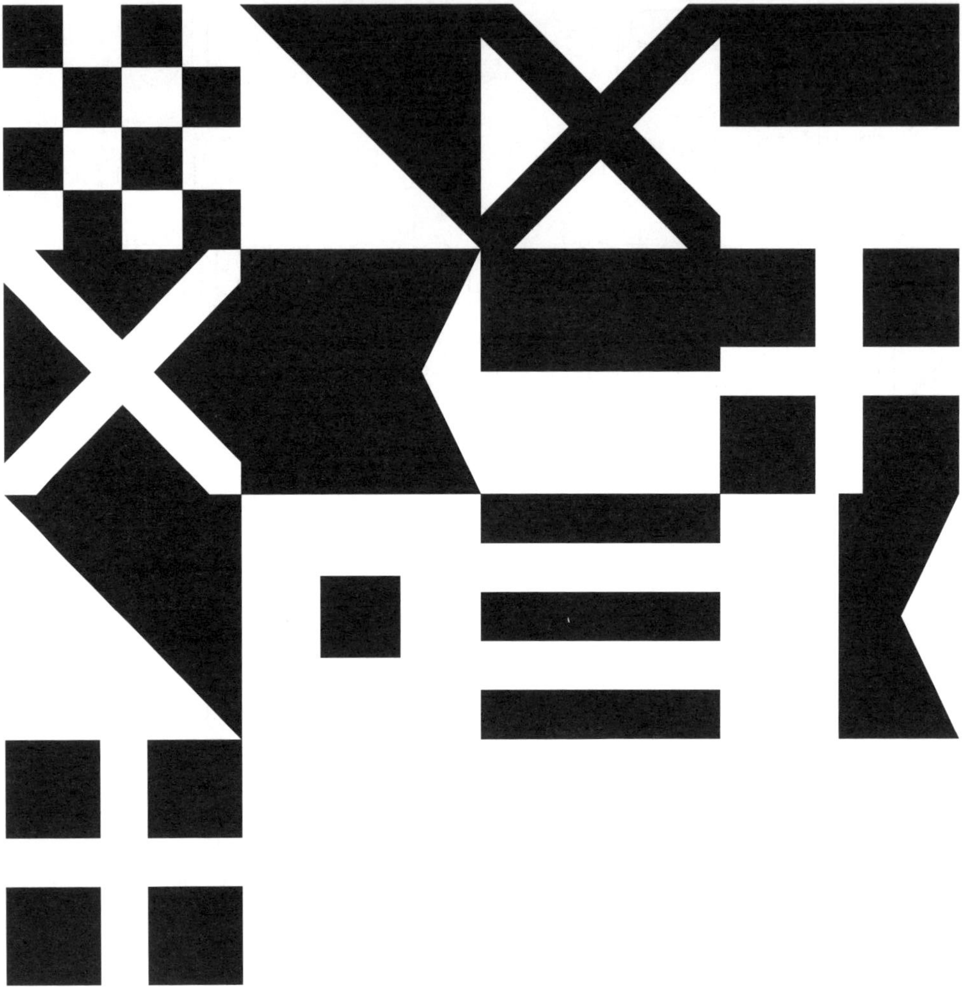

P.C An alphabet formed of its letter's Flaghoist communication flag*

November Oscar

s. 92
l. 92
t. 0

P.C

A–Z

s. 61
l. 61
t. 0

P.D An alphabet formed of its letter's semaphore positioning

November Papa

s. 92
l. 92
t. 0

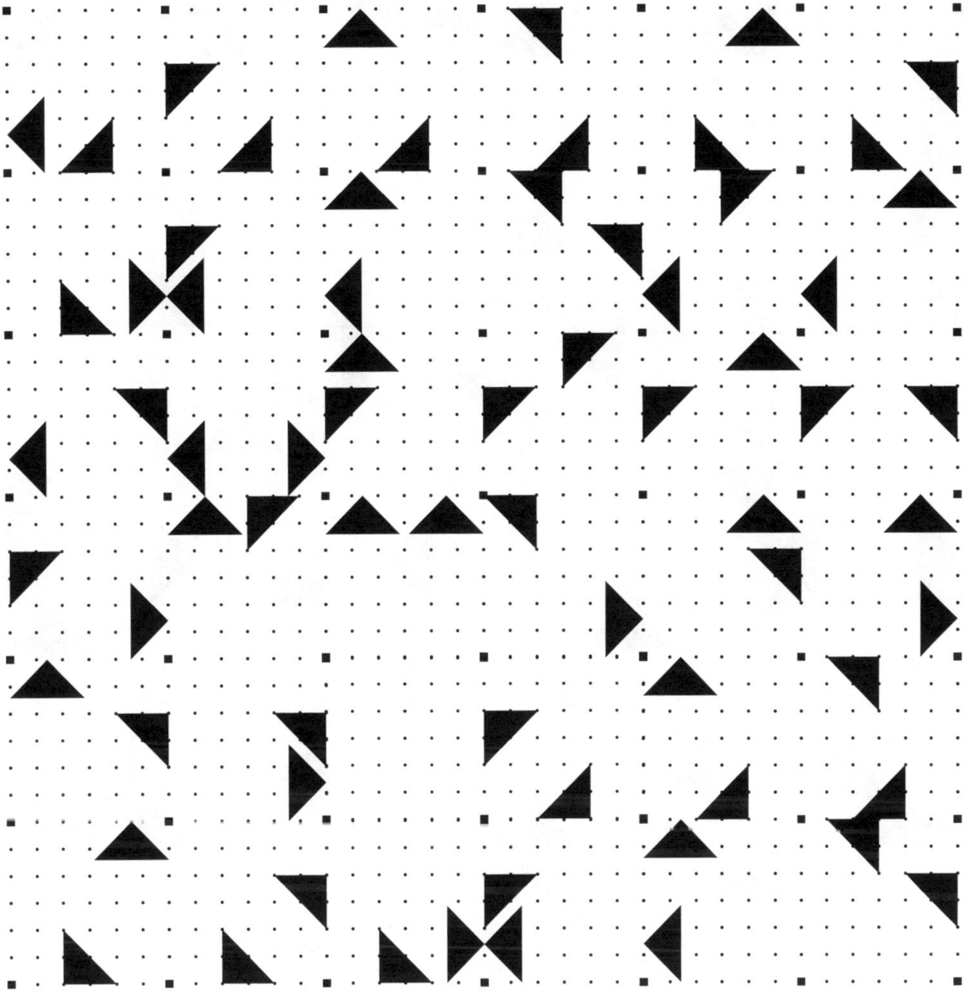

P.D

A–Z

s. 61
l. 61
t. 0

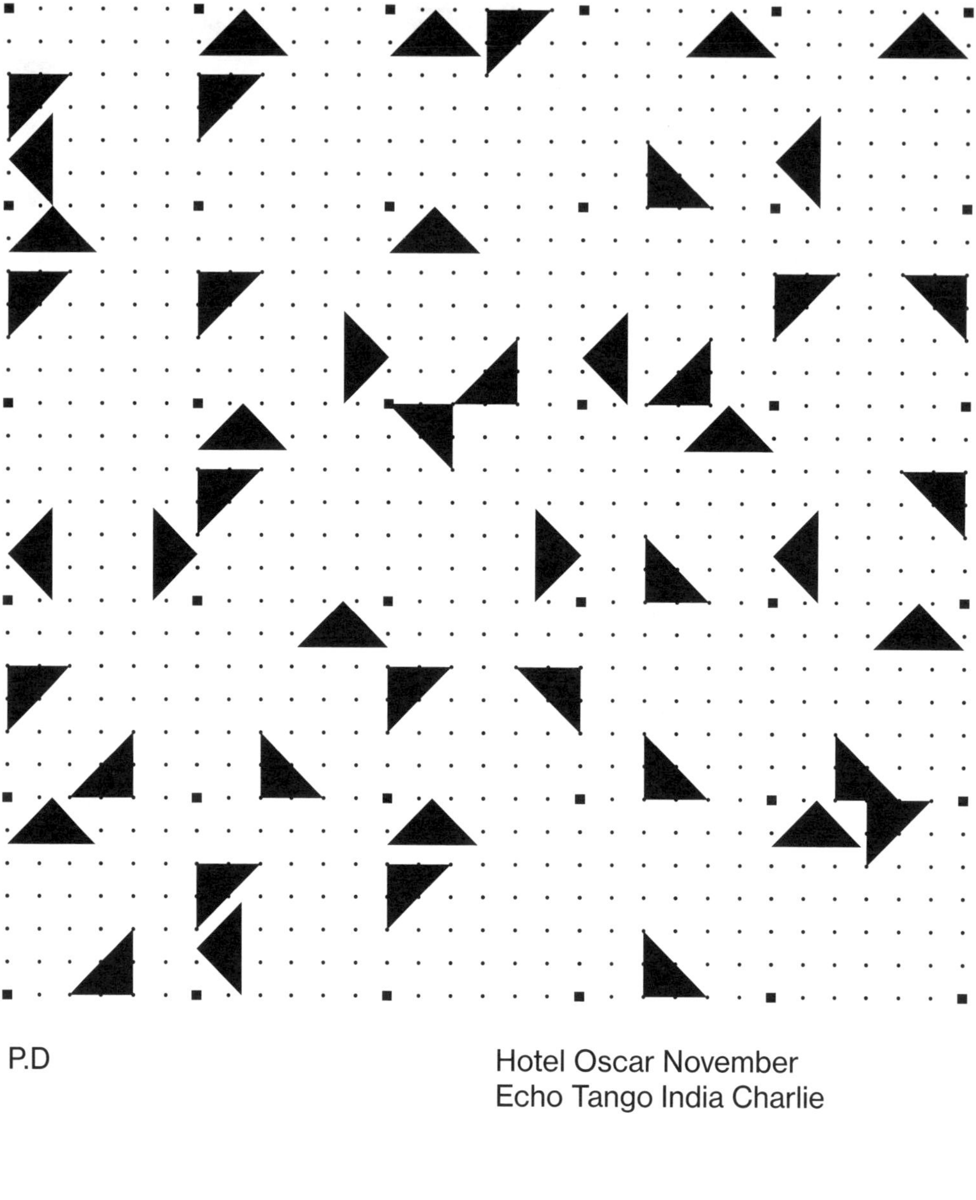

P.D

Hotel Oscar November
Echo Tango India Charlie

s. 74
l. 74
t. 0

P
Phonetic

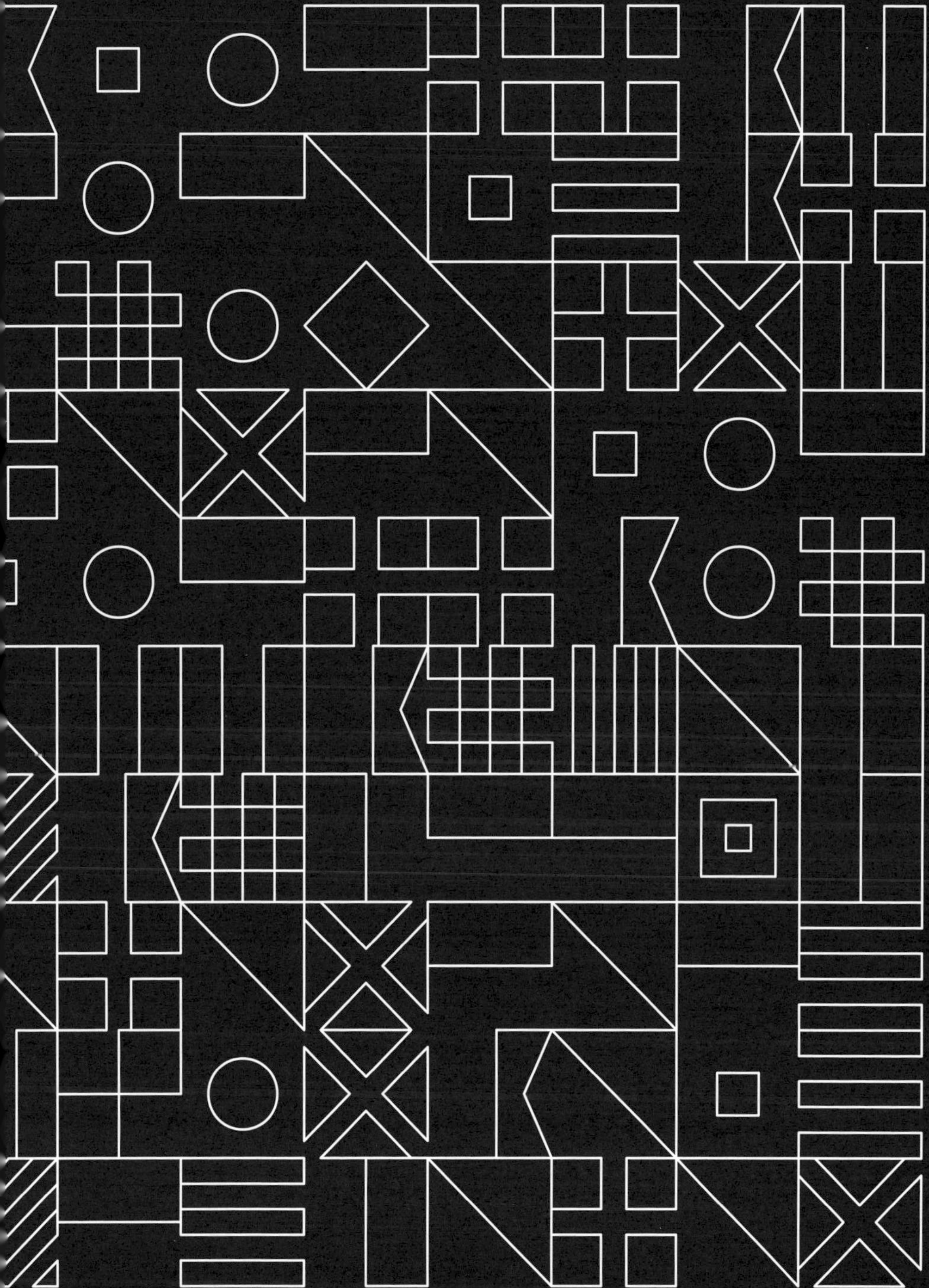

Section Notes:

Created in Glyphs, the original sources for the alphabets in the Phonetic section are either the International Phonetic Alphabet or the NATO Standardisation Office. These sources have been adapted, redrawn, and recontextualised. P.A and P.B are based on a monoline grotesque alphabet developed for use across different sections of Alphabetical Playground.

Quadrisect is a set of alphabets where every letterform is constructed from four equal, congruent shapes that are mirrored or rotated versions of the same module, all identical in form and size to ensure strict uniformity across each design. Following this constraint, texts are distilled into a pattern-based composite of elemental forms. The elimination of letter-spacing further dissolves verbal clarity, shifting the outcome towards asemic writing, a cultural tradition where text serves as an exclusively visual code rather than a linguistic one.

Q.A

An all-caps quadrisected alphabet with letters formed of 4 equal congruent rectangles

A–Z 0–9 .,-

s. 50
l. 50
t. 0

Q.B An all-caps quadrisected alphabet with letters formed of 4 equal congruent stadium shapes

A–Z.,-

s. 50
l. 50
t. 0

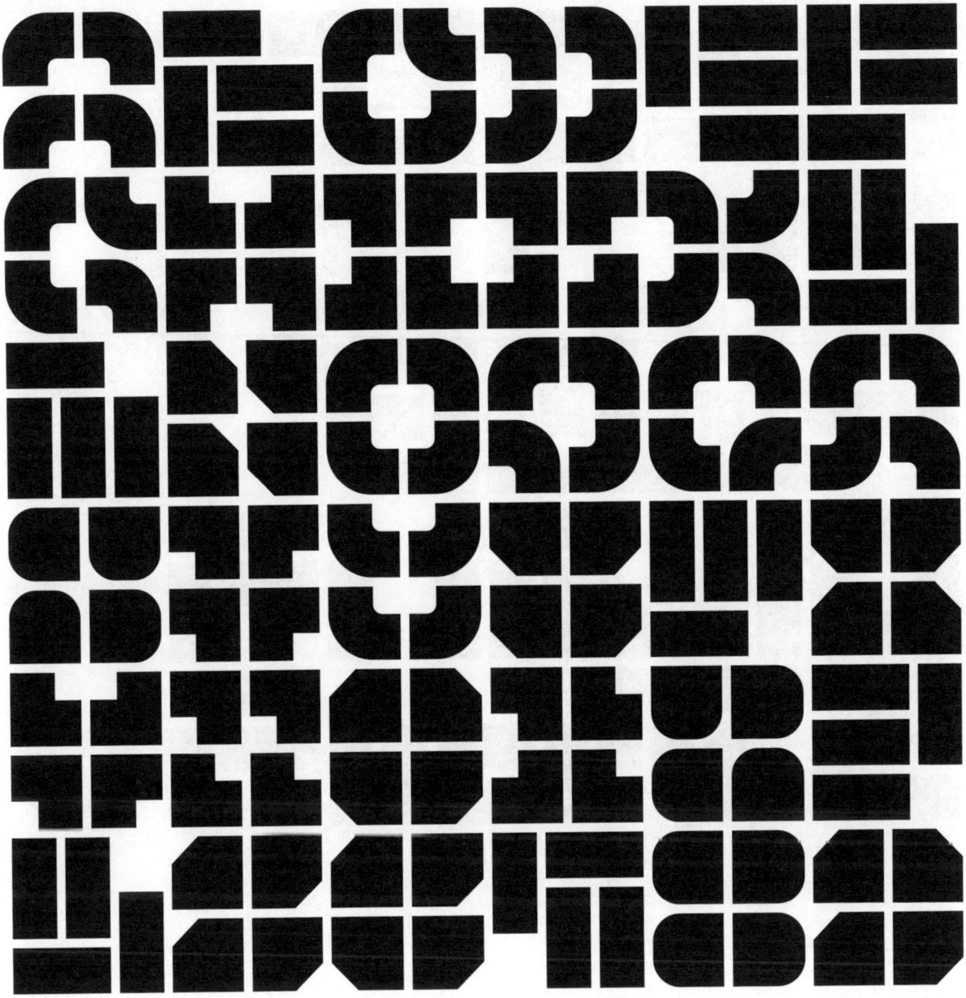

Q.C An all-caps quadrisected alphabet with letters formed of 4 equal congruent shapes

A–Z 0–9

s. 62
l. 62
t. 0

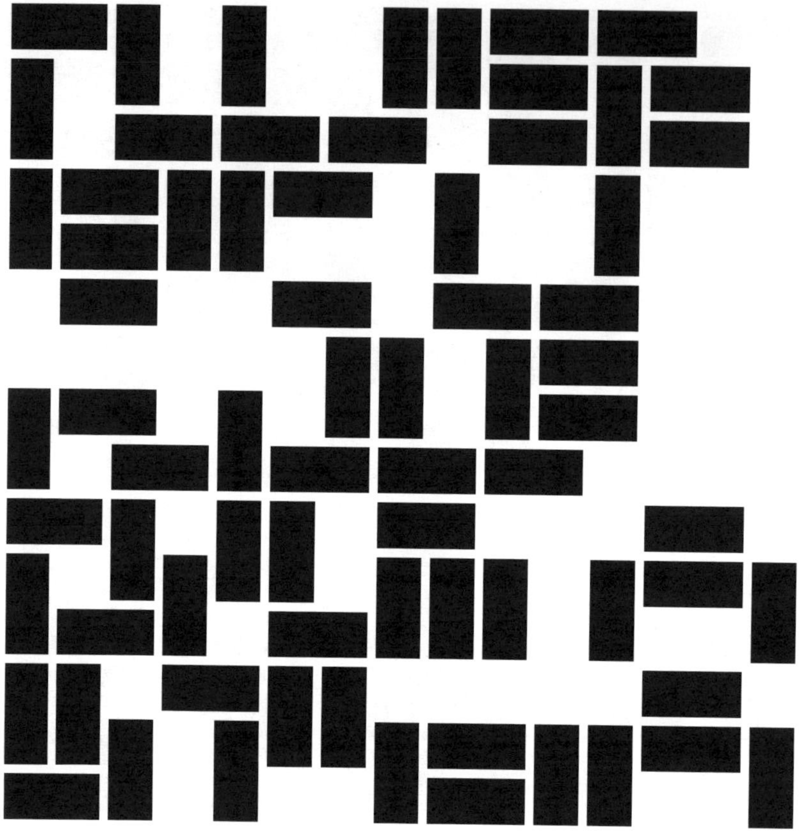

Q.A

Quebec Uniform Alpha

s. 62
l. 62
t. 0

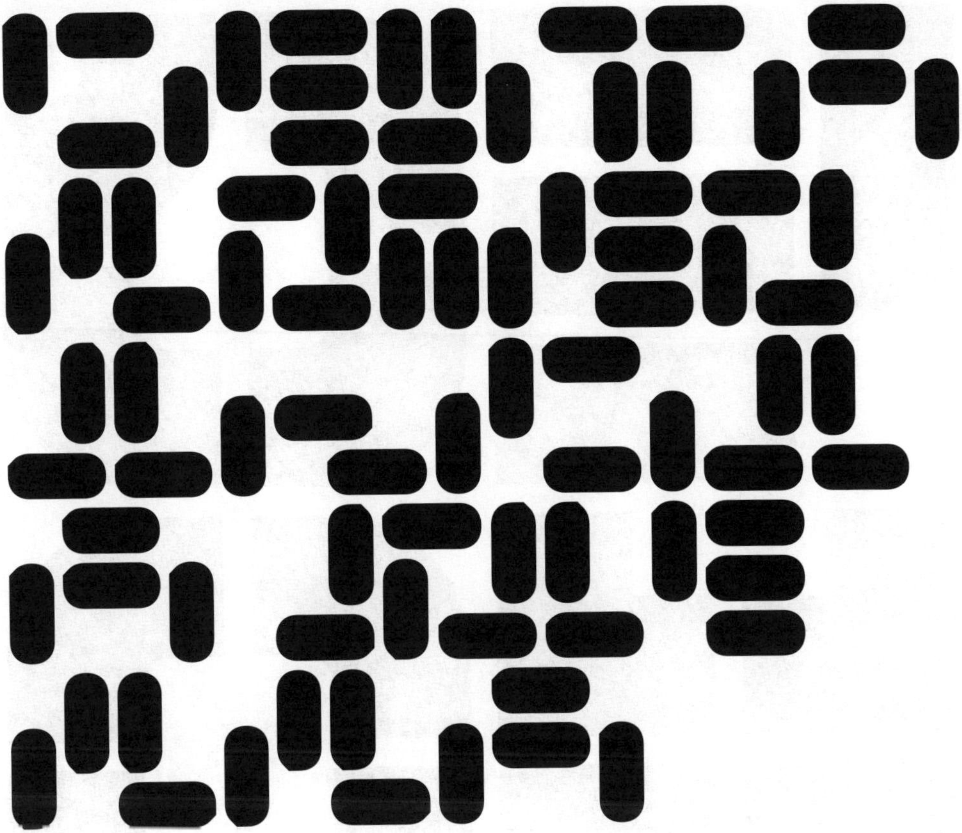

Q.B

Delta Romeo India Sierra

s. 62
l. 62
t. 0

Q.C

Echo

s. 189
l. 189
t. 0

Q.C

Charlie Tango

s. 94
l. 94
t. 0

Q Quadrisect

Q Quadrisect

Section Notes:

All alphabets within Quadrisect were created using Glyphs and consist of single weight font files that include uppercase letters, numerals, and basic punctuation.

R

A set of three alphabets that draw freely from a range of historic scripts such as Arabic, Armenian, Burmese, Chinese, Coptic, Ethiopic, Greek, Hebrew, Hiragana, Javanese, Katakana, Malayalam, Runic, Tamil, Thai and Tibetan. Every character, symbol and sign is a re-appropriation of an original source glyph, offering a new perspective on familiar writing systems. Recontextualised explores how changing the cultural context of letterforms can reshape their relationships and meanings.

ROMEO ECHO- CHARLIE OSCAR NOVEMBER TANGO

R.A A Roman all-caps alphabet formed of characters recontextualised from other modern alphabets

Romeo Echo - Charlie
Oscar November Tango

s. 39
l. 43
t. 20

R.A

A–Z 0–4

s. 56
l. 59
t. 10

R.B Another Roman all-caps alphabet formed of characters recontextualised from other modern alphabets

A–Z 5–9

s. 56
l. 59
t. 10

R.A+B

Echo

s. 175
l. 187
t. 75

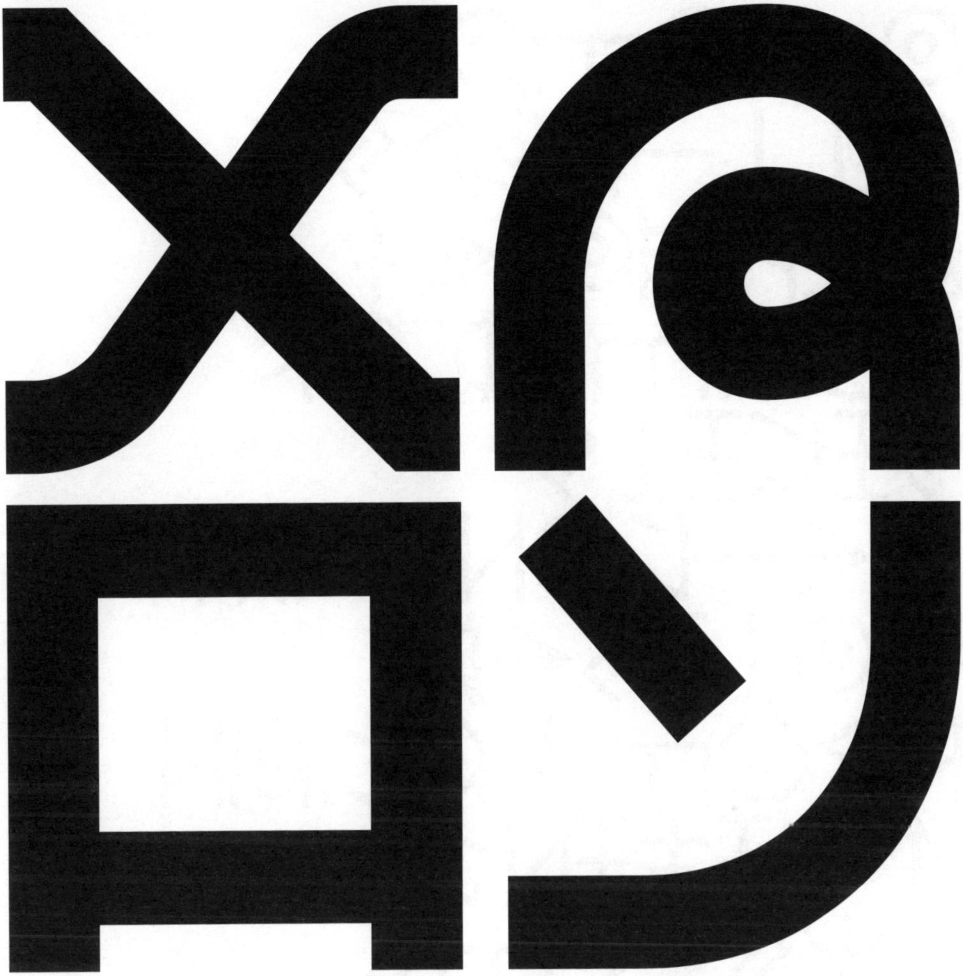

R.A+B

Xray

s. 175
l. 187
t. 75

A ROMAN
ALL—CAPS
ALPHABET
FORMED ON
SIGILS
RE—CONTEXT—
UALISED
FROM PAGAN
WRITING
SYSTEMS

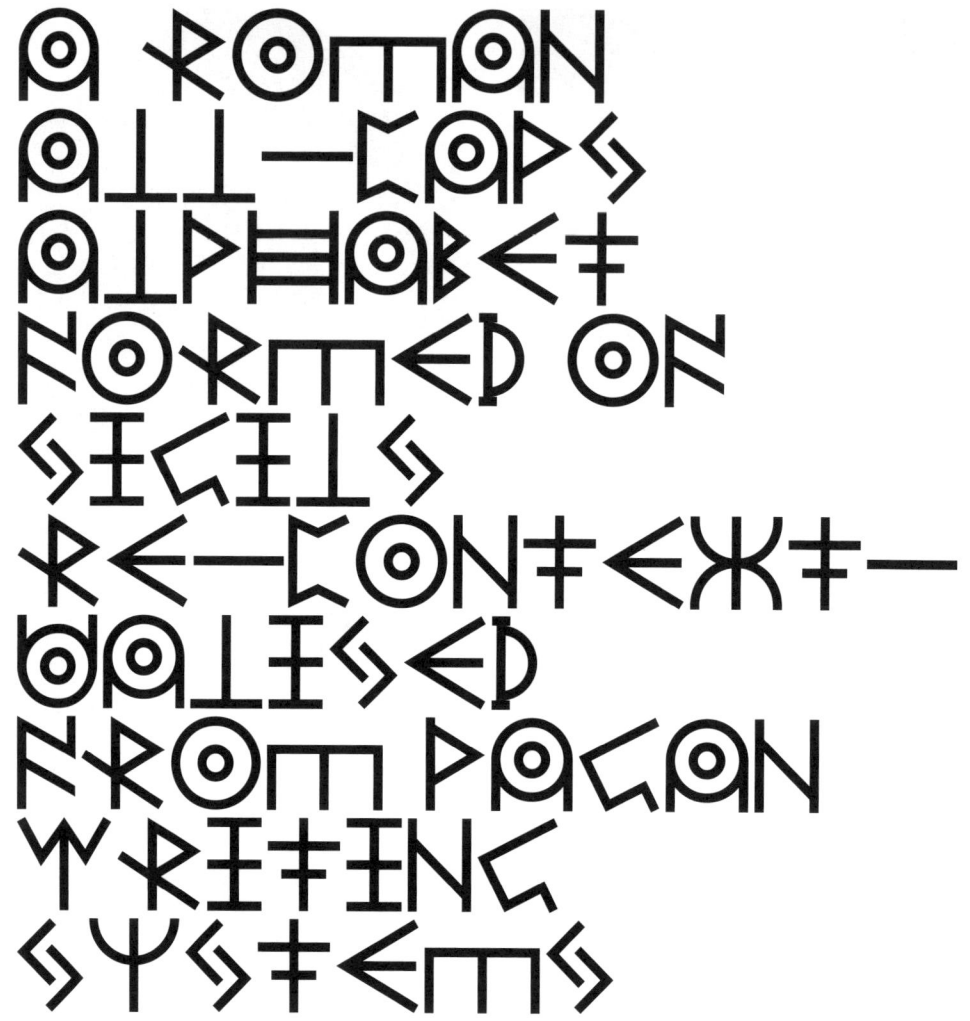

R.C A Roman All-caps alphabet formed of sigils recontextualised from Pagan writing systems

*

s. 35
l. 38
t. 10

R.C

A–Z

s. 66
l. 74
t. 50

TANGO
UNI-
FORM
ALPHA
LIMA

R.C

Tango Uniform Alpha Lima

s. 66
l. 74
t. 50

INDIA
SIE—
RRA
ECHO
DELTA

India Sierra Echo Delta

s. 66
l. 74
t. 50

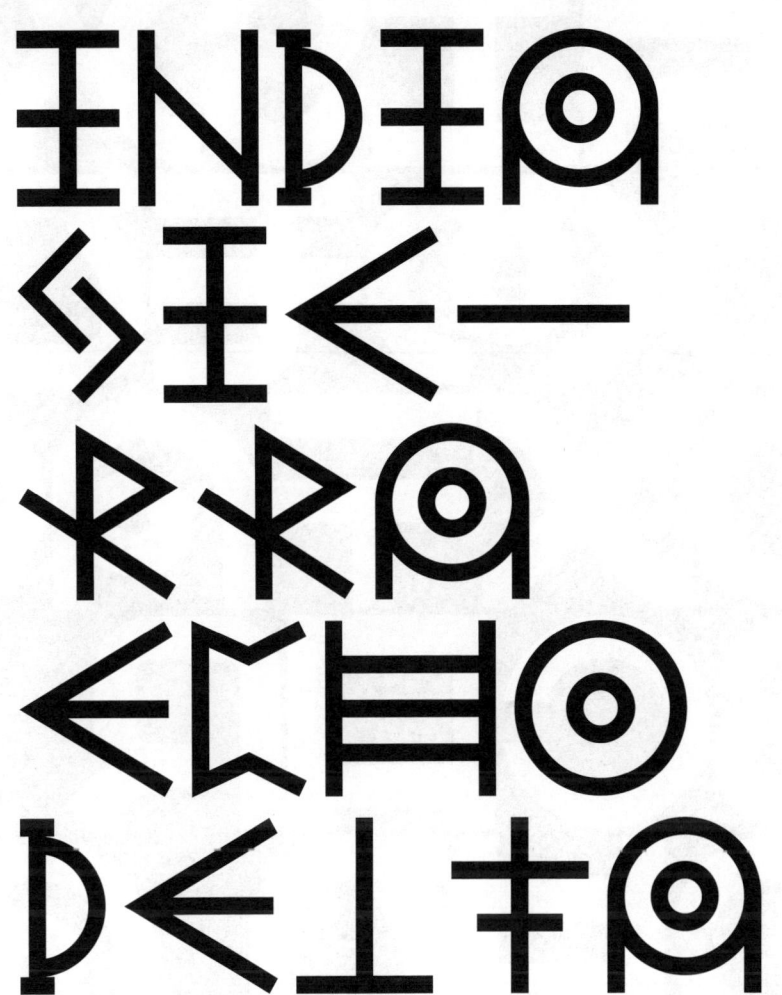

R Recontextualised

Section Notes:

All alphabets in Recontextualised were created using Glyphs. Each is a single-weight font containing only uppercase letters. Sourced and redrawn from various writing systems, their calligraphic features have been removed to create monoline forms, unifying them into cohesive alphabets. Below is a list of character origins.

*ancient/
not in current use

† sourced from *Pagan Sigils* MB Jackson (Green Magic, 2022)

R.A

A: Thai kho khwai
B: Malayalam bha
C: Burmese ng
D: Hebrew mem
E: Katakana mo
F: Armenian ben
G: Khmer tô
H: Korean yae
I: Chinese tŭ
J: Katakana u
K: Gujarati jha
L: Tamil ta
M: Malayam ta
N: Bermese la
O: Malayalam ṭha
P: Ge'ez y
Q: Tamil uw
R: Armenian t^{h}o
S: Malayalam ṭa
T: Katakana te
U: Tamil pa
V: Tibetan pa
W: Thai ph
X: Coptic kh/khi
Y: Katakana so
Z: Devanagari ṭ-

R.B

A: Chinese ZH kǒu
B: Latin h*
C: Hiragana ku
D: Chinese moon*
E: Tibetan zha
F: Kanji down
G: Bengali ḍhô
H: Ge'ez z
I: Kanji king
J: Arabic lam
K: Hiragana ni
L: Armenian lyan
M: Javanese ga
N: Hebrew aleph
O : Hebrew samek
P: Malayalam ḻa
Q: Malayalam u
R: Tibetan the
S: Khmer r
T: Chinese ZH ten
U: Thai kh/k
V: Greek Euboea khi*
W: Malayalam dha
X: Greek theta*
Y: Hebrew ayin
Z: Hiragana ro

R.C

A: Pictish I*†
B: Runic*†
C: Viking Runic Th*†
D: Runic*†
E: Runic*†
F: Runic Ac*†
G: Bardic Rune G*†
H: Runic*†
I: Etrustcan*†
J: Pictish J*†
K: Runic*†
L: Runic*†
M: Runic*†
N: Bardic U*†
O: Runic*†
P: Viking Runic W*†
Q: Adulrunen M*†
R: Runic safe travel*†
S: Ur-Runen J*†
T: Etruscan Z*†
U: Pictish U*†
V: Pecti Wita U*†
W: Runic Ear*†
X: Runic*†
Y: Galdrastafir energy*†
Z: Runic*†

A series of experimental alphabets investigating how disruption, distortion, and irregularity can generate foundations for letterforms. Each alphabet begins with a core structural element that is split, shifted, mirrored, fragmented or partially eliminated, revealing the underlying architecture of each character. Legibility emerges either by discerning the anomalies that disrupt the anticipated pattern or through an understanding of the overarching system.

S.A An all-caps shifting pattern alphabet formed of a shifted hazard stripe pattern*

*

s. 32
l. 32
t. 0

S.A

Golf

s. 184
l. 184
t. 0

S.B An all-caps shifting pattern alphabet formed of a shifted square grid pattern*

Papa

s. 189
l. 189
t. 0

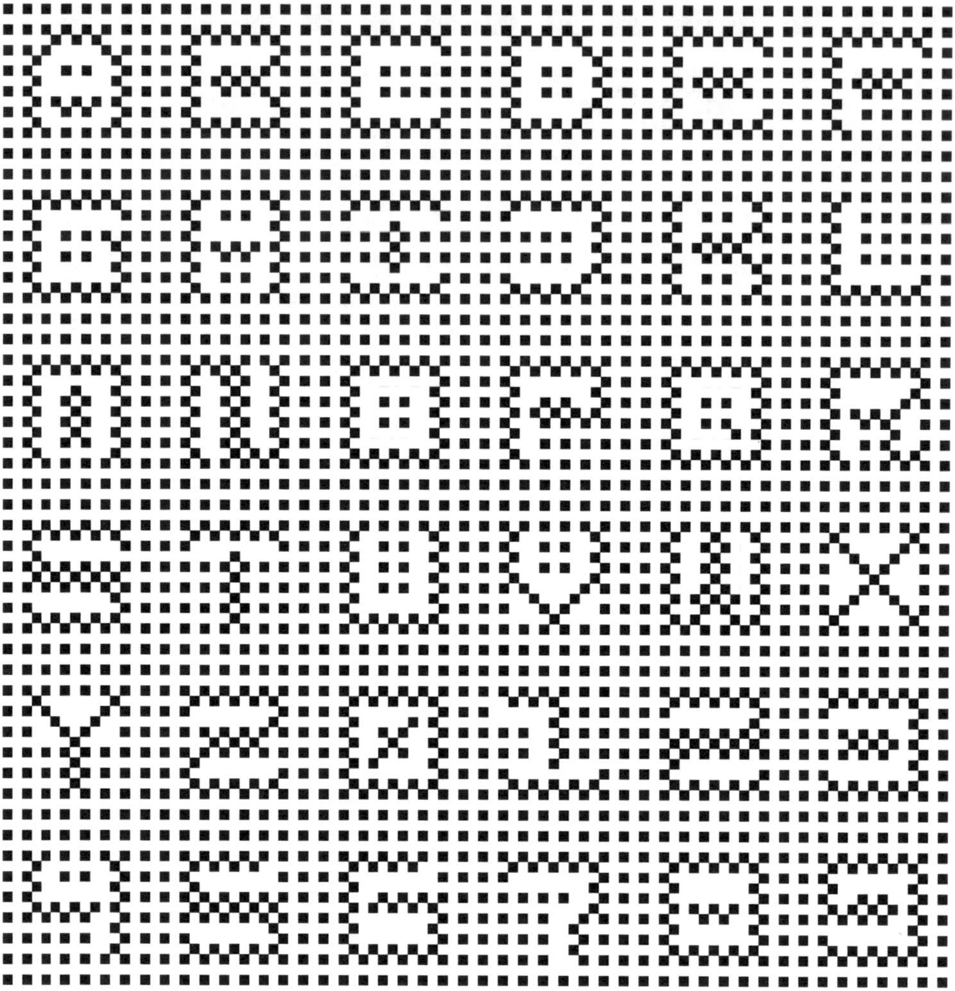

S.B

A–Z 0–9

s. 62
l. 62
t. 0

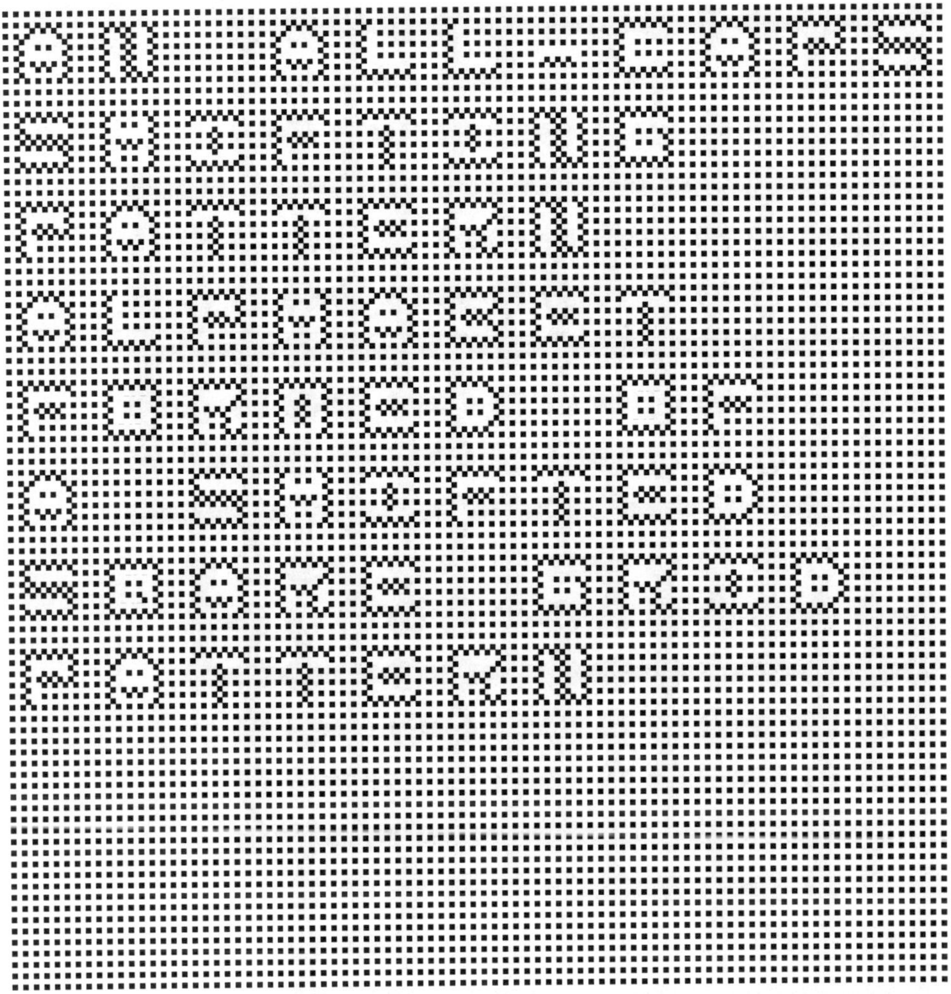

S.B

*

s. 33
l. 33
t. 0

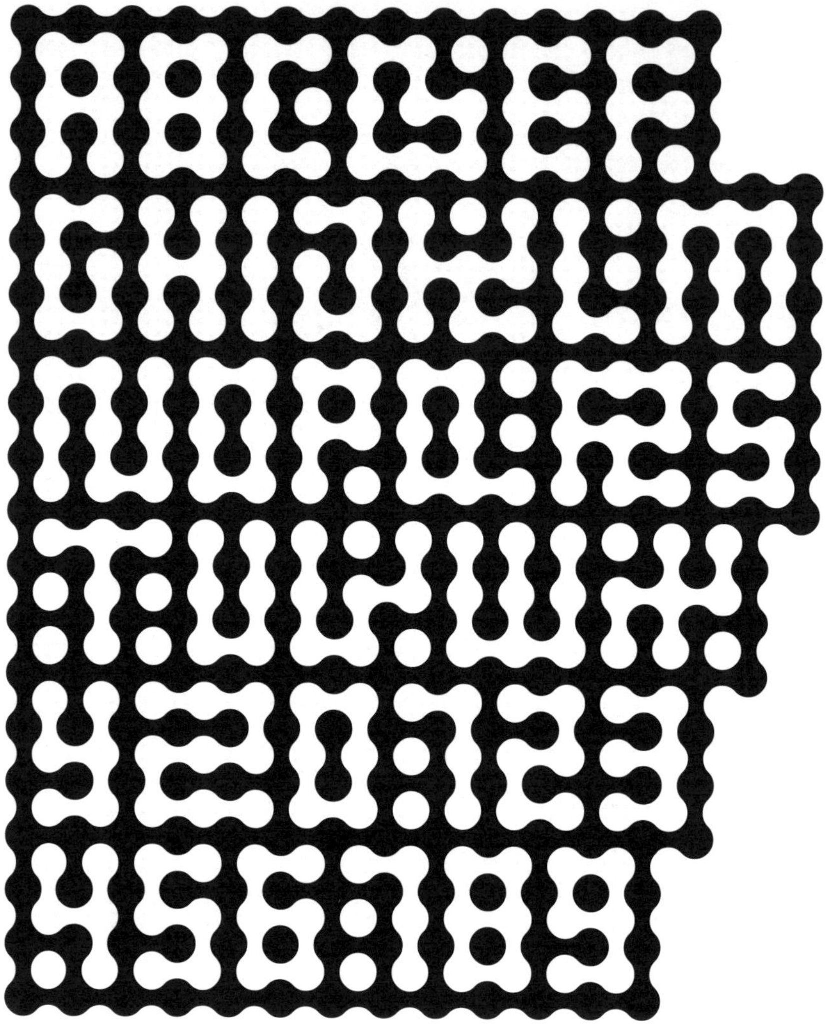

S.C A shifting pattern alphabet formed of a rounded diagonal chequerboard pattern

A–Z 0–9

s. 81
l. 61
t. 0
w. 100

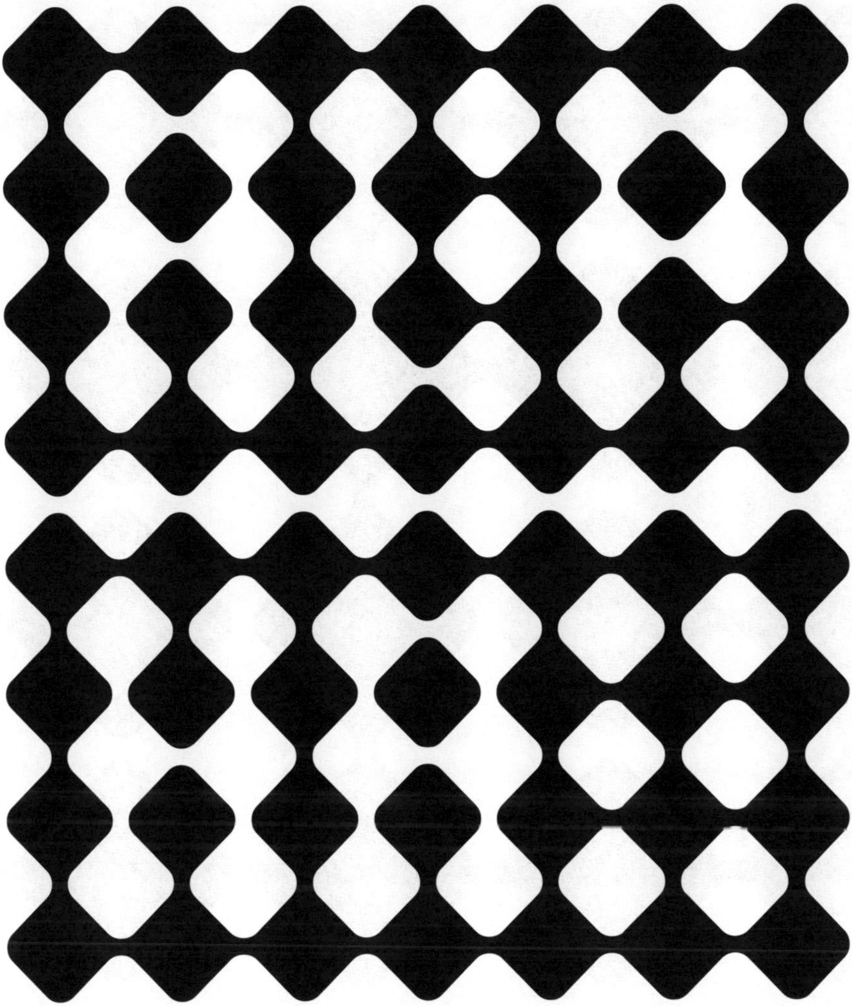

S.C

Alpha

s. 190
l. 190
t. 0
w. 550

S.C

529

s. 377
l. 377
t. 0
w. 700

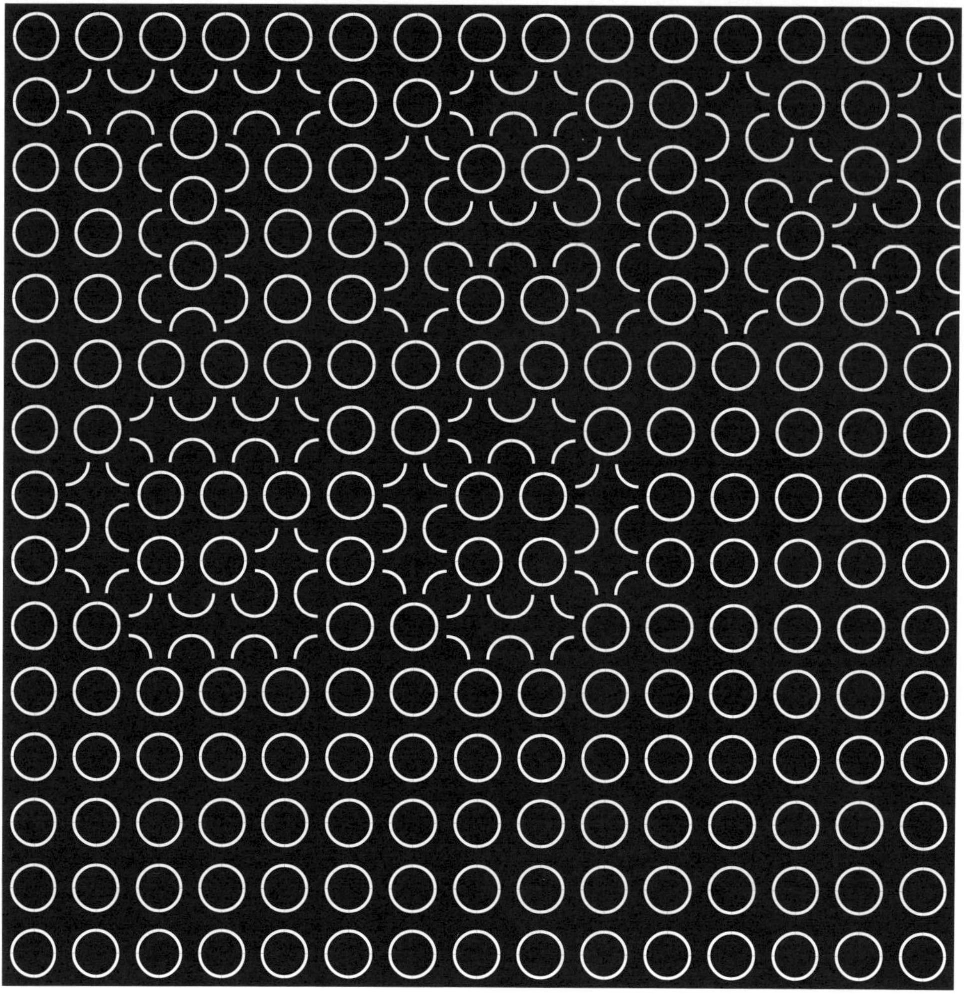

S.D A shifting pattern alphabet formed of a rotated quarter circle pattern

Tango

s. 123
l. 123
t. 0
w. 250
wd.900

S.D

Tango

s. 123
l. 123
t. 0
w. 900
wd. 100

S.D

A–Z 0–9

s. 61
l. 61
t. 0
w. 500
wd.900

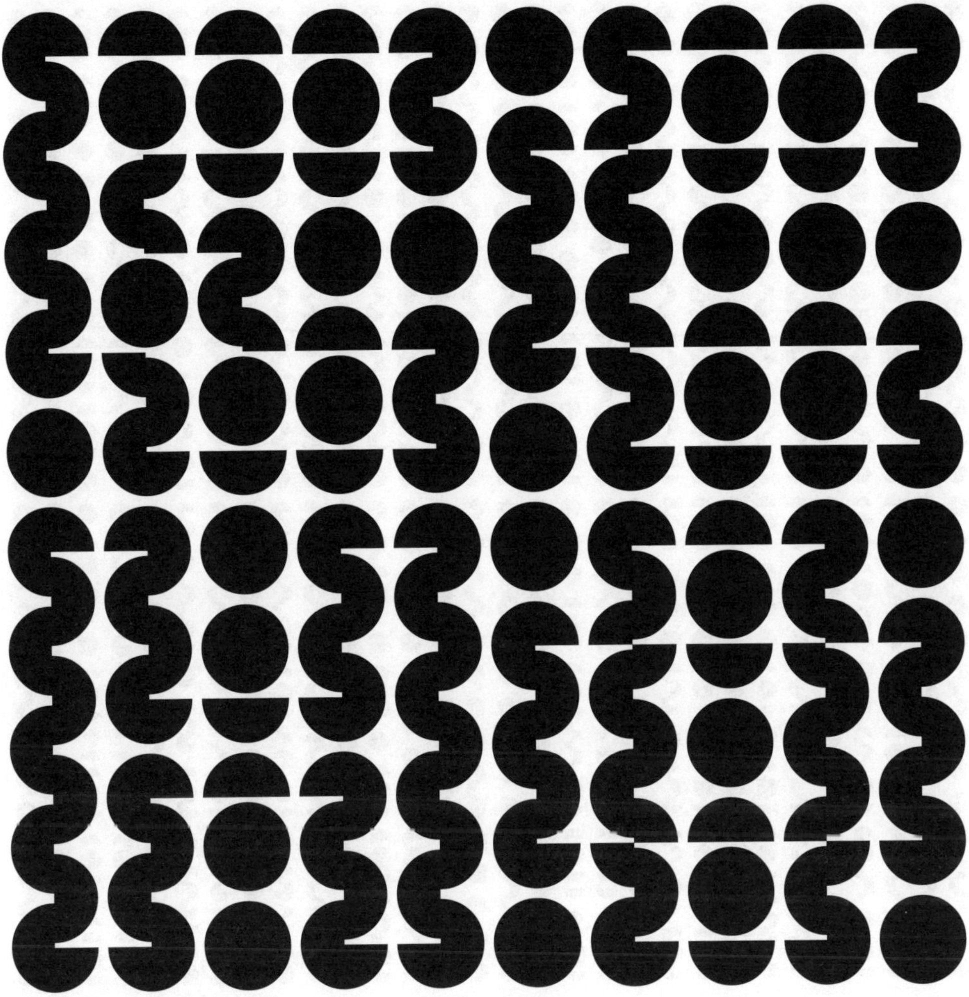

S.E A shifting pattern alphabet formed of a shifted dot pattern

Echo

s. 168
l. 168
t. 0
w. 900

S.E

A–Z 0–9

s. 62
l. 62
t. 0
w. 400

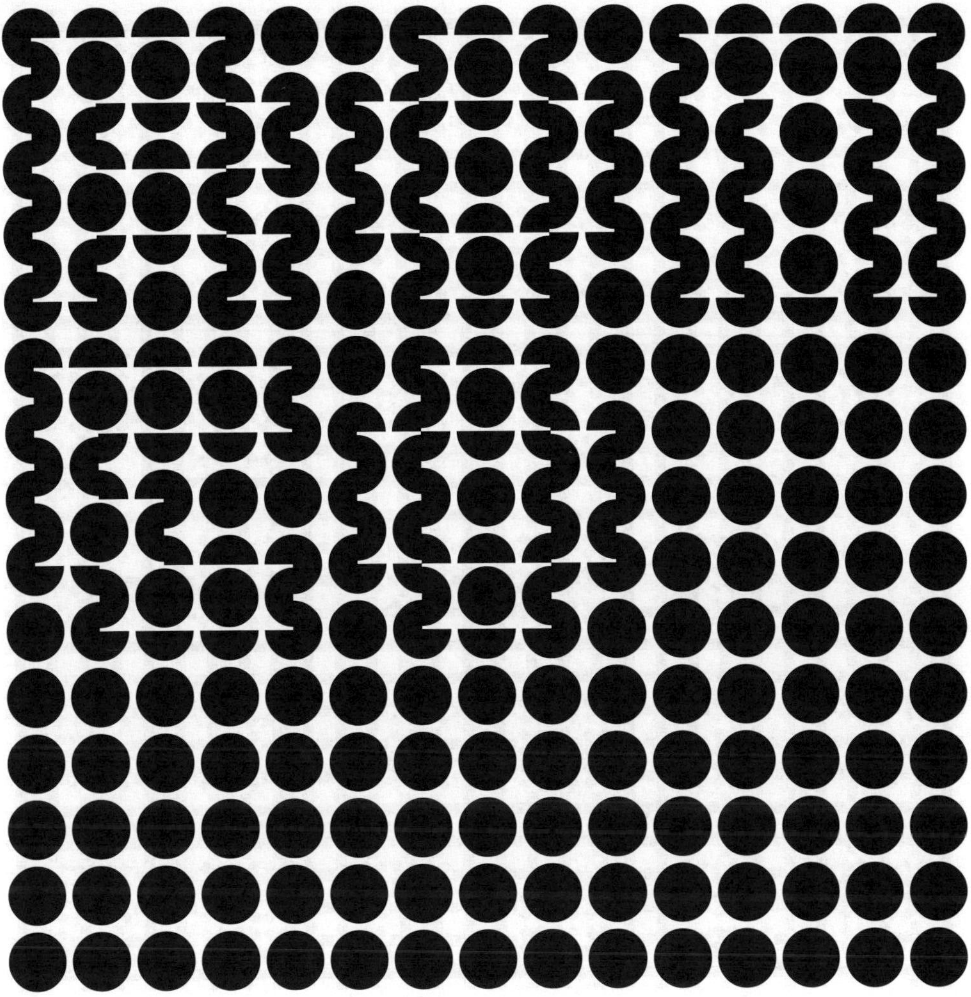

S.E

Romeo

s. 124
l. 124
t. 0
w. 900

S.F A shifting pattern alphabet formed of a rotated cross pattern

A–Z 0–9

s. 61
l. 61
t. 0
w. 900
wd.900

S.F

November

s. 123
l. 123
t. 0
w. 100
wd.900

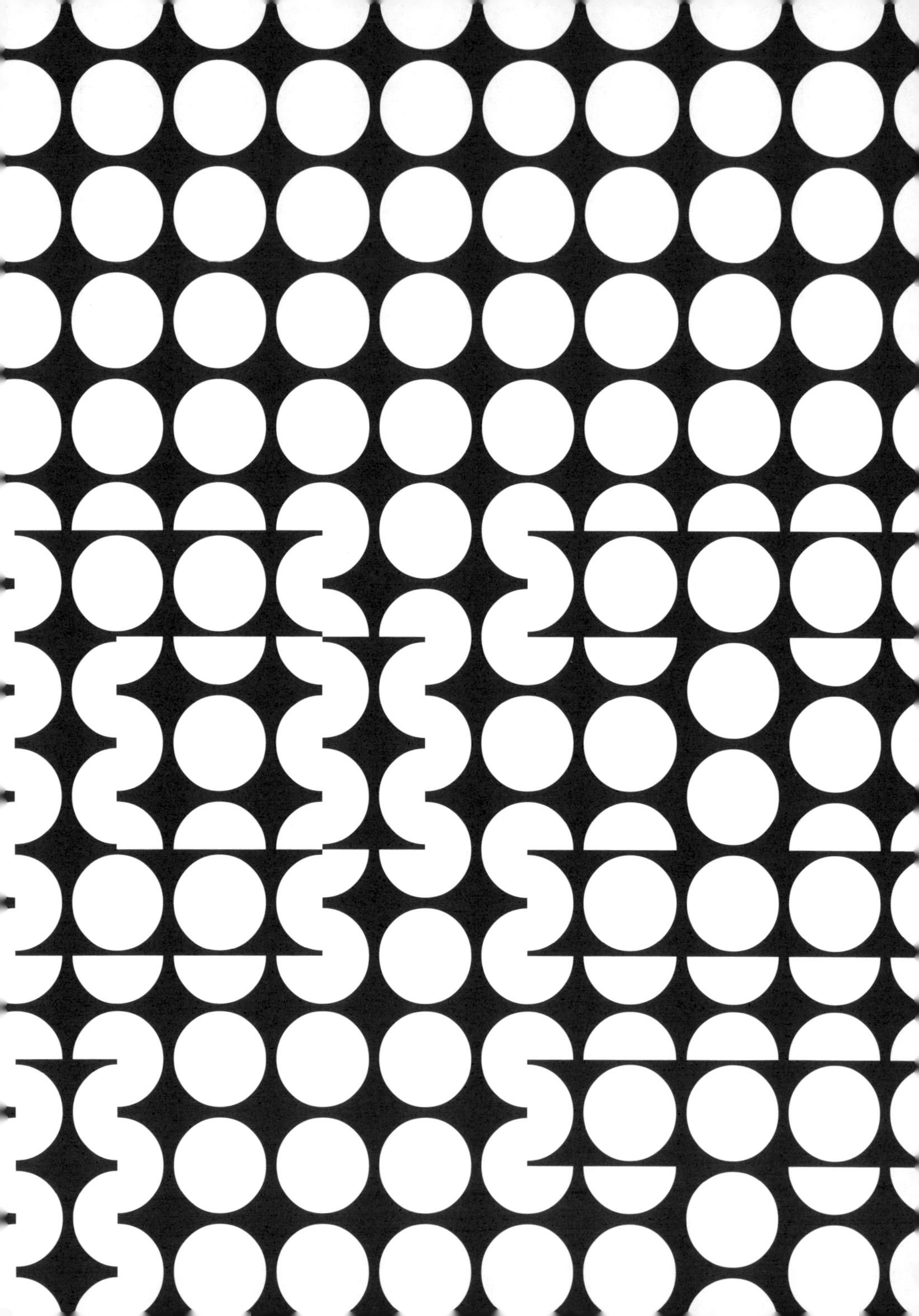

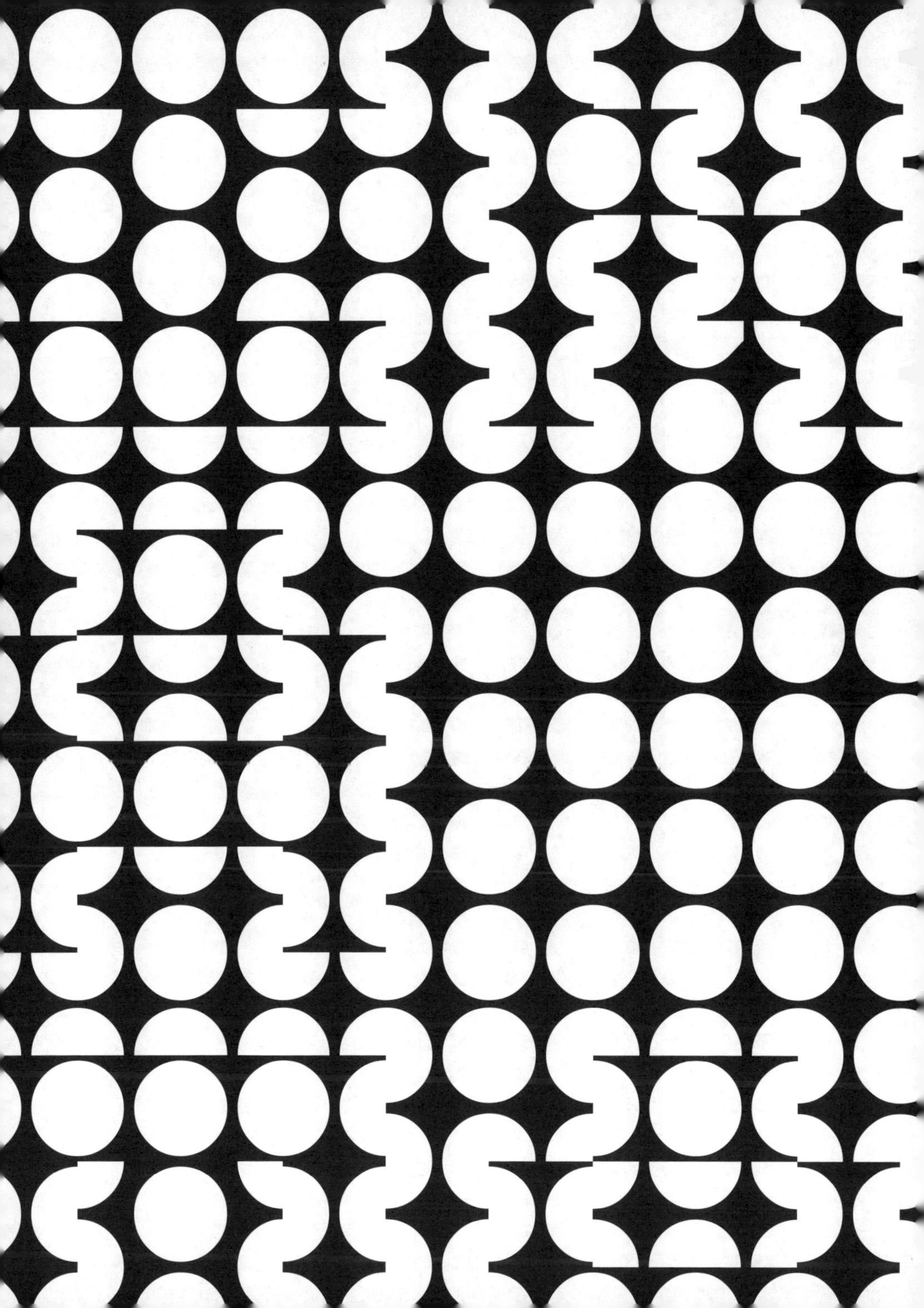

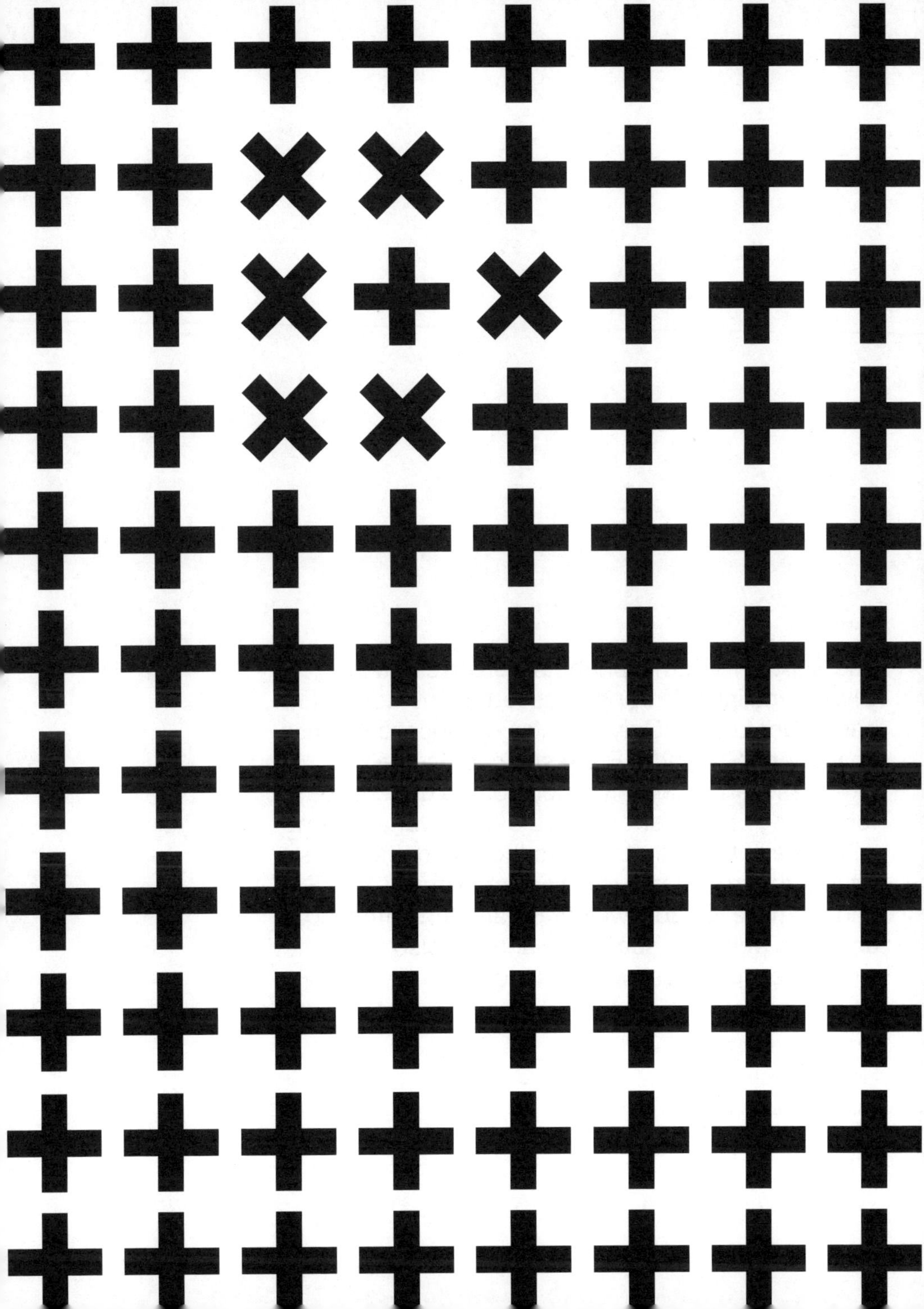

Section Notes:

The Shifted Pattern alphabets were created in Glyphs and include uppercase letters, numerals, and basic punctuation. Only S.C also includes lowercase characters. S.A and S.B are static fonts; in S.A, lowercase letters are inversions of the uppercase set for varying character contrast. S.C is a variable font with a weight axis that adjusts the roundness of its chequerboard pattern to reveal letterforms. S.D, S.E, and S.F have variable weight parameters affecting unit form weight or scale; S.D and S.F also feature width axes for adjusting unit spacing.

S.A has been redrawn from Process-Pattern Hazard Alphabet released in 2020
S.C has been redrawn from Process-Pattern Clandestine Polka-dot Variable released in 2024

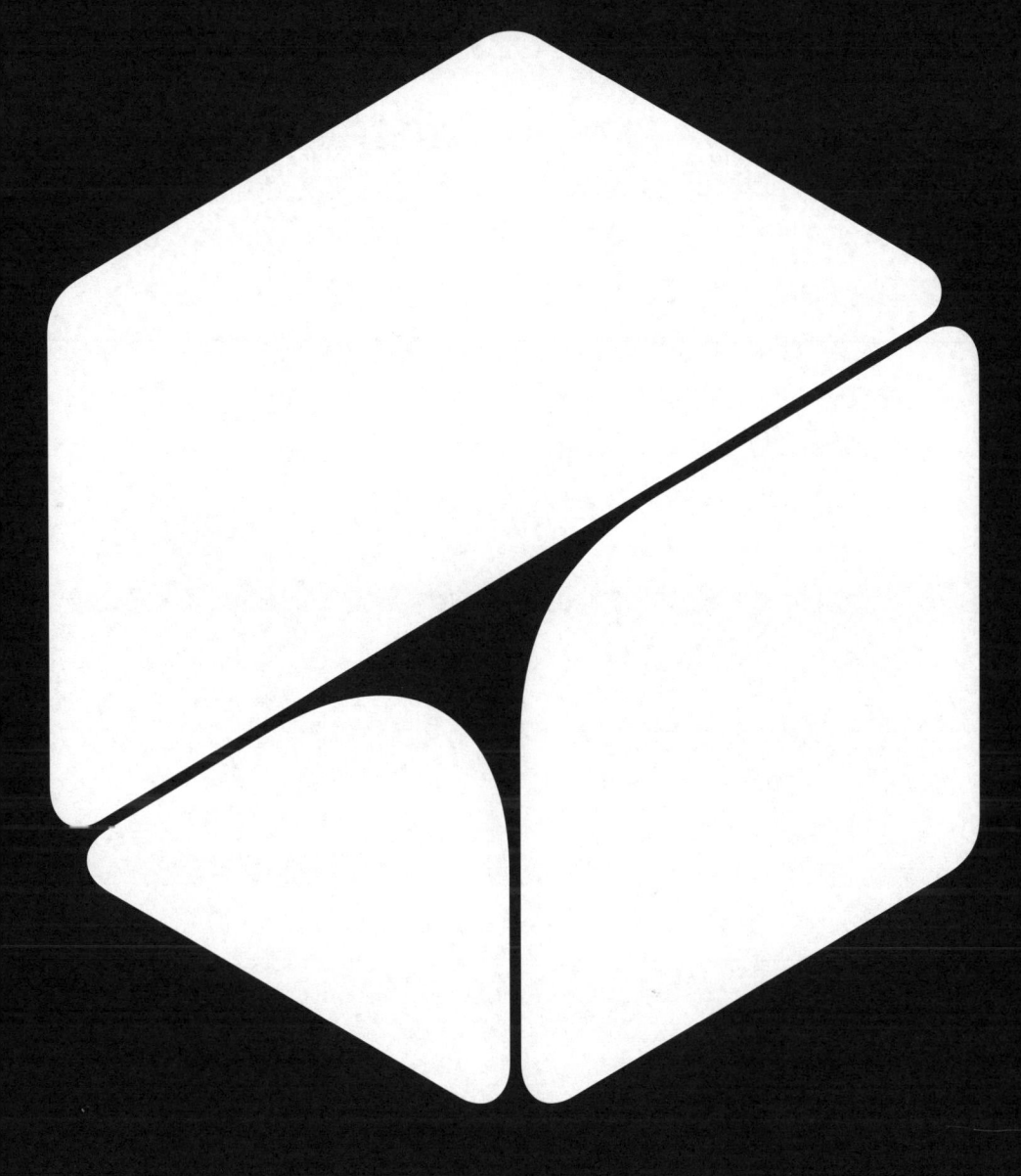

T Tessellation

A set of type systems designed to tessellate, fitting together seamlessly within a hexagonal grid. Each letterform is built from discreet segments of the base hexagon, allowing for a variety of visual expressions within a consistent modular system. The system also features inverted versions of each alphabet, where letterforms are defined by the negative space around and within them, subverting text into a rhythmic, pattern-like structure.

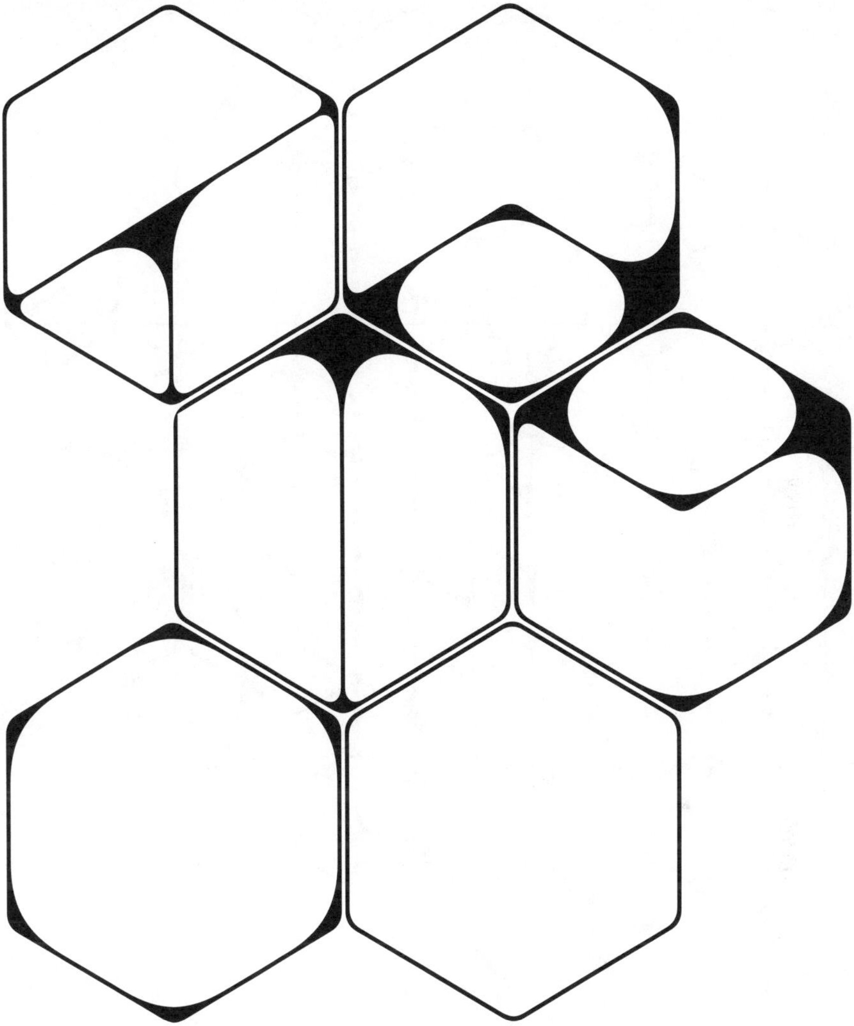

T.A A tessellating type system formed of hexagonal letterforms

Tango

s. 116
l. 116
t. 0

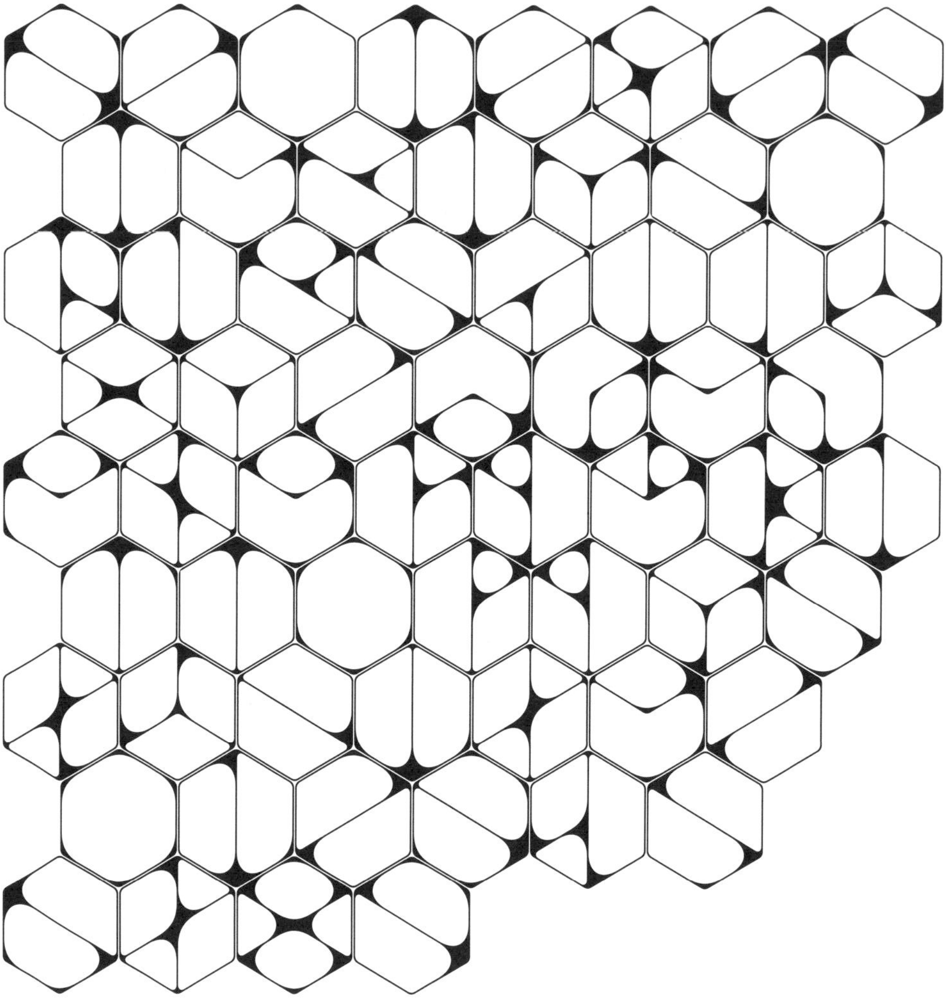

T.A

A-Z a-z 0-9

s. 40
l. 40
t. 0

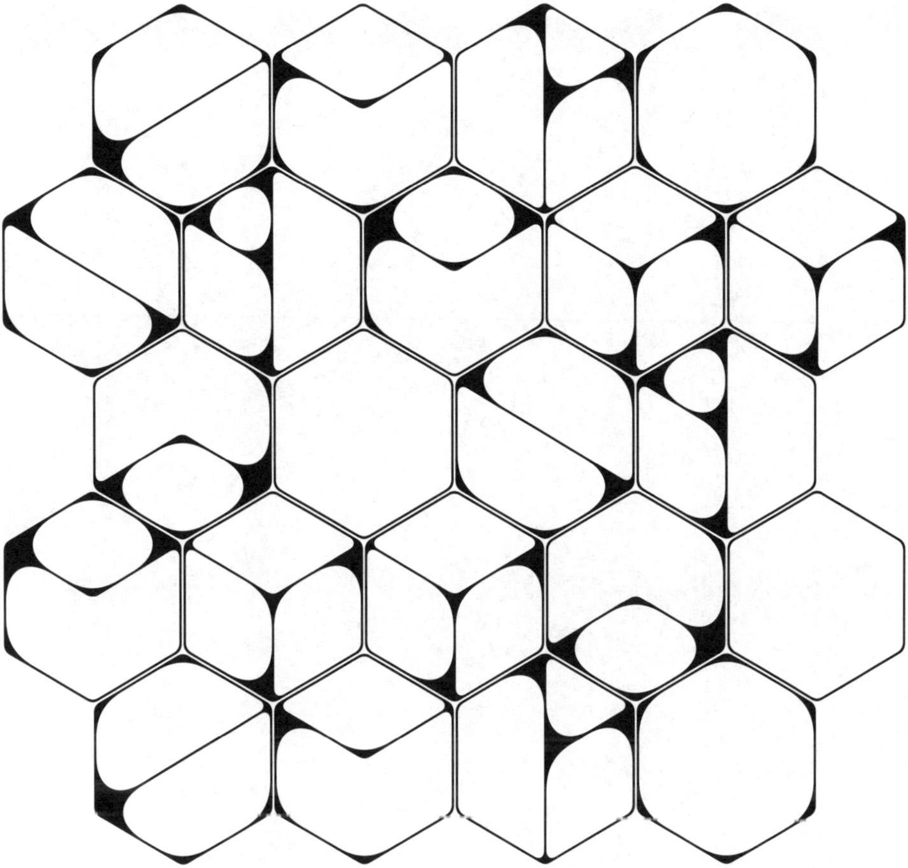

T.A

Echo Sierra
Sierra Echo

s. 61
l. 61
t. 0

T.B	A negative space tessellating type system formed of hexagonal letterforms	A-Z a-z 0-9	s. 40 l. 40 t. 0

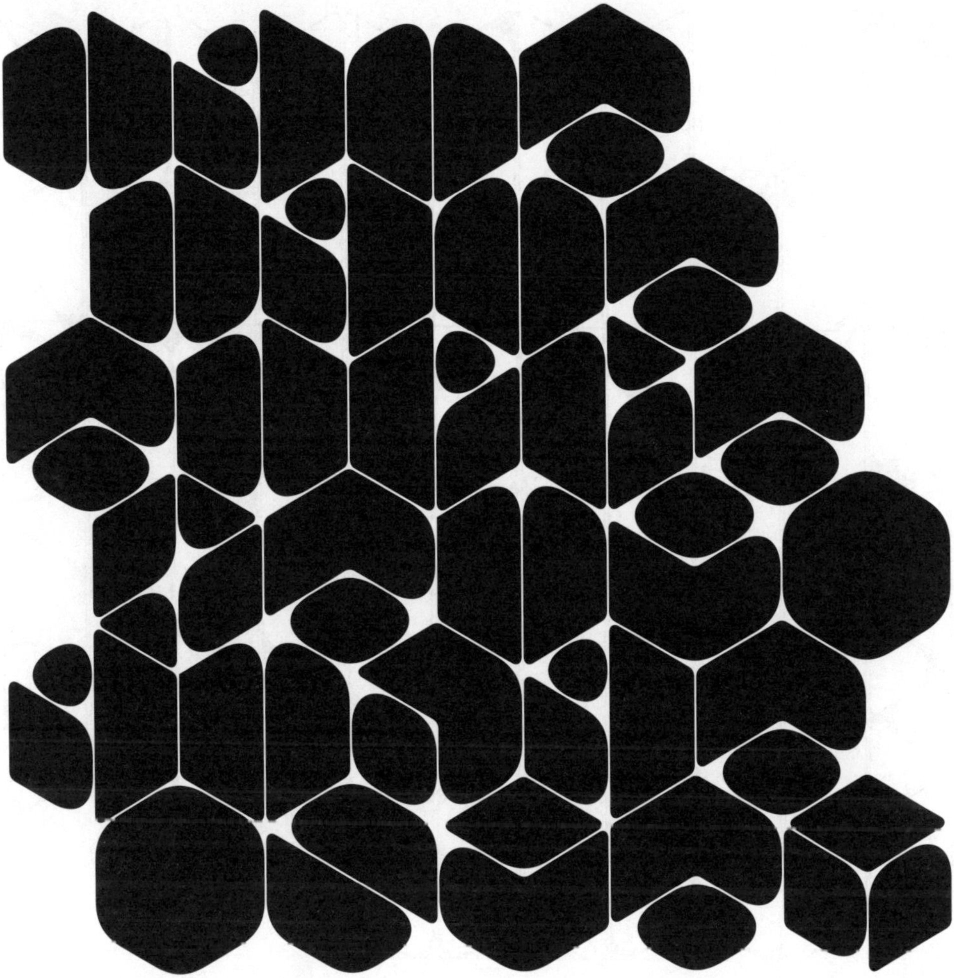

T.B

Lima Lima Alpha
Tango India Oscar

s. 58
l. 58
t. 0

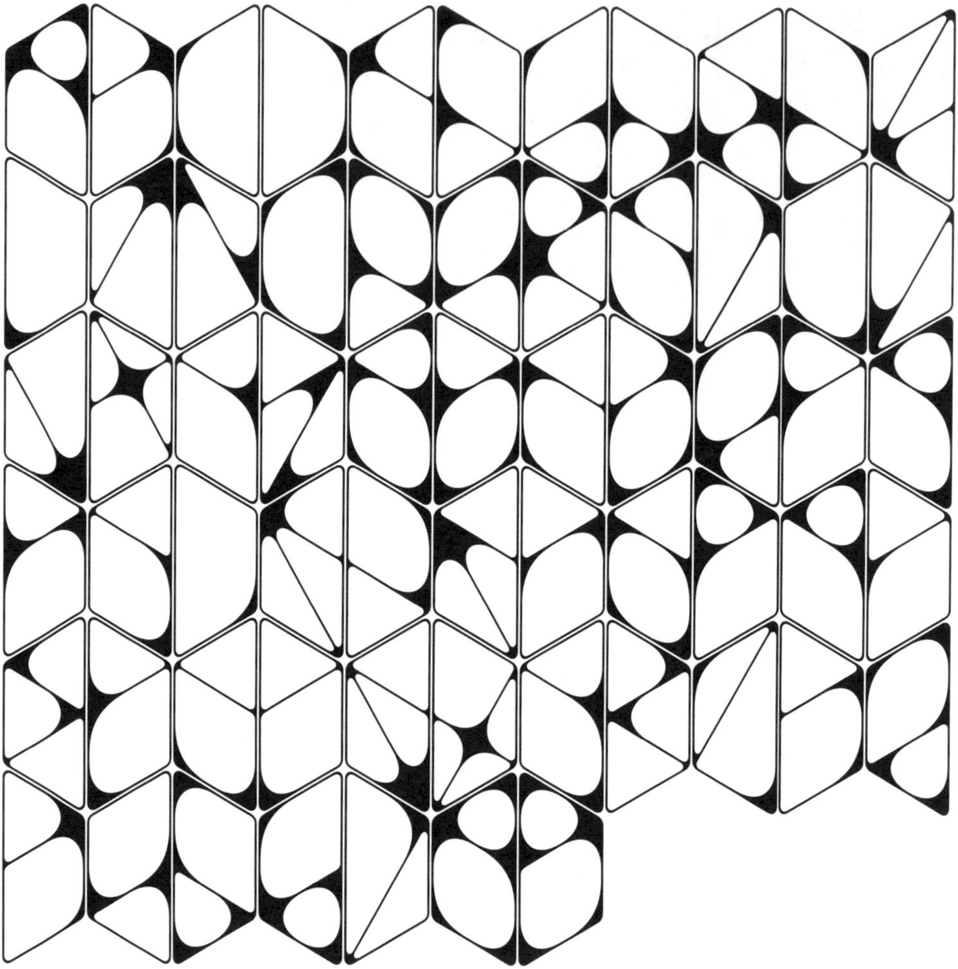

T.C A tessellating type system formed of trapezoid letterforms on a hexagonal grid

A-Z a-z 0-9

s. 58
l. 58
t. 0

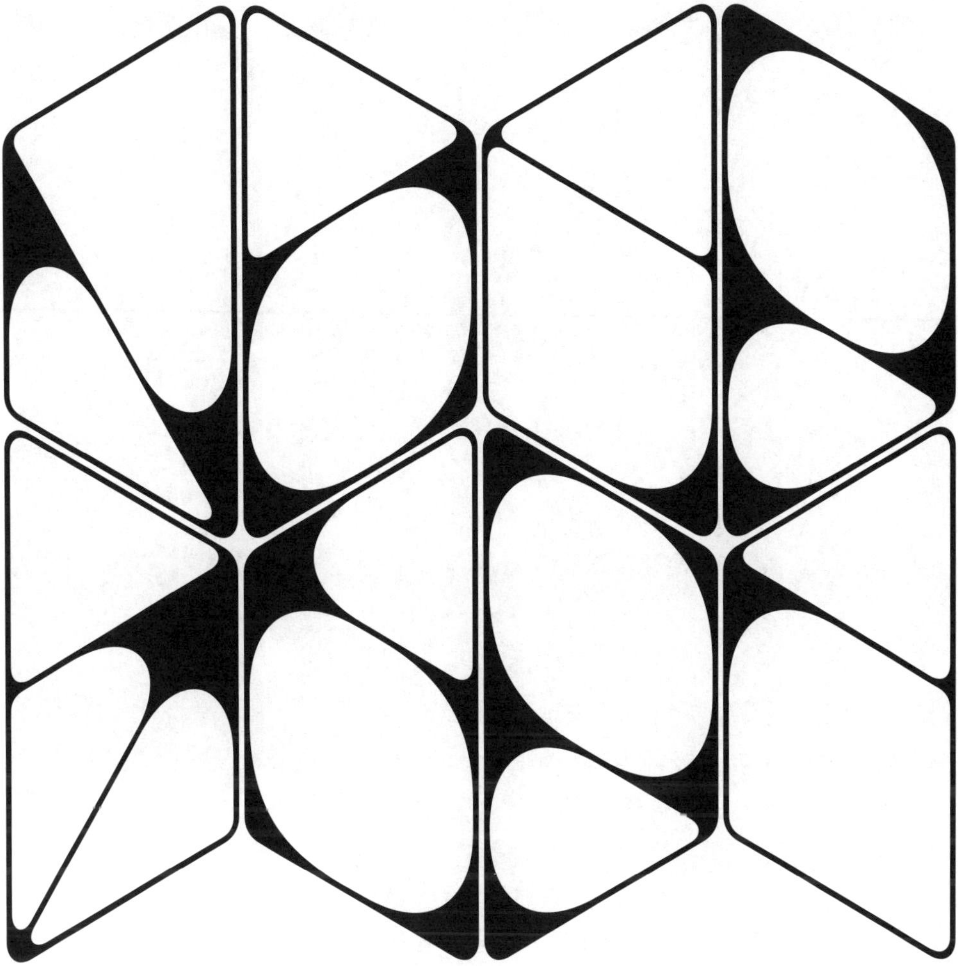

T.C

November

s. 158
l. 158
t. 0

T.D

A negative space tessellating type system formed of trapezoid letterforms on a hexagonal grid

A-Z a-z 0-9

s. 58
l. 58
t. 0

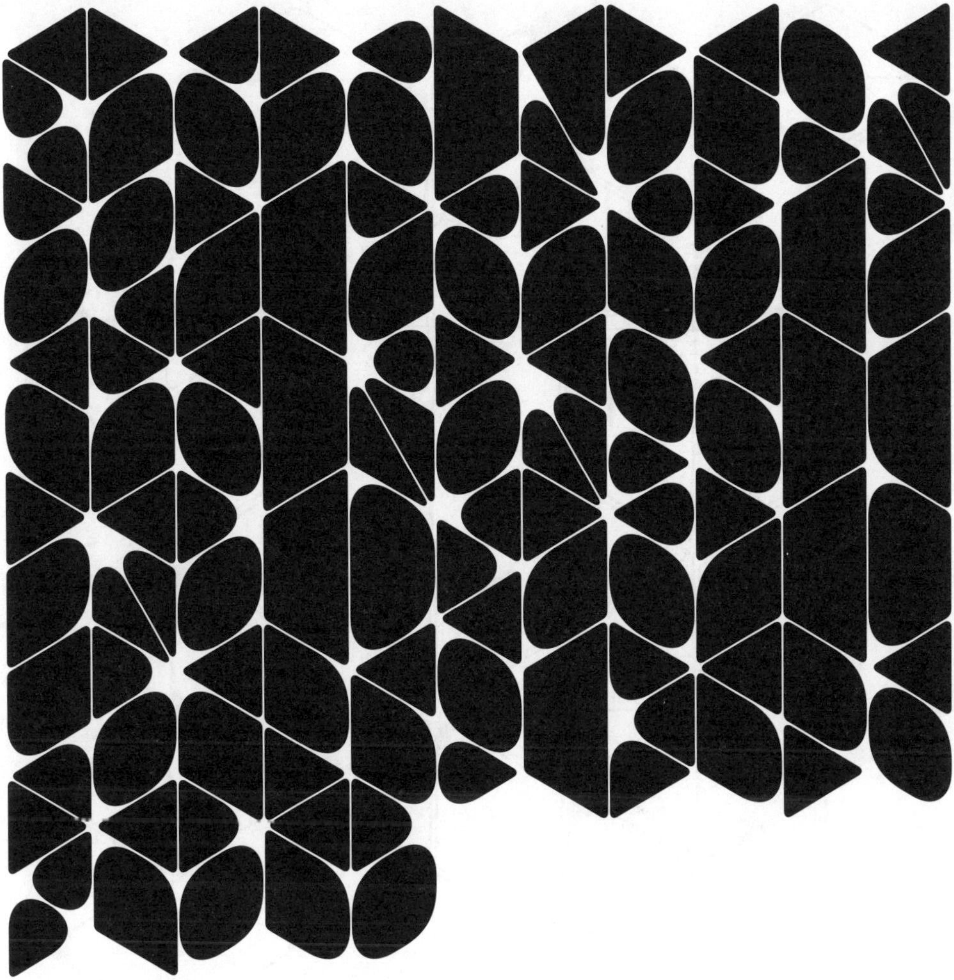

T.D

India November
Tango Echo Romeo
Lima Oscar Charlie
Kilo India

s. 58
l. 58
t. 0

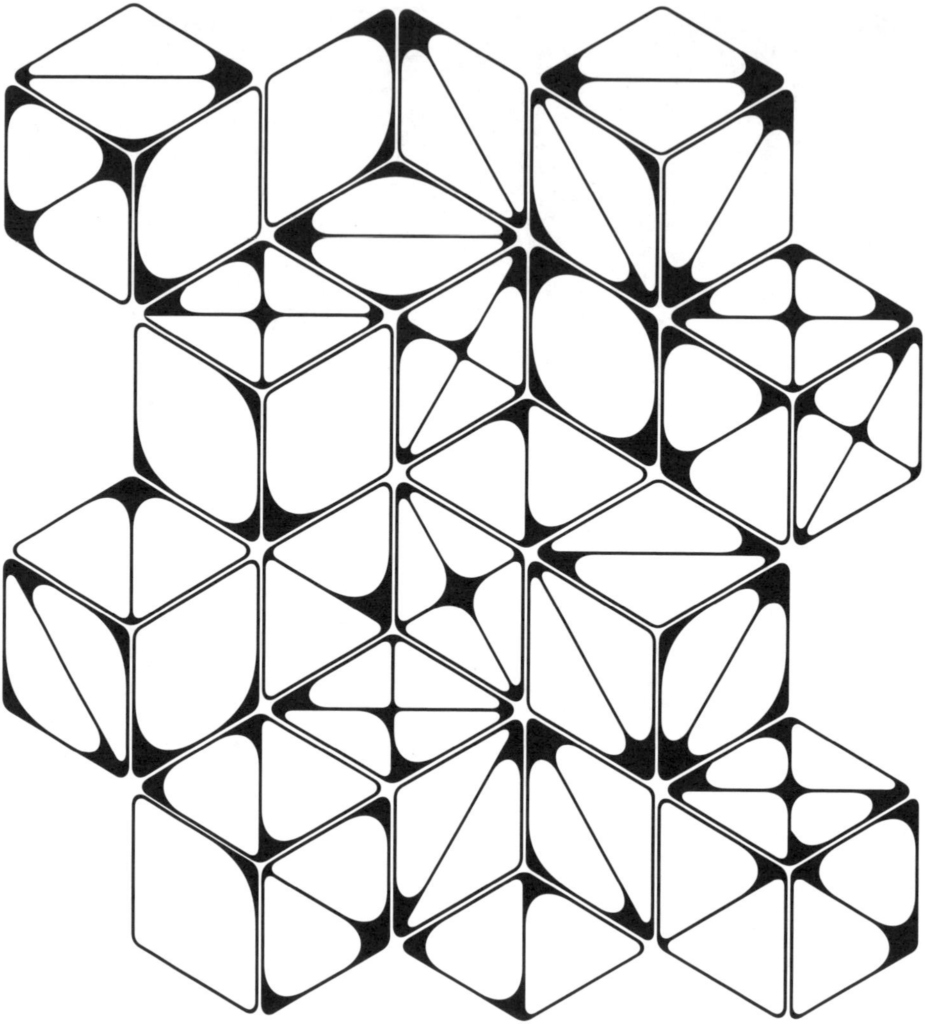

T.E A tessellating type system formed of rhombus letterforms on a hexagonal grid

A-Z 0-9

s. 86
l. 86
t. 0

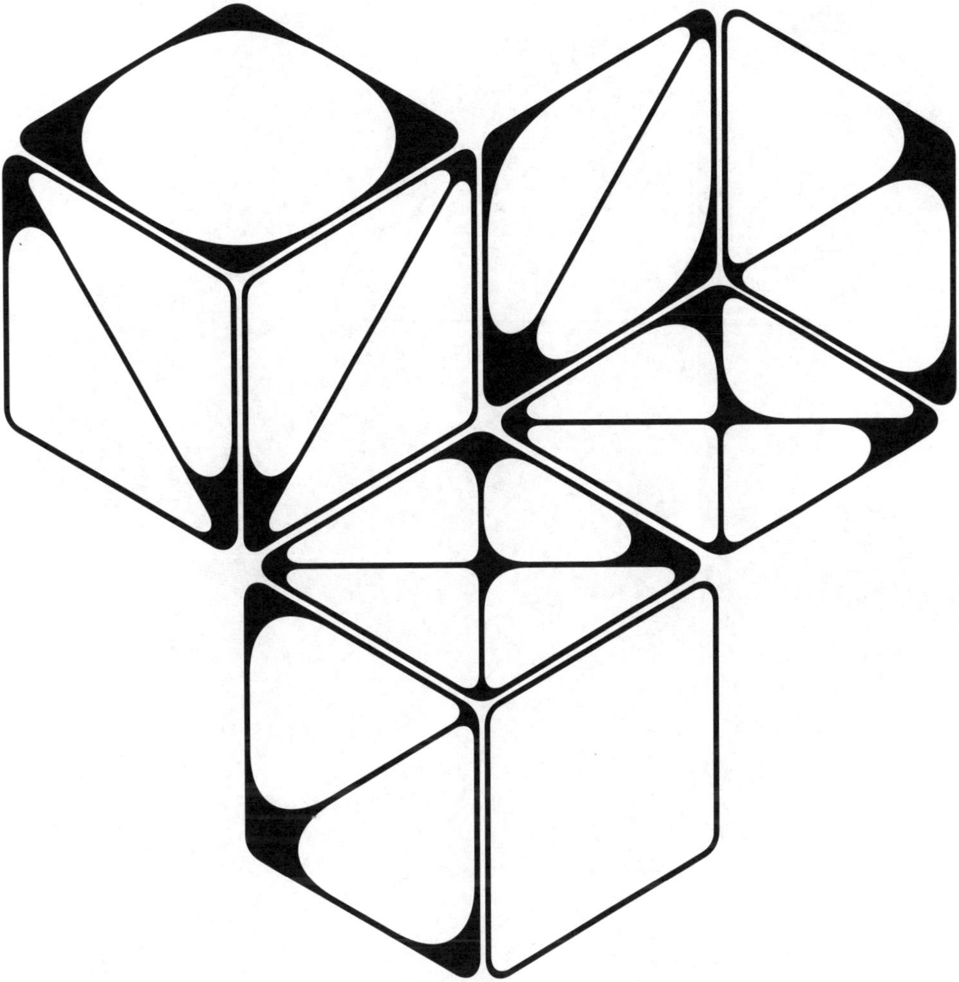

T.E

November

s. 158
l. 158
t. 0

T.F

A negative space tessellating type system formed of rhombus letterforms on a hexagonal grid

A-Z a-z 0-9

s. 88
l. 88
t. 0

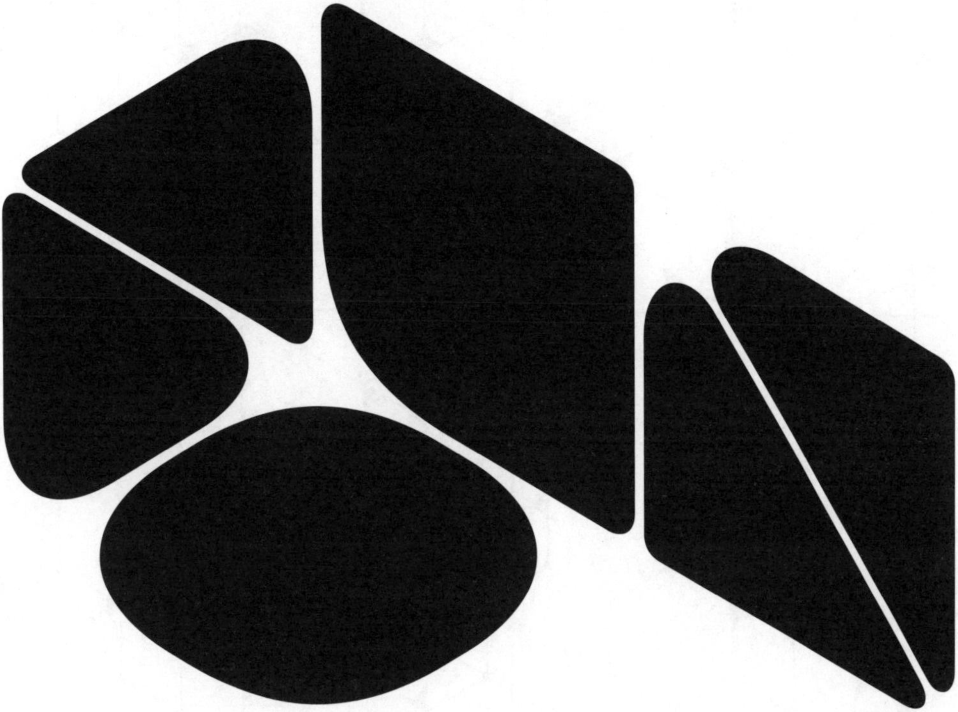

T.F

Golf

s. 213
l. 213
t. 0

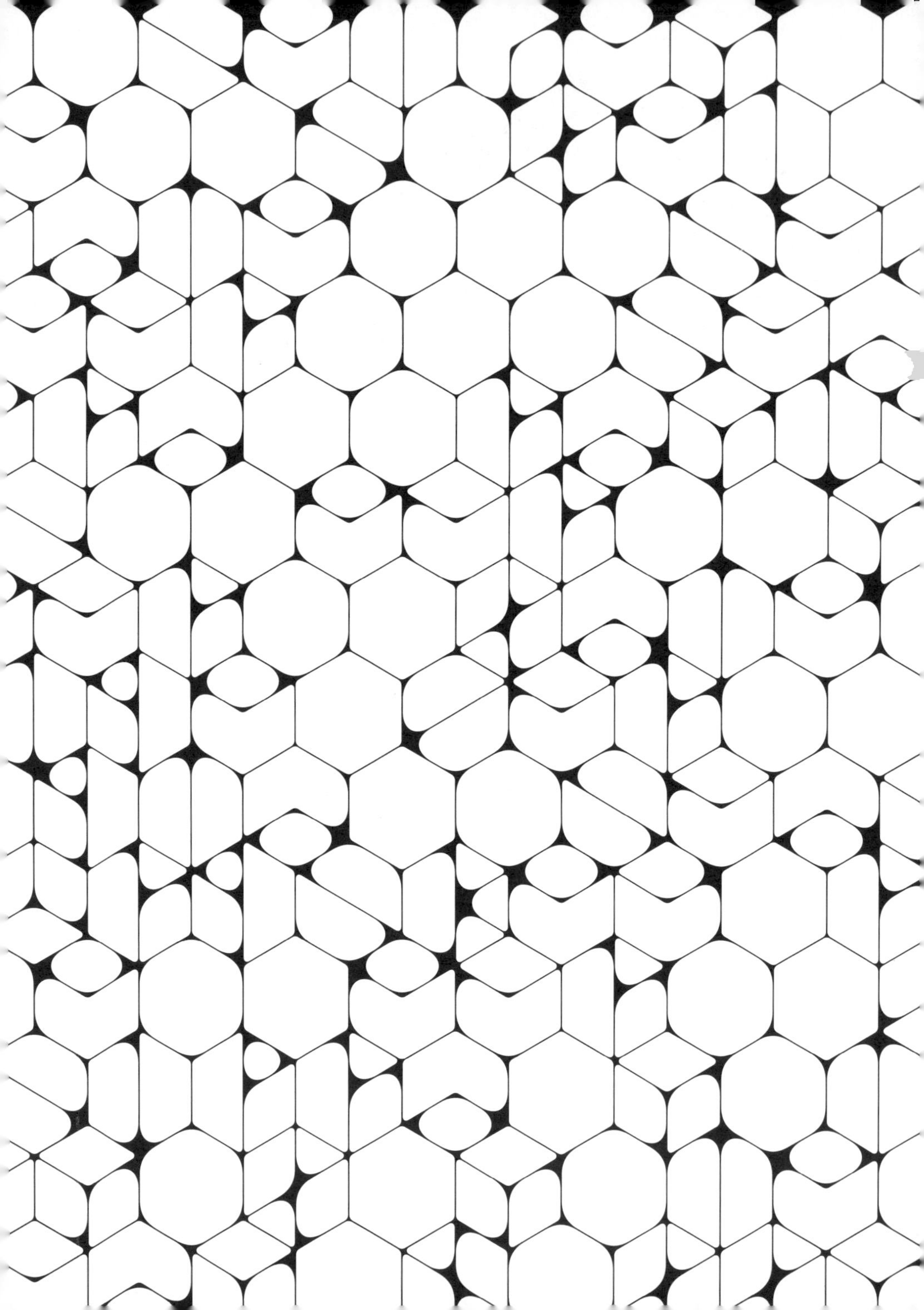

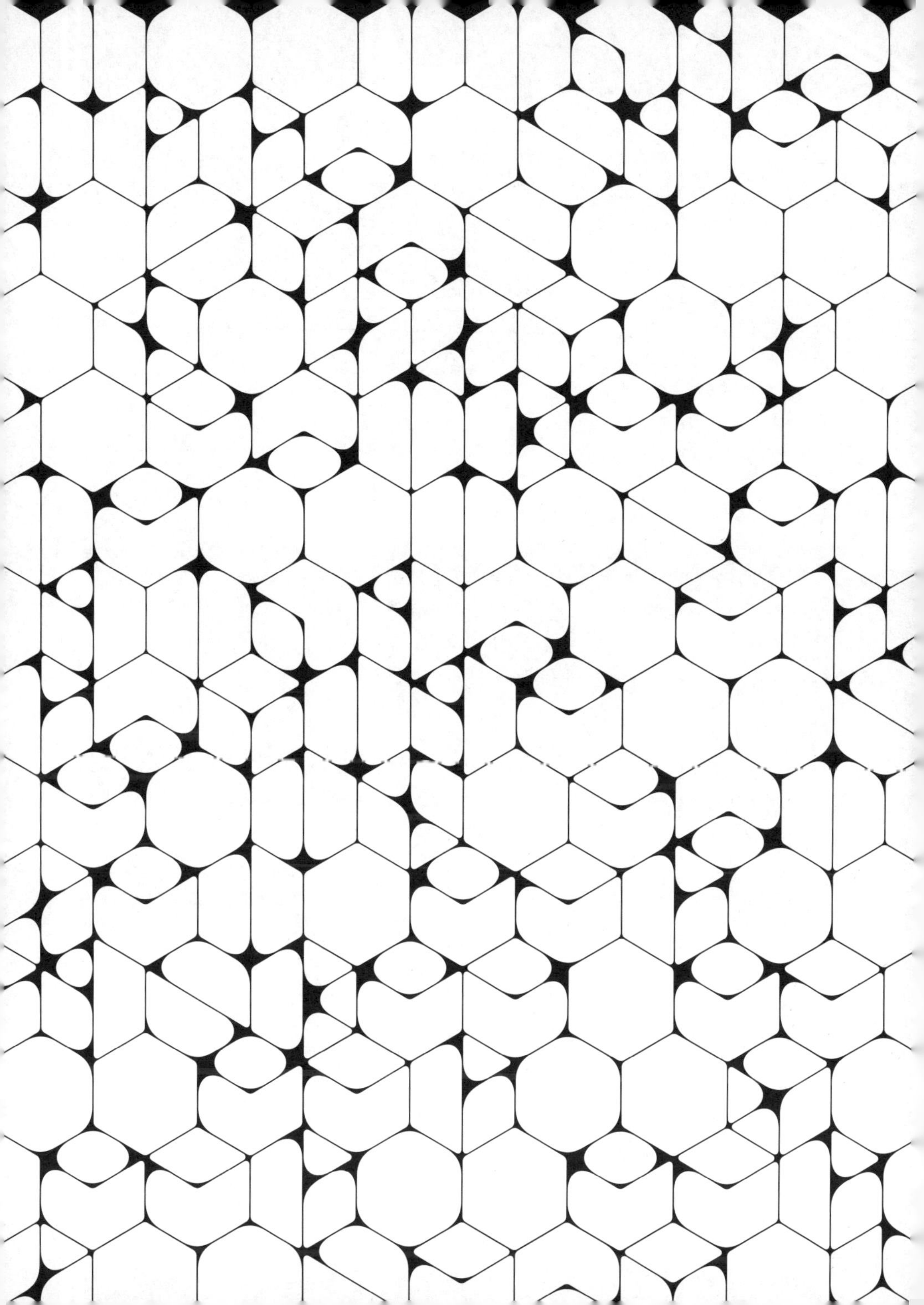

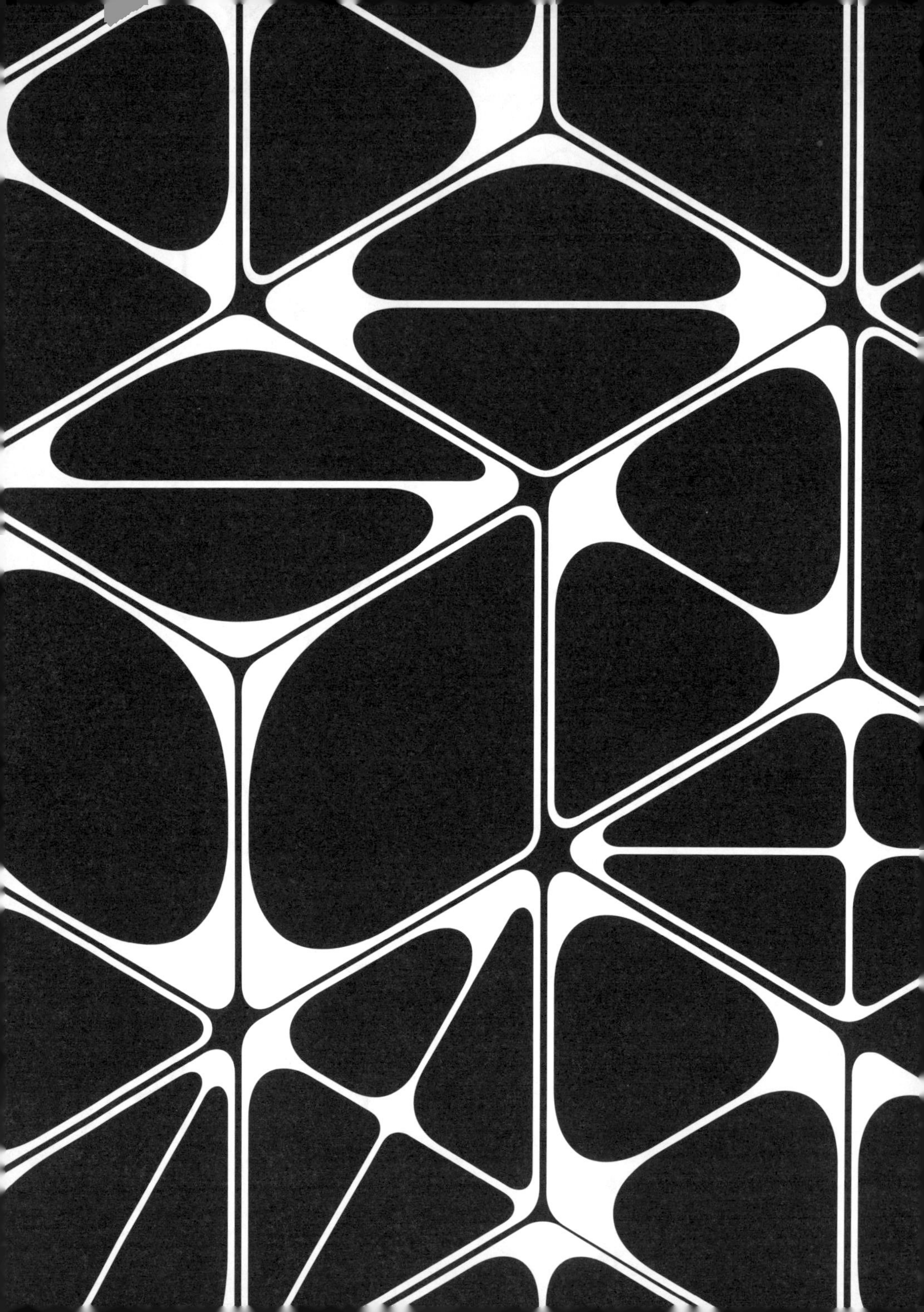

T Tessellation

T Tessellation

Section Notes:

All Tessellated alphabets were created in Glyphs as static fonts and include uppercase letters, numerals, and basic punctuation. Only T.A also includes lowercase characters. T.C and T.D feature two stylistic sets and contextual alternates that alternate the left and right sides of the hexagonal unit from character to character. T.E and T.F offer six stylistic sets, enabling segments of two alternative hexagonal perspectives to form sides within text.

The Ultra system comprises three alphabets that extend to the outermost limits of traditional typographic weight and width classifications. The set includes an Ultra-Black, an Ultra-Hairline, and an Ultra-Condensed variant. Each design serves as an extreme exaggeration of its respective class, intended to exceed the structural limits of conventional typographic systems.

UNIFORM

U.A An extreme ultra-black sans serif alphabet

Uniform

s. 90
l. 74
t. 0
w. 600

UC

ABCD
EFGH
IJKL
MN
OPQR
STUV
WX
YZ,/?

U.A

A–Z,/?

s. 54
l. 44
t. 0
w. 600

abcde
fghijk
lmnop
qrstu
vwx
yz012
345
6789

U.A

a–z 0–9

s. 54
l. 44
t. 0
w. 600

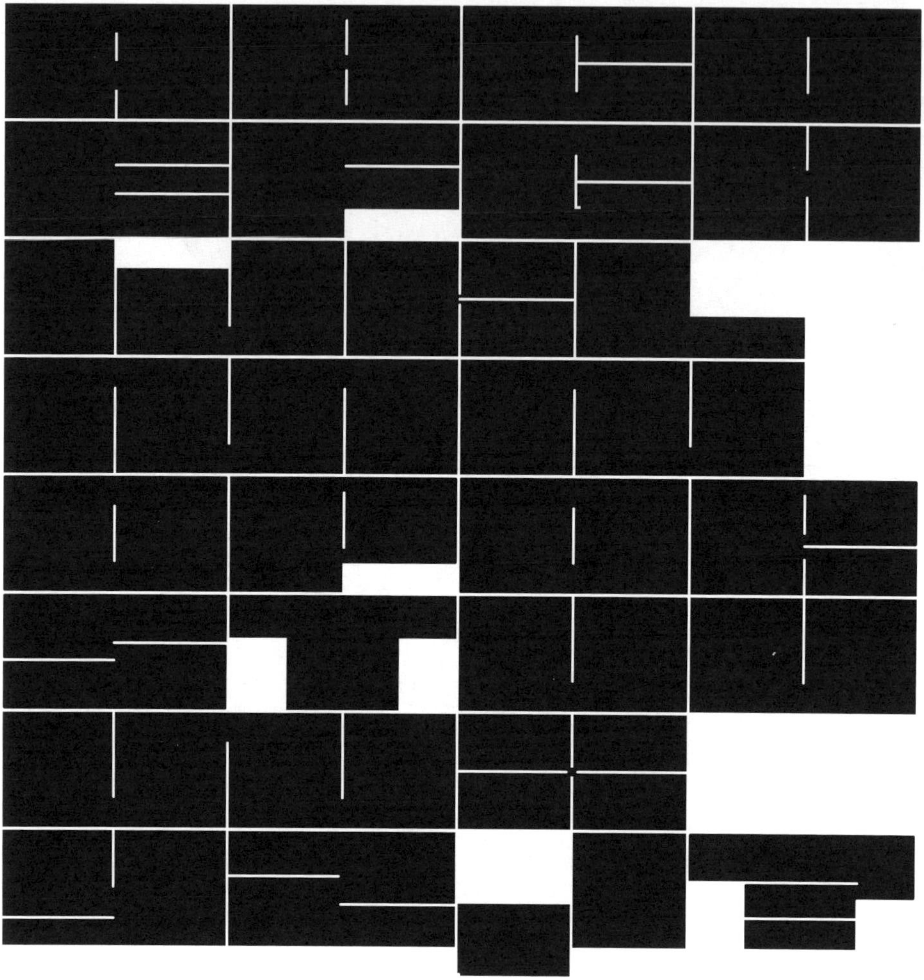

U.A

A–Z,/?

s. 54
l. 44
t. 0
w. 800

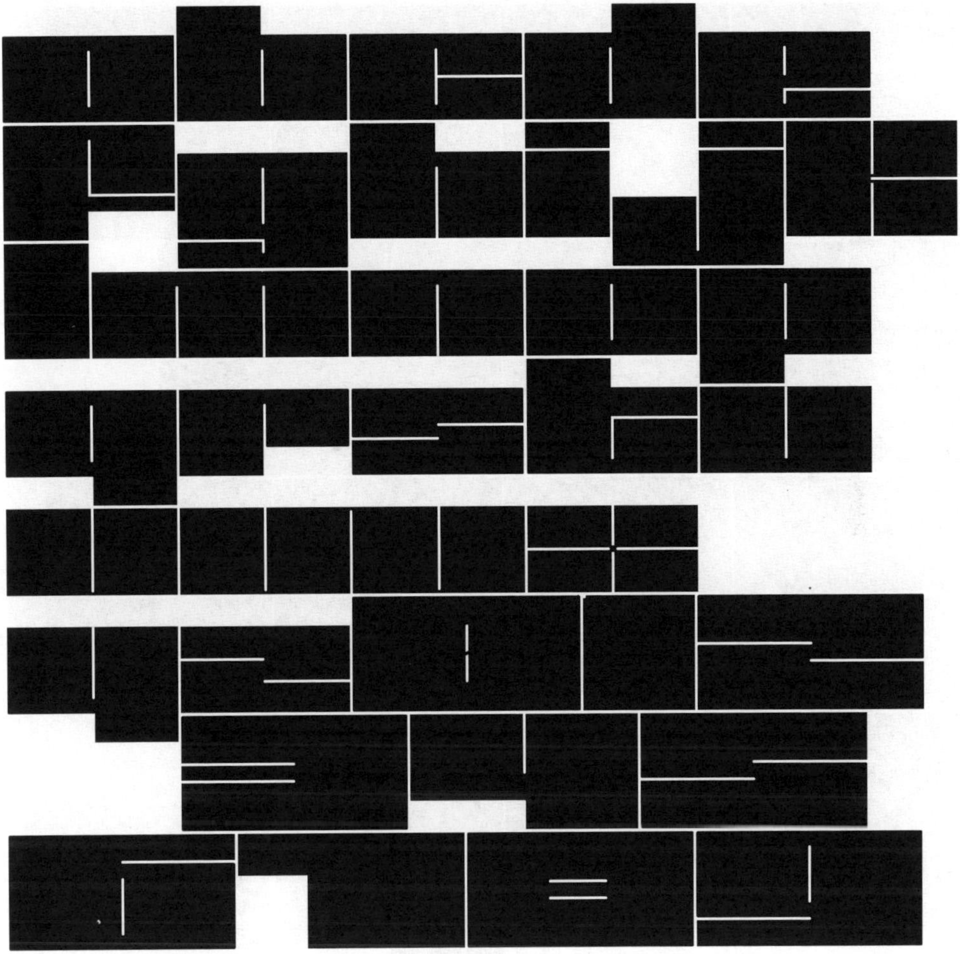

U.A

a–z 0–9

s. 54
l. 44
t. 0
w. 800

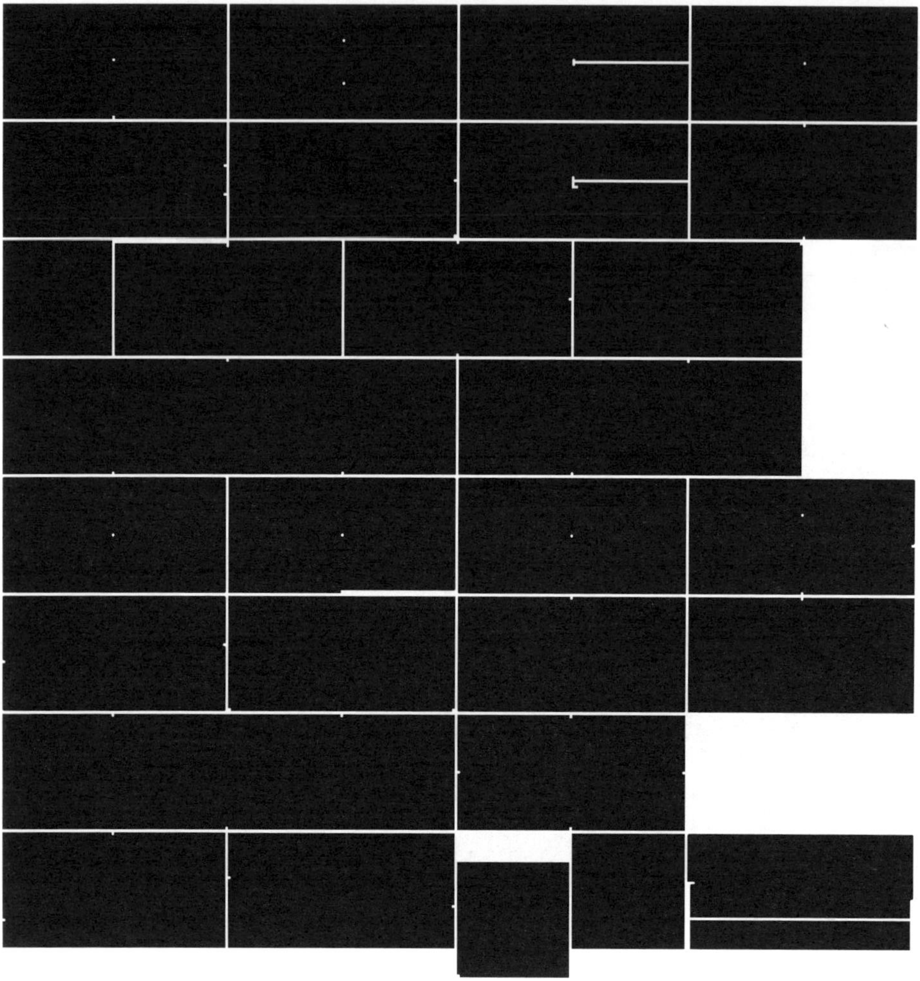

U.A

A–Z,/?

s. 54
l. 44
t. 0
w. 900

U.A

a–z 0–9

s. 54
l. 44
t. 0
w. 900

Alpha
nove
mber
Uni
form
lima
tango
romeo
alpha

U.A

Alpha november
Uniform lima tango
romeo alpha

s. 45
l. 37
t. 0
w. 600

Bravo
lima
alpha
charlie
kilo
Sierra
alpha
nove
mber
sierra

U.A

Bravo lima alpha
charlie kilo Sierra
alpha november sierra

s. 45
l. 37
t. 0
w. 600

580
580
580
580
580
580

U.A 580

s. 75
l. 62
t. 0
w. ±

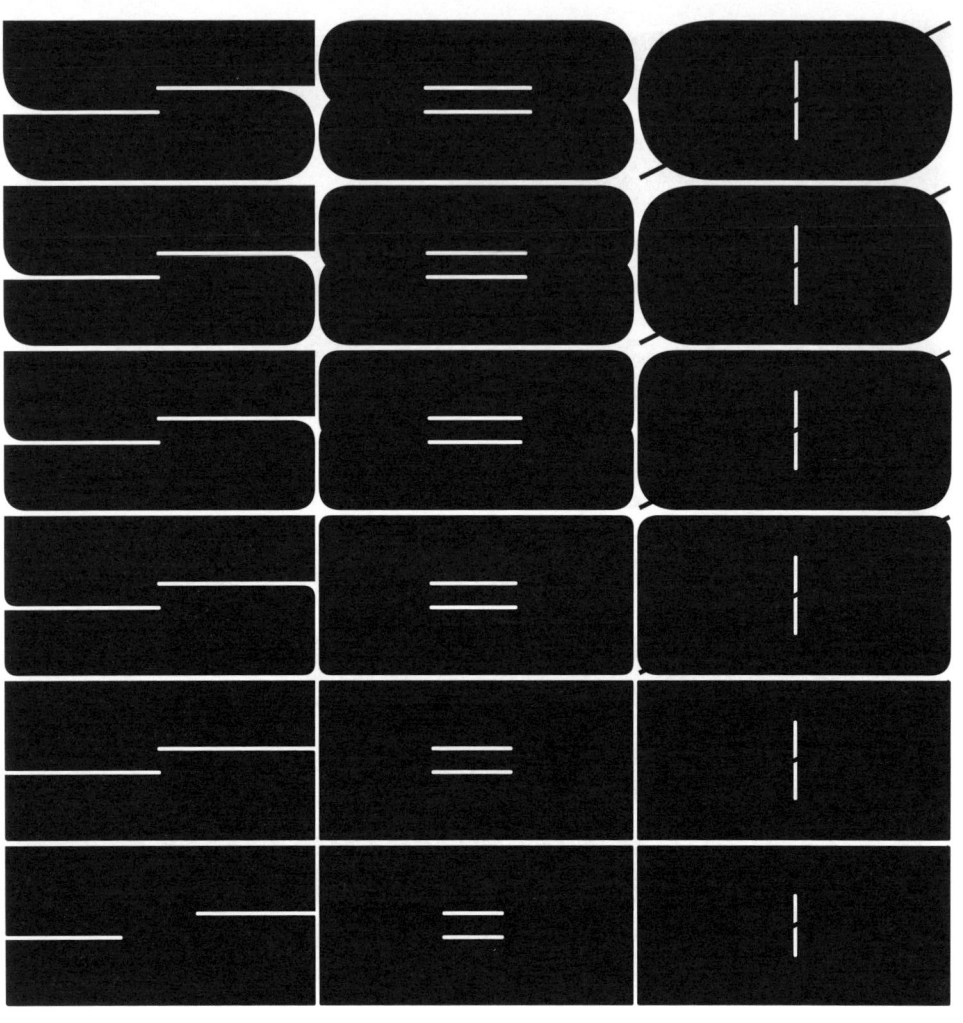

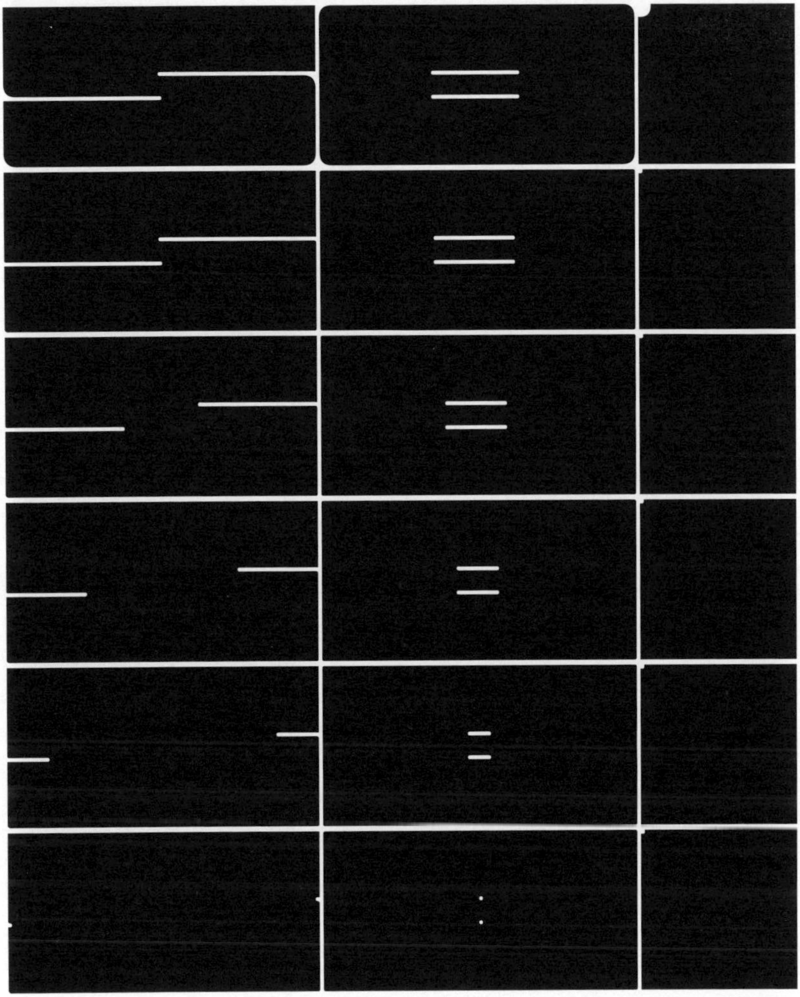

U.A

581

s. 45
l. 37
t. 0
w. ±

ABCDEF
GHIJKLN
MOPQR
STUVW
XYZ-.,

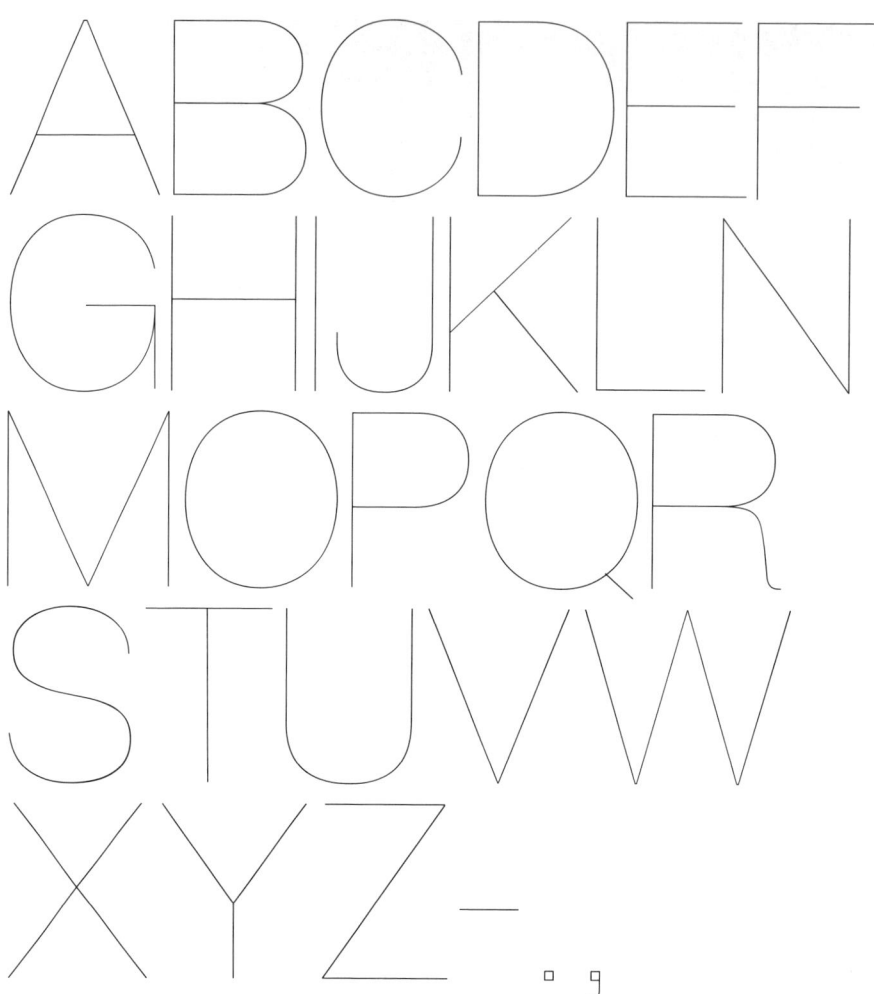

U.B An extreme ultra-hairline sans serif alphabet

A–Z -.,

s. 93
l. 73
t. 0
w. 100

abcdefgh
ijklmnopq
rtuvwxyz
0123456
789

U.B

a–z 0–9

s. 93
l. 73
t. 0
w. 100

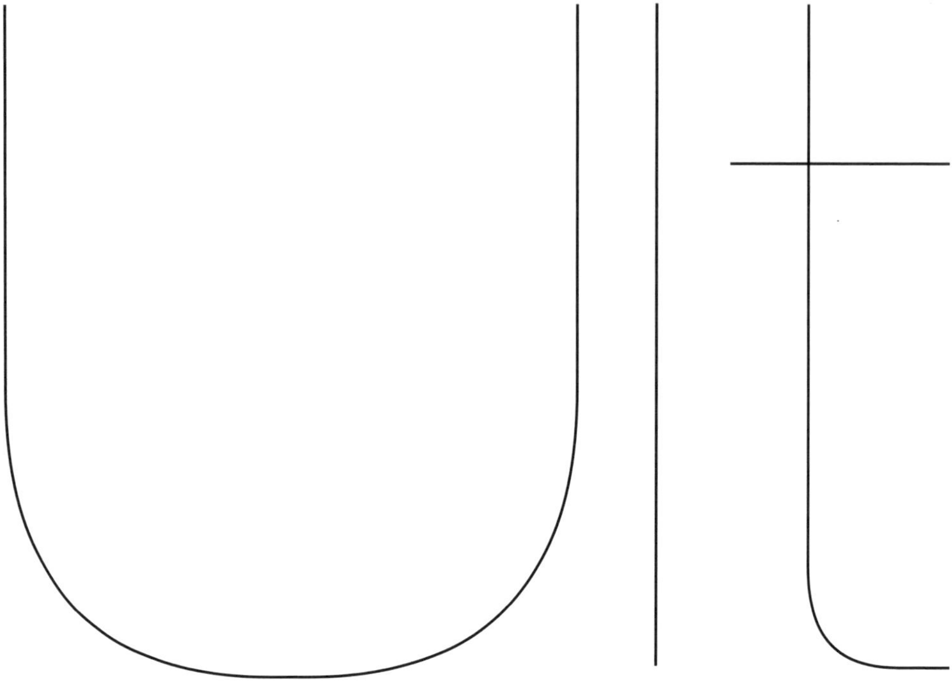

U.B Ultra

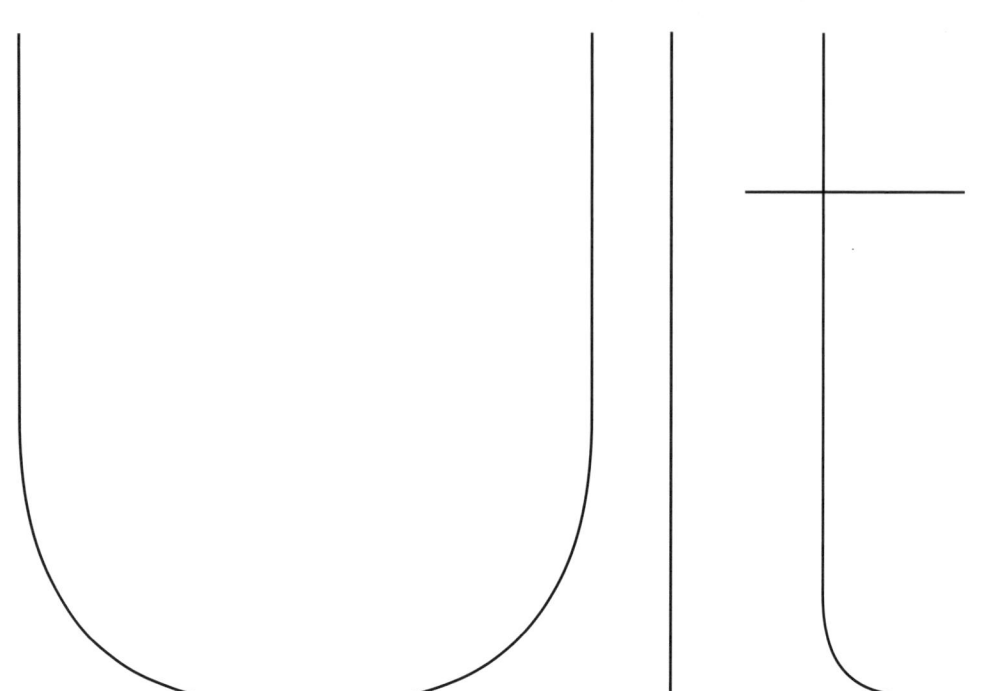

ra

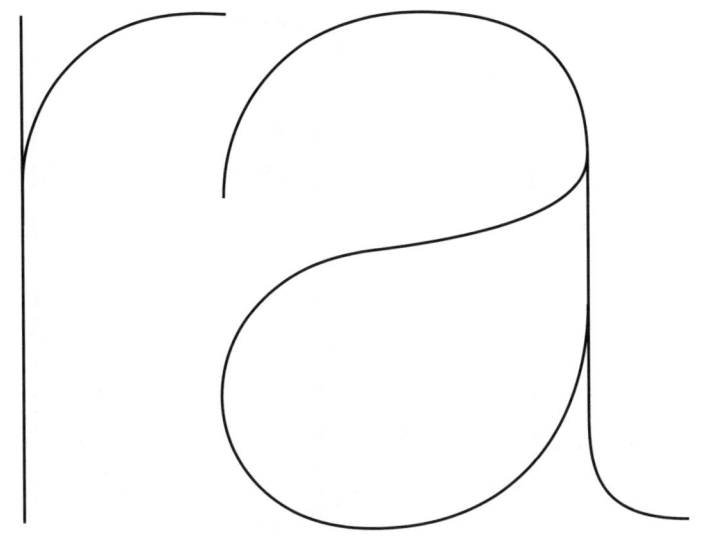

s. 380
l. 380
t. 0
w. 40

-lig

U.B

-light

ht

s. 380
l. 380
t. 0
w. 40

123

U.B

123

s. 320
l. 320
t. -40
w. 40

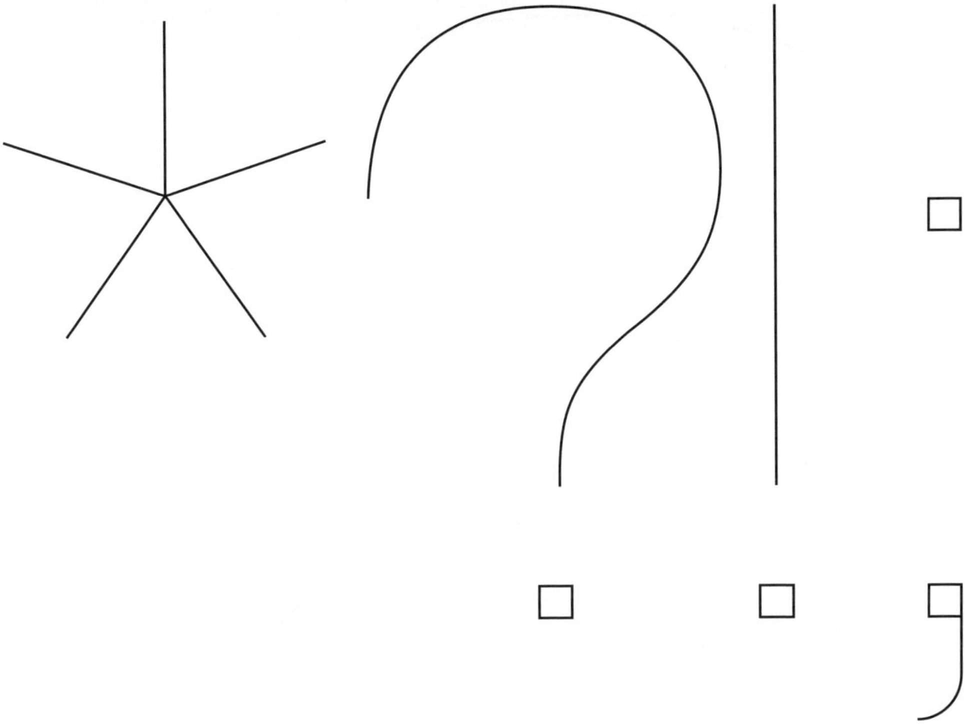

U.B

*?!;

s. 320
l. 320
t. -40
w. 40

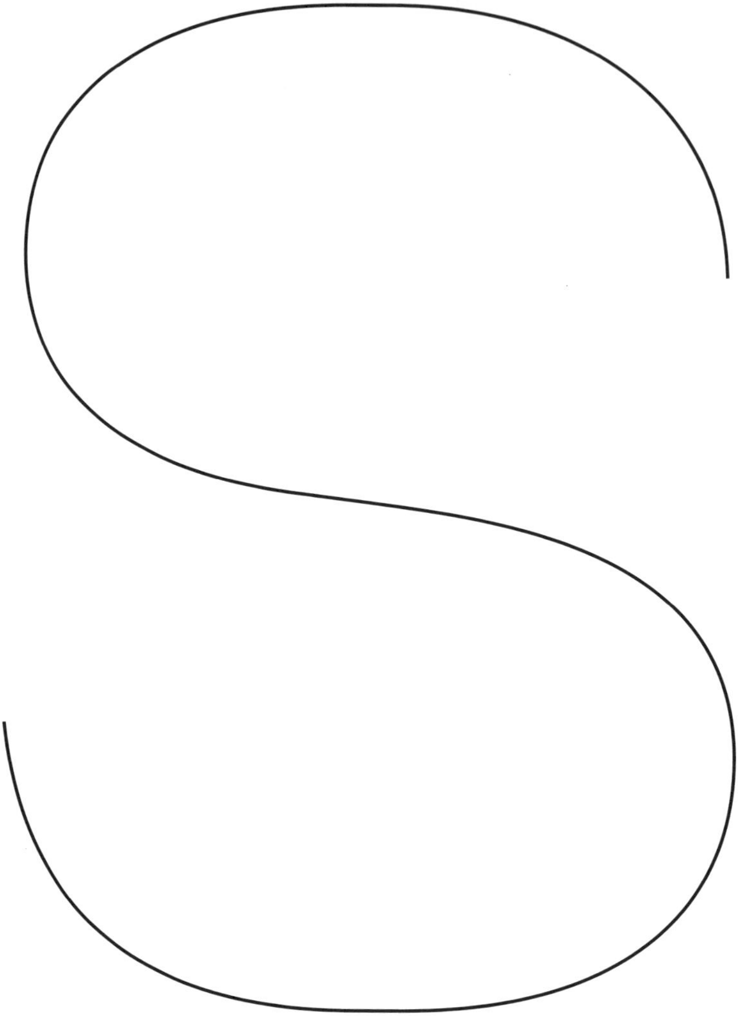

U.B

S

s. 540
l. 540
t. 0
w. 40

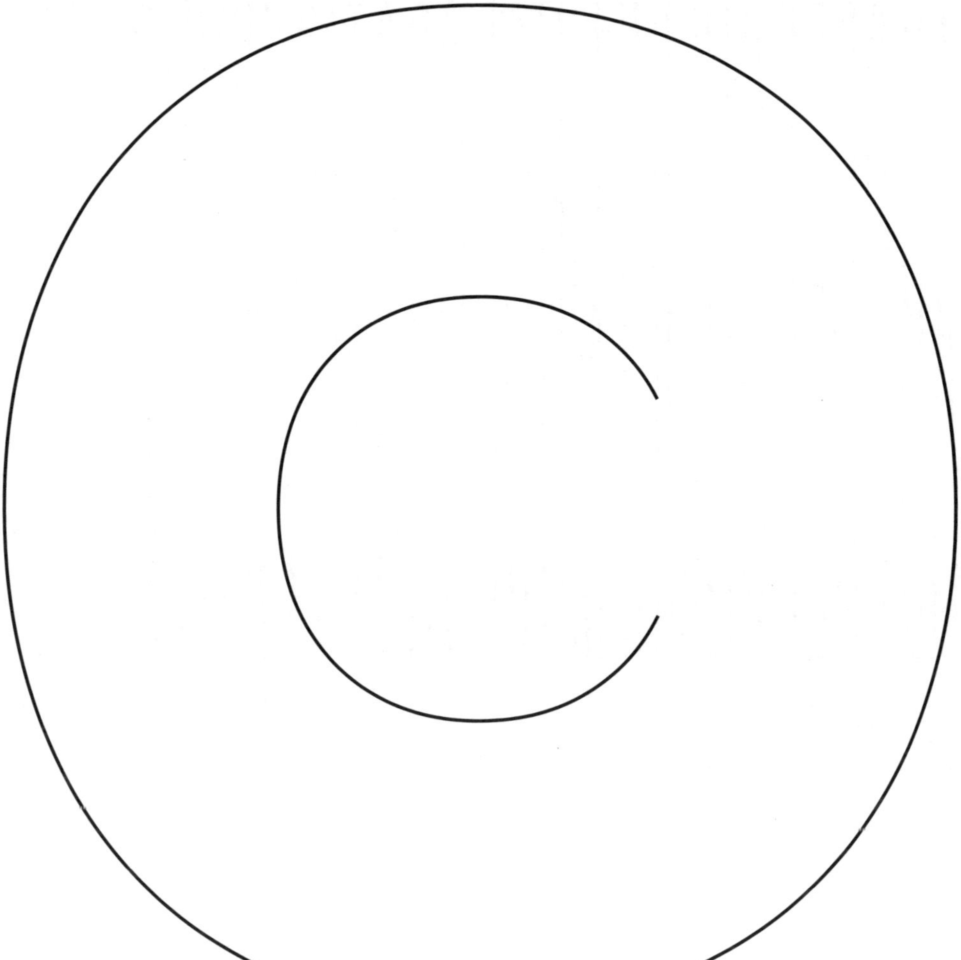

U.B

©

s. 540
l. 540
t. 0
w. 40

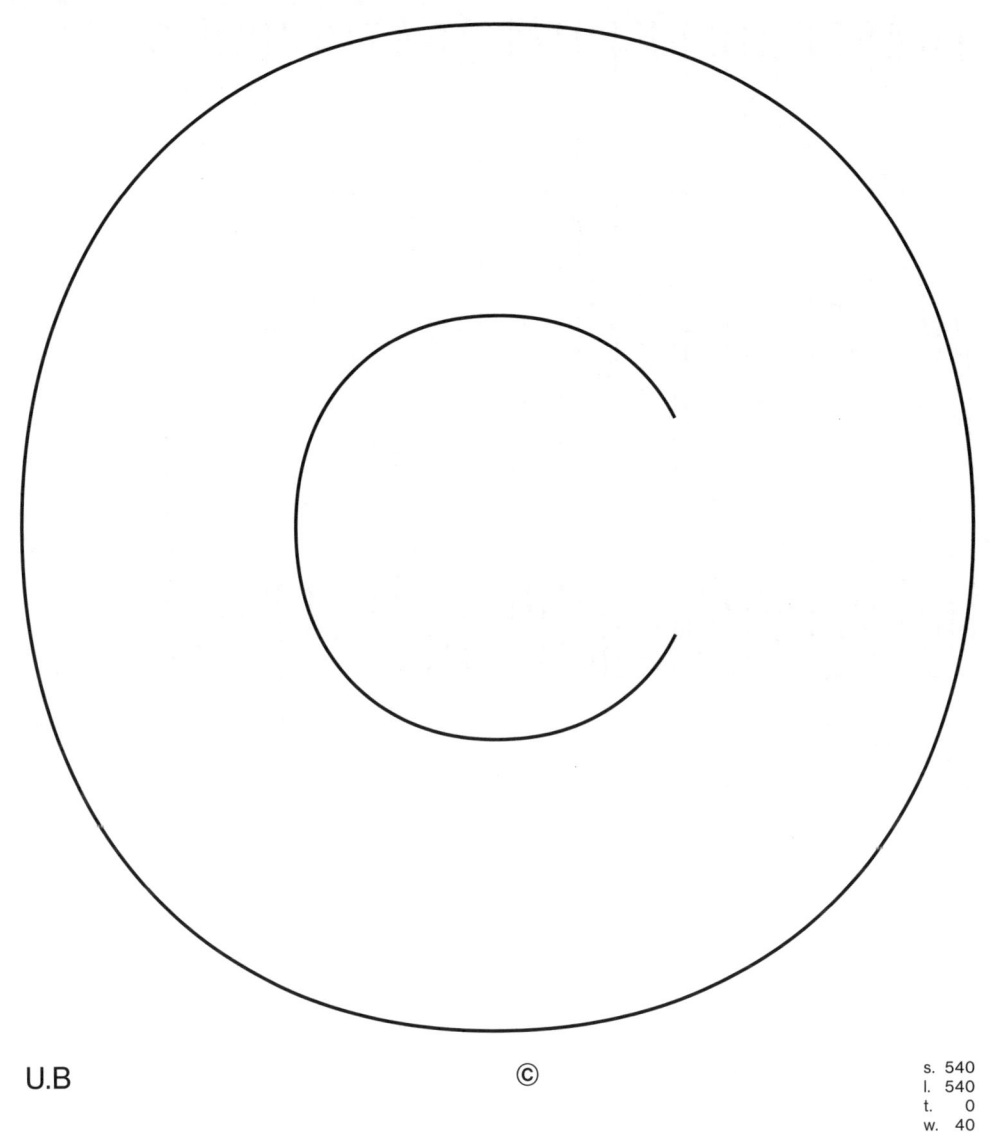

ABCDEFGHIJKLMNOPQRSTUVWXYZ

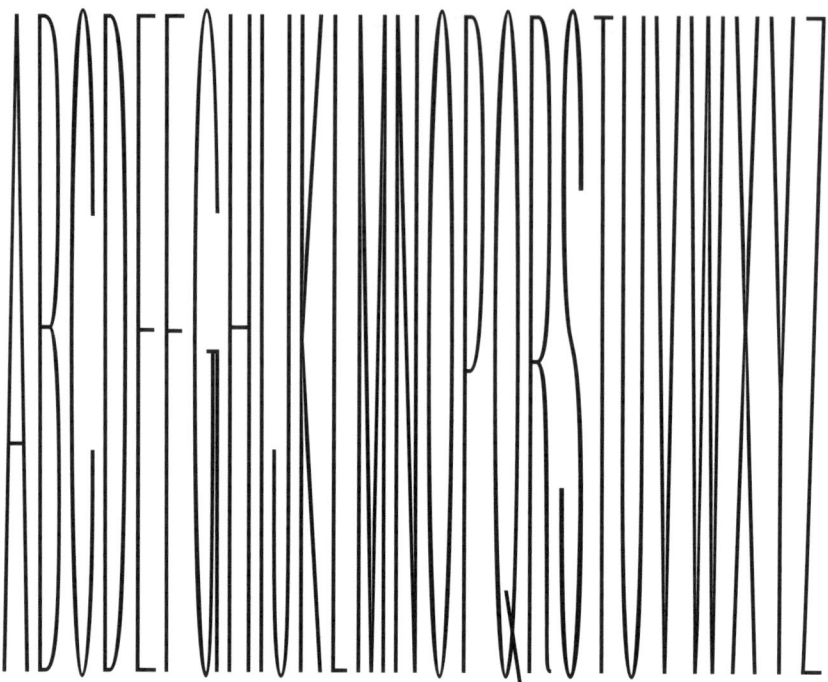

U.C An extreme ultra-condensed sans serif alphabet A–Z

s. 353
l. 353
t. 0

abcdefghijklmnopqrstuvwxyz0123456789

U.C

a–z 0–9

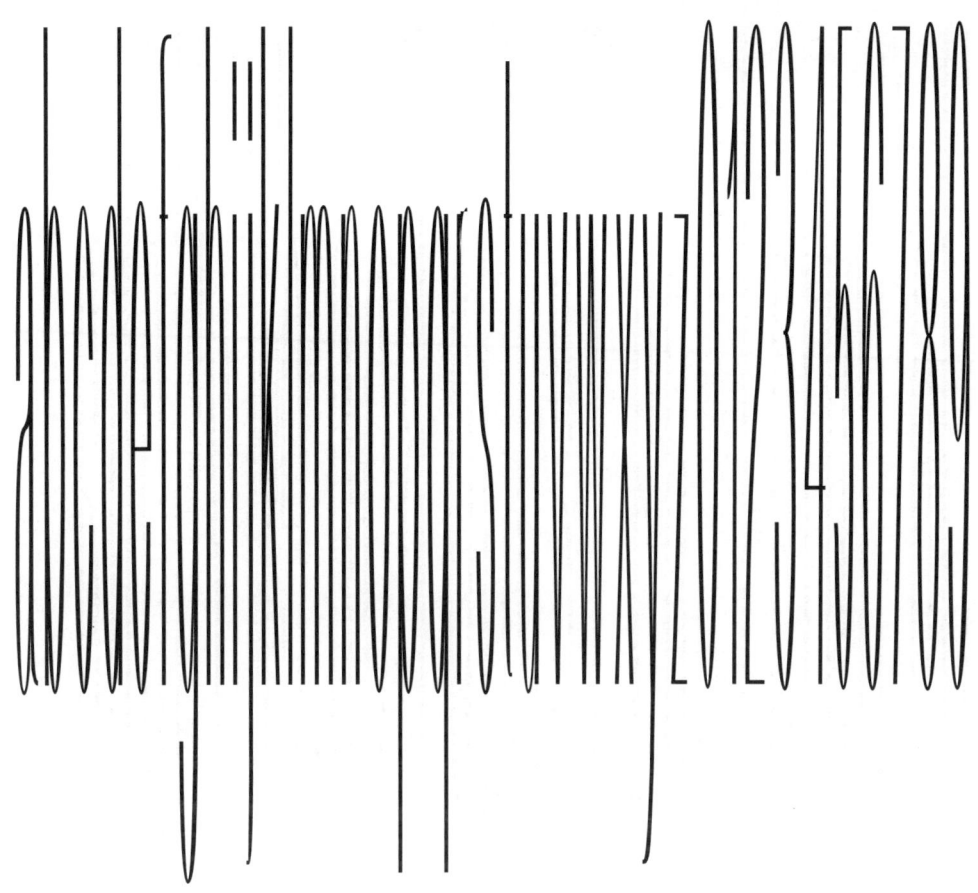

s. 353
l. 353
t. 0

Uniform Lima Tango Romeo Alpha

U.C

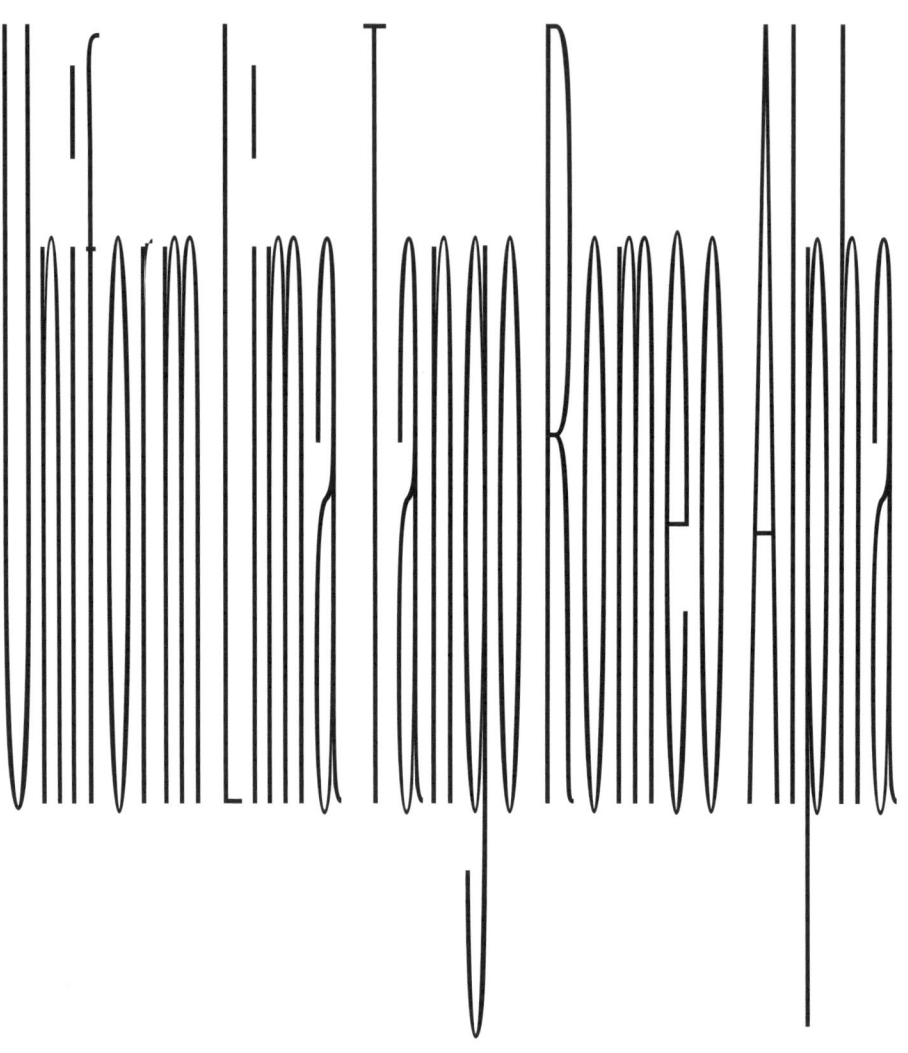

Unifrom Lima Tango
Romeo Alpha

s. 420
l. 420
t. 0

Charlie Oscar November Delta Echo

November Charlie Echo Delta

U.C

Charlie Oscar
November Delta Echo
November Charlie
Echo Delta

s. 262
l. 190
t. 0

U Ultra

Section Notes:

All Ultra alphabets were created in Glyphs as varibale fonts with paramters for weight and containing both uppercase and lowercase characters, numerals, and basic punctuation, with the exception of U.C which consists of a static font with no parameters.

As a counterpart to Horizontal, Vertical shares the same structural foundation — a reductive type system built entirely from vertical lines arranged on a 5×5 unit grid. Both systems employ identical variable parameters: foreground line weight, background line weight, width, and focus. The result here is a similarly minimal output, distinguished by its uniquely vertical orientation.

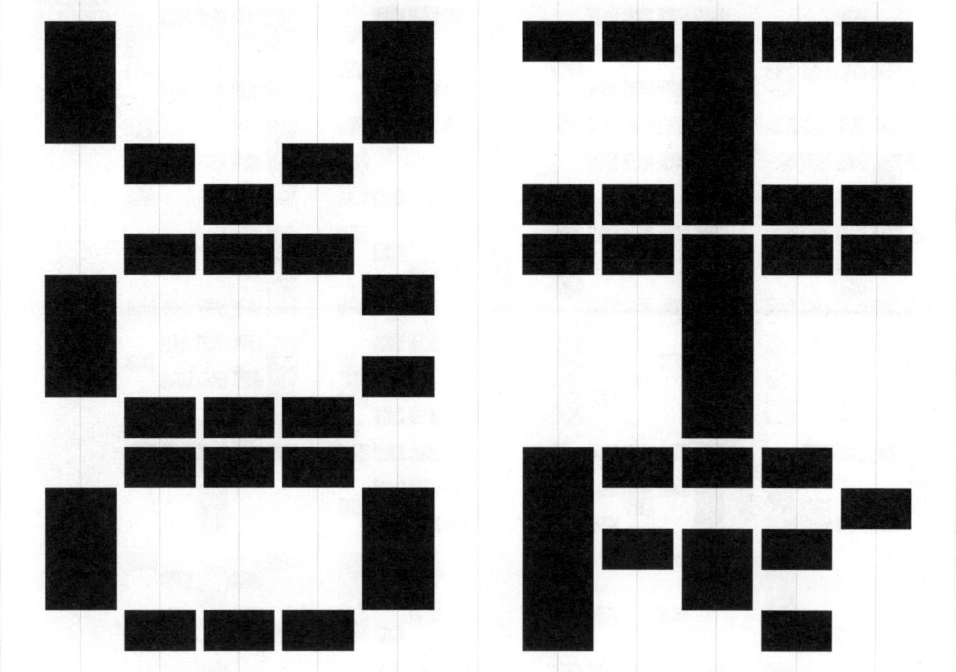

V.A A

A wide width alphabet formed of vertical lines, bold in foreground weight

Victor

s. 92
l. 80
t. 0
fw. 800
bw. 100
wd. 900
b. 0

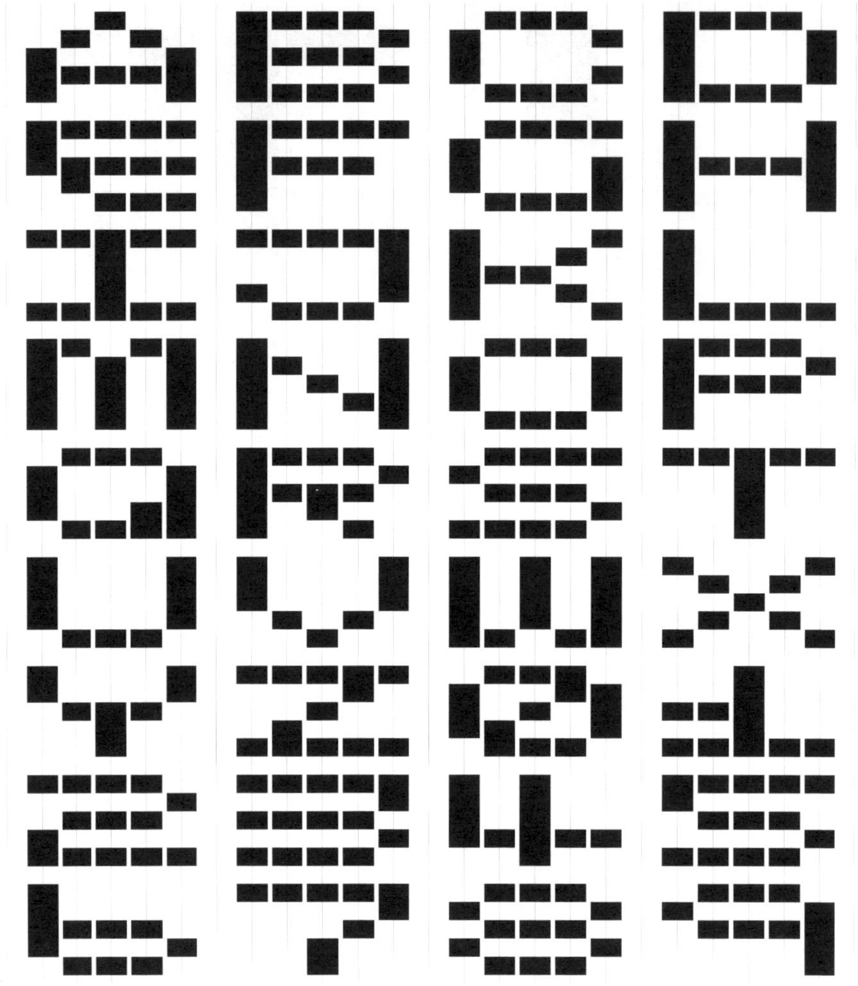

V.A A

A–Z 0–9

s. 41
l. 41
t. 0
fw. 800
bw. 100
wd. 900
b. 0

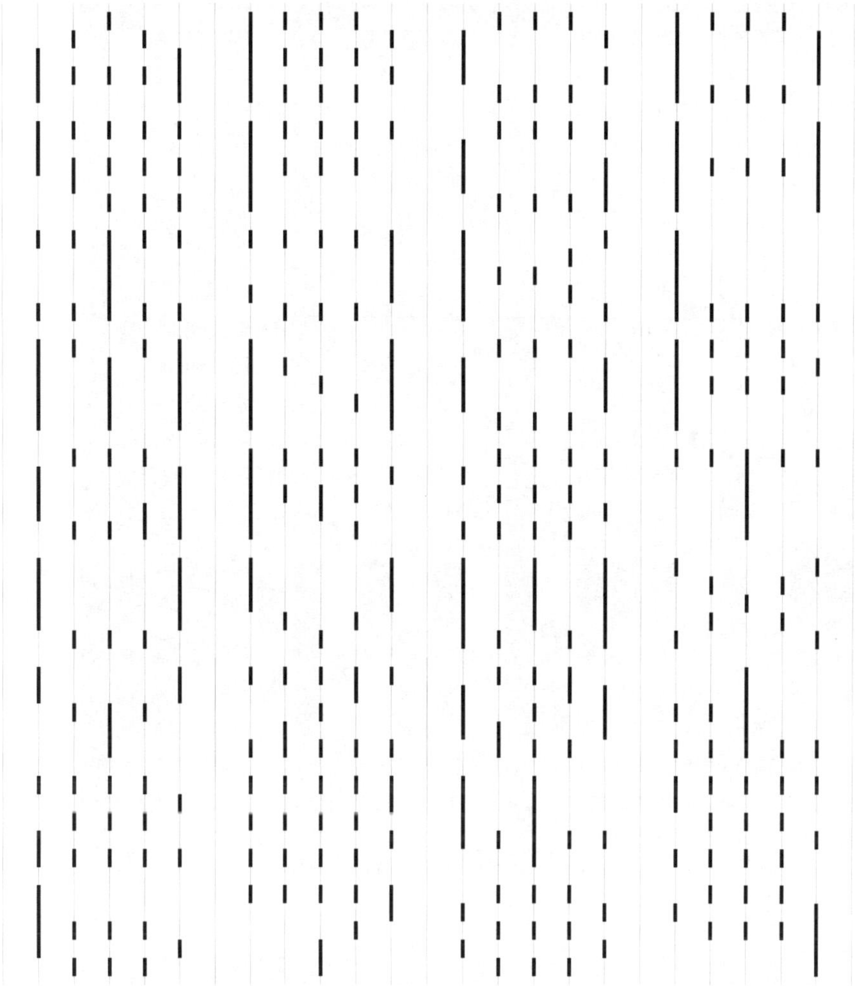

V.A B

A wide width alphabet formed of vertical lines, light in foreground weight.

A–Z 0–9

s. 41
l. 41
t. 0
fw. 100
bw. 100
wd. 900
b. 0

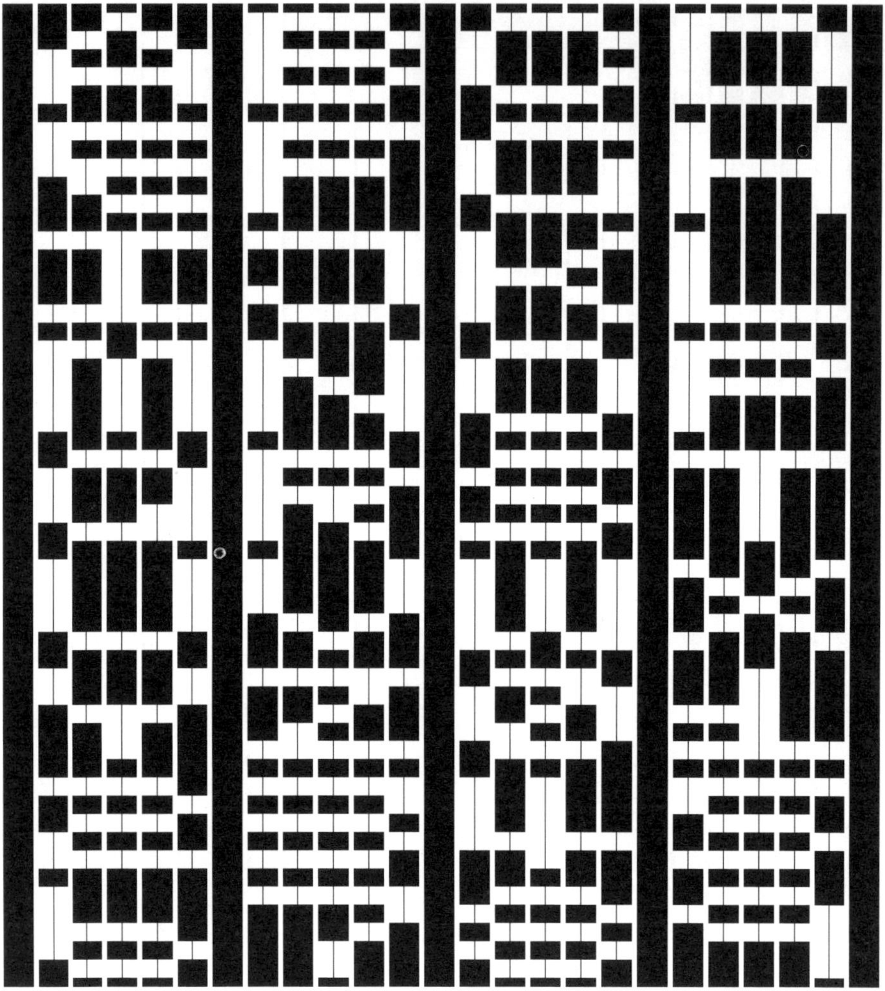

V.A C

A wide width alphabet formed of vertical lines, bold in background weight

A–Z 0–9

s. 41
l. 41
t. 0
fw. 100
bw. 800
wd. 900
b. 0

V.A D

A wide width alphabet formed of vertical lines, bold in foreground weight and bold in background weight

A–Z 0–9

s. 41
l. 41
t. 0
fw. 800
bw. 800
wd. 900
b. 0

V.A E

A blurred wide width alphabet formed of vertical lines, bold in foreground weight and light in background weight

A–Z 0–9

s. 41
l. 41
t. 0
fw. 800
bw. 100
wd. 900
b. 100

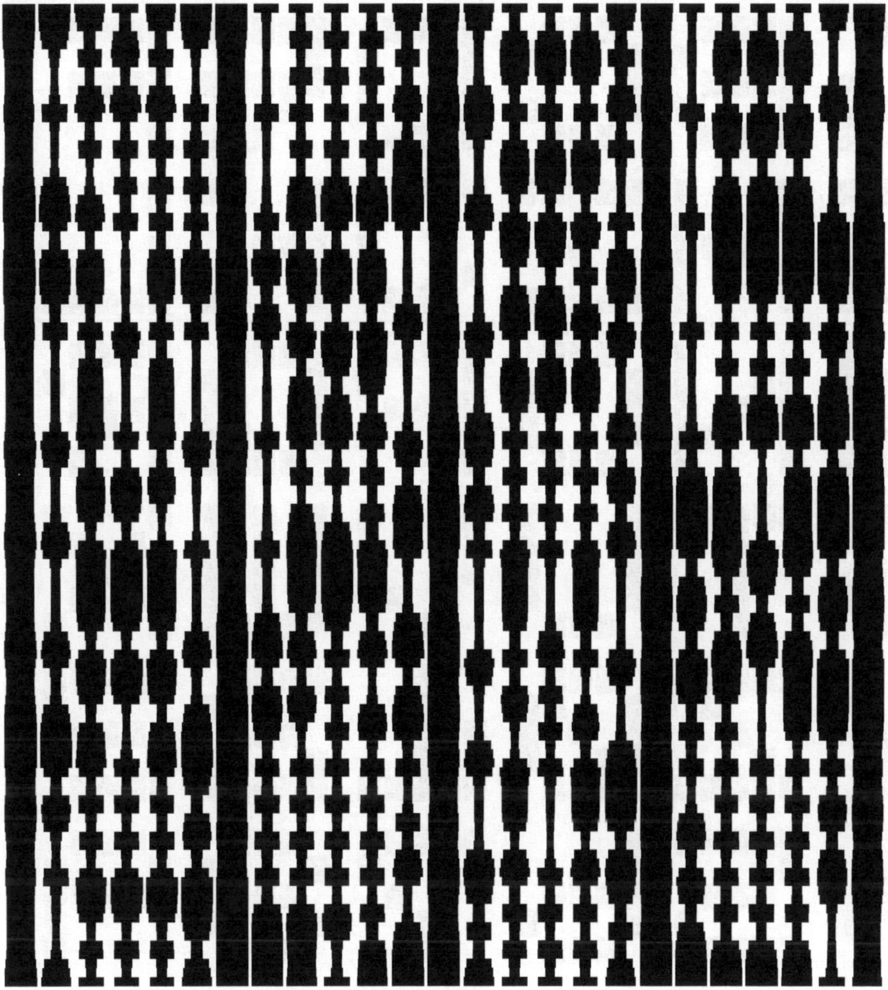

V.A F

A blurrred wide width alphabet formed of vertical lines, light in foreground weight and bold in background weight

A–Z 0–9

s.	41
l.	41
t.	0
fw.	100
bw.	100
wd.	900
b.	100

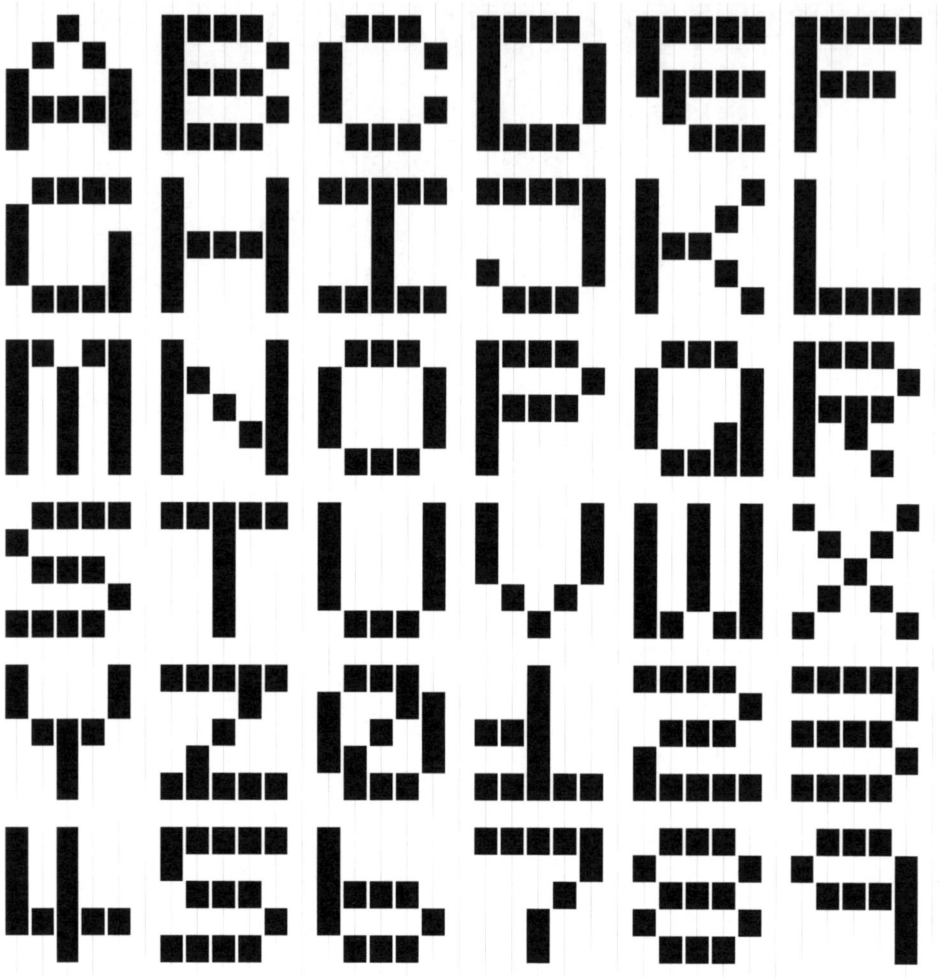

V.A G

A regular width alphabet formed of vertical lines, bold in foreground weight

A–Z 0–9

s. 61
l. 61
t. 0
fw. 800
bw. 100
wd. 500
b. 0

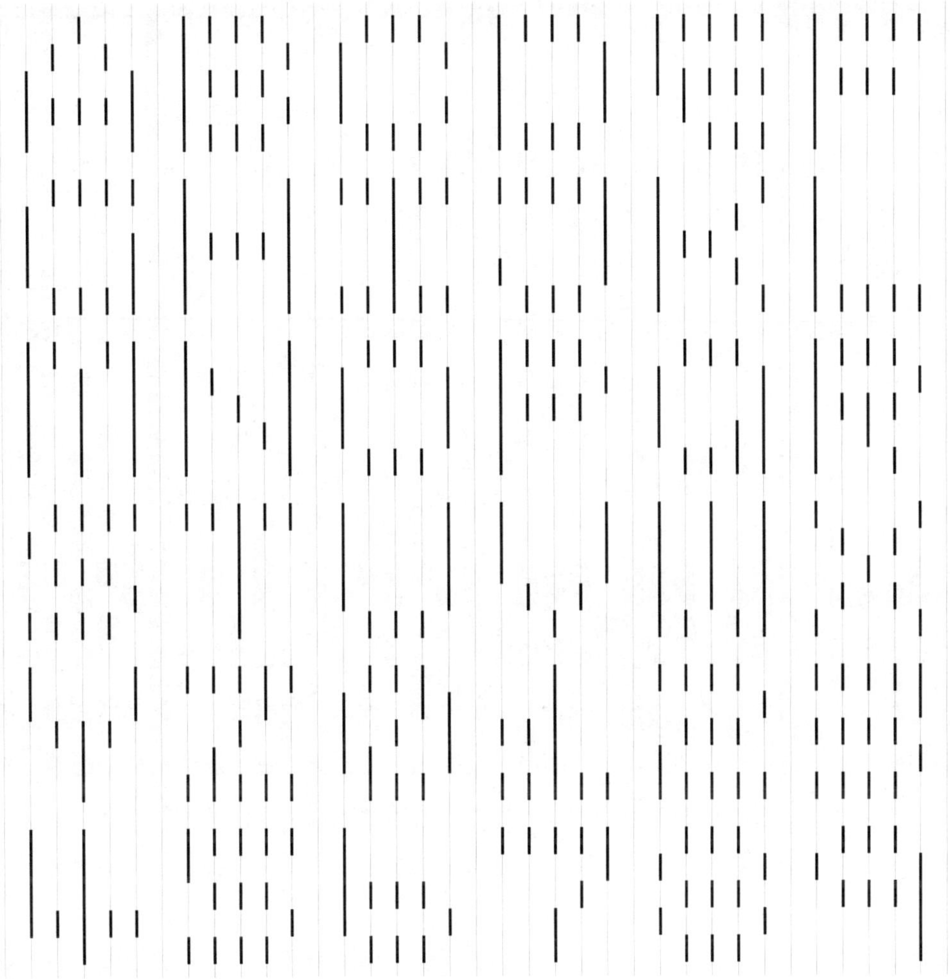

V.A H

A regular width alphabet formed of vertical lines, light in foreground weight

A–Z 0–9

s. 61
l. 61
t. 0
fw. 100
bw. 100
wd. 500
b. 0

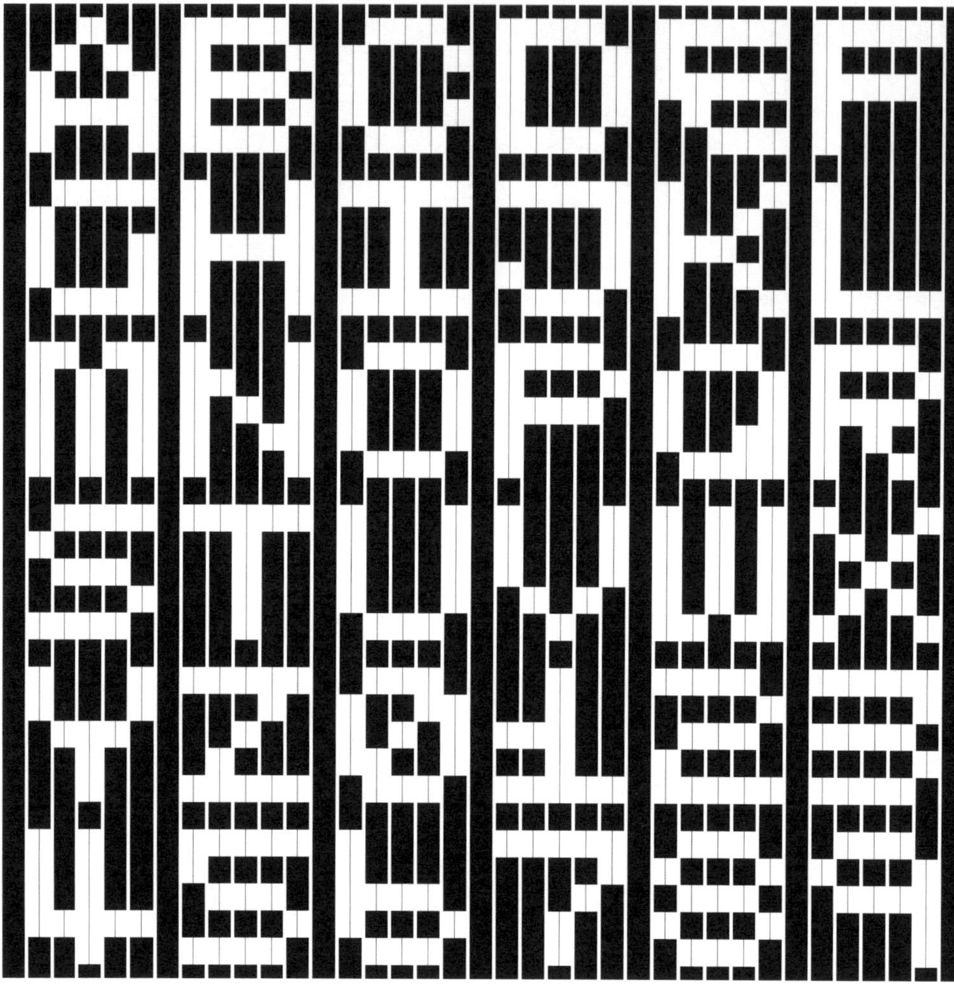

V.A I

A regular width alphabet formed of vertical lines, bold in background weight

A–Z 0–9

s. 61
l. 61
t. 0
fw. 100
bw. 800
wd. 500
b. 0

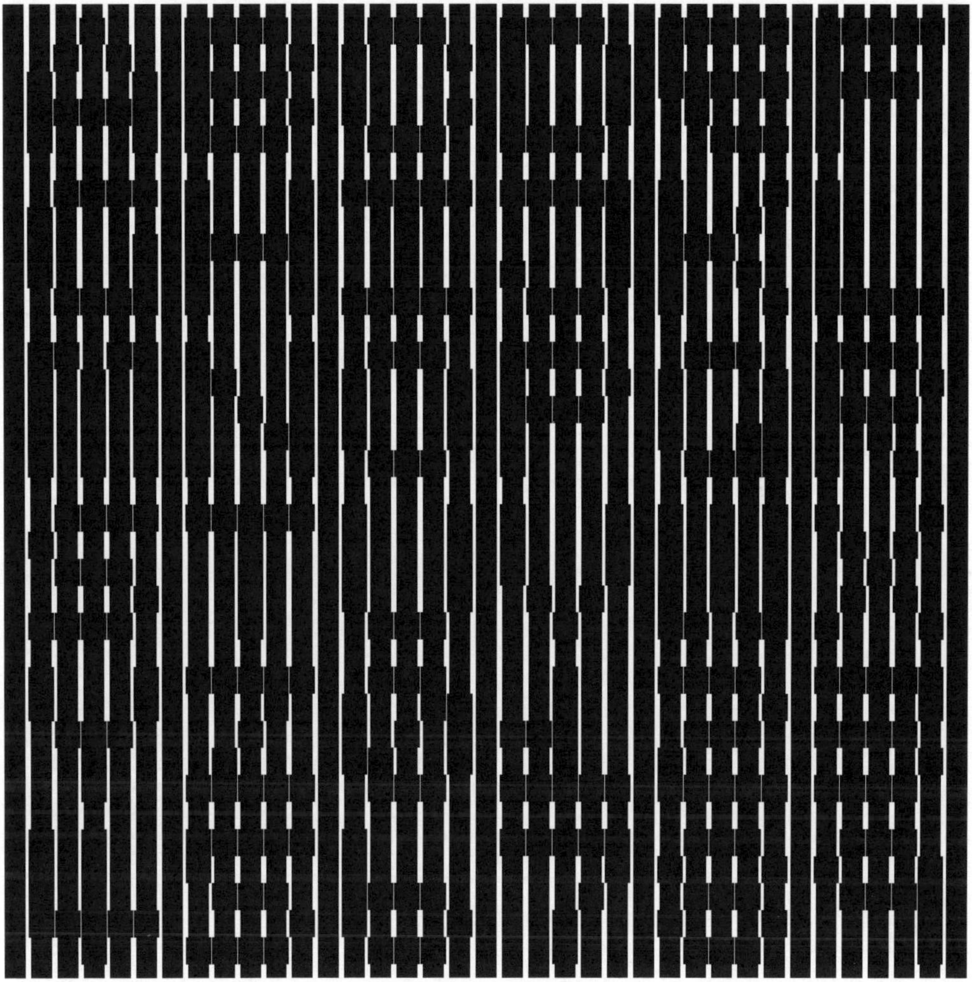

V.A J

A regular width alphabet formed of vertical lines, bold in foreground weight and bold in background weight

A–Z 0–9

s. 61
l. 61
t. 0
fw. 900
bw. 800
wd. 500
b. 0

V.A K

A blurred regular width alphabet formed of vertical lines, bold in foreground weight and light in background weight

A–Z 0–9

s. 61
l. 61
t. 0
fw. 900
bw. 100
wd. 500
b. 100

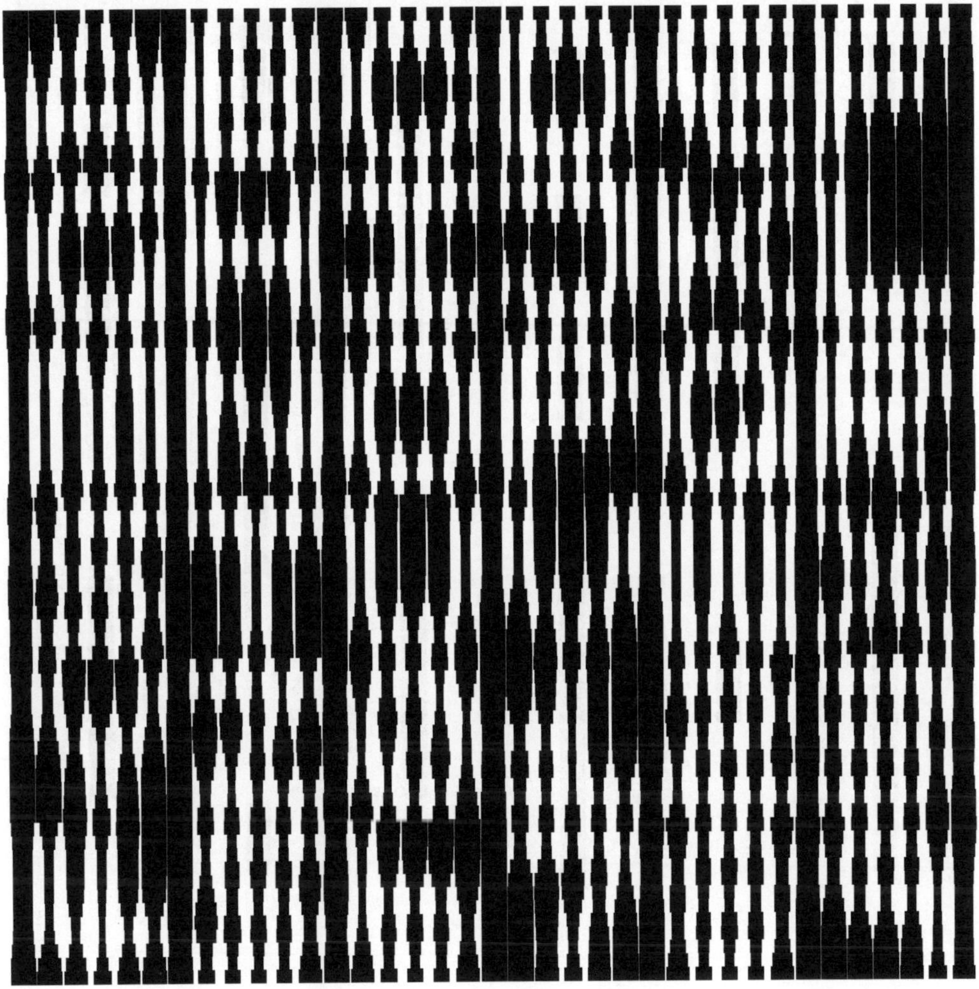

V.A L

A blurred regular width alphabet formed of vertical lines, light in foreground weight and bold in background weight

A–Z 0–9

s. 61
l. 61
t. 0
fw. 100
bw. 900
wd. 500
b. 100

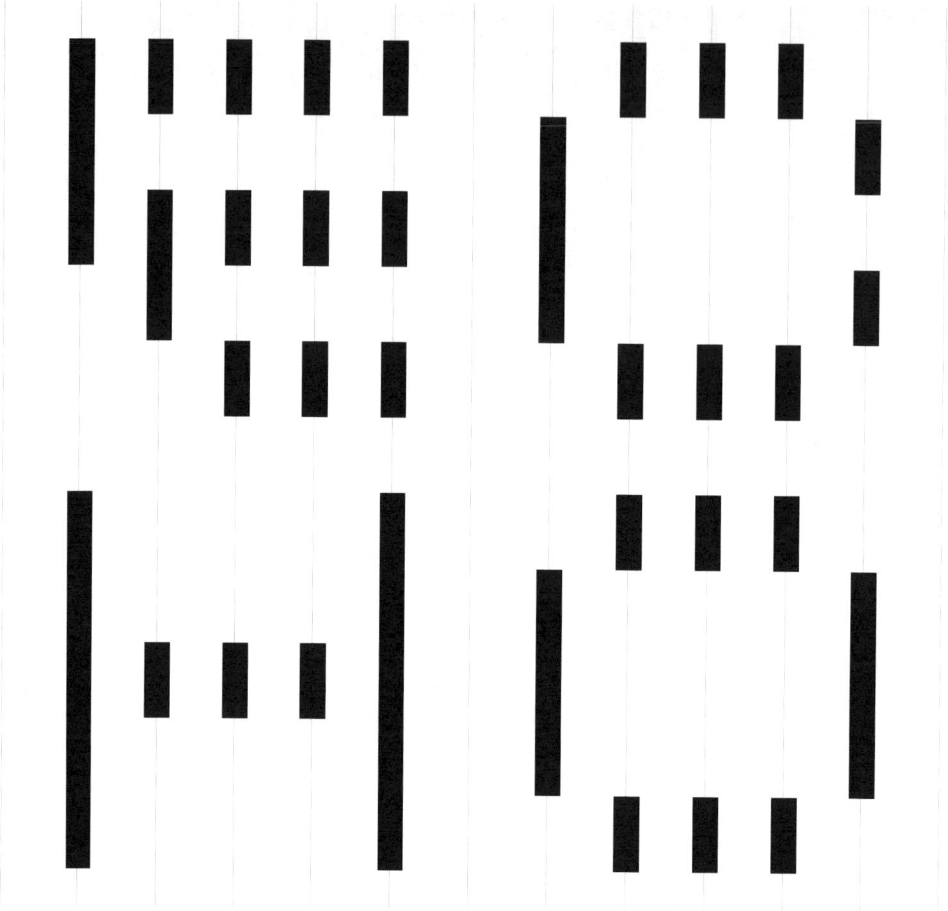

V.A

Echo

s. 170
l. 170
t. 0
fw. 300
bw. 100
wd. 500
b. 0

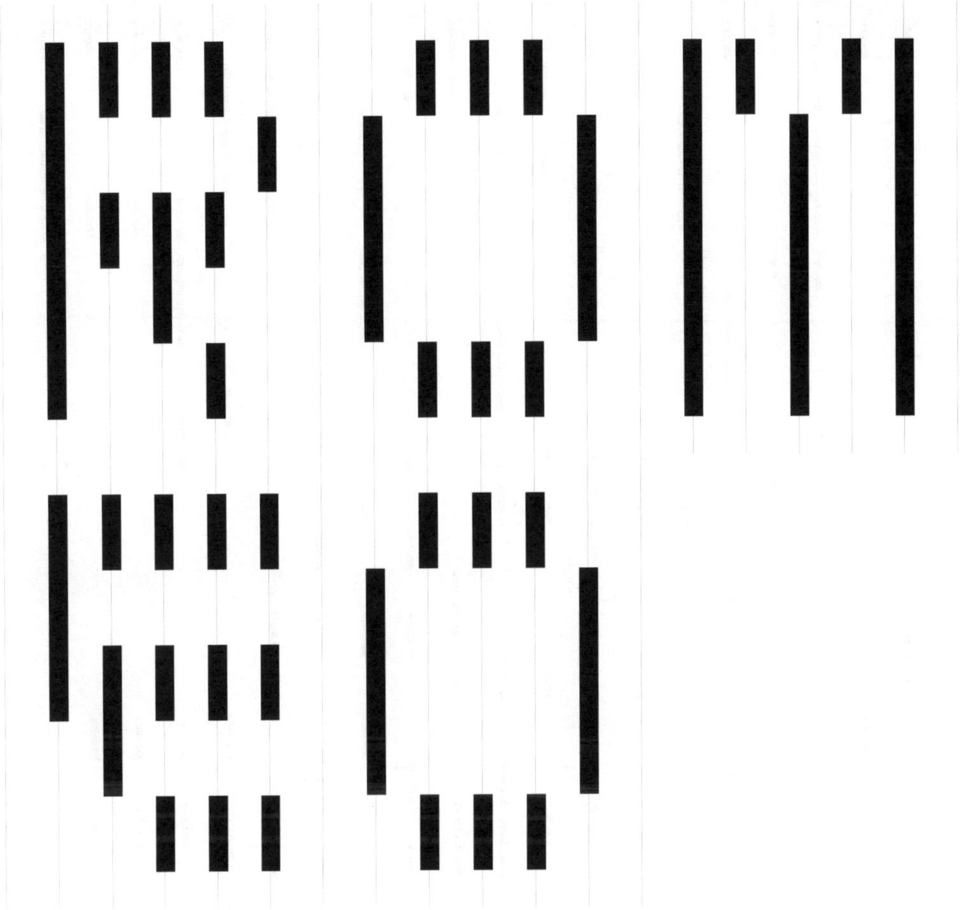

V.A

Romeo

s. 170
l. 170
t. 0
fw. 300
bw. 100
wd. 300
b. 0

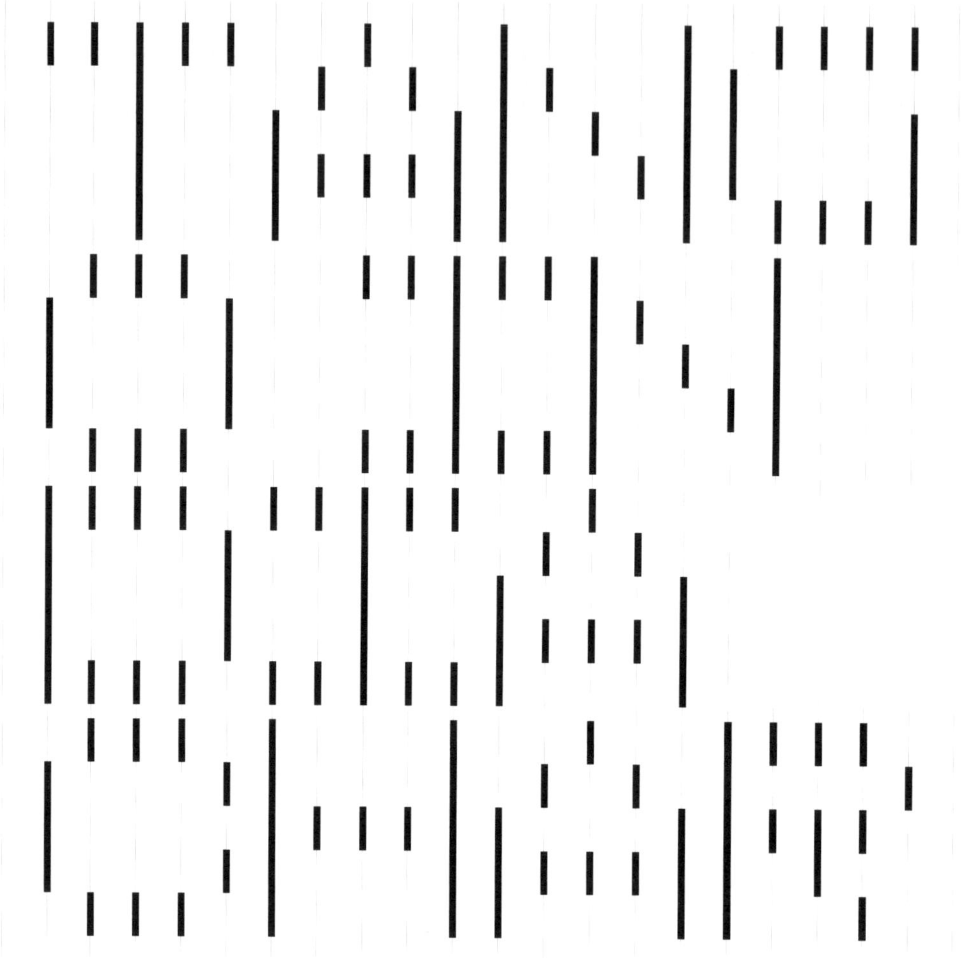

V.A

Tango India Charlie
Alpha Lima

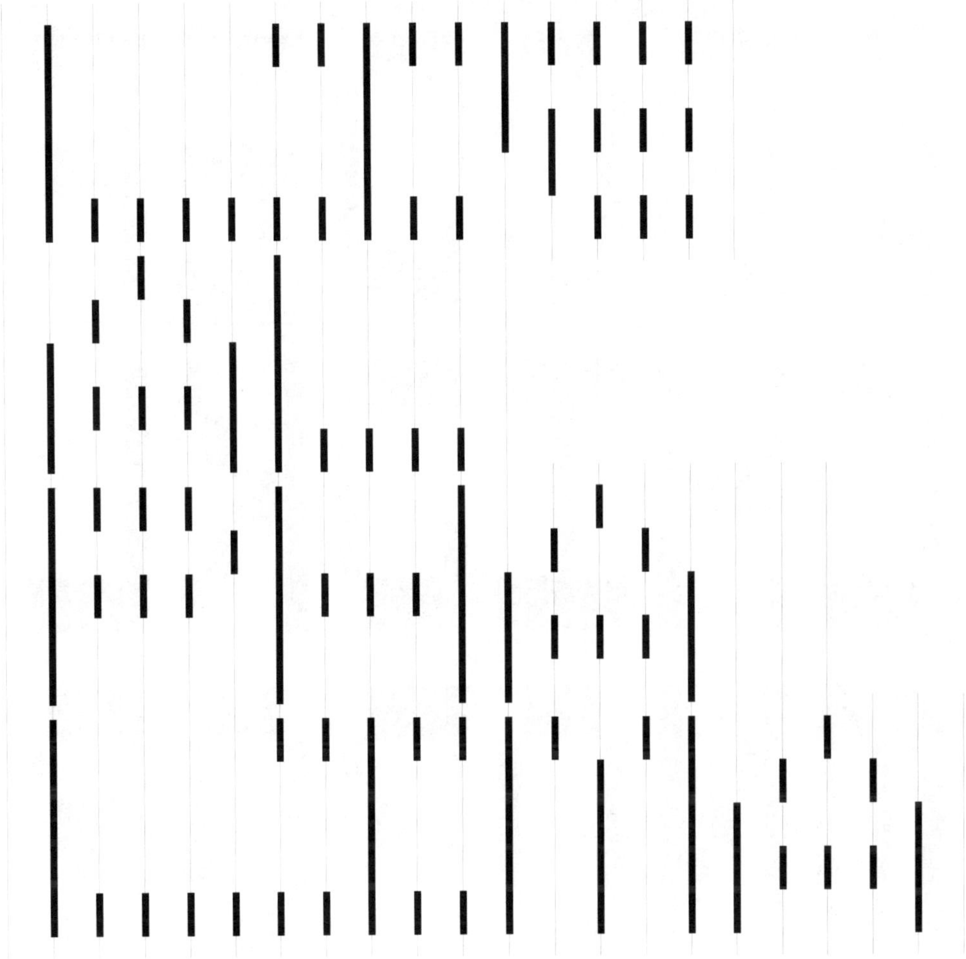

s. 98
l. 86
t. -180
fw. 200
bw. 100
wd. 500
b. 0

V.A M

A narrow width alphabet formed of vertical lines, bold in foreground weight

A–R

s. 123
l. 123
t. 0
fw. 800
bw. 100
wd. 100
b. 0

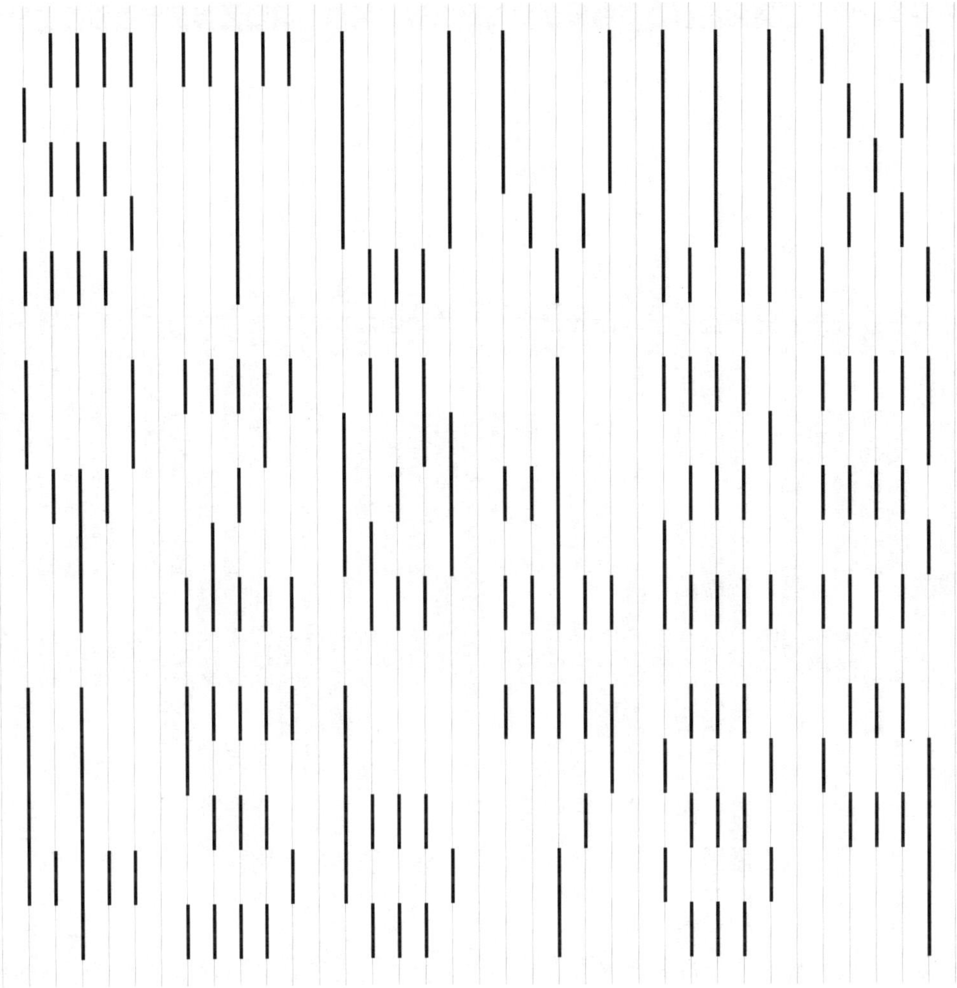

V.A N

A narrow width alphabet formed of vertical lines, light in foreground weight

S–Z 0–9

s. 123
l. 123
t. 0
fw. 100
bw. 100
wd. 100
b. 0

V.A O

A narrow width alphabet formed of vertical lines, bold in background weight

A–R

s. 123
l. 123
t. 0
fw. 100
bw. 800
wd. 100
b. 0

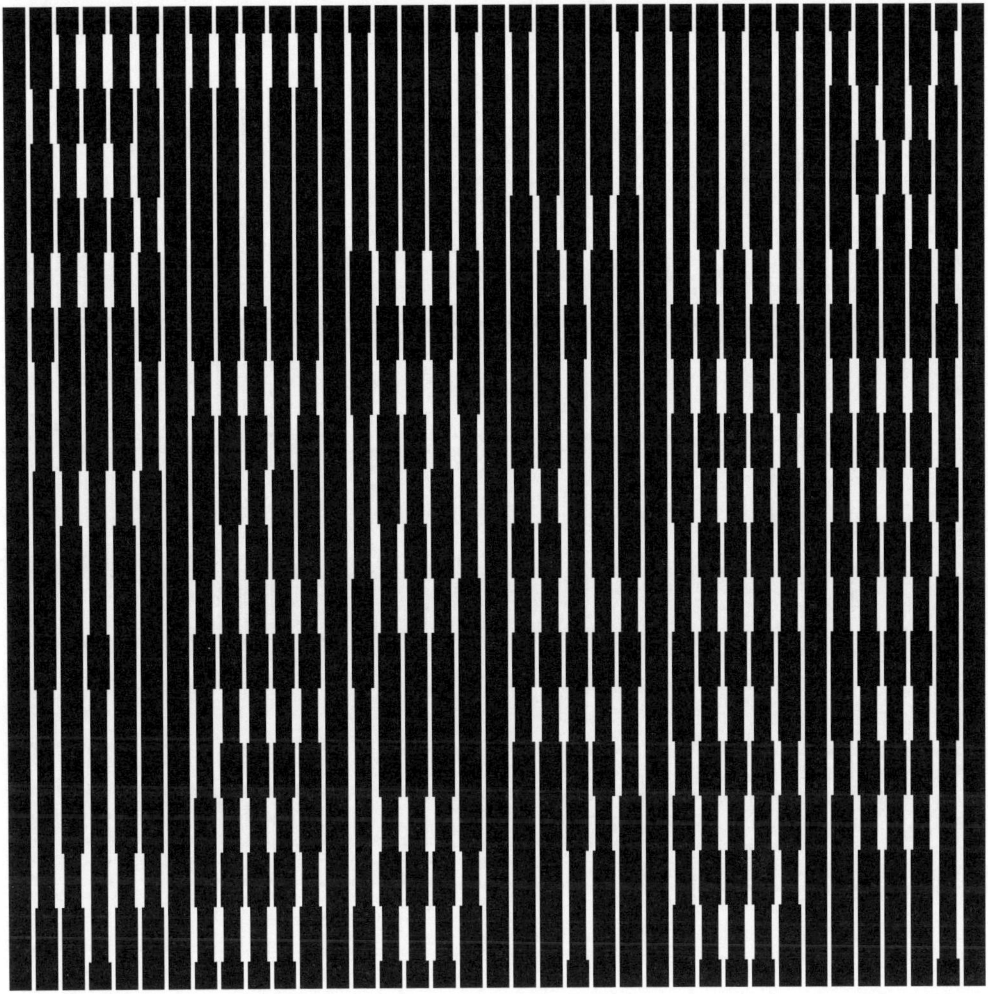

V.A P

A narrow width alphabet formed of vertical lines, bold in foreground weight and bold in background weight

S–Z 0–9

s. 123
l. 123
t. 0
fw. 800
bw. 800
wd. 100
b. 0

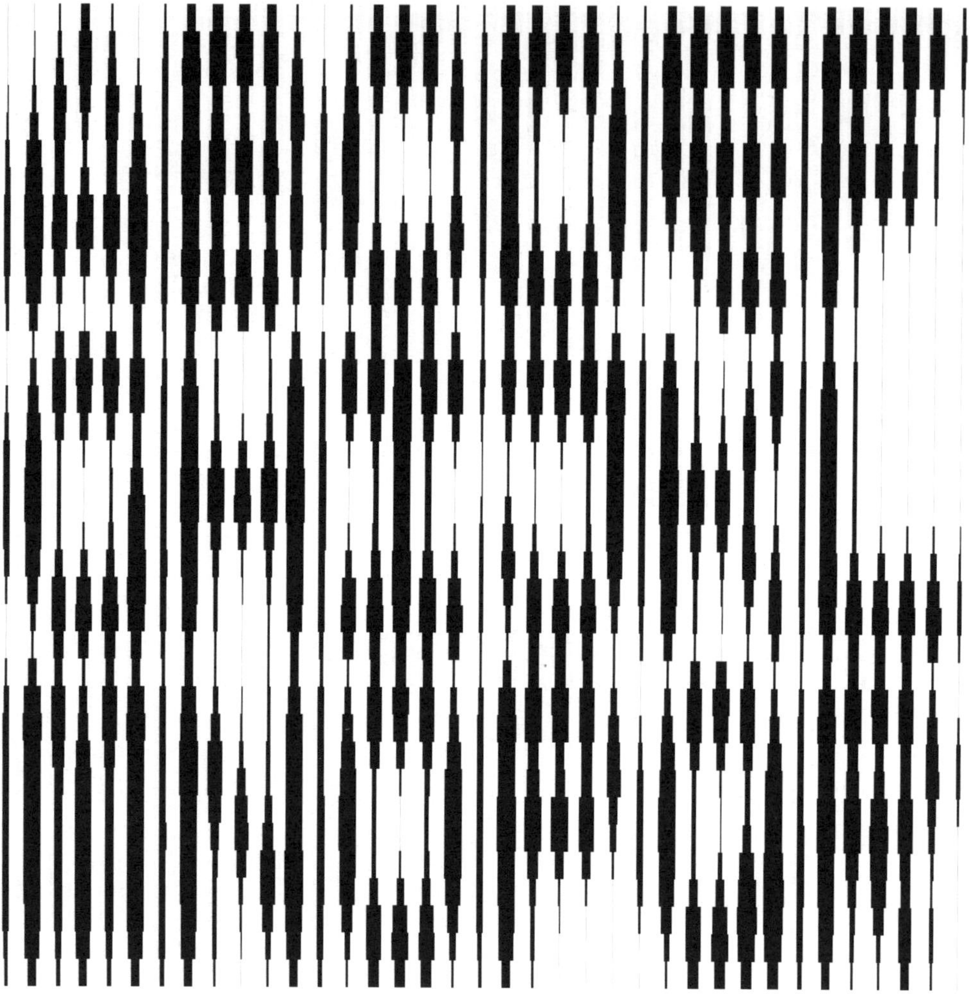

V.A Q

A blurred narrow width alphabet formed of vertical lines, bold in foreground weight and light in background weight

A–R

s. 123
l. 123
t. 0
fw. 800
bw. 100
wd. 100
b. 100

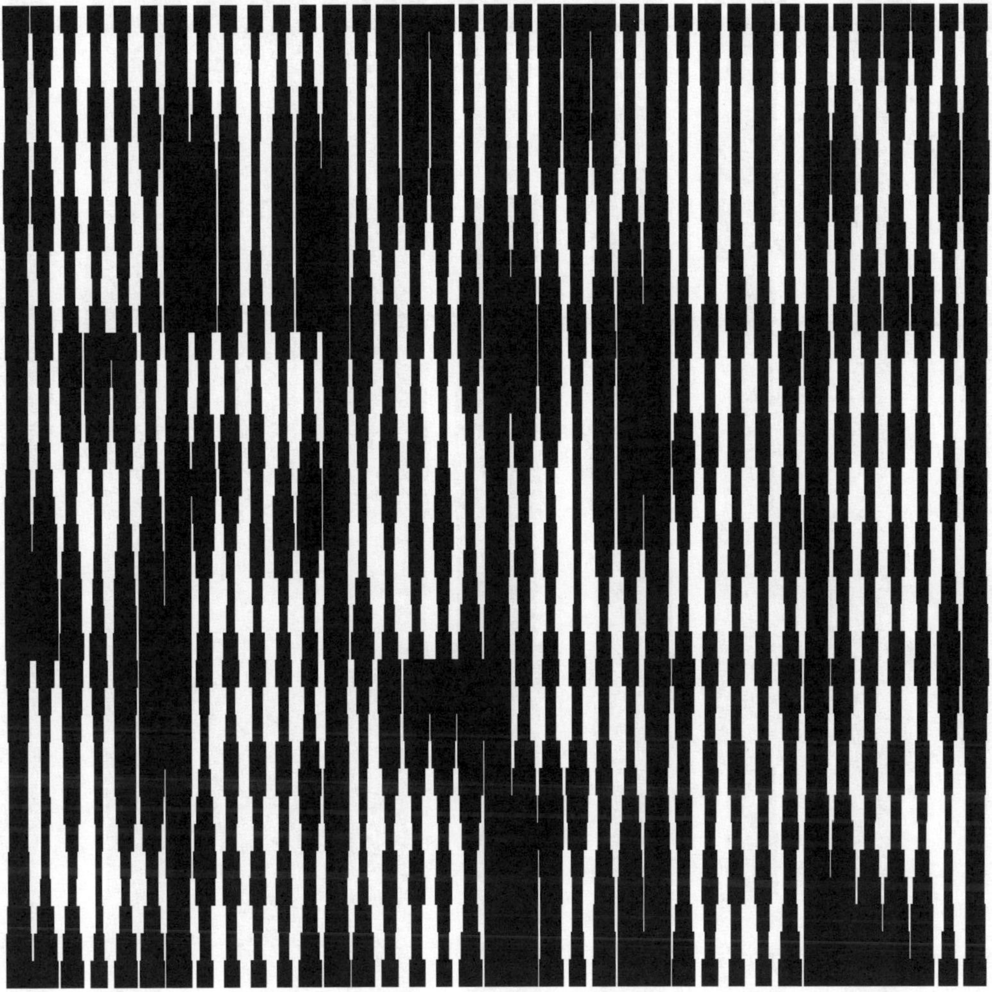

V.A R

A blurred narrow width alphabet formed from vertical lines, light in foreground weight and bold in background weight

S–Z 0–9

s. 123
l. 123
t. 0
fw. 100
bw. 800
wd. 100
b. 100

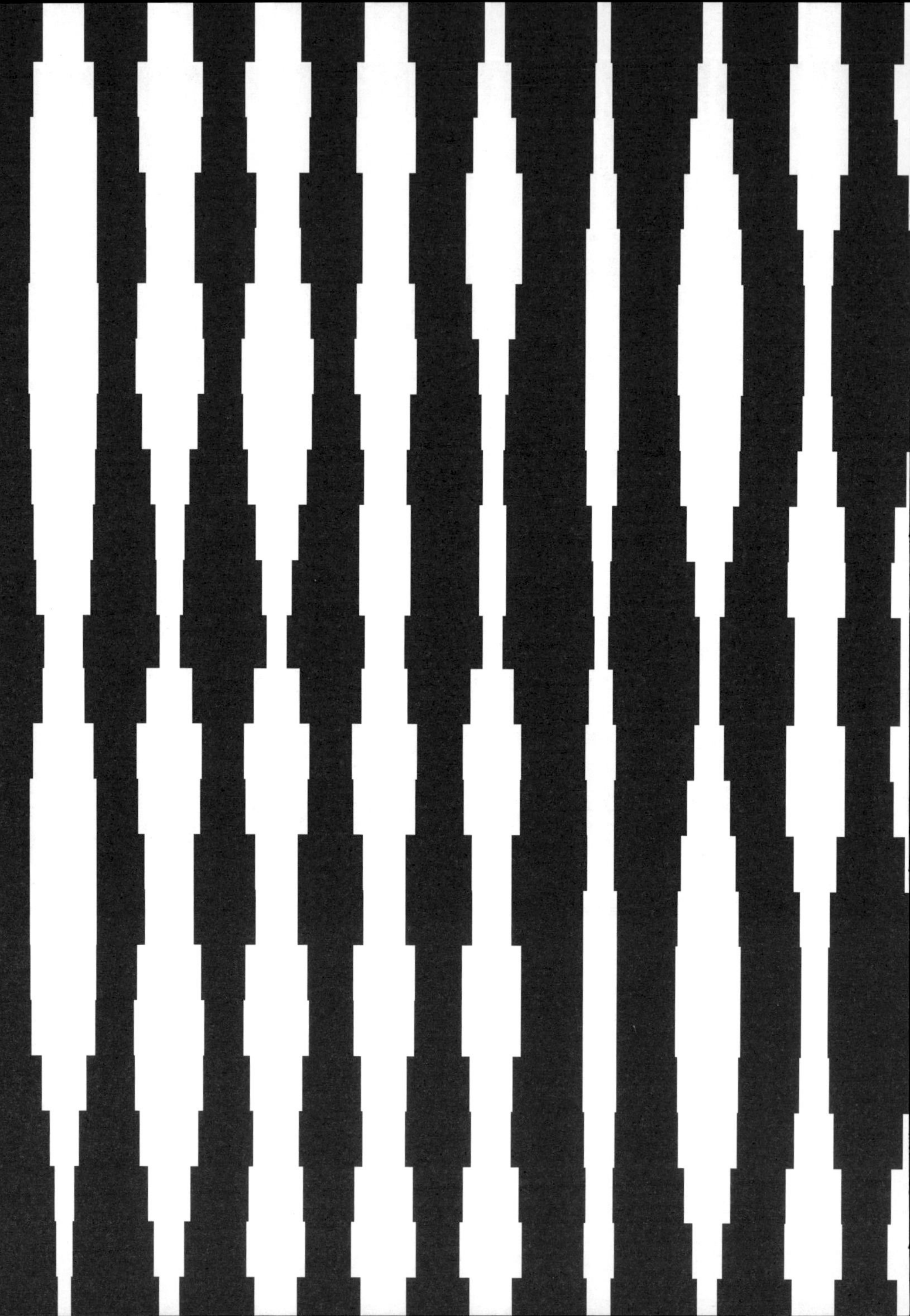

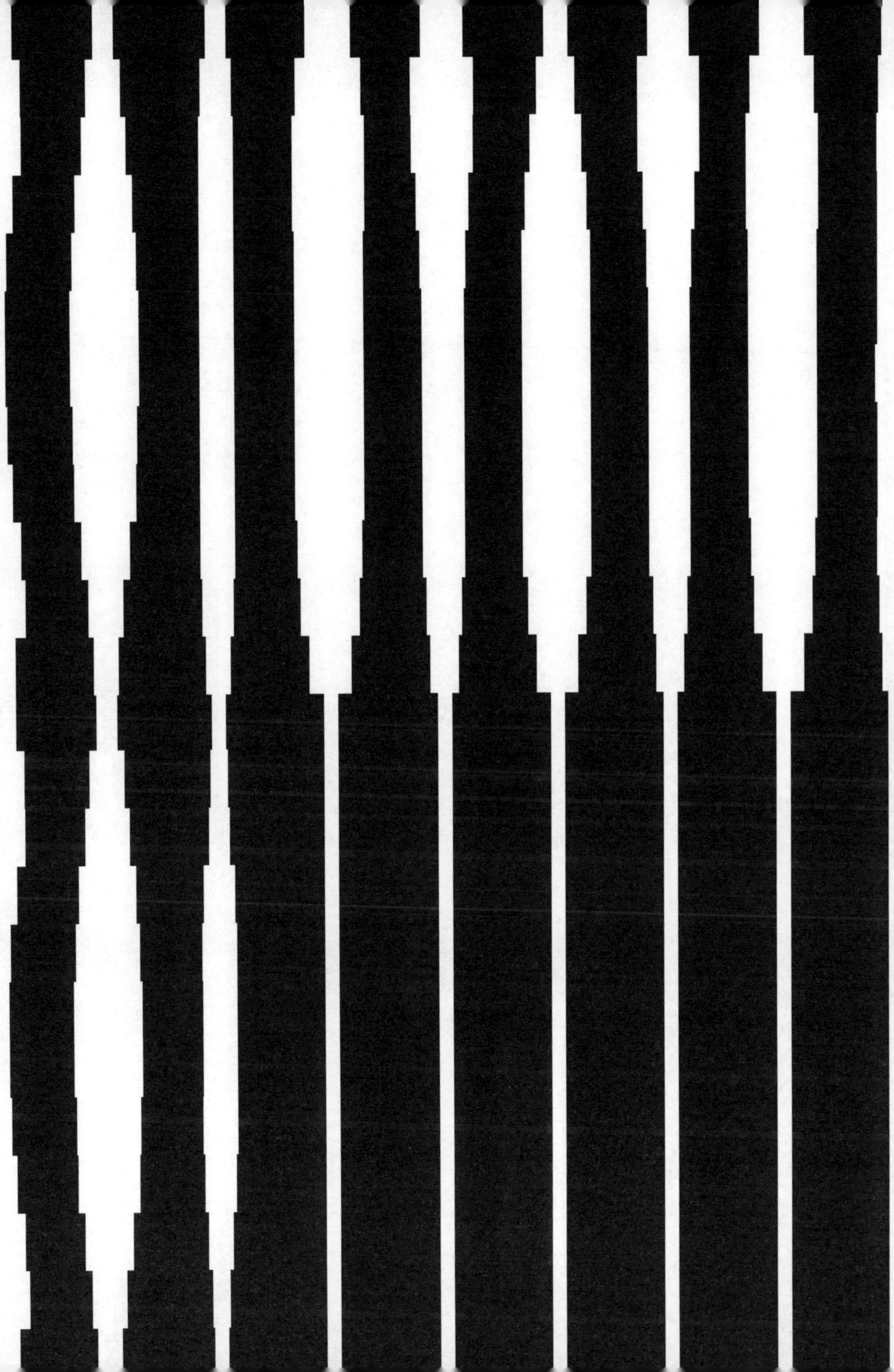

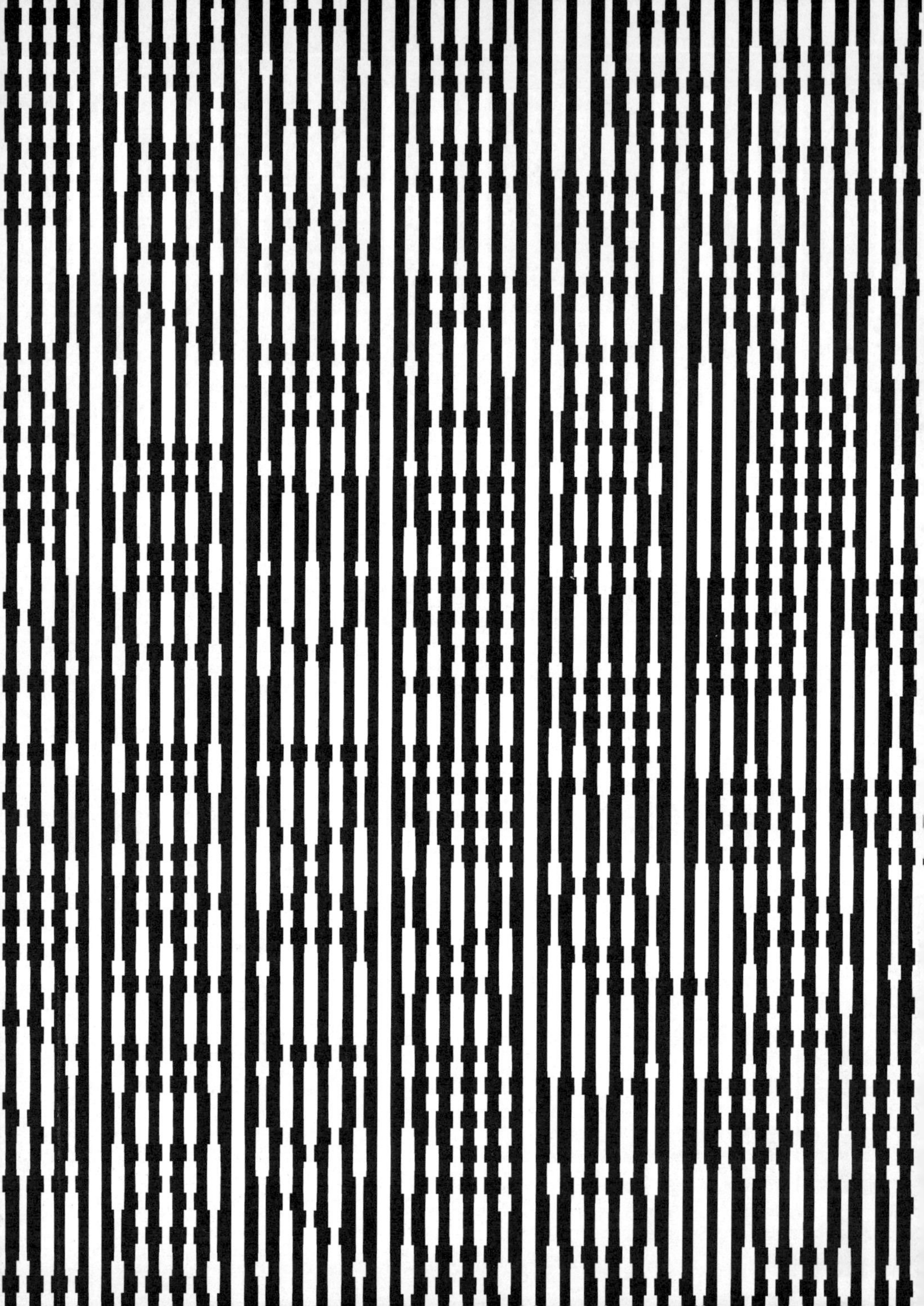

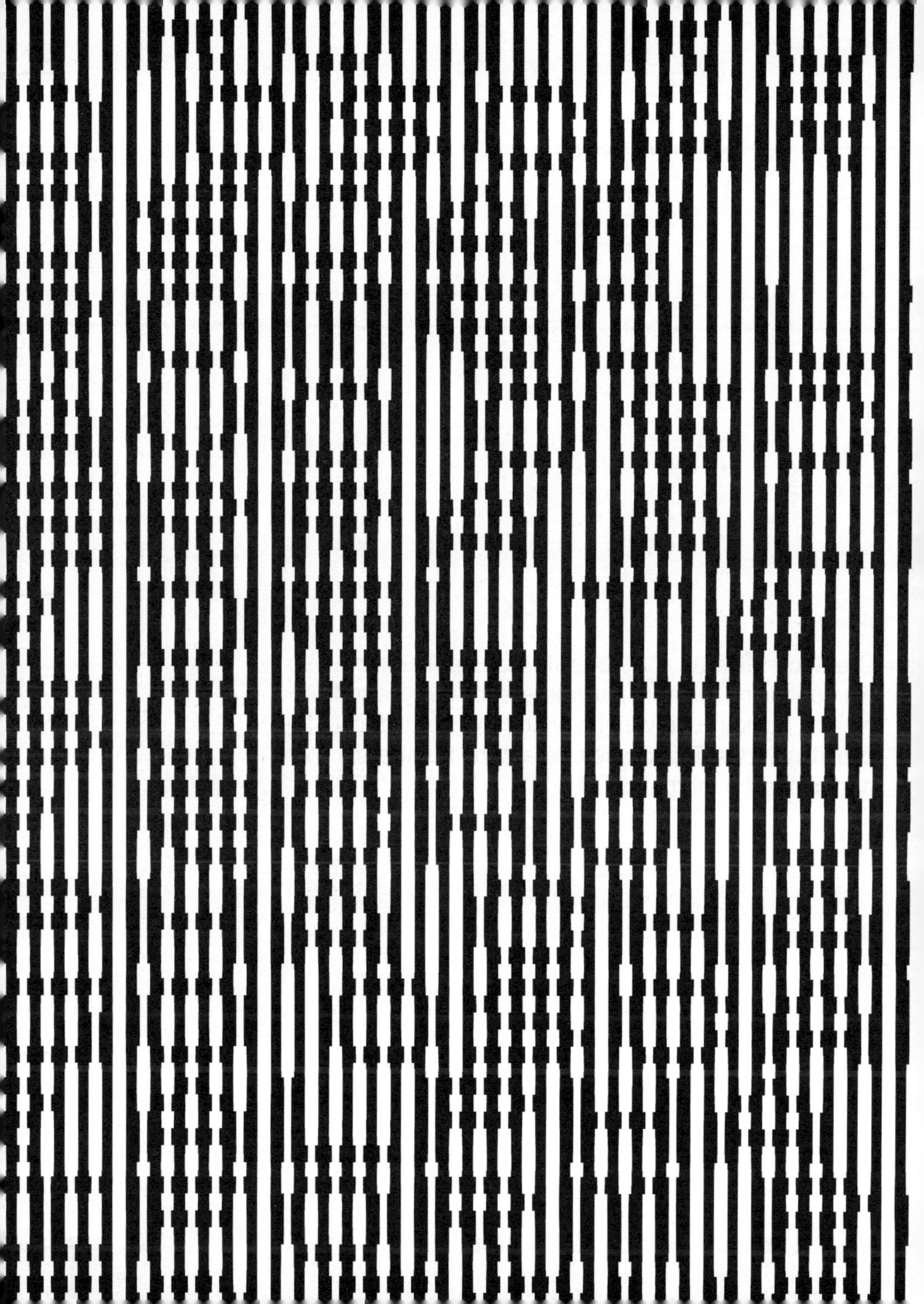

Section Notes:

Created in Glyphs, V.A consists of a single font file containing variable parameters for foreground weight, background weight, width and simulated blur, it includes uppercase characters, numbers, and minimal punctuation.

An amalgamation of both the Horizontal and Vertical type systems shown in earlier sections, this approach interweaves standard-width alphabets aligned along each axis. Additionally, two supplementary alphabets are introduced, with the underlying grid structure doubled and tripled in resolution respectively. In these high-resolution variants, the weave pattern takes on a more representative character, increasingly resembling the texture and structure of fabric.

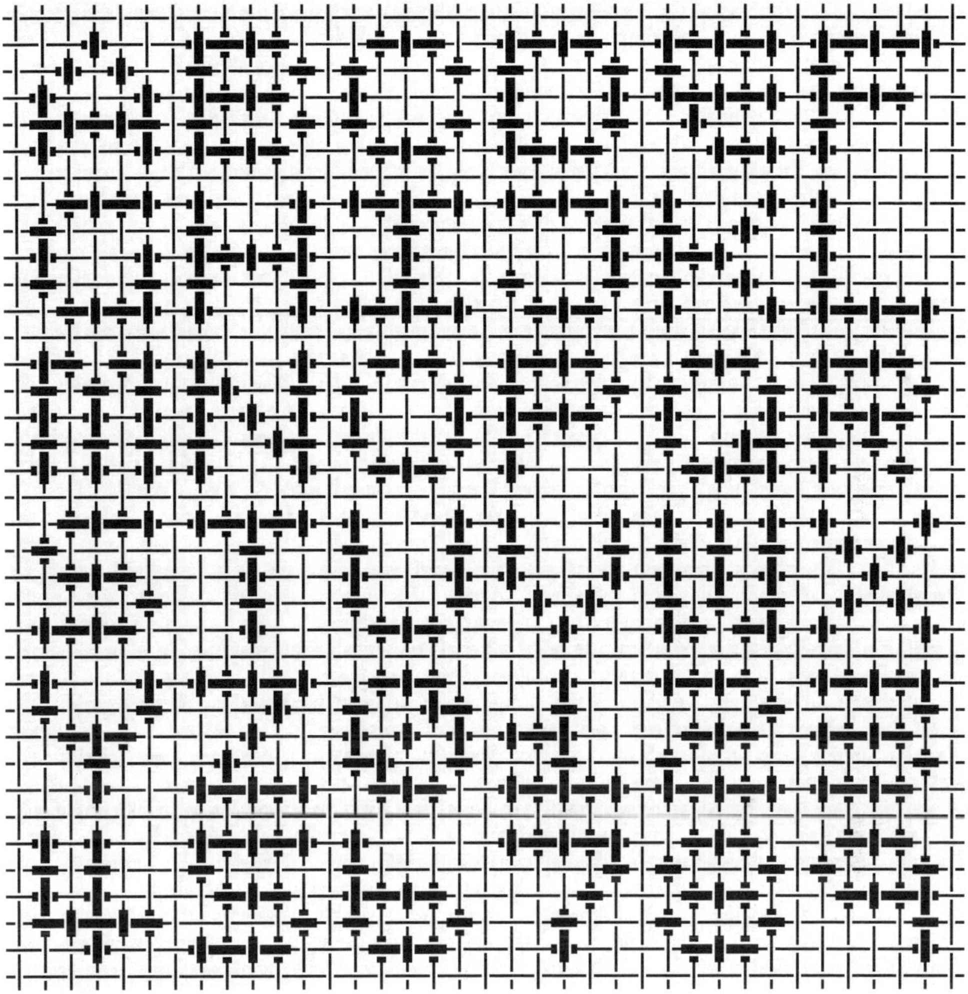

W.A A

A woven alphabet formed of meshing vertical and horizontal lines, bold in foreground and light in background weight

A–Z 0–9

s. 60
l. 60
t. 0
fw. 500
bw. 100

W.A B

A woven alphabet formed of meshing vertical and horizontal lines, light in foreground and bold in background weight

A–Z 0–9

s. 60
l. 60
t. 0
fw. 100
bw. 900

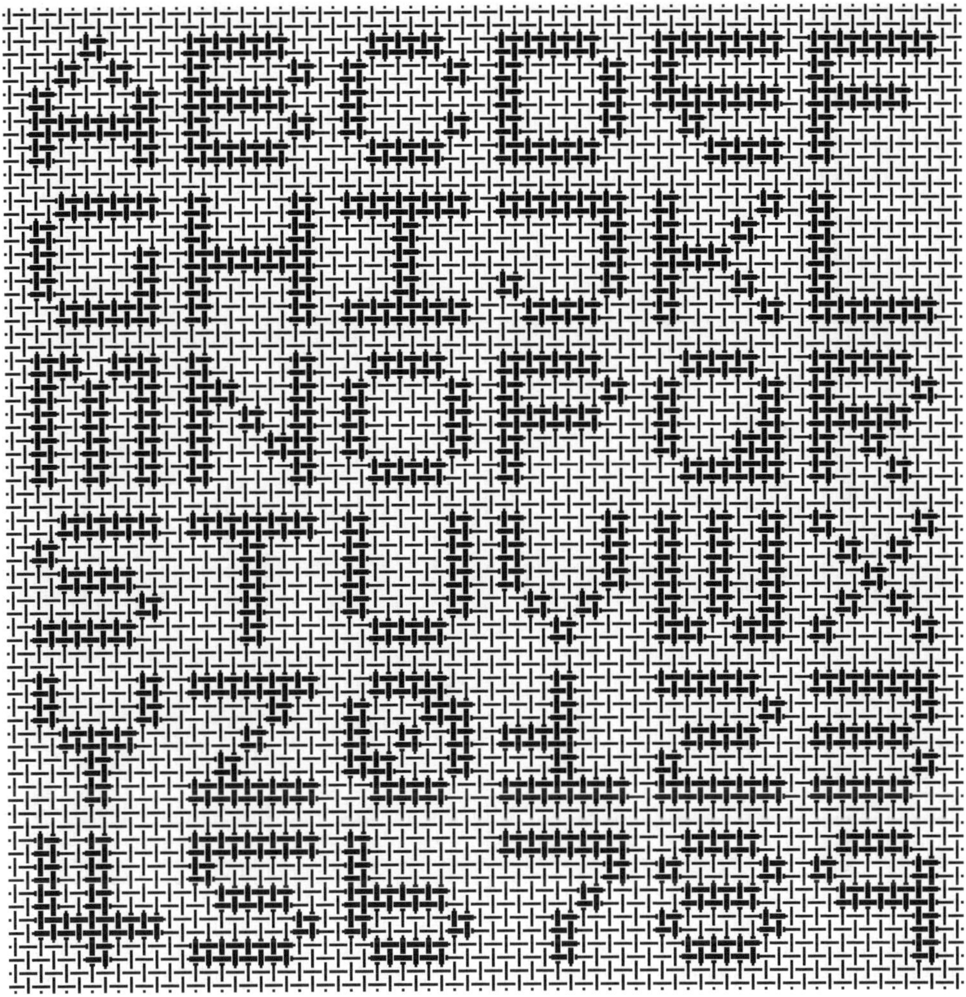

W.B A

A woven alphabet formed of detailed meshing vertical and horizontal lines, bold in foreground and light in background weight

A–Z 0–9

s. 60
l. 60
t. 0
fw. 900
bw. 100

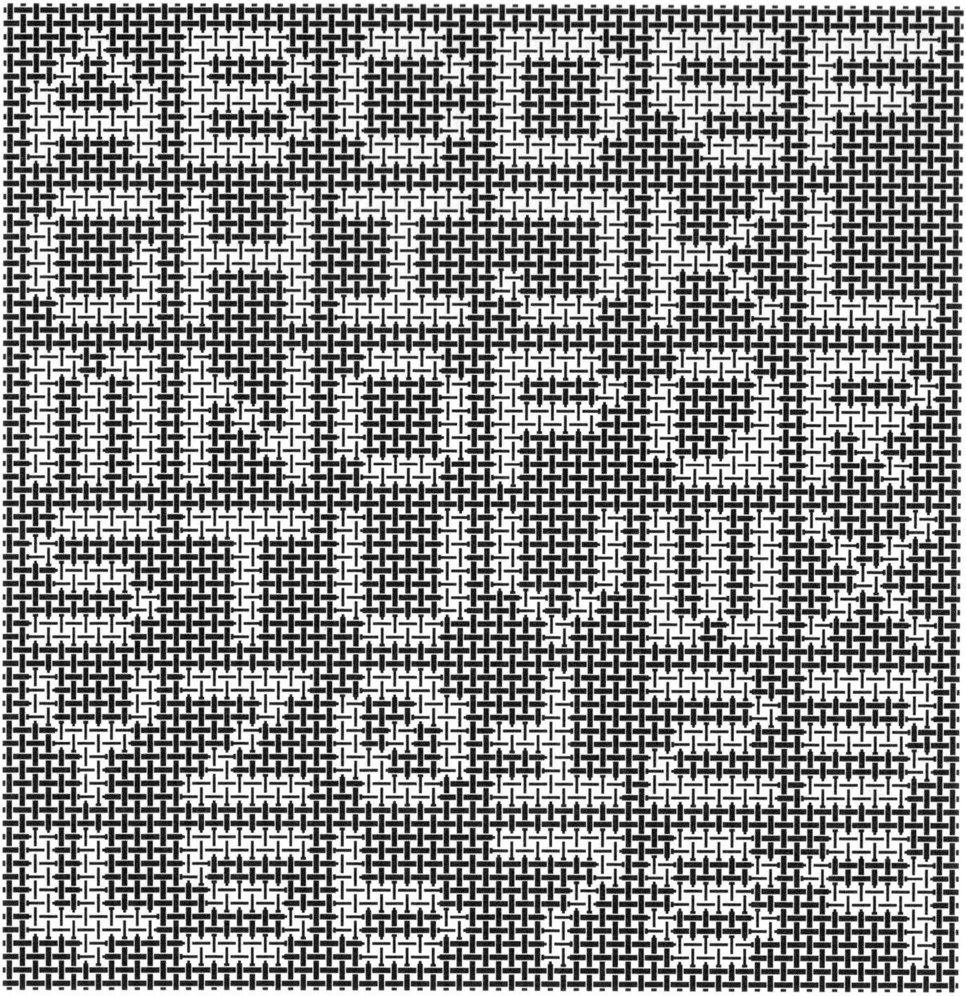

W.B B

A woven alphabet formed of detailed meshing vertical and horizontal lines, light in foreground and bold in background weight

A–Z 0–9

s. 60
l. 60
t. 0
fw. 100
bw. 900

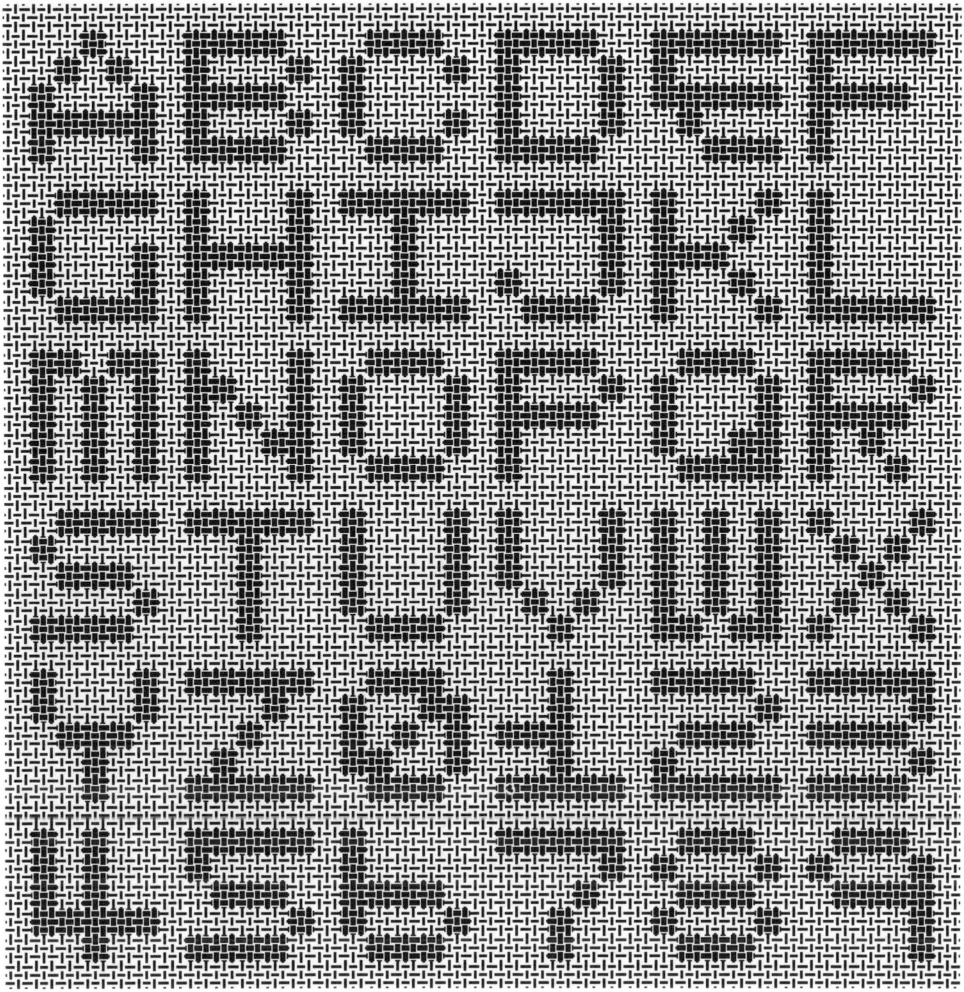

W.C A

A woven alphabet formed of intricate meshing vertical and horizontal lines, bold in foreground and light in background weight

A–Z 0–9

s. 60
l. 60
t. 0
fw. 900
bw. 100

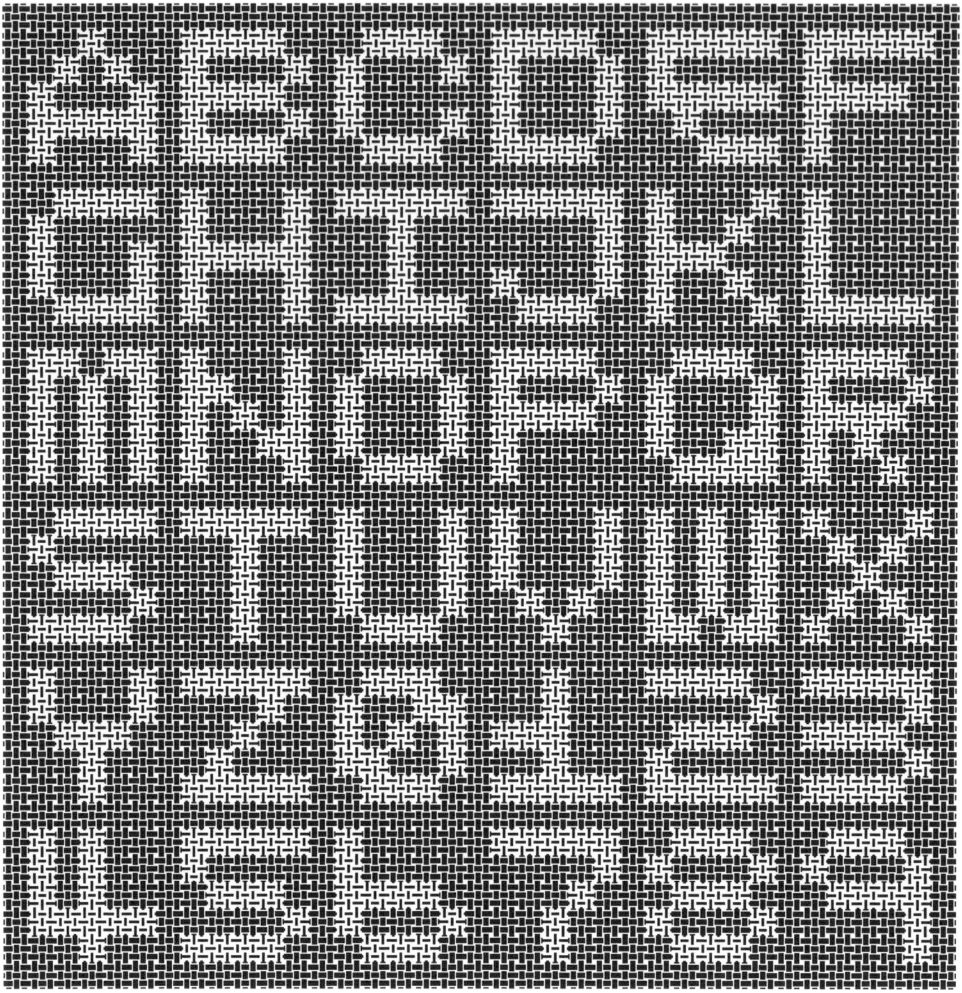

W.C B

A woven alphabet formed of intricate meshing vertical and horizontal lines, light in foreground and bold in background weight

A–Z 0–9

s. 60
l. 60
t. 0
fw. 100
bw. 900

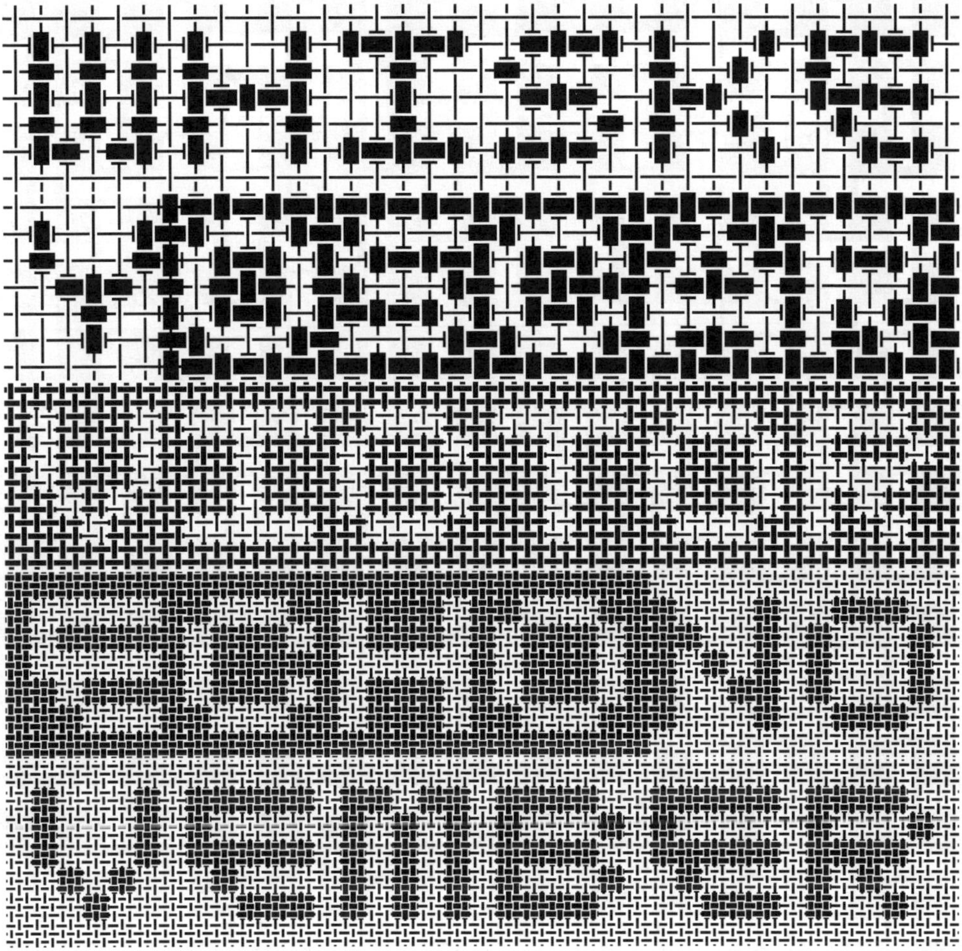

W.A–C

Whiskey Oscar Victor
Echo November

s.	60
l.	71
t.	0
fw.	±
bw.	±

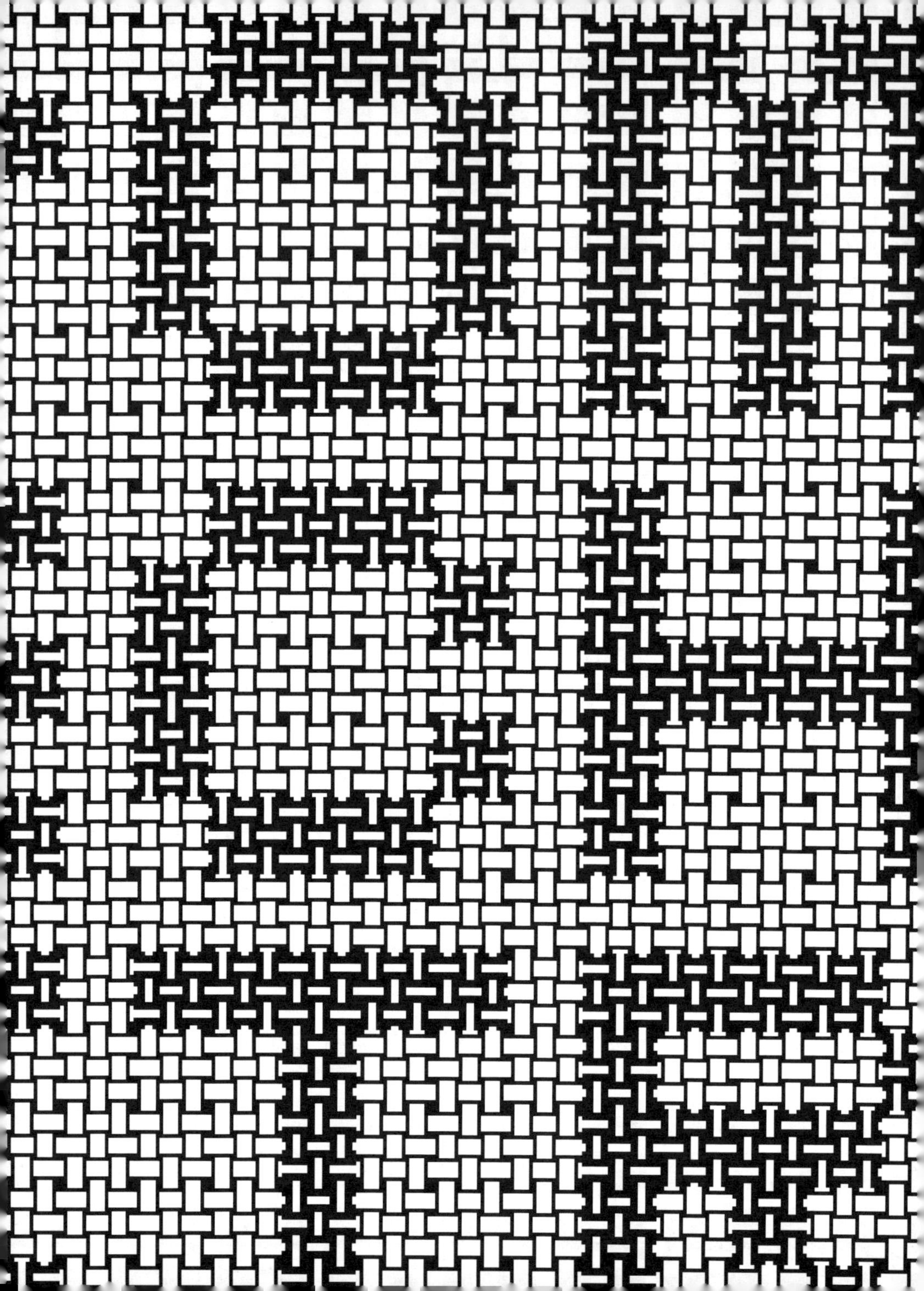

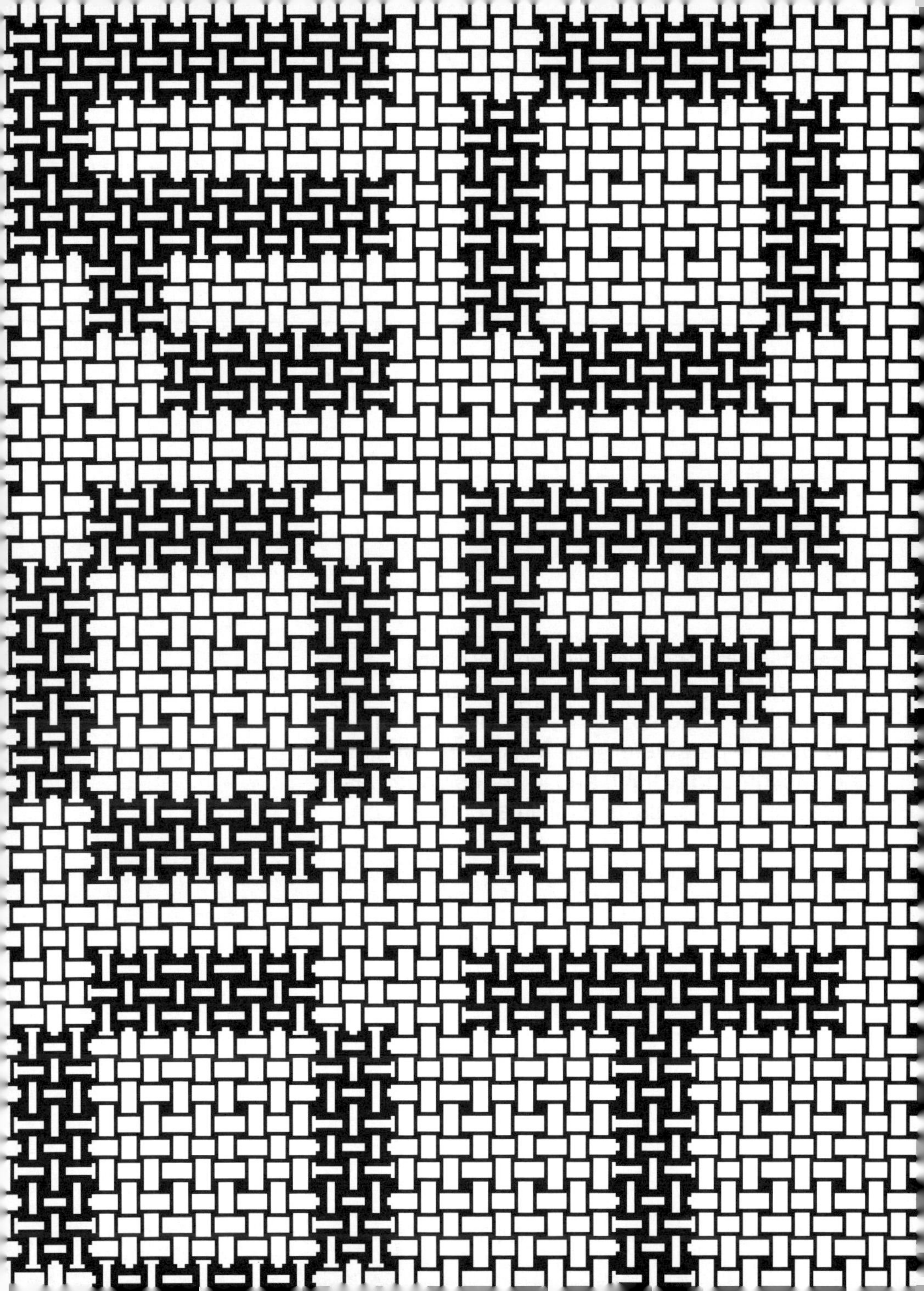

Section Notes:

Created in Glyphs, W.A, W.B, and W.C are an amalgamation of both the Horizontal and Vertical type systems. Each is a single font file with variable parameters for foreground weight and background weight, and includes uppercase characters, numerals, and minimal punctuation.

The final section extends the ideas explored throughout Alphabetical Playground by amalgamating combinations of any three themes into individual letterforms. The result is a series of experimental typographic alphabets that challenge conventional legibility while emphasising the esoteric nature of the design spaces they occupy. They illustrate the enormous creative potential of multilayered combinatoric systems, yielding a diverse range of unexpected outcomes.

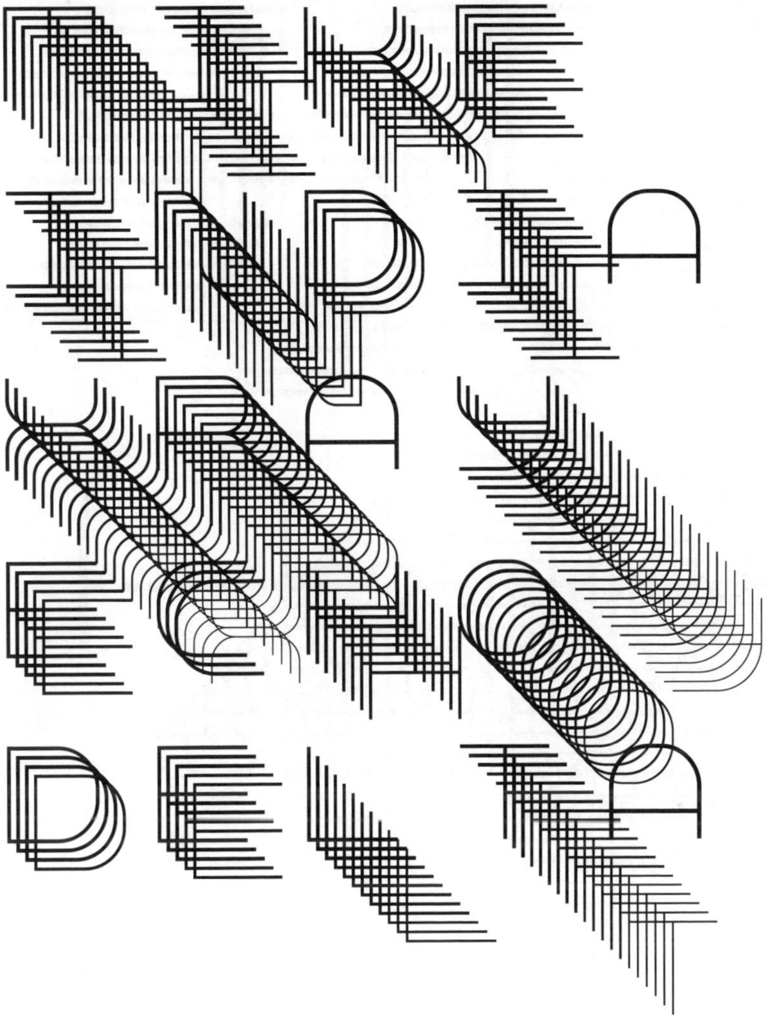

XYZ. A

Gradated × Alphanumeric × Dimensional. An alphabet formed of letterforms gradated in weight, repeated based on each letter's alphanumeric code through a cavalier projection

Mike India Xray
Echo Delta

s. 116
l. 70
t. 150

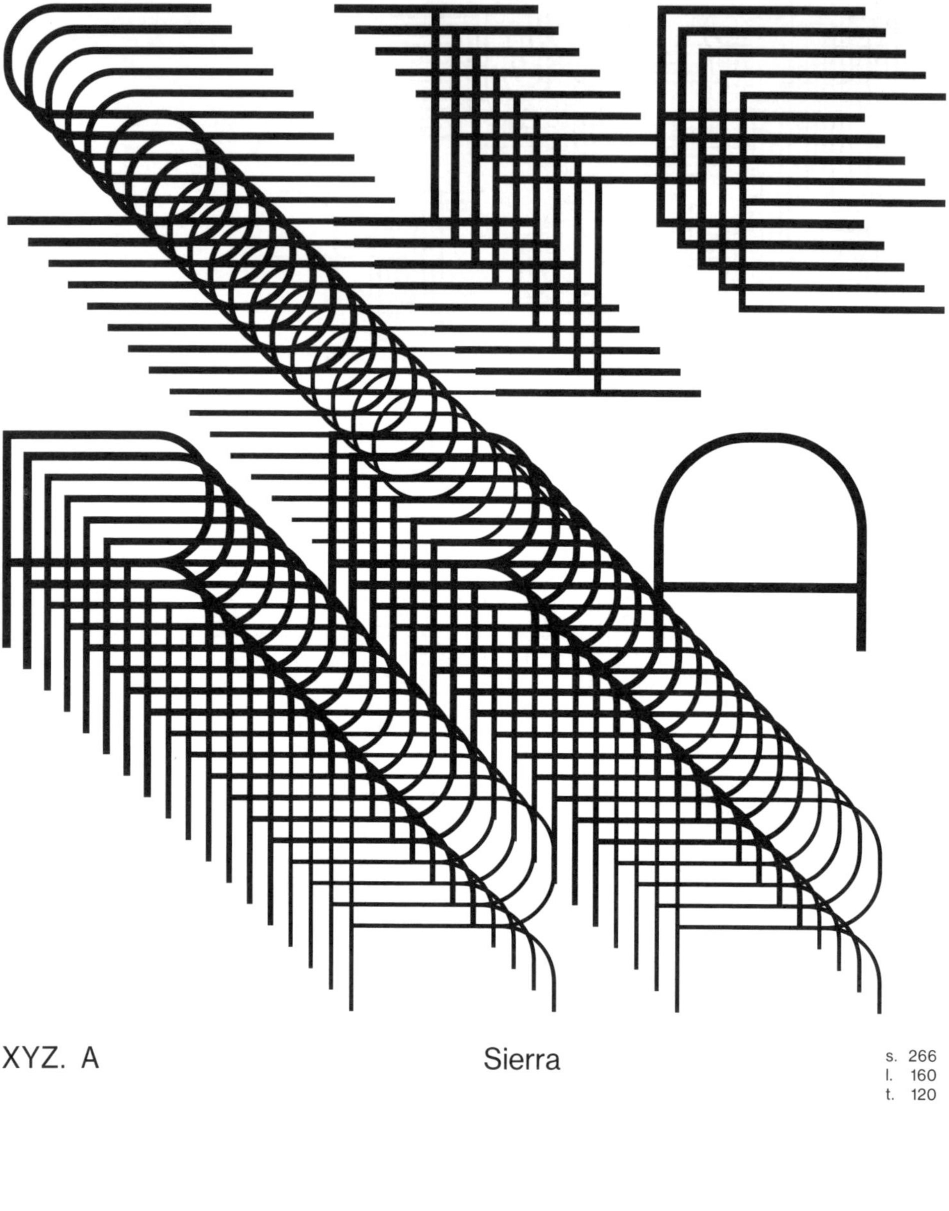

XYZ. A

Sierra

s. 266
l. 160
t. 120

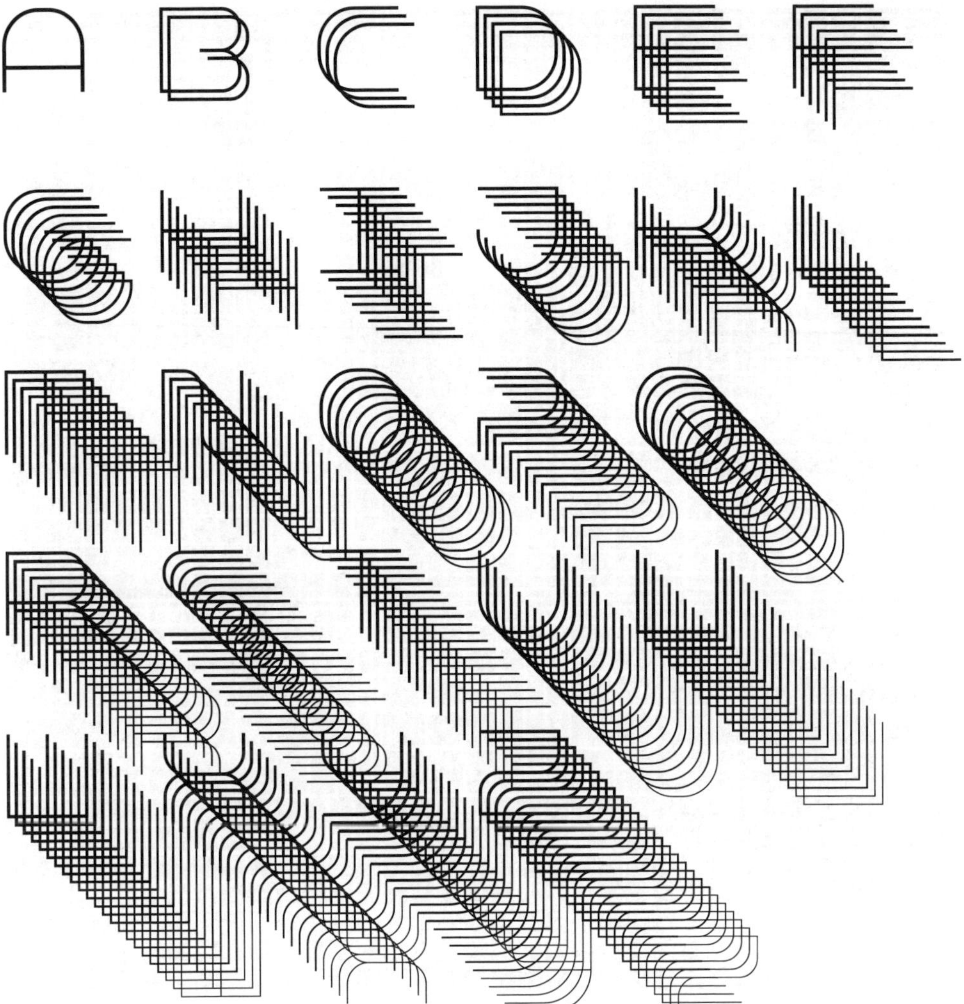

XYZ. A

A–Z

s. 103
l. 68
t. 240

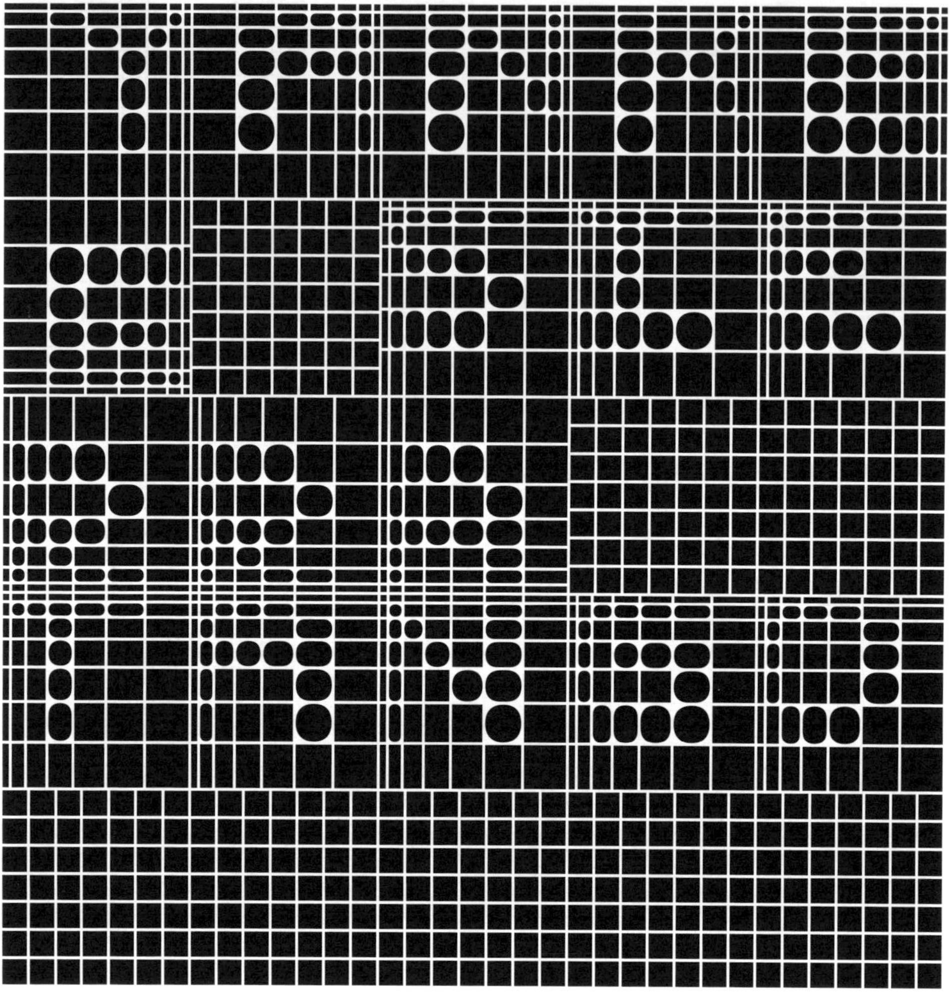

XYZ. B

Kinetic × Shifting Pattern × Gradated. An optically shifting alphabet formed of a rounded gradated square grid

Yankee Sierra Tango

s. 92
l. 92
t. 0
h. ±
v. ±

XYZ. B

A–Z 0–9

s. 61
l. 61
t. 0
h. ±
v. ±

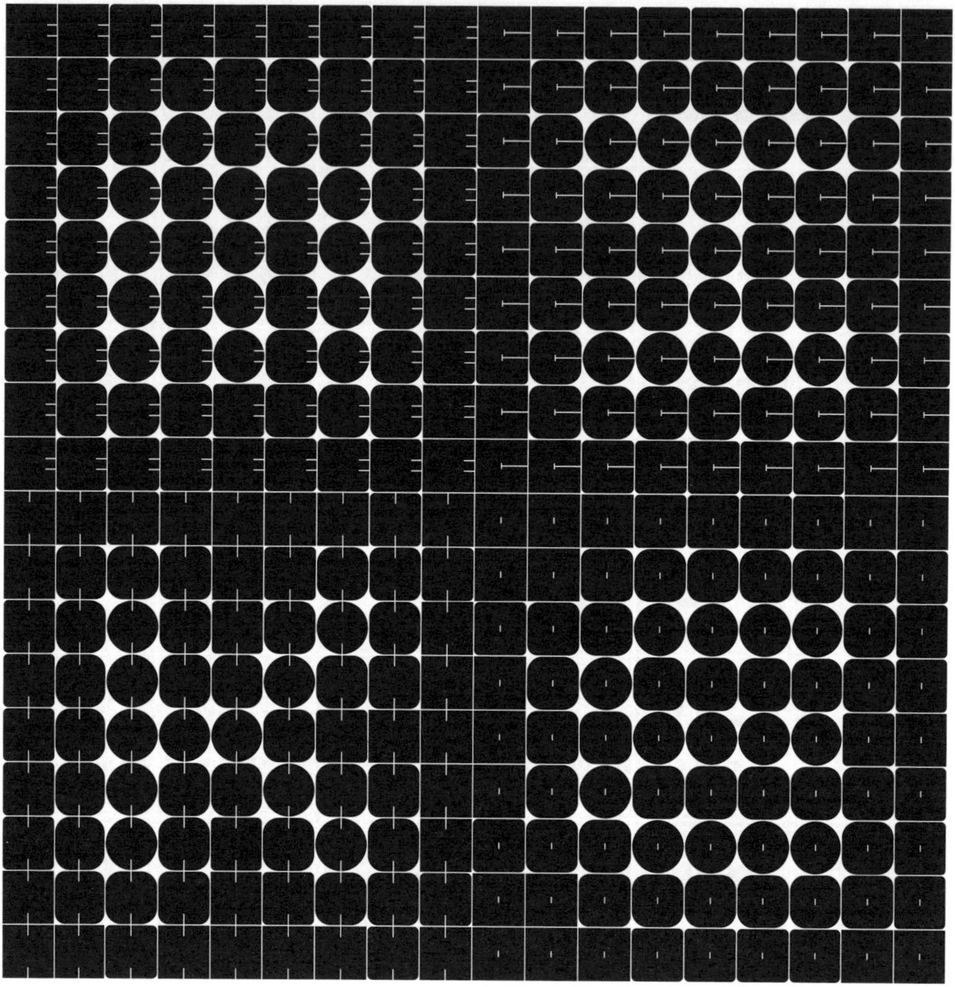

XYZ. C

Letters within letters × Embedded geometry × Dimensional.
A 2 layer letters within letters writing system with a macro layer formed of superellipse curves with a blurred effect

Echo Mike

s. 184
l. 184
t. 0

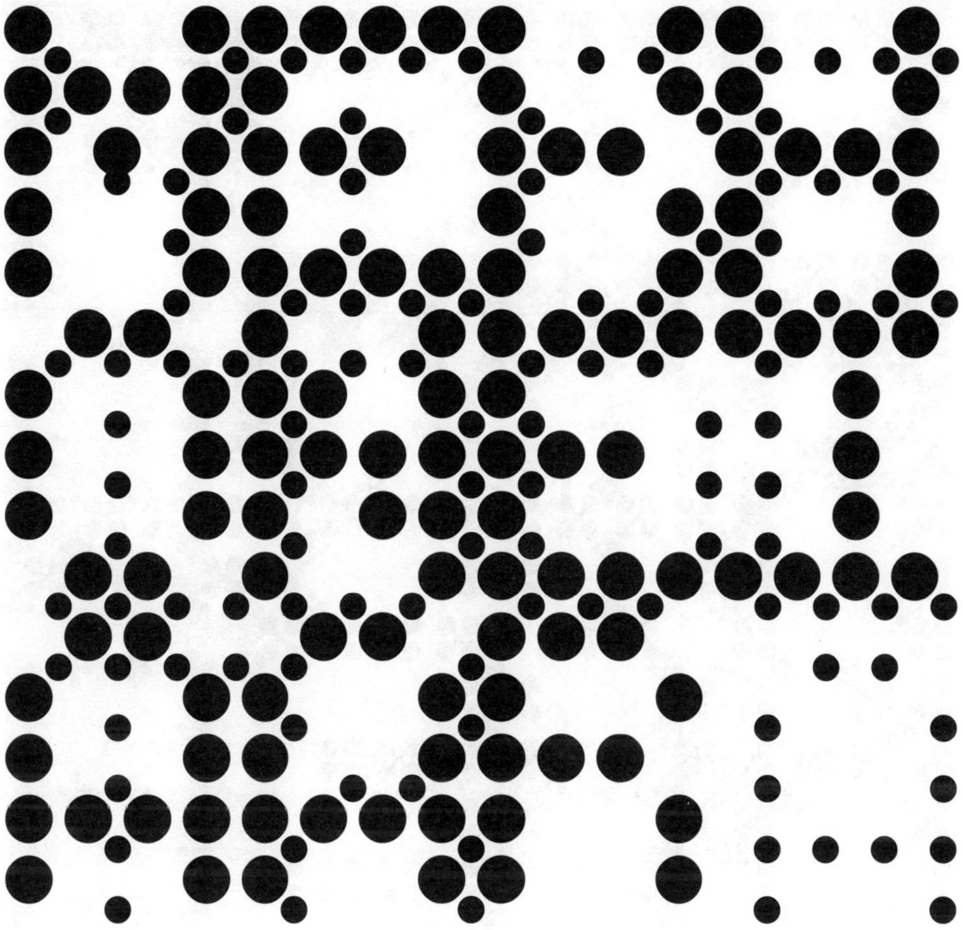

XYZ. D

Inverting × Letters-within-Letters × Matrix.
An inverting in prominence, 2 layer letters within letters matrix writing system formed of a range of shapes

Mike India Xray Echo Delta

s. 114
l. 114
t. 0

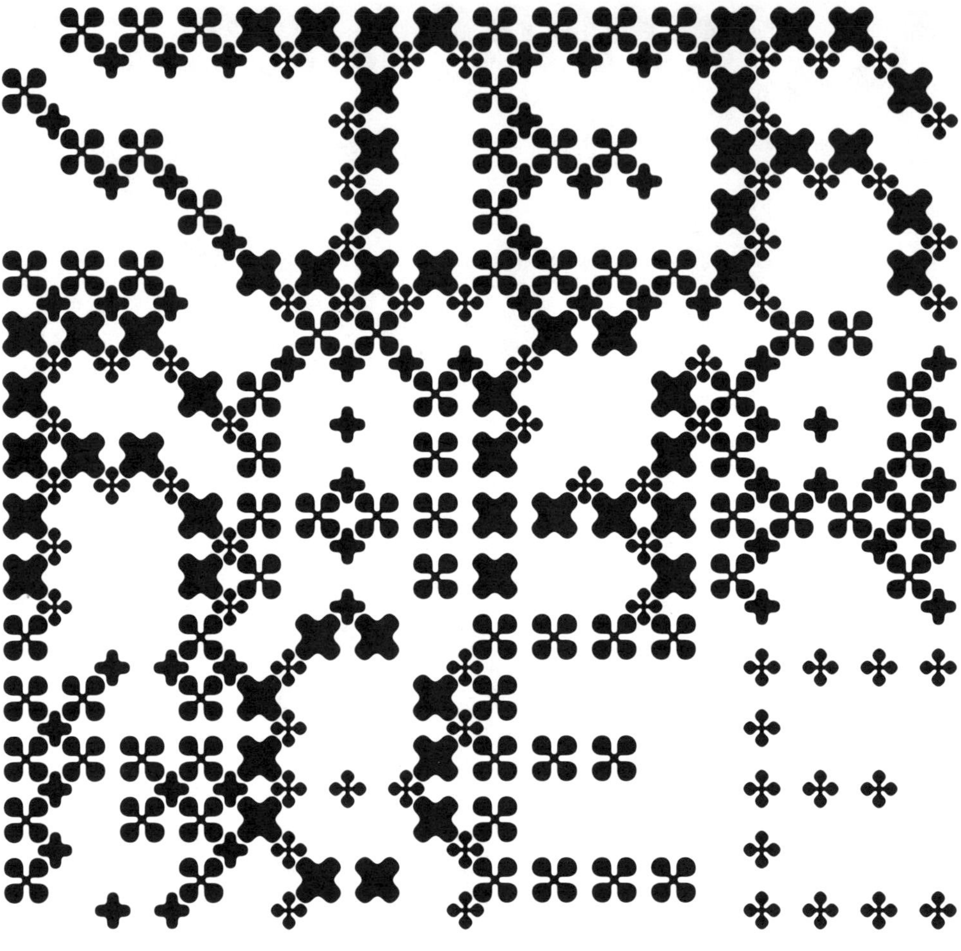

XYZ. D

Sierra Yankee Sierra Tango

s. 114
l. 114
t. 0

XYZ. D

Echo Mike

s. 185
l. 185
t. 0

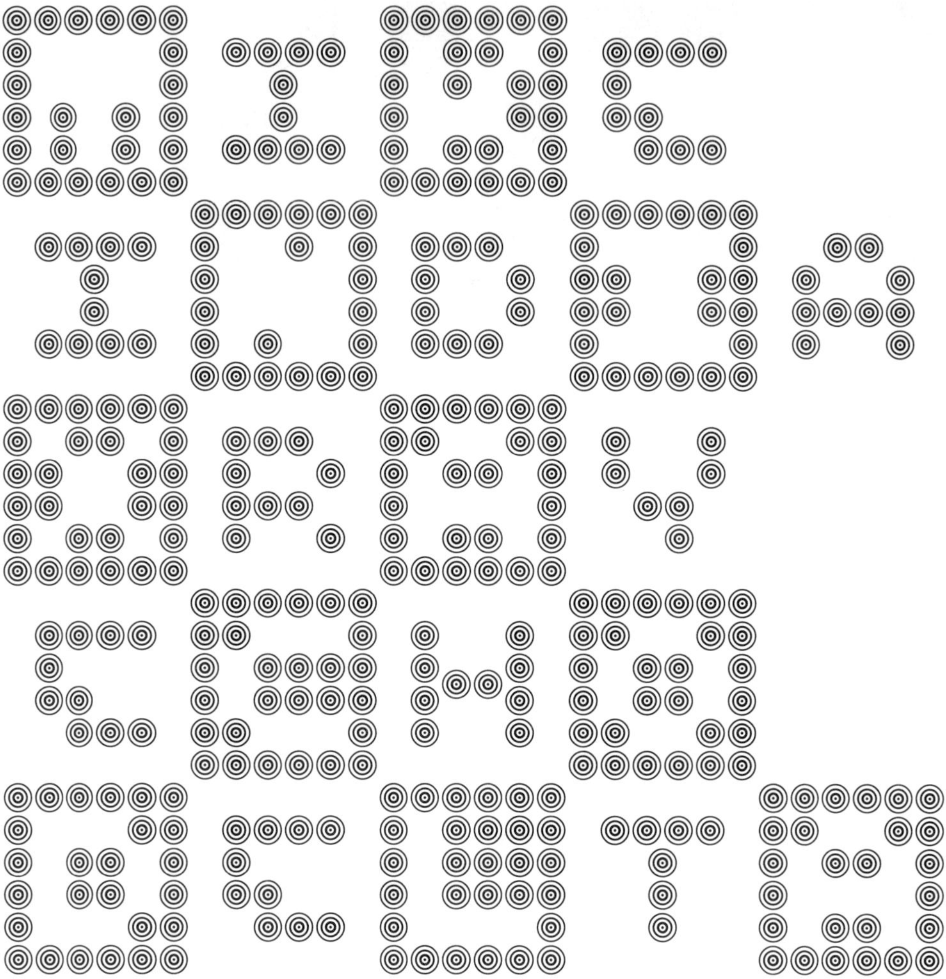

XYZ. E

Matrix × Gradated × Inverting.
A matrix alphabet formed of circles gradating in weight, alternating between negative and positive space from character to character

Mike India Xray Echo Delta

s. 73
l. 73
t. 0

XYZ. F

Neo-Matrix × Gradated × Inverting.
A Neo-Matrix alphabet formed of conjoining circles gradating in weight, alternating between negative and positive space from character to character

Sierra Yankee Sierra Tango

s. 73
l. 73
t. 0

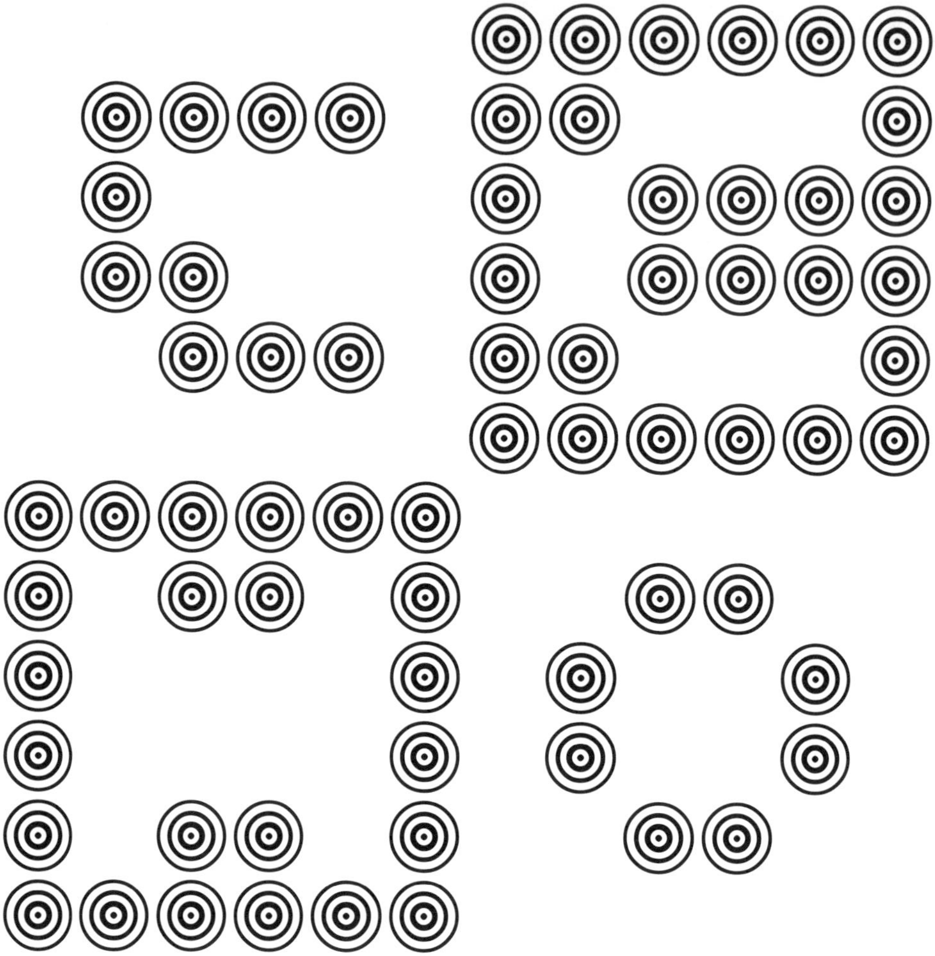

XYZ. E

Echo

s. 180
l. 180
t. 0

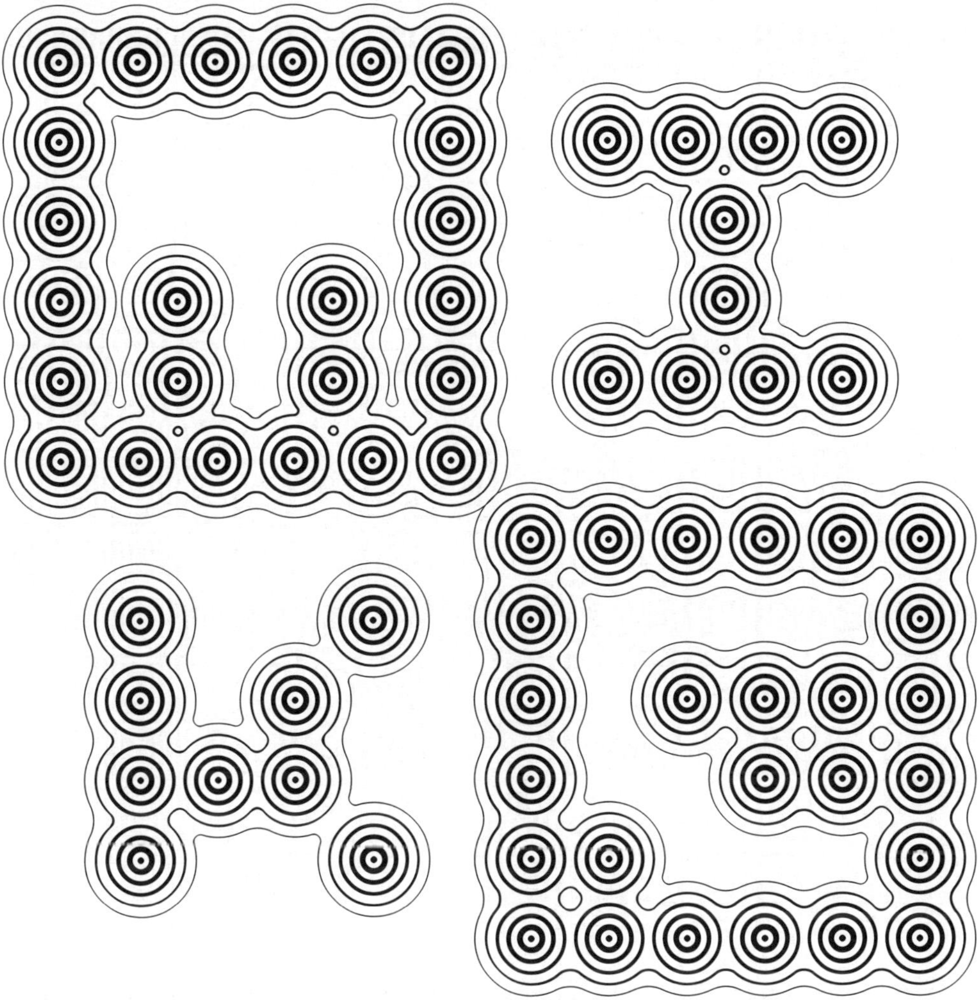

XYZ. F

Mike

s. 180
l. 180
t. 0

XYZ. G

Shifting Pattern × Gradated × Inverting.
A shifting pattern alphabet formed of a gradating cross pattern alternating between negative and positive space from character to character

Mike India Xray Echo Delta

s. 74
l. 74
t. 0

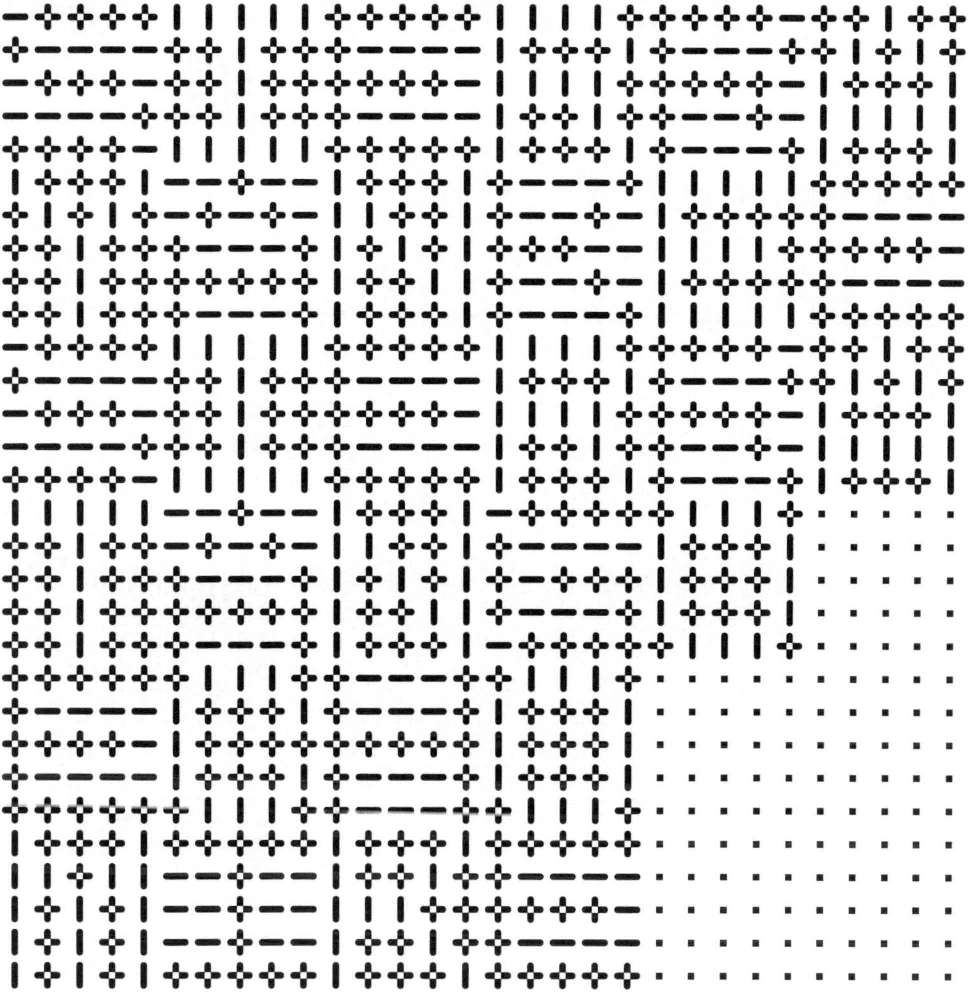

XYZ. H

Neo-Matrix × Shifting Pattern × Inverting. A Neo-Matrix shifting pattern alphabet formed of a rotated stadium curve cross pattern alternating between negative and positive space from character to character

Sierra Yankee Sierra Tango Echo Mike

s. 62
l. 62
t. 0

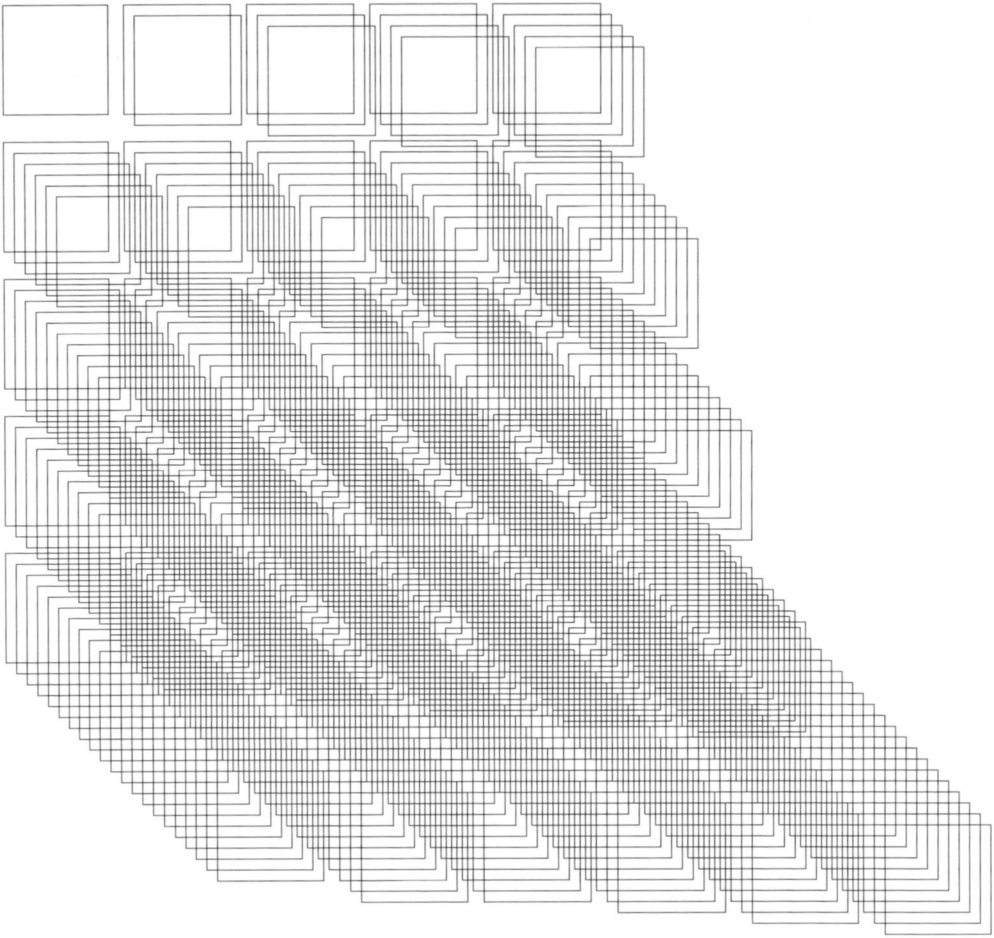

XYZ. I

Alphanumeric × Gradated × Dimensional. An alphabet formed of gradated outline squares repeated based on its letter's alphanumeric code through a cavalier projection

A–Z

s. 137
l. 51
t. -15

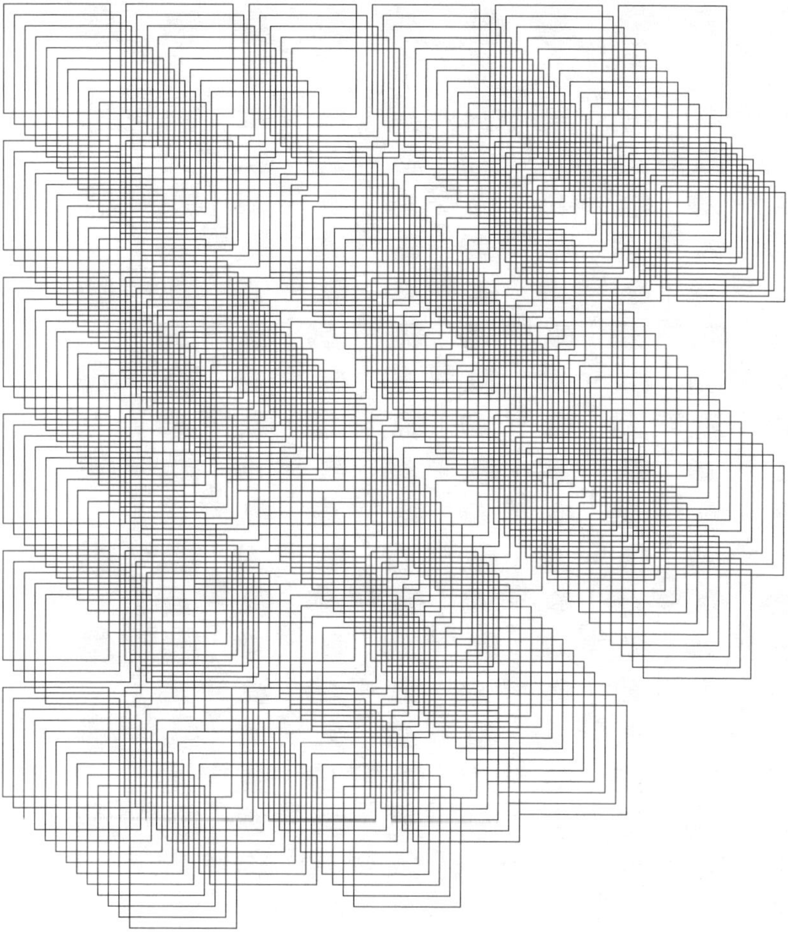

XYZ. I

Sierra Yankee Sierra
Tango Echo Mike

s. 137
l. 51
t. -15

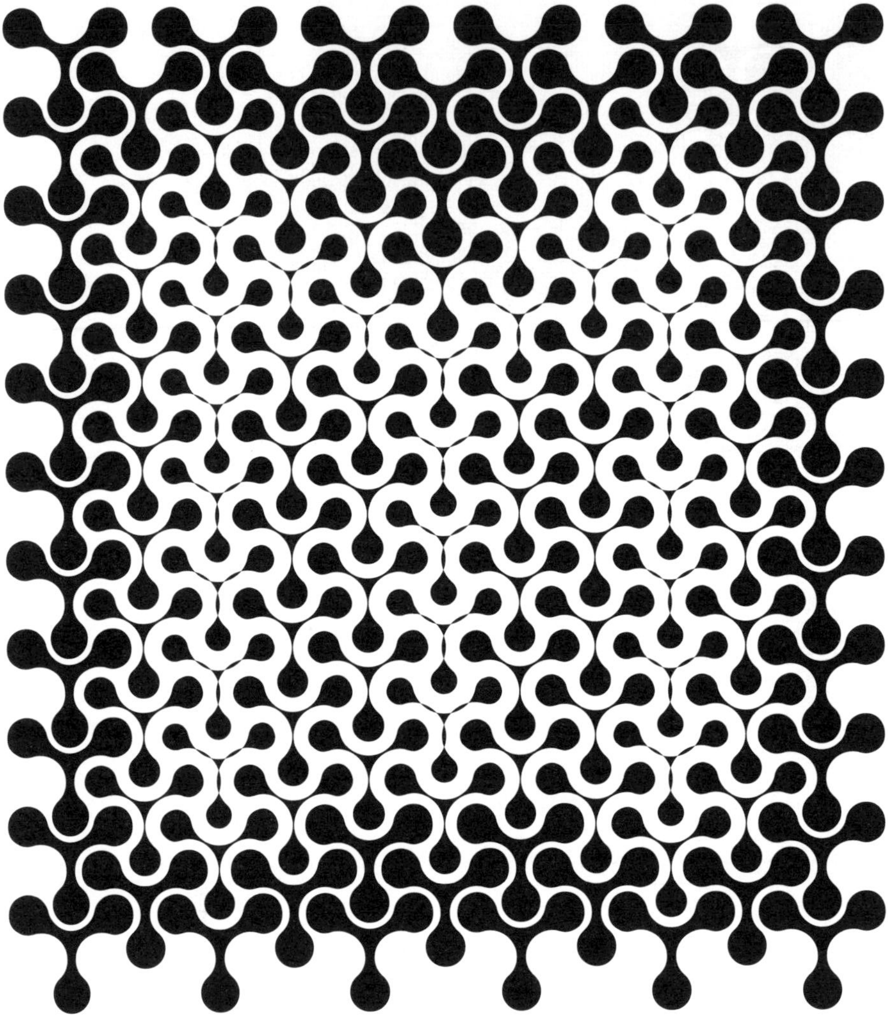

XYZ. J

Dimensional × Matrix × Tessellation.
A blurred alphabet formed of tessellating pinched trefoils

M

s. 333
l. 333
t. 0

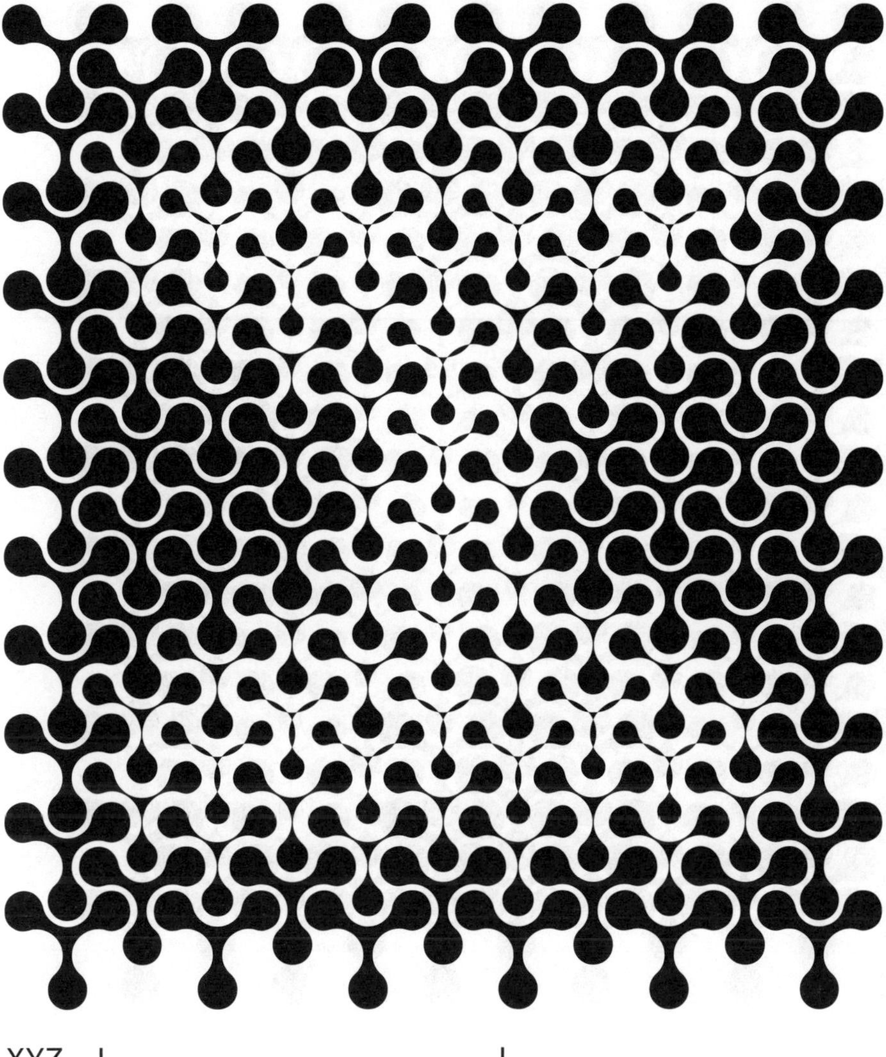

XYZ. J I

s. 333
l. 333
t. 0

XYZ. J K

s. 333
l. 333
t. 0

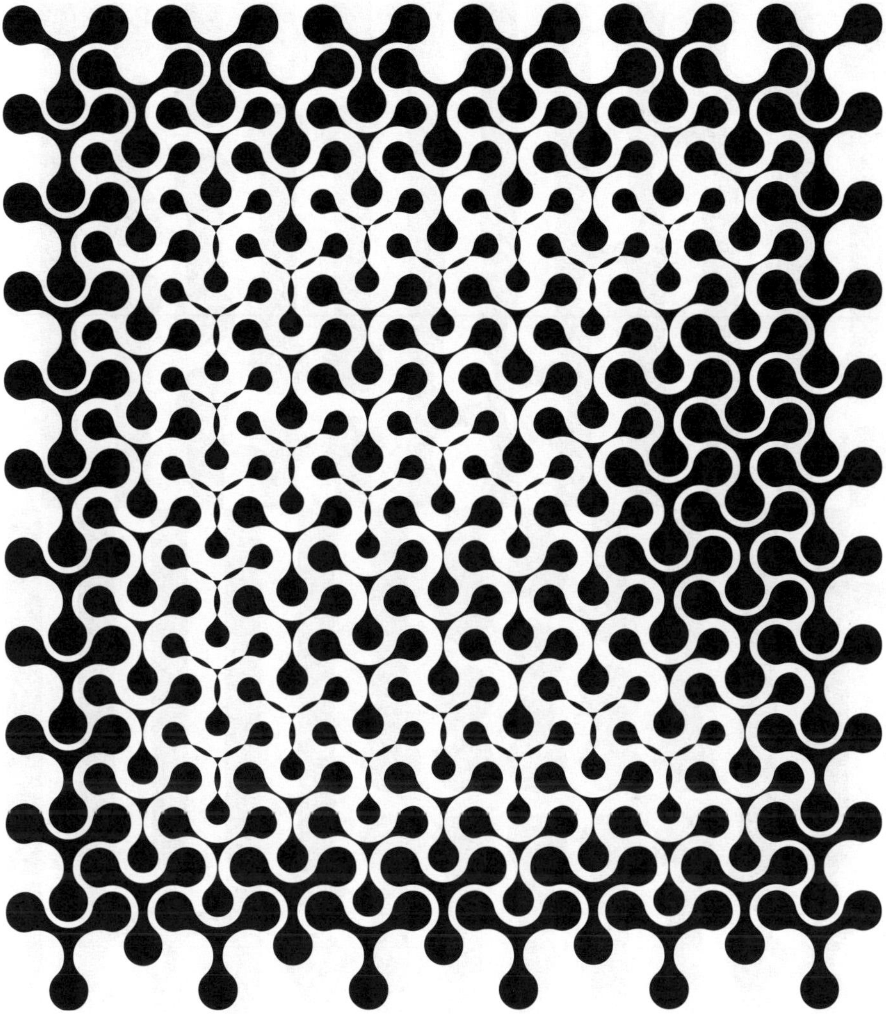

XYZ. J

E

s. 333
l. 333
t. 0

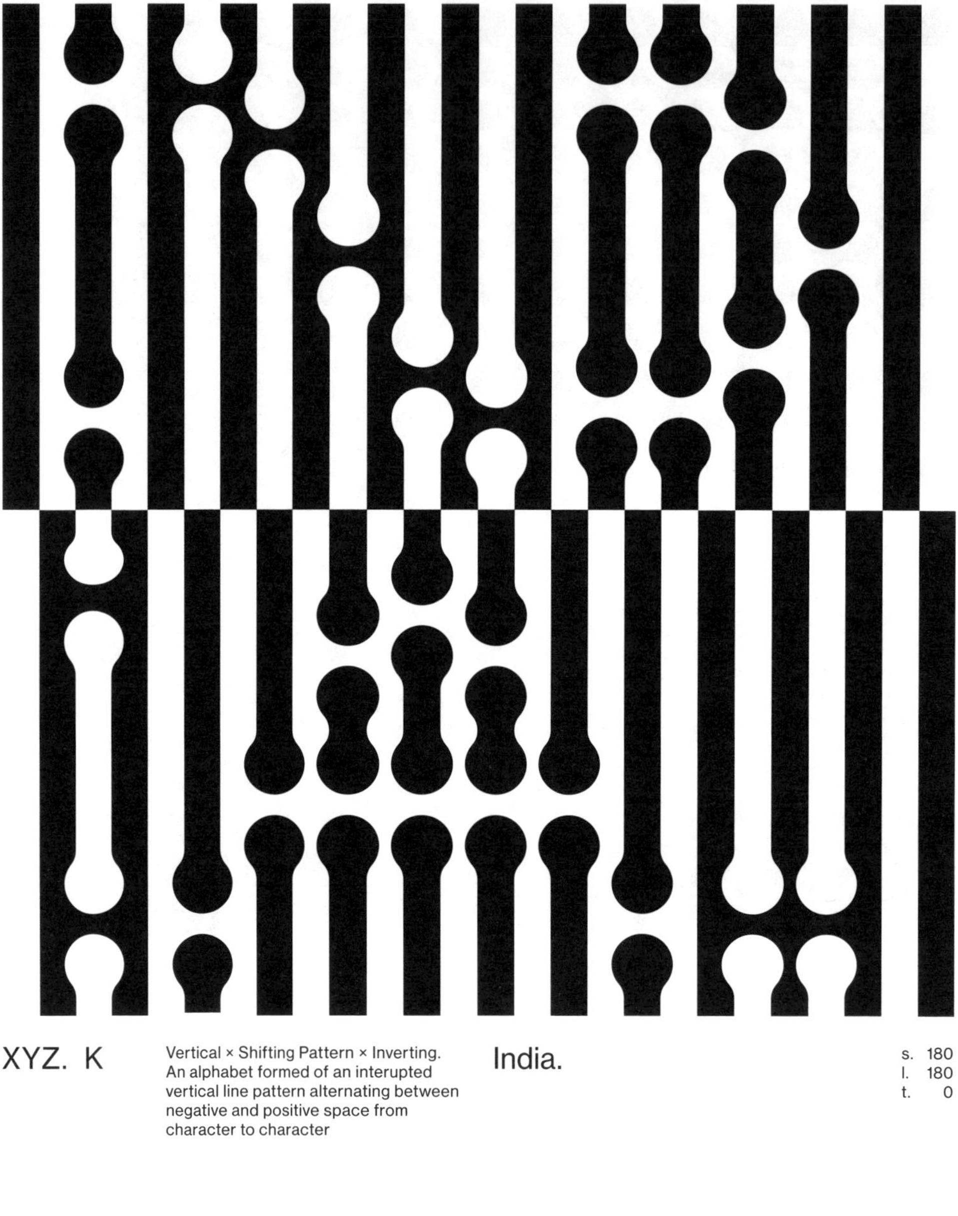

XYZ. K

Vertical × Shifting Pattern × Inverting.
An alphabet formed of an interupted vertical line pattern alternating between negative and positive space from character to character

India.

s. 180
l. 180
t. 0

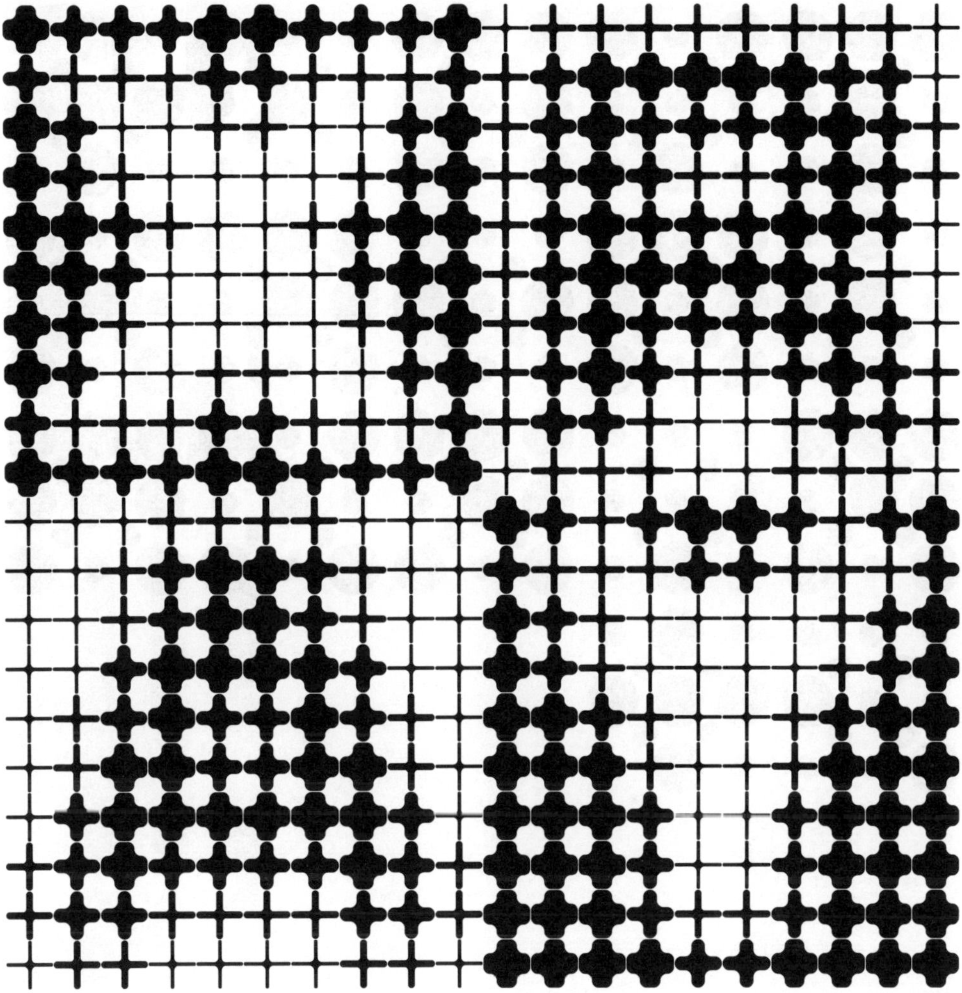

XYZ. L

Dimensional × Matrix × Inverting.
A blurred Matrix alphabet formed of rounded crosses alternating between negative and positive space from character to character

Xray

s. 185
l. 185
t. 0

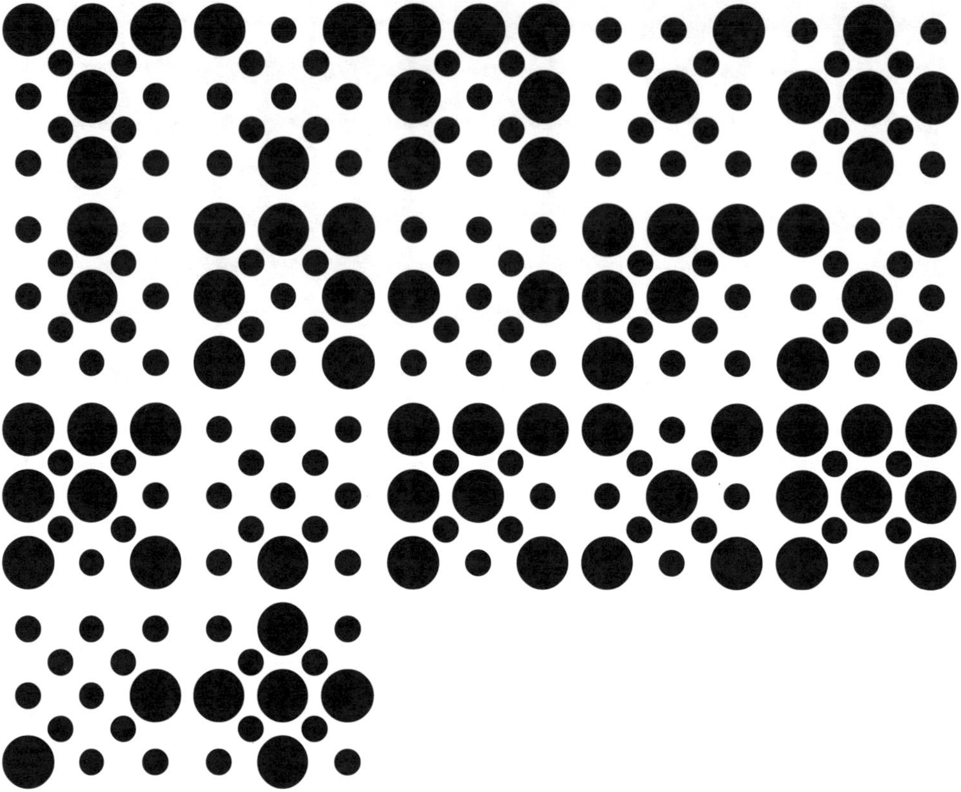

XYZ. M

Kinetic × Shifting Pattern × Inverting.
An optically shifting alphabet formed of scaled dots on a diagonal grid alternating between negative and positive space from character to character

Tango Uniform Romeo

s. 75
l. 75
t. 0

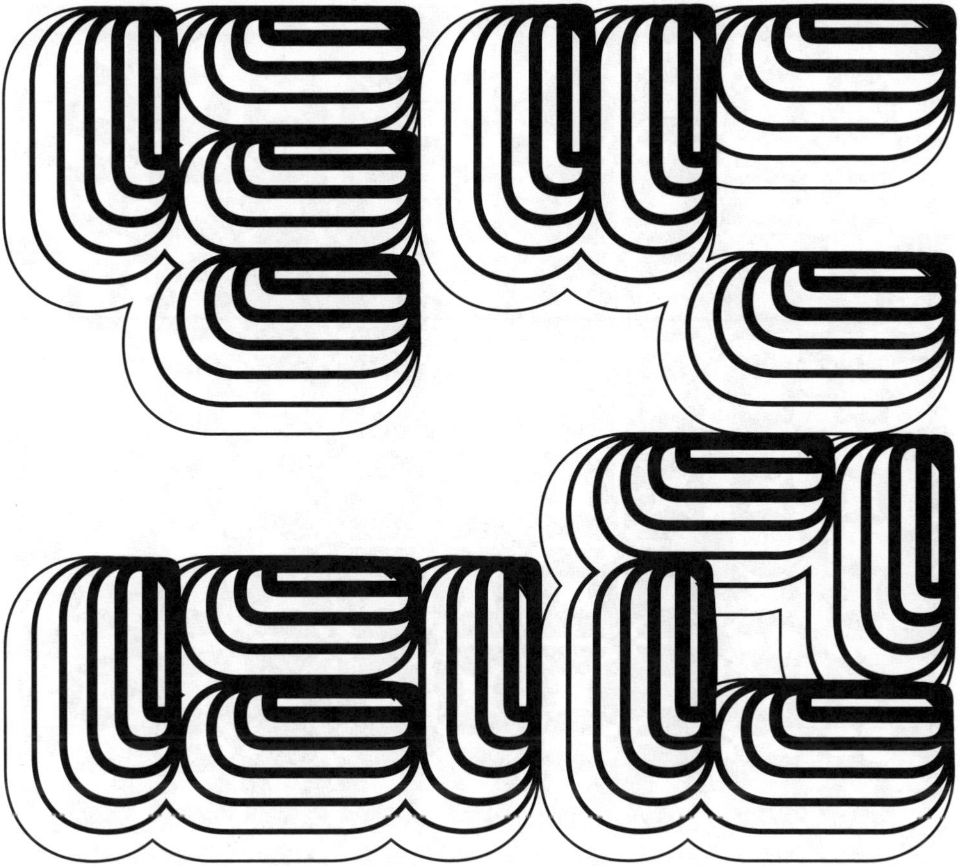

XYZ. N

Gradated × Dimensional × Quadrisect.
An alphabet with repeated gradated letters through a cavalier projection from 4 equal outline stadium curves

Echo

s. 185
l. 185
t. 0

XYZ. O

Dimensional × Neo-Matrix × Inverting.
A blurred Neo-Matrix alphabet formed of rounded crosses with inverting dot nodes alternating between negative and positive space from character to character

X

s. 370
l. 370
t. 0

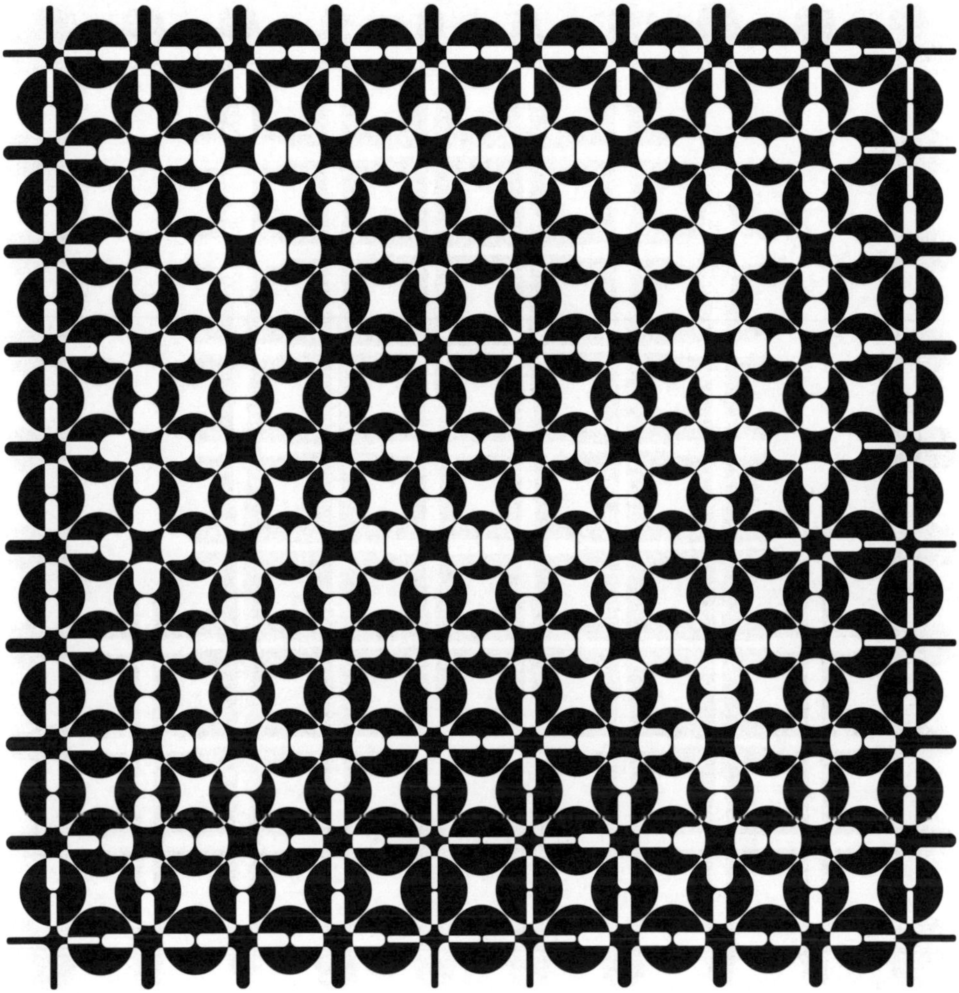

XYZ. O

R

s. 370
l. 370
t. 0

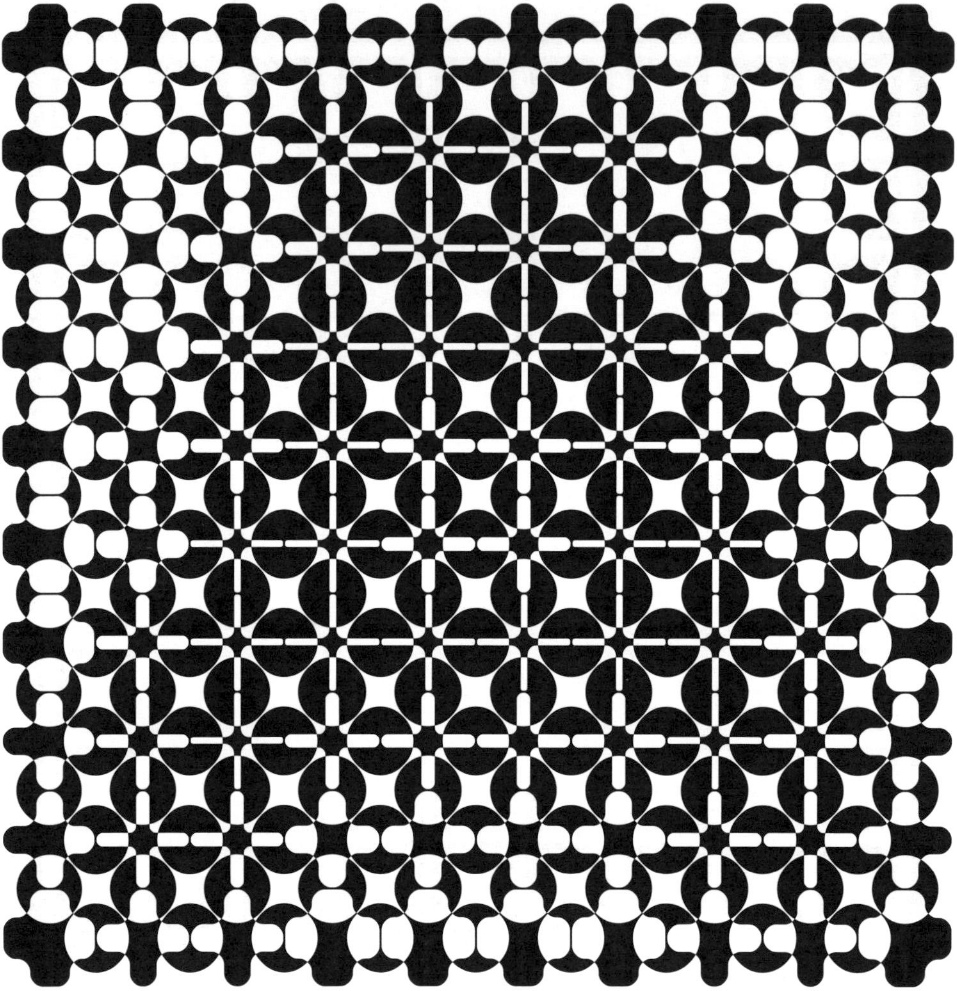

XYZ. O A

s. 370
l. 370
t. 0

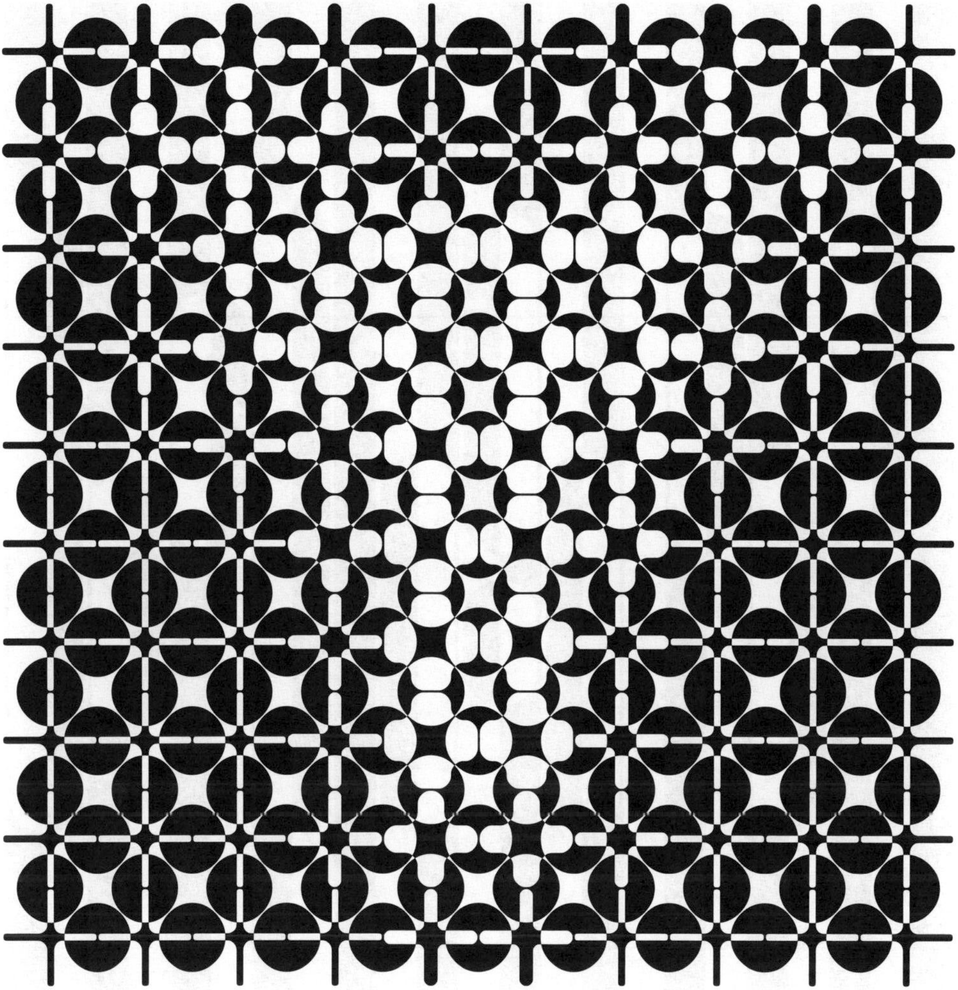

XYZ. O Y

s. 370
l. 370
t. 0

XYZ. P

Vertical × Shifting Pattern × Kinetic. An alphabet formed of a vertical line pattern shifted within units to reaveal modular letterforms with an optical kinetic effect

Yankee

s. 370
l. 370
t. 0

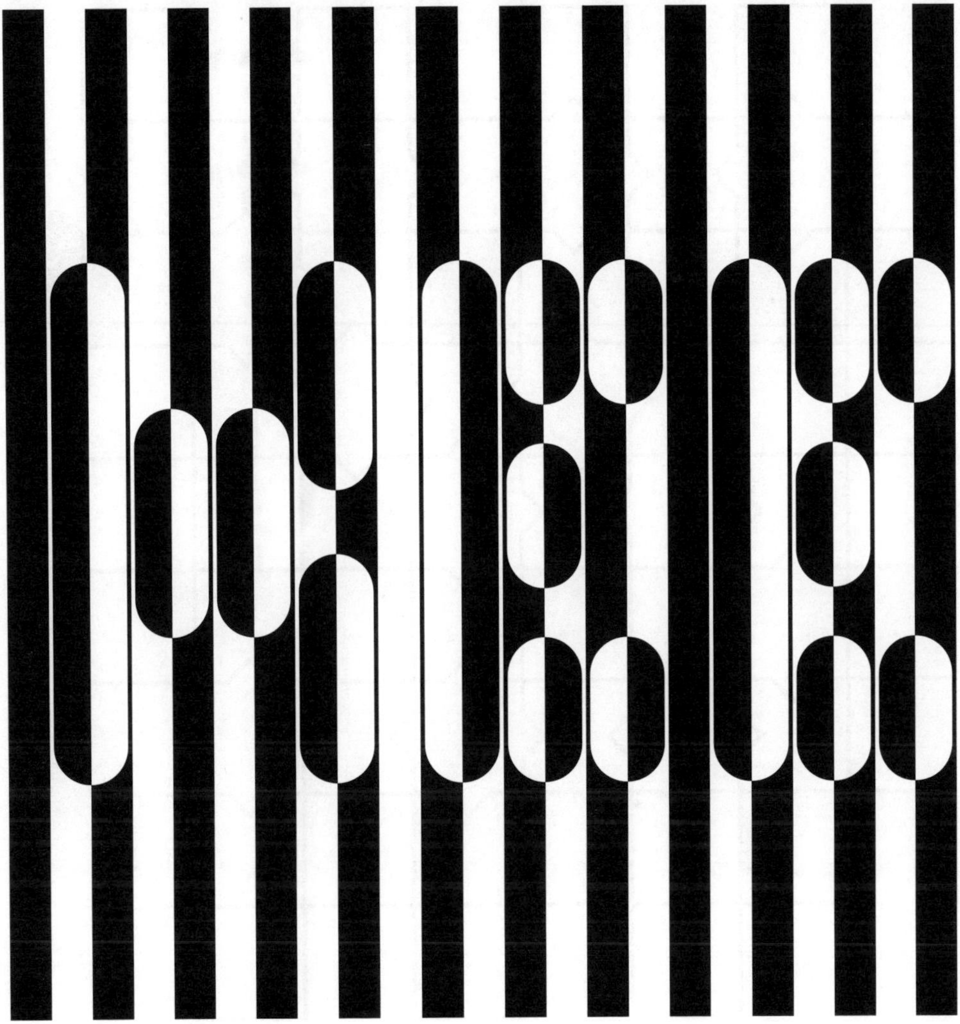

s. 370
l. 370
t. 0

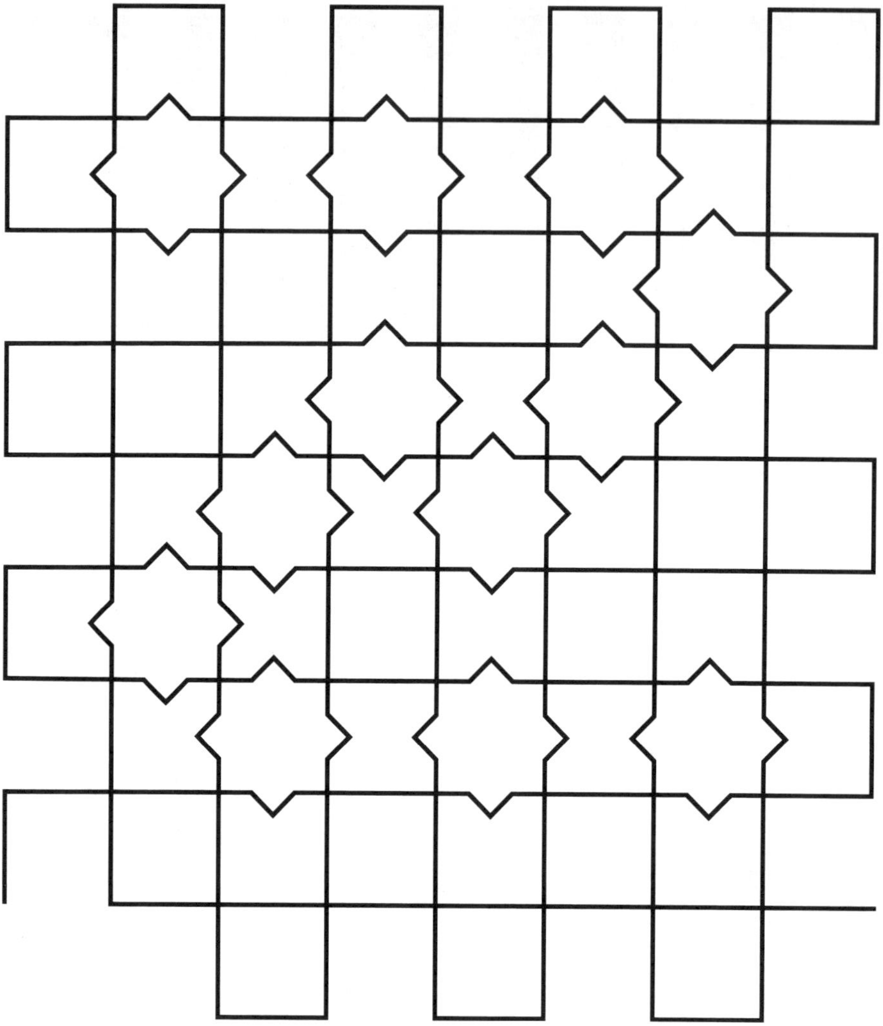

XYZ. Q

Cursive × Shifting Pattern × Gradated.
A cursive alphabet formed of a square pattern with rotated diagonal units revealing letterforms with gradated strokes

Z

s. 422
l. 422
t. 0

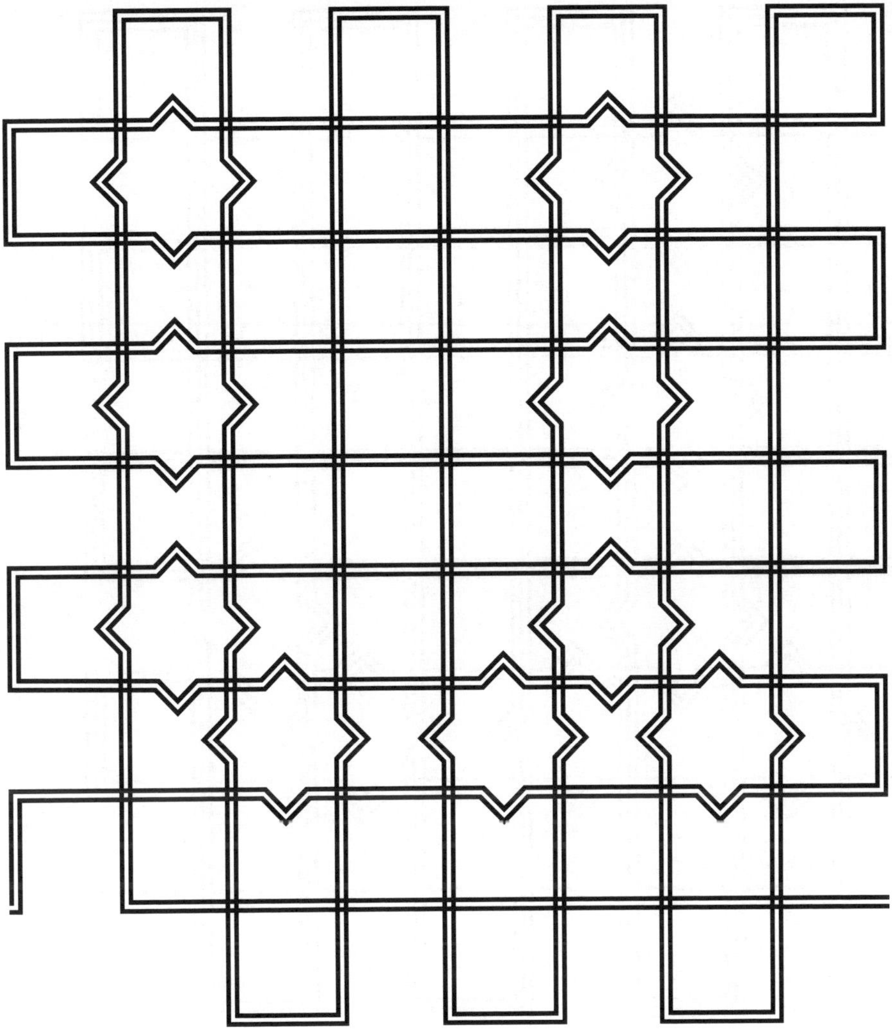

XYZ. Q

U

s. 422
l. 422
t. 0

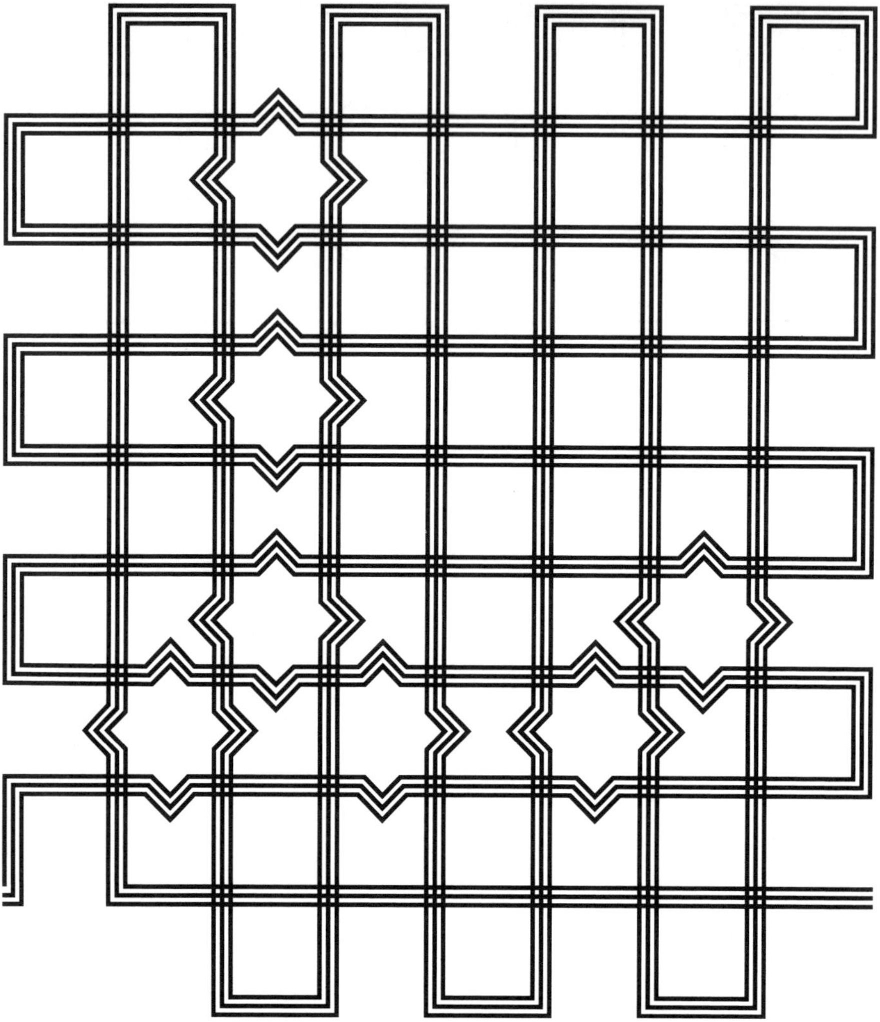

XYZ. Q L

s. 422
l. 422
t. 0

XYZ. Q U

s. 422
l. 422
t. 0

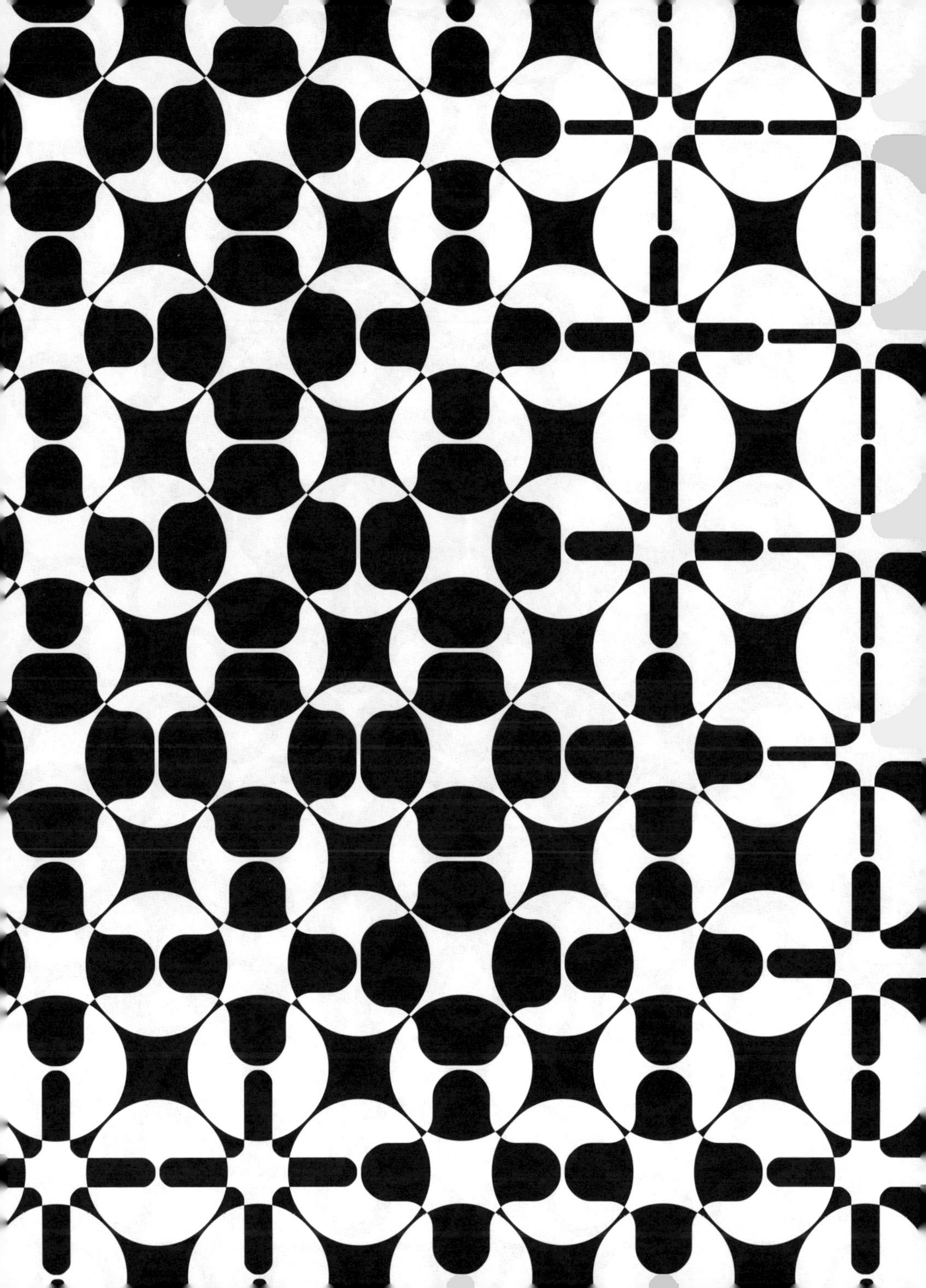

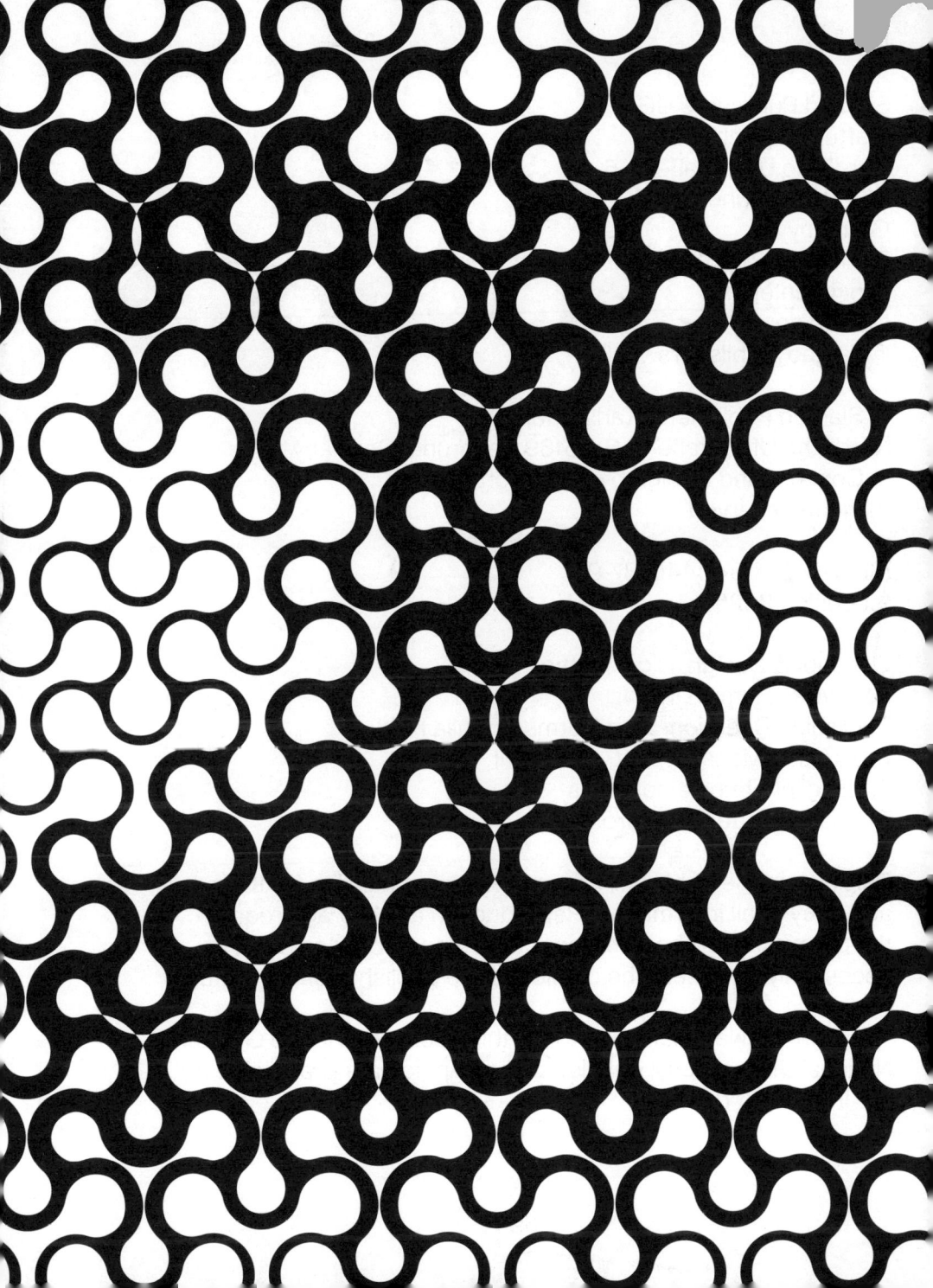

Imprint

Slanted Publishers UG
(haftungsbeschränkt)
Nördliche Uferstraße 4–6
76189 Karlsruhe
Germany
T +49 (0) 721 85148268
info@slanted.de
slanted.de
@slanted_publishers

© Slanted Publishers, Karlsruhe, 2025
Nördliche Uferstraße 4–6, 76189 Karlsruhe, Germany
© Concept and Design by Nigel Cottier
All rights reserved.

ISBN: 978-3-948440-87-9
1st edition 2025

Concept & Design: Nigel Cottier
Foreword: Hamish Muir
Publishing Direction: Lars Harmsen, Julia Kahl
Production Management: Julia Kahl
Printing: printmedia solutions
Typeface: Neue Haas Grotesk

Disclaimer: The publisher assumes no responsibility for the accuracy of all information. Reproduction and storage require the permission of the publisher. Signed contributions do not necessarily represent the opinion of the publisher or the editor.

The German National Library lists this publication in the German National Bibliography; detailed bibliographic data is available on the Internet at dnb.de.

Slanted Publishers is an independent design, publishing and media house founded in 2014 by Lars Harmsen and Julia Kahl. They publish the award-winning print magazine Slanted biannually featuring global design and culture. Since 2004, the daily blog highlights international design and showcases inspiring video interviews. Slanted Publishers initiates and creates publications, focusing on contemporary design and visual culture, working closely with editors and authors to produce outstanding publications with meaningful content and high quality. Slanted was born from great passion and has made a name for itself across the globe. Its design is vibrant and inspiring—its philosophy open-minded, tolerant, and curious.

Nigel Cottier is a designer and experimental typographer with an ongoing interest in creating work of beauty using formulae, hidden systems, and data as tools for creation. As a designer and director, he has led notable commercial projects for Apple, BMW, Google, Nike, NASA, and Rapha. In 2021, he published his first book with Slanted. Letterform Variations is a playful study of letterform construction using basic grid- and shape-based systems, and its potential to generate vast numbers of varying alphabetical outcomes.

alphabeticalplayground.com
@process.pattern